Biblical Lexicology: Hebrew and Greek

Beihefte zur Zeitschrift für die alttestamentliche Wissenschaft

———

Edited by
John Barton, Reinhard G. Kratz
and Markus Witte

Volume 443

Biblical Lexicology: Hebrew and Greek

Semantics – Exegesis – Translation

Edited by
Eberhard Bons, Jan Joosten
and Regine Hunziker-Rodewald

With the collaboration of
Romina Vergari

DE GRUYTER

G

ISBN 978-3-11-031206-5
e-ISBN (PDF) 978-3-11-031216-4
e-ISBN (EPUB) 978-3-11-038311-9
ISSN 0934-2575

Library of Congress Cataloging-in-Publication Data
A CIP catalog record for this book has been applied for at the Library of Congress.

Bibliographic information published by the Deutsche Nationalbibliothek
The Deutsche Nationalbibliothek lists this publication in the Deutsche Nationalbibliografie;
detailed bibliographic data are available on the Internet at http://dnb.dnb.de.

© 2015 Walter de Gruyter GmbH, Berlin/Boston
Printing and binding: CPI books GmbH, Leck
♾ Printed on acid-free paper
Printed in Germany

www.degruyter.com

MIX
Papier aus verantwor-
tungsvollen Quellen
FSC
www.fsc.org   FSC® C083411

Table of Contents

Part III: **Greek**

Part IV: **Projects**

Preface

The study of word meaning in ancient languages is fraught with difficulty. On dead languages, there are no "native speakers" one can interrogate. Only the texts can inform one about the words they contain. Etymology and the study of cognate languages may be of help; traditional interpretation—ancient translations or commentaries—may also be useful. At best, however, these additional sources of information will provide an approximation of word meaning. And at worst, they may lead one astray. In the final analysis only the context is a sure guide to what a given word means. But some contexts are too sparse or too enigmatic to do this effectively. And if the corpus attesting the ancient language is small, or made up of a collection of old and late texts, poetry and prose, and different local dialects, all this may increase the difficulty. In addition, the texts cannot always be taken at face value. In some cases, the texts may result from the combination of different literary strata thus giving words a context they weren't originally intended for. In other cases, they may have suffered corruption in the course of scribal transmission, or they may have been "updated" linguistically by later editors.

In spite of all these obstacles, interpreters of ancient texts do not abandon the pursuit. The stakes are too high. Without a tolerably precise appreciation of word meaning, any understanding of old texts will remain out of reach. Complex and sophisticated procedures are devised, and refined over long periods of time, to determine the meaning of words in ancient languages.

Both the difficulty and the necessity of research on word meaning are excellently illustrated in the field of biblical studies. The biblical texts make up a rather limited corpus. They have come down to us in late manuscripts that show much variation. The writings stem from different periods and locations, and many of them are widely regarded as being composite. Determining what the words of the Bible mean is at times a near-impossible task. Many generations of scholars have spent their best efforts trying to achieve it nonetheless. In our own generation, many exciting developments are creating new possibilities, some of which merit to be briefly mentioned:

a) The discovery of Hebrew texts in the Dead Sea area, notably in Qumran, has had a profound and durable effect on biblical lexicology. Although the majority of texts were discovered more than sixty years ago, their decipherment, analysis and interpretation is still going on. The Dead Sea scrolls show how the vocabulary of the biblical texts was interpreted in the Hellenistic period, and how it continued to be actively used. The corpus also sheds light on the literary processes that produced the Hebrew Bible as we know it. Although many results of scrolls research have been integrated into biblical studies, many other observations still await critical reception.

b) The discovery of the Qumran texts has also reinvigorated historical study of the Hebrew language, and in various ways. The Dead Sea scrolls fill in an important gap in the attestation of literary Hebrew, between the last books of the biblical corpus and the earliest Tannaitic sources. They show that Hebrew continued to be practiced, at least in writing but almost certainly also in living speech. As a result, Hebraists nowadays are much more receptive to the idea that early and late phases of the language need to be studied together in mutual illumination. Similarly, Qumran Hebrew has transformed scientific approaches to the various traditions transmitting the biblical text. The Tiberian tradition is no longer considered the unique standard. The value of other traditions—manuscripts with Babylonian pointing, the oral tradition of the Samaritans, Origen's second column—is increasingly being recognized.

c) Biblical studies have in recent decades opened up to anthropological questions, and to the social sciences in general. These approaches have enriched historical critical exegesis of the classic type. The impact on lexicology is profound, as word meanings are related to socio-political and cultural representations.

d) Over the last thirty years or so, Septuagint studies have developed enormously. From being a useful tool in textual criticism, the Greek version has grown into an object of research in its own right. Study of the Septuagint, in comparison with the Hebrew Bible, leads to a "binocular" approach that lends additional perspective to the biblical text. Lexicology of the Septuagint is itself a burgeoning field with lots of unresolved questions. Nevertheless, it is already clear that Septuagint philology and philology of the Hebrew Bible are intimately related.

From 9 to 12 September 2012 a conference devoted to lexicological research and its relations to exegesis and translation was held in Strasbourg. The organizers were, and are, actively engaged in lexicological research: Regine Hunziker-Rodewald was collaborating on Walter Dietrich and Samuel Arnet's *Konzise und aktualisierte Ausgabe des Hebräischen und Aramäischen Lexikons*, which has appeared in the meantime (Brill, 2013), Eberhard Bons and Jan Joosten are directing the *Historical and Theological Lexicon of the Septuagint*. Several other large-scale lexical projects were also represented, notably the recently completed *Sheffield Hebrew Dictionary*, the *Semantics of Ancient Hebrew Database*, and the *Lexicon of Samaritan Hebrew*. Other scholars addressed methodological issues or presented elaborate case studies illustrating at once the progress and the remaining challenges in this domain of research.

Our thanks go to the Catholic and Protestant Faculties of the University of Strasbourg and to their respective research groups, EA 4377 and 4378, as well as to the Scientific Council of the same university. The lion's share of the budget of the conference was provided by the *Institut Universitaire de France*. Our research assistant, Phoebe Woods, was instrumental in organizing the conference. The publication of the papers was prepared by Romina Vergari. Last but not least, we thank all the participants in the conference for their contributions.

Eberhard Bons
Jan Joosten
Regine Hunziker-Rodewald

Part I: **Hebrew**

Mark S. Smith
Words and Their Worlds*

For Jonas, again (and again)

I. Introduction

In this essay, I offer my reflections on the study of words. My primary research does not lie in lexicography, but in textual commentary, literature and religion. Of course, words and their study are indispensable and foundational for all of these areas.

To locate my own experience and sensibility about words, I would say that my work in this area finds its greatest resonance with the encyclopedic knowledge and proven intuitions of my teacher, Jonas C. Greenfield[1]. I would say about myself, just as Greenfield himself wrote for a symposium on semantics also organized by this university two decades ago[2], "I am not a theoretician, nor do I consider myself a trained linguist, but rather a philologist by training and inclination"[3]. I would also recommend the article from which this quote comes; it is indicative of an inductive approach with a laser-like precision that Greenfield used to attack the study of words. This is not to say that I have not found more thoughtful exercises about words helpful. At Yale, graduate students were introduced to the first edition of James Barr's *Comparative Philology and the Text of the Old Testament*[4]. I later encountered J. F. A. Sawyer, *Semantics in Bib-*

---

* I thank the conveners of this symposium for their invitation to reflect on lexicography. I also wish to thank Moshe Bernstein, Steven Fassberg, David Goldenberg, Aaron Koller, Shalom Paul and Richard Steiner, for their comments on an earlier version of this essay.

1 See Greenfield, *'Al Kanfei Yonah: Collected Studies of Jonas C. Greenfield on Semitic Philology* (ed. Shalom M. Paul, Michael E. Stone and Avital Pinnick; two vols.; Leiden/Boston/Köln: Brill; Jerusalem: Magnes, 2001).

2 Under the aegis of the Semantics of Ancient Hebrew Database project; see http://www2.div.ed. ac.uk/research/sahd/descript.html (accessed 8 August 2012). The proceedings of the 1992 symposium appeared in ZAH VI/1 (1993).

3 Greenfield, "Etymological Semantics," in *'Al Kanfei Yonah*, 2.821. Greenfield expressed these sentiments in a letter to me dated 25 May 1992.

4 Barr, *Comparative Philology and the Text of the Old Testament* (Oxford: Oxford University, 1968); see also Barr, *Comparative Philology and the Text of the Old Testament: With Additions and Corrections* (Winona Lake, IN: Eisenbrauns, 1987). See also Barr's well-known book, *The Semantics of Biblical Language* (Oxford: Oxford University, 1961).

lical Research[5], as well as Arthur Gibson's *Biblical Semantic Logic*[6] (itself no less sharp than Barr in its critique of philological practice). In the meantime, I have taken some interest in proposals for work on semantic domains, as found inter alia in John Lübbe's writings[7]. More recently, I have been mulling over the proposals of Ellen van Wolde in her impressive 2009 collection of essays, *Reframing Biblical Studies: When Language and Text Meet Culture, Cognition, and Context*[8]. As you will see, some concerns of mine that I mention below relate to what van Wolde expresses in her subtitle. Still, my focus falls on the practical side in asking what words mean in context. In his survey of European dictionaries of Biblical Hebrew in the twentieth century a decade ago, Michael Patrick O'Connor drew a distinction between "applied or practical linguistics" and "theoretical linguistics" as they bear on the lexicon[9]. Clearly I work in a "practical" mode[10].

There is a theoretical reason involved in my emphasis on the applied or practical. The use of modern linguistics concepts (such as word fields) by modern students of biblical (or ancient Hebrew) lexicography has been vitally important for the study of words, but at times it does not account for what we might call the ancient thinking about language or words. This is not to deny the tremendous value of the use of modern theory; it is only to ask that ancient understandings be included in our modern search for the meaning of ancient words. While it might be thought that the first task of lexicography is to capture the intuitions of ancient users about words and language, I find a good deal work in semantics of ancient Hebrew disengaged from its users and their specific linguistic and cultural contexts. Lexicography includes the ancients' operating assumptions. How

---

5 Sawyer, *Semantics in Biblical Research: New Methods for Defining Hebrew Words for Salvation* (London: SCM, 1972).

6 Gibson, *Biblical Semantic Logic: A Preliminary Analysis* (1981; second edition; The Biblical Seminar 75; Sheffield: Sheffield Academic Press, 2001). Note also his subsequent volume, *Text and Tablet: Near Eastern Archaeology, the Old Testament and New Possibilities* (Aldershot/Burlington USA/Singapore/Sydney: Ashgate, 2000).

7 For example, a number of articles by John Lübbe, "An Old Testament Dictionary of Semantic Domains," *Zeitschrift fur Althebraistik* 9/1 (1996) 52–57, "Semantic Domains and the Difficulties of a Paradigm Shift in Old Testament Lexicography," *Journal for Semitics* 11/2 (2002) 245–55, and "Semantic Domains, Associative Fields and Hebrew Lexicography", *Journal for Semitics* 12/1 (2003) 128–42.

8 Van Wolde, *Reframing Biblical Studies: When Language and Text Meet Culture, Cognition, and Context* (Winona Lake, IN: Eisenbrauns, 2009).

9 O'Connor, "Semitic Lexicography: European Dictionaries of Biblical Hebrew in the Twentieth Century," in *Israel Oriental Studies XX. Semitic Linguistics: The State of the Art at the Turn of the 21st Century* (ed. Shlomo Izre'el; Winona Lake, IN: Eisenbrauns, 2002) 174–75.

10 To quote a letter of Greenfield (dated 21 June 1992), commenting on his contribution to the 1992 Strasbourg symposium.

did they think about words? West Semites did not write ancient treatises or modern dissertations, books or articles on the subject. Instead, what they thought about words is embedded in what they did with words. So that is where I begin.

II. Indigenous Information about Words

I do not wish to focus on any number of theoretical issues, such as the problem of defining the term, "word" or "words" as such, much less the definition of roots[11] or the problem of classifying words for lexicographical purposes according to their parts of speech[12]. However, I would mention the Levantine expression about words, as known from ancient lists, sometimes given in multiple languages. For example, under the influence of the Mesopotamian scribal tradition as practiced in northern Syria[13], lexical lists from Ugarit have Sumerian, followed by comparands in Akkadian, Hurrian, and finally Ugaritic (in syllabic form); the lists include verbs, nouns, pronouns, prepositions and other particles[14]. So we can surmise that the ancient scribes engaged in "the structural segregation of the units"[15] that would constitute available vocabulary. In other words, there was linguistic material recognized by scribes that would comport to the modern usage of the term, words. In short, we might say that such lists embed an early form of lexicographic delimitation with a comparative aspect. While the scribal craft entailed considerable specialized skills and resources (such as the ability to write as well as the linguistic data for comparative listings), it presumably built upon understandings of words shared in the larger culture.

---

11 See the modern history of the term laid out by Gregorio del Olmo Lete, *Questions of Semitic Linguistics: Root and Lexeme. The History of Research* (trans. Wilfred G. E. Watson; Bethesda, MD: CDL Press, 2008) 5–15. See also the discussion of BH roots by Douglas Leonard Penney, "Towards a Prehistory of Biblical Hebrew Roots: Phoneme Constraints and Polymorphism" (Ph.D. diss., University of Chicago, 1993).

12 See Terry C. Falla, "A New Methodology for Grammatical Classification in Hebrew and Syriac Lexicography," in *Hamlet on a Hill: Semitic and Greek Studies Presented to Professor T. Muraoka on the Occasion of his Sixty-Fifth Birthday* (edited by M. F. J. Baasten and W. Th. van Peursen; OLA 118; Leuven: Peeters, 2003) 165–90.

13 The Akkadian in these lists represents what John Huehnergard calls a northern variety of "Western Peripheral Akkadian," with some substrate of Ugaritic. See Huehnergard, *Ugaritic Vocabulary in Syllabic Transcription: Revised Edition* (HSS 32; Winona Lake, IN: Eisenbrauns, 2008) 4–5.

14 For the Ugaritic multi-language word-lists, see John Huehnergard, *Ugaritic Vocabulary in Syllabic Transcription: Revised Edition* (HSS 32; Winona Lake, IN: Eisenbrauns, 2008).

15 O'Connor, "Semitic Lexicography", 178.

Another form of word comparison available (though relatively rarely) involves parallel versions of texts, such as the well-known cases of Psalms 14// 53 and 2 Samuel 22//Psalm 18. Such texts show an implicit sense of semantic word fields or semantic nuance. Psalm 14:1 uses *'ălîlâ*, where Psalm 53:2 uses *'awel*. Similarly, the second line of 2 Samuel 22:32 shows *mibbal'ădê*, where the same slot in Ps 18:32 attests to *zûlātî*[16]. Or, we may see semantic nuance of a fairly broad term confirmed by noting its more specific parallel word, for example *ûmôṣî'î* in 2 Sam 22:49 compared with *mĕpallĕṭî* in Ps 18:49. Of course, other cases are not what we would call synonyms, but descriptive comparands, such as *miśbĕrê-māwet* in 2 Sam 22:5 and *ḥeblê-māwet* in Ps 18:5[17], or *wā'ašmiddēm* in 2 Sam 22:38 versus *wĕ'assîgēm* in Ps 18:38. Thus this sort of work comparing words in parallel slots requires considerable caution.

For understanding how words were defined in the post-exilic context, we might compare the replacement of words in the books of Chronicles compared with their apparent correspondences in the Former Prophets[18]. The famous substitution of *mĕpazzēz ûmĕkarkēr* in 2 Sam 6:16 by *mĕraqqēd wmĕśaḥēq* in 1 Chron 15:29 may suggest how the earlier words later on were understood[19]. Similarly, the replacement of a word in texts that are supposed to be the same is illustrated by the replacement of the rare *yāhēllû* by the more common *y'yrw* by 1QIsa at Isa 13:10[20]. Given its scope, I expect that the *Semantics of Ancient Hebrew Database* is including these matters. I would add that these cases of substitutions would support relative chronologies for specific words, even if distinct phases may be harder to define for the history of Biblical Hebrew[21].

---

16 Even if a text-critical error is involved, it would still show the semantic proximity but at a later point in the textual tradition. See further Murray H. Lichtenstein, "Idiom, Rhetoric and the Text of Genesis 41:16", *JANES* 19 (1989 = Semitic Studies in Memory of Moshe Held) 87, for *zûlātî* in Deut 1:34–36 compared with *bal'ădê* in Gen 14:24.

17 According to Frank Moore Cross, Jr., and David Noel Freedman, an error is involved in Ps 18:5, given the same word in v. 6. See Cross and Freedman, *Studies in Ancient Yahwistic Poetry* (second ed.; The Biblical Resources Series; Grand Rapids, MI/Cambridge, UK: Eerdmans; Livonia, MI: Dove Booksellers, 1997) 96 n. 4.

18 I thank Moshe Bernstein for reminding me of this material and for providing these particular suggestions.

19 For these terms, see Mayer I. Gruber, "Ten-Dance Derived Expressions in the Hebrew Bible," in *The Motherhood of God and Other Studies* (South Florida Studies in the History of Judaism 57; Atlanta, GA: Scholars Press, 1992) 149–72, esp. 164–65 and 171.

20 See E. Y. Kutscher, *The Language and Linguistic Background of the Isaiah Scroll (I Q Isaᵃ)* (STDJ VI; Leiden: Brill, 1974) 32–33 and 216–17 for this substitution, and 32–33 and 216–315 for other cases of substitution.

21 In this formulation, I am responding on the one hand to critics of dating by linguistic means and on the other hand to its supporters, especially Avi Hurvitz, whose work is particularly strong

III. The Internal World of Words

Such comparisons of texts in different books are not entirely different from reading a word within its immediate context at various levels of complexity. We may attempt to understand a word's meaning according to these multiple levels: within itself for its form and sound; within a syntactical phrasing[22] within a prose clause or poetic line; within a series of clauses, or within a colon of poetry[23] (I hasten to add that *BDB* at times and *DCH* as well as Kaddari do provide parallelism of poetic terms. Perhaps surprisingly, some of the entries in the *Semantic of Ancient Hebrew Database*[24] delve into parallelism sometimes in a minimal manner and with little of the context of such parallelism). Poetic parallelism in particular may furnish an indigenous sense of word-fields not entirely unlike some comparisons of words in parallel versions of the same texts, as noted above. Syntactical parallelism within prose contexts may clarify the mean-

when it comes to specific vocabulary items. This matter lies beyond the scope of this discussion. For now, see Avi Hurvitz, "The Recent Debate on Late Biblical Hebrew: Solid Data, Experts' Opinions, and Inconclusive Arguments," *Hebrew Studies* 47 (2006) 191–210; Jan Joosten, "Diachronic Aspects of Narrative wayhi in Biblical Hebrew", *Journal of Northwest Semitic Languages* 35/2 (2009) 43–61, esp. 58–59; Jacobus A. Naudé, "Linguistic Dating of Biblical Hebrew Texts: The Chronology and Typology Debate", *Journal of Northwest Semitic Languages* 36/2 (2010) 1–22, esp. 15–18; Jan Joosten, Review of Ian Young and Robert Rezetko, with the assistance of Martin Ehrensvärd, *An Introduction to Approaches and Problems*, Babel und Bibel 2011 (in press). See also Robert Holmstedt and John Cook, on http://ancienthebrewgrammar.wordpress.com/; and Ronald Hendel, "Unhistorical Hebrew Linguistics: A Cautionary Tale", at http://www.bible interp.com/opeds/hen358022.shtml. See the rejoinder by Robert Rezetko, Ian Young, and Martin Ehrensvärd, "A Very Tall 'Cautionary Tale': A Response to Ron Hendel", at http://www.bible interp.com/articles/rez358028.shtml. For further discussion, see Mark S. Smith, *Poetic Heroes: The Literary Commemorations of Warriors and Warrior Culture in the Early Biblical World* (Grand Rapids, MI: Eerdmans, 2013), 211–33, chapter eight.

22 See John Lübbe, "The Use of Syntactic Data in Dictionaries of Classical Hebrew", *Journal for Semitics* 5 (1993) 89–96.

23 For recognition of this feature for lexicographical purposes by Held and his students, see Cohen Chaim, "The 'Held Method' for Comparative Semitic Philology", *JANES* 19 (1989 = Semitic Studies in Memory of Moshe Held) 12–13; and Chaim Cohen and Elisha Qimron, "Modern Biblical Lexicography", *Jewish Studies* 32 (1992) 69–77, here 70. Cohen has announced the *Companion to the Hebrew and Aramaic Lexicon of the Old Testament* (ed. Chaim Cohen et al.; Leiden: Brill, forthcoming), in his article, "New Directions in Modern Biblical Hebrew Lexicography", in *Birkat Shalom: Studies in the Bible, Ancient Near Eastern Literature, and Post-Biblical Judaism Presented to Shalom M. Paul on the Occasion of His Seventieth Birthday: Volume 1* (ed. Chaim Cohen et al.; Winona Lake, IN: Eisenbrauns, 2008) 441–73.

24 http://www2.div.ed.ac.uk/research/sahd, accessed 15 August 2012. For the list of words treated thus far, see http://www2.div.ed.ac.uk/research/sahd/lexeme_index.html.

ing of a word or particle[25]. We might look to see if the word is repeated, whether in part or whole in the construction of a passage, within a paragraph of prose or across poetic cola (key in this examination is repetition with variation). And we look to see its larger context, to the kind of prose or poetic genre, of literary *topos* or type-scene, as well as the concern, perspective or ideology that words help to create. Is a given word key to such matters, or is it a bit player in the textual drama before us? In short, how does the word mean within that drama?

At this point, it becomes important to consult parallel contexts *beginning* with the distinction between prose or poetry within the same language corpus, although this distinction between prose and poetry is not as hard and fast as it may have once seemed. Indeed, "prosaic parallelism" remains an important desideratum of modern research. Consideration of such parallel contexts should also ideally involve the same genre, *topos* or type-scene, within the same language corpus. This approach triangulates the search for the meaning of words. It helps to see what words have been used in similar slots, if they are available. Here the issue is what other words are similar to a given word and how they are different. What is specific about a word that it is used here and not another similar term? So I might be looking at a group of terms that seem to belong to a semantic field and are used in a given group of similar contexts. In moving into parallel contexts, we move into the intersection of different passages or texts and their internal worlds. In a sense, we are asking about how these worlds intersect.

IV. The External World of Words, with Five Examples

At this point, the examination of words may move from their internal worlds to the world postulated outside the text, the cultural associations and sensibility that a given word brings to the text for its author and audience (though these, of course, may vary and may be part of the negotiation between author and au-

---

25 For an example of prosaic parallelism, in Ezek 36:23 the first and longer part of the quoted oracle parallels loosely the second and shorter part (after "oracle of Yahweh God"): "I will sanctify my name"//"when I am sanctified"; "among the nations"//"in their sight"; and "among whom you have caused it to be profaned"//"among you (*bākem*)". If correct, the final phrase cited, namely *bākem*, would not be instrumental, i.e. "through you" (so NJPS), but "among" (more locative in sense). This may hold implications for the other uses of *bākem* with the same root in Ezek 20:41, 28:22, 38:16, and 39:27 (these cases were brought to my attention by Dale Launderville, whom I thank).

dience). Words not only help to create the world inside the text; they also evoke a world outside of their text for their authors and audiences. There is, of course, a complex hermeneutical circle (or, a series of such circles) between the world inside the text and what might be posited as lying outside the text, since that external world is largely lost to us, despite appeals to iconography and archaeology. Arguably within their "grammars"[26], pictorial materials and material culture still involve learning the different "languages" of these divergent media and their interconnections of space and usage. For all the problems, they point to experience that words may have evoked. I will return to this point shortly.

This leads me to my basic point, that we cannot study words (here I have in mind verbs, nouns and adjectives, considerably less so particles and prepositions) without their cultural context, information insufficiently undertaken in our currently available lexica. Central to this work is classic historical and comparative lexicography[27]; I would defend these as foundational for our work. It is absolutely necessary, as demonstrated by the comparative work of fine scholars, particularly Greenfield (whom I mentioned at the outset of my remarks), Baruch A. Levine and Shalom M. Paul (especially with respect to Akkadian)[28], Moshe Held and many of his students (again, with particular appeal made to Akkadian)[29], as well as Richard C. Steiner and his student Aaron J. Koller[30]. As I have

---

26 The use of grammatical terminology as analogies for iconography appears in Othmar Keel and Christoph Uehlinger, *Gods, Goddesses, and Images of God* (trans. Thomas H. Trapp; Minneapolis: Fortress, 1998): The gender elements represented on cultic stands are characterized on p. 169 as "a paratactic collection of substitute entities". The image of a bull is said on p. 120 not to be "an 'isolated' vocable,... but is used in the context of 'sentences'". Cf. "complex constellations in iconography is analogous to "the syntax of sentences" (p. 13). Elsewhere, a more literary characterization obtains, such as "narrative sequence" (p. 12).

27 To be clear, I am not referring at this point to the complementary task of comparative Semitic lexicography in the broad sense, as realized in the useful volumes of Alexander Militarev and Leonid Kogan, *Semitic Etymological Dictionary: Vol. I. Anatomy of Man and Animals* (AOAT 278/1; Münster: Ugarit-Verlag, 2003) XXXIII-CLIV, and *Semitic Etymological Dictionary: Vol. II. Animal Names* ((AOAT 278/2; Münster: Ugarit-Verlag, 2005) XLIII-XCI. For discussion of comparative lexicography, see also del Olmo Lete, *Questions of Semitic Linguistics*, 87–125.

28 For Levine, see his essays in *In Pursuit of Meaning: Collected Studies of Baruch A. Levine. Volume II: Law, Society, and Language* (ed. Andrew D. Gross; Winona Lake, IN: Eisenbrauns, 2011); and Paul, *Divrei Shalom: Collected Studies of Shalom M. Paul on the Bible and the Ancient Near East 1967–2005* (CHANE 23; Leiden/Boston: Brill, 2005).

29 For a synthesis of Held's approach, see Cohen Chaim, "The 'Held Method' for Comparative Semitic Philology", *JANES* 19 (1989 = Semitic Studies in Memory of Moshe Held) 9–23; and Hayim ben Yosef Tawil, *An Akkadian Lexical Companion for Biblical Hebrew: Etymological-Semantic and Idiomatic Equivalents with Supplement on Biblical Aramaic* (Jersey City, NJ: KTAV, 2009) ix-xiv. Tawil's book provides a listing of words according to Held's approach; see Victor

tried to indicate above, there is some indigenous basis for this approach. In some instances, comparative textual work between corpora even of different languages has become indispensable for biblical lexicography. For example, in their comparative approach Moshe Held and his students (especially under the influence of Benno Landsberger) identify semantically comparable words (and even phrases) in comparable contexts across different languages (what they have called "interdialectal distribution" of terms) and not only etymologically related words. This provides a measure of method, and it would increase the fund of comparative material worth including in such an encyclopedic approach. I would like to see the contexts of such parallel usage cited in the *Semantics of Ancient Hebrew Database* or in any sort of encyclopedia of BH words. To illustrate this point, let me refer very briefly to some cases, which progressive from the better-known instances to less known ones. Accordingly, the discussions become progressively more involved.

i. The World of Statuary in *ṣelem* ("image") and *dĕmût* ("likeness") in Gen 1:26

I begin with a well-known case, involving the Tell Fekheriyeh inscription's use of "image" (*ṣlm*)/"his image" (*ṣlmh*) in lines 12 and 16, respectively, and "likeness" (*dmwt*') in lines 1 and 15. These terms in the inscription, used for the representation of the speaker on the statue on which it was incised, was heralded not only for having the same combination of etymologically related terms in Gen 1:26 (note also v. 27, and Gen 5:1, 3), but also for providing a useful linguistic

---

(Avigdor) Hurowitz, "'Can Two Walk Together?' A Look at a New Akkadian Companion to the Hebrew and Aramaic of the Bible"; Review article of Hayim ben Yosef Tawil, *An Akkadian Lexical Companion for Biblical Hebrew: Etymological-Semantic and Idiomatic Equivalents with Supplement on Biblical Aramaic*", *Leshonenu* 72 (2012) 359–82 (Heb.). See also E. L. Greenstein, "Trans-Semitic Idiomatic Equivalency and the Derivation of Hebrew *ml'kh*", *UF* 11 (1979) 329–36. The studies of Shalom M. Paul have likewise been informed by this approach; see Paul, *Divrei Shalom: Collected Studies of Shalom M. Paul on the Bible and the Ancient Near East 1967–2005* (CHANE 23; Leiden/Boston: Brill, 2005), essays #15 and 40 among others.

30 For Steiner, see for example his monograph, *Stockmen from Tekoa, Sycomores from Sheba: A Study of Amos' Occupations* (CBQMS 36; Washington, DC: The Catholic Biblical Association of America, 2003); Koller, *The Semantic Field of Cutting Tools in Biblical Hebrew: The Interface of Philological, Semantic and Archaeological Evidence* (CBQMS 49; Washington, DC: The Catholic Biblical Association of America, 2013). See further below.

and cultural analogue for the biblical terms[31]. This usage of statuary for the human person, provided by the *editio princeps* of this Aramaic inscription in 1982, is not in *DCH* as to be expected from its principles; nor does it appear in Kaddari (even in its second printing of 2007) though his entry of *ṣelem* mentions Akkadian *ṣalmu*; nor in *KB* (fourth edition), in either its 1994 volume with *dĕmût* or its 1996 volume with *ṣelem* (Tawil's *An Akkadian Lexical Companion for Biblical Hebrew*, which sometimes does include Aramaic, does not do so in this case). I would like to see an encyclopedia include this sort of information, which holds considerable potential for illuminating the use of BH words and combinations of words. Such a listing should not only include this kind of information such as can be expected on the *Semantics of Ancient Hebrew Database*. Yet in order to show the force of the comparison for readers, it is not enough to list the words; it is necessary also to quote them in context and make appropriate comments showing their relevance for understanding the biblical terms.

ii. The Political World of *yiqqĕhat* ("obedience") and *šîlōh* ("tribute to him") in Gen 49:10

The next case involves etymologically related words in culturally analogous contexts, in this case political in nature. As is well known to scholars of Ugaritic, KTU 1.2 I offers a lexicon of terms pertaining to political tribute and vassalage. These terms include **'armgn*- and **mnḫy*- in 1.2 I 37–38 (with *ṯ'*- commonly reconstructed as the third direct object in this tricolon), as well as **tqh//*tqynh* in

---

31 The correspondences have spurred considerable commentary. For the inscription's editio princeps, see Ali Abou-Assaf, Pierre Bordreuil and Alan R. Millard, *La statue de Tell Fekherye et son inscription bilingue assyro-araméenne* (Etudes Assyriologiques; Paris: Editions Recherche sur les civilizations, 1982). Many commentators tend to view the two terms as near equivalents; see J. C. Greenfield and A. Schaffer, "Notes on the Curse Formulae of the Tell Fekherye Inscription", *RB* 92 (1985) 47. W. Randall Garr's discussion notes how one of these terms opens the first section, *dmwt'* in line 1 (for Garr, focusing on the speaker's petitionary role), while *ṣlm* opens the second section in line 12 (expressive of the speaker's commanding presence and authoritative status; see also *ṣlmh* in line 16). Garr would see this sense of *dmwt'* also in the second section, in line 15. See Garr, *In His Own Image and Likeness: Humanity, Divinity, and Monotheism* (CHANE 15; Leiden/Boston: Brill, 2003) 121–22, 150–51; and "'Image' and 'Likeness' in the Inscription from Tell Fakhariyeh", *IEJ* 50 (2000) 227–34. On this approach, note the cautionary remark of Alan R. Millard and Pierre Bordreuil, "A Statue from Syria with Assyrian and Aramaic Inscriptions", *Biblical Archaeologist* 45/3 (1982) 140. For the basic point of the human person as living statuary representing God in Gen 1:26–27, see also Bernd Janowski, "Die lebendige Statue Gottes: zur Anthropologie der priesterlichen Urgeschichte", in *Gott und Mensch im Dialog. Volume I* (Berlin/New York: de Gruyter, 2004) 183–214.

1.2 I 34 – 35. This field of terms may be brought to bear on Gen 49:10. In this verse, *yiqqĕhat*, "obedience," appear to be cognate with **tqh//*tqynh* ("whom you obey") in 1.2 I 34 – 35[32]. Accordingly, I hazard to mention this contextual evidence in support of the old proposal that *šay*, as known from Pss 68:30, 76:12 and Isa 18:7 (for example in *KB* fourth edition, p. 1476)[33], is to be read in the infamous crux of Gen 49:10, more specifically **šay lōh* as antecedent for MT *šîlōh*[34]. Rashi endorsed the proposal as he knew it from midrashic sources[35]. In modern scholarship, it was defended in 1958 by William L. Moran and in 2010 by Richard C. Steiner[36]. It has also been accepted by NRSV, NJPS and NABRE, and it is noted in *DCH* (VIII:334). In any case, the parallelism with BH *yiqqĕhat* comports with this reading. Moreover, the political thrust of the expressions is evident in both the Ugaritic and biblical contexts: poetic praise is offered to a superior political force. The political connotation of these words hardly comes through in the list format in *KB* 2.430. The Ugaritic usage **tqh//*tqynh* in 1.2 I 34 – 35 should be laid out in parallelism for a BH encyclopedia entry for BH *yiqqĕhat*, and this word's context in Gen 49:10 should be also laid out in parallelism so that readers can see the force of this reading for MT *šîlōh*. Because of the long and difficult history of the interpretation of Gen 49:10, the Ugaritic information in tandem with the political usage of elsewhere of BH *šay* might be questioned as the right solution to the crux here, but in order to gauge its value in any listing of alternatives, it nonetheless would be helpful to include the contextual information.

---

32 For discussion, see Mark S. Smith, *The Ugaritic Baal Cycle: Volume 1. Introduction with Text, Translation and Commentary of KTU 1.1 – 1.2* (VTSup 55; Leiden: Brill, 1994) 290 – 91.

33 Ugaritic **ty*, "gift", is sometimes claimed for KTU 2.13.14 and 2.30.13, e. g., Daniel Sivan, "Final Triphthongs and Final yu/a/i – wu/a/i, in Diphthongs in Ugaritic Nominal Forms", *UF* 14 (1982) 211 and noted by *KB*). By contrast, the letters of this putative word is also read as part of a place name, *ṯynḏr*, by *DULAT* 939 and Cunchillos, *TO* 2.289 and 322. However, the two elements of the GN may be read with Dennis Pardee as "the tribute that they vowed" (discussed among the proposals reviewed in *TO* 2.289 n. 9 and 323 n. 10).

34 Richard C. Steiner, "Poetic Forms in the Masoretic Vocalization and Three Difficult Phrases in Jacob's Blessing", *JBL* 129 (2010) 209 – 35, here 219 – 26. To explain the difference of vowel, Steiner notes the contraction of **ayy-* in Old Canaanite to long *i*. Thus for Steiner, no emendation needs to be posited.

35 For citations from Genesis Rabbah as well as Yalqut Shim'oni (to Isa 18:7), see Steiner, "Poetic Forms", 219 – 20. For a convenient edition for Rashi's comment, see M. Rosenbaum and A. M. Silbermann, *Pentateuch with Targum Onkelos, Haphtaroth and Rashi's Commentary: Genesis* (Jerusalem: published by the Silbermann Family, 1972) 245.

36 Moran, "Genesis 49,10 and Its Use in Ez 21,32", *Biblica* 39 (1958) 405 – 25; and Steiner, "Poetic Forms", 219 – 26.

I would suggest further that in the case of Gen 49:10, the Ugaritic evidence offers a particular challenge to the standard approach of lexicography confined to a single language corpus. Indeed, it is arguable that the Ugaritic and early biblical poetic traditions at times may stand in a close linguistic and literary relationship[37]. In an instance such as this, the lexical work may not be simply comparative in the traditional sense; instead, the usages may reflect a shared or overlapping cultural matrix. And this, I would suggest, poses an intellectual challenge to traditional notions of language delineation in demarcating corpora for dictionaries.

iii. The Cultic World of *ʾmr ("to be seen, appear") in Ps 29:9c

A third case involves *ʾmr in Ps 29:9c. Usually this line is translated along the lines of "and in his temple all say 'glory'" (see NRSV, NJPS, NABRE). It is arguable that the root here may not refer to speech but to visual perception. In *ûbĕhêkālô kullô ʾōmēr kābôd*, *kullô* may be post-positional relative to *ûbĕhêkālô*[38],

---

37 For different formulations of this view, see Michael D. Coogan and Mark S. Smith, *Stories From Ancient Canaan* (second revised and expanded edition; Louisville, KY: Westminster John Knox, 2012) 3; Edward L. Greenstein, "Texts from Ugarit Solve Biblical Puzzles", *Biblical Archaeological Review* 36/6 (2010) 48–53; Simon B. Parker, *The Pre-Biblical Narrative Tradition* (SBLRBS 24; Atlanta: Scholars Press, 1989) 3–4; Dennis Pardee, *The Ugaritic Texts and the Origins of West Semitic Literary Composition* (The Schweich Lectures of The British Academy 2007; Oxford: Oxford University Press, 2012) 79–80; and Mark S. Smith, "Biblical Narrative between Ugaritic and Akkadian Literature: Part I: Ugarit and the Hebrew Bible: Consideration of Recent Comparative Research", *Revue Biblique* 114/1 (2007) 5–29.
38 So already Mitchell J. Dahood, *Psalms 1–50: Introduction, Translation, and Notes* (AB 16; New York: Doubleday, 1966) 175, 179, but without reference to post-positional *kol-* plus third person suffix for places: 2 Sam 2:9, Isa 16:7, Jer 18:31, Ezek 29:2, 35:15; Job 34:13; so J. C. de Moor and P. van der Lugt, "The Spectre of Pan-Ugaritism", *BO* 31 (1974) 9. For Ugaritic examples, see KTU 1.3 VI 14//1.17 V 21, 31 and 1.6 I 37; and for Aramaic cases, see KAI 215:17, 222 A 5, etc. For these references, see Mark S. Smith, *The Ugaritic Baal Cycle: Volume 1. Introduction with Text, Translation and Commentary of KTU 1.1–1.2* (VTSup 55; Leiden: Brill, 1994) 166 n. 90; and Mark S. Smith and Wayne T. Pitard, *The Ugaritic Baal Cycle: Volume 2. Introduction with Text, Translation and Commentary of KTU 1.3–1.4* (VTSup 114; Leiden: Brill, 2009) 366 n. 4. Frank Moore Cross would delete *kullô* in Ps 29:9c as prosaic and metrically impossible; see Cross, *Canaanite Myth and Hebrew Epic: Essays in the History of the Religion of Israel* (Cambridge, MA/London: Harvard University, 1973) 154 n. 39. However, the Ugaritic cases are in poetry.

and following Frank Moore Cross, the verb may be *G*-stem stative (**qatul-*[39]), "to be seen, appear". These would issue in a translation: "and in his temple all of it glory is seen (or, appeared)". While **'mr*, "to speak", is attested in Ugaritic (KTU 1.2 I 31)[40], the visual sense of the root is attested in Akkadian[41] and Ugaritic (KTU 1.3 I 22; cf. 1.2 I 32), including PNs possibly denoting the perception of Baal (*a-mur-*[d]*ba'al* and *'amrb'l*)[42]. The perception of *kābôd* seems to be at home in the Israelite milieu (Exod 16:7, Num 14:22, Isa 35:2, 62:2, 66:18–19, Ps 63:3, 97:6; see *DCH* IV:354), apparently more than saying it. In Ps 145:11, the only other example of **'mr* plus *kābôd* for speech noted by *DCH* (IV:354), the meaning is "to speak of" God's glory. This is not impossible for Ps 29:9c, but it does not seem likely; this sense "speak of" appears in late contexts (e.g., Neh 6:19, Ben Sira 45:26)[43]. In addition, the translations putting "glory" in quotation marks assume that that verse 9c is a response to the theophany, not a discussion of it ("to speak of"). In sum, the balance of evidence, it may be argued, would favor a visual interpretation for **'mr* in Ps 29:9c. In some instances such as this, Ugaritic and what has called early Hebrew poetry may be more proximate than what has been labeled early and late Hebrew.

---

39 Following Cross, *Canaanite Myth*, 154 nn. 39–40, noting the PN *a-mur-*[d]*ba'al*, "Baal is seen", or "better" (in Cross' view), "Baal appeared", which is not mentioned by Dahood. The visual sense of the root in Akkadian and Ugaritic has been long noted; see W. F. Albight, "Northwest-Semitic Names in a List of Egyptian Slaves from the Eighteenth Century B. C.", *JAOS* 74 (1954) 229 n. 47, with the further claim that "the original meaning of Hebrew 'MR, 'to say', was 'to see'". Based on the Akkadian and Ugaritic usages, Dahood (*Psalms 1–50*, 175, 179) read a nominal clause here: "While in his temple – all of it, a vision of the Glorious One". This translation, according to Cross (*Canaanite Myth*, 154 n. 39), is "awkward, prosaic as well as metrically impossible".
40 *DULAT* 72.
41 *CAD A* / 2:5–27. Note Akkadian *nanmuru*, "to be seen, appear" in CAD A/2:23–24.
42 *DULAT* 72. For the names at Ugarit, see F. Gröndahl, *Die Personnamen der Texte aus Ugarit* (Studia Pohl 1; Rome: Päpstiliches Bibelinstitut, 1967) 41, 99. For the corresponding name Amur-Ba'ala in EA 170:38, see W. L. Moran, *The Amarna Letters* (Baltimore, MD: The Johns Hopkins University Press, 1992) 380. The root **'mr* in this name was taken as the verb of speaking ("Speak, Lord/Haddu") by Richard S. Hess, *Amarna Personal Names* (Winona Lake, IN: Eisenbrauns, 1993) 33–34. For both possibilities, see Michael Patrick O'Connor, "The Onomastic Evidence for Bronze-Age West Semitic", *JAOS* 124 (2004) 452, 456.
43 *DCH* I.323. Cf. **ngd* in the C-stem governing *kābôd* in Gen 45:13 and Isa 66:19, and **spr* also governing *kābôd* in Pss 19:2, 96:3//1 Chron 16:24, and Esther 5:11, in *DCH* 4:354. For other features in Ps 145:11 considered late, see Avi Hurvitz, *The Transition Period in Biblical Hebrew: A Study in Post-Exilic Hebrew and its Implications for the Dating of Psalms* (Jerusalem: Bialik, 1972) 79–88 (Heb.).

iv. Agricultural and Magical Words in the Elijah-Elisha Corpus: *šns ("to gird"); bṣql ("sprout"); 'ōrōt (greens); *ghr ("to make a loud noise" with the mouth)

A comparable point might be made for Ugaritic cognates for lexica in pre-exilic BH prose sources. I draw here on lexical items attested in episodes from the Elijah-Elisha material. Here I only mention the famous case from the Elijah material of the *hapax legomenon*, * šns, "to gird," in 1 Kgs 18:46, known also from Ugaritic, in KTU 1.3 II 11–13[44], but this example bears mentioning as some commentaries with philological notes do not cite it[45]. The first item, bṣqln in 2 Kgs 4:42, has long been recognized as cognate with Ugaritic bṣql, "a sprout" (*KB* 1.148)[46], although I think it would help readers to see both the prose context of the Hebrew attestation and the poetic context of the Ugaritic usage in KTU 1.17 II 13–14, 16–17, 23–24. Then it would be also possible for readers to see the parallelism of Ugaritic bṣql with the Ugaritic cognate for the second lexical item for plants, namely Ugaritic 'ur, in 1.17 II 16–17, 23–24, a word related to 'ōrōt in

---

44 See Gary A. Rendsburg, *Israelian Hebrew in the Book of Kings* (Bethesda, MD: CDL Press, 2002) 54–55; and William Schniedewind and Daniel Sivan, "The Elijah-Elisha Narratives: A Test Case for the Northern Dialect of Hebrew", *JQR* 87 (1997) 331.

45 For example, John Gray, *I & II Kings: A Commentary* (second, fully revised edition; OTL; Philadelphia: Westminster, 1970) 404–5; and Mordecai Cogan, *I Kings: A New Translation with Introduction and Commentary* (AB 10; New York: Doubleday, 2000) 445.

46 The suggestion goes back to Umberto Cassuto according to Rendsburg, *Israelian Hebrew*, 94–95. See also Gray, *I & II Kings*, 501; Harold R. (Chaim) Cohen, *Biblical Hapax Legomena in the Light of Akkadian and Ugaritic* (SBLDS 37; Missoula, MT: Scholars Press, 1978) 112–13 n. 16; and Mordechai Cogan and Hayim Tadmor, *II Kings: A New Translation with Introduction and Commentary* (AB 11; New York: Doubleday, 1988) 59. Gray would emend the text to reverse the word order; this seems unnecessary. Citing the article of R. Weiss, "On Ligatures in the Hebrew bible (*nw* = *-m*)", *JBL* 82 (1963) 188–94, Rendsburg cleverly reads the final *-nw* as the plural ending *-m*. Cohen rightly that in the Ugaritic contexts, bṣql is gathered into a granary, and translates, "corn stalk"; cf. "ears of grain" as rendered by Cogan and Tadmor (*II Kings*, 59); note also Ugaritic bṣql 'rgz in KTU 1.85.5). According to Wilfred G. E. Watson, the Ugaritic word "may denote a dry measure on the model of the Akk. measures še'u(m) and uṭṭa/etu(m), which also denote grain"; Watson, *Lexical Studies in Ugaritic* (Aula Orientalis – Supplementa 19; Barcelona: Editorial AUSA, 2007) 72. The final consonant seems to be the afformative *-l* (cf. BH gib'ōl, karmel, 'ărāpel and šim'ōl, cited in Joüon-Muraoka, para. 88Mm, with some having Ugaritic cognates cited in Tropper, *Ugaritische Grammatik*, 276; for other possible examples, see Militarev and Kogan, *Semitic Etymological Dictionary: Vol. I*, CXLVIII, and *Semitic Etymological Dictionary: Vol. II*, LXXXVIII); the noun is derived from *bṣq, "to sprout" (see *DULAT* 241). Israel Knohl cites 2 Kgs 4:42 in connection with the grain first fruits composed of "parched spring grain and grits" in priestly material. See Knohl, *The Sanctuary of Silence: The Priestly Torah and the Holiness School* (Minneapolis: Fortress, 1995) 24.

the preceding episode in 2 Kgs 4, in v. 39; the cognate for the former, but neither its context nor the parallelism in Ugaritic, is noted in *KB* 1.25[47]. The rural context of both passages is also suggestive for understanding the words in both the Ugaritic and biblical contexts, a point not made readily evident for readers of the lexica. These sorts of deeper lexical relationships are not readily seen without citation of the texts along with their contexts and further discussion.

The third lexical item, **ghr* in 1 Kgs 18:42 and 2 Kgs 4:34–35[48], has a cognate in Ugaritic, though this is not well known[49]. The translation for **ghr* in 2 Kgs 4:34–35 is given as "he bent over" (NRSV), "bend, bend down, crouch" (*BDB* 155; *KB* 1.182; *DCH* 2.328); or the like ("*procubuit* ["he leaned or bent forward"] ... super cadaver", in Zorell 145; *hyṯh 't hgwp qdymh, htkpp* ["to incline the body forward, bend/crouch down," in Kaddari 147); sometimes this view is supported by appeal to Aramaic **ghn* (Zorell 145; *KB* 1.182). In context, this translation is not without difficulty. Before the root **ghr* appears (in its *waw*-consecutive form, *wayyighar*), the prophet Elisha "rose and lay upon the child and set his mouth on his mouth, his eyes on his eyes and his hands on his hands"[50]. At this point, the prophet is already lying on top of the child before the verb **ghr*. Thus, the word in context might not seem to refer to this sort of bodily action. Instead, from context **ghr* in 2 Kgs 4:34–35 would appear to represent an action that takes place after the holy man is on top of the child. The problem seems to be recognized by *BDB*, which marks **ghr* as parallel with **škb* in this context[51] (if correct, this would hold interesting implications for understanding the prose storytelling style here)[52].

47 See the discussion in Rendsburg, *Israelian Hebrew*, 92–93, which includes later Hebrew citations.

48 For this case, see Dennis Pardee, *Les textes rituels: Fascicle 2* (RSO XII; Paris: Éditions Recherche sur les Civilisations, 2000) 832 n. 20; and Mark S. Smith, "Recent Study of Israelite Religion in Light of the Ugaritic Texts", in *Ugarit at Seventy-Five* (edited by K. Lawson Younger Jr.; Winona Lake, IN: Eisenbrauns, 2007) 1–25, here 12–13.

49 So, as of 1997, in Schniedewind and Sivan, "The Elijah-Elisha Narratives", 330.

50 NJPS and NABRE obviate the sequence of *waw*-consecutive verbs here (including *wayyighar*) by breaking the sequence and rendering the clause with *wayyighar*: "as he bent over it" (NJPS); "As Elisha stretched himself over the child... " (NABRE). In this approach, however, it is unclear whether the clause with *wayyighar* goes with the preceding clause or with the following clause, as shown by the difference between these two translations.

51 So, too, Dennis Pardee, *Les textes rituels: Fascicle 2* (RSO XII; Paris: Éditions Recherche sur les Civilisations, 2000) 832 n. 20.

52 Commentators (such as Cogan and Tadmor, *II Kings*, 58) compare *wayyitmōdēd* in 1 Kgs 17:21 in the revival story associated with Elijah.

There is etymological support for another possibility. The root *ghr in the Ugaritic incantation, RS 92.2014.8b–15 (published in 2000), refers to the word of anyone, "when it sounds forth in their mouth/on their lips"[53]. Lines 8b–15 read (with the relevant Ugaritic terms transliterated), according to Dennis Pardee[54]:

> So may the tormentors (*dbbm*), the sorcerers (*kšpm*) not give ear
> To the word of the evil man,
> To the word of any man (lit. son of the people"):
> When it sounds forth (*ghrt*) in their mouth (*phm*),
> on their lips (*wšpthm*)
> May the sorcerers, the tormentors
> Then pour it to the earth (*'arṣ*).
> For Urtenu, for his body, for his members.

The understanding of *dbbm* is disputed[55]; whatever it means, the passage describes sorcerers who are to divert the effect of malicious, quite likely magical, speech directed against Urtenu. To judge from *ghrt* in this text, it might be inferred that in Elisha's situation he is taking some sort of action with his mouth[56]. The result of this action seems to be the resuscitation of the boy, in context expressed by means of his mouth ("and he sneezed", *wayzôrēr*)[57]. Whether or not

---

53 For the text, translation and discussion, see Dennis Pardee, *Les textes rituels: Fascicle 2* (RSO XII; Paris: Éditions Recherche sur les Civilisations, 2000) 829–33; Pierre Bordreuil and Dennis Pardee, "Une incantation", in *Études ougaritiques I: Travaux 1985–1995* (ed. Marguerite Yon and Daniel Arnaud; Paris: Éditions Recherche sur les Civilisations, 2001) 387–91; and Dennis Pardee, *Ritual and Cult at Ugarit* (SBLWAW 10; Atlanta: Society of Biblical Literature, 2002) 159. This discussion largely follows Pardee's.

54 Pardee, *Ritual and Cult*, 159.

55 See DULAT 261: "just as sorcerers do not listen to the demons... so the sorcerers spill to the ground the demons".

56 Pardee (*Les textes rituels*, 832) notes the cognate with Arabic. See Arabic *jahura*, "be loud (of voice)," *jahir*, "high, loud, vehement" (of voice)" in Lane 2.475, Dozy 1.227, and Wehr 143. The following supportive Aramaic data is cited courtesy of David Goldenberg: Jewish Babylonian Aramaic *ghr in the aphel means "to extinguish": '{n}<g>hryh lšrgh, "[the wind] extinguished the lamp" in bT. Berakot 60b, listed in Michael Sokoloff, *A Dictionary of Jewish Babylonian Aramaic of the Talmudic and Geonic Periods* (Dictionaries of Talmud, Midrash and Targum III and Publications of the Comprehensive Aramaic Lexicon Project; Ramat-Gan: Bar-Ilan University; Baltimore/London: The Johns Hopkins University, 2002) 263. For the rendering of *ghr by *lht, "to pant," in Targum Jonathan of 2 Kgs 4:34–35, see Menahem Moreshet, *A Lexicon of the New Verbs in Tannaitic Hebrew* (Ramat-Gan: Bar-Ilan University, 1980) 201 n. 1** (Heb.); and Sokoloff, *A Dictionary of Jewish Palestinian Aramaic of the Byzantine Period* (Dictionaries of Talmud, Midrash and Targum II; Ramat-Gan: Bar-Ilan University, 1990) 278.

57 Schniedewind and Sivan, "The Elijah-Elisha Narratives", 331.

this is a case of mouth-to-mouth resuscitation, this biblical passage seems to involve the magical work of a holy man, not entirely unlike the Ugaritic context, which involves an incantation against words of sorcery. While this Ugaritic evidence came to light only after their commentary, Mordecai Cogan and Hayim Tadmor suggested the possibility that an incantation may be involved in Elisha's actions in this context[58]. Both contexts evoke the world of magical personnel[59], which seems rather removed from many, if not most, prophets as represented in the Hebrew Bible.

The context of *ghr in 1 Kgs 18:42 seems to conform less readily to the traditional interpretation of the root, "to bend over". As a possible alternative based on Ugaritic *ghr and the reading here of the root in 2 Kgs 4:34–35, Elijah may be making a "rumbling sound" with his mouth, perhaps corresponding to the approaching *qôl haggešem* in v. 41. It is to be noted that in this passage Elijah makes this sound "to the earth" ('*arṣâ*), perhaps not entirely unlike the pouring of the word to the earth ('*arṣ*) in RS 92.2014.12. In other words, some sort of magical action may be involved, perhaps along the lines of T. H. Robinson's old suggestion that this was an act of "imitative magic" where the prophet simulates a rain-cloud ("crouching into the shape of a rising cloud")[60]. However, the magical praxis here involves not a matter of form as Robinson would have it, but sound. Contextually, this case for *ghr in this sense might seem to be more difficult case to make than what is being suggested for 2 Kgs 4:34–35, but it is a possibility.

v. The Economic World of *nětîbôt* ("roads") in Judges 5:6

The final example is the word, *nětîbôt* in Judges 5:6. Occurring 21 times and only in poetry[61], the word *nětîbâ* is neither particularly rare nor exceedingly common. The following dictionaries provide the following glosses for the word: "path" (*BDB* 677; *KB* [fourth ed.] 2.732); "via, semita ["narrow path, footpath,

---

58 Cogan and Tadmor, *II Kings*, 58.

59 See Alexander Rofé, *The Prophetical Stories: The Narratives about the Prophets in the Hebrew Bible. Their Literary Types and History* (Jerusalem: Magnes, 1988) 17–18. Such "holy men" as Elisha and perhaps Elijah may be compared with the holy men described by E. B. Reeves, *The Hidden Government: Ritual, Clientalism, and Legitimation in Northern Egypt* (Salt Lake City: University of Utah Press, 1990).

60 Robinson, *A History of Israel: Vol. I. From the Exodus to the Fall of Jerusalem, 586 B.C.* (Oxford: At the Clarendon, 1932) 306. Cf. Gray, *I & II Kings*, 404.

61 See Even Shoshan 1467; and the discussions in Klaus Koch, "derekh", *TDOT* 3:280, noted by Philip J. King and Lawrence E. Stager, *Life in Biblical Israel* (Library of Ancient Israel; Louisville/London: Westminster John Knox, 2001) 178.

footway"]"[62] (Zorrell 538); "path, pathway" (*DCH* V:783); "derek, šabil; 'oraḥ" (Kaddari 738); and perhaps the best for Judges 5:6, "caravan route" (*TDOT* 3:280)[63]. For etymological information, *BDB* offers Arabic *nataba*, "swells forth, become prominent, protuberant", citing Lane 2760. This etymological information does not seem terribly helpful for elucidating the sense of the word in West Semitic languages. *KB* mentions Ugaritic *ntb* (after the masculine BH form) as well as MHeb (without giving its meaning, "highway, road", as in Jastrow 943). *TDOT* 3:280 mentions the masculine and feminine forms in Ugaritic, with no reference to their contexts. So this is the information we learn from Hebrew dictionaries when it comes to the word and its etymology[64].

This etymological data is to be amended in a number of respects. First, one inscribed Hebrew seal bears the root in the PN, *ntybyhw*, according to Nahman Avigad[65]. Second Aramaic *nātîbtā'* in the same meanings as MHeb (Jastrow 943) is to be noted, although it may be a borrowing from Hebrew given its attestation in the Targum to Proverbs and given the lack of attestation of the word in other Aramaic dialects (such as Syriac). Third, Ebla provides a place name NI-*ti-ba*[ki66]. Fourth, the Ugaritic attestations offer considerable more information, which we will return to below. An observation may be offered concerning the word's distribution: it is attested in Biblical Hebrew poetry and its derivatives in contrast to its lack in first millennium West Semitic epigraphic sources or

---

62 This word was used in some passages for the Vulgate translation of *nĕtîbâ, for example in Prov 8:2 and Isa 43:16. It was also loaned into Jewish Bablyonian and Palestinian Aramaic as *symṭ'*, according to Sokoloff, *A Dictionary of Babylonian Aramaic*, 805.

63 See also David A. Dorsey, *The Roads and Highways of Ancient Israel* (Baltimore/London: The Johns Hopkins University, 1991) 226–28.

64 In *TDOT*'s defense, it does not have a separate entry for this word, but directs readers' attention to the entry on "derekh" in *TDOT* 3.

65 Avigad, *Corpus of West Semitic Stamp Seals* (revised and completed by Benjamin Sass; Jerusalem: The Israel Academy of Sciences and Humanities/The Israel Exploration Society/The Institute of Archaeology, The Hebrew University of Jerusalem, 1997) 59, #26 for the seal in question, 24 for the comparison with Ps 119:35, and 12 for the issue of authenticity. Another seal (#1157) is read as *nt(b)b'l*(?) (Avigad, Corpus, 438–39).

66 ARET 3 87, in Kilian Butz, "Zur Terminologie: Der Viehwirtschaft in den Texten aus Ebla", in *La lingua di Ebla: Atti del convegno internazionale (Napoli, 21–23 aprile 1980)* (ed. L. Cagni; Naples, 1981) 337 n. 90, cited in *DULAT* 651. Jeremy Black, Andrew George and Nicholas Postgate (*A Concise Dictionary of Akkadian* [2nd (corrected) printing; SANTAG 5; Wiesbaden: Harrassowitz, 2000] 251) note Mari Akkadian *netbītum*, "mobilization place" following 204, 205. The editors derive this noun from *tebû*, "to depart", which would preclude an etymological relationship to West Semitic *ntb. Charpin ARM 26/2 205 "Versammlungsort (aufgebotener Truppen)"?

later Aramaic[67]. If it is sound to generalize about the distribution of *ntb in West Semitic sources based on the relatively small base of data, it would appear that in the second millennium sources such as Ugaritic, the nominal forms appear in both prose material (ntbt in KTU 2.36.15, 4.288.6, 4.336.7, 4.388.10; see below) and poetic contexts (ntb in 1.17 VI 43–44, and ntbt in KTU 1.82.37 and 1.119.33), while in the first millennium context the two forms of the noun seem more at home in BH poetry. As a possible corollary, the root is used more metaphorically than literally in the BH and epigraphic corpus (in the one PN, ntybyhw)[68], rather different from the situation in the Ugaritic texts where the literal (KTU 2.36.15, 4.288.6, 4.336.7, 4.388.10, 1.119.33) predominates over the metaphorical (KTU 1.17 VI 43–44; 1.82.37 is unclear).

As for context, KB and Zorell offer little help for BH attestations of the word. By contrast, the more contextually oriented dictionaries provide some further information. BDB (677) notes the parallelism of *nĕtîbâ with derek elsewhere, while DCH (V:783) and Kaddari (738) refer to the parallelism of nĕtîbâ with 'ōraḥ here and with derek elsewhere[69]. BH derek may suggest a route that is *drk, "tread underfoot" by human and animal traffic[70] (which would comport with the root's usage in Deut 2:5 and 11:24 = Josh 1:3)[71]. Bringing this point to bear on Judges 5, this observation fits with the mention of persons apparently going on foot

---

67 There is no entry for the word in DNWSI, nor in the Canaanite in the Ugaritic-Canaanite lexicon of Issam K. H. Halayqa (see below), nor in the Phoenician-Punic Dictionary of Charles Krahmalkov or the listings of words by Jongeling's Handbook of Neo-Punic Inscriptions, nor in the lexica of Michael Sokoloff.

68 According to Dorsey (The Roads and Highways of Ancient Israel, 227), the BH root "does not seem to lend itself readily to metaphorical extension, and even when it does (Isa. 69[sic]:8; Ps 119:35; Prov. 1:15; 3:17; 8:20), the image of a physical road or course of travel is usually still there... ". By comparison, Dorsey notes, the synonyms 'ōrāḥ and derek are used more in biblical metaphor. Perhaps as a corollary, 'ōrāḥ is also used more in poetic texts than in prose (cf. Gen 18:11). By contrast, BH derek commonly appears in both prose and poetic contexts. Note also the distinction made for derek between "common" and sacred, in 1 Sam 21:6.

69 For these terms, see Klaus Koch, "derekh", TDOT 3:278; and Philip J. King and Lawrence E. Stager, Life in Biblical Israel (Library of Ancient Israel; Louisville/London: Westminster John Knox, 2001) 178.

70 Koch, "derekh", TDOT 3:278; and Philip J. King and Lawrence E. Stager, Life in Biblical Israel (Library of Ancient Israel; Louisville/London: Westminster John Knox, 2001) 178. Note in a postbiblical Hebrew inscription, "the great road leading to the desert" (wdrk hgdwlh hhwlkt lmydbr) cited in DNWSI 1.261. See further below.

71 See BDB 204. Cf. the semantics of *'qb, discussed by Menaḥem Zevi Kaddari, "Homonymy and Polysemy in the New Modern Hebrew Lexicon of the Hebrew Bible", in Biblical Hebrew in Its Northwest Semitic Setting: Typological and Historical Perspectives (ed. Steven E. Fassberg and Avi Hurvitz; Jerusalem: The Hebrew University Magnes Press; Winona Lake, IN: Eisenbrauns, 2006) 151–52.

as well as riding of animals (see vv. 6 and 10). Per their practice, the dictionaries provide little further context for the word, and it is this aspect of the word, namely its internal and external worlds that, it seems to me, are in need of some redress.

In the immediate context of *nětîbôt* in Judges 5:6, the dominant term is *'ōrāḥôt*, which appears both in the preceding line, *bîmê yā'ēl ḥādēlû 'ōrāḥôt*, and also in the same sentence as *nětîbôt: wěhōlěkê nětîbôt yēlěkû 'ōrāḥôt 'ăqalqallôt*. The first mention of *'ōrāḥôt* appears unqualified by an adjective, while the second is qualified by *'ăqalqallôt*. The phrase *hōlěkê nětîbôt* pertains to persons who would use either sort of *'ōrāḥôt* depending on conditions. The first and unqualified usage of *'ōrāḥôt* appears to be the norm, while the second, which is qualified, is not the norm and apparently the less preferable situation (cf. *nětîbôtêhem 'iqqěšû lāhem* in Isaiah 59:8, which also uses *derek* in parallelism; *derek 'iqqēš* in Prov 22:5, etc.). The verbal use of **ḥdl*[72] suggests the loss of the routes used regularly for travel, leaving by default *'ōrāḥôt 'ăqalqallôt*. The verb **ḥdl* is repeated at the head of v. 7, which describes another loss of what seems to be the traditional situation with Israel that obtained until the appearance of Deborah. Whatever the precise meaning of v. 7 (especially the word, *pěrāzôn*, which I take as "village militia"[73]), this verse along with v. 6 portrays Israel's negative situation. The agency of this negative situation goes unnamed in these verses.

The larger context of v. 6 suggests one additional expression pertinent to *nětîbôt*, and that is the third party named in v. 10, *wěhōlěkê 'al-derek*. It is the same participle heading the phrase in v. 6, *wěhōlěkê nětîbôt*. We need not be detained by the other participles heading the parallel expressions in v. 10, although they all indicate human parties that travel in various modes. Verse 10 is further interesting for the overall sense of vv. 6–7, as the attention of the travelling parties in this verse is invoked for the accomplishment of the military action presumably taken on their behalf. In other words, travel may be represented implicitly as the *casus belli*[74].

For the sense of the complaint in Judges 5:6–7, interpretation may also draw on parallel contexts in the biblical corpus, which through comparison and contrast might provide some sense of the situation. Isaiah 33:7–13 provides just such

---

[72] For this root, see Theodore J. Lewis, "The Songs of Hannah and Deborah: ḤDL-II", *JBL* 104 (1985) 105–8.

[73] I defend this translation in my forthcoming book, *Poetic Heroes: The Commemoration of Warriors and Warrior Culture in the Early Biblical World* (Grand Rapids, MI: Eisenbrauns, 2013, in press).

[74] See J. David Schloen, "Caravans, Kenites, and *Casus Belli:* Enmity and Alliance in the Song of Deborah", *CBQ* 55 (1993) 18–38.

a parallel context. Verses 7–9 (despite the *setuma* between vv. 12 and 13) first describes negative conditions ("depopulation, social breakdown, and devastation of the environment" in the wake of enemy attack[75]), which Jerusalem's inhabitants lament. Then verses 10–13 quote a divine declaration of the town's destruction as well as the burning of the peoples. More specifically in v. 8, the inhabitants decry how *nāšammû mĕsillôt šābat ʿōbēr ʾōraḥ*, "Highways are desolate, a wayfarer has ceased". The conditions involving the roads in both passages are markers of the bad situation in each of the two texts[76]. In both passages enemies seem to be the source of the problem with highways (note the destroyer in Isa 33:1). The comparison may be extended to a more specific verbal level. In Isa 33:8 *ʿōbēr ʾōraḥ* compares with *wĕhōlĕkê nĕtîbôt* in Judg 5:6, while the verb *šābat* recalls the use of **ḥdl* in Judg 5:6. The descriptions of the roads then are followed by a divine response, in Judges 5 one of help and in Isa 33:10–13 one of destruction. Here the conditions of the highways signal the situation of the people who depend on them for economic well-being; in this respect, Judg 5:6–7 seems little different.

At this point, we may turn to the external world of the word. In other words, what might this word evoke in the world of ancient Israelites? I will turn to three sets of sources that may add various dimensions to understanding *nĕtîbôt* in Judg 5:6. We will begin with the most proximate to the least proximate, and perhaps ironically from the least helpful to the most. We begin with a small piece of possibly pertinent evidence in the Hebrew Bible. Given the poetic use of the word, it might be expected that the usage might tend to the more metaphorical than the literal, and in fact this is the case. The Hebrew Bible offers relatively "real-life" information about *nĕtîbôt* in addition to what has been noted little up to this point. Apart from the parallelism with various terms, one apparent "real-life" usage may appear in Prov 8:2, which belongs to the introduction to

---

75 Joseph Blenkinsopp, *Isaiah 1–39: A New Translation with Introduction and Commentary* (AB 19; New York: Doubleday, 2000) 440. For the question of the historical context in the Neo-Assyrian situation of Hezekiah, see also J. J. M. Roberts, "Isaiah 33: An Isaianic Elaboration of the Zion Tradition", in *The Word of the Lord Shall Go Forth: Essays in Honor of David Noel Freedman in Celebration of His Sixtieth Birthday* (ed. Carol L. Meyers and M. O'Connor; American Schools of Oriental Research Special Volume Series 1; Winona Lake, IN: Eisenbrauns, 1983) 15–25.

76 To judge from these biblical texts as well as the following Phoenician text, problems with roads may constitute a Levantine trope. In KAI 26 A ii 4–5 (but missing from the parallel Hieroglyphic Luwian text), Azatiwada boasts that road safety improved against the enemy Danunians who had threatened "even in places which formerly were feared, where a man feared to walk the road (*llkt drk*), but in my days, (especially) mine, a woman can walk alone with her spindles". So K. Lawson Younger, Jr., "The Phoenician Inscription of Azitawada", *JSS* 43/1 (1998) 11–47, here 17, 24 and 32–33.

the invitation issued by personified Wisdom. The verse names the locations where she takes up her address:

bĕrō'š-mĕrômîm 'alê-derek   At the top of heights on the way,
bêt nĕtîbôt niṣṣābâ   (at) the house of roads, she stands.

The context is difficult. *KB* 732 and NJPS render *bêt nĕtîbôt* as "crossroads" (so too Modern Hebrew *parashat* ["crossroad"] in Kaddari). This gloss would smooth out the sense with the first line, but it might also erase the possibly literal sense of *bêt*, as "house of". *KB* and apparently *DCH* V:783 would emend here from *bêt* to **bên*, though without citing text-critical evidence in support. This view is essentially followed by the commentaries of Richard D. Clifford, Michael V. Fox and Bruce K. Waltke[77]. In the face of this apparent *opinio communis*[78], perhaps this passage should not be pressed, but it should be noted that the lack of philological argument for *bêt* as crossroad, or for the proposed emendation to **bên* is notable; and the even more striking proposal to read *bêt* as a feminine form of the preposition *bên*[79] does not inspire confidence. Perhaps there is some further basis adduced elsewhere in the secondary literature, but thus far I see little or no effort among the dictionaries or these commentaries to read the verse as it might seem to suggest at first glance, namely as "house of roads". Unnoted in these discussions is Job 38:20, which may compare with this use of the two words, "that you may understand the ways of its house... ". The cosmic usage may be founded on a more mundane usage perhaps as attested in Prov 8:2, as a house or building where roads come together. Here Clifford in speaking of Prov 8:2–3 perhaps comes the closest: "Like Absalom attempting to win a following in 2 Sam 15:2, she stands by the *road* leading through the *gate* and *calls* to people passing by (words appearing in both passages are italicized)"[80]. It is no wonder that the expression in Prov 8:2 is translated as crossroads, but

77 Clifford, *Proverbs: A Commentary* (OTL; Louisville, KY: Westminster John Knox, 1999) 90, 94; Fox, *Proverbs 1–9: A New Translation with Introduction and Commentary* (AB 18 A: New York: Doubleday, 2000) 265–66; and Waltke, *The Book of Proverbs: Chapters 1–15* (NICOT; Grand Rapids, MI/Cambridge, UK: Eerdmans, 2004) 386, 394. See also Dennis Pardee, *The Ugaritic Texts and the Origins of West-Semitic Literary Composition: The Schweich Lectures of the British Academy 2007* (Oxford/New York: Oxford University Press, 2012) 95. Contextual support for this view might be derived from v. 20, with its use of *bĕtôk nĕtîbôt* (could *bên* in v. 2 be an error for *bĕtôk*, as seen in v. 20?).
78 For a dissenting voice, see Dorsey, *The Roads and Highways of Ancient Israel*, 45–46.
79 Waltke (*The Book of Proverbs*, 386 n. 3) cites *HALOT* 1:129 for *bêt* here as a feminine form of the preposition *bên*. The use of *bên* in post-biblical Hebrew in the meaning "part", remains a desideratum of research, as Aaron Koller has pointed out to me.
80 Clifford, *Proverbs*, 94.

there is no reason why some sort of building at this putative crossroads at a town could not be included in the referent. Indeed, there may be a vocabulary of places associated with roads, whether at crossroads located at towns or on the road (*mĕlôn 'ōrāḥîm*, "lodging-place of travelers," in Jer 9:1; cf. Gen 42:27, 43:21; Exod 4:24; 2 Kgs 19:23)[81]. The *bêt nĕtîbôt* of Prov 8:2 may be a building or part of one located by a town's walls (perhaps at "the heights" as mentioned in the preceding line in Proverbs 8:2). While it cannot be demonstrated that *bêt nĕtîbôt* in this context is a "hostel" at a crossroads despite a later Aramaic parallel[82] (much less a "toll-house"),[83] this approach including some sense of "house" in this expression is no less well supported by context or philology than "crossroads".

As the next proximate source for *nĕtîbôt* in ancient Israel after the Hebrew Bible itself, we may turn briefly to what archaeology may offer. This is not a customary resource for dictionaries and lexica, but to my mind this remains a great desideratum for an encyclopedia of words in Biblical Hebrew. This is not to suggest that lexicographers have been entirely disinterested in using material culture for understanding biblical vocabulary[84]. Indeed, I am most impressed by the recent study of Aaron J. Koller, *The Semantic Field of Cutting Tools in Biblical Hebrew: The Interface of Philological, Semantic and Archaeological Evidence*[85]. The archaeological evidence for the material reality of roads is relatively meager,

---

81 Cf. caravans lodging in the steppe in Isa 21:13; lodging in the mountains in 2 Kgs 19:23 versus Isa 37:24. For discussion, see Dorsey, *The Roads and Highways of Ancient Israel*, 45–46.

82 Cf. later Palestinian Aramaic *byt dh d'wrḥwtyh*, "this hostel of his"; see Joseph A. Fitzmyer and Daniel Harrington, *A Manual of Palestinian Aramaic Texts* (Biblica et Orientalia 34; Rome: Pontifical Biblical Institute, 1978), Appendix #48, cited in *DNWSI* 1.159.

83 For this proposal, see Kevin McGeough, *Exchange Relationships at Ugarit* (Ancient Near Eastern Studies Supplement 26; Leuven/Paris/Dudley, MA: Peeters, 2007) 132 n. 302. For an effort at the "archaeology of tolls" in Iron II Israel, see the studies of John S. Holladay, Jr., "Toward a New Paradigmatic Understanding of Long-Distance Trade in the Ancient Near East: From the Middle Bronze II to Early Iron II – A Sketch", in *The World of the Arameans II: Studies in History and Archaeology in Honour of Paul-Eugène Dion* (ed. P. M. Michèle Daviau, John W. Wevers and Michael Weigl; JSOTSup 325; Sheffield: Sheffield Academic Press, 2001) 136–73, and "Hezekiah's Tribute, Long-distance Trade, and the Wealth of Nations ca. 1000–600 BC: A New Perspective ('Poor Little [Agrarian] Judah' at the End of the 8th Century BC: Dropping the First Shoe", in *Confronting the Past: Archaeological and Historical Essays on Ancient Israel in Honor of William G. Dever* (ed. S. Gitin, J. E. Wright and J. P. Dessel; Winona Lake, IN: Eisenbrauns, 2006) 309–31.

84 For "archaeology in lexicography", see Aaron J. Koller, *The Semantic Field of Cutting Tools in Biblical Hebrew: The Interface of Philological, Semantic and Archaeological Evidence* (CBQMS 49; Washington, DC: The Catholic Biblical Association of America, 2012) 1–4.

85 Koller, *The Semantic Field of Cutting Tools in Biblical Hebrew: The Interface of Philological, Semantic and Archaeological Evidence* (CBQMS 49; Washington, DC: The Catholic Biblical Association of America, 2013).

but hardly without interest: "Archaeology provides only limited and indirect evidence with respect to ancient roads. Open roads were not paved in the Iron Age, in contrast to the main streets of towns, which were paved with stones"[86]. These roads outside of towns were designed to handle human and animal traffic, but wheeled vehicles less so[87]. To this information might be added sites that have been thought to be lodging for travelers, such as Kuntillet ʿAjrud[88]. Such sites may be disputed, but they do point to the need for more archaeological work on ancient roads, which in turn may prove helpful for relevant biblical lexicography[89].

As a third external source for *nĕtîbôt* in Judg 5:6, I would return to Ugaritic *ntbt*[90]. As noted above, this cognate was not entirely overlooked by the dictionaries; it was listed in the entries in *KB* and *TDOT* III. However, neither makes any mention of its usage, which may be pertinent to Judg 5:6[91]. First, we may note its usage in KTU 4.288.6. KTU 4.288 is an administrative listing for *spr blblm*, "record of transporters," as stated in line 1. Lines 2–6 demarcated by scribal lines lists four *skn* (a high-ranking official) of four places, followed in line 6 by *rb. tntnbt š*, "head of sheep (?) paths"[92]. This line suggests paths perhaps used for animal shepherding, as well as an interest in their administration, as signaled by the mention by *rb*. The find-spot of this tablet in the eastern archive of the royal palace would suggest in addition a specifically royal interest.

---

86 King and Stager, *Life in Biblical Israel*, 177, citing Avraham Biran, "Dan", *NEAEHL* 1.323–32. See also Dorsey, *The Roads and Highways of Ancient Israel*, 28–32.

87 See King and Stager, *Life in Biblical Israel*, 178, citing Edward Robinson on this point.

88 The northern and southern pottery as well as its isolated location have recommended this interpretation of Kuntillet ʿAjrud. See the discussion in Zeʾev Meshel, *Kuntillet ʿAjrud (Ḥorvat Teman): An Iron Age II Religious Site on the Judah-Sinai Border* (Jerusalem: Israel Exploration Society, 2012) 65–69. The sites of Qitmit or Ein Hasevah are forts, but they are also sometimes considered to be stopover places. See Yifat Thareani-Sussely, "Ancient Caravanserais: An Archaeological View from ʿAroer'", *Levant* 39 (2007) 123–41.

89 For a study of roads in ancient Israel based largely on biblical references and an examination of topography, see Dorsey, *The Roads and Highways of Ancient Israel*.

90 See *DULAT* 651; note also Issam K. H. Halayqa, *A Comparative Lexicon of Ugaritic and Canaanite* (AOAT 340; Münster: Ugarit-Verlag, 2008) 244

91 Kevin McGeough, *Exchange Relationships at Ugarit* (Ancient Near Eastern Studies Supplement 26; Leuven/Paris/Dudley, MA: Peeters, 2007) 132 n. 302.

92 For this approach, see *DULAT* 651; Kevin McGeough, *Ugaritic Economic Tablets: Text, Translation and Notes* (ed. Mark S. Smith; Ancient Near Eastern Studies Supplement 32; Leuven/Paris/Dudley, MA: Peeters, 2011) 151–52. The final consonant has been taken alternatively as the Hurrian abstract ending -*šše* (Tropper, Ugaritische Grammatik, 107). For discussion, see Watson, Lexical Studies in Ugaritic, 132.

A number of other Ugaritic texts point to another sense of *ntbt* that may provide a helpful comparison with its BH cognate in Judg 5:6. We begin with KTU 4.336[93]:

[1]*bym ḥdṯ*	On the day of the new moon,
[2]*b.yrḫ.pgrm*	in the month of *pgrm*,
[3]*lqḥ.'iwrpzn*	PN,
[4]*'argḏd*	PN,
[5]*ḳṯkn*	PN,
[6]*ybrk*	(and) PN took
[7]*ntbt*	the route(s)
[8]*b.m'itm* [9]*'šrm*	for 220
[10]*kbd.ḫrṣ*	total in gold.

The phrase rendered literally "took the route(s)," has been generally understood to refer to purchase of trading concessions for traveled routes[94]. The economic situation in this text seems to involve individuals who have bought the rights from the royal authority to exact tolls from traders or travelers.

KTU 4.388, while quite broken, appears to offer an example of the same subgenre[95]:

[1]*x*[	...
[2]*b*[	On[96] (?) [...
[3]*b*[	On (?) [...
[4]*lq[ḥ*	[PN...] took
[5]*mx*[	PN
[6]*bn*[	PN
[7]*bn*[	PN
[8]*w.yn*[	and PN

---

93 For a convenient presentation of text with translation, see McGeough, *Ugaritic Economic Tablets*, 175.

94 See Jack M. Sasson, "Canaanite Maritime Involvement in the Second Millennium B.C.", *JAOS* 86 (1966) 136; M. Dijkstra, "Ugaritic Stylistics. 1 Ugaritic Prose", in *Handbook of Ugaritic Studies*, 146; D. M. Clements, *Sources for Ugaritic Ritual and Sacrifice. Vol. I: Ugaritic and Ugarit Akkadian Texts* (AOAT 248/1; 2001) 352; *DULAT* 651; and McGeough, *Exchange Relationships at Ugarit*, 132, and *Ugaritic Economic Tablets*, 175. Sasson compared Akkadian *ḫarrānu* and Sumerian KASKAL, which mean both "road" and "business venture". For a different view, see Mario Liverani, "La dotazione dei mercanti di Ugarit", *UF* 11 (1979 = C. F. A. Schaeffer Festschrift) 495–503. Liverani takes *ntbt* as "donations", but the putative cognate with Akkadian *nadānu*, "to give", would involve an irregular correspondence of consonants.

95 McGeough, *Ugaritic Economic Tablets*, 220.

96 In theory, lines 2–3 could contain dating the formulary as seen in the example above (and following); if so, line 1 may contain some sort of additional subscription or label.

[9]*bn.ʿdr*[	son of[97] PN
[10]*ntb*[t	rout[e(s)]
[11]*b.ʾarb*[ʿ	for 40[0...][98]
ḫr[ṣ	in go[ld].

The same situation obtains in KTU 4.266[99], but with one crucially different term, in line 5:

[1]*b.ym.ḥdṯ*	On the day of the new moon,
[2]*b.yr*<*ḫ*>.*pgrm*	in the month of *pgrm*,
[3]*lqḥ.b ʿlm ʿdr*	PN took
[4]*w.bn.ḫlp*	and PN
[5]*m ʾiḫd*	GN/the harbor
[6]*b.ʾarbʿ* [7]*m ʾat.*	for 400
[7]*ḫrṣ*	in gold.

This text uses the same formulary as KTU 4.336, except that instead of *ntbt* in the former, the sale of trading rights in the latter involves *ma ʾḫd*, literally the harbor serving Ugarit[100]. In both cases, the text concerns financial arrangements for trade. The word *ntbt* applies to land-routes, and *ma ʾḫd* to the sea-route stop-over[101].

Finally, one Ugaritic letter bears on *nĕtîbôt* in Judg 5:6. At the same time, it is important to mention that this passage is poorly preserved and its precise context is debated. KTU 2.36 evidently concerns Egypt's *ntbt* through the kingdom of Ugarit. The letter is an Ugaritic copy of a letter sent by the queen, Puduhepa, to the king of Ugarit. In the pertinent but rather broken section, in lines 14–22,

---

97 The preceding *w-* in line 8 would suggest that the name that follows may be the last PN, hence *bn* in line 9 is not a separate PN but the further specific of the name of the person presumably mentioned in line 8.

98 Note the price in the following document.

99 For a convenient presentation of text with translation, see McGeough, *Ugaritic Economic Tablets*, 198–99. See also the nearly identical text, KTU 4.172, in McGeough, *Ugaritic Economic Tablets*, 200.

100 See Jack M. Sasson, "Canaanite Maritime Involvement in the Second Millennium B.C.", *JAOS* 86 (1966) 136, followed by Michael Astour, "Maʾhadu, the Harbor of Ugarit", *Journal of the Economic and Social History of the Orient* 13 (1970) 120; and Cohen, *Biblical Hapax Legomena*, 70 n. 127. Note also E. Y. Kutscher, "[mḥwz] = Harbour in the DSS", *IEJ* 25 (1961) 160–61. For options, see M. Dietrich and O. Loretz, "Ugaritisch *mi/aḫd* 'Hafen' und *m(i/a)ḫdy* 'Hafenbewohner'", *UF* 32 (2000) 195–201. See also *DULAT* 514, citing 4.172.6 and 4.266.5. Note also the older study of Michael Astour, "Maʾaḫadu, the Harbor of Ugarit", *JESHO* 13 (1970) 113–27, here 120.

101 For the BH use of this word-field for sea routes, see 1 Kgs 18:43; Ps 8:9; Prov 30:19; cf. Hab 3:15.

the king has expressed his desire that caravans going to Egypt would pass through Ugarit[102]:

> [14]Concerning (?) the message that you sent to the royal palace: [15]"[and no]w (?)[103], as for Egypt's (right of) way (ntbt), [16]Egypt's (right of) [wa]y (ntbt) should stop(?)[104] in the land of Ugarit.

It is feasible to understand the word *ntbt*, attested in lines 15–16 as "the caravans of Egypt"[105], but it has been argued that it more specifically involves the "right of way" of Egypt[106]. The latter would be in keeping with the other attestations of *ntbt* in these documents, but the text is admittedly very broken and difficult at this point. The lines that follow in this section of the letter are even more broken.

These Ugaritic passages offer considerably more about *ntbt* than what the BH dictionaries tell us about this cognate with *nĕtîbôt* in Judg 5:6. If we only took the sense of the word from these sources, this would be little indication beyond a general meaning. As mentioned in the discussion above, the following is what was offered for the BH word: "path" (*BDB* 677; *KB* [fourth ed.] 2.732); "via, semita" (Zorrell 538); "path, pathway" (*DCH* V:783); "derek, šabil; ʾoraḥ" (Kaddari 738); and perhaps the best for Judges 5:6, "caravan route" (*TDOT* 3:280). For the listing for the Ugaritic cognate, the word receives a mention in two of these BH resources, though without a separate gloss. More telling, none of these sources for BH *nĕtîbôt* offers any indication of what the Ugaritic information might provide for interpreting the biblical word. These Ugaritic texts evoke an economic world of trade, both on land and by sea, which involves not only the physical platform for this activity (roads and harbor), but also the economic practice of control that informs it. It also entails a local authority vis-à-vis those engaged in trade and travel. It is the combination of the physical reality, its mechanism

---

102 See Jesús-Luis Cunchillos, *TO* 2.404–6, and "The Correspondence of Ugarit", in *Handbook of Ugaritic Studies*, 368.

103 Commentators generally following Pardee's reconstruction of the particle *w-* plus [*h*]*t*; see Cunchillos, *TO* 2.404 n. 182.

104 The interpretation of *ʾušbtm* is most difficult. If the form is not a verb (initial *ʾu* representing a significant difficulty), perhaps it is to be taken as a *ʾu-* preformative noun of *šbt, in effect "there is a stop (?)". However, as indicated by the controversy rehearsed in *TO* 2.405–6 n. 185 (note also *DULAT* 806–7), the interpretation remains uncertain, and the same form in KTU 2.3.10 hardly clarifies the matter.

105 See Cunchillos, *TO* 2.404–6.

106 M. Dietrich and O. Loretz, "Ugaritisch *mi/aḫd* 'Hafen' und *m(i/a)ḫdy* 'Hafenbewohner'", *UF* 32 (2000) 195–96; and the discussion in *DULAT* 651.

of economic exchange and the parties that interact in it that appears to be central not only to the Ugaritic contexts, but also to Judg 5:6. I am not suggesting that the word in Judg 5:6 refers to (or "means") precisely the same economic practice as what appears in these Ugaritic passages (although in its historical context this could be the issue involved for Judg 5:6); what can be reasonably discerned is that both Judg 5:6 and the Ugaritic passages noted here concern economic control of roads significant to their users as well as the physical reality of these roads. Further comparison and contrast help to refine the sense of the word in the two corpora.

The Ugaritic texts point to concerns about trade routes by members of Ugarit's elite. The parties involved in trade appear also to be elites, operating at an international scale. In contrast, Judges 5 may register a local complaint over the lack of access to trade routes by Israelites, which may involve both less well-to-do as well as relative elites, though hardly the international elites apparently envisioned in the Ugaritic texts. The Ugaritic texts, especially KTU 2.36, and Judges 5 may provide two sides of the picture in the conditions involving trade routes. The Ugaritic texts point to the financial management of trading routes and rights of ways, while Judges 5 suggest a complaint of the loss of such rights of use or rights of way on the part of local users of such routes. The poem at this point in v. 6 may understand the cause of battle as Israel's loss of the use of the trade route or right of way through the Jezreel Valley[107].

Although separate from the lexical focus of this discussion, it is to be noted that such a situation may fit better in the Iron I period than in the Iron II when the Israelites controlled the Jezreel Valley[108]. If so, then the Ugaritic sources would not be so far in time from the situation evoked in Judges 5:6[109].

---

107 See J. David Schloen, "Caravans, Kenites, and *Casus Belli*: Enmity and Alliance in the Song of Deborah", *CBQ* 55 (1993) 18–38. For related topography, see Dale W. Manor, "The Topography and Geography of the Jezreel Valley as They Contribute to the Battles of Deborah and Gideon", *Near Eastern Archaeological Society Bulletin* ns 28 (1987) 25–33.

108 Such control would be a major goal of the monarchy in the north, as reflected in the description of Solomon's activity in the north. Even if 1 Kgs 9:15, with its reference to Hazor, does not prove to be historical, control of major routes across Israel would be a goal for the early northern monarchy. For this point, see Israel Finkelstein and Nadav Na'aman, "Shechem of the Amarna Period and Rise of the Northern Kingdom of Israel", *IEJ* 55 (2005) 182.

109 For other reasons, I would see the verse as part of the Iron IIA contribution of the composer's construction of the poems's introduction. See my book, *Poetic Heroes*.

V. General Considerations

These examples show the rich potential of cognates for elucidating BH words. In addition to offering cognates, the contexts of the BH words and their extra-biblical contexts are interesting to compare. In the case of the words in the Elijah-Elisha corpus, these instances also offer some inkling of differences in northern versus southern dialects of Hebrew[110], which lexical resources could include in their discussions of these words. As all of these examples illustrate, dictionaries of biblical Hebrew or "classical Hebrew" delimited by language risk incurring some loss of valuable information about words.

The sort of comparative consideration represented by the Ugaritic-Hebrew cases is given little or no place in the current state of BH dictionaries or lexica, even though in these cases Ugaritic stands closer in time and cultural proximity than post-exilic Hebrew. Some of the more recent lexical resources stay within Hebrew (e.g., *The Dictionary of Classical Hebrew*, Kaddari), while others that do consider comparative data keep their discussions at a fairly general level of comparison of individual words in other languages, with little indication of their usage (e.g., Zorrell, *KB* fourth edition, *TDOT* and some entries in the *Semantics of Ancient Hebrew Database*). While these works offer wonderful resources, on the comparative score they arguably operate at a certain cost to understanding words more concretely. Some might say that dictionaries should not or cannot do such in-depth comparison of words in other languages in their contexts, that such work falls beyond the parameters of what it means to produce a dictionary. To be sure, the field could indeed benefit from updated versions of traditional dictionaries, such as *BDB*[111].

At the same time, what I think the field could truly use is an encyclopedia of words and their usages that include the specific cultural context of the word, whether it is political, economic, social or material. As a field, we need a more encyclopedic approach to what dictionaries ought or can do, ones that will present not only more exegetical context inside a text (this task the *Semantics of Ancient Hebrew Database* does do, although to my mind with not enough

---

110 For proper procedures, see William Schniedewind and Daniel Sivan, "The Elijah-Elisha Narratives: A Test Case for the Northern Dialect of Hebrew", *JQR* 87 (1997) 303–37, largely a critical review of Rendsburg, *Israelian Hebrew in the Book of Kings*.

111 See the note along these lines in Jo Ann Hackett and John Huehnergard, "Revising and Updating BDB", in *Foundations for Syriac Lexicography III: Colloquia of the International Syriac Language Project* (ed. Janet Dyk and W. T. van Peursen; PSL 4; Piscataway, NJ: Gorgias, 2008) 227–33. The authors are planning to produce a new BH dictionary based on BDB at some point in the not-too-distant future (John Huehnergard, personal communication).

citation of contexts of the words in parallelism or with reference to the literary *topoi* or genres); it will also include the relevant material from outside of the text, whether that means other textual corpora, material culture or iconography. What I have in mind is a tool of and for research (and not primarily for purposes of translation)[112]. This project should be informed by the comparative approach of Moshe Held and his students, as mentioned earlier. In identifying semantically comparable words (and even phrases) in comparable contexts across different languages and not only etymologically related words, this approach would increase the fund of comparative material worth including in such an encyclopedic project. It should also include relevant iconographic and archaeological information.

My major concern involves the meanings of words at the intersection of their internal and external worlds, between their contexts within and across texts and the contexts in their cultures that words relate to, refer to and evoke. Generally I think of words as evoking all kinds of worlds, of different realms of experience and worldview. At the most basic level, the modern scholarly study of individual words, it appears to me, sometimes misses the basic consideration of what words meant in the experience of ancient authors and audiences. What were words' basic denotations and connotations for them? What experience of life and the world did words draw on and conjure up? I have given discussions that illustrate this point about cultural context: one involving the language and practice of statuary (*ṣelem* and *dĕmût*); another entailing a political coinage (*yiqqĕhat*); a third set of terms for plants in rural settings (**biṣqalôn* and *'ōrōt*), with a fourth for magical praxis (**ghr*); and a fifth about economic practice (*nĕtîbôt*).

When lexical investigation is configured according to a notion of the word that does not consider its cultural context, then linguistic reasoning has omitted what is potentially some of its most informative help. Words may be quite specific in terms of their material reality or their social, political or economic backgrounds. Without material or cultural context, scholarship on biblical lexicography may gloss over particulars crucial for understanding a word and its worlds. So this, I suppose, is my basic point: a word without their worlds, without their internal literary contexts and external cultural realities, is not a word, as any user would have understood it.

---

112 For a proposal for a tool for translators, see John Lübbe, "An Old Testament Dictionary of Semantic Domains", *ZAH* 9 (1996) 52–57.

Ingo Kottsieper

„Was du ererbt von deinen Vätern ... "

Eine Randbemerkung zur hebräischen Lexikographie

1. Einleitung

Seit der lateinischen Ausgabe der 3. Auflage von Gesenius' „Hebräisches und chaldäisches Handwörterbuch" begleitet der Satz „Dies diem docet" – „der Tag lehrt den Tag" – die vielfältigen Neuauflagen dieses epochemachenden Werkes und darf durchaus als ein Mottosatz der jüngeren hebräischen Lexikographie gelten. Offensichtlich wollte Gesenius mit dieser klassischen Phrase, die auf die Sentenz *Discipulus est prioris posterior dies* („Schüler des vorigen ist der folgende Tag") des Publilius Syrus zurückgeht, auf den rasanten Fortschritt hinweisen, den die hebräische Lexikographie gerade mit seiner eigenen, unermüdlichen Forschertätigkeit nahm und der sich in den immer neuen erweiterten und überarbeiteten Wörterbüchern niederschlug.[1] In der Tat war diese wissenschaftliche Entwicklung revolutionär: durch die Etablierung der Semitistik und beständige Neufunde standen nun für das Verständnis der hebräischen Texte und ihres

---

1 Im Weiteren werden die verschiedenen Ausgaben des Handwörterbuches mit Ges und die Nummer der Ausgabe als Index angegeben: Ges$_0$: Wilhelm Gesenius, *Hebräisch-Deutsches Handwörterbuch über die Schriften des Alten Testaments I*. Leipzig: Friedrich Christian Wilhelm Vogel, 1810; Ges$_2$: Wilhelm Gesenius, *Hebräisches und chaldäisches Handwörterbuch über die Schriften des Alten Testaments I*. Leipzig: Friedrich Christian Wilhelm Vogel, 1823; Ges$_{17}$: Frants Buhl, *Wilhelm Gesenius' Hebräisches und aramäisches Handwörterbuch über das Alte Testament. 17. Auflage*. Berlin, Göttingen und Heidelberg: Springer, 1915; Ges$_{18}$: Rudolf Meyer (†) und Herbert Donner, *Wilhelm Gesenius Hebräisches und aramäisches Handwörterbuch über das Alte Testament. 18. Auflage*. Berlin u. a.: Springer, 1987–2012. Weitere Abkürzungen für gebräuchliche Wörterbücher sind: AHw: Wolfram von Soden, *Akkadisches Handwörterbuch I – III*. Wiesbaden: Otto Harrassowitz, 1965–1981; CAD I/1: A. Leo Oppenheimer u. a., The Assyrian Dictionary 1/I, Chicago: Oriental Institute 1964; HAL: Walter Baumgartner, *Hebräisches und aramäisches Lexikon zum Alten Testament I– V + Suppl. 3. Auflage*. Leiden: Brill, 1967–1996; KBL: Ludwig Köhler und Walter Baumgartner, *Lexicon in Veteris Testamenti Libros. 2. Auflage*. Leiden: Brill, 1958; KAHAL: Walter Dietrich und Samuel Arnet (Hg.), *Konzise und aktualisierte Ausgabe des Hebräischen und Aramäischen Lexikons zum Alten Testament*. Leiden: Brill, 2013; *Thesaurus*: Wilhem Gesenius, *Thesaurus philologicus criticus linguae Hebraeae et Chaldaeae Veteris Testamenti I*. Leipzig: Friedrich Christian Wilhelm Vogel, 1835; Soweit nichts anderes angegeben ist, beziehen sich die Verweise auf Wörterbücher grundsätzlich auf den Eintrag des gerade behandelten Lemmas.

Wortschatzes neue Quellen und fundiertere Methoden zur Verfügung, mit denen die alt ererbten Traditionen der traditionellen Bibelübersetzungen und der jüdischen Gelehrten des Mittelalters kritisch evaluiert und die hebräische Wortforschung auf eine breitere und solidere Basis gestellt werden konnten. Gesenius selbst macht dies in der 2. Auflage seines Handwörterbuches von 1823 deutlich, in dessen Einleitung er unter dem Titel „Von den Quellen der hebräischen Wortforschung nebst einigen Regeln und Beobachtungen über den Gebrauch derselben" dezidiert Rechenschaft über die Grundlagen seiner lexikographischen Arbeit ablegt. Darin führt er aber auch aus, dass neben dem sich aus dem Kontext ergebenden Sinn der Wörter, dem Zeugnis der frühen Übersetzungen – und hier insbesondere der LXX – und den Hinweisen des Sprachvergleiches immer noch die mittelalterliche jüdische lexikographische Tradition eine wertvolle Quelle bleibt, die vor seiner Zeit neben dem berühmten, hebräisch abgefassten Sefær Haš-Šorāšîm von David (ben Josef ben) Qimḥī im Wesentlichen über ihre Aufnahme in die jüdischen Kommentare zugänglich war.[2] Die ursprünglich judeo-arabischen Texte der jüdischen Sprachwissenschaftler des Mittelalters wurden erst ab der Mitte des 19. Jahrhunderts der westlichen europäischen Hebraistik in halbwegs verlässlichen Editionen zugänglich. Gesenius war auch hierin bahnbrechend, dass er bei seiner lexikographischen Arbeit umfassende Exzerpte insbesondere aus der Oxforder Handschrift des *Kitāb al-ʾUṣūl* des Abū-l-walīd Merwān ibn Ǧanāḥ zu Rate zog, dessen Arbeit er ausdrücklich lobt.[3] Aber auch das spätere Sefær Haš-Šorāšîm von Qimḥī wurde von Gesenius[4] (und anderen Lexikographen) als Quelle herangezogen.

Die mittelalterliche hebräische Lexikographie ist jedoch ein Produkt der Bestrebungen, nach dem Aussterben des Hebräischen als gesprochene Sprache diese als literarische Hochsprache in der Form des klassischen Biblisch-Hebräischen wieder zu beleben. Seinen Anfang hatte dieser Neuansatz in den Piyyutim, die bewusst – aber auch kreativ – an das Biblisch-Hebräische anknüpften. Bestärkt wurde das Interesse an der „klassischen" Sprachform zudem durch den hohen Stellenwert, den das „klassische" Arabische insbesondere des Korans und dann auch der Dichtung für den arabischen Kulturraum gewann und dessen Beherrschung Ausweis kultureller und intellektueller Höhe wurde. Der jüdische Uni-

---

2 Im Folgenden wird die Ausgabe von Johannes H. R. Biesenthal und F. Lebrecht, ספר השרשים לרבי דויד בן יוסף קמחי הספרדי [*Rabbi Davidis Kimchi radicum liber sive hebraeum bibliorum lexicon*] (Berlin: G. Bethge, 1847), zugrunde gelegt. Ein weiteres, einflussreiches Wörterbuch war auch die Maḥbæræt des Ben Parḥôn; benutzt wurde die Ausgabe von Salomo Gottlieb Stern, מחברת הערוך [*Salomonis Ben Abraham Aragonensi Lexicon Hebraicum*] (Pressburg: Anton von Schmid, 1844).
3 Vgl. Ges$_2$ 12–14.
4 Vgl. Ges$_2$ 14–15.

versalgelehrte Saadja Gaon, der im 9. Jh. n. Chr. mit seinen sprachlichen Arbeiten am Anfang der (uns erhaltenen)[5] sprachwissenschaftlichen Tradition des mittelalterlichen Judentums steht, verweist ausdrücklich in der arabischen Einleitung zu seinem *Kitāb al-ʾuṣūl aš-šiʿr al-ʿibrānī*, der von ihm selbst besorgten arabischen Edition seines älteren, hebräisch verfassten *Hā-ʾÆgrôn* (trad. Egron), auf diese Vorbilder aus der arabischen Umwelt. Und das Werk selbst war in seiner hebräischen Urfassung ein Reimwörterbuch, das den Dichter bei der Abfassung von Poesie in klassischer Sprache unterstützen sollte und das erst durch seine arabische Fassung auch zu einem Bedeutungswörterbuch wurde.[6]

Natürlich spielten auch exegetische Interessen bei der Herausbildung der jüdischen Sprachwissenschaft im Mittelalter eine wichtige Rolle, wobei die Auseinandersetzung zwischen den Karäern und den Rabbaniten um das rechte Verständnis des nun durch die masoretische Arbeit im Detail festgestellten Textes der hebräischen Bibel ein nicht zu unterschätzendes Motiv gewesen sein dürfte. Karäische Gelehrte, die dezidiert rabbanitische Traditionen abwiesen, mussten ihr Verständnis der biblisch-hebräischen Texte ebenso nachvollziehbar belegen, wie rabbanitische Exegeten ihre Tradition als textgerecht verteidigen. So dürfte es kein Zufall sein, dass das zweite lexikographische Werk Saadjas (*Kitāb as-sabʿīn lafẓa al-mufrada*) Hapax legomena bzw. sehr seltene Wörter der hebräischen Bibel mittels rabbinischem Wortgebrauch erklärt.[7]

---

5 Natürlich ist nicht auszuschließen, dass schon vor Saadja andere, insbesondere karäische Gelehrte, die ihre Auslegungen allein auf den Text der hebräischen Bibel stützten, hebraistische Studien betrieben und vielleicht auch schon Beiträge zur „klassischen" hebräischen Sprache schrieben; diese wären aber dann völlig verloren gegangen.

6 Dass dabei der auch dichterisch tätige Saadja eine Wiederbelebung der „heiligen Sprache, die unser Gott von alters her erwählt hat und in der seine heiligen Engel ihn besingen (Sela) und in der ihn alle Söhne des Höchsten verehren" (vgl. Saadjas hebräisches Vorwort zum Egron in Neḥemya Allony, האגרון. כתאב אצול אלשער אלעבראני *[Ha'Egron. Kitāb ʿuṣūl al-shiʿr al-ʿibrānī]* (Jerusalem: The Academy of the Hebrew Language, 1969), 156–163, der hebräische Text des Zitats auf S. 156.), als Hochsprache der jüdischen Gemeinschaft im Sinn hatte, entspricht ebenfalls der arabischen Sprachideologie des „klassisch-koranischen" Arabischen als der von Gott gewählten Reinform der Sprache. Dieser religiös-ästhetische Zugang zum Hebräischen wird auch in dem Titel deutlich, den Saadja seinem grammatischem Werk gab: *Kitāb faṣīḥ luġat al-ʿibrāniyyīn* „Buch des Korrekten in der Hebräischen Sprache". فصيح bezeichnet im Arabischen insbesondere die sprachliche Korrektheit und Reinheit eines sprachlichen Ausdruckes und konnotiert dabei auch die darin sich manifestierende Schönheit; vgl. Aron Dotan, אור ראשון בחכמת הלשון. ספר צחות לשון העברים לרב סעדיה גאון *[The Dawn of Hebrew Linguistics. The Book of Elegance of the Language of the Hebrews] I – II* (Magnes: Jerusalem, 1997), I 30.

7 Saadja selber datierte das Ende des „klassischen" Hebräischen als gesprochene Sprache unter Bezugnahme auf Neh 13 und dem *Sedær ʿÔlām Rabbā* an das Ende der persischen Zeit: „Im Jahr 101 nach der Zerstörung der Stadt unseres Gottes fingen wir an, die heilige Sprache aufzugeben

Dies führt zu der Frage, auf welcher Grundlage die lexikographischen Arbeiten des Mittelalters die Bedeutung der Lemmata des Biblisch-Hebräischen bestimmten. Die Vorgehensweise der späteren dezidierten Lexikographen mutet durchaus modern an und ist nicht allzu weit von den „Quellen der hebräischen Wortforschung" im Sinne Gesenius' entfernt. Ein wesentlicher Schritt bestand darin, die einzelnen Lemmata und ihren Bedeutungshorizont dadurch zu bestimmen, dass man sie in Bedeutungsgruppen aufteilte und entsprechende Belegstellen im Kontext anführte. Die Bedeutung kann dabei auch mit Verweis auf externe Informationen begründet sein. Als Beispiel sei hier zunächst der Eintrag zu כלב aus einem der ersten in dieser Form abgefassten Wörterbüchern geboten, die Maḥbæræt (Menaḥem) des Menaḥem (ben Josef) ibn Sarūq (910 – 970)[8]:

> כלב teilt sich in drei Abteilungen auf:
> Die erste: והנה כלוב קיץ (Am 8,1), ככלוב מלא עוף (Jer 5,27): Diese weisen die Bedeutung „Korb"
> auf.
> Die zweite: לא יחרץ כלב לשונו (Ex 11,7), והכלבים עזי נפש (Jes 56,11), לשית עם כלבי צוני (Hi 30,1):
> entsprechend ihrer (üblichen) Bedeutung.
> Die dritte: והאיש קשה ורע מעללים והוא כלב (1 Sam 25,3): aus der Sippe Kalebs; und deshalb
> beginnt das Wort mit *Kaf*.

Bei Sarūq werden externe Informationen noch sehr zurückhaltend geboten und beschränken sich in unserem Beispiel auf den zweiten Teil, in dem er auf die allgemein bekannte Bedeutung des Wortes כֶּלֶב „Hund" verweist. Dabei bleibt offen, ob Sarūq mit diesem Verweis sagen will, dass diese Bedeutung aus der (arabischen) Umgangssprache seiner Leser abzuleiten, oder aber, dass diese dem gebildeten jüdischen Leser aus den ihm bekannten Texten geläufig sei. Wahrscheinlich hat sich diese Frage, die kontrovers zwischen den Schülern Sarūqs und Dunāš ibn Labrāṭ (920 – 990) und dessen Anhängern diskutiert wurde und auch

---

und die Sprachen der landfremden Völker zu sprechen – 3 Jahre bevor der König von Griechenland seine Herrschaft antrat. In den Tagen des Statthalters Nehemia und seiner Männer mussten wir fürwahr solche sehen, die Aschdoditisch sprachen. Und er zürnte darüber und schalt sie und stritt mit ihnen." (Vorwort des Egron, hebr. Text bei Allony, האגרון, 158) Nach dem *Sedær 'Ôlām Rabbā* betrug die Zeit der Perser 104 Jahre = 70 Jahre Exil + 34 Jahre während des 2. Tempels. Wenn er im *Kitāb as-sabʿīn* aber insbesondere das tannaitische Hebräische heranzieht, so wird deutlich, dass er damit eine Kontinuität zwischen diesem und dem klassischen Hebräischen voraussetzt und damit zugleich deutlich macht, dass seiner Meinung nach die rabbanitische Tradition auf einer ausreichenden Kenntnis selbst der schwierigsten klassisch-hebräischen Wörter beruht.

8 Vgl. Ángel Saénz-Badillos, *Menahem ben Saruq: Mahberet. Edición crítica e introducción* (Granada: Universidad de Granada, 1986).

später noch zu akademischen Auseinandersetzungen führte,[9] Sarūq selbst nicht in dieser Form gestellt. Für die Bestimmung der Bedeutung eines Lemmas spielte aber die targumische Tradition von Anfang an eine große Rolle. Dabei sind zwei Verfahren zu unterscheiden: Zum einen konnte die targumische Übersetzung eines Wortes zur Klärung herangezogen werden, zum anderen konnte auch ein in den Targumen belegtes und nach Ansicht des Lexikographen identisches Wort, das aber im Targum für ein anderes hebräisches Wort benutzt wird, zur Gleichung zwischen beiden Lemmata herangezogen werden.[10]

Das erste Verfahren – die Ableitung der Bedeutung eines Wortes aus der targumischen Übersetzung – bildet dabei ein Hauptfundament der mittelalterlichen Lexikographie, wie z. B. der Eintrag כלב in dem späteren *Kitāb al-'uṣūl* des Ibn Ǧanāḥ *expressis verbis* zeigt:

הכלב אנכי (1 Sam 17,43): bekannt.

כלוב קיץ (Am 8,1): Korb; *und von diesem sagt das Targum* מאן מלי ביזפי קיטא.

ככלוב מלא עוף (Jer 5,27): Käfig; *und von diesem sagt das Targum* דמלי עופא כבית פטימא; und R. Hai sagt in Bezug auf die Phrase in der Mischna האקון והרטוב והכלוב (mKel 23,5) „Käfig" und führt ככלוב מלא עוף (Am 8,1) an.[11]

והוא כלבי (1 Sam 25,3): Einer, der mit Kaleb verbunden ist.

---

9 Vgl. A. Maman, *Comparative Semitic Philology in the Middle Ages. From Saʿadiah Gaon to Ibn Barūn (10th – 12th C.)* (Studies in Semitic Languages and Linguistics XL; Leiden: Brill, 2004), 276 – 279.

10 Die Targume werden wie folgt abgekürzt: TgO = Targum Onqelos; TgJ = Targum Jonatan; TgPsJ = Targum Pseudo-Jonatan; TgN = Targum Neofiti; TgF = Fragmenten Targum; MS.E = Manuskript E nach Michael L. Klein, *Genizah Manuscripts of Palestinian Targum to the Pentateuch I – II* (Cincinnati: Hebrew Union College Press, 1986); TgS[A/J]= Ms. A bzw. J des samaritanischen Targums; vgl. die Ausgabe von Abraham Tal, התרגום השומרוני לתורה *[The Samaritan Targum of the Pentateuch]* I – III, (Tel-Aviv: Tel-Aviv University, 1980 – 1983).

11 Der Mischnahkommentar des Hai Gaon (bar Šerīrā; 939 – 1038) hat sich nicht erhalten und ist wohl kaum identisch mit dem anonymen Kommentar(teil), den 1856 Alexander Rosenberg in seiner Edition Hai zugeschrieben hat, vgl. A. Rosenberg, ספר קובץ מעשי ידי הגאונים קדמונים (Berlin: Friedländer'sche Buchdruckerei, 1851), Teil 1: פירוש רבינו האי גאון על סדר טהרות. So findet sich diese Deutung ebenso wenig in diesem dann später erneut auf einer breiteren Manuskriptbasis und korrekter von Epstein edierten Text (J.N. Epstein, פירוש הגאונים על סדר טהרות מיוחס לרב האיי גאון ז"ל I – II [Schriften des Vereins Mekize Nirdamin 3/21+23; Berlin: Zwi Hirsch Itzaqowski, 1921/24]; vgl. auch ders. ״פירוש הגאונים״ תשלום, *Tarbiẓ* 16 [1945]: 71– 134) wie die übrigen bei Ibn Ǧanāḥ angeführten Zitate; vgl. ders., *Der gaonäische Kommentar zur Ordnung Toharot. Eine kritische Einleitung zu dem R. Hai Gaon zugeschriebenen Kommentar* (Berlin: Mayer & Müller, 1915), 1– 35, zu den Zitaten aus Ibn Ǧanāḥ 4 – 10, zu unserer Stelle S. 6 – 7. Interessanterweise findet sich diese Deutung aber im Mischnakommentar des Maimonides *ad. loc.*, der zwar keine Quelle angibt aber diese ebenfalls aus dem Kommentar Hais entnommen haben könnte: והכלוב, אלקפץ ככלוב מלא עוף.

Dass aber auch schon für Sarūq das Targum eine autoritative Quelle war, auch wenn er es normalerweise nicht ausdrücklich anführt, macht z. B. der Eintrag zu איתן deutlich:

איתן מושבך (Num 24,21), נחל איתן (Dtn 21,4; vgl. Am 5,24),לאיתנו (Ex 14,27); וישב הים לפנות בקר והאתנים מוסדי ארץ (Mi 6,2), ותשב באיתן קשתו (Gen 49,24): eine einzige Deutung haben sie. Sie weisen die Bedeutung „Kraft" und „Stärke" (תוקף) auf.

Schon die targumische Tradition gibt in den meisten Fällen איתן mit der Wurzel תקף wieder,[12] woraus nicht nur Sarūq wohl geschlossen hat, dass das Wort grundsätzlich etwas mit Stärke (תוקף) zu tun hat. Dabei spricht für den targumischen Hintergrund nicht nur, dass Sarūq das Wort תוקף sonst kaum benutzt,[13] sondern auch, dass er am Ende dieses Lemmaeintrags ausdrücklich auf TgO zu Gen 49,24 verweist und klarstellt, dass das Targum dort ותשב באיתן קשתו mit ושוי תוקפא רוחצניה übersetzt und der im Targum vorangehende Text eine kommentierende Zufügung ist. Somit kann davon ausgegangen werden, dass auch schon die frühen Lexikographen wie Sarūq das Targum als wichtige Quelle benutzten, auch wenn es nur dann ausdrücklich erwähnt wird, wenn der Bezug nicht offensichtlich ist.[14]

---

12 So in drei der vier auch bei Sarūq aufgeführten Torabelege: Gen 49,24; Ex 14,27; Num 24,21; vgl. weiterhin Jer 5,15; Ps 74,15; Hi 12,19; 33,19; Prov 13,15; vgl. auch Am 5,24, wo נחל איתן im TgJ mit נחל מגבר wiedergegeben wird. Dtn 21,4 bietet TgO mit ביר דלא יתפלח ביה ולא יזדרע offenkundig eher eine Interpretation des folgenden אשר לא יעבד בו ולא יזרע und somit war erkennbar, dass mit ביר hier nicht eine wörtliche Übersetzung von איתן vorlag. Ähnliches gilt auch für die Paraphrase von Jer 49,19 ‖ 50,44, wobei aber wohl kaum zufällig das Wort תקיף, wenn auch am Ende des Verses und nicht an der Stelle von איתן vom Targumisten in die Aussage eingebracht wurde, und schließlich Mi 6,2, wo die Wiedergabe mit עיקריא sich von der Apposition מסדי ארץ herleitet, die im hebr. Text איתן näher bestimmt.

13 Soweit ich sehe, begegnet תוקף textlich sicher nur noch zweimal: 1) Als Bedeutungsangabe für חסן, wo Sarūq neben biblisch-aramäisch Dan 2,37 + 4,27 nur Jes 1,31 und 33,6 zitiert und TgJ an beiden Stellen auch תקוף hat. Diese Stelle ist somit auch von der targumischen Tradition abhängig; 2) In der langen exegetischen Ausführung zum Bund, der mit dem Hindurchgehen zwischen zwei Tierhälften geschlossen wird, die Sarūq s.v. בתר bietet, findet sich die Phrase תוקף מעוזה als nahezu hymnische Bezeichnung der zwingenden Kraft des göttlichen Bundes, dem menschliche Bünde nicht vergleichbar sind (כי זאת הברית אין כמוה ואין כתוקף מעוזה), eine Phrase, die sonst nur noch bei Dunaš parallel zu עוצם כוח in Bezug auf das göttliche Einschreiten gemäß Jes 63,1 ff. benutzt wird (ועל כן הביא המגפה הזאת הנביא). להודיע תוקף מעוזם ועוצם כוחם וכבוד האלה׳ים עשה (באמרו "חסדי יי אזכיר תהילות יי". und offenkundig als elativischer Ausdruck zur Zeit der Gaonim geläufig war, vgl. Ángel Saénz-Badillos, *Teshubot de Dunash ben Labrat* (Granada: Universidad de Granada 1980), 72. Ein weiterer Beleg s.v. בלג ist nur in einem Teil der Manuskripte belegt und wohl nicht ursprünglich.

14 Entsprechend führt Sarūq Onqelos noch s.v. טח an und diskutiert dort, dass dessen Übersetzung von Gen 21,16 nicht der Interpretation von כמטחוי mit משך widersprechen würde.

Auch die zweite Form des Gebrauchs insbesondere des TgO findet sich schon bei Sarūq, wie z. B. der Eintrag zu כפן deutlich macht:

בחסר ובכפן גלמוד (Hi 30,3), כפנה שרשיה עליו (Hes 17,7): Ein Ausdruck der Hungersnot (רעבון) sind sie. Und jedes רעב ist im Aramäischen כפנא.

Das Wort כפן begegnet nicht in der Tora und wird im TgJ zu Hes 17,7 durchaus sachgerecht nicht mit כָּפָן ”Hunger“, sondern mit der Verbalwurzel כפן ”sich zu-wenden“ identifiziert und mit כפי wiedergegeben. Das Targum zu Hiob hat sowohl in 30,3 als auch in 5,22 אולצן für כָּפָן. Das targumische כְּפַן ist aber bei Onqelos die übliche Übersetzung für hebräisch רָעָב, woraus Sarūq die Gleichung hebr. כָּפָן = aram. כְּפַן = hebr. רָעָב ableitet.

Dass insbesondere die babylonisch-targumische Tradition des TgO zur Tora eine autoritative Rolle für die mittelalterliche jüdische Sprachwissenschaft besaß, ist angesichts des autoritativen Charakters dieses Targums nicht verwunderlich. Es wies wie die hebräische Bibel sogar eine eigene Masora auf,[15] und seine Sprache, die ein früher Abkömmling des Jüdisch-Literarisch-Aramäischen aus der Zeit des 2. Tempels ist,[16] wirkt gegenüber dem rabbinischem und späterem ga-onäischem Aramäischen ähnlich „klassisch“ wie das Biblisch-Hebräische.

Diese kurzen Hinweise sollen genügen zu verdeutlichen, dass die mittelal-terliche jüdische Lexikographie an vielen Stellen die Deutung des Targums vertritt, auch wenn dies häufig nicht explizit gesagt wird. Insbesondere TgO wurde als kaum zu überbietende Autorität bei der Deutung hebräischer Wörter angesehen. Mithin ist bei jedem Verweis auf die mittelalterlichen Quellen zu prüfen, inwieweit diese etwas Neues in die Diskussion einbringen oder inwieweit sie die targumische Deutung eines Textes wiedergeben und diese dann gegebenenfalls mit weiteren Argumenten unterfüttern, in dem z. B. auf (scheinbar) parallele arabische Wörter verwiesen wird.

Sowohl das Targum als auch die mittelalterliche lexikographische Tradition trat als explizit aufgenommene Quelle in der modernen Lexikographie des Bib-lisch-Hebräischen mehr und mehr wieder zurück, und heute würde kaum ein Lexikograph die lobenden Worte eines Gesenius gegenüber dem Wert des Targum und eines Lexikons wie das des Ibn Ǧanāḥ finden.

---

15 Vgl. Michael L. Klein, *The Masorah to Targum Onqelos* (Binghamton: Binghamton University, 2000).

16 Vgl. Ingo Kottsieper, „Das Aramäische als Schriftsprache und die Entwicklung der Targume“, in *The Targums in the Light of Traditions of the Second Temple Period* (ed. Thierry Legrand and Jan Joosten; JStJ.S 167; Leiden: Brill, 2014), 27–37.

Der folgende Beitrag möchte aber darauf hinweisen, dass die Ursprünge der hebräischen Lexikographie und ihre Rezeption insbesondere durch Gesenius bis heute ihre Spuren hinterlassen haben, obwohl oder gerade weil dies den späteren Bearbeitern der Lexika nicht mehr bewusst war. Mancher Verweis auf diese Tradition wurde gestrichen oder nur noch unvollständig bzw. fehlerhaft weiter tradiert, so dass zuweilen nicht mehr klar ist, woher die eigentlich angenommene Deutung eines Lemmas eigentlich stammt.

Die folgenden zwei Beispiele aus den jüngsten deutschsprachigen und einflussreichen Lexika sollen dies illustrieren. Dabei geht es dem Verfasser nicht darum, die Ergebnisse der mühevollen Detailarbeit, die eine Überarbeitung eines Lexikons mit sich bringt, in Misskredit zu bringen. Vielmehr sollen diese Beispiele in Erinnerung rufen, dass eine Forschungsgeschichte eine im positiven Sinne kritische Funktion haben kann. Sie ruft in Erinnerung, auf welchen Daten unsere zuweilen als sicher geglaubten Ansichten jeweils de facto beruhen und leitet zu einer beständigen kritischen Aneignung dessen an, was wir „von den Vätern ererbt" haben.

Gerade im Hinblick auf die Lexikographie kann diese Rückbesinnung auf die Forschungsgeschichte heilsam sein. Es gehört zu den Merkmalen der Gattung des Wörterbuches, dass es oftmals eine nicht oder nur kaum hinterfragte Autorität aufweist. Man benutzt eben ein Wörterbuch normalerweise nicht, um eine Diskussion über den Bedeutungshorizont eines Lemmas zu eröffnen, sondern um zu erfahren, was es bedeutet. Und die knappen Auskünfte, die ein Wörterbuch normalerweise bietet, lassen den Nutzer leicht vergessen, dass diese eben auch nur ein Ergebnis einer zum Teil längeren Forschungsgeschichte sind, die als wissenschaftliche Aussagen eben grundsätzlich auch falsifizierbar und eben keine letzten Wahrheiten sind. Indem diese Bedeutungen in die Texte, für deren Verständnis das Wörterbuch benutzt wird, eingetragen werden, erzeugt das Wörterbuch zuweilen seine eigenen Belege. Gerade für die wissenschaftlichen hebräischen Lexika gilt darüber hinaus, dass sie mit ihren häufig informationsreichen etymologischen Abschnitten auch für die Erarbeitung anderer semitischer Wörterbücher als Quelle dienen. Deren Ergebnisse wiederum fließen in die Neubearbeitung der hebräischen Wörterbücher ein. Hier besteht somit die Gefahr des Zirkelschlusses, der den Blick auf andere, möglicherweise sachgerechtere Deutungen verstellen kann. Die forschungsgeschichtliche Rückbesinnung kann helfen, diese Zirkelschlüsse zu durchbrechen, indem sie aufzeigt, auf welcher Basis eigentlich alle folgenden Schlüsse beruhen, die somit einer kritischen Evaluierung zugänglich werden.

2. אֵל/אֱיָלוּת‎‎‎‎‎, אֵל und die Erfindung der Wurzel ’*WL* „stark, kräftig sein"

In Ps 88 fleht ein Mensch, der am Ende seiner Kräfte ist, um die Hilfe Gottes, der schon in V. 2 als „Gott meines Heils/meiner Hilfe" (אֱלֹהֵי יְשׁוּעָתִי) angesprochen wird. Der Beter beschreibt sich dabei als jemand, der wie ein Toter von der Einflusssphäre Gottes abgeschnitten ist:

> (4) Ja, satt vom Übel ist meine Seel,
> und mein Leben hat die Scheol erreicht.

> (5) Ich werde zu denen gerechnet, die in die Grube hinabgehen,
> ich bin geworden wie ein Mann ohne אֱיָל,

> (6) einer der unter die Toten entlassen wurde wie Erschlagene, [die im Grab liegen],
> derer du nicht mehr gedenkst,
> und sie sind abgeschnitten von deiner Hand.

Im Fortgang des Psalms schildert der Beter sich dann entsprechend als ein Mensch, der völlig allein in seinem Leiden ist, da Gott ihn seiner Umwelt entfremdet habe (8 f. + 19), und als von Gott Geschlagener darum fleht, dass Gott sich ihm wieder zuwende.

Das in V. 5 belegte, von den Masoreten aramäisch punktierte אֱיָל begegnet in der erweiterten, ebenfalls aramäisch vokalisierten Form אֱיָלוּת noch einmal in dem thematisch ähnlichen Ps 22:

> (2) Mein Gott, mein Gott, warum hast du mich verlassen,
> fern von meiner Hilfe (מישועתי) sind die Worte meines Stöhnens.
> ...

> (12) Sei nicht fern von mir,
> denn meine Not ist nah,
> ja, da ist kein Helfer!
> ...

> (16) Meine Kraft (כֹּחִי) ist vertrocknet wie eine Scherbe
> und meine Zunge klebt an meinem Gaumen,
> und in den Todesstaub legtest du mich.
> ...

> (20) Du aber, Jahwe, sei nicht fern,
> meine אֱיָלוּת, eile mir zu Hilfe!

Dieses offenkundig aus dem Aramäischen entlehnte Wortpaar findet nicht nur in syrisch *'ayālā* > *'īyālā*[17] bzw. *'īyālūṯā* „Hilfe" ein entsprechendes Pendant, sondern auch das neuassyrisch/jung-/neubabylonische *ayālu* „Hilfe" dürfte ebenfalls auf eine Entlehnung eines aramäischen *'ayāl* zurückgehen.[18] Dieselbe Wortwurzel ist schließlich auch aus dem Qumranaramäischen bekannt:

אל רבא באילה | הוא ועבד לה קרב עממין ינתן בידה וכלהן | ירמה קדמוהי

> „Der große Gott wird als sein איל da sein und für ihn Krieg führen. Völker wird er in seine Hand geben und sie alle vor ihm niederwerfen" (4Q246 frag. 1 ii 7–8).

Die Aussage bezieht sich auf das endzeitliche Israel, das nach der Überwindung der bösen Herrschaft die Macht über die gesamten Völkerschaften bekommt. Sie hat eine Parallele in 1QM 17,6–8, wo davon die Rede ist, dass Gott in der entscheidenden letzten Schlacht „ewige Hilfe (עזר עולמים) der Gefolgschaft seiner Erlösung durch die Macht eines Engels" sendet, was dazu führt, dass Israel die Macht über die Menschheit erringt. Angesichts dieser Parallele und der auch sonst aramäisch belegten Bedeutung von איל kann kein Zweifel bestehen, dass auch in 4Q246 איל mit dieser Konnotation begegnet.[19] Dem entspricht die Schilderung Gottes als desjenigen, der letztlich den Kampf selber durchführt und die Feinde in Israels Hand gibt, d.h. als entscheidender Helfer im Endkampf selbst auftritt.

Dass die Bedeutung „Hilfe" in den beiden Psalmen ebenfalls ausgezeichnet passt, ist evident und wird zudem auch von der LXX (21,20: βοήθειάν μου; 87,5: ἀβοήθητος) und der Vulgata[LXX] (22,20: *auxilium tuum*; 87,5: *sine adiutorio*) bezeugt.[20]

Umso überraschender ist es, dass Ges[18] für אֱיָל zwar sowohl die aramäische Herkunft des Wortes als auch die entsprechende Übersetzung durch die Versionen angibt,[21] sich aber dann doch für die Bedeutung „Kraft" entscheidet. Und für אֱיָלוּת

---

17 Vgl. Carl Brockelmann, *Grundriß der vergleichenden Grammatik der semitischen Sprachen I. Laut- und Formenlehre* (Berlin: Reuther & Reinhard, 1908), 69.

18 Vgl. ABL 222 (SAA XV 199) r 19; 1114 (SAA XVIII 87) r 17; 1215 (SAA XVIII 204) 19; 1286 r 2; 1311 27; 1335+ (SAA XVII 120) 11.16; CT 53 29 (SAA XV 172) 7; 454 (SAA V 131) 5; PRT 110 (SAA IV 324) r 5; CAD I/1 *sub voce* ajalu B; Simo Parpola und Robert Whiting, *Assyrian-English-Assyrian Dictionary* (Helsinki: Neo Assyrian Text Corpus Project, 2007), *sub voce* aiālu.

19 Vgl. dazu auch weiter unten, S. 56–57.

20 Vgl. auch die Peschitta, die an beiden Stellen *'yl(')* bietet.

21 Ges[18] verweist zudem noch auf Alfred Guillaume, „Hebrew, and Arabic Lexicography. A Comparative Study," *Abr Nahrain* 1 (1959), [6,] 18 f., der אֱיָל mit arabisch وَأَل „Zuflucht" vergleicht und ausdrücklich betont, dass auch das hebräische Wort nicht mit „Kraft" o. ä. zu übersetzen sei.

bietet Ges$_{18}$ dann ebenfalls die etymologische Verbindung zum syrischen Wort für „Hilfe", um dann aber als Bedeutung „Stärke, Hilfe" anzugeben.

Der Grund für diese Entscheidungen bleibt dem Nutzer verborgen und es wird lediglich angeführt, dass in Ps 88,5 אֱיָל אֵין כְּגֶבֶר parallel zu יוֹרְדֵי בוֹר sei. Dass aber in diesem Psalm das Hinabsteigen in die Grube ein Bild für die Kraftlosigkeit wäre, ist alles andere als zwingend. So wird in V. 6 das Motiv gerade dahingehend ausgeführt, dass man im Grab nicht mehr die Zuwendung Gottes erfährt, was eher ein Bild für die Hilflosigkeit ist.

Auch die übrigen Literaturangaben helfen hier nicht weiter: Sowohl Paul Haupt als auch Max Wagner, auf die Ges$_{18}$ zu אֱיָל verweist, geben keinerlei Grund an, warum das Lemma trotz seiner Eigenschaft als Aramaismus „Kraft" und nicht wie im Aramäischen „Hilfe" bedeuten soll. So postuliert Haupt[22] lediglich, dass das aramäische Wort ursprünglich „Stärke" bedeutet habe, „Beistand" also erst eine sekundäre Bedeutung sei.[23] Dies setzt die Ansicht *voraus*, dass das Hebräische die Grundbedeutung des Wortes bewahrt habe. Auch bei Wagner[24] wird nicht deutlich, worauf sich seine Annahme stützt, dass das Hebräische für diese Lemmata die Bedeutung „Kraft" hat. Er verweist lediglich auf syr. *'iyālā/-ūtā*, für das er die Bedeutung „Kraft, Hilfe" annimmt, wobei aber die Konnotation Kraft für das Syrische schlicht nicht nachweisbar ist.[25] So bleibt für den Semitisten eigentlich nur, wie schon Lagarde und dann deutlich auch Brockelmann den Schluss zu ziehen, dass diese aus dem Aramäischen entlehnten Wörter natürli-

---

22 Vgl. Paul Haupt, Der Name Jahwe, *OLZ* 12 (1909), 214.

23 "*El* gehört zu dem aram. *ijâla*, Beistand, ursprünglich Stärke. Die Bedeutungsentwicklung ist wie in dem assyr. *tukultu*." Der Verweis auf akk. *tukultu* „Vertrauen, Hilfe" beruht seinerseits auf der Annahme, dass akk. *takālu*/aram. *tkl* „vertrauen" eine Nebenform zu *WKL* sei und diese auch arab. mit der Bedeutung „anvertrauen" belegte Wurzel dem hebr./aram. יכל „können" entsprechen würde. Ob aber יכל auf *WKL* oder eher *YKL* zurückgeht oder auch nur eine Nebenform zu *KHL* ist, muss ebenso offenbleiben wie die Annahme, dass „können" dann die Grundbedeutung der Wurzelgruppe *WKL/TKL* war. Die Argumentation von Haupt zeigt aber mit wünschenswerter Deutlichkeit, wie das hebräische Wörterbuch unhinterfragt als Grundlage für die Bestimmung semitischer Semantiken dient.

24 Max Wagner, *Die lexikalischen und grammatikalischen Aramaismen im alttestamentlichen Hebräisch* (BZAW 96; Berlin: De Gruyter, 1966), 23 f.

25 Man fragt sich, woher Wagner diese Angabe genommen hat. Eine Möglichkeit wäre, dass dies aus der Tatsache geschlossen wurde, dass die Peschitta die Lexeme zur Wiedergabe der hebräischen Wörter benutzt, womit aber wieder ein Zirkelschluss gegeben wäre. Oder sollte Wagner – wie später auch Puech (vgl. unten, S. 56–57) – KBL, das ebenfalls von der Bedeutung „Kraft" ausgeht und dabei das syrische Pendant unübersetzt anführt, dahingehend verstanden haben, dass dieses „Kraft" bedeuten könne?

cherweise mit ihrer aramäischen Bedeutung „Hilfe" entlehnt wurden,[26] was zudem ihrem Kontext und ihrer Bezeugung in der LXX und anderen Versionen entspricht.[27]

Aber nicht nur Ges[18] präferiert die Bedeutung „Kraft", sondern auch HAL, wo neben der dort ebenfalls als gegeben angesehenen Ableitung der hebräischen Wörter aus dem Aramäischen nun auch die Ableitung von einer Wurzel *'WL „vorn, stark sein" angeführt wird, zu der nach den Angaben *sub voce* אול II auch Lemmata wie אַיִל I „Widder", II „mächtiger Baum", אֵל IV „Kraft, Macht" und V „El, Gott", אַלֹן „wie אֵלָה zunächst grosser Baum, ‚Gottesbaum'", אַלֹן „urspr[ünglich] jeder stattliche Baum" und vielleicht מוּל „Vorderseite" zu stellen seien. Auffälligerweise fehlt aber bei אֵל IV und V jeglicher Rückverweis auf אול II und zu אֵל IV notiert das Wörterbuch „Bedeutung klar, Etym[ologie] strittig; prob[abiliter] = V אֵל".

Die Wurzel ’WL hat jedoch die positionale Bedeutung „vorderste, erster sein" und nicht eine qualitative wie „stark sein". Dies geht aus sämtlichen eindeutig dieser Wurzel zuzuordnenden Belegen hervor. So findet sich im Arabischen آلَ/يَؤُولُ bzw. أَوِلَ/يَأْوَلُ „vorangehen, der erste/vorderste sein" und أَوَّلُ „erste, frühere", zu dem das targumische אולא „Anfang, Beginn"[28], syr. ’wl „erste, das was früher war"[29] sowie mand. (< arab.?) awal „erste (Monat/Tag)" zu stellen sind.[30] Dabei steht wahrscheinlich die Konnotation des Ursprungs im Hintergrund, so dass sich eine Verbindung zur Bedeutung „zurückkehren"[31] ergibt, die für آلَ/يَؤُولُ auch

---

26 Vgl. Carl Brockelmann, אל ידי, *ZAW* 26 (1906), 30: „אֱיָל Ps 88,5 heißt nicht ‚Kraft', sondern ‚Hilfe', wie das aramäische Wort, aus dem es entlehnt ist", wobei er auf Paul de Lagarde, *Orientalia. 2. Heft* (Göttingen: Dieterische Verlags-Buchhandlung, 1880), 7, verweist.

27 Vgl. auch MidrTeh zu Ps 22,20: אותה קפיצה שקפצתה כאיל על אבותי בים והושעתים כן תקפוץ עלי היום ותפלטיני „Denselben Sprung, den du als Hirsch für meine Vorväter am Meer getan und sie damit gerettet hast, den springe auch für mich heute und rette mich." Sprachlich verbindet der Midrasch hier אֱיָלוּת mit אַיָל (vgl. die Überschrift zu Ps 22!), aber dem Ausleger ist offenbar völlig bewusst, dass es hier um „Hilfe" und Rettung geht. So erklärt der Midrasch auch אֱיָל in 88,5 mit פטרון „Beschützer".

28 TgJ Jes 1:26; 40,21; 41,26; 43,18; Jer 13,21; 17,12; Ez 16,55; 36,11; Hos 9,10; Am 7,1; TgPsJon Gen 1,1; 13,3; Tg Ps 37,20; Tg Hi 20,4; aramTobit 11 (Adolf Neubauer, *The Book of Tobit* (Oxford: Clarendon, 1878), 15, 13)

29 So wohl in Ms Harvard Syr 42 118 v 2:30; vgl. Matthias Henze, *The Syriac Apocalypse of Daniel* (Studien und Texte zu Antike und Christentum 11; Tübingen: Mohr Siebeck, 2001), 39; Comprehensive Aramaic Lexicon Project (cal1.cn.huc.edu) *sub voce* ʔwl adj. „first".

30 Vgl. auch Bo Utas, *Frahang I Pahlavīk* (Wiesbaden: Harrassowitz, 1988), II 0 (S. 41, 62).

31 Vgl. Edward William Lane, *An Arabic-English Lexicon*, (London: Williams and Norgate, 1863 ff.), 127c: „namely [to] a thing [of any kind; the thing or place, whence he or it, originated, or came; his, or its, origin or source; his, or its, original state, condition, quantity, weight, &c; ...]".

belegt ist.[32] Für dieses Verb findet sich aber noch unter dem Eintrag als آلَ رَعِيَّةً im Arabischen auch die Bedeutung „fürsorglich leiten", „einer Gruppe vorstehen und sich um ihre Angelegenheiten zum Guten kümmern", „sich um seine Tiere dergestalt kümmern, dass sie in gutem Zustand sind".

Es ist offensichtlich, dass die Konnotation „Kraft, Stärke" hier fehlt. Wenn אַיִל „Widder" und dann in übertragener Bedeutung „Führer eines Landes/einer Gruppe" zu dieser Wurzel gehören sollte, so ließe sich dies leicht von der Bedeutung des Leitens und Führens ableiten.[33] Inwieweit auch die Baumbegriffe entweder als die „ersten" Bäume, die schon am Anfang da waren, oder als die „vorstehenden Bäume", die sozusagen die Führungspositionen unter den Bäumen einnehmen, auch hierzu zu stellen sind, ist nicht abschließend zu entscheiden, würde aber eben auch keine größere Abstraktion von der Grundbedeutung der Wurzel bedeuten, wie die Annahme, dass sie als „Kraft-Bäume" verstanden wurden.

Da nun der Gottesbegriff אֵל der Nominalklasse *qil*[34] und damit nicht einer Wurzel ʾW/YL zuzuordnen ist, ist dieses Wort auf jeden Fall aus der Diskussion auszuscheiden.[35] Aber auch der scheinbar so eindeutige Kandidat für die Annahme der Bedeutung „Kraft" – אֵל in der Phrase יֶשׁ/הָיָה/אֵין לְאֵל יָד־, die die Möglichkeit zu einer Handlung bezeichnet – ist nicht so eindeutig, wie es auf den ersten Blick erscheint. Schon allein die Tatsache, dass es sich hier um eine feststehende Phrase handelt, sollte davor warnen, allzu naiv die semantische Funktion der einzelnen Elemente der Phrase einzelnen Elementen einer Phrase aus einer Übersetzungssprache eins zu eins zuzuordnen – ein solches Vorgehen führt

---

32 Möglicherweise ist auch „(auf seine Essenz) reduziert werden" > „eindicken" hiermit zu verbinden.

33 Vgl. z. B. schon *Thesaurus*, 43. Natürlich bleibt dies nur eine Möglichkeit; aber die Skepsis von Alexander Militarev und Leonid Kogan, *Semitic Etymological Dictionary II* (AOAT 278/2; Münster: Ugarit-Verlag, 2005), 36, gegenüber dieser Annahme trifft nur zu, wenn man den Bedeutungsraum von ʾWL auf „to be first, foremost" einschränkt. Denkbar wäre aber auch, dass die arabisch bezeugte Konnotation „fürsorglich führen" von dem Tierbegriff auf die Wurzel übertragen wurde.

34 Vgl. Hans Bauer und Pontus Leander, *Historische Grammatik der hebräischen Sprache des Alten Testaments 1* (Halle: Max Niemeyer, 1922), § 61i; Rudolf Meyer, *Hebräische Grammatik 2* (Berlin: de Gruyter, 3. Aufl. 1969), § 33,3a. Der Kurzvokal ergibt sich nicht nur aus dem semitischen Sprachvergleich, sondern auch daraus, dass in Eigennamen häufig das Sere zu Segol oder Hatef-Segol reduziert wird, wenn es völlig unbetont ist bzw. zusätzlich noch in offener Silbe steht, vgl. z. B. אֶלְדָּד und אֱלְדָד.

35 Dass Gesenius es unter der Wurzel ʾW/YL mitbehandelt, beruht auf seiner Annahme, dass das /e/ von Haus aus lang sei, wozu er auf Pleneschreibungen im Arabischen und Syrischen verweist, vgl. schon Ges₀, 39. Jedoch war schon ihm die Fragwürdigkeit dieser Ableitung durchaus bewusst, wie seine lange Diskussion, in der er auch andere Deutungen nicht ausschließen will, im *Thesaurus*, 49, zeigt.

leicht zu Fehlern.[36] Mithin wäre selbst dann, wenn eine Übersetzung der Phrase mit „es steht (nicht) in der Macht der Hand des ... " sachlich der hebräischen Aussage entsprechen würde, nicht gesichert, dass auch im Hebräischen das Lemma אֵל „Macht" bedeuten und dies zudem „Macht" im Sinne von „Kraft" meinen würde. Dass diese Bedeutung auf Grund des alttestamentlichen Befundes *möglich* ist, ist wissenschaftlich gesehen kein *Beweis*, dass damit das Richtige getroffen wurde.

Das Wort אֵל begegnet aber auch in der Phrase מא(י)ל + Sf., die im Mittelhebräischen gut belegt ist. Dass dieses א(י)ל nicht, wie von der älteren Lexikographie angenommen wurde, zur Präposition אֶל zu stellen ist,[37] hat schon 1964 Hanoch Yalon erkannt[38] und ist auf Grund seiner häufigen Schreibung mit י auch in den Formen, in denen bei אֶל der Vokal reduziert wäre, und seiner durchgehenden Vokalisation mit Sere in vielen Manuskripten evident.[39] א(י)ל markiert den Verursacher einer Handlung, wobei die intentionale Konnotation so stark ist, dass mit diesem Ausdruck zugleich impliziert wird, dass kein anderer für die Handlung verantwortlich ist. Wenn auch an vielen Stellen die deutsche Übersetzung „von selbst" durchaus angemessen erscheint, so intendiert die Aussage jedoch nicht, dass die so charakterisierte Handlung auf Grund der eigenen Kraft oder Fähigkeit

---

36 Ein Beispiel für eine entsprechende Fehldeutung findet sich in der Analyse der Phrase אחז אבות, die in 1QS 2,9 belegt ist und eine Parallele in akk. *abbūta ṣabātu* hat und auch im Syr. als ʾḥd ʾabūṭā belegt ist. Wie AHw *sub voce abbūtu(m)* korrekt ausführt, bedeutet das Wort natürlich „Vaterschaft" und auch „väterliche Gesinnung", so dass die Phrase *abbūta ṣabātu* wörtlich „die Vaterschaft ergreifen" im Sinne „eine väterliche Gesinnung gegenüber jemandem einnehmen" bedeutet und damit die positive Handlung bildlich umschreibt, für das so als Kind anerkannte Gegenüber einzutreten. Mithin hat auch syr. ʾabūṭā nicht die Bedeutung „defence, protection" (so z. B. Michael Sokoloff, *A Syriac Lexicon* [Winona Lake: Eisenbrauns und Piscataway: Gorgias, 2009], 3 zum Syrischen), und noch weniger kann aus 1QS 2,9 geschlossen werden, dass im Qumran-Hebräischen אבות allgemein im Sinne von „Fürsprache" benutzt wurde, wie manche Ausleger es in dem fragmentarischen Stück 4Q369 frag. 2,1 ohne zwingenden Kontext in ומשר מלאך אבות ש- annehmen wollen (so z. B. H. Attridge und J. Strugnell in DJD XIII, 359: „]and prison of an angel of intercessions" = Florentino García Martínez und Eibert J.C. Tigchelaar, *The Dead Sea Scrolls Study Edition* (Leiden: Brill und Grand Rapids: Eerdmans, 2000), 731; anders z. B. Johann Maier, *Die Qumran-Essener: Die Texte vom Toten Meer II* (Uni-Taschenbücher 1863; München und Basel: Ernst Reinhardt 1995), 315, der das Wort mit „Väter" übersetzt). Eine Deutung dieses Fragments ist auf Grund des fehlenden Kontexts zwar nicht möglich, die Annahme eines „Engels der Fürsprache" beruht aber auf einem methodologischen Fehler.

37 Zu diesem Missverständnis dürfte beigetragen haben, dass es vor Suffixen wie die Präposition אֶל ein י einfügt. Offenkundig wurde מאיל als eine Art Präposition verstanden und, wie es bei solchen präpositional gebrauchten Wörtern üblich ist, vor Suffixen als Pseudoplural gebildet.

38 Vgl. Hanoch Yalon, מבוא לניקוד המשנה (Jerusalem: Bialik, 1964), 25.

39 Vgl. auch Gabriel Birnbaum, לשון המשנה בגניזת קהיר: הגה וצורות (Sources and Studies 10; Jerusalem: The Academy of the Hebrew Language, 2008), 35.

geschieht (dies ist lediglich eine logische Folgerung aus dieser Aussage), sondern dass der Handelnde dies aus eigenem Antrieb, freiwillig bzw. intentional tut und kein anderer dafür verantwortlich ist. Folgende Beispiele sollen dies illustrieren:

a) Im Kontext der Diskussion der Verantwortung eines Hirten für den Verlust von Tieren durch Raubtiere unterscheidet die Mischna in mBM 7,9 (12) unter anderem dazwischen, ob ein Löwe oder ein anderes Raubtier מאליהם zur Herde kam, oder ob der Hirte die Tiere selbst an einen Ort gebracht hat, der von Wildtier- oder Räuberbanden bevölkert ist:[40]

האריה והדוב והנמר והפרדלס והנחש הרי אילו אנסים. אמתי. בזמן שבאו מאליהם. אבל אם הוליכן למקום גדודי
ח>יי<ה וליסטי?ס/ם? אין אלו אנסים

Löwe, Wolf, Panther, Leopard und Schlange: Siehe, diese gelten als Gewalttäter. Wann? Wenn sie aus eigenem Antrieb kommen! Aber wenn er (der Hirte) sie (die Herde) an einen Ort bringt, wo Wildtiere oder (ein) Räuber hausen, dann gelten sie nicht als Gewalttäter.

Im ersten Fall gelten die Tiere als die verantwortlichen Gewalttäter, und der Hirte ist folglich nicht verantwortlich. Die Weisen wollten aber sicherlich nicht ausdrücken, dass im zweiten Fall die Tiere oder Räuber zu schwach waren, um an die Herde zu gelangen und der Hirte sie ihnen deshalb quasi servieren musste, sondern, da es in ihrer Natur liegt, dass sie Tiere reißen, wenn sie vor ihnen auftauchen, derjenige die Verantwortung trägt, der sie ihnen nahebringt. Der Fokus liegt also auf der Frage, wer in diesem Fall initiativ wurde.

b) Sifre Num 12 legt die Anweisung von Num 5,19.21, dass der Priester im Ehebruchordal die Frau schwören lassen soll, dahingehend aus, dass die Frau nicht מאליה "aus eigenem Antrieb" schwören darf.

"והשביע אותה הכהן". הכהן משביעה. ואינה נשבעת מאליה. שהיה בדין. נא' כאן "שבועה". ונא' לה]ל[ן
"שבועה". מה שבועה האמור להלן היא נשבעת מאליה. אף שבועה האמורה כאן היא נשבעת מאליה. ת"ל
"והשביע אותה הכהן". הכהן משביעה. ואין נשבעת מאליה. והשביע אותה הכהן.

Der Priester lässt sie schwören, aber sie schwört nicht aus eigener Initiative. Denn man könnte folgende Schlussfolgerung ziehen: Hier heißt es „Schwur"[41] und dort heißt es „Schwur".[42] Was bedeutet „Schwur", der dort genannt wurde? Sie schwor aus eigener In-

---

40 Alle Zitate nach dem Text der Ma'ªgārîm, vgl. http://maagarim.hebrew-academy.org.il.
41 Der Num 5,21 fährt fort: בשבעת האלה.
42 Dies dürfte sich auf 30,11 beziehen: ואם בית אישה נדרה או אסרה אסר על נפשה בשבעה.

itiative.[43] So sollte auch „Schwur", der hier genannt wird, bedeuten, dass sie aus eigener Initiative schwört. Die Stelle lehrt (aber dagegen ausdrücklich): „Und es beschwört sie der Priester." Der Priester lässt sie schwören, aber sie schwört nicht aus eigener Initiative.

Für das Verfahren ist wichtig, dass die Initiative vom Priester ausgeht, obwohl natürlich die Frau in der Lage wäre, aus eigener Kraft die Schwurformel über sich selbst zu sprechen und in der Antwort „Amen, Amen", mit der die Frau auf die Beschwörung reagieren soll (V. 22), *de facto* eine aktive Zustimmung zu dem Schwur vorliegt.[44] Wenn es prinzipiell nicht in der Macht der Frau läge, einen entsprechenden Schwur zu leisten, wäre die Diskussion an dieser Stelle völlig überflüssig, ob die zweifache Nennung des Schwurs im biblischen Text nicht im Sinne der גְּזֵירָה שָׁוָה dahingehend auszulegen ist, dass die Frau selber den Schwur leistet.[45]

c) Im Jerusalemer Talmud findet sich mehrfach die Phrase מאיליהן קיבלו עליהן als Ausdruck dafür, dass man eine Verpflichtung aus freien Stücken, aus eigener Initiative auf sich nimmt und nicht, weil sie einem auferlegt wurde.[46] Dabei entspricht diese Aussage der Formulierung קיבלו עליהן דברים שלא היו חייבין עליהן „sie nahmen diese Dinge auf sich, zu denen sie nicht verpflichtet waren" (jScheb 36b).

d) bZeb 116a[47] diskutiert die Frage, wie in der Zeit, als die Tora noch nicht gegeben worden war, man wissen konnte, welche Tiere rein und welche unrein waren. Wie war es z. B. möglich, dass von den reinen Tieren sieben, von den unreinen aber nur zwei jeweils in die Arche gelangten. Zunächst wird die Ansicht von R. Ḥisda angeführt, dass Noah die Tiere an der Arche vorbeiführte (העבירן לפני התיבה), diese dann die reinen Tiere aufnahm, und man so aus der Reaktion der Arche ersehen

---

43 Num 30,4–16 handelt von Gelübden, die eine Frau selbständig ablegt, der Schwurcharakter wird in V. 11 mit בשבועה zum Ausdruck gebracht.

44 Vgl. mSoṭ 2,5; ySoṭ 18b; bSoṭ 17b; Ibn Ezra und Seforno zu Num 5,19.

45 Vgl. den Kommentar von Menahem I. Kahana, ספרי במדבר: מהדורה מבואר II (Jerusalem: Magnes, 2011), 139. Die Anwendung der Regel der גְּזֵירָה שָׁוָה zwischen Num 5,21 und 30,11 wäre theoretisch deswegen möglich gewesen, weil nur an diesen beiden Stellen in der Tora בשבועה im Kontext des Eides einer Frau begegnet und eigentlich an beiden Stellen diese Erwähnung der שבועה nicht unbedingt nötig ist. Sifre erklärt die explizite und gleich zweimal in V. 19 und 21 zu findende Aussage, dass der Priester die Frau schwören lässt (und die nach mSoṭ 2,4 auch nicht in das in Num 5,23 genannte Schriftstück aufzunehmen ist), also als bewusst hinzugefügte Aussage der Tora, die damit zum Ausdruck bringen wollte, dass hier der Schluss nach גְּזֵירָה שָׁוָה nicht angebracht ist.

46 Zumeist wird dies im Hinblick auf den Zehnten gesagt, vgl. jDem 23c; jJeb 8a; 13d; jJoma 45b; jMaas 49c; jQid 61c; jTer 40c; 48a.

47 Vgl. auch die kürzere Version in bSan 108b.

konnte, welche als rein gelten. Als abweichende Erklärung wird dann die Meinung
R. Abahus zitiert, der aus הבאים זכר ונקבה (Gen 7,16) den Schluss zieht: הבאין מאיליהן
„sie (die Tiere) kamen aus eigenem Antrieb", d. h. sie wurden nicht von Noah
gebracht, sondern Noah selbst lernte erst daraus, dass manche in Gruppen von
sieben und andere paarweise kamen, welche rein und welche unrein waren. Der
logische Gegensatz zu מאיל wäre also hier: „nicht aus eigener Initiative, sondern
auf Grund eines äußeren Einflusses". Der Aspekt der „Kraft" ist hier sicher völlig
fern, da die unversehrten und gesunden Tiere[48] natürlich in jedem Fall „aus eigener Kraft" kommen konnten.

e) In bEruv 20b – 21 bezeichnet die Phrase שותה מאיליה in der Bedeutung „es (das
Vieh) möge aus eigenem Antrieb trinken" das Gegenteil des Vorgangs, das man ein
Tier dazu drängt, zu trinken, was im Kontext des Sabbats natürlich verboten ist.

f) In bNid 51a begegnet der Gegensatz zwischen Pflanzen, die „von Beginn" als
Futter ausgesät wurden (דזרעינהו מתחלה לבהמה/לאדם) und denen, שעלו מאיליהן „die
aus eigenem Antrieb hochwachsen", also sich selbst ausgesät haben.

Die Maʾᵃgārîm der Academy of the Hebrew Language[49] stellen wohl mit Recht
dieses mittelhebräische Wort zu biblisch-hebräisch אֵל in der Phrase יָד־לְאֵל, auch
wenn die Bedeutungsangabe כוח zumindest für den mittel-hebräischen Gebrauch
sich nicht nahelegt und nur die traditionelle Deutung des biblisch-hebräischen אֵל
widerspiegelt.[50] Diese *Identifikation* bestätigt sich nun auch darin, dass die
Konnotation der Intention bzw. des intentionalen Ausgangspunkts einer Handlung an allen Belegstellen von יָד־לְאֵל nicht nur ebenfalls guten Sinn gibt, sondern
sogar sich besser in die Kontexte einfügt.
      Besonders deutlich ist dies im Hinblick auf die negative Aussage יָדְךָ לְאֵל אֵין/
יָדֵנוּ in Dtn 28,32 und Neh 5,5, die ohne eine Fortsetzung zum Ausdruck bringt, dass
man nichts gegen die vorher geschilderten Übergriffe tun kann, sondern, wie es
Dtn 28,32 ausdrücklich betont, man tatenlos zusehen muss. Geht man von der
Bedeutung „Kraft" für אֵל aus, so würde man eher אֵין אֵל לְיָדְךָ/לְיָדֵנוּ „es gibt keine
Kraft für deine/unsere Hand" erwarten.[51] Dagegen würde „nichts ist da für/in

---

48 Dass natürlich die Tiere der Arche gesund waren, wird nebenbei ausdrücklich im vorangehenden Text diskutiert.
49 http://maagarim.hebrew-academy.org.il
50 Yalon hat unter Aufnahme eines Vorschlages von Ginsberg an eine Verbindung zu אֱיָל gedacht,
dem sich Birnbaum mit Fragezeichen anschließt, vgl. Anm. 38 – 39.
51 Entsprechend übergeht die LXX in Neh 5,5 die Präposition einfach: καὶ οὐκ ἔστιν δύναμις
χειρῶν ἡμῶν.

Bezug auf die Kraft deiner/unserer Hand", de facto bedeuten, dass diese Kraft zwar vorhanden, aber die Situation selbst nicht den Bereich der Kraft der Hand erreicht. Dies wäre eine zwar denkbare, aber sicher auch recht komplexe und indirekte Formulierung für die Aussage, dass man in der gegebenen Situation nichts von dem tun kann, was man eigentlich tun wollte. Ein Wort jedoch, dass die Intentionalität des Handelnden bzw. den Ausgangspunkt einer selbständigen Handlung konnotiert, passt in diesem Kontext ausgezeichnet: „Da ist nichts im Hinblick darauf, was für eine intentionale Handlung deiner/unserer Hand in Frage käme" im Sinne von „da kannst du/können wir nichts tun, auch wenn wir es wollen". אֶל in dieser Funktion würde exakt den Aspekt des Handelns nach der eigenen Intention einbringen, der in diesen Kontexten ja angesprochen wird, während der Aspekt der Handlungsfähigkeit durch יָד „Hand" eingetragen wird.

Angesichts der bisherigen Beobachtungen wird man es nicht als Zufall abtun können, dass die verbleibenden Belege für יָד־אֶל לְ sich alle auf Handlungen beziehen, die zu tun oder zu unterlassen sich der Handelnde bewusst entscheidet.

So entscheidet sich in Gen 31,29 Laban deswegen dagegen, Jakob und seiner Familie etwas Böses anzutun, weil Gott ihn davor gewarnt hat. Im Mittelpunkt von Mi 2,1–2 steht der Gedanke, dass die ausbeuterische Oberschicht bei ihrem asozialen Tun ihren Plänen und Wünschen hemmungslos folgt. Auf der andere Seite lehrt Prov 3,27, dass man, wenn es zu den eigenen Handlungsmöglichkeiten gehört, demjenigen, dem Gutes zukommt, dieses Gutes auch tun und ihm nicht vorenthalten soll, d.h., sich für das Tun entscheiden soll.

Auch die Belege bei Jesus Sirach lassen sich in dieses Bild einordnen. So warnt Sir 5,1 davor, dass man sich nicht auf seine Macht (חיל) stützen und sagen soll: יש ידי לאל! Diese Aussage wird in V. 2 dann wie folgt variiert: „Nicht stütze dich auf deine Kraft (כוח), um deinen eigenen Begierden zu folgen." Dabei sind die beiden Verse offenkundig zueinander parallel aufgebaut, wobei der jeweils zweite Versteil den Aspekt einträgt, dass es hier nicht einfach darum geht, bei seinem Tun sich nur auf die eigene Kraft zu verlassen. Vielmehr hebt Sirach auf die arrogante Haltung dessen ab, der im Bewusstsein seiner eigenen Stärke sich alles das erlauben zu können meint, was er tun will. יש לאל ידי dürfte hier also durchaus als „es steht in meiner Macht!" sachgerecht übersetzt sein, aber in dem Sinn von „das zu tun, was ich will/intendiere!"[52] Dementsprechend thematisiert Sirach dann im Fortgang nicht die Frage, ob die Kraft zum Handeln ausreichen würde oder ob man damit an einer Aufgabe scheitern kann, sondern dass man sich letztendlich vor

---

52 LXX: Αὐτάρκη μοί ἐστιν. Dass dies gemeint ist, hat z. B. auch Moshe Zwi Segal, ספר בן סירא השלם (Jerusalem: Bialik, 2. Aufl. 1958), 31 korrekt gesehen, wenn er לאל ידי mit כלומר בכוחי לעשות שלבי חפץ paraphrasiert.

Gott für sein Handeln *verantworten* muss. Und V. 3a bietet wohl mit אל תאמר מי יוכל
כחו[53] „Nicht sage: „Wer kann ‚meine' Kraft überwinden?" eine weitere sachliche
Variante zu V. 1, die aufweist, dass hier der Aspekt der Auto*nomie* konnotiert wird.

Sir 14,11 hingegen warnt vor zu großer Knauserigkeit, bei der man sich nichts
selber gönnt. Man wird aber fragen müssen, ob Sirach mit der Aussage ולאל ידך
הדשן wirklich so etwas wie „und soweit du es vermagst, labe dich"[54] oder „und
pflege dich, soweit du kannst"[55] meint – zumal wenn man noch Kap. 5 im Ohr hat.
Es geht nicht darum, dass man es sich gut gehen lässt, sich „mästet", *soweit* man
kann, sondern dass man sich seine eigenen Wünsche durchaus erfüllen sollte,
wenn man es vermag.

Schließlich sei noch auf 4Q179 frag. 1 i 2 verwiesen, wo in einem unklaren
Kontext die Phrase אין לאל ידנו begegnet:

כֹּל עוונותינו ואין לאל ידנו כי לא שמעֹנֹ[ו

„.... all unsere Sünden – und wir können nichts tun, denn nicht haben wir gehört [...

Da der Kontext zerstört ist, lässt sich nicht sagen, worum es hier im Detail geht,
aber die Fortführung „denn wir haben nicht gehört", sowie die folgenden Zeilen
lassen an einen Kontext wie Dtn 28,32 (s. o.) denken.

Es ergibt sich mithin, dass auch für אל die Bedeutung „Kraft, Macht" sich nicht
vom Sprachgebrauch her belegen lässt, sondern mit diesem Wort in der biblisch-
hebräischen Phrase לְאֵל יָד־ der Aspekt eingetragen wird, dass die schon mit יָד
referenzierte Handlungsfähigkeit durch die Möglichkeit, initiativ zu werden,
komplettiert wird, so dass hier der Aspekt begegnet, dass etwas zu den Hand-
lungs*optionen* gehört, aus denen man bewusst auswählen und so entsprechend
seines Willens handeln kann – und also auch dafür verantwortlich ist.[56]

Wenn die LXX diese Phrase in der Tora mit ἰσχύει ἡ χείρ μου (Gen 31,29) bzw.
verneint mit οὐκ ἰσχύσει ἡ χείρ σου wiedergibt, so belegt auch sie nicht die Bedeutung „Kraft" für אל, sondern übersetzt eine Phrase mit einer anderen, die
sachlich durchaus korrekt ist. Lediglich in Neh 5,5 hat LXX אל mit δύναμις übersetzt, wobei aber das Fehlen einer Wiedergabe der Präposition zeigt, dass eine
adäquate Übersetzung der Phrase mit dieser Deutung kaum möglich ist: καὶ οὐκ
ἔστιν δύναμις χειρῶν ἡμῶν. Dass die unterschiedlichen griechischen Übersetzer

---

53 L. mit LXX כחי.
54 So Ges₁₈ *sub voce* דשן.
55 So Ges₁₈ *sub voce* 1 אֵל.
56 Letztendlich hat hier schon Lagarde, *Orientalia*, 9, insoweit richtig gesehen, wenn er אֵל mit
„das was in reichweite liegt" wiedergibt, wenn auch seine Gleichung mit אֵל „Gott" sicher falsch ist.

mit der hebräischen Phrase ihre Probleme hatten, zeigt die Wiedergabe der LXX in Mi 2,1, wo der Übersetzer אֵל im Sinne von „Gott" versteht (διότι οὐκ ἦραν πρὸς τὸν θεὸν τὰς χεῖρας αὐτῶν). Mithin lässt sich auch von der LXX her die Bedeutung „Kraft, Macht" nicht belegen.

Damit stellt sich die Frage, woher die von vielen Autoren als so sicher angesehene Annahme kommt, dass אֵל und אֱיָל/אֱיָלוּת die Bedeutung „Kraft, Stärke, Macht" hätten? Die Antwort ist simpel: Dies beruht auf der Deutung des kanonischen TgO zur Tora bzw. TgJ zu den Propheten. So hat TgO zu Gen 31,29 אית חילא בידי und zu Dtn 28,32 ולית חילא בידך. TgJ zu Mi 2,1 bietet אית חילא בידהון und das Targum zu Prov 3,27 hat entsprechend כל אית חילא בידך. Dabei zeigt schon die Umformulierung von לְאֵל יָד zu חילא ביד, dass die Phrase in ihrer ursprünglichen Form mit אֵל im Sinne von Kraft nicht der aramäisch-hebräischen Phraseologie entsprechen würde.

Die Tradition der palästinischen Targume ist dagegen nicht eindeutig. Lediglich TgS^A übersetzt in Gen 31,29 die hebräische Phrase לְאֵל יָדִי Wort für Wort und אֵל mit „Kraft": ליכלת אדי. TgN/F und Ms. E interpretieren sie jedoch als Ausdruck, dass Laban eine große Streitmacht (חי(י)ל ואוכלסין) gehabt habe. Dass dies eine Deutung aus dem Kontext ist und kaum eine direkte Übersetzung zeigt sich in Dtn 28,32 wo TgN die Phrase völlig anders interpretiert: ולא אלהה על ידיכון למפרוק יתכם „aber Gott wird nicht an eurer Seite sein, um euch zu befreien". TgPsJ/F bietet eine lange Paraphrase, die sowohl den Aspekt der Kraft einträgt, als auch die Deutung von אֵל als „Gott" (vgl. TgN), die TgS^J für Gen 31,29 (יית לאל אדי) und 28,32 (ולית לאל אדי) sowie LXX zu Mi 2,1 haben: ולית בידיכון עבדין טובין דתיתוקפן ידיכון בצלו קדם אבוכון דבשמיא דיפרוק יתכו „und keinerlei gute Taten sind in euren Händen, so dass ihr eure Hände im Gebet vor eurem Vater, der im Himmel ist, stärken könntet, so dass er euch rette." TgPsJ hingegen deutet אֵל in Gen 31,29 durchaus in dem oben aufgezeigten Sinn: אית ספיקא בידי „die Möglichkeit ist in meiner Hand".

Der Wiedergabe von אֵל im TgO/J entspricht, dass diese Targumtradition auch אֱיָל־ von אֱיָל „Widder" in der Bedeutung „Führer, Machthaber" normalerweise mit תקיף „Starker" wiedergibt (Ex 15,15; Ez 31,11[57]; 32,21) und nur einmal (Ez 17,13) רב begegnet. Angesichts der Tatsache, dass schon zur Zeit des 2. Tempels in der Aussprache des Hebräischen und wohl auch in vielen aramäischen Dialekten auf Grund der allgemeinen Schwächung der Laryngale und Pharyngale diese miteinander verwechselt werden konnten,[58] ist es durchaus nachvollziehbar, dass

---

57 Codex Reuchlinianus תקוף.
58 Vgl. z. B. für das Hebräische Edward Yechezkel Kutscher, *The Language and Linguistic Background of the Isaiah Scroll (1QIsaᵃ)* (STDJ VI; Leiden: Brill), 505–511; Elisha Qimron, *The Hebrew of the Dead Sea Scrolls* (HSS 29; Atlanta: Scholars Press, 1986), 25; für das Aramäische Klaus Beyer, *Die aramäischen Texte vom Toten Meer* (Göttingen: Vandenhoeck & Ruprecht, 1984), 103.

aramäische Übersetzer bei אֵיל(י) (st.cs.) חֵיל = st.cs. von חַיִל assoziierten und die in diesen Kontexten durchaus ebenfalls nicht gänzlich unpassende Deutung als „Kraft, Macht" annahmen.[59] Wie dem auch sei, es war die autoritative Targumtradition des TgO/J, die in die jüdische Auslegungstradition die Gleichung אֵיל(י) = חֵיל eingebracht hat, die dann auch auf das im Mittelhebräischen ungebräuchliche אֱיָל/אֱיָלוּת übertragen wurde. Der älteste Beleg dafür ist die Psalmenübersetzung des Hieronymus aus dem hebräischen Text, die für אֱיָל אֵין in Ps 88,5 *invalidus* und für אֱיָלוּתִי in Ps 22,20 *fortitudo mea* bietet und damit diese Deutung für das Ende des 4. Jh. n.Chr. auch in Palästina bezeugt. Da die Traditionen, auf denen TgO/J beruhen, wohl schon früher in Palästina bekannt waren[60] und diese Deutung auch in den meisten palästinischen Targumen rezipiert wurde (s.o.), ist es nicht verwunderlich, dass Hieronymus diese Tradition kannte und nutzte.[61] Diese kanonische Deutung wird dann von den Pajtanim rezipiert, die diese im Mittelhebräischen ungebräuchlichen Wörter dann in der Bedeutung „Stärke" für ihre Dichtungen wieder beleben,[62] wobei auch hier die von den Dichtern empfundene phonetische Nähe zu חיל deutlich wird.[63] Das recht späte Targum zum Psalter, das in seiner jetzigen Gestalt erst in gaonäischer Zeit vorlag, übersetzt ebenfalls אֱיָל mit חילא und אֱיָלוּתִי mit תקוף חילי, das in einigen Manuskripten dann zu תקופי verkürzt wurde.[64]

Dementsprechend hat diese von der targumischen Tradition vorgegebene Deutung dann Eingang in die jüdische Lexikographie gefunden. So werden schon in der Maḥbæræt des Ibn Sarūq אֱיָלוּת (Ps 22,20), אֱיָל (Ps 80,5) mit אֵילֵי מוֹאָב (Ex 15,15) und אֵילֵי נְבָיוֹת (Jes 60,7) zusammen einem Eintrag (איל II) zugeordnet und als Bedeutung כח ומעוז „Kraft und Schutz" angegeben, wobei Ibn Sarūq es auch für möglich hält, dass hierzu ebenso אַיֶּלֶת in der Überschrift zu Ps 22,1 zu stellen wäre,

---

59 Es sei hier noch einmal daran erinnert, dass die Beobachtung, dass eine Übersetzung in einem Kontext Sinn ergibt, noch lange nicht bedeutet, dass sie das trifft, was der Autor wirklich intendierte.

60 Vgl. dazu jetzt auch Ingo Kottsieper, *Aramäische*, 24–27

61 Mithin könnte die Deutung im MidrTeh (vgl. Anm. 27), der in seiner Letztgestalt relativ jung ist, aber viel altes palästinisches Material verwertet, hier auf eine ältere, tannaitische Tradition zurückgehen.

62 Als Beispiel sei hier Jannai (6./frühes 7. Jh.) genannt, der z. B. איילות לרגליים „Kraft für die Füße" u. a. mit חוזק לבירכיים „Kraft für die Knie", מעמד קרסוליים „Stand für die Knöchel" und זרועות אומץ „Stärke für die Arme" parallelisiert (וגבוהים משמים, CUL T.S.-H 2.1 v [= FGP No. C241975] Z. 31); vgl. ferner ולאייל לאומץ in תלויים לתהלה = JTS: ENA 2672.19 frag. 1r (= FGP No. C22772) 31 u. a.

63 Vgl. z. B. den Piyyut איילים חיילים = T-S NS 249.7 frag. 1r (= FGP No. C387284) I 26 (palästinisch als אֱיָלִים punktiert).

64 Möglicherweise verdankt sich die doppelte Aussage תקוף חיל dem Versuch des Targumisten die Erweiterung von אֱיָל mit der Abstraktendung -/ūt/ widerzuspiegeln.

das nebenbei im TgPs auch mit תקוף wiedergegeben wird.[65] Da Ibn Sarūq noch keine Vorstellung von grundsätzlich dreiradikaligen Wurzeln hatte, sondern seine Wörter nach ihrer Oberflächenform einordnet, erwähnt er hier natürlich nicht אֵל, sondern bringt dies unter dem Eintrag אֵל I zusammen mit dem Gottesnamen, wobei er aber auch hier ganz im Sinne des Targums als Bedeutung „Kraft und Stärke" (כח ואונים) angibt.

Die Idee, dass diese Wörter von einer schwachen Wurzel abstammen können, hat dann der Begründer der Theorie der dreiradikaligen Wurzeln, Juda ibn Daud al Fāsī, der auch unter dem Namen Ḥayyūǧ bekannt ist, in seinem *Kitāb al-'afʿāl ḏawāt ḥurūf al-līn* „Das Buch der Verben mit schwachen Lauten" eingeführt. Der entsprechende Eintrag lautet in Übersetzung:

> יֵשׁ לְאֵל (stammt auch) יֵשׁ לְאֵל (Ps 22,20) – und von diesem Wort (stammt auch) כְּגֶבֶר אֵין אֱיָל (Ps 88,5), אֱיָלוּת לְעֶזְרָתִי חוּשָׁה
> יָדִי (Gen 31,29), כִּי יֵשׁ לְאֵל יָדָם (Mi 2,1). Zwischen dem Alef und dem Lamed steht ein schwacher Laut, und dieser ist Jod, welches in אֱיָל (und) אֱיָלוּתִי ist. Und manchmal wird das Eigenschaftswort mit Jod geschrieben: אֵילֵי גִבּוֹרִים (Ez 32,21).[66]

Hier sind nun אֵל, אֱיָל, אֱיָלוּת und der Plural אֵילִים von אַיִל unter einer Wurzel zusammengefasst. Ibn Ǧanāḥ greift diese Verbindung ausdrücklich auf, fügt ihr aber dann noch das Wort אֵל als Gottesbezeichnung in הָאֵל יהוה (Jes 42,5; Ps 85,9) hinzu.

> כגבר אין איל (Ps 88,5) Dies wurde schon im *Kitāb ḥurūf al-līn* erwähnt. Und von diesem Wort und von dieser Bedeutung ist auch י האל (Jes 42,5; Ps 85,9). Und dies ist ein Eigenschaftswort. Und ihm gleicht ואתנהו ביד אל גוים (Ez 31,11). Jedoch ist (אל in) יש לאל יד ein Nomen. Die Quieszierung, welche zwischen dem Alef und dem Lamed ist, verweist auf die Tätigkeit. Und der Plural (von) אל גוים (findet sich in) ידברו לו אלי גבורים (Ez 32,21). Und dies ist ohne Jod. Und die Masora hat darüber לית כת' חסר („Nur einmal defektiv geschrieben"). Aber Abū Zakarja (= Ḥayyūǧ) gibt an, dass es mit Jod geschrieben sei, so es jenes ואת אילי הארץ לקח (Ez 17,13) sei, und er verwechselt es.

Schließlich geht Qimḥi, der dann in seiner breiten Behandlung von איל immer wieder auch auf die Wiedergabe im Targum verweist, soweit, auch אול hier zuzuordnen.

---

65 Der Eintrag אילת III = arab. טאקה (طاقة) im Egron, den Alony, האגרן, 190, vorschlägt, ist jedoch zu streichen. In der Handschrift CUL T.S: NS 302.75 1v = FGP No. C409911 ist deutlich עיר : אֱיָלַת zu lesen. Saadjas arabische Übersetzung von Ps 22,20 und 88,5 bietet jedoch dieses Wort als Übersetzung für אֱיָל und אֱיָלוּת.

66 Vgl. Ali Wated und Daniel Sivan, שלושה חיבורי הדקדוק של ר' יהודה חיוג' במקורם הערבי ובתרגומם לעברית חדשה [Three Treatises on Hebrew Grammar by R. Judah Ḥayyuj] (Jerusalem: Bialik, 2012), 124, 125.

Und ein Nomen mit anderer Form ist אוּל nach der Bildung von אוּר: וּבְרִיא אוּלָם אָבְרִיא (Ps 73,4) und seine Erklärung ist „und stark ist ihre Kraft".

Die jüdische Tradition zeigt also, ausgehend von der targumischen Deutung die Tendenz, einen Großteil der Lemmata א(ו/י)ל unter eine Wurzel mit der Bedeutung „stark, kräftig" zu vereinen.

Von dieser Ausgangslage her ist es nicht verwunderlich, dass dann auch Gesenius in seinem Thesaurus diese Verbindungen aufgreift:

> אוּל et אֵיל rad. Hebraeïs inusitata. 1) *praecessit, anterior, primus fuit*, ut in arab. وَأُوَلَ, unde أَوَّلُ primus, آيَّلَ praecesse, regere, administrare. Hinc derivata אוּל, Plur. אוּלִים, אוּלָם, אוּלִי, אֵיל, אֱיָל, אֵילִים, et אֵילֻת Prov. XIV, 24. De significatione *crassitudinis*, quam nonulli primarium esse statuunt, vidimus s. אוּל q.v.
> 2) *fortis, potens fuit*. Hinc אֵל robustus, robur, Deus, אוּל corpus a robore dictum, אֵיל, אֵלוֹן, אֵלָה, arbor robustam et cum Jod mobili אֵיָל, אֵיָלוּת אֵיָלֹת robur, auxilium.
> Utraque significatio cognata est, et aliquoties in eodem nomine derivato locum habet, ut in אוּלִים et אֵילִים promores, potentes.[67]

Deutlich ist, dass Gesenius durchaus noch das Problem gesehen hat, dass die arabische Wurzel eben nicht „stark, kräftig" bedeutet, aber durchaus als Ausgangspunkt für Begriffe wie אֵיָל dienen kann. So rechtfertigt er die Verknüpfung beider Bedeutungsebenen mit dem Hinweis auf אוּלִים und אֵילִים. Dies beruht jedoch einerseits auf der Annahme, dass das Ketib אוּלִים in 2 Kön 24,15, für das das Qere אֵילִים bietet, ein real existierendes Wort wiedergibt,[68] andererseits darauf, dass er in Aufnahme der jüdischen Tradition ein eigenständiges אֵיל „fortis, potens" annimmt, das mit אֵל vergleichbar sei und dem die אֵילֵי Belege in Ex 15,15 und Ez 17,13 zuzuordnen wären. Beide Annahmen werden heute zurecht nicht mehr geteilt, so dass damit diese Verbindung schlicht hinfällig wird.

Wie stark Gesenius hier von der jüdischen Tradition abhängig ist, zeigen auch die Einträge im Thesaurus zu אֵיָל und אֵיָלוּת, wo er selbst auf den Sachverhalt verweist, dass LXX und das Syrische eher auf die Bedeutung „Hilfe" führen, aber dennoch die Ableitung von אוּל in der zweiten Bedeutung mit Hinweis auf das Targum und Qimḥī vertritt.[69]

Es ergibt sich somit, dass die Wurzel ʾW/YL „stark, kräftig sein" ein Konstrukt ist, das auf der Annahme beruht, Wörter wie אֵל oder אֵיָל würden die Konnotation

---

67 So bezeichnet Gesenius das Qere als „forma ... vulgaris", vgl. *Thesaurus*, 42.
68 Ebd.
69 Vgl. *Thesaurus*, 46 f.

„Kraft" aufweisen.[70] Diese Annahme geht aber letztlich auf eine targumische Deutung zurück, die für die mittelalterliche Hebraistik kanonisch wurde, aber wohl nur auf der phonetischen Affinität von אֵיל/אֵל zu חַיִל/חֵיל beruht. Die Information über diese Herkunft aus der targumischen Deutung hat aber keinen Eingang in die gebräuchlichen Wörterbücher gefunden, was wohl begünstigte, dass die darauf aufbauenden etymologischen Spekulationen bis in die Neuzeit immer wieder Auferstehung feiern konnten.

So hat schon Ges₁₇ s.v. אול bezweifelt, dass all diese Wörter hier auf eine einzige Stammwurzel zurückzuführen seien, und stand insbesondere der Annahme eines אול im Sinne von „stark sein" skeptisch gegenüber. Deren Bedeutung könne man „am ehesten in אֵל IV finden" – d. h. in dem אֵל der oben behandelten Phrase לְאֵל יַד־ – „dag[egen] kaum in אֱיָל u[nd] אֱיָלוּת". Entsprechend übernimmt Ges₁₇ für אֱיָל und אֱיָלוּת die vom Kontext, dem Sprachvergleich und den Versionen nahegelegte Deutung als „Hilfe". Ges₁₈ folgt Ges₁₇ nicht nur in der Ablehnung dieser etymologischen Vermutungen, sondern streicht sogar jeden Hinweis auf eine Wurzel 'WL, um dann aber doch überraschenderweise bei der Deutung von אֱיָל und אֱיָלוּת zur alten targumisch-mittelalterlichen Tradition zurückzukehren und diese traditionelle Deutung auch für אֵל IV beizubehalten. Es steht zu vermuten, dass, wenn den Herausgebern von Ges₁₈ der forschungsgeschichtliche Hintergrund bewusst gewesen wäre, sie diese Entscheidung wohl kaum getroffen hätten.

Dass solche lexikographischen Entscheidungen ihre ganz eigene Dynamik entwickeln und dabei zu Ergebnissen führen können, die eine Korrektur eher verhindern und sogar noch falsche Argumente liefern, lässt sich auch an den beiden Wörten, von denen unsere Diskussion ihren Ausgang nahm – אֱיָל und אֱיָלוּת – exemplarisch studieren.

Benutzt man KBL, so findet man bei אֱיָל und אֱיָלוּת nicht nur keinerlei Hinweise darauf, dass die Bedeutung „Kraft" in irgendeiner Weise problematisch sein könnte, sondern das Wörterbuch notiert zu אֱיָל als etymologische Daten neben dem Verweis auf die Wurzel אול nur kommentarlos ܐܰܝܠܐ. Dies erzeugt den Eindruck, dass es im Syrischen ein solches Wort mit der Bedeutung „Kraft" gibt und dass dieses Wort unzweifelhaft im Hebräischen vorliegt. Ausdrücklich auch auf Grund von KBL hat dann Émile Puech aram. איל in 4Q246 frag. 1 ii 7 als „Kraft" gedeutet. Dabei ist seine Diskussion in DJD XXII, 177 bezeichnend: Zum einen argumentiert er, dass die Peschitta in Ps 88,5 dasselbe Wort wie der hebräische Text habe und dass dies vom Targum mit חילא wiedergegeben werde: „synonyme,

---

70 So besonders deutlich in KBL 19b: „Wörter wie ... אֵל, אֱיָל ... führen auf *אול vorn stark sein". Dagegen lässt sich sowohl אֱיָל/אֱיָלוּת als auch אֵל mit arab. آلَ in der Bedeutung „fürsorglich leiten" verbinden, wobei ersteres den Aspekt der Fürsorge, letzteres den Aspekt der Leitung, die eine Handlung verantwortlich initiiert, betonen würde.

ou confusion des lettres *ḥet*, et *'aleph* dans l'ecriture de l'epoque?" Zum anderen weist er den Hinweis von Guillaume auf das Syrische und Arabische[71] schlicht mit dem Hinweis zurück, dass KBL dem Wort die Bedeutung „Kraft" „de'apres le syriaque" gegeben habe und auch Wagner in seiner Behandlung der Aramaismen[72] das Wort so übersetzen würde. De facto bestimmt Puech somit in der Bearbeitung eines aramäischen Textes die Bedeutung eines aramäischen Wortes nicht mit Hilfe aramäischer Wörterbücher wie die des Syrischen, sondern auf Grund der Hinweise in hebraistischen Arbeiten. Dass dabei ein aramäisches Wort kreiert wird, das seinerseits nun scheinbar die hebraistische Deutung unterstützt,[73] könnte leicht zur Grundlage eines Zirkelschlusses werden, bei dem dann die hebraistische Deutung mit einem Hinweis auf diese scheinbare aramäische Parallele begründet wird.[74]

Auch für das Ugaritische hat man bei der Deutung von Wörtern wie *ulny*, *ul* oder auch *awl* die Existenz einer Wurzel *'WL* „stark sein" auf Grund der hebräischen lexikographischen Tradition als gesichert vorausgesetzt und die ugaritischen Wörter entsprechend interpretiert. So findet sich in KTU 1.2 IV 5 die Phrase *larṣ ypl ulny* || *wl'pr ʻẓmny*. Weitverbreitet ist hierfür die Deutung von *ul(n)* als „Kraft".[75] Da es in diesem Zusammenhang aber um das konkrete Versinken Baals im Meer geht[76] und zuvor vom drohenden Tod Baals die Rede ist, ist die Annahme, dass in dem vorliegenden Bikolon von dem Fall nur der *Kraft* Baals die Rede sei, sachlich zwar nicht unmöglich, aber auch nicht gerade zwingend. Besser passt aber eine Verbindung mit hebr. אוּל „Leib", wobei das -n- sowohl bei *ul* als auch bei *ʻẓm* entweder eine Erweiterung vor dem Sf.1.c.sg. ist[77] oder aber als Bildungselement zu den Nomina gehört, die dann hier in erweiterter Form begegnen:[78] „Zur Erde wird fallen mein Leib, und zum Staub mein Gebein." Ein anderer Beleg für *ul*

---

71 Vgl. Anm. 21.

72 Vgl. Anm. 24.

73 Und das dann auch Eingang in weit verbreitete Übersetzungen qumranischer Texte gefunden hat, vgl. z. B. García Martínez und Tigchelaar, *Study Edition*, 493; A. Steudel, *Die Texte aus Qumran II* (Darmstadt: Wissenschaftliche Buchgesellschaft, 2001), 173.

74 Dass natürlich איל in diesem aramäischen Text „Hilfe" bedeutet, wurde schon von anderen erkannt; vgl. z. B. Klaus Beyer, *Die aramäischen Texte vom Toten Meer 2*, Göttingen: Vandenhoeck & Ruprecht, 2004, 149; Maier, *Qumran-Essener*, 191.

75 Vgl. z. B. Gregorio del Olmo Lete und Joaquín Sanmartín, *A Dictionary of the Ugaritic Language in the Alphabetic Tradtion I* (HdO 67/I; Brill: Leiden, 2003), 52; Issam K.H. Halayqa, *A Comparitive Lexicon of Ugaritic and Canaanite* (AOAT 340; Münster Ugarit-Verlag, 2008), 68.

76 Vgl. Z. 6 f.: „Er wird sinken unter den Thron des Fürsten Jam!"

77 Vgl. Josef Tropper, *Ugaritische Grammatik* (AOAT 273; Münster: Ugarit-Verlag, 2000), 219.

78 Das Ugaritische kennt viele mit -n erweiterte Nomina mit konkreter Bedeutung, vgl. Tropper, *Grammatik*, 271–273.

findet sich in KTU 1.14 II 35 im Kontext der Beschreibung eines zahlreich aus-
ziehenden Heeres. Dass mit *ul mad* dort eine „zahlreiche" Macht"[79] gemeint sei,
wäre in diesem Kontext nur sinnvoll, wenn konkret an eine „Streitmacht" gedacht
wird, nicht aber an „Kraft, Macht" als Qualität. Da aber der Text danach einzelne
Soldatenklassen nennt, die ohne Zahl ausziehen (*ḫpṯ dbl spr / ṯnn dbl hg* „Söldner
ohne Zahl, Bogenschützen ohne Berechnung"), kann hier ebenso gut *ul* von der
arab. bezeugten Bedeutung „vorne sein, vorangehen" als *terminus technicus* für
die Soldaten, die vorweg gehen oder einen Angriff ausführen, verstanden werden.
Und schließlich ist *awl* in KTU 1.12 II 56 mit derselben Wurzel zu verbinden und im
Sinne von „Anführer, Erster" zu verstehen.[80]

Schließlich dürfte es auch auf den grossen Einfluss der deutschsprachigen
hebräischen Wörterbücher im nicht anglo-amerikanischen Raum zurückzuführen
sein, dass bei all diesen Diskussionen das gut belegte akk. *ayālu* völlig übergangen
wird. Es begegnet weder in den etymologischen Abschnitten der hebräischen
Wörterbücher noch in dem deutschsprachigen und einflussreichen Akkadischem
Handwörterbuch von Wolfram von Soden (AHw). Warum dieser das akkadische
Wort nicht erkannt hat, sondern es als *ajjalu II* „Verbündeter o. ä." bietet,[81] lässt
sich zwar nicht mit Sicherheit feststellen, aber die Tatsache, dass insbesondere
KBL, an dessen Neubearbeitung (HAL) von Soden als Berater mitgearbeitet hat,
jeden Hinweis auf die Existenz eines vergleichbaren semitischen Wortes mit der
Bedeutung „Hilfe" verschweigt und sogar, wie oben gesehen, den Eindruck er-
weckt, dass auch das syrische *'īyālā* „Kraft" bedeutet, könnte zumindest mitge-
wirkt haben, dass von Soden in den Belegen des akkadischen Wortes nicht das
Wort für „Hilfe, Beistand" erkennen konnte. Dass umgekehrt dann die späteren
deutschsprachigen hebräischen Wörterbücher ihrerseits dieses akkadische Wort
übersahen,[82] ist angesichts seines Fehlens im AHw verständlich, illustriert aber
auf das Trefflichste, wie sich die Entscheidungen der Lexikographen gegenseitig
beeinflussen – und wie hilfreich es sein kann, hin und wieder für das eine oder
andere Wort seine Forschungsgeschichte kritisch zu erheben und nachzufragen,
worauf sich eigentlich die vorgeschlagenen Deutungen stützen.

---

79 So z. B. Manfried Dietrich und Oswald Loretz, *Mythen und Epen IV* (TUAT III/6; Gütersloh:
Gütersloher Verlagshaus, 1997), 1222.
80 Vgl. Dietrich und Loretz, *Mythen*, 1211.
81 Vgl. AHw I *sub voce* ajjalu II, wo von Soden es mit a'lu „Beduinenstamm?" verbindet; auch in
den Nachträgen von 1981 korrigiert von Soden diesen Eintrag nur dahingehend, dass er nun das
Wort jālūtum „Bündnis" zum Vergleich heranzieht, vgl. AHw 1542 u. 1565.
82 Da von Soden sowohl für das HAL als auch für Ges₁₈ als akkadistischer Berater gewirkt hat,
verwundert es nicht, dass das akkadische Wort dort fehlt; aber man sucht es auch vergeblich in der
Neubearbeitung von HAL, dessen etymologischer Teil von Grund auf erneuert worden ist (KAHAL,
vii).

3. אַט/אוֹט – von der „Sanftheit" zur „Angemessenheit"

Auch das zweite Beispiel illustriert, dass etymologische Theorien zuweilen den Blick auf die Daten verstellen können und einer kritischen Validierung gerade hinsichtlich der Frage bedürfen, auf welcher Grundlage sie eigentlich selbst stehen.

An mehreren Stellen der hebräischen Bibel begegnet das Lemma אַט, das nach Ges[18] ein „leises, sanftes, gemächliches Verhalten" bezeichnet, während HAL „gedrückte Stimmung, Sanftheit" als Grundbedeutung angibt.

Die Belege in der hebräischen Bibel sind wenige, zeigen aber eine erstaunliche Bandbreite:

Gen 33,14 begegnet אֶתְנָהֲלָה לְאִטִּי, was wörtlich übersetzt mit „und ich will mich führen/versorgen[83] in Bezug auf mein אַט" übersetzt werden kann und die Art und Weise beschreibt, in der Jakob hinter Laban mit Rücksicht auf den „Schritt der Viehherde" und dem „Schritt der Kinder" herziehen will.

2 Sam 18,5 wird mit לְאַט־לִי לַנַּעַר לְאַבְשָׁלוֹם König Davids Befehl zitiert, Absalom zu schonen bzw. auf ihn zu achten (vgl. V. 12!). Wörtlich fordert David, dass für Absalom das sei, was ein אַט für ihn selbst ist.

In 1 Kön 21,27 gehört die Phrase הלך אַט neben dem Zerreissen der Kleider, Fasten und in Sacktuch Schlafen zu den Beschreibungen der Selbstminderungsriten, die Ahab nach dem Tod Nabots auf sich nimmt. Dabei ist es möglich, dass das abschließende וַיְהַלֵּךְ אַט entweder einen weiteren Aspekt dieser Riten beschreibt oder das Verhalten des Königs zusammenfassend charakterisiert.

Jes 8,6 charakterisiert הלך לְאַט die Art und Weise, wie die Wasser von Siloa fließen, wobei dies in V. 7 mit mächtigen Wassern kontrastiert wird, die zerstörerisch über die Ufer treten.

Schließlich charakterisiert לָאַט עִמָּךְ in Hi 15,11 ein Wort (דָּבָר), wobei der Ausdruck im Parallelismus membrorum zu תַּנְחֻמוֹת אֵל „Tröstungen Gottes" steht.

Die LXX hilft bei diesen Belegen nicht viel weiter und zeigt nur, dass sie die Belege jeweils nach ihrem Kontext deutet. So bietet sie in Gen 33,14 ἐν τῇ ὁδῷ „auf

---

83 נהל bedeutet „leiten, führen", aber auch „versorgen" (Gen 47,17), wobei „leiten, führen" grundsätzlich im Kontext der Fürsorge gebraucht wird und den Geführten zu dem von ihm Benötigten führt und damit auch versorgt, vgl. Ex 15,13; Jes 40,11; 49,10; 51,18; Ps 23,2; 31,4; 2 Chron 28,15. Das hier gebrauchte Dt ist singulär; zur Deutung im Sinne von „sich versorgen" vgl. bes. TgS[A] ואנה אסתובר (Var. אסובנה, אסובר) „und ich versorgte mich", aber auch LXX ἐγὼ δὲ ἐνισχύσω „ich aber will mich stark machen".

dem Weg",[84] in 2 Sam 18,5 aber Φείσασθέ μοι τοῦ παιδαρίου τοῦ Αβεσσαλωμ· „Verschont mir den Jungen, den Absalom!" In 1 Kön 21,27 hat LXX offenbar einen völlig anderen Text oder interpretiert den Schluss des Verses ohne näheren Anhalt an den hebräischen Text: ἐν τῇ ἡμέρᾳ, ᾗ ἐπάταξεν Ναβουθαι τὸν Ιεζραηλίτην „an dem Tag, da er den Jesreeliter Nabot zerschlagen hatte". Jes 8,6 deutet LXX im Sinne von „ruhig fließen": τὸ πορευόμενον ἡσυχῇ, während in Hi 15,11 die LXX wiederum ein völlig anderes Verständnis des Verses zeigt, das, wenn die LXX hier wirklich dasselbe Wort gelesen hat, genau zum Gegenteil führen würde: μεγάλως ὑπερβαλλόντως λελάληκας „du hast absolut übermäßig gesprochen". Mithin würde Gen 33,14 und Hi 15,11 auf die Bedeutung „stark, heftig" führen, während 2 Sam 18,5 und Jes 8,6 die Bedeutung „sanft" unterstützen würden.[85]

Die targumische Tradition von TgO/J zieht hingegen die Bedeutung „Ruhe, Gelassenheit, Freundlichkeit" vor und übersetzt entsprechend אָט in Gen 33,14 (= TgPsJ) und Jes 8,6 mit ניח, das dann auch das Targum zu Hi 15,11 bietet. Möglicherweise steht diese Deutung auch hinter 1 Kön 21,27, wo TgJ וַיְהַלֵּךְ אַט mit והליך יחיף „und er ging barfuss" paraphrasiert, was eine Ausdeutung von „und er ging ruhig" sein könnte. In 2 Sam 18,5 übernimmt das TgJ die sachliche Deutung der Anweisung, die in V. 12 zu finden ist (שְׁמָרוּ־מִי בַּנַּעַר בְּאַבְשָׁלוֹם) und übersetzt an beiden Stellen mit אסתמרו לי בעוליִמא באבשלום.

Die palästinische Tradition hat für Gen 33,14 eine andere Deutung parat. TgN gibt אֶתְנָהֲלָה לְאָטִי mit להוני „אדבר יתהון „ich will sie führen mit Bedacht" wieder, was eine Parallele in BerR 78,14 hat: אני מהלך היך דאת אמר ההולכים לאט „להוני: „ich will gehen mit Bedacht', wie das (die Schrift) sagt: ההולכים לאט (Jes 8,6)". Das hier „mit Bedacht" übersetzte להונ־ bedeutet wörtlich „entsprechend des Verstandes von ...". הן konnotiert auch im palästinischen Aramäischen die Überlegung und Sorgfalt im Hinblick auf eine Handlung, die dementsprechend bewusst, bedacht und überlegt ausgeführt wird.[86] Dass diese Bedeutung auch hier vorliegt, wird durch den Kontext der Stelle belegt, die die so interpretierte Aussage Jakobs als Antwort auf Labans Frage präsentiert, ob er sich nicht vor den Militärs Labans fürchten würde: „Ich werde mit Bedacht gehen." Dem entspricht auch der Gebrauch von להונך in LevR 26,8 (par.), mit dem Gott eine Rede an den Engel Gabriel eröffnet, die

---

84 Dies entspricht auch der Deutung in den samaritanischen Targumen, die u. a. לאלכה (TgSʲ) oder למהכה (TgSᴬ) bieten.

85 Wollte man dies unter einen Hut bringen, so müsste man allenfalls annehmen, dass LXX in 2 Sam 18,5 und Jes 8,6 haplographisch לא לאט gelesen hätte, was den Schluss erlauben würde, dass LXX אַט im Sinne von „Kraft, Macht" verstanden hätte.

86 Vgl. die Beispiele bei Michael Sokoloff, *A Dictionary of Jewish Palestinian Aramaic* (Ramat Gan: Bar Ilan University, 1990), *sub voce* הן und im Comprehensive Aramaic Lexicon Project (http://cal1. cn.huc.edu/) *sub voce* hwn, hwnʾ.

diesen davon abbringt, aus Wut über Israel glühende Kohlen auf das Volk zu werfen. לְהוּנָךְ „Zu deinem הוּן!" bedeutet hier, dass Gabriel zu seinem Verstand (zurück)kommen und bedächtig erst die Situation[87] durchschauen soll, bevor er handelt.[88] Auffällig ist, dass die palästinische Tradition darin mit TgO/J übereinstimmt, dass sie den Gebrauch von לְאָט in Gen 33,14 analog zu Jes 8,6 versteht, dabei aber die Konnotation der Angemessenheit einträgt. So wie die Wasser von Siloa im Gegensatz zu den mächtigen Wassern in ihrem Bett bleiben und so mit Bedacht und angemessen fließen, so will Jakob mit Bedacht und seiner Situation angemessen handeln, wie es sich aus dem Schritttempo seiner Herden und Kinder ergibt.

Die von der palästinischen Tradition gewiesene Richtung führt auf eine mögliche Deutung aller Belegstellen von אָט. An jeder dieser Stellen ergibt die Konnotation der Angemessenheit einen guten Sinn und erklärt zugleich auch, warum das Wort teils mit Suffix, teils absolut gebraucht wird. Im absoluten Gebrauch bezieht sich אָט auf das, was in diesem Kontext allgemein angemessen ist, mit Suffix drückt es aus, was insbesondere für die Person angemessen ist, wobei auch der Aspekt mitschwingt, dass das Angemessene auch das ist, was sich als notwendig erweist und gebraucht wird.

Dass dies für Gen 33,14, und Jes 8,6 eine für den jeweils gegebenen Kontext sinnvolle Aussage ergibt, hat die Besprechung der palästinischen Targumtradition gezeigt. Mit dieser Deutung von אָט ist dann 1 Kön 21,27 dahingehend zu verstehen, dass Ahab in seinen Trauerriten sich „angemessen" verhält. In Hi 15,11 wäre das tröstende Wort eben angemessen in Bezug auf Hiob. Schließlich klärt sich von hier auch die auffällige Formulierung in 2 Sam 18,5. Mit לְאַט־לִי לַנַּעַר לְאַבְשָׁלוֹם drückt David den Befehl aus, dass man Absalom gemäß dem, was David selbst angemessen wäre, behandeln soll. Absalom soll also immer noch als königliche Person und nicht als einfacher Putschist behandelt werden, was die Diener dann in V. 12 durchaus korrekt dahingehend auslegen, dass sie auf Absalom achthaben sollen.

Aber auch hier gilt der Grundsatz, dass die Tatsache, dass eine bestimmte Bedeutung in den vorliegenden Kontexten sinnvoll ist, noch lange nicht bedeutet,

---

87 Diese wird im anschließenden Satz geschildert: יש בהם בני אדם שעושין צדקה אלו עם אלו „Es gibt bei ihnen Menschen, die untereinander wohltätig handeln."
88 Vgl. Mordecai Margoulies, מדרש ויקרא רבה [*Midrash Wayyikra Rabbah*] III (Jerusalem: American Academy for Jewish Research, 1956), 609:6; Parallelen: EchR 1,41; Tanḥ Emor 3; MidrSam 24,8. Von daher ist es irreführend, wenn Sokoloff, *Dictionary*, diese Stellen unter dem eigenständigen Eintrag להונ־ bucht und als Bedeutung „at ... 's leisure" angibt. Dass Jakob angesichts der Bedrohung, die in BerR den Kontext der Aussage gibt, „in Muße" oder „gemächlich" oder „so, wie es ihm passt" wandern will, ist ebenso absurd, wie die Annahme, dass Gott auf Gabriels wütende Reaktion gegen Israel mit einem „At yours leisure!" antworten würde.

dass dies auch der Intention der Autoren entsprach. Jedoch lässt sich eine zusätzliche Evidenz aufweisen.

Weisheitliche Texte aus Qumran bieten mit אוט ein Lemma, das offenkundig eine ganz ähnliche Konnotation aufweist. Die Bedeutung dieses אוט, das zweimal (4Q424 frag. 1,6; 4Q418 frag. 8,13) auch defektiv geschrieben wird, ist lange kontrovers diskutiert worden,[89] aber eine Übersicht über die Belege, für die ein, wenn auch nicht immer klarer Kontext erhalten ist, zeigt, dass an allen Stellen die Konnotation „Angemessenheit" insbesondere auch im Sinn von „angemessener Bedarf" sinnvoll ist:[90]

4Q417 frag. 2 ii + 23,3 ‖ 4Q416 frag. 2 ii1
כול מחסורי אוטו [... ... all der Bedarf, der ihm angemessen ist,
ולתת טרף לכ̇[ו]ל חי ... und zu geben Nahrung für alles Leben ...

4Q418 frag. 126 ii 2
או [-]י̇[-] באמת מיד כול אוט ... in Wahrheit durch alles den Menschen Angemessene.
אנשים

4Q418 frag. 126 ii 12–13
ובידכה אוטהו [...] ... und in deiner Hand ist das ihm Angemessene/sein Bedarf
ומטנאכה ידרוש חפצו und aus deinem Korb fordert er sein Begehr.
... ...
ואם לוא תס̇ⁱⁱג ידו Und wenn seine Hand nicht vermag,
למחסורכה ומחסור אוטו[...] für deinen Bedarf oder dem Bedarf, der ihm angemessen ist ...

4Q418 frag. 127,5
כי אל עשה כול חפצי אוט Denn Gott hat gemacht alles, was angemessen erstrebenswert ist,
ויתכ̇נם באמת[...] und es festgesetzt in Wahrheit ...

4Q424 frag. 1,6
ביד עצל אל תפקד אט Der Hand eines Trägen vertraue nichts Notwendiges[91] an,
כי לא יצניע מלאכתך denn er wird nicht sorgsam mit deinem Geschäft umgehen.

---

89 Vgl. etwa die Übersicht bei Antoon Schoors, „The Language of the Qumran Sapiential Works", in *The Wisdom Texts from Qumran and the Development of Sapiential Thought*, (ed. Charlotte Hempel, Armin Lange & Herrmann Lichtenberger; BEThL 159; Löwen: University Press und Peeters, 2002), 77, 78, und John Kampen, *Wisdom Literatur* (Eerdmans Commentaries on the Dead Sea Scrolls; Grand Rapids & Cambridge: Eerdmans, 2011), 50 f.; Michel Becker, Art. אוט 'wṭ, in *Theologisches Wörterbuch zu den Qumrantexten I* (hg. von Heinz-Josef Fabry und Ulrich Dahmen; Stuttgart: Kolhhammer, 2011), 84–86.
90 Weitere Stellen ohne ausreichenden Kontext sind 4Q415 frag. 18,2; 4Q418 frag. 79,2; 101,3; 177,8; 4Q423 frag. 1–2 i 5.
91 אט hier im Sinne des das der Situation angemessene, d. h. das, was wirklich wichtig zu tun ist.

4Q418 frag. 81+81a,16

אוט לכול הולכי אדם [...   ... das Angemessen für alle, die unter den Menschen wandeln.

ומשם תפקוד טרפכה ז̊[ה...]   Und von dort her wirst Du anvertrauen/dich kümmern um deine Nahrung und ...

4Q418 frag. 103 ii 6

כמקור מים ח̊יים   ... wie eine Quelle lebendigen Wassers.

אשר הכיל א[ו]ט̊-[...]   die enthält, das was angemessen ist für/den Bedarf von ...

4Q418 frag. 107,4

א̊וטב̊ית̊ם [...   ~~was dir angemessen ist~~ Angemessenes

מסחורכה ופעולתכה בחפצי   dein Handel und dein Tun bezüglich der Belange ...
[...]

4Q418 frag. 138,4

אוטכה [92](https://...) וכל חפציכה[...]   ... was dir angemessen ist/dein Bedarf und all dein Begehr ...

4Q416 frag. 2 ii 12 ‖ 4Q418 frag. 8,13

א̊ם ברצונו תחזיק עבודתו   Wenn Du nach seinem Wohlgefallen an seinem Dienst festhältst,

וחכמת[93](https://...)   wirst Du weise sein.

אוטו [94*/] –   Was ihm/mir angemessen ist ...

Dass dieses Wort Eingang in die weisheitliche Terminologie erhalten hat, ist wenig verwunderlich, da „Angemessenheit" ja ein zentrales weisheitliches Thema ist.

Dass hier dasselbe Wort wie biblisch-hebräisch אָט und nicht nur eine andere Ableitung von derselben Wurzel vorliegt, legt die Wiedergabe von אָט (Jes 8,6) in 1QIsaa VII 26 mit אוט nahe. Das Wort wurde wohl, wie auch die vereinzelten defektiven Schreibungen אט nahelegen, in Qumran als *qutl* gesprochen, das auch sonst in der hebräischen Sprachgeschichte gerne mit *qatl* wechselt.[95]

Von diesen Beobachtungen her hat man guten Grund, für das Biblisch- und Qumran-Hebräische die Existenz eines אָט/אֹט anzunehmen, das „Angemessenheit" im Sinne von „was einer Situation angemessen oder in ihr notwendig ist" bedeutet. Der Grund, warum diese Verbindung zwischen den Texten aus Qumran und der hebräischen Bibel bisher nicht erkannt wurde, obwohl immer wieder Ausleger versucht haben, eine Beziehung zwischen beiden Wörtern herzustel-

---

92 So korrekt vgl. Eibert J. C. Tigchelaar, *To Increase Learning for the Understanding Ones* (STDJ 44; Leiden: Brill, 2001), 105; das nächste Wort weist aber gegen Tigchelaar keine Schreiberkorrektur auf.

93 Entgegen der landläufigen Deutung dürfte וחכמת nicht st.cs.sg. von חכמה sein, sondern ein perf.cons. von חכם G. Mit אוטו beginnt dann ein neuer Satz/Spruch, so dass Überlegungen, was eine „Weisheit seines אוטו" bedeuten könnte, überflüssig sind.

94 4Q418 frag. 8,13: defektiv אטו[י].

95 Vgl. Kutscher, *Language*, 390.459 – 462; Qimron, *Hebrew*, 65.

len,[96] liegt auf der Hand. Solange man davon ausgeht, dass biblisch-hebräisch אַט etwas mit „Langsamkeit", „Sanftheit" oder auch „Stille" zu tun hat, wie es die Wörterbücher suggerieren, ist kaum eine überzeugende Verbindung zu den Belegen aus Qumran zu ziehen.[97]

Auch hier empfiehlt sich somit die Frage, worauf eigentlich diese Bedeutungsbestimmung beruht. Wie אֱיָל/אֱיָלוּת ist dieses Wort im Mittelhebräischen ungebräuchlich und wird erst in späterer Zeit wiederbelebt. Wie zu erwarten, greifen dabei die Lexikographen die kanonische Tradition insbesondere des TgO und TgJ auf.[98] Für unsere Fragestellung nach den Quellen der modernen Wörterbücher kommt hier zunächst das Wörterbuch von Ibn Ǧanāḥ in Frage.[99]

---

96 Vgl. z. B. André Caquot, „Les Textes de sagesse de Qoumrân (Aperçu préliminaire)", *RHPhR* 76 (1996), 11, 26, der entsprechend das Wort in 4Q417 frag. 2 ii + 23,3 mit „indulgence" und in 4Q418 frag, 126,2 mit „lenteur (?)" wiedergibt, aber die übrigen Stellen nicht mit einbezieht, oder Tzvi Novick, „The Meaning and Etymology of אוט", *JBL* 127 (2008), 339 – 343, dessen Bedeutungsbestimmung von אוט als „property, affair" unserer durchaus nahekommt. Jedoch ist seine Argumentation, dass die oben (S. 60 – 61) diskutierte Wiedergabe von לְאָטִי mit להוני im TgN auch für das Hebräische einen Übergang von der Bedeutung „Muße" zu „Besitz" belegen würde, sicher nicht korrekt: „As Biblical Hebrew הון reflects a shift from 'leisure' to 'property', so אוט underwent the same shift in the Hebrew of the Qumran wisdom texts" (342).

97 Vgl. z. B. Becker, אוט, 85: „Die Unsicherheit [hinsichtlich der Bedeutung von אוט, I.K.] hat gute Gründe, da weder in der bibl[ischen] noch in der frühjüd[ischen] oder rabb[inischen] Literatur ein entsprechendes Nomen belegt ist. Einen Anhaltspunkt für eine Interpretation könnten zwar der adverbiale Gebrauch von אט mit und ohne ל, seine mögliche Verbindung mit der Wurzel אטט ... bieten, doch legt ein Vergleich der Wortfelder nahe, den bibl[ischen] Sprachgebrauch nicht zur Herleitung heranzuziehen."

98 Dass die Übernahme der targumischen Interpretation alles andere als sachlich zwingend war, zeigt die karäische Adaption von אט als religionsphilosophischer Begriff, der offenkundig אֶתְנַהֲלָה לְאִטִּי aus Gen 33,14 aufgreift. So bezeichnet Phrase אטים ונהולים die Opfer als Vorbereitung und Hinleitung zur Umkehr oder die Gebote der Tora als Grundlage der Vernunftgebote, die von diesen sich ableiten (vgl. die Belege Eliezer Ben Yehuda, *A Complete Dictionary of Ancient and Modern Hebrew* (New York und London: Thomas Yoseloff, 1960,) *sub voce* אט ב). Daneben begegnet es auch mehrfach allein bzw. neben Begriffen wie תקון im Sinne von „Grundlage, Hinleitung" o. ä. (Belege in den Maʾ'ᵃgarîm [http://maagarim.hebrew-academy.org.il] *sub voce* בספרות הקראים (הדרכה) (אטאט))). Sollte sich hier ein Nachhall der ja auch in der palästinischen Tradition erhaltenen ursprünglichen Bedeutung etwa in dem Sinne finden, dass das, wofür eine Sache ein אט ist, auch das ist, was dieser Sache angemessen ist?

99 Die Diskussion der hier behandelten Wörter in den mittelalterlichen Wörterbüchern ist recht komplex, da einerseits sich das Konzept der schwachen Wurzeln als ursprünglich dreiradikalig erst allmählich herausbildete, andererseits unser Lemma einschließlich der häufig mit diesem auftretenden Präposition ל sich in seiner Oberflächenform mit Ableitungen von anderen Wurzeln wie לאט/לוט überschneidet und so die Lexikographen verwirrte. Dazu kam auch die uneinheitliche Wiedergabe in den kanonischen Targumen. So ordnet z. B. Sarūq (Maḥbæræt) Gen 33,14, 2 Sam 18,5 und Jes 8,6 zusammen mit בלאט in Ri 4,21 unter der Wurzel לאט II ein, der er die Bedeutung

אט וַיְהַלֵּךְ (1 Kön 21,27) „und er ging langsam einher, [das heißt] in Ruhe. Und von diesem Wort und von dieser Bedeutung stammt auch לָאט לִי לַנַּעַר (2 Sam 18,5) „behandelt den Knaben milde"; הַהֹלְכִים לְאַט (Jes 8,6); אֶתְנָהֲלָה לְאִטִּי (Gen 33,14). Und das *Lamed* bei diesen ist ein Zusatz mit der Bedeutung des Umstands. Und ebenso ist das Jod ein Zusatz bei לְאִטִּי. Aber es ist nicht ein Pronomen der 1. Pers. sg. Aber Abū Zakarja zog es vor, dass diese Lameds wurzelhaft seien.[100]

Im Anschluss daran behandelt Ibn Ǧanāḥ dann die אִטִּים (Jes, 19,3; modern: „Totengeister" < akkadisch *eṭemmu*), wobei er hier einerseits *expressis verbis* auf das Targum verweist, andererseits für dieses Wort arabisch اطيط anführt:

וְדָרְשׁוּ אֶל הָאֱלִילִים וְאֶל הָאִטִּים: Eine Art von den feinen verborgenen Kunstfertigkeiten, von welchem ihre Besitzer ein verborgenes Zeichen gemäß ihrer Behauptung suchen; und man sagt, dass sie Astrologen seien. Und sein Targum ist וּמִן חָרָשַׁיָּא („und von den Zauberen").

Und meiner Meinung nach ist es nicht fernliegend, dass es eine Affinität zu dem arabischen Wort اطيط für den Laut hat, (das) in Bezug auf jeden Laut (gebraucht wird): Es entspricht dem Laut eines neuen Sattels oder eines getwisteten Leders.

Als Begründung führt Ibn Ǧanāḥ dann Jes 29,4 (כְּאוֹב מֵאֶרֶץ קוֹלֵךְ) an und erklärt, dass diese Zauberer Stimmen ertönen lassen, wobei ihr Ächzen dem Laut der Kamele (اطيط الابل) entsprechen würde.

Mithin geht Ibn Ǧanāḥ von zwei unterschiedlichen Wörtern aus, wobei das erste, unser אַט, mit dem Targum im Sinne von Ruhe, Gelassenheit verbunden wird, was aber nichts mit Stille zu tun hat. Das Wort für die Mantiker wäre aber mit اطيط

בנחת zuordnet. Der Einfluss des autoritativen TgO, das für die einzige Torastelle dieser Gruppe ניח bietet, dem zudem TgJ zu Jes 8,6 entspricht, dürfte hier unübersehbar sein. Dagegen ist 1 Kön 21, 27 der einzige Beleg für אט I, den Sarūq aber wiederum nach TgJ deutet (אט כמו יחף). Letzteres findet sich auch bei dem Karäer Dāwd ibn 'Ibrāhīm Al-Fāsī in seinem *Kitāb ǧāmi' al-alfāẓ* (hg. von. Solomon L. Skoss, *The Hebrew-Arabic Dictionary of the Bible known as Kitāb Jāmi' Al-Alfāẓ (Agrōn) of David Ben Abraham Al-Fāsī I – II* (YOS XX – XXI; New Haven: Yale University Press, 1936–45), der 2 Sam 18,5; Jes 8,6 und Gen 33,14 dem Lemma לאט (entsprechend seiner Vorgehensweise unter dem Obereintrag לא) zuordnet, für das er die Bedeutung „sanft, freundlich" angibt. Die Behandlung von 1 Kön 21,27 in diesen beiden Lexika ist für den Einfluss des Targum auch von daher von Bedeutung, da sie damit explizit von der Deutung durch Saadja abweichen, der im Egron unter dem Eintrag אָט (sic!) dies zur Bedeutung „sanft, milde, freundlich" stellt: וַיְהַלֵּךְ אט תפסֹ רפֹ'ק (= تفث رفيق/رفق); Allony, האגרון, 166).

100 Dies bezieht sich auf den *Kitāb al-'af'āl ḏawāt ḥurūf al-līn* des Juda ibn Daud al-Fāsī (= Abū Zakarija), der die genannten Stellen unter לוט לוט subsumiert, aber dort auch schon angesichts des אַט in 1 Kön 21,27 anmerkt: „Und vielleicht kann man sagen, dass dieses Lamed eine Ergänzung ist (und) nicht von der Wurzel kommt" (vgl. Wated / Sivan, שלושת חיבורי הדקדוק, 145).

vergleichbar, einem Wort für jede Art von Laut und hier insbesondere von Lauten, die Kamele erzeugen.[101]

Dieser Verweis auf das arabische Wort war der europäischen Welt über den viel benutzen Sefār haš-Šorāšîm von David Qimḥī zugänglich, der im Wesentlichen eine verkürzte Version von Ibn Ǧanāḥs Eintrag bietet. Entscheidend ist aber, dass Qimḥī nun eine direkte Verbindung zwischen beiden Teilen zieht und den Verweis auf das Arabische abkürzt. So entspricht der erste Teil sachlich Ibn Ǧanāḥ, wobei Qimḥī nur noch Hi 15,11 nachträgt. Die weitere Ausführung lautet dann:

ודרשו אל האלילים ואל האטים: Eine Art von den Arten der Zauberer, die im Stillen (בנחת) gewirkt wird. Und angesichts des Dageš' in באטים ist es möglich, dass *ihre* Wurzel אטט ist. Und so hat mein Herr Vater ז"ל geschrieben und er sagte, dass man es in der arabischen Sprache الاطوط nenne.

In dem Qimḥī die „feinen verborgenen Kunstfertigkeiten" (الصناعات اللطيفة الخفيّة) zu solchen, die in der Stille (בנחת) getan werden, macht, greift er die Hauptbedeutung auf, die er für die Belege im ersten Teil in Aufnahme der älteren Tradition gibt (עניינו בנחת) und subsumiert beide Wörter zugleich unter einer Wurzel. Und indem er nur das arabische اطوط > اطيط ohne jegliche Deutung zitiert, ergibt sich der Eindruck, dass אטט und أَطّ beide etwas mit Stille zu tun hätten.

Ein weiterer Schritt war dann der Versuch von Albert Schultens, den Beleg aus Hi 15,11 zu erklären.[102] Er plädierte dafür, diesen mit אט in 1 Kön 21,27; 2 Sam 18,5 und Jes 8,6 zu verbinden und als Bedeutung „sanft" anzunehmen. Dabei verweist auch er auf arabisch أَطّ, das seiner Meinung nach „*Teneriore amoris* vel *commiserationis adfectu ductus fuit*" bedeuten könne, aber die Grundbedeutung „sanft murmeln" habe, die auch in Jes 8,6 zu finden sei. Schultens sagt leider nicht, woher er diese Bedeutung des Arabischen nimmt. Wahrscheinlich aber beruht die Annahme, dass die Wurzel auch „Mitleid" konnotieren könne, auf von den klassischen arabischen Lexika gebotenen Beispielsätzen wie (أَطّت لَهُ رَحِمِي). Dies

---

101 Vgl. auch die Aufnahme dieser Ansicht bei Ibn Barūn, der zur Begriffsbestimmung von اطيط noch den Laut anführt, den Kamele wegen der Schwere der Ladung ausstoßen; vgl. Paul Kokovzov, יתר הפליטה מן כתאב אלמואזנה אללגה אלעבראניה ואלערביה (Petersburg: Elieser Behrman und Zvi Rabbinowitz, 1890), 32; Pinchas Wechter, *Ibn Barūn's Arabic Works on Hebrew Grammar and Lexicography* (Philadelphia: The Dropsie College for Hebrew and Cognate Learning, 1964),, 66. Dass Ibn Barūn dieses Wort von unserem אט trennt, zeigt sich daran, dass er das אט in 1 Kön 21,27 mit einem ganz anderen arabischen Wort verbindet; s.u. S. 68.

102 Vgl. Albertus Schultens, *Liber Jobi cum nova versione I* (Leiden: Johannes Luzac, 1737), 372–3.

bedeutet aber wörtlich schlicht „mein Leib schrie, stöhnte nach ihm".[103] Die Konnotation des Affekts eignet hier der gesamten Phrase, wobei der Begriff des „Leibes" als Sitz des Gefühles den emotionalen Aspekt einträgt. Hier liegt ein typisches Beispiel für den methodischen Fehler vor, direkte Beziehungen zwischen Einzelgliedern von Phrasen aus unterschiedlichen Sprachen anzunehmen.

Gesenius schließlich verband den Ansatz des Ibn Ǧanāḥ mit dem von Schultens: Die Grundbedeutung von אטט sei „murmeln, knarren, knurren" (für das er Ibn Ǧanāḥ anführt), das im Zusammenhang mit Gewässern aber „sanft fließen" bedeute (Jes 8,6), um schließlich auch „sanftes Gehen/Treiben" bezeichnen zu können: „Translatum est vocabulum a sono ad fluxum, a fluxu ad incessum."[104]

Wie aber schon die Angaben des muttersprachlich Arabisch sprechenden Ibn Ǧanāḥ zeigen, konnotiert أَطَّ jede Art von Lautäußerung und ist sicherlich kein spezieller Begriff für leise Laute oder „Murmeln" – so bezeichnet es z. B. auch das Schreien hungriger Kamele oder solcher, die nach ihren Jungen rufen.[105] Und ausgerechnet auch die Stelle aus den Maqāma des al-Ḥarīrī (1054–1122), auf die Gesenius zur Unterstützung der Ansicht, dass أَطَّ „lenem sonum edidit" bedeute, belegt das Gegenteil. Ḥarīrī beschreibt dort mit هَدَأَ بها لَأطِيطُ والغطِيطُ ، سَمِعْتُ صَيْتًا من الرِّجالِ[106] eine Szene, in der der Erzähler erst, nachdem der Lärm, den eine Karawane bei ihrem Niederlassen erzeugt, aufgehört hatte, eine Unterhaltung mithören kann, die ein anderer Mann mit lauter Stimme führt.[107] Ibn Ǧanāḥ, der darauf verzichtet hat, die אֹטִים aus Jes 19,3 mit dem אט der anderen Stellen in einen direkten Zusammenhang zu stellen, konnte durchaus auf diese arabische Wurzel verweisen, um die Mantiker als Leute zu kennzeichnen, die irgendwelche Laute von sich geben – dass das Wort ein akkadisches Lehnwort ist, das wohl seinerseits auf sumerisch g i d i m zurückgeht, konnte er natürlich nicht wissen. Aber es führt kein Weg von dieser Wurzel zu einem Wort, dass in besonderem Maße ein ruhiges Murmeln eines Flusses und dann noch ein sanftes Gehen bezeichnen könnte. Ein Fluss, der أَطَّ macht, wäre ein Fluss, der sich gerade dadurch auszeichnet, dass er zu hören ist, was kaum zu einem sanften Fließen passen will.

---

103 Vgl. z. B. den *Al-Qāmūs (al-muḥīṭ)* des al-Fīrūzābādī (1326–1414), der der europäischen Lexikographie als eine Hauptquelle gedient hat und u. a. zu أَطَّ folgendes anführt: له رَجِمي: رَقَّتْ وتحرَّكتْ „… mein Leib nach ihm: (mein Leib) bekam Mitleid (mit ihm) und war erschüttert".

104 *Thesaurus* 76.

105 Vgl. Lane, *Lexicon*, 66a–b.

106 „Und als das Stöhnen und Schreien in ihr (*scil.* der Karawane) verstummt war, da hörte ich die laute Stimme von dem Mann … ".

107 Vgl. den Text bei Silvestre de Sacy, *Les Séances de Hariri* (Paris: Imprimerie Royale, 1822), arab. Text 34.

Es zeigt sich also, dass die Konnotation der Ruhe oder Gelassenheit sich insbesondere aus der targumischen Interpretation des autoritativen TgO zu Gen 33,14 ableitet, die zusammen mit TgJ zu Jes 8,6 (und Tg zu Hiob 15,11) Schritt für Schritt in der mittelalterlichen Lexikographie nicht nur auf alle unsere Belegstellen ausgeweitet wurde. Spätestens bei David Qimḥī traten die אֵטִים dazu, die zuvor Ibn Ǧanāḥ mit der arabischen Wurzel اَلَ in Verbindung gebracht hat. Parallel dazu hat auch Schultens diese Wurzel in einer sachlich nicht überzeugenden Form in das Spiel gebracht, und schließlich Gesenius daraus den folgenschweren Schluss gezogen, dass all diese irgendwie miteinander etymologisch verbunden seien.

Der Blick auf die Forschungsgeschichte zeigt somit, dass die bei Ges₁₈ gegebene etymologische Begründung für die Annahme, dass אט ein „leises, sanftes, gemächliches Verhalten" bezeichne, nicht zu halten ist – die Aussage „ar. ʾaṭṭa – murmeln, leise knarren" hat sich als ein Konstrukt der Forschungsgeschichte erwiesen, die über die Deutung der mit diesem Wort nicht verbundenen אֵטִים in die Diskussion geraten ist.

HAL war somit gut beraten, auf diese Etymologie zu verzichten – dass es dabei aber an der traditionellen Übersetzung des Wortes grundsätzlich festhält, zeigt den starken Einfluss der letztlich bis auf das Targum zurückgehenden lexikographischen Tradition. Dass dagegen der Verweis auf arabisch طَأْطَأَ die Bedeutungsangabe „gedrückte Stimmung, Sanftheit" stützen könnte, wie HAL es durch seinen etymologischen Hinweis suggeriert, ist nicht überzeugend. Es handelt sich um eine völlig andere Wurzel mit umgekehrter Reihenfolge der Wurzelkonsonanten, und die Wurzel bedeutet auch nicht „beugen", sondern „herabsenken, herunterlassen" (auch von Vorhängen, Brunneneimern, Schleier o. ä.) oder „erniedrigen.[108] Semantisch passt dies allenfalls zu 1 Kön 21,27.[109] Wie dies dann aber auf die übrigen Stellen einschließlich Gen 33,14 und Hi 15,11 zu übertragen wäre, bleibt fraglich. Aus „erniedrigen" oder „herablassen" lässt sich die Bedeutung „sanft" oder „gemächlich" kaum ableiten.

Aber auch hier folgt die Lexikographie der mittelalterlichen Forschung, da diese Gleichung auf Ibn Barūn zurückgeht. Dieser schlägt sie jedoch allein in Bezug auf 1 Kön 21,27 vor und vergleicht korrekter تَطَأْطَأَ: משא מתמאטיא, was von Kokovzov wohl zu Recht zu משי מתטאטיא = مشي متطأطنا „er ging als einer, der erniedrigt war" emendiert wird.[110] Dass KAHAL diesen Verweis im HAL streicht, ist

---

108 Vgl. Lane, *Lexicon*, 1819a–b.
109 Vgl. auch Ges₁₈, der zu dieser Stelle ebenfalls auf dieses Wort verweist.
110 Vgl. יתר, 32. Nebenbei, schon Ibn Barūn hat selber davor gewarnt, seine Sprachvergleiche zu einer Stelle auf alle anderen Belege eines Wortes auszuweiten, vgl. Kokovzov, יתר, 24; Wilhelm

somit sicher zu begrüßen, dass es aber seinerseits dann wieder auf أَطْ zurückgreift, ein Rückschritt.

Man wird also konstatieren müssen, dass auch in diesem Fall die Bedeutungsangaben unserer Wörterbücher letztlich eine mittelalterliche Tradition fortführen, deren Ursprung und damit auch Verlässlichkeit aber kaum deutlich wird. Dies führte in unserem Fall dazu, dass die Verbindung zu neuen Belegen in neuen Texten verschleiert wurde. Erst wenn man diese traditionellen Deutungen beiseite lässt und die nun angewachsene Zahl der Belege im Ganzen studiert, ergibt sich ein neues Ergebnis, dass der Beleglage besser gerecht wird.

4. Fazit

Es dürfte deutlich geworden sein, dass eine forschungsgeschichtliche Erarbeitung der modernen hebräischen Lexikographie durchaus einen heuristischen Wert hat. Sie öffnet die Augen dafür, worauf letztlich die Entscheidungen unserer Wörterbücher im Einzelnen beruhen, und damit auch dafür, wo eine Analyse, die noch einmal von vorne beginnt, erfolgversprechend ist. Sie verhindert zudem, dass das, was wir ererbt haben, den Blick auf das verstellt, was die Daten wirklich hergeben. Das Zitat, das diesem Beitrag seinen Titel gegeben hat – „Was Du ererbt von deinen Vätern... " – geht bekanntlich so weiter: „... erwirb es, um es zu besitzen." Die Mühe des Erwerbs der Tradition lohnt sich anscheinend wirklich, um damit in dem Sinne wahrer Besitzer der Tradition zu werden, dass man sich ihrer bedienen kann, ohne von ihr in die Irre geleitet zu werden.

Bacher, „Die hebräisch-arabische Sprachvergleichung des Abû Ibrahîm Ibn Barûn", *ZAW* 14 (1894), 240.

David J.A. Clines
The Recovery of the Ancient Hebrew Language: The Astonishing Wealth of its Unrecognized Vocabulary[1]

The project for the recovery of the ancient Hebrew language aims to restore to the Hebrew lexicon words that had been forgotten by Masoretic times and remained unknown to Hebrew lexicography, but that can now be reconstructed, thanks to new texts and our expanded knowledge of the Semitic languages.

There is a myth around that, in recent decades, (1) scores of words have been added to the Hebrew lexicon, (2) unnecessarily, (3) by some few eccentric scholars, (4) on the basis of supposed cognates mainly in Arabic and Ugaritic. I will show this myth to be untrue on all counts, and will present some highlights of the more than 2500 new words that are now known (or, at least, proposed) but are not to be found in BDB.

To end the paper, I discuss some practical implications for lexicography of the existence of these many proposals for new words.

On 30 January 1939, David Winton Thomas gave his inaugural lecture as Regius Professor of Hebrew in the University of Cambridge under the title "The Recovery of the Ancient Hebrew Language"[2]. It was published later that year as a pamphlet by Cambridge University Press[3]. Its title referred to the project of Winton Thomas and his teacher, G.R. Driver of Oxford, to restore to the Hebrew lexicon words that had, by Masoretic times, become forgotten and had subsequently remained unknown to Hebrew lexicography, but that could nevertheless be inferred, partly on the basis of cognates in other Semitic languages. It was an issue, Thomas said, that "above all others is claiming the attention of Hebraists at the present time"[4]. I am not sure that claim was true at the time, and it certainly has not been true of the course of Hebrew scholarship throughout the last century. Nevertheless, I am suggesting that his title be adopted as a name for this philo-

---

1 A shorter version of this paper was first read to the Language and Linguistics Section of the Society of Biblical Literature International Meeting, Groningen, The Netherlands, 28 July 2004.
2 I might mention that although Thomas is generally referred to as Winton Thomas (and I will follow that custom here), Winton was not part of his surname.
3 David Winton Thomas, *The Recovery of the Ancient Hebrew Language: An Inaugural Lecture* (Cambridge: Cambridge University Press, 1939), 43 pp.
4 Thomas, *The Recovery of the Ancient Hebrew Language*, 5. I should note that all of Winton Thomas's articles on Hebrew philology have been reprinted in an edition by John Day, together with Day's own evaluative assessments of Winton Thomas's proposals; see John Day, *The Recovery of the Ancient Hebrew Language: The Lexicographical Writings of D. Winton Thomas*, Hebrew Bible Monographs 20 (Sheffield: Sheffield Phoenix Press, 2013).

logical enterprise that has been pursued throughout the twentieth century and that even now shows no signs of slackening.

Admittedly, another speech that day was of greater moment. It concluded:

> In the course of my life I have very often been a prophet, and have usually been ridiculed for it ... [I]t was in the first instance the Jewish race which only received my prophecies with laughter when I said that I would one day take over the leadership of the State, and with it that of the whole nation, and that I would then among many other things settle the Jewish problem ... Today I will once more be a prophet: If the international Jewish financiers in and outside Europe should succeed in plunging the nations once more into a world war, then the result will not be the Bolshevization of the earth, and thus the victory of Jewry, but the annihilation of the Jewish race in Europe! ... The nations are no longer willing to die on the battlefield so that this unstable international race may profiteer from a war or satisfy its Old Testament vengeance. The Jewish watchword "Workers of the world unite" will be conquered by a higher realization, namely "Workers of all classes and of all nations, recognize your common enemy!"[5]

Hitler was celebrating the sixth anniversary of his chancellorship in a speech to the Reichstag. On the day he was calling, more unambiguously than ever before, for the extermination of the Jewish people, Winton Thomas was proposing the recuperation of the Hebrew language.

At the time, I was unaware of either speech, being an infant of some nine weeks, on the other side of the globe. But 23 years later, I found myself in the classroom of Winton Thomas in Cambridge, beginning my personal induction into his programme for the recovery of the ancient Hebrew language. Even then, I did not imagine that I ever would become part of that project. But now, with the completion of *The Dictionary of Classical Hebrew*[6], I am eager to bring to the attention of scholars the manifold contributions to Hebrew lexicography that have been made in the course of recent decades, and which have been incorporated in *DCH* to the best of my ability.

Not everyone is equally enthusiastic about the proposals that have been made for new words in the Hebrew lexicon. I identify a myth that has grown up around it in recent decades, that (1) scores of words have been added to the Hebrew lexicon, (2) unnecessarily, (3) by some few eccentric scholars, (4) on the basis of supposed cognates mainly in Arabic and Ugaritic. In this paper I intend to show this myth to be untrue on all counts.

---

5 Adolf Hitler, "Speech before Reichstag, January 30, 1939", in *The Speeches of Adolf Hitler, April 1922–August 1942*, ed. Norman H. Barnes (London: Oxford University Press, 1942), vol. 1, 737–41.
6 David J.A. Clines (ed.), *The Dictionary of Classical Hebrew*, 8 vols. (vols. 1–5: Sheffield: Sheffield Academic Press, 1991–2001; vols. 5–8: Sheffield: Sheffield Phoenix Press, 2007–2011). Hereafter referred to as DCH.

The Fourfold Myth

1. Scores of New Words?

In *The Dictionary of Classical Hebrew* I have identified some 3580 "new words", meaning thereby words that are not to be found in the standard English-language lexicon of Brown–Driver–Briggs (BDB)[7]. Since the successive volumes of the *Dictionary* were published, I have identified a further 621, bringing my current total to 4201. BDB contained, by my reckoning, some 8424 words (lemmas), which means that the new words have increased the Hebrew vocabulary by almost exactly 50 %.

If the myth is that "scores" of new words have emerged in recent decades, the myth is wildly inaccurate. If it were true, we would certainly need to take account of them, but we would not be greatly troubled by them. Scores of mosquitoes might be a nuisance, but not a major calamity. But there are not scores of these new words, there are not hundreds, there are thousands. They cannot be swept under the carpet, and they will not go away. Sooner or later they will rise up to bite us – if we do not identify them, classify them and assess them.

The extent of the corpus of new words is unknown to most biblical scholars, even to linguistically oriented biblical scholars. The only attempt I am aware of to collect such words was made by James Barr in the appendix to his *Comparative Philology and the Text of the Old Testament*. There he catalogued 334 new words, which he admitted were "only a selection from the total number of philological treatments known to me"[8]. Their number, he reckoned, ran to "many hundreds, if not thousands, even if one discounts obviously incompetent or fantastic solutions"[9]. Barr was right, and it is a pity he did not make known all the examples he was aware of.

---

7 Francis Brown, S.R. Driver and Charles A. Briggs (eds.), *A Hebrew and English Lexicon of the Old Testament with an Appendix Containing the Biblical Aramaic, Based on the Lexicon of William Gesenius as Translated by Edward Robinson* (Oxford: Clarendon Press, 1906), hereafter BDB. The Lexicon was published in parts, the first being issued in Boston in 1891 and in Oxford in 1892. The last part appears to have been published in 1901, and the whole work produced as a single volume in 1906 (more commonly, but apparently erroneously, 1907 is given as the publication date; current editions of the work say 'first edition 1907').

8 James Barr, *Comparative Philology and the Text of the Old Testament* (Oxford: Clarendon Press, 1968), 320 – 37, here 320.

9 Barr, *Comparative Philology and the Text of the Old Testament*, 9.

I must immediately remark that there are two very different sources for Classical Hebrew words that are not to be found in BDB, and thus two kinds of new words.

(1) The first group are those that occur in texts not known to BDB or not used by BDB. A few occasional texts, like the Siloam Inscription, known since 1880, and the Hebrew Ben Sira, a first edition of which was published in 1899 when BDB was not yet complete, were not used by BDB since it was specifically a Hebrew and English lexicon *of the Old Testament*. The great majority of new texts, however, have been discovered since the publication of BDB; most important have of course been the texts belonging to the Qumran literature, and, secondarily, the many inscriptional and occasional texts found in archaeological excavations.

These new words are indubitably present in the extant texts (even if the reading or the meaning of every one of them is not beyond dispute). By my reckoning, there are 675 such words in the Dead Sea Scrolls, 277 in Ben Sira, and 440 in the Inscriptions, a total of 1392 (I am including proper names, since it is traditional in Hebrew lexicography to treat such items as words for the dictionary).

(2) The second kind of new words (2232 of them) is quite different. I will give first an example. In addition to the well-known עֵמֶק I "valley", which occurs some 72 times in Classical Hebrew, we now have the proposal of a עֵמֶק II "strength", which has been identified in six passages of the Hebrew Bible. In one of them, Jer 49:4, where the Masoretic text has מַה־תִּתְהַלְלִי בָּעֲמָקִים ... הַבַּת הַשּׁוֹבֵבָה the RSV has "Why do you boast of your valleys, O faithless daughter?" The NRSV, on the other hand, has adopted the proposal to understand עֲמָקִים as "strength," thus "Why do you boast in your strength?", and so also similarly NJPS, NAB, NEB, and REB. The proposal rests on the Ugaritic cognate *'mq* "strength"; it was first made by Gordon, and then adopted by Driver, Dahood, Albright and many others; it is to be found also in Koehler–Baumgartner's *HALOT*[10]. It is in

---

10 The following is a reasonably complete list of the key proponents of this new word: C.H. Gordon, *Ugaritic Grammar: The Present Status of the Linguistic Study of the Semitic Alphabetic Texts from Ras Shamra* (Rome: Pontificium Institutum Biblicum, 1940), 105 no. 624; G.R. Driver, "Difficult Words in the Hebrew Prophets", in *Studies in Old Testament Prophecy Presented to Professor Theodore H. Robinson*, ed. H.H. Rowley (Edinburgh: T. & T. Clark, 1950), 52–72, here 61; W.F. Albright, "Some Canaanite-Phoenician Sources of Hebrew Wisdom", in *Wisdom in Israel and in the Ancient Near East, Presented to Professor Harold Henry Rowley ... in Celebration of his Sixty-Fifth Birthday, 24 March 1955*, ed. M. Noth and D. Winton Thomas, VTSup 3 (Leiden: E.J. Brill, 1955), 1–15, here 14; M. Dahood, "The Value of Ugaritic for Textual Criticism", *Bib* 40 (1959), 160–70, here 166; Arnold A. Wieder, "Ugaritic–Hebrew Notes", *JBL* 84 (1965), 160–64, here 162–63; Jonas C. Greenfield, "Ugaritic Lexicographical Notes", *JCS* 21 (1967), 89–93, here 89; G. Rinaldi, "Nota ['mq]", *BeO* 10 (1968), 196; Wilfred G.E. Watson, "Archaic Elements in the Language of Chroni-

my view, certainly correct, though not necessarily in every place where it has been suggested. When, for example, the war horse in Job 39:21 paws בָּעֵמֶק, some think he paws "with force" (NJPS) or "he paws fiercely" (NIV) or "violently" (Pope, Andersen) or "vigorously" (Guillaume); but I think, remembering that עֵמֶק I properly means "plain" or "lowland" (rather than "valley", as many are taught it does) and that plains are the natural place for the deployment of chariots drawn by horses, that it is probably "paws the plain". But this is no argument against the existence of עֵמֶק II "strength" in other references.

Here is a brief sample of queries and suggestions raised by other proposals for new words:

סְפִינָה   II *hold (of ship)*. Did Jonah go down into the ship, or into its hold (Jonah 1:3)[11]?

סַפֵּר   *barber*. Did Jehoiakim cut Baruch's scroll up with a scribe's knife or with a barber's knife (Jer 36:23)[12]?

סֵפֶר   II bronze. Did Job wish that his words were written in a book or inscribed in bronze (Job 19:23)[13]?

עֲבֻדָּה   II *cattle*. Did Job have many servants (Job 1:3) or many cattle[14]?

עלף   III *perfume*. In order to seduce Judah, did Tamar wrap herself up or perfume herself (Gen 38:14)[15]?

פְּדוּת   II *separation*. Did Yahweh put a ransom between the Hebrews and the Egyptians, or a separation (Exod 8:19)[16]?

שׂמח   II *be high, make a loud noise*. At Solomon's anointment as king, did the people rejoice greatly or make a very loud noise (1 Kgs 1:40)[17]?

---

cles", *Bib* 53 (1972), 191–207, 196; Ludwig Koehler and Walter Baumgartner *et al.*, *Hebräisches und aramäisches Lexikon zum Alten Testament* (5 vols.; Leiden; E.J. Brill, 1967–94), vol. 3 (1983), 803a (hereafter *HALAT*); Ludwig Koehler and Walter Baumgartner *et al.*, *The Hebrew and Aramaic Lexicon of the Old Testament*, trans. M.E.J. Richardson (5 vols.; Leiden: E.J. Brill, 1994–2000), vol. 2 (1995), 848b (hereafter *HALOT*).

11 Martin Mulzer, "ספינה (Jona 1,5) '(gedeckter) Laderaum'", *BN* 104 (2000), 83–94.

12 See Felix Perles, "The Fourteenth Edition of Gesenius-Buhl's Dictionary", *JQR* 18 (1906), 383–90, here 385.

13 See M. Dietrich, "Akkadisch *sipparu* "Bronze", ugaritisch *spr*, *ġprt* und hebräisch *spr*, *'prt*", *UF* 17 (1986), 401.

14 See Arnold B. Ehrlich, *Randglossen zur hebräischen Bibel*, vol. 1 (Leipzig: J.C. Hinrichs, 1908), 123–24.

15 See Godfrey R. Driver, "Problems of Interpretation in the Heptateuch", in *Mélanges bibliques redigés en l'honneur de André Robert*, Travaux de l'Institut catholique de Paris 4 (Paris: Bloud & Gay, 1957), 66–76, here 70–71.

16 See A.A. Macintosh, "Exodus viii 19, Distinct Redemption and the Hebrew Roots פדה and פדד", *VT* 21 (1971), 548–55.

17 Jonas C. Greenfield, "Lexicographical Notes. The Root שׂמח", *HUCA* 30 (1959), 141–51, here 149.

שׁרף	II *anoint.* Were the bones of Saul and his sons burned or anointed (1 Sam 31:12)[18]?
שׁבח	III *muzzle.* Does Yahweh still the waters of the sea or muzzle them (Psa 89:10)[19]?
שָׁחַל	II *serpent* and III *leopard.* Is the path beneath the earth untrodden by lions, or by serpents or by leopards (Job 28:8)[20]?
שׁנן	II *repeat.* Are Israelites to 'sharpen' (? 'teach incisively') the commandments to their children or to 'repeat' them (Deut 6:7)[21]?

Examples like these show that the identification of new words is not an esoteric undertaking to be reserved to professional lexicographers; every group of Bible translators across the globe has now to reckon with them, and in some 2200 cases to make a choice among meanings of Hebrew homonyms. A hundred, or even 50 or 60 years ago, they did not have to do that.

What are the characteristics of this group of new words? First, they all occur in the Hebrew Bible. Secondly, they all have the status of proposals or suggestions. Thirdly, they all attempt to improve upon lexicographical material we already have in our dictionaries. Fourthly, there can be several proposals for the same passage of the Bible, i.e. several explanations of a given word in a given text; in that sense, a large number of the proposals for new words are mutually exclusive: only one of them can be right in each case[22]. Nevertheless, in many of those cases it is impossible to tell which one is right; so the lexicographical situation is as if they were all right. Each has a claim to appear in a dictionary of Classical Hebrew.

---

18 G.R. Driver, "A Hebrew Burial Custom", *ZAW* 66 (1954), 314–15.

19 Mitchell J. Dahood, *Psalms I: 1–50,* Anchor Bible 16 (Garden City, NY: Doubleday, 1966), 279.

20 In favour of שָׁחַל II is Sigmund Mowinckel, 'שַׁחַל', in *Hebrew and Semitic Studies Presented to Godfrey Rolles Driver in Celebration of his Seventieth Birthday, 20 August 1962,* ed. D. Winton Thomas and W.D. McHardy (Oxford: Clarendon Press, 1963), 95–103. In favour of שָׁחַל III is E. Dhorme, *A Commentary on the Book of Job* (London: Thomas Nelson, 1967; orig. 1926), 47, 152–53, 404.

21 Godfrey Rolles Driver, "Problems of the Hebrew Text and Language", in *Alttestamentliche Studien Friedrich Nötscher zum sechzigsten Geburtstage 19. Juli 1950 gewidmet,* ed. Hubert Junker and Johannes Botterweck; BBB, 1 (Bonn: Hanstein, 1950), 46–61, here 48; Matitiahu Tsevat, 'Alalakhiana', *HUCA* 29 (1959), 109–36, here 125 n. 112; Ludwig Koehler and Walter Baumgartner (eds.), *Lexicon in Veteris Testamenti libros* (Leiden: E.J. Brill, 1953), 998–99; M. Dahood, *Ugaritic-Hebrew Philology: Marginal Notes on Recent Publications,* BibOr 17 (Rome: Pontifical Biblical Institute, 1965), 74; Dahood, 'Hebrew-Ugaritic Lexicography VIII', *Bib* 51 (1970), 391–404, here 391; *HALOT* (1999; orig. 1990), 1606a.

22 I use the example of מִשְׁפְּתַיִם, which may mean *fireplaces, saddle-bags, divided sheepfolds, double wall,* or *grazing places* – or perhaps something else altogether different – but it cannot mean more than one of those things. Thus, at least four out of the five proposals in *The Dictionary of Classical Hebrew* (*DCH,* vol. 5, 564–65) for this word must be wrong, but I do not know which they are.

This overview of the places where new words occur may be summarized in this chart, which analyses occurrences according to four corpora of Classical Hebrew, namely the Hebrew Bible, Ben Sira, the Dead Sea Scrolls, and the Inscriptions.

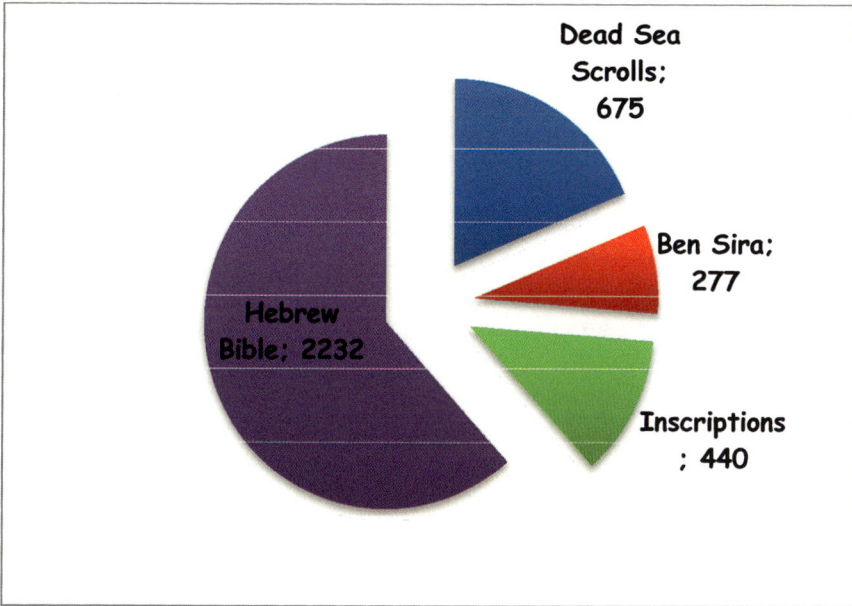

Fig. 1 Numbers of New Words by Corpus

2. Unnecessarily?

The myth is that many, if not most, of these new proposals are unnecessary – meaning that the Masoretic text is satisfactory enough if only we will work at it, and that our knowledge of Hebrew was by 1906 (BDB) or 1915 (Gesenius-Buhl[23]) as good as we are likely to get.

I notice that those who keep BDB or Gesenius–Buhl on their desk as their tool of reference for Biblical Hebrew do not expect their surgeons or auto mechanics to operate according to the textbooks of 1906 or 1915. Even in principle,

---

23 *W. Gesenius' hebräisches und aramäisches Handwörterbuch über das Alte Testament in Verbindung mit H. Zimmern, W. Max Müller und O. Weber; bearbeitet von Frants Buhl* (Leipzig: F.C.W. Vogel, 16th edn, 1915).

before we get to examine individual cases, I myself would suppose that BDB and Gesenius-Buhl, wonderful works though they were, must be out of date in thousands of particulars, and that revisions of their lexicographical decisions are not only desirable but necessary. As for the Masoretic text, and its thousands of difficult, odd, questionable and downright unintelligible readings, I remark that there is not one of those readings that cannot be justified by scholarly ingenuity, for scholars are in business to invent interpretations and explanations. But the mere fact that someone somewhere has offered an explanation of an apparently corrupt Hebrew text is no reason for preferring the Masoretic text to a simple philological solution to a problem text.

I have been much impressed in reading the philological literature (and I have read the whole of G.R. Driver's and M.J. Dahood's lexical work at least five times over, in addition to the work of some hundreds of others) by the overwhelming extent to which new proposals are made in response to perceived difficulties in the Hebrew text. Contrary to some accounts that are given of the practice of comparative Semitic philology, it has by no means been a matter of trawling through the dictionaries of Arabic and of other Semitic languages to see how many alternative renderings one can propose for the Hebrew Bible. Rather, the sequence of research steps has typically been that philologians have fastened on some oddity or problem in the Hebrew text, and have gone looking for a solution to it in the range of Semitic languages (including Hebrew itself). Reviewing their proposals, we may differ over whether the difficulty perceived is a real difficulty or not, or whether there may be other or better ways of dealing with it, but there is no doubt in my mind that the procedure adopted by the great majority of those who have proposed new words has been a responsible one. This has been an area of scholarly study where the rhetoric of abuse has been very prevalent, and charges that comparative philologians have been reckless, incautious and undisciplined abound. I have seen no special reason to conclude that philologians are more prone to such faults than other scholars, and I can only suppose that those who urge caution are troubled, perhaps at an unconscious level, by what the philologians are telling us about the stability of our knowledge of the Hebrew language.

3. Some few eccentric scholars?

One of the myths about new philological proposals is that they are mostly the creation of a few scholars with a comparative Semitic bee in their bonnet (everyone thinks first of G.R. Driver and Mitchell Dahood). My database of information about all these new words would give the lie to such a suggestion. Here is an analysis of the proposers of the 493 new words I have identified for Samekh to Pe in Biblical Hebrew (I have not made a similar analysis for the Hebrew vocabulary as a whole):

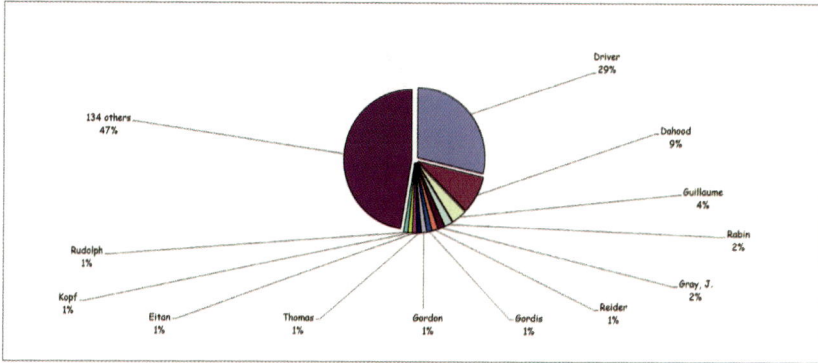

Fig. 2 Proponents of New Words Beginning Samekh-Pe for Biblical Hebrew

From this table it would appear that the proposal of new Hebrew words, that is, the project for the recovery of the ancient Hebrew language, has not been the work of a small band of scholars. Driver and Dahood may have together contributed over a third of the suggestions, but for this segment of the Hebrew vocabulary I have located over 300 other proposals in the name of more than 140 other scholars, not all of whom could be called eccentric – certainly not de Moor, Dhorme, Dietrich, Elliger, Emerton, Fohrer, Gese, Greenfield, Koehler, Moran, Pope, Rudolph, Talmon, and Zimmerli, to name only a dozen or so.

4. On the basis of supposed cognates mainly in Arabic and Ugaritic?

The final myth about the recovery of the ancient Hebrew language project is that it has been carried out simply by looking up the Arabic dictionaries for roots resembling the Hebrew or by plundering the Ugaritic lexicon. If we actually look at the new words proposed for Samekh to Pe, however, we find a quite different picture:

The table shows that of all the new words proposed for Biblical Hebrew beginning Samekh to Pe more than half depended not on a cognate from another Semitic language but upon the Hebrew vocabulary we already know. The proposed word may be another noun from a root that is already recognized, or per-

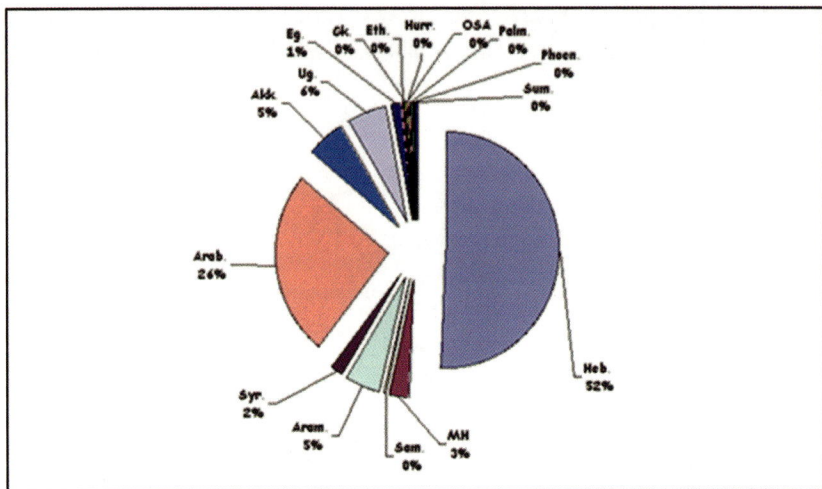

Fig. 3 Semitic Cognates Invoked for New Words in Biblical Hebrew (Samekh-Pe)

haps an occurrence of a verb that is not attested in Biblical Hebrew but may be inferred from nouns that are "derived" from it. It is the same principle that is used in explaining new words in Qumran Hebrew or in the Hebrew of Sirach, by reference principally to the Hebrew language itself. One quarter of the proposed words depend mainly on a cognate in Arabic, it is true, and 10 % upon later forms of Hebrew or upon Aramaic or Syriac. It would be interesting to know how these proportions correspond to those we find in the traditional lexica such as those of BDB and Gesenius-Buhl or KB, but as far as I know, no one has ever asked how dependent their knowledge of the Hebrew language is upon cognates in the other Semitic languages. Certainly the eighteenth-century revolution in Arabic learning made a deep impression on the linguistic researches of a Schultens[24] and the lexica of Castell[25] and Michaelis[26] and Gesenius[27], to

---

24 Albert Schultens, *Disputatio theologico-philologica de utilitate linguæ Arabicæ in interpretanda S. Scriptura* (Groningen, 1689), together with his commentaries such as his *Versio integra Prouerbiorum Salomonis et in eadem commentarius quem in compendium redegit et obseruationibus criticis* (Halle: J.J. Curtius, 1769) and his two-volume *Commentarius in librum Iobi* (Halle: J.J. Curtius, 1773–1774).

25 Edmund Castell, *Lexicon heptaglotton: hebraicum, chaldaicum, syriacum, samaritanum, aethiopicum, arabicum, conjunctim, et persicum, separatim* (2 vols.; London: Thomas Roycroft, 1669).

26 Johann David Michaelis, *Supplementa ad lexica hebraica* (3 vols.; Göttingen: G. Rosenbusch, 1792).

which our BDB and *HALOT* are heirs. There is nothing remotely odd about basing our knowledge of Hebrew words to some extent on the Arabic lexicon: we are all doing it all the time, even when we do not know that is what we are doing.

Conclusion

I conclude that it is more than time that the popular myths about new words in Hebrew are exposed, and that the dramatic impact the recovery of such words are having upon our understanding of the language is recognized. Though the project for the recovery of the ancient Hebrew language is nothing new methodologically speaking, the very size of its contribution to our knowledge of the language unsettles our certainties about the language and about our standard lexica and presents a inescapable challenge to every commentator and Bible translator[28].

Beyond a Conclusion

It is one thing to bring a scholarly paper to a conclusion. It is another to attempt to deal with the practical consequences of a scholarly paper. Here I want to reflect on how the existence of the plethora of proposals for new words in the Classical Hebrew vocabulary is to be best translated into lexicographical practice, that is, the creation of real-world dictionaries of the language.

I often think that because of my enthusiasm for researching and identifying the multitude of proposals for new words I may have wrongly estimated what role they should play in a dictionary of the language. I have often had in my mind the remark of James Barr somewhere that while it is worthwhile to search out the proposals that have been made for new words, it would be better to present the results of such research in a printed list quite separate from any dictionary of the language. He was very displeased by Dahood's incorporation of many of his proposals in his Anchor Bible commentary on the Psalms, supposedly for the general public, without first submitting them to the judgment of his scholarly

---

27 Wilhelm Gesenius, *Thesaurus philologicus criticus linguae hebraeae et chaldaeae Veteris Testamenti* (3 vols.; Leipzig: F.C.W. Vogel, 1829–1858).

28 I like to think of Hebrew lexicography as a challenge, above all; see my paper, "The Challenge of Hebrew Lexicography Today", in *Congress Volume, Ljubljana 2007*, ed. André Lemaire, VTSup 133 (Leiden: Brill, 2009), 87–98.

peers, and he would not doubt have disapproved equally of the reporting of them in a dictionary alongside words that everyone recognizes.

But I had to decide in creating *The Dictionary of Classical Hebrew* whether new words should be included or not. I was pretty clearly not in a position to make a judgment on the validity of all the proposals I encountered. I reckoned it could take on average a day's work to consider any such proposal adequately. Certainly, when I undertook to review the arguments for a few such words, I was spending up to 100 hours to write up my results on each word[29]; I did not have 150 years free (2200 words x 100 hours, 1500 working hours a year) to judge the merits of all the proposals I knew of, and even if I did, they would be just my judgments. Who made me a ruler and a judge over the work of hundreds of my peers? Yet even though I could not judge the validity of the proposals I had found, I could not in all conscience leave out all such words just because they were not in another Hebrew dictionary 100 years old.

I decided to include all the new words I could find. But since the new words were novelties, on the whole, it would be wrong to present them as if they were universally accepted. So I prefaced each such word with an asterisk, to warn readers that they were voyaging in uncharted waters.

When I came to prepare *The Concise Dictionary of Classical Hebrew*[30], I had to think the issue through afresh. Was it right to set before the users (no doubt many of them students and beginners) of a brief dictionary, only 10 % of the length of *The Dictionary of Classical Hebrew*, all these new words, many of them mutually exclusive and most of them having attracted no more than a handful of adherents (in print at least)? And yet, on what ground would I exclude them? And what would I do with the cases I thought were well supported? If I included them, and omitted the rest, how would I decide which were which? In the end, I did exactly as I did for the larger dictionary.

Now that I am contemplating a *Pocket Dictionary of Classical Hebrew*, with barely more than the principal senses of each word following the lemma, what shall I do?

---

29 I refer to my papers: "Was There an *'bl* II 'be dry' in Classical Hebrew?", *VT* 42 (1992), 1–10; reprinted in my *On the Way to the Postmodern: Old Testament Essays, 1967–1998*, vol. 2, JSOTSup 293 (Sheffield: Sheffield Academic Press, 1998), 585–94; and "Was There a ברח II 'vex' or ברח III 'wound, bruise, pierce' or ברח IV 'bar' in Classical Hebrew?," in *Shai le-Sara Japhet: Studies in the Bible, its Exegesis, and its Language*, ed. Moshe Bar-Asher, Dalit Rom-Shiloni, Emanuel Tov and Nili Wazana (Jerusalem: The Bialik Institute, 2007), 285–304.
30 David J.A. Clines (ed.), *The Concise Dictionary of Classical Hebrew* (Sheffield: Sheffield Phoenix Press, 2011).

Leonid Kogan
Semitic Etymology in A Biblical Hebrew Lexicon: the Limits of Usefulness[1]

1. Introdution

The role of etymology in the lexicographic description of a dead language has been differently assessed in the two major branches of the Western philological scholarship – Indo-European and Semitic.

Nearly all (pre-)Modern standard dictionaries of classical Indo-European languages (such as Greek, Latin, Sanskrit or Hittite) are strictly descriptive in their approach: etymological glosses are either altogether absent or restricted to a handful of occasional laconic observations. Incidentally, almost every Indo-European language can boast a fully-fledged etymological dictionary.

The situation in the Semitic domain is exactly the opposite: until very recently, etymology has been almost universally recognized as an integral element of any large-scale project in Semitic lexicography. At the same time, there is only one ancient Semitic language (Classical Ethiopic) that possesses an etymological dictionary in the strict sense of this concept. As far the Biblical lexicography is concerned, *Hebrew and Aramaic Lexicon of the Old Testament* by Koehler, Baumgartner and their followers can be deservedly considered a culmination of the traditional approach: there is hardly any other Semitic dictionary where the comparative evidence from other languages (both Semitic and non-Semitic) would be so prominently represented. At the same time, a real etymological dictionary of Biblical Hebrew is still unwritten and, to the best of my knowledge, not even scheduled for preparation.

Most colleagues would probably agree that to have such a wealth of comparative information under one cover with the synchronic lexicographic facts – as is the case of HALOT – is *interesting* or at least *nice*. Yet it is equally certain that, in modern times, epithets like *interesting* and *nice* can scarcely match such a huge amount of time and energy (let alone money and paper) that a comprehensive and up-to-date inquiry into the history of the Hebrew vocabulary would certainly require – it should not be forgotten that, however extensive and detailed

1 This article has been written in the framework of the projects 12–06–00182-a (RFBR/РФФИ) and 12–04–00164 (RFH/РГНФ). I am glad to extend my gratitude to these institutions for their financial support.

the etymological information provided by HALOT may be, it is still very far from the present-day standards of Semitic etymology in terms of both completeness and precision.

In other words, one can legitimately wonder about the practical output of the comparative aspect of Biblical Hebrew lexicography: is etymology not only *interesting* and *nice*, but also *useful* in a present-day fundamental dictionary of Biblical Hebrew?

The answer to this question will critically depend on the basic methodological premises of the lexicographer, more concretely, on his attitude towards the necessity of justifying the meaning ascribed to a given Hebrew word. As long as the necessity of semantic justification is denied, the uselessness of etymology becomes almost self-evident[2].

It may be argued, however, that providing arguments in favor of a given semantic decision *is* the primary task of a dictionary of any dead language with a relatively restricted text corpus, and Biblical Hebrew is no exception to this principle. Now it is no big secret that relevant arguments at our disposal are not many:

- Extant attestations in the Biblical texts;
- Renderings of the ancient versions;
- Traditional Jewish lexicography and exegesis;
- Etymology.

There is no need to emphasize that there are scores of widely attested Hebrew lexemes whose fundamental meaning can be safely deduced from the contexts. One may doubt that exhaustive lists of cognates for such ubiquitous lexemes as $ḳārab$ 'to be close', $šāmaʕ$ 'to hear', or $rō(ʔ)š$ 'head', occupying from one to almost two columns each on the pages of HALOT, can add anything substantial to our understanding of the basic meaning of these verbs and nouns. As long as the criterion of usefulness applies, this evidence can be safely omitted from the lexicographic analysis.

There remains, however, quite a substantial body of lexemes whose meanings cannot be adequately described from the contexts alone. Within a strictly synchronistic methodology, such words must be either described in very broad terms (such as 'a kind of bird', 'a kind of tree', 'a milk product', 'a disease', 'a verb of movement') or just left without translation. This approach is by no

---

2 "We have not, in fact, seen it as our task to justify the meanings we propose for the Hebrew words; that is too complex a task to be accomplished within the confines of a dictionary" (preface to the first volume of DCH, p. 18).

means illegitimate *per se* and has been carried out with admirable consistency in such a titanic lexicographic enterprise as the recently completed *Chicago Assyrian Dictionary*. However, as long as Hebraists are willing to preserve the familiar *terebinths*, *weasels*, *kites* and *eczemas* on the pages of our dictionaries, it seems desirable to justify our choice at some length, however circumstantial and contradictory the pertinent extra-context information may be.

Within such a methodology, the *potential* usefulness of etymology for the Hebrew lexicography can scarcely be doubted. The debate thus shifts to a different register, namely, the *practical realization* of this potential. In other words: how to assess the impact of etymology on each concrete problematic case? The answer to this question will depend on multiple factors, such as the amount of comparative evidence, its reliability and internal consistency as well as the possibility to correlate it with other types of primary and secondary data at our disposal.

2. Types of etymological evidence

Before proceeding to a few case-studies, intended to illustrate the positive potential of comparative evidence side by side with its limitations and drawbacks, it seems convenient to deal briefly with the types of etymological data available to us. An important, yet often neglected fact is that, by its very nature, etymology has to deal with the origin of a given word (or, indeed, all words of a given language) whatever this origin may be. Accordingly, neither the etymological evidence nor the etymological procedure can be typologically and methodologically homogeneous. Rather, three substantially different types of situations can be detected.

- De-verbal or de-nominal derivation within the history of the language under scrutiny;
- Borrowing from a foreign source;
- Derivation from a proto-form going back to one of the stages of the language's prehistory.

When scholars speak of "Semitic etymology" in the Hebrew lexicography, they typically mean the third option, that is, looking for cognate lexemes in other Semitic languages which presumably go back to the same proto-Semitic source, but may preserve its original meaning more transparently than the extant Biblical attestations. This kind of etymological evidence will be, therefore, the main subject of this presentation. However, the importance of the remaining two aspects of the Hebrew etymology is not to be neglected, and it seems appropriate to briefly deal with them in the present context.

2.1 Loanword

I shall start with the loanwords, where the situation appears to be rather straightforward. Differently from many other Semitic languages – both ancient and modern – Biblical Hebrew proved to be highly conservative as far as the acceptance of loanwords is concerned. According to my raw calculations, there are about 300 lexical items of foreign origin in the Old Testament corpus, which constitutes less than 4 % of the total amount of Hebrew words. Nevertheless, etymological investigation of this relatively restricted body of lexical material has traditionally played quite a significant role in Hebrew lexicography and, it seems, on good grounds.

Firstly, loanwords are often rare lexemes (including *hapax legomena*) and the extant contexts tend to be too scarce and/or opaque to allow the lexicographer to establish their meanings with a sufficient degree of precision. A quest for the origin of such words is thus quite natural.

Secondly, the chronological distance between the act of borrowing and the written attestation is usually not very broad if compared with the cognate relationship, which often implies many hundreds, sometimes even millennia of independent linguistic history. This puts the semantic identification on a safer footing: an attempt to elicit the meaning of an Akkadian *loanword* in the book of Hosea through an inquiry into the meaning of the Akkadian *source-word* is a priori less risky than a semantic identification of an obscure *autochthonous* lexeme in the same book with its hypothetic Akkadian *cognate*. All this does not mean, of course, that drastic and bizarre semantic shifts cannot take place in the course of the borrowing process or during the independent existence of the borrowed lexeme in the recipient language.

Finally, many groups of loanwords are of great extra-linguistic value, and the recently resumed debate on the linguistic dating of Biblical texts provides abundant proof thereof. For example, an up-to date etymological discussion of true and alleged Iranian loanwords in the Old Testament would certainly be helpful to save scholars from premature conclusions on the supposed presence of Iranisms in "Early Biblical Hebrew"[3]. As long as we believe that the readership of

---

3 Including such lexemes as *yāšəpē* 'jasper', whose Akkadian equivalent *yašpû* is attested as early as in Amarna and Boğazköy (AHw. 413, CAD I/J 328), or *šūˁāl* 'fox', whose Semitic origin

Hebrew dictionaries is not restricted to linguists, the omission of this type of information from the pages of our lexicographic treaties will undoubtedly turn out to be quite damaging for their potential audience.

In view of these circumstances, careful and sufficiently detailed annotations about the origin of loanwords in the Hebrew Bible become highly desirable, perhaps even mandatory for any future project in the field of Biblical lexicography. This holds true, I believe, even if all other types of etymological evidence are disregarded as useless. As a good example of such a minimalist approach to comparative data one can mention M. Sokoloff's comprehensive dictionaries of Jewish Aramaic and Syriac, where Semitic etymology is restricted to transparent parallels in other Aramaic idioms, but the origin of loanwords (Iranian, Akkadian, Greek and other) is analyzed with a notorious degree of consistency.

2.2 Internal derivation

It is an important, yet generally neglected fact that tracing back substantives and adjectives to the respective verbal (more rarely, nominal) roots is also an etymological procedure. Indeed, by its very nature lexical derivation occupies the border area between synchrony and diachrony: on the one hand, derivational patterns, together with their meanings and functions, are usually transparent enough on the synchronic level and many of them may have been productively used when Biblical Hebrew was still a spoken language; on the other hand, most of the commonly attested Hebrew substantives and adjectives were certainly produced already in the (presumably, not very deep) prehistory of this language.

Most cases of such "derivational etymology" are quite transparent and hardly need any deep lexicographic treatment: a brief cross-reference from *ḥokmā* 'wisdom' to *ḥākam* 'to be wise' or from *bōkēr* 'cowherd' to *bāḳār* 'large cattle' is clearly sufficient.

The situation is not always so straightforward, however. A good example to be considered is *śāʿîr* 'he-goat', whose derivation from *śēʿār* 'hair' is universally recognized. Yet this derivation – however probable it may be – remains purely intuitive and, for all practical purposes, is not too different from another widespread etymological speculation, viz. the derivation of *śəʿōrā* 'barley' from the same primary noun *śēʿār*. A practicing Hebrew lexicographer must take a certain methodological stance towards this category of cases, especially since for many

---

is beyond doubt (SED II No 237), against Ian Young and Robert Rezetko, *Linguistic Dating of Biblical Texts* (London: Equinox, 2008), p. 309.

decades this type of etymological (or quasi-etymological) procedure was one of the principal sources of semantic identification for many of the obscure Biblical *realia*, particularly in the field of the natural environment. The well-known inquiries into the meaning of obscure Biblical bird names by G. R. Driver and I. Aharoni[4] readily come to mind, where *šālāk* is thought to indicate 'some kind of bird that darts on to its prey' because of the hypothetic derivation from *šlk* 'to throw'[5], *taḥmās* is translated as 'owl' "because its name means robber" (< *ḥms*)[6], *šaḥap* is likely the long-eared owl, said to be 'very thin' because "the root *šḥp*... implies something thin"[7] and so forth. That this type of exercise does not entirely belong to the history of Biblical scholarship is eloquently demonstrated by a recent study on the Biblical fauna[8], whose basic premise is a somewhat naïve belief that, due to the particular closeness of the ancient man to the animal world (both domestic and wild), most of faunal terms of ancient languages (in our case, Biblical Hebrew) can be analyzed as descriptive terms derived from synchronically attested non-faunal lexemes ("Wie der Mensch jedes Tier nennen würde, so sollte es heißen")[9]. (this is just the title of one of the chapters, recycled from the article you refer to. i do not think we need any special reference for it, it is just a kind of motto)

3. Comparison beyond etymology

Let us, stress, finally, that the comparative dimension of Biblical lexicography is not limited to etymology in the strict sense. Structural and semantic parallels from other Semitic languages and text corpora can be no less useful for eliciting the meaning of difficult Hebrew words and passages and may, therefore, occupy a legitimate place on the pages of Hebrew dictionaries, side by side with immediate, "material" cognates. The essence of this aspect of comparative research, prominently associated with the name of M. Held and even labeled "the Held

---

4 Godfrey Rolles Driver, Birds in the Old Testament. I. Brids in Law. *Palestine Exploration Quarterly* 87 (1955), 5–20 and Israel Aharoni, "On Some Animals Mentioned in the Bible", Osiris 5 (1936), 461–478.
5 See Driver, *op.cit.*, p. 15.
6 See Driver, *op.cit.*, p. 13 and I. Aharoni, *op.cit.*, p. 471.
7 See Driver, *op.cit.*, p. 13 and I. Aharoni, *op.cit.*, p. 470.
8 See Peter Riede, *Im Spiegel der Tiere* (Freiburg: Universitätsverlag, 2002), pp. 165–212.
9 Most of the identifications proposed by Driver and Aharoni and the etymological arguments behind them (many of them eventually going back to Rabbinic exegesis) are still considered probable in today's standard reference commentaries, such as Jacob Milgrom, *Leviticus 1–16*, New York: Doubleday, 1991, p.663.

method" by some of his pupils, has been conveniently summarized in Ch. Cohen's summary article of 1989 and need not be repeated here[10]. I will limit myself to one particularly illuminating case put forward by Cohen, i. e. the expression *ṭabbūr hā-ʾāräṣ*, perhaps designating "the intersection of north-south and east-west routes east of Shechem"[11] (DCH 339) in Judg 9:37 and Ezek 38:12. As is well known, both the ancient versions and the Jewish tradition strongly support the translation 'navel' for *ṭabbūr*. The ensuing concept of the "navel of the earth" has attracted lots of scholarly attention because of its potential cultural-historical relevance, yet there is, of course, no internal evidence whatsoever for such a translation, and the etymology is, in this particular case, not helpful either[12]. It is rather the structural Akkadian parallel *abunnat mātim* (AHw. 9, CAD A₁ 89) that prompts one to take seriously the traditional interpretation[13]. As I will try to demonstrate below, the potential of this aspect of comparative research in Hebrew lexicography is far from exhausted.

4. Some case-studies

4.1. *šāpān* 'hyrax'

I shall begin my presentation with a case admittedly more important for the history of the Biblical lexicography than for its present-day stage. The animal name *šāpān* occurs four times in the Bible, twice in the food prohibitions of Lev 11:5 and Deut 14:7 (where it is described as ruminant but having no divided hoofs) as well as in two poetic passages (Ps 104:18 and Prov 30:26) where the rocky habitat of the animal is described. For a present-day Hebraist, familiar with modern zoological descriptions of the Middle Eastern mammals, these scanty data are probably enough to identify *šāpān* with the rock hyrax (*Procavia syriaca*), a translation gradually establishing itself in the standard reference tools from

---

10 See Chaim Cohen, "The "Held Method" for Comparative Semitic Philology", *Journal of the American Near Eastern Society* 19 (1989), 9–23, here pp. 16–17.
11 Cohen, *op.cit.*, pp. 16–17.
12 See Shemaryahu Talmon, "*har*; *gibhʿāh*," TDOT III (1978), 427–441, here p. 438.
13 But not the alleged mythological connotations: the Akkadian contexts simply refer to military penetration into the enemy's land (*mātu* would not normally designate 'earth', but rather 'land', 'country'). As pointed out in a recent article by I. Khait, Akkadian divination texts make use of a whole array of similar expressions, such as *zibbat mātim* 'the tail of the country', *kutal mātim* 'the backside of the country' and even *šubur mātim* 'the anus of the country', see Ilya Khait, "The Old Babylonian Omens in the Pushkin State Museum of Fine Arts, Moscow", *Babel und Bibel* 6 (2012), 31–59, here p. 46.

the beginning of the 20th century, even if still incapable to oust completely the rather misleading "coneys" (NJB) and "badgers"[14].

Let us not forget, however, that the first appearance of this identification on the pages of a Hebrew dictionary is due to a splendid etymological discovery by the French orientalist F. Fresnel, to whom we owe the first European description of a Modern South Arabian language labeled Jibbali by today's Semitists. In his remarks on the Jibbali vocabulary, published as early as in 1838[15], Fresnel reveals his keen interest towards the output of the newly discovered language for Biblical scholarship. Comparison between *šāpān* and Jibbali *thofoun* (Fresnel's transcription), which his informant rendered by the familiar Arabic lexeme *wabr-*, is one of his key examples[16]. The importance of Fresnel's discovery was immediately recognized by E. Rödiger and W. Gesenius[17] and, eventually, found its way into BDB 1050[18] and other standard dictionaries.

Fresnel's intuition has been amply confirmed by the present-day research into Modern South Arabian languages: the Jibbali cognate *t̠ɔ́fun* (JL 283) has been supplemented by the corresponding Mehri form *t̠ōfən* (ML 416) by T. M. Johnstone, whose brief remarks on the animal's status among the modern Mahra are not without interest for a Biblical scholar. On the one hand, Johnstone observes that "rock hyrax is eaten by all but a few women". That means that its explicit inclusion into the list of potentially eatable, yet forbidden mammals (together with camel, hare and pig) could be motivated by practical reasons and not merely by the priestly endeavor at completeness[19]. On the other hand, Johnstone's remark "it is *believed* to chew the cud" (my italics) is in striking agreement with the following observation of a modern Biblical scholar: "It is not a true ruminant, but only resembles one because in chewing it moves its jaws from side to side. Thus the attribution of cud-chewing to this animal was

---

14 See Michael Fox, *Proverbs 10–31* (New Haven: YUP, 2009), p. 878.

15 Fulgence Fresnel, "Sur la langue hhymiarite", *Journal asiatique* 6 (1838), pp. 79–84.

16 See now Antoine Lonnet, "La découverte du sudarabique moderne: le *eḥkili* de Fresnel (1838)", *Matériaux arabes et sudarabiques* 3 (1991), 15–89, here p. 30.

17 See Emil Rödiger, "Fresnel über die himjaritische Sprache", *Zeitschrift für die Kunde des Morgenlandes* 3 (1840), 288–293, here p. 293 and Wilhelm Gesenius, "Himjaritische Sprache und Schrift, und Entzifferung der letzteren", *Allgemeine Literatur-Zeitung* 123 (1841), 369–376, here p. 374.

18 Quoted as "Ar[abic]" and adduced in Arabic letters. The formulation of HALOT 1633 is also quite infelicitous ("The creature was known as *t̠afan* by the South Arabians"): almost every word in this statement is fully or partly misleading.

19 Cf. Milgrom, *Leviticus 1–16*, p. 416: "Moreover, the fact that this animal is wild ... indicates that the criteria of chewing the cud and of cloven hoofs came first and that at a later period the environment was scoured to find the animals that bore one of the two criteria".

made by observing its chewing habits rather than by dissecting it to determine whether it has multiple stomachs, the characteristic anatomical feature of the ruminant".

4.2. ʕarʕār (ʕărōʕēr) 'tamarisk' or 'juniper'

This word is twice attested in the Old Testament, and in both cases the information of the context appears to be minimal:

> wə-hāyā kə-ʕarʕār ba-ʕărābā   'He will become like an ʕarʕār in a desert' (Jer 17:6)
> tihyänā ka-ʕărōʕēr ba-mmidbār   'You will become like ʕărōʕēr in a steppe' (Jer 48:6).

In fact, the only clear-cut piece of identification data one can get from these two passages is the prototypical connection of ʕarʕār with steppe or desert. Otherwise, ʕarʕār (ʕărōʕēr) could be just everything: a human, a mammal, a bird, a plant or an element of the landscape. An appeal to external evidence is, in this case, almost mandatory.

The ancient traditions have opted for the tamarisk tree (LXX ἀγριομυρίκη[20]) in agreement with part of the etymological evidence, which, until recently, was almost entirely restricted to the Syriac word ʕarʕūrā 'tamarisk resin' and the clearly related non-reduplicated noun ʕarrā 'tamarisk' (LSyr. 544, SL 1141, 1133).

Today, the Syriac form can be supplemented by a nice formal and semantic cognate from a living Semitic idiom, namely ʕarʕeyr in the Modern South Arabian language Jibbali just mentioned above. The word is missing from the standard dictionary of that language by T. M. Johnstone, but the scientific information accumulated in the botanic encyclopedia of Dhofar by A. Miller and M. Morris[21] together with the beautiful pictures accompanying it do not leave any room for doubt: we are faced with a species of tamarisk (*Tamarix aphylla*).

Finally, the translation 'tamarisk' has become almost standard in Ugaritology. In the Ugaritic corpus, ʕrʕr is attested three times (DUL 178). Two examples are found in in the snake incantation KTU 1.100: 64–65:

> ydy b ʕṣm ʕrʕr   'Il rejette le tamaris (de) parmi les arbres,
> w b šḥt ʕṣ mt   et la "plante de la mort" (de) parmi les buissons:

---

20 In Jer 17:6. As kindly pointed out to me by J. Joosten, in Jer 48:6 (LXX 31:6) the Greek text has ὥσπερ ὄνος ἄγριος ἐν ἐρήμῳ 'like a wild ass in a wilderness', with ʕayir (or ʕārōd?) in the *Vorlage*.
21 See Anthony Miller and Miranda Morris, *Plants of Dhofar* (Oman: Diwan of Royal Court, 1988), p. 282.

ʿrʿrm ynʿrnⁱh   au moyen du tamaris il l'éloigne
ssnm ysynh   au moyen de la grappe de dattier il le chasse'[22].

The third, somewhat less transparent attestation is found in the ritual KTU 109:29–30: l bʿl ṣpn b ʿrʿr p²amt tltm 'Pour bʿl ṣpn, (l'offrande) dans le(s) tamaris, trente fois'[23].

According to Pardee, the identification of ʿrʿr with tamarisk is certain "parce que le tamaris (bīnu) joue un grand rôle dans les namburbi mésopotamiens, et parce que le ʿrʿr est une plante du désert"[24]. These arguments are scarcely compelling, however: the desert as the habitat of ʿrʿr does not seem to surface from the Ugaritic passages themselves, only from the Biblical parallels we are dealing with, whereas the alternative identification possibility, i.e. juniper, is far from alien to steppes and deserts[25]. Finally, tamarisk is certainly not the only plant that can be used in exorcism. It is not surprising; therefore, that some scholars preferred to identify ʿrʿr with juniper[26] whereas Pardee himself speaks of "un arbre du type des genévriers"[27].

The evidence in favor of the meaning 'juniper' is of more or less equal weight.

Traditionally, the nuclear element of this identification has been the Arabic cognate ʿarʿar-, for which this meaning can be solidly established on the basis of the traditional lexicography (LA 4 644, Lane 1990) and the modern dialectal usage (Behnstedt 819). It is certainly the Arabic cognate that has prompted an almost universal recognition of the translation 'juniper' in (pre-)Modern Hebrew lexicography (BDB 792, HALOT 887).

Today, the Arabic evidence can be supplemented by the data from another Modern South Arabian language, Mehri: ʿarʿōr 'Juniperus'[28], missing from the standard Mehri dictionary by Johnstone. Finally, there are good reasons to believe that Akkadian erēnu, traditionally interpreted as cedar (AHw. 237, CAD E

---

22 Translation from Dennis Pardee, *Les textes para-mythologiques de la 24ᵉ campagne (1961)* (Paris: Recherche sur les civilisations, 1988), pp. 215–216.

23 Translation from Dennis Pardee, *Les Textes Rituels*, Fascicules 1–2 (Ras Samra Ougarit XII, Paris: Éditions Recherche sur les Civilisations 2000), pp. 602–604.

24 See Dennis Pardee, *Les textes para-mythologiques*, p. 216.

25 See Immanuel Löw, *Die Flora der Juden*. III (Wien: R. Löwit, 1924), p. 37.

26 See Juan Antonio Belmonte, "Los productos vegetales de KTU 1.100:64–67", *Aula Orientalis* 11 (1993), 114–115.

27 See Dennis Pardee, *Les Textes Rituels*, p. 611.

28 See Alexander Sima, *Mehri-Texte aus der jemenitischen Ṣarqīyah* (Wiesbaden: Harrassowitz, 2009), p. 200.

274), actually designated a kind of juniper[29], whereas an etymological connection between *erēnu* and *ᶜarᶜār*, even if not completely certain, seems to be rather likely.

Vacillation between 'tamarisk' and 'juniper', sometimes observable even within very narrow Semitic subgroups (Jibbali vs. Mehri), is certainly not accidental. As is well known, the two trees are completely different from the point of view of scientific botany, yet the external similarity between tamarisk and some species of juniper can be quite striking, which is partly due to the fact that the "leaves" of tamarisk are "minute, grey green ... abruptly and sharply pointed"[30], "très petites, alternes et écailleuses, un peu semblables à celles de certains conifères" (http://fr.wikipedia.org/wiki/Tamaris).

A Semitic etymologist can be comforted and even encouraged by this conclusion: it confirms the well-known (yet often forgotten) fact that biological difference between *signifiés* is no obstacle for an etymological relationship of the phonologically comparable *signifiants*. In other words, etymology is no safe guide for botanic or zoological identification of obscure *realia* from ancient texts, only a rough approximation to it.

For an Ancient Near Eastern philologist (and a Biblical scholar in particular) all this is certainly bad news: while the array of options can be reasonably reduced to two tree species, a meaningful choice between them is scarcely possible. The external evidence helps, but the limits of its potential are not to be overestimated.

In order to close this case-study in a more positive pitch, I would like to draw the reader's attention to another, rather unexpected dimension of comparative research, namely, the morphological discrepancy between *ᶜarᶜār* and *ᶜărōᶜēr*.

With no appeal to comparative Semitics, this pair looks a strange morphological doublet without any internal justification. However, a quick look at the Arabic cognate shows that the pair *ᶜarᶜār* – *ᶜărōᶜēr* is a phonologically exact reflex of *ᶜarᶜar-* – *ᶜarāᶜir-* in Arabic, where this opposition has a well-known morphological meaning: singular vs. plural. One would not attach too much importance to this circumstance if not for the striking distribution of the two Hebrew forms: when *ᶜarᶜār* is used, the verbal predicate is in the singular (*wə-hāyā*), whereas *ᶜărōᶜēr* is found in combination with the plural verbal form *tihyānā*.

There is no ready diachronic explanation for this remarkable distributional pattern. The broken plural *$^*C_1aC_2\bar{a}C_3iC_4$*- is well known to be a specifically

29 See Jacob Klein and Kathleen Abraham, "Problems of Geography in the Gilgameš Epics: the Journey to the 'Cedar Forest'", In *Landscapes. Territories, Frontiers and Horizons in the Ancient Near East*, eds. Lucio Milano et al. (Padova: Sargon, 2000), pp. 64–73.
30 See Miller and Morris, *op.cit.*, p. 282.

"South Semitic" feature with no clear parallels elsewhere in Hebrew. This circumstance, together with the prominent desert connotations of the Biblical passages in question, would make feasible an early North Arabian morpholexical infiltration into Biblical poetic language. A powerful argument against such a possibility is the "Canaanite shift" which affected the long $\bar{a}$ in *ʕărōʕēr:* this pre-Hebrew vocalic mutation could scarcely remain operative when the supposed North Arabian borrowing would take place. An alternative possibility is to treat the $*C_1aC_2\bar{a}C_3iC_4$- plural as a PWS phenomenon otherwise lost in Hebrew, but somewhat mysteriously preserved in this particular plant name.

4.3. ḥämʔā 'clarified butter'

The problem of semantic identification of Biblical Hebrew words and its subsequent justification does not pertain exclusively to designations of plants and animals. Other, at first sight much less specific and more commonly attested *realia* can also be in need of such a procedure. A well-known example is the milk product *ḥämʔā,* for which the standard dictionaries and translations provide a bewildering variety of alternative interpretations: 'curds', 'sour milk', 'cream' and, finally, 'butter'.

With its nine Biblical attestations, this lexeme cannot be said to be particularly rare, yet a fair analysis of the relevant contexts with no appeal to external data can scarcely provide anything beyond the most general definition 'a milk product'. As soon as the general association with milk is taken for granted, some of the contexts turn out to be not informative at all (Gen 18:8, Deut 32:14, 2 Sam 17:29, Isa 7:15), while a few other suggest a liquid, flowing substance (Job 20:17) which can be used for "drinking" (Judg 5:25) and even "washing" (Job 29:6). The famous passage Prov 30:33 (*mīṣ ḥālāb yōṣī ḥämʔā wū-mīṣ ʔap yōṣī dām wū-mīṣ ʔappayim yōṣī rīb*) is now commonly interpreted as referring to the butter production, but the popularity of this understanding (reflected already in Saadiyah's rendering *zubd*) is undoubtedly due to the Akkadian etymology (*māṣu* 'to churn', AHw. 621, CAD M₁ 350); one must acknowledge, furthermore, that even in the light of the Akkadian cognate the general meaning of this passage remains quite problematic[31]. The prototypical smoothness of *ḥämʔā* in the

---

31 As rightly observed by Marten Stol, "Milch(produkte). A. In Mesopotamien", RlA 8 (1993–1997), 189–201, here p. 194: "nowadays churning in a bag made of goat skin is the rule … but this is not attested in the ancient texts"; *contra* Moshe Held, "*mḫṣ/*mḫš in Ugaritic and Other Semitic Languages", *Journal of the American Oriental Society* 79 (1959), 169–176, here p. 171: "The process of churning (milk) in primitive cultures does not involve beating but rather

emended attestation from Ps 55:22 (*ḥāləkū maḥmā²ōt pīw* || *rakkū dəbārāw miššämän*) is probably better compatible with butter than with any other milk product, but this is, again, hardly more than a feasible conjecture.

In summary, the available internal evidence does not allow us to establish the exact meaning of *ḥäm²ā*, and the divergent translations adopted by the scholars up to this date are a telling witness of this. Yet, as aptly observed by A. Caquot, this term "cannot be ambiguous and refer to the results of two very different processes"[32], i.e. coagulation of milk protein and churning, "which separates the fat particles and then combines them".

In his vigorous defense of the meaning "butter", Caquot, following Dalman[33], only obliquely refers to the etymological data, relying mostly on the LXX translation βούτυρον as well as on the internal evidence – as we have just seen, sorely inconclusive. This is in part understandable, as the cognates from the classical Semitic languages are (or at least were a few decades ago) almost as inconclusive as the Biblical data themselves. In Ugaritic, *ḥm²at* is attested only once, in the well-known passage KTU 1.23:14 (*gd b ḥlb ²annḫ b ḥm²at*) from which nothing concrete can be inferred. The same is true of the lone Sabaic attestation of *ḥm²t* in CIH 540:96–97 where this word appears, as its Hebrew cognate often does, in combination with *dbs₁* 'honey'[34]. The Akkadian cognate *ḫimētu* is, of course, well attested (AHw. 346, CAD Ḫ 189), but, as far as I can see, truly

---

shaking". In Mesopotamia at least, butter was churned in a jar, and it is hard to see how the Hebrew root *myṣ* could be applied to such a procedure if, as generally acknowledged, its meaning is 'to press, to squeeze'. The alternative translation 'to beat' = 'to churn' would fit well *mīṣ ḥālāb* and *mīṣ ²ap*, but probably not *mīṣ ²appayim* ("churning of anger" in Fox, *op.cit.*, pp. 881– 882, appears rather strained). The translation "For as the churning of milk produces ghee, and the pressing of the nose produces blood, so the stirring up of wrath produces strife" in Moshe Held, "Marginal Notes to the Biblical Lexicon", In *Biblical and Related Studies Presented to Samuel Iwry*, eds. Ann Kort and Scott Morschauser, Winona Lake: Eisenbrauns, 1985, 93–103, here p. 10, presupposes, *de facto*, three rather different meanings for *mīṣ* in each of the three comparisons: 'to churn' (which, in Held's perception at least, amounts to 'to shake'), 'to press' and 'to stir up'.

32 André Caquot, "*chālābh*; *gᵉbhīnāh*; *chem'āh*", TDOT IV (1980), 386–391, here p. 390.

33 See Gustaf Dalman, *Arbeit und Sitte in Palästina*. Vol. VI (Gütersloh: C. Bertelsmann, 1939), pp. 310–311.

34 In his recent comprehensive treatment of the Sabaic term, A. Sima opts for clarified butter (*Butterschmalz*), using a variety of comparative evidence including etymology, see Alexander Sima, *Tiere, Pflanzen, Steine und Metalle in den altsüdarabischen Inscrhiften* (Wiesbaden: Harrassowitz, 2000), p. 240. The Sabaic lexeme reappears in a recently published document on wood, but the context is not very informative as far as the identification of the foodstuff in question is concerned, see Peter Stein, *Die altsüdarabischn Minuskelinschriften auf Holzstäbchen aus der Bayerischen Staatsbibliothek in München*, (Tübingen: Ernst Wasmuth, 2010), p. 383.

diagnostic contexts justifying the meaning 'clarified butter' are not easy to find. It is mostly from its Sumerian equivalent Ì.NUN, copiously attested in the sources (including economic documents), that this translation has been established with a reasonable degree of certainty[35]. Another piece of indirect etymological evidence comes from the Akkadian loanword *ḥewtā* in Syriac[36], rendered into Arabic as *zubd* 'fresh butter' or *samn* 'clarified butter' in the traditional Syriac lexicography (PS 1166).

A more direct and unambiguous piece of etymological evidence comes from the modern South Arabian language Soqotri, where *ḥámʔi* (LS 179) designates exactly this – clarified butter, *ghee* or *samn*, by far the most precious substance in the traditional economy based on animal husbandry. In Soqotri, fresh milk is called *ŝḥaf*, whereas *ḥélob*, the etymological equivalent of Hebrew *ḥālāb*, is applied specifically to the fermented milk from which fresh butter (*ḳáṭməhim*) is prepared via shaking in a butter-skin. The clumps of fresh butter are then boiled and refined with the help of ground barley, wheat or rice. The outcome is called *ḥámʔi*, the clarified butter whose expiry date is practically unlimited in whatever climatic conditions and without refrigerators. Needless to say, this is the most natural (in fact, almost the only) way of preserving the surplus of milk in the Middle Eastern natural environment, and it is not by chance that in the oral literature of Soqotra "shaking the butter-skin" is tantamount to "abundance of milk", a topos finding an interesting parallel in Isa 7:21–22: *wə-hāyā ba-yyōm ha-hū yəḥayyā ʔiŝ ʕáglat bāḳār wū-štē ṣōn wə-hāyā mē-rōb ʕăŝōt ḥālāb yōkal ḥämʔā* "On that day one will raise (just) one young cow and a couple of sheep, yet they will give so much milk that he will be able to feed on clarified butter".

We may conclude that, in this particular case, the etymological (and, more broadly, comparative) evidence should be taken rather seriously. It is only in the light of this evidence that the unified translation 'butter' for all attestations of *ḥämʔā*, advocated by Dalman, Caquot and others, appears strong enough to definitely oust such alternatives as 'curds' or 'cream'. As far as I can see, the potential objections to this approach are more apparent than real. Thus, clarified butter is of course solid rather than liquid when stored in room temperature and, as such, may not be described as a flowing substance as is commonly the case in the Old Testament. However, it *is* actually flowing (and being poured) at the two most crucial stages of its life: immediately after preparation and at the moment

---

35 See M. Stol, *op.cit.*, pp. 194–198.
36 See Steven Kaufman, *The Akkadian Influences on Aramaic* (Chicago: University of Chicago, 1974), pp. 55–56.

of consumption. A more serious objection would come from Judg 5:25 where *ḥämʔā* is offered to Sisera who is willing to quench his thirst. Needless to say, in the ordinary life clarified butter would never be "drunk", but there are good reasons to believe that in this poetic passage the climactic parallelism with "value" as its dominant feature (*mayim* 'water' > *ḥālāb* 'milk' > *ḥämʔā* 'clarified butter') overrides the requirements of the common sense.

4.4. ʿ*am* 'grandfather'

The idea that the Hebrew word ʿ*am* can be used not only with the collective meaning 'people', but also as a term of kinship is by no means new and goes back to the last decades of the 19th century at the latest. The survey of early (and not so early) literature by Good[37] makes it clear that the origin and development of this idea – essentially correct, as I will try to demonstrate below – is inseparable from the analysis of the comparative-etymological perspective of the Hebrew word. And, as very often in the history of the Hebrew etymology, it was the meaning of the Arabic cognate, the well-known ʿ*amm*- 'paternal uncle' (Lane 2149), that heavily dominated the discussion.

However, as early as in 1898 the French orientalist Ch. Clermont-Ganneau was able to state that the original meaning of **ʿamm*- was rather 'grand-father' or, more generally, 'forefather', "une acceptation ancienne et probablement générale chez les Sémites"[38]. Today, one cannot but admire the intuition of the great scholar who was able to achieve such a far-reaching conclusion on the basis of very scanty evidence, i.e. two Nabatean inscriptions where the meaning great-grandfather for ʿ*m* (obviously an early North Arabian loanword) can be safely established on prosopographic grounds.

During the recent years, the amount of direct and unmistakable evidence for the meaning 'grandfather', 'forefather' for the proto-WS kinship term **ʿamm*- has grown remarkably. The new data come, paradoxically, from two geographic and chronological extremes of the Semitic-speaking world – Old Babylonian Akkadian and Modern South Arabian.

---

37 Robert McClive Good, *The Sheep of His Pasture. A Study of the Hebrew Noun* ʿam(m) *and Its Semitic Cognates* (Chico: Scholars, 1983), pp. 3–12.

38 Charles Clermont-Ganneau, *Recueil d'archéologie orientale*, vol. 2 (Paris: Émile Bouillon, 1898), pp. 372–373.

As rightly observed by J.-M. Durand[39], the meaning 'grand-father' (rather than 'paternal uncle') has to be ascribed to the earliest attestations of ⁵amm-(ḥammu) as a WS loanword in the Akkadian texts from Mari. The clearest piece of evidence comes from the unpublished text A.405 (ll. 12–13) adduced by Charpin and Ziegler: *pattīya [ša] ḫa-am-mi a-pil-*ᵈEN.ZU *iš-ku-nu*[40]. This text, translated by the editors as "ma marche qu'a institué mon grand-père Apil-Sin", alludes to a well-known prosopographic chain: Apil-Sin as the grand-father of Hammu-rabi. In a similar vein, Yagid-Lim is mentioned as the "grand-father" of Zimri-Lim in M.9597:8–9: *[pa-n]a-nu-um-ma ḫa-am-ma⌈ʳni li im⌉]-[k]a* ˡ*ḫa-ad-ni-li-im ik-⌈ʳx⌉}[d]i* "autrefois Hadnî-Lîm avait assuré la protection de ton grand-père"[41]. The same allusion is found in ARMT 26, 449:18–19: *panānum abūšu u ḫa-am-ma-šu ṭēmšunu ana bītim annîm ul ugammirūnim* "Auparavant son père et son aïeul ne faisaient pas des rapports complets à cette maison".

In view of this recently published evidence, a few other, better known passages where *ḥammu* is attested must be reconsidered. Thus, in the famous Old Babylonian hymn to Ishtar published by F. Thureau-Dangin in *Revue d'assyriologie* 22 we read: *imtallikū šī u ḫa-am-mu-uš* "they take counsel from each other, she and her *ḥammu*". This line alludes to the heavenly god Anum who, according to the most widespread genealogy of Ishtar, is her great grand-father. Finally, the meaning 'ancestor, forefather' fits admirably the context of the OB incantation YOS 11, 12:8: *u₄-ta-mi-ka er-ṣe-tam ù ḫa-am-mi-e* "I adjure you with the Earth and the Forefathers" (that is, the spirits of the dead).

As far as Modern South Arabian is concerned, the meaning 'grand-father' for the reflexes of *⁵amm- can be easily located in the standard dictionaries: Mhr. ʔōm (ML 36) and Jib. ⁵om (JL 19).

As early as in 1906, T. W. Juynboll was able to observe that the meaning 'grand-father' (rather than 'paternal uncle' or, indeed, any other meaning) is

---

39 Jean-Marie Durand, "Unité et diversités au Proche-Orient à l'epoque amorrite", In *La circulation des biens, des personnes et des idées dans le Proche-Orient ancien*, ed. Dominique Charpin and Francis Joannès (Paris: Editions Recherche sur les Civilisations, 1992), 97–128, here p. 120.
40 Dominique Charpin and Nele Ziegler, *Mari et le Proche-Orient à l'époque amorrite. Essai d'histoire politique* (Paris: SEPOA, 2003), p. 228.
41 See Michaël Guichard, "Le Šubartum occidental à l'avènement de Zimrî-Lîm," In *Recueil d'études à la mémoire d'André Parrot*, eds. Dominique Charpin and Jean-Marie Durand (Paris: SEPOA, 2002), 119–168, here p. 126; Charpin and Ziegler, *op.cit.*, pp. 35 and 54.

the most fitting one for at least two groups of Biblical passages where *ʿam* is attested[42].

The first one is the etiological name *bēn ʿammī* which Lot's younger daughter gave to her son in Gen 19:38: the meaning "(I am) the son of my grandfather" fits admirably the boy's difficult family background.

The second one is the "burial formula" *nä²ăsap ²äl-ʿammāw* 'to be gathered to one's forefathers'[43] in Gen 25:8, 17, 35:29, 49:29, 33, Num 20:24, 27:13, 31:2, Deut 32:50[44], structurally parallel to and, with all probability, semantically identical with *nä²ăsap ²äl-²ăbōtāw*. As far as I can see, the linear relationship ('grandfathers') is much more natural in such an expression than the collateral one ('paternal uncles').

This meaning is, finally, not incompatible with the "banishment formula" *wə-nikrətā ha-nnäpäš ha-h(ī)² mē-ʿammāhā*: as reasonably argued by J. Milgrom[45], it can well mean that the sinner "is not permitted to rejoin his ancestors in the afterlife" and/or is banned from "the family sepulcher in which his kin has been gathered".

As for the more general meaning 'relatives, kin, clan' codified by HALOT 837, it seems to be compelling only for a rather small group of passages: *lə-näpäš lō(²) yiṭṭamma(²) bə-ʿammāw* (Lev 21:1[46], and cf. Lev 21:4), *bətūlā mē-ʿammāw yikkaḥ ²iššā* (Lev 21:14[47]) and *²ăšär lō(²) ṭōb ʿāśā bə-ʿammāw* (Ezek 18:18[48]).

4.5. *ṭūb ṣawwārāh* (Hos 10:11)

In Hos 10:11 we read: *wa-²ănī ʿābartī ʿal-ṭūb ṣawwārāh*. Following the ancient versions[49], modern translators mostly render *ṭūb ṣawwārāh* as 'her fine neck' (or similar)[50], but since *ṭūb* 'goodness' is never applied to body parts, the collocation

---

42 See T. W. Juynboll, "Über die Bedeutung des Wortes 'amm", In *Orientalische Studien Theodor Nöldeke zum siebzigsten Geburtstag (2. März 1906) gewidmet von Freunden und Schülern*, ed. Carl Bezold (Giessen: A. Töpelmann), 353–356.

43 See Good, *op.cit.*, pp.90–92.

44 See Edward Lipiński, "'am", *TDOT* XI (2001), 163–177, here pp. 170–171.

45 Milgrom, *Leviticus 1–16*, p. 460.

46 See Milgrom, *Leviticus 17–22*, pp. 1796–1798.

47 See Milgrom, *Leviticus 17–22*, pp. 1819–1820.

48 See Daniel Block, *The Book of Ezekiel. Chapters 1–24* (Grand Rapids: Eerdmans, 1997), p. 579.

49 LXX: ἐπὶ τὸ κάλλιστον τοῦ τραχήλου αὐτῆς, Vulg. *super pulchritudinem colli eius.*

50 For a summary of syntactic problems see Hans Walter Wolff, Hosea (Philadelphia: Fortress Press, 1974), p. 179.

has often been considered strange or even "unintelligible"[51]. However, the correctness of the received text finds a striking confirmation in the materially different, yet structurally almost identical parallel from the Ugaritic Baal myth (KTU 1.4 iv 13–15):

yḥbḳ ḳdš w ʾamrr   "Qudšu-wa-ʾAmruru grasps (her)
yštn ʾaṯrt l bmt ʿr   puts ʾAṯiratu on the donkey's back,
l **ysmsmt** bmt pḥl   on the ass's beautiful back" [52].

According to Pardee, "the Ugaritic expression consists of a substantivized adjective preceding the nouns in question, literally, 'the most beautiful (part[s] of) the thorax of the male equid'"[53]. However, a more straightforward interpretation as a substantive accepted in DUL 984 ('handsomeness, the best part') is by no means inferior, perhaps even preferable in view of the parallel passage in KTU 1.19 ii 10 where we find ysmsm bmt with no feminine ending. In such a case, the parallelism between ṭūb ṣawwārāh and ysmsmt bmt pḥl becomes nearly perfect[54].

4.6. ʾāḥaztā šəmūrōt ʿēnāy (Ps 77:5)

In spite of its rather transparent syntactic alignment, the interpretation of this passage has been rather hotly debated (cf. HALOT 1586 for a summary of opinions). It has been apparently neglected that this fragment has a fine structural parallel in one of the most ancient monuments of Semitic literature, i.e. the famous Old Akkadian love incantation MAD 5, 8. The lines 13–14 of this text read:

---

51 With a rather unsophisticated emendation to *ʿōl ṭūb 'a fine yoke'; see Francis Anderson and David Noel Freedman, *Hosea* (New York: Doubleday, 1980), p. 567.
52 Translation from Dennis Pardee, "The Baʿlu Myth", In *The Context of the Scripture*. I. *Canonical Compositions from the Biblical World*, ed. W. Hallo (Leiden: Brill, 1997), 241–274, here pp. 258–259.
53 So also Josef Tropper, *Ugaritische Grammatik* (Münster: Ugarit, 2000), p. 842.
54 It is hard to say to what extent the Ugaritic text can bear on our interpretation of Hos 10:11 as a whole. The parallel predicates ʿābartī ʿal ‖ ʾarkīb are usually understood as 'I passed by' ‖ 'I harnessed' (as in Wolff, *op.cit.*, p. 179; Anderson-Freedman, *op.cit.*, p. 560 and elsewhere), but this is fraught with difficulties: one can hardly "pass by" a heifer's neck whereas the root rkb "has to do with mounting and riding" (see Anderson–Freedman, *op.cit.*, 568), not harnessing. Since mounting and riding is exactly the topic of the Ugaritic passage, one may dare to wonder whether, in a somewhat eccentric poetic image, Hosea actually presents God as *riding* on the stubborn heifer. One has to admit that, within this interpretation, the use of the causative stem for rkb remains problematic, whereas ṣawwār 'neck' does not seem to be the right place for the rider to sit on.

a-ḫu-EŠ *bu-ra-ma-ti e-ni-ki* "I hold the iris of your eyes"[55].

The general context of the Akkadian passage is of course quite different from the Biblical one: here the incantation priest "holds" or "seizes" the eyes of a young lady he has to enchant, side by side with her "mouth full of spittle" and "vagina full of urine". It seems, nevertheless, that there are several lessons we can learn from the Akkadian text for a better understanding of Ps 77:5.

On the one hand, it casts doubt on the widespread assumption that *šəmūrā* actually means 'eyelid'. If this noun is indeed derived from the common verbal root *šmr*, one may legitimately wonder why eyelid as "guarding the eye" (BDB 1037) should be designated by the passive participle, whose most natural reading would rather be "the guarded one". Now, what is guarded, protected and cherished is certainly not the eyelid, but the eye itself – the eyeball in general, the iris or the pupil, as brilliantly shown by Ps 17:8: *šomrēnī kə-ʔīšōn bat ʕayin* 'Guard me as the pupil of your eye'. In such conditions, the meanings 'eyeball', 'iris' or 'pupil' for *šəmūrā* should, in my opinion, be seriously considered[56].

On the other hand, it shows that the meaning of *ʔāḥaz* in this passage can be rather straightforward and makes unnecessary such exaggerations as "God himself has torn open his eyelids", rightly qualified as "a singular expression"[57]. "Seizing" or "holding" the eyes of a person would just amount to having an unconditioned power over his or her vision, an exclusive right on his attention.

5. Conclusion

As I have tried to demonstrate, our attitude towards the comparative evidence in a Hebrew lexicon has to be sober and modest in its expectations, but certainly not a priori negative. Practical usefulness of etymology for each and every concrete case has to be carefully assessed. It is on the basis of such an assessment that the amount of comparative evidence assigned to a given lexicographic entry has to be measured, from laconic observations à la AHw. ("Semitic") to rather lengthy digressions. It is clear to everybody that the working team of a future comprehensive dictionary of Biblical Hebrew will be unable to afford any special

---

55 Brigitte Groneberg, "Die Liebesbeschwörung MAD V 8 und ihr literarischer Kontext", *Revue d'assyriologie* 95 (2001), 97–113, here p. 104.

56 The meaning 'iris' for the Akkadian word *burāmu* (or *burāmtu*) has been mostly derived from the cognate lexeme *burmu* (AHw. 140, CAD B 330) as well as from the general meaning of the verb *barāmu* 'to be variegated, multicolored'.

57 See Frank-Lothar Hossfeld, Erich Zenger, *Psalms 2* (Philadelphia: Fortress Press, 2005), p. 277.

"etymological department" whose staff would meticulously collect the entire amount of etymological parallels to Hebrew words from Ebla to Soqotra. Such a task is appropriate for another, completely different type of project, namely, a comparative-historical dictionary of Biblical Hebrew, which remains one of the most important desiderata of Semitic studies in general. At the same time, it is my conviction that a successful achievement of any major project in "synchronic" lexicography of Biblical Hebrew can hardly be carried out without an active collaboration with specialists in comparative Semitics, including etymologists.

Walter Dietrich
Hebräische Hapaxlegomena in den Samuelbüchern

Die Untersuchung der Hapaxlegomena in den Samuelbüchern verspricht einerseits lexikographisch und sprachgeschichtlich interessant, andererseits aber auch exegetisch, d. h. für das Verständnis und die Auslegung der Texte, nützlich zu sein.

Die Samuelbücher weisen 131 nur einmal in der Hebräischen Bibel begegnende Lexeme auf[1]. Diese lassen sich in vier Sparten aufteilen: In dreizehn Fällen scheinen Textfehler die Ursache für das Entstehen nur einmal belegter Wörter zu sein (1). Sodann kommen 32 Personen- oder Gruppennamen (2) und 35 Orts- oder Regionalnamen (3) nur in den Samuelbüchern vor. Schliesslich gibt es 51, wenn man so sagen darf, ‚normale' Hapaxlegomena (4), also hebräische Wörter, die sich einzig in den Samuelbüchern und auch in diesen nur einmal finden.

Damit ist die Gliederung der folgenden Ausführungen vorgegeben. Die Hapaxlegomena (bzw. eine Auswahl aus ihnen) sollen auf der einen Seite auf ihre lexikalischen Eigenheiten untersucht werden, was anhand des „Hebräischen und Aramäischen Lexikons zum Alten Testament" (HALAT) geschieht[2]. Auf der anderen Seite soll die Untersuchung der betreffenden Wörter für die Exegese, insbesondere die Literargeschichte, der Samuelbücher nutzbar gemacht werden, könnte doch die Streuung und Dichte von Hapaxlegomena Aufschlüsse über die sprach- und entstehungsgeschichtlichen Hintergründe der jeweiligen Texte geben.

Es mag nützlich sein, dazu die von mir bisher gewonnene Vorstellung von der Textdiachronie der Samuelbücher vorab zu skizzieren, damit die nachfolgend vorgenommenen Zuordnungen besser verfolgt werden können. Nach meinem

---

1 Ich danke Samuel Arnet (Bern/Zürich), der mit mir zusammen das (mittlerweile erschienene) Lexikon KAHAL („Konzise und aktualisierte Version des Hebräischen und Aramäischen Lexikons zum Alten Testament", Leiden: Brill, 2013) herausgegeben hat. Dank seiner ausgeprägten Computerkenntnisse war er in der Lage, mir eine erste grobe Auflistung der betreffenden Lexeme zusammenzustellen.

2 Zunächst 5 Faszikel, dann 2 Bände, Leiden: Brill, 1974–1995 bzw. 1995. Das von dem Zürcher Alttestamentler Ludwig Köhler und dem Basler Walter Baumgartner begonnene Lexikon wurde von dem Berner Johann Jakob Stamm (in Zusammenarbeit mit Benedikt Hartmann) zu Ende geführt. Es sei mir verziehen, wenn ich aus rein pragmatischen, vielleicht auch ein wenig lokalpatriotischen Gründen nicht mit HAHAT (Gesenius. Hebräisches und Aramäisches Handwörterbuch über das Alte Testament, 18. Auflage, Gesamtausgabe, Springer: Berlin/Heidelberg 2013) abgeglichen habe.

Dafürhalten sind die Samuelbücher im Wesentlichen auf sechs Stufen entstanden[3]. Von hinten nach vorne sind dies:

6) eine recht weit verzweigte *Textgeschichte*, die einsetzte, nachdem der Textbestand der Samuelbücher (etwa in der spätpersischen Zeit) so weit verfestigt war, dass die Verfasser der Chronik nicht mehr daran rührten, und aus der als Hauptformen die Textfassungen der Septuaginta (bzw. ihrer hebräischen Vorlage), der Handschriften von Qumran und der Bibel der Masoreten resultierten (wobei diese Hauptzweige sich noch weiter verästeln);

5) *spätnachexilische Ergänzungen* namentlich am Anfang der Samuelbücher (das Hanna-Lied) und an ihrem Schluss (der grosse Appendix 2Sam 21–24), die freilich auch ältere Textbestandteile in sich aufgenommen haben können;

4) die *deuteronomistische Redaktion* (bzw. deren mehrere), die im 6. und 5. Jh. den bis dahin vorliegenden Samuelstoff ins dtr Geschichtswerk integriert und auf bestimmte Weise kommentiert hat (bzw. haben);

3) das sog. *„Höfische Erzählwerk"*, das im ausgehenden 8. oder frühen 7. Jh. die Geschichte der frühen Königszeit Israels erstmals im Zusammenhang darstellte und bereits beträchtliche Bestandteile des jetzt in 1Sam 1 bis 1Kön 2 (oder 12) zu Lesenden enthalten hat; es ist dies die wichtigste formative Phase in der Buchentstehung.

2) ältere *Teildarstellungen* (mündlicher oder schon schriftlicher Natur), die in das Höfische Erzählwerk Eingang fanden: über Samuel und Saul, über die heilige Lade, über das Schicksal der Sauliden, über David als Freibeuter, über den Abschalom-Aufstand sowie über die dubiosen Umstände der Geburt und der Machtergreifung Salomos;

1) *Einzelüberlieferungen*, die in diesen Teilsammlungen oder Novellen, teilweise auch abseits davon (etwa im Anhang 2Sam 21–24), aufbewahrt sind und deren Wurzeln teilweise bis ins 10. Jh. zurückreichen mögen.

1. Textfehler

Eine Reihe von nur einmal und nur in den Samuelbüchern belegten Wörtern scheint durch Versehen der Tradenten und Abschreiber zustande gekommen zu sein: also faktisch erst auf Stufe 6 der Textentwicklung – oder noch danach, in der

---

3 Nähere Informationen und Begründungen zum Folgenden finden sich in: Walter Dietrich, *Die frühe Königszeit in Israel. 10. Jahrhundert v. Chr.* (Biblische Enzyklopädie 3), Stuttgart: Kohlhammer, 1997, 18–33. 229–273. – Walter Dietrich, *David. Der Herrscher mit der Harfe* (Biblische Gestalten 14), Leipzig: Evangelische Verlagsanstalt, 2006, 26–65. – Walter Dietrich, *Samuel, Teilband 1, 1Sam 1–12* (BKAT 8.1), Neukirchen-Vluyn: Neukirchener, 2011, 38*–58*.

langen Geschichte immer neuen Abschreibens der biblischen Texte. Da diese Art von „Hapaxlegomena" für die Ziele dieser Untersuchung nicht sehr ertragreich ist, genügt es, sich, gleichsam zu Demonstrationszwecken, auf drei Fälle zu beschränken.

– In der Weissagung eines „Gottesmannes" gegen Eli bzw. das elidische Priesterhaus (1Sam 2,27–36) findet sich, nach der Ankündigung mancherlei Ungemachs, die folgende Drohung: „Und Einen will ich dir nicht ausrotten von meinem Altar, um seine Augen überfließen und seine Kehle austrocknen zu lassen. Und die große Mehrzahl deines Hauses wird im besten Mannesalter sterben" (2,33). Was hier mit „austrocknen lassen" wiedergegeben ist, hat zur Grundlage das Hapaxlegomenon וְלַאֲדִיב. Dies sieht nach dem Infinitiv Hif. eines Verbs אדב aus, bei dem das ה entfallen wäre. HALAT (11) führt zwar gleich zwei homonyme Verben mit dieser Konsonantenfolge auf, doch das eine ist nur aus dem Arabischen erschlossen, um den Namen „Adbeël" zu etymologisieren, und zum anderen wird lediglich unsere Stelle angegeben – anders gesagt: Es gibt keine positiven Belege für ein solches Verb im Hebräischen. Anscheinend liegt eine Vertauschung des ersten und des zweiten Buchstaben vor. דאב Qal nun bedeutet „schmachten" (HALAT 199); das an unserer Stelle vorausgesetzte Hif. in Verbindung mit נפש, „Kehle", meint etwas wie „austrocknen lassen"[4], wofür es einen Beleg auch in Jer 31,25 gibt.

– In 1Sam 13,20 f wird eine Art Metallbearbeitungsmonopol der Philister beschrieben, das die Israeliten zwingt, abgenutzte oder beschädigte Werkzeuge in die Küstenebene hinunter zu tragen und dort warten oder reparieren zu lassen. In meinem Kommentar ist der Passus so übersetzt: „Und ganz Israel stieg hinab zu den Philistern, jeder, um seine Pflugspitze und seine Pflugschar und seine Axt und seine Sichel schärfen zu lassen. Und der Preis war ein Pim für Pflugspitzen und Pflugscharen und ein Drittelschekel für das Schärfen der Äxte und das Richten eines Rindersteckens"[5]. Die Wendung „ein Drittelschekel für das Schärfen" beruht auf einer Konjektur. Im hebräischen Text steht: שְׁלֹשׁ קִלְּשׁוֹן. Die Vulgata hat im ersten dieser beiden Wörter die Zahl „drei" gesehen und von da aus auf „Dreizack" getippt. Die LXX schreibt: τρεῖς σίκλοι εἰς τόν ὀδόντα, „drei Schekel für den Zahn". Auch hier ist das Zahlwort „drei" erkannt und werden die letzten Buchstaben von קִלְּשׁוֹן auf שֵׁן, den „Zahn", gedeutet: eine Fehldeutung. Interessant aber ist das Auftauchen von σίκλος, „Schekel". Das passt zu dem zuvor erwähnten „Pim", einem alten Gewichtsmass, das ca. zwei Drittel eines Schekels ausmachte. Tatsächlich findet sich inmitten der Zeichenfolge שלשקלשון das Wort שקל. Nimmt man

4 Siehe Dietrich, *Samuel* (Anm. 3), 110. 116.
5 Walter Dietrich, *Samuel* (BKAT 8.2/1), Neukirchen-Vluyn: Neukirchener, 2011, 25.

einmal für dessen ersten und letzten Buchstaben eine Haplographie an – geboren aus der Not bzw. dem Unverständnis eines Abschreibers –, zeichnen sich drei Wörter ab: שלש שקל לשׁן. Die ersten beiden meinen kaum „drei Schekel", das wäre im Kontext ein zu hoher Betrag, sondern „ein Drittel eines Schekels". Und lässt man beim dritten Wort die – wohl wiederum aus Not hinzugekommene – *mater lectionis* weg, erhält man einen Infinitiv Qal + ל von שׁנן, „um zu schärfen", zusammen also: „ein Drittelschekel für das Schärfen". Demnach hätten zu dem Hapaxlegomenon קלשׁון, einem laut HALAT völlig „unsicheren Wort" (1034), gleich mehrere Textfehler geführt.

– In 1Sam 15,9 wird berichtet, wen und was Saul und seine Soldaten bei der Razzia gegen Amalek verschont und was sie, scheinbar im Gehorsam gegen den göttlichen Bannbefehl, vernichtet haben. Dies Letztere hat im Hebräischen den Wortlaut: נְמִבְזָה וְנָמֵס אֹתָהּ הֶחֱרִימוּ. Hier ist נְמִבְזָה ein Hapaxlegomenon, das mit dem zweiten Wort נָמֵס offenbar einen Stabreim auf *Nun* bildet, ähnlich wie das deutsche „niet- und nagelfest". Auch im Hebräischen könnte es sich um eine gleichsam sprichwörtliche Redewendung handeln. Laut HALAT (662) ist sie von zwei wohlbekannten Verben herzuleiten: בזה, „verachten", und מאס, „verwerfen" (jeweils im Nif.), also: „das Verachtete und Verworfene". Ich habe übersetzt: „minderwertige und unbrauchbare Ware: die bannten sie"[6].

Die weiteren auf Text- bzw. Schreibfehlern beruhenden Hapaxlegomena sind (in alphabetischer Reihenfolge): אֵצֶל 1Sam 20,19; אִין 1Sam 21,9; בֵּרִים 2Sam 20,14; כֻּלְּבוּ 1Sam 25,3; לוּשׁ 2Sam 3,15; מַגְדִיל 2Sam 22,51 (Ketib); קלה 2Sam 20,14; עַמִּיחוּר 2Sam 13,37; עָצְנִי/עֵצֶן 2Sam 23,8; שִׁיבָה 2Sam 19,33; תַּחְכְּמֹנִי 2Sam 23,8.

2. Personen- und Gruppennamen

Die einzig in den Samuelbüchern belegten Personen- und Gruppennamen könnten in mehrfacher Hinsicht aufschlussreich sein: Häufen sie sich an bestimmten Stellen? Sind sie aus dem sonst bekannten hebräischen Wortschatz etymologisierbar? Sind etwa fremdländische Namen darunter? Wie verhalten sich diese Namen zum übrigen biblischen Onomastikon (insbesondere auch zu etwaigen Parallelen in der Chronik)?

Gehäuft finden sich einmalige Namen vor allem in den Ahnenreihen Samuels und Sauls, also eher am Anfang, sowie in den Anekdotensammlungen und Kriegerlisten im Anhang der Samuelbücher.

---

6 Walter Dietrich, *Samuel* (BKAT 8.2/2), Neukirchen-Vluyn: Neukirchener, 2011, 132.

– Für תֹּחוּ, laut 1Sam 1,1 ein Vorfahr Samuels bzw. Elkanas, findet sich in 1Chr 6,19 die Schreibweise תּוֹחַ (also eine Metathesis des zweiten und des dritten Radikals). Beide Namensformen lassen sich innerhebräisch nicht etymologisieren. HALAT (1563) vermutet, im Hintergrund könne ein akkadisches Wort *taḫu* II stehen, das so viel wie „Jungtier" bedeutet; auch die Verbindung zu einem ugaritischen *nomen locale Tu-ḫi-ya* wird erwogen – beides immerhin innersemitische Ableitungsversuche.

– Gleich drei singuläre Namen finden sich unter den Vorfahren Sauls. In 1Sam 9,1 werden אֲפִיחַ und צְרוֹר erwähnt, der eine zu deuten als „der mit (grossem) Vorderkopf" (HALAT 76), der andere wohl herzuleiten von צֻר, „Fels, Stein" (HALAT 987). In der Szene von der Auslosung Sauls aus der versammelten Mannschaft Israels begegnet zudem der Sippenname מַטְרִי (1Sam 10,21); laut HALAT (544) bedeutet er so viel wie „zur Regenzeit geboren". Bis auf den ersten sind dies alles ‚gut hebräische', auffälligerweise freilich überhaupt nicht theophore Namen. Nichts deutet darauf, dass sie aus einer späten Zeit stammten (wie das bei vielen Namen in der Chronik der Fall ist), eher im Gegenteil. Das Auftauchen des in der Ahnenliste 1Sam 9,1 nicht genannten Namens „Matri" in 10,21 weist auf vermutlich recht frühe, separate literarische Entwicklungen[7].

Im *Anhang zu den Samuelbüchern* sind zwei Anekdotenreihen über herausragende Taten von Kriegern Davids und eine Namensliste seiner „dreissig" Elitekrieger enthalten. In den Anekdoten finden sich drei, in der Liste der „Dreissig" dreizehn singuläre Personennamen. Das ist umso bemerkenswerter, als die Anekdotenreihe 2Sam 23,8 – 23 in 1Chr 11,10 – 25 und die Dreissiger-Liste 2Sam 23,24 – 39 in 1Chr 11,26 – 47 aufgenommen sind und daher eigentlich überhaupt keine *Hapax*legomena enthalten sollten.

Zunächst die Anekdotenreihen.

– Ein besiegter philistäischer Recke heisst סַף (2Sam 21,18). HALAT (720) führt als Parallele den babylonischen Namen *Sippē/ai* an. Tatsächlich schreibt die Chronik (1Chr 20,4) סִפַּי. Über eine mögliche Etymologie schweigt sich HALAT aus. Es gibt ein Nomen סַף, „Schwelle", und ein Verb ספה in den Bedeutungen „wegnehmen" und „hinschwinden"; einen Reim auf den Namen „Sap(pai)" vermag ich mir nicht zu machen.

– Der Name des ersten von „drei" besonders hoch gerühmten Kriegern Davids ist יֹשֵׁב בַּשֶּׁבֶת (2Sam 23,8). In 1Chr 11,11 heisst er Jaschâb'am, was hebräisch weniger

---

7 Konkret gehören die Überlieferungen zum Sauliden-Erzählkranz und zur Samuel-Saul-Geschichte.

auffällig klingt. HALAT (425) hält den Namen für eine Deformation aus Jischbaal, was zuerst zu Jischboschät und dann eben zu „Joscheb-baschäbät" geworden sei. Stimmte das, dann läge hier kein (unabsichtlicher) Textfehler, sondern eine beabsichtigte Textumformung vor.

– Der dritte der grossen „Drei" heisst Schamma' (2Sam 23,11): ein nicht einmaliger, etymologisch gleichwohl ungesicherter Name. In 1Chr 11 ist er – nach Jaschâb'am, dem ersten, und Elasar, dem zweiten der drei grossen Helden – einfach weggelassen. Sein Vater soll ein „Harariter" gewesen sein: gemäss HALAT (246) ein „gentilicium incertum", das laut Amarna-Brief 256 jedenfalls „im Süden" zu suchen sei. Der Vater des „Harariters Schamma'" – und jetzt kommt das eigentliche Hapaxlegomenon – heisst אָגֵא. HALAT (10) führt als keilschriftliche Analogie einen gleichnamigen König von Aschkelon (um 600 v.Chr.) auf. Auch Aschkelon liegt bekanntlich „im Süden", gehört aber zur philistäischen Pentapolis. Doch dürfte es sich kaum um einen ägäischen Namen handeln; denn es gibt eine gleichlautende semitische Bezeichnung für den „Kameldorn", eine Steppenpflanze. Dann wären der „Age'" aus der Davidzeit und sein jüngerer königlicher Namensvetter in Aschkelon nicht griechischstämmige, sondern gewissermassen autochthone Gestalten gewesen.

Nun zur Liste der „dreissig" Elitekrieger in 2Sam 23,24–39. Sie findet sich in 1Chr 11,26–47 wieder. Über zwei Dutzend der Namen sind in beiden Texten identisch bzw. nur leicht unterschiedlich geschrieben. Vier kommen in der Sam-, nicht aber in der Chr-Version vor, umgekehrt achtzehn nur in der Chr-Version. Diese hat denn auch insgesamt 47 Namen im Vergleich zu 31 in 2Sam 23; vor allem gegen Ende hin ist die Chr- gegenüber der Sam-Liste deutlich ausgeweitet. Lag dem Chronisten eine eigene, von derjenigen in 2Sam 23 abweichende Tradition vor, oder hat er von sich aus erweitert?

2Sam 23,24–39	1Chr 11,26–47
24 עֲשָׂה־אֵל אֲחִי־יוֹאָב בַּשְּׁלֹשִׁים אֶלְחָנָן בֶּן־דֹּדוֹ בֵּית לָחֶם:	26 וְגִבּוֹרֵי הַחֲיָלִים עֲשָׂה־אֵל אֲחִי יוֹאָב אֶלְחָנָן בֶּן־דּוֹדוֹ מִבֵּית
25 שַׁמָּה הַחֲרֹדִי אֱלִיקָא הַחֲרֹדִי: ס	לָחֶם: ס
26 חֶלֶץ הַפַּלְטִי עִירָא בֶן־עִקֵּשׁ הַתְּקוֹעִי: ס	27 שַׁמּוֹת הַהֲרוֹרִי חֶלֶץ הַפְּלוֹנִי: ס
27 אֲבִיעֶזֶר הָעַנְּתֹתִי מְבֻנַּי הַחֻשָׁתִי: ס	28 עִירָא בֶן־עִקֵּשׁ הַתְּקוֹעִי אֲבִיעֶזֶר הָעַנְּתוֹתִי: ס
28 צַלְמוֹן הָאֲחֹחִי מַהְרַי הַנְּטֹפָתִי: ס	29 סִבְּכַי הַחֻשָׁתִי עִילַי הָאֲחוֹחִי: ס
29 חֵלֶב בֶּן־בַּעֲנָה הַנְּטֹפָתִי ס אִתַּי בֶּן־רִיבַי מִגִּבְעַת בְּנֵי	30 מַהְרַי הַנְּטֹפָתִי חֵלֶד בֶּן־בַּעֲנָה הַנְּטוֹפָתִי: ס
בִנְיָמִן: ס	31 אִיתַי בֶּן־רִיבַי מִגִּבְעַת בְּנֵי בִנְיָמִן ס בְּנָיָה הַפִּרְעָתֹנִי:
30 בְּנָיָהוּ פִּרְעָתֹנִי הִדַּי מִנַּחֲלֵי גָעַשׁ: ס	32 חוּרַי מִנַּחֲלֵי גָעַשׁ ס אֲבִיאֵל הָעַרְבָתִי: ס
31 אֲבִי־עַלְבוֹן הָעַרְבָתִי עַזְמָוֶת הַבַּרְחֻמִי:	33 עַזְמָוֶת הַבַּחֲרוּמִי אֶלְיַחְבָּא הַשַּׁעַלְבֹנִי: ס
32 אֶלְיַחְבָּא הַשַּׁעַלְבֹנִי בְּנֵי יָשֵׁן יְהוֹנָתָן:	34 בְּנֵי הָשֵׁם הַגִּזוֹנִי יוֹנָתָן בֶּן־שָׁגֵה הַהֲרָרִי: ס
33 שַׁמָּה הַהֲרָרִי אֲחִיאָם בֶּן־שָׁרָר הָאָרָרִי: ס	35 אֲחִיאָם בֶּן־שָׂכָר הַהֲרָרִי אֱלִיפַל בֶּן־אוּר: ס
34 אֱלִיפֶלֶט בֶּן־אֲחַסְבַּי בֶּן־הַמַּעֲכָתִי ס אֱלִיעָם בֶּן־אֲחִיתֹפֶל	36 חֵפֶר הַמְּכֵרָתִי אֲחִיָּה הַפְּלֹנִי: ס

2Sam 23,24–39	1Chr 11,26–47
הַגִּלֹנִי׃ ס	37 חֶצְרוֹ הַכַּרְמְלִי נַעֲרַי בֶּן־אֶזְבָּי׃ ס
35 חֶצְרוֹ הַכַּרְמְלִי פַּעֲרַי הָאַרְבִּי׃ ס	38 יוֹאֵל אֲחִי נָתָן מִבְחָר בֶּן־הַגְרִי׃ ס
36 יִגְאָל בֶּן־נָתָן מִצֹּבָה ס בָּנִי הַגָּדִי׃	39 צֶלֶק הָעַמּוֹנִי נַחְרַי הַבֵּרֹתִי נֹשֵׂא כְּלֵי יוֹאָב בֶּן־צְרוּיָה׃ ס
37 צֶלֶק הָעַמֹּנִי נַחְרַי הַבְּאֵרֹתִי נֹשְׂאֵי כְּלֵי יוֹאָב בֶּן־צְרֻיָה׃ ס	40 עִירָא הַיִּתְרִי גָּרֵב הַיִּתְרִי׃ ס
38 עִירָא הַיִּתְרִי גָּרֵב הַיִּתְרִי׃ ס	41 אוּרִיָּה הַחִתִּי זָבָד בֶּן־אַחְלָי׃ ס
39 אוּרִיָּה הַחִתִּי כֹּל שְׁלֹשִׁים וְשִׁבְעָה פ	42 עֲדִינָא בֶן־שִׁיזָא הָראוּבֵנִי רֹאשׁ לָראוּבֵנִי וְעָלָיו שְׁלוֹשִׁים׃ ס
	43 חָנָן בֶּן־מַעֲכָה וְיוֹשָׁפָט הַמִּתְנִי׃ ס
	44 עֻזִּיָּא הָעַשְׁתְּרָתִי שָׁמָע וִיעוּאֵל בְּנֵי חוֹתָם הָעֲרֹעֵרִי׃ ס
	45 יְדִיעֲאֵל בֶּן־שִׁמְרִי וְיֹחָא אָחִיו הַתִּיצִי׃ ס
	46 אֱלִיאֵל הַמַּחֲוִים וִירִיבַי וְיוֹשַׁוְיָה בְּנֵי אֶלְנָעַם וְיִתְמָה הַמּוֹאָבִי׃
	47 אֱלִיאֵל וְעוֹבֵד וְיַעֲשִׂיאֵל הַמְּצֹבָיָה פ

Bei den *nur* in 2Sam 23 begegnenden Namen handelt es sich um drei Gentilicia und zehn Personnamen. Zuerst die Gentilicia:

– In 23,26 begegnet חֶלֶץ הַפַּלְטִי Nach HALAT (880) zeigt פַּלְטִי entweder die Herkunft aus Bet-Pelet, einer judäischen Ortschaft (Jos 15,27; dann wäre es ein *nomen locale*), oder die Zugehörigkeit zu einer Sippe Pelet an (vgl. 1Chr 2,47). Die Chr-Parallele in 11,27 spricht indes von „Helez dem *Peloniter*"; diese Angabe wiederholt sich in 11,36. Vielleicht konnte der Chronist mit diesem Namen mehr anfangen als mit פַּלְטִי.

– In 2Sam 23,31 lesen wir von עַזְמָוֶת בַּרְחֻמִי. In der Chronik haben wir den gleichen Personennamen, doch statt „Barchumiter" heisst es dort „Bacharumiter": eine Metathesis der Buchstaben Resch und Chet. In HALAT (115) wird eine Konjektur gegenüber beiden Fassungen vorgeschlagen, und zwar zu „Bachurmiter", d. h. zu „einem aus Bachurim", einem auch aus den Samuelbüchern wohlbekannten Ort nahe Jerusalem. Demnach resultierte dieses Hapax aus einem Textfehler – sowohl in Sam als auch in Chr –, und wieder hätten wir es ursprünglich mit einem *nomen locale* zu tun.

– Ein echtes und besonders interessantes Gentilicium findet sich in 2Sam 23,35. Mit ihm zusammen ist auch gleich noch der zugehörige Eigenname ein Hapax: פַּעֲרַי הָאַרְבִּי. HALAT (81) zögert nicht, אַרְבִּי von אֲרַב herzuleiten; es handelt sich also um einen Araber. Die Chronik macht ihn zu einem בֶּן־אֶזְבָּי; vielleicht störte sie die Zugehörigkeit eines Arabers zu Davids Elitetruppe. Womöglich aus gleichem Grund unterschlägt sie zwei Aramäer[8]: einen „Maachatiter" (23,34) und

---

8 Den Ammoniter Zeleq freilich übernimmt sie (2Sam 23,37 = 1Chr 11,39), und der Moabiter Jitma begegnet in ihrem Eigentum (1Chr 11,46).

einen Mann aus „Zoba" (23,36)[9]. Zum Namen jenes Arabers liesse sich auf ein hebräisches Verb פָּעַר verweisen, das etwas wie „aufsperren" bedeutet: meist in einem unangenehmen Sinn (etwa vom Rachen der Scheol, Jes 5,14: HALAT 898). Das wirkt bei einer Namengebung merkwürdig, und HALAT (ebd.) setzt zu dieser Ableitung denn auch ein Fragezeichen. Martin Noth habe die Lesung der Chronik bevorzugt: נַעֲרַי, was wieder gut hebräisch ist. In Wahrheit dürfte es sich eben um einen Ausländer mit fremdländischem Namen gehandelt haben.

Was die weiteren einmaligen Namensformen der Liste in 2Sam 23 betrifft, so sind sie oft hebräisch schwer ableitbar und innerhalb des hebräischen Onomastikons erratisch und archaisch. Womöglich war eben dies der Grund, dass dem Chronisten (oder schon den Tradenten, die auf dem Traditionsweg zwischen der Sam- und der Chr-Fassung allenfalls anzunehmen sind) Fehlschreibungen unterlaufen oder Neuschreibungen sinnvoll erschienen sind. Im Einzelnen:

– אֱלִיקָא (2Sam 23,25) fehlt in der chronistischen Parallele völlig. Das zugehörige *nomen locale* חָרֹד („der Haroditer") hat die Chronik (11,27) einem anderen Mann namens Schammot übertragen – aus welchen Gründen auch immer. Der Name אֱלִיקָא soll laut HALAT (54) eine Kurzform von אֱלִיקָם sein, „G[ott] hat sich (z. Kampf) erhoben". Allerdings ist eine „Kürzung" nicht wirklich zu erkennen, so dass der Name rätselhaft bleibt[10].

– Aus מְבֻנַּי dem Huschatiter (2Sam 23,27) machen einige LXX-Handschriften und die Chronik „Sibbechai den Huschatiter"; genau so heisst der Held einer Anekdote in 2Sam 21,18 (die freilich in der Chronik nicht überliefert ist). HALAT (515) erklärt dies ohne Begründung für die richtige Namensform; diejenige in 2Sam 21,18 sei „corr.[upt]". Ich würde wieder sagen: Sie ist rätselhaft.

– Für צַלְמוֹן in 2Sam 23,28 hat die Chronik עִילַי. Laut HALAT (772) könnte das eine Verschreibung aus צִילַי sein und dieses wieder eine Kurzform von צַלְמוֹן. Dann wäre dieser Name also ursprünglich. Er soll sich entweder von dem (konjizierten!) Verb צלם, „dunkel, schwarz sein", oder von dem Nomen צֶלֶם, „Ebenbild" (eines verstorbenen Verwandten, 964) herleiten.

– Für den Namen חֵלֶב in 2Sam 23,29 haben einige hebräische Handschriften, der Targum, die Vulgata und auch 1Chr 11,30 „Heled". HALAT (302) fordert, dieser Lesung zu folgen, und leitet den Namen von I חלד, einem aufgrund einer arabischen Analogie postulierten Verb mit der Bedeutung „lebendig sein", ab. Läge

---

9 Auch wenn hier etwas anders geschrieben, handelt es sich um das in 1Sam 14,47; 2Sam 8,3.5.12; 10,6.8; 1Kön 11,23; 1Chr 18,3.5.9; 19,6 erwähnte aramäische Fürstentum.
10 Eine pikante Einzelheit: HALAT macht zu dem Wort die verkehrte Stellenangabe 2Sam 23,35; das ist jetzt in KAHAL korrigiert.

aber nicht eine Verbindung der in MT belegten Namensform mit חֵלֶב, dem damals so hoch geschätzten „Fett", viel näher?

– Der הַדָּי von 2Sam 23,30 heisst in Chr חוּרַי. Hier soll man gemäss HALAT (287) der Sam-Fassung folgen. In dieser stecke möglicherweise das Nomen הוֹד, „Hoheit", das um einen Gottesnamen zu ergänzen wäre.

– Der seltsame Name אֲבִי־עַלְבוֹן in 2Sam 23,31 wird in Chr durch das leicht verstehbare „Abi'ël" ersetzt. HALAT (783) erwägt für אֲבִי־עַלְבוֹן zwei Erklärungen: es könne sich um eine Verballhornung von ursprünglich Abi-Baal oder um ein Derivat aus einem arabischen Etymon der Bedeutung „überwinden" handeln; in Palmyra sei ein analoger Name belegt. Wäre das Zweite richtig, dann wäre dies ein weiterer Fall von Tilgung ausländischer Spuren durch den Chronisten.

– Martin Noth hatte den Namen יָשֵׁן in 2Sam 23,32 schlicht von ישן herleiten wollen: „der Schläfrige" – originell, und gar nicht so fernliegend bei einem Baby. Die in HALAT (427) vorgeschlagene Konjektur zu „Schanah" erscheint mir dagegen recht freihändig.

– Der Vater eines gewissen Ahiam heisst laut 2Sam 23,33 שָׁרָר, laut Chr שָׂכָר. Letzteres ist der Name auch eines korachitischen Türhüters (1Chr 26,4) und hängt gewiss mit dem gleichlautenden Nomen für „Lohn" zusammen. Die Namensform in 2Sam 23,33 führt HALAT (1528) auf ein im Ugaritischen belegtes Verb שרר zurück, das etwas wie „fest sein" bedeute; dies wirkt bedeutend archaischer als der Name in Chr.

– Auch der Vater des Elifelet von 2Sam 23,34 hat einen auffälligen Namen: אֲחַסְבַּי. In der Chronik heisst der Krieger Elifal und sein Vater Ur. Letzterer Name hat natürlich mit dem geläufigen Nomen אוּר, „Licht(schein)", zu tun. Zu אֲחַסְבַּי wagt HALAT (33) gar keine Etymologie. Die Vierradikalität fällt ins Auge, und selbst wenn das א ein Präfix wäre, gäbe es keine Wurzel חסב.

Abschliessend seien noch vier weitere interessante Personennamen aus dem zweiten Samuelbuch näher betrachtet.

– Der Zweitgeborene Davids und Sohn der bekannten Abigajil (1Sam 25) soll nach 2Sam 3,3 כִּלְאָב gewesen sein. HALAT (453) deutet den Namen als *kål-'āb*, „ganz der Vater". Es ist erstaunlich, dass die Kunde von diesem Davidsohn erhalten geblieben ist, obwohl sein Träger in den nachfolgenden Erzählungen keinerlei Rolle spielt. Ist er vielleicht früh verstorben?

– Natan gibt in 2Sam 12,25 dem frisch geborenen Salomo den Beinamen יְדִידְיָה, „Jahs Liebling". Da dieser Name hernach nie mehr vorkommt, könnte es sich entweder um eine sehr alte, im Übrigen verschollene Information handeln – oder um eine gezielte Leserlenkung durch den „Höfischen Erzähler", der frühzeitig einen Hinweis geben wollte, wer aus den nachfolgenden Irrungen und Wirrungen im Hause Davids als Nachfolger des Dynastiegründers hervorgehen werde.

– Im Kontext des Abschalom-Aufstandes wird in 2Sam 17,25 der Name des Mannes genannt, den der Aufrührer als kommandierenden General eingesetzt hat: Amasa, Sohn eines gewissen יִתְרָא הַיִּשְׂרְאֵלִי. Der Name hängt gewiss mit der hebräischen Wurzel *j-t-r* zusammen und bezeichnet etwas wie „Überschuss, Vorrang". Die gut hebräische Etymologie passt zu der Herkunftsbezeichnung „Israelit". Die Chronik (in 1Chr 2,17) und in ihrem Gefolge viele Versionen, angefangen mit LXX[A], machen daraus einen „Ismaeliter", und viele moderne Exegeten folgen ihnen. Doch der Name des Mannes klingt so gar nicht arabisch. Offenbar konnte man sich schon früh nicht mehr vorstellen, dass inmitten der Daviderzählungen ein Mann als „Israelit" bezeichnet wird, als wäre dies etwas Besonderes und gar Fremdes. Es *war* aber etwas Besonderes, dass Abschalom einen israelitischen General bestellte[11]; dessen Gegenspieler (und späterer Mörder) Joab war selbstverständlich Judäer. Abschaloms Aufstand wurde offenbar nicht zuletzt von den israelitischen Nordstämmen getragen[12] (was nach seiner Niederschlagung zu schweren Spannungen zwischen Judäern und Israeliten führte, 2Sam 19,10 – 16.42 – 44). Wenn Abschalom die Heeresführung also einem *Israeliten* anvertraute, war damit durchaus eine Signalwirkung beabsichtigt.

– Schliesslich noch Elhanan, Sohn des יַעְרֵי אֹרְגִים in 2Sam 21,19. Der zweite Teil der Wortfügung, „Weber", könnte aus der nachfolgenden Angabe, Goliats Lanzenschaft sei „wie ein Weberbaum" (כִּמְנוֹר אֹרְגִים) gewesen, herübergedrungen sein – wenn sich nicht darin der Beruf des Namensträgers abzeichnet. Für יַעְרֵי schreibt die Chronik יָעִיר (1Chr 20,5), was laut HALAT (404 bzw. 401) die ursprüngliche Namensform und „Kf. v. VI עִיר" sein soll. Hier scheint ein Irrtum vorzuliegen, unterscheidet HALAT (s.v., 777) doch nur vier Homonyme dieser Lautung. Ernster zu nehmen ist der Hinweis auf „ug. *ġr* schützen". Wäre aber nicht – gerade in der in 2Sam bezeugten Namensform – auch ein Zusammenhang mit יַעַר, „Wald" bzw. „Honig", denkbar? Kostbar ist dieses Hapaxlegomenon deswegen, weil der Mann mit dem schwer erklärbaren Vatersnamen König David die Ehre streitig macht, Goliat von Gat erschlagen zu haben. Bekanntlich hat die Chronik das Problem dadurch zu entschärfen versucht, dass sie „Elhanan ben Jair" lediglich „Lachmi, den Bruder Goliats" als Opfer zugestand. Die Wahrheit dürfte sein, dass der Goliatsieg Davids eine Fiktion ist[13].

---

11 Vgl. Ernst Axel Knauf, Ismael. Untersuchungen zur Geschichte Palästinas und Nordarabiens im 1. Jahrtausend v.Chr. (ADPV), Wiesbaden: Harrassowitz, [2]1989, 12f.

12 So etwa Albrecht Alt, „Die Staatenbildung der Israeliten in Palästina", in A. Alt, Kleine Schriften zur Geschichte Israels, Bd. 2, München: Beck, [3]1964, 1– 65, hier 57; auch Dietrich, Frühe Königszeit (s. Anm. 3), 199f.

13 Vgl. das (von einem Studenten übernommene) Diktum Steven L. McKenzie's („David's Enemies", In *König David – biblische Schlüsselfigur und europäische Leitgestalt*, ed. Walter Dietrich /

Weitere, nur in den Samuelbüchern begegnende Personennamen sind: אַרְמֹנִי 2Sam
21,8; יָרָבְשֶׁת 2Sam 11,21; מָעוֹךְ 1Sam 27,2; שֹׁבִי 2Sam 17,27; שִׁיָא 2Sam 20,25.
Die weiteren Stammes- und Volksnamen sind: גִּרְזִי/גֶּזְרִי 1Sam 27,8; יָאֵרִי 2Sam
20,26.

3. Orts- und Regionalnamen

35 hebräische Orts- und Regionalnamen begegnen in der Bibel nur einmal und nur
in den Samuelbüchern. Die Belege ballen sich an vier Stellen in auffälliger Weise.
Ihnen möchte ich nachgehen und ein besonderes Augenmerk auf die doppelte
Frage richten, welche *siedlungs-* und *literar*historischen Hinweise sich aus dem
Phänomen ergeben.

Drei geographische Hapaxlegomena finden sich in der Erzählung von Sauls
Salbung durch Samuel in 1Sam 9,1–10,16. Gemäss 9,4 f durchstreift Saul auf der
Suche nach den entlaufenen Eselinnen seines Vaters eine Reihe von Landschaf-
ten. Die Häufung von Territorialnamen und ihre teilweise Unbekanntheit erhöhen
das Gefühl der Ziel- und Hilflosigkeit, das sich seiner bei der langen, vergeblichen
Suche bemächtigt. Das „Gebirge Efraim" und das „Land Benjamin" sind zwar
bekannt, vor allem ersteres freilich ist von erheblicher Ausdehnung. Das „Land
Zuf"[14], in das Saul mit seinem Knecht schliesslich gelangt, ist kaum lokalisierbar.
Dürfte man es mit dem Namen des in 1Sam 1,1 erwähnten Vorfahren Samuels „Zuf,
der Efratiter" verbinden, gelangte man ins südliche Efraim. Die Toponyme שַׁעֲלִים
und שָׁלִשָׁה (9,4) machen ganz und gar ratlos. In meinem Kommentar habe ich dazu
geschrieben[15]: „Die topographischen Bezeichnungen Schalischa und Schaalim
kommen nur hier vor, weshalb eine Lokalisierung schwierig bis unmöglich ist.
Eine Identifizierung von Schalischa mit dem in 2Kön 4,42 genannten, aber wiederum nicht näher lokalisierten Baal-Schalischa führt nicht viel weiter[16]. Schaalim
könnte eine Verschreibung aus Schaalbim sein, was ausweislich von Ri 1,35 und
1Kön 4,9 in den Südwesten Efraims wiese[17]." Man tappt mit derlei Versuchen im

---

Hubert Herkommer [Fribourg/Stuttgart: Universitätsverlag/Kohlhammer, 2003], 33–47, hier 47):
„So basically David killed everyone except Goliath."
14 G^{BA} haben die leicht abweichende Namensform Σειφ.
15 Dietrich, *Samuel* (Anm. 3), 409.
16 Diana Edelman („Saul's Journey," *ZDPV* 104 [1988], 44–58, hier 50–53) wagt immerhin eine
Lokalisierung: westlich von Jericho.
17 Neben Schaalbim wird in 1Kön 4,9 Bet-Schemesch im philistäisch-israelitischen Grenzland
genannt. P. Kyle McCarter (*I Samuel* [AnB 8], New York a.o.: Doubleday, 1980, 174) befürwortet
demgegenüber eine Gleichsetzung mit *šû'al*, was aufgrund von 1Sam 13,17 in die Gegend nördlich
von Bet-El führte.

Nebel – wie seinerzeit Saul. Weckten diese Toponyme in den Ohren des Erzählers (und auch seiner Hörer oder Leserinnen) konkrete Vorstellungen – oder waren sie nur mehr sagenhafte Relikte einer früheren Siedlungsgeschichte?

Saul trifft schliesslich, von Gott gelenkt, doch auf Samuel, und dieser salbt ihn überraschend zum נגיד, zu Jhwhs „Bevollmächtigtem" über Israel. Um ihn dessen zu versichern, dass wirklich Gott hinter dieser Wahl steht, kündigt er dem Frischgesalbten drei Zeichen an, dessen erstes „beim Grab Rahels, im Gebiet Benjamins, bei Zelzach" in Erfüllung gehen soll (1Sam 10,2). Das Gebiet (bzw. die [Nord-]Grenze, גבול) Benjamins ist von diesen Angaben noch die klarste, wenn auch keine punktgenaue. Sie verbietet es, das Rahelgrab mit einem Glossator in Gen 35,19 f. (und einer langlebigen Pilgertradition) in der Nähe Betlehems zu suchen. צֶלְצַח wäre, wenn man darin einen Ortsnamen sehen darf, ganz in der Nähe gelegen. Freilich haben einige Forscher gemeint, das Hapaxlegomenon per Konjektur beseitigen zu sollen: Statt צלצח solle man etwa בצלצלים („mit Zimbeln") oder בצל צור („im Felsschatten") lesen oder als ursprüngliche Textvorlage בצלחים במקלות annehmen („when they are setting fire to roasting places / a roasting place"[18]). Doch dürfte solchen Gewaltsamkeiten die Annahme vorzuziehen sein, dass man es mit einer alten, irgendwann aufgegebenen und dann nur noch dem Namen nach bekannten Ortschaft zu tun hat.

Ein weiterer Schwerpunkt geographischer Hapaxlegomena ist die Erzählung von Sauls erster Philisterschlacht, 1Sam 13 f. Bei der Kommentierung habe ich einen in beiden Kapiteln zu greifenden alten Erzähler festgestellt, in dem Saul die Haupt- und Heldenfigur war (1Sam 13,4.5a.15b; 14,2.*3a.15b.16.18a.19 f.46). Diese Version wurde durch eine andere überlagert, die Jonatan in den Mittelpunkt rückt (13,2f.5b–7a.*16.17–23; 14,4–15a.21–23.31)[19]. Alle geographischen Hapaxlegomena finden sich in dieser jüngeren, gleichwohl noch recht alten Textschicht[20]. Laut 13,17 f. schickten die Philister nach ihrem Aufmarsch im benjaminitischen Kernland Plünderertrupps in verschiedene Richtungen: einen „in Richtung Ofra, zum Land Schual", einen anderen „in Richtung aufs Grenzland, das hinunterblickt aufs Tal Zeboïm". Ofra „liegt ca. 6 km nördlich von Michmas und wird in Jos 18,23 zu Benjamin gerechnet. Das ‚Land Schual' (wohl … ‚Fuchsland') ist unbekannt. Manche bringen es mit dem ‚Land Schaalim' … von 9,4 in Verbindung, das sich freilich geographisch ebenfalls nicht einordnen lässt"[21];

---

18 So T. Harviainen, „Ṣelṣaḥ in 1 Sam. 10:2," *StOr* 51 (1979), 3–11. Es wäre dies ein Beleg für Grillplätze in der Antike!

19 Vgl. Dietrich, *Samuel* (BK 8.2/1), Neukirchen-Vluyn: Neukirchener, 2011, 36.72 f.

20 Immerhin hat bereits der „Höfische Erzähler" (wohl im ausgehenden 8. Jh.) die beiden Versionen kombiniert.

21 Dietrich, *Samuel* (BK 8.2/1), Neukirchen-Vluyn: Neukirchener, 2011, 48 mit Anm. 91.

davon war vorhin die Rede. Beim הַצְּבֹעִים גֵּיא, dem „Hyänental", handelt es sich offenbar um eines der in den Ostabhang des benjaminitischen Berglandes ein- gekerbten Wadis: das Wadi es-Suwenit (steckt in ‚Suwenit' noch ‚Zeboʻim'?) oder das von Norden in es einmündende Wadi Abu Dabaʻ oder das beide vereinende Wadi Qilt[22].

In 1Sam 14,4 werden die Namen der beiden Felsen genannt, zwischen denen hindurch Jonatan seine Attacke auf den Philisterposten bei Michmas führen wollte. Der eine heisst בּוֹצֵץ, „der Dürre"[23], der andere סֶנֶּה, wohl „der Stachelige". Vor dem Auge des Lesers „entsteht der Eindruck einer abweisenden Unwegsam- keit, aber auch einer gewissen Unübersichtlichkeit des Geländes, die einem ver- deckten Angriff zugute kommen könnte"[24]. Vermutlich haben wir es hier mit alten, im Zug der weiteren biblischen Überlieferung gleichsam versunkenen Gelände- bezeichnungen zu tun.

Die nächste Häufung nur einmal begegnender Ortsnamen bietet die Liste der Orte, denen David nach seiner erfolgreichen Razzia gegen die Amalekiter Beute- anteile geschickt haben soll (1Sam 30,26–31). Soweit erkennbar (und teilweise auch archäologisch nachweisbar), führen alle hier versammelten Toponyme – abgesehen von einem einzigen, Bet-El, bei dem es sich aber um eine Verschreibung handeln dürfte[25] – in die Gegend zwischen Hebron und Beerscheba. Bei Israel Finkelstein, einem gewiss nicht des Biblizismus verdächtigen Archäologen, finden sich die folgenden bemerkenswerten Feststellungen: „Die Ortsnamen und geo- graphischen Angaben in den David-Geschichten im ersten Buch Samuel ... be- kunden ... Vertrautheit mit den damaligen Machtverhältnissen". „Wie Fossilien" sind sie „eingeschlossen im Felsgestein der biblischen Überlieferung". „Die geographische Beschreibung Judas in der David-Geschichte stimmt tatsächlich mit den naturräumlichen Bedingungen, der Topographie und dem Siedlungs- muster der frühen Eisenzeit im 10. Jh. v. Chr. überein"[26]. Meines Erachtens kann dies grundsätzlich auch für die Liste 1Sam 30,26–31 gelten[27]. Sie wird eröffnet und

---

22 Vgl. Dietrich, ebd. 49.
23 Von בצץ, s. HALAT 142.
24 Vgl. Dietrich, *Samuel* (BK 8.2/2), Neukirchen-Vluyn: Neukirchener, 2011, 81 mit Anm. 45.
25 Die LXX schreibt βαιθσουρ, ein Kodex der Vetus Latina *Bethor*, s. BHS. In Anlehnung an Jos 19,4 konjiziert Hans Joachim Stoebe (*Das erste Buch Samuelis* [KAT 8.1], Gütersloh: Gütersloher Ver- lagshaus, 1973, 508) in Betul (also בתול statt בית־אל), eine Ortschaft, die er nach dem Vorschlag anderer mit dem heutigen *qaryetein* 30 km nordöstlich von Beerscheba gleichsetzt.
26 Israel Finkelstein / Neil A. Silberman, *David und Salomo. Archäologen entschlüsseln einen Mythos*, München: Beck, 2006, 34 f.
27 Im Blick auf sie ist im genannten Buch von Finkelstein und Silberman freilich ein Widerspruch zu verzeichnen: Einmal werden, im zitierten Zusammenhang und zum Nachweis historischer Verlässlichkeit, Namen aus 1Sam 30,26–28 mit modernen Ortsbezeichnungen identifiziert

abgeschlossen durch zwei wohlbekannte Namen: Bet-El und Hebron. Bet-El erscheint als eine Art – beabsichtigter oder unbeabsichtigter – ,Ausrutscher', da in der Einleitung zur Liste ausdrücklich die „Ältesten Judas" als Adressaten genannt werden, Bet-El aber immer klar zu Benjamin gehört hat. Hebron dürfte angefügt sein, um die in 2Sam 2 berichtete Übersiedlung Davids und seiner Leute dorthin vorzubereiten[28]. Dazwischen finden sich elf Toponyme. Die Nennung zweier Stammesgebiete – der Jerachmeeliter und der Keniter – dürfte dem Umstand geschuldet sein, dass diese Verbände nicht in festen Siedlungen, sondern in Beduinenzelten lebten. Möglicherweise liegt hier auch ein redaktioneller Rückverweis auf 1Sam 27,10 vor[29]. Vier Ortsnamen – Jattir, Aroër, Eschtemoa und Horma – sind selten, aber immerhin auch anderswo belegt. Fünf dagegen begegnen einzig hier: רָמֹות נֶגֶב (30,27), שִׂפְמֹות (30,28), רָכָל (30,29), בּוֹר־עָשָׁן und עָתָךְ (beide 30,30). Schon dieses pure Faktum weist auf Altertümlichkeit. Dem tut es keinen Abbruch – eher im Gegenteil! –, dass zwei oder drei dieser Namen in leicht anderer Form auch anderswo belegt sind: Bor-Aschan dürfte mit dem Aschan identisch sein, das in Jos 15,42 Juda und in Jos 19,7 Simeon zugewiesen wird; laut HALAT (112) ist der Name in dem der Ruinenstätte (Chirbet) 'Asan, 2 km nordöstlich von Beerscheba, noch erhalten. Zu Ramot-Negev (mit Plene-Schreibung des ô!) gibt es in Jos 19,8 das Äquivalent Ramat-Negev; die Ortslage wird in der Forschung meist für nicht lokalisierbar gehalten, doch bringt Volkmar Fritz[30] sie mit el-Ghazze, 9 km südöstlich von Arad, in Verbindung. Zu Sifmot, Rachal und Atach gibt es in der grossen Enzyklopädie NEAEHL keine Einträge oder Verweise, und HALAT vermerkt jeweils lapidar „ign."[31].

Kurzum: Die geographischen Hapaxlegomena der Ortsliste von 1Sam 30,26 – 31 stellen entweder abweichende Schreibweisen auch sonst (freilich selten!) belegter Namen dar, oder sie bezeichnen gleichsam versunkene oder vergessene Ortschaften. Kaum verdanken sie sich blühender literarischer Phantasie, vielmehr wohl alter archivarischer Tradition. Wie alt diese Tradition ist, muss hier nicht festgelegt werden. Nur so viel kann vorausgesetzt werden, dass sie dem Höfischen

---

(Eschtemoa = Es-Semu'a, Jattir = Chirbet 'Attir: 36), einmal wird die gesamte Liste als Spiegelung einer (angeblichen) Expansion Joschijas (spätes 7. Jh.!) in Richtung Philisterland interpretiert (172).
28 So mit Recht Alexander A. Fischer, Von Hebron nach Jerusalem. Eine redaktionsgeschichtliche Studie zur Erzählung von König David in II Sam 1–5 (BZAW 335), Berlin/New York: de Gruyter, 2005, 44.
29 So mit guten Gründen Alexander A. Fischer, „Beutezug und Segensgabe. Zur Redaktionsgeschichte der Liste 1 Sam. XXX 26–31," VT 53 (2003), 48–64, hier 51 f.
30 Volkmar Fritz, Israel in der Wüste. Traditionsgeschichtliche Untersuchung der Wüstenüberlieferung des Jahwisten (Marburger Theologische Studien 7), Marburg: N.G. Elwert, 1970, 104.
31 Bei Rachal könnte es sich indes um einen Textfehler handeln: Die LXX schreibt hier Καρμήλ, fand also möglicherweise in ihrer Vorlage כרמל vor, vgl. Jos 15,55 und 1Sam 25,2.

Erzähler um 700 v.Chr. vorlag. Anscheinend hat er sie durch die beiden rahmenden Verse in den jetzigen Kontext eingepasst[32]. Woher er sie genommen haben mag, ist unklar. Es liegt nahe, an königliche Archive in Jerusalem zu denken.

Lange Zeit nahm man an, die Liste sei davidzeitlich und ein Beleg für einen grösseren, um Hebron zentrierten politischen Verband „Grossjuda", der David zum König erhoben habe (2Sam 2,4)[33]. Einer solchen Annahme steht einiges entgegen. Unserer Liste ist Hebron, wie bemerkt, erst sekundär angefügt worden. Nur wenige der übrigen Ortschaften sind einigermassen sicher identifiziert, und eher nur im Ausnahmefall weisen sie archäologisch greifbare Spuren aus dem späten 11. oder frühen 10. Jh. auf[34]. Insgesamt ist die literarische wie die archäologische Beweislage für ein vordavidisches Juda derart schütter, dass man besser mit der Gründung eines politischen Verbandes „Juda" erst durch David rechnet.

Der letzte, hier zu behandelnde Schwerpunkt sind die Kapitel 2Sam 2f. Sie vereinen mehrere nordisraelitische, genauer: benjaminitische Überlieferungen, die m.E. zu der vom „Höfischen Erzähler" benutzten Sammlung „Erzählungen über Aufstieg und Niedergang der Sauliden" gehört haben[35].

– 2Sam 2,9 umreisst das von Sauls Sohn und Nachfolger Eschbaal (und dann wohl auch von Saul selbst) beherrschte Gebiet: „Gilead, die/der Aschuriter, Jesreel, Efraim, Benjamin – kurz: ganz Israel". Die Aufzählung ist so glaubwürdig wie historisch aufschlussreich. Der Einflussbereich (Sauls und) Eschbaals umfasste im Wesentlichen nur das mittelpalästinische mit einer Ausbuchtung ins ostjordanische Bergland. In diesem Rahmen schwer unterzubringen ist das Wort הָאֲשׁוּרִי, ein Hapaxlegomenon. Sollte es identisch sein mit dem Stamm Ascher (der freilich nie plene mit einem ו geschrieben wird), dann hätte zumindest teilweise Galiläa zu Sauls Reich gehört. Dies würde freilich weder zu den anderen Toponymen noch zu

---

32 Die literarkritischen Argumente bei Fischer, Beutezug (s. Anm. 29), 50f. Plausibel legt Fischer (53–55) auch dar, dass dieser Einbau durch Zusätze in 1Sam 30,14aβ.16aβb vorbereitet wurde.
33 So Albrecht Alt, „Beiträge zur historischen Geographie und Topographie des Negev," In A. Alt, *Kleine Schriften zur Geschichte Israels*, Band 3, München: Beck, ²1968, 382–459, hier 418.
34 Vgl. Fischer, Beutezug (s. Anm. 29), 57–61, der aber m.E. zu zielstrebig auf eine Spätdatierung (in die ausgehende Königszeit) zusteuert. Der in 1Sam 30,26–31 verschiedentlich gebrauchte Terminus „Stadt" (עיר) könnte erst auf den Höfischen Erzähler zurückgehen, der die Verhältnisse zu seiner Zeit zurückprojiziert haben mag. In Horma (Tel Māśōś) und Rama/ot Negev (Tel 'Ira) wurden nach Fischers eigenen Feststellungen (Beutezug 57–61) Siedlungsspuren mindestens nahe dem 10. Jh. nachgewiesen. Und kleine Dörfer oder gar Zeltsiedlungen – wie die meisten der genannten Orte es zur damaligen Zeit gewesen sein dürften – können, wenn überhaupt, dann archäologisch nur schwer nachweisbare Spuren hinterlassen.
35 Vgl. Dietrich, *Frühe Königszeit* (s. Anm. 3), 242–249.

der Erzählung 1Sam 31 passen, der zufolge sich das Schicksal Sauls auf den Bergen von Gilboa erfüllt hat: in Blickweite von „Jesreel" und offenbar an der äussersten nordöstlichen Ecke seines Herrschaftsgebietes, wo die Philister ihn stellten. Nun hat Diana Edelman[36] den gewinnenden Vorschlag gemacht, bei „Aschuri" handle es sich um eine ascheritische Sippe, die im efraimitischen Bergland siedelte. Wäre das richtig, dann verlöre diese Angabe ihre Anstössigkeit.

– Laut 2Sam 2,16 erhielt die Stätte nahe Gibeon, wo der in einem schaurigen Blutvergiessen endende Stellvertreterkampf von je zwölf Kriegern Eschbaals und Sauls stattfand, den Namen חֶלְקַת הַצֻּרִים. Der erste Namensteil ist leicht zu erklären – חֶלְקָה bedeutet „Feldstück" –, der zweite schwieriger. Ihn mit dem Substantiv צוּר, „Fels", zu verbinden, macht wenig Sinn, spiegelte sich darin doch nicht das dramatische Geschehen. Ginge es um eine Verbform, dann wohl um ein Partizip (masc. pl.), doch ist die konkrete Zuordnung problematisch: Wollte man eines der Verben I, II, III צור („binden, einschliessen", „bedrängen, bekämpfen" bzw. „formen, giessen", vgl. HALAT 951 f) zugrunde legen, würde die korrekte Partizipialform צָרִים lauten. Und bei I oder II צרר („umhüllen, festbinden" bzw. „anfeinden, befehden", vgl. HALAT 990 f) erwartete man צוֹרְרִים. Immerhin führen zwei dieser Verben, II צור und II צרר, auf eine Namensdeutung als „Feld der Feinde". Man hätte dann entweder eine Fehlvokalisation oder eine Haplographie (des Buchstabens ר) – oder aber eine altertümliche Aussprache- bzw. Schreibweise anzunehmen.

– In 2Sam 2,24, im Kontext des Kampfes Abners mit den Zerujasöhnen, begegnen zwei topographische Hapaxlegomena nebeneinander: „der Hügel Amma (אַמָּה) gegenüber Giach (גִּיחַ)". Zu beiden Toponymen gibt es bei NEAEHL keinerlei Hinweise. Nach HALAT lassen sich beide zwar etymologisieren (60: „Kanal"; 161: „Sprudel"), lokalisieren jedoch nur insoweit, als sie vom literarischen Kontext her in der Nähe Gibeons zu suchen sind.

– Laut 2Sam 3,26 hatte Abner nach den Verhandlungen mit David Hebron wieder verlassen und war bis בּוֹר הַסִּרָה gelangt, als Joab ihn zurückholen liess, um ihn am Ende zu ermorden. HALAT deutet den Namen als „Dornbrunnen, Dornzisterne" (726 bzw. 710 f) und erwägt vorsichtig eine Verbindung mit dem Bergrücken ṣirat al-ballāʿi (112), der sich 4 km nördlich von Hebron erhebt (und eine Zisterne getragen haben mag). Außer dieser Lage dürfte die Lautähnlichkeit zwischen dem biblischen und dem arabischen Toponym zu dieser Annahme geführt haben.

Auch bei dieser zuletzt behandelten Gruppe geographischer Hapaxlegomena stellt sich der Eindruck alter, lokal situierter und ortskundiger Überlieferung ein.

---

[36] Diana Edelman, „The ‚Ashurites' of Eshbaal's State," *PEQ* 117 (1985), 85–91.

Weitere, nur in den Samuelbüchern vorkommende Orts- und Regionalnamen sind:

בַּעַל 1Sam 7,11; בֵּית כָּר 1Sam 7,1; אֶפֶס דַּמִּים 1Sam 8,8; בֶּטַח 2Sam 10,6; אֲרַם בֵּית־רְחוֹב 2Sam 13,23; חָצוֹר 1Sam 22,5; חֶרֶת 2Sam 6,6; גֹּרֶן נָכוֹן 2Sam 8,8; בֵּרֹתַי 2Sam 6,2; בַּעֲלֵי יְהוּדָה 1Sam 15,4; טְלָאִים 1Sam 23,28; סֶלַע הַמַּחְלְקוֹת 2Sam 6,8; פֶּרֶץ עֻזָּה 1Sam 1,1; צֹפִים צֵלָע 2Sam 24,6; תַּחְתִּים חָדְשִׁי 1Sam 7,12; שֵׁן 1Sam 19,22; שֶׂכוּ 2Sam 21,14.

4. Übrige Lexeme

Abschliessend wenden wir uns den Hapaxlegomena im eigentlichen Sinne zu: „normalen" Lexemen, die in der Hebräischen Bibel nur einmal und nur in den Samuelbüchern vorkommen. Ich werde dabei im Prinzip der kanonischen Anordnung folgen – verfeinert freilich durch eine literarhistorische Untergliederung, die auf meiner eingangs skizzierten Gesamtsicht der Entstehung der Samuelbücher beruht. Dabei werden mehrere Fragen zu bedenken sein: Gibt es zu den betreffenden Wörtern alternative Schreibweisen namentlich in der hebräischen und der griechischen Textüberlieferung? Wie sind die betreffenden Lexeme etymologisch zu erklären? Welches ist ihre ‚Textpragmatik', d. h. ihre Funktion im jeweiligen Aussagezusammenhang?

4.1. Die Samuel-Saul-Geschichte

Diese 1Sam 1–3; *7; *10,17–27; 11; 14,47–52 umfassende Quelle weist lediglich zwei (bzw. eineinhalb) Hapaxlegomena auf, und zwar gleich im ersten Kapitel, genauer: in dessen kritisch zu ermittelndem Grundbestand, einer am Heiligtum von Schilo haftenden Samuel-Legende.

– Peninna, die zweite, kinderreiche Frau Elkanas und Kontrahentin der kinderlosen Hanna, wird in 1Sam 1,6 als צָרָה bezeichnet. HALAT führt den Beleg unter einem eigenen Lexem II צָרָה auf (neben I צָרָה, "Not")[37]. Man könnte freilich bezweifeln, ob dieser Eintrag nötig ist. Sicher leitet sich das Nomen vom Verb צרר, „gehemmt, beklemmt, beengt sein", ab. Es gibt davon auch die Nominalbildung II צַר, „Feind". Nähme man an, צָרָה wäre ein Femininum zu diesem Maskulinum, dann bedeutete es einfach "Feindin" (oder "Rivalin", wie ich in BK übersetzt ha-

---

37 In KAHAL ist dies aus einer gewissen Pietät gegenüber HALAT so geblieben. Dort (486) findet man unter II צָרָה die Informationen: 1. Mitfrau, Nebenfrau eines Mannes, der noch eine andere Frau hat, die in ihrer Beziehung zu dieser anderen Frau als Feindin gesehen ist 1S 1₆; – 2. Feindschaft, als *abstractum pro concreto* = Feind Ps 54₉ 143₁₁.

be[38]) – und jener Eintrag wäre überflüssig. Immerhin, in der weiblichen Form bleibt das Wort doch ein halbes Hapaxlegomenon.

- Das zweite, volle Hapaxlegomenon ist das Nomen שֵׁלָה in 1Sam 1,17. HALAT vermerkt dazu lapidar: "< שְׁאֵלָה" (1393), will sagen: Es handelt sich um eine Abwandlung des gewöhnlichen Worts für „Bitte". Es ist der Priester Eli, der Hanna wünscht, ihre (leise vor Gott geäusserte) "Bitte" möge in Erfüllung gehen (1,17). Später, als sie tatsächlich einen Sohn zur Welt gebracht hat, nennt sie ihn שְׁמוּאֵל, "denn von Jhwh habe ich ihn erbeten" (1,20). Einige Jahre später übergibt sie den Knaben Eli mit den Worten: "Jhwh hat mir gegeben, was ich in meiner Bitte von ihm erbeten habe. Und nun habe auch ich ihn zu etwas von Jhwh Erbetenem gemacht. Alle Tage seines Lebens sei er ein Erbetener für Jhwh" (1,27f)[39]. שְׁאֵלָה/ שאל ist offensichtlich das Leitwort der Erzählung. Wenn es an der ersten Belegstelle um ein א verkürzt wird, dann wohl in der Absicht, dieselbe Konsonantenfolge herzustellen wie im Namen des Heiligtums, an dem die Geschichte spielt und an dem Eli und schliesslich auch Samuel Dienst tun: שִׁלֹה. Stimmt dies, dann ist hier ein Hapaxlegomenon absichtsvoll konstruiert worden.

4.2. Die Ladegeschichte

Diese Quelle des „Höfischen Erzählwerks" hat ihren Ursprung unverkennbar in Nordisrael (wo die Lade ursprünglich beheimatet war). Die Erzählung von ihrem Verlust (1Sam *2; 4) wird jetzt aber fortgeführt mit einer ‚Rundreise' der Lade durch Philistäa und über Bet Schemesch nach Jerusalem, wo sie im Salomonischen Tempel ihren endgültigen Platz findet (1Sam 5f; 2Sam 6; 1Kön 8). In diesen späteren Teilen zeigt sie unverkennbar judäischen Einfluss und datiert kaum vor dem 8. Jh. Die Ladegeschichte weist sechs Hapaxlegomena auf[40], von denen hier drei – zwei aus den älteren, eines aus den jüngeren Partien – näher ins Auge gefasst seien.

- Die Erzähler erklären sich den Verlust der Lade damit, dass sie zuvor nicht angemessen behandelt worden sei. Nicht nur, dass sie einigermassen respektlos in die Schlacht gegen die Philister geschleppt wurde (1Sam 4,3f): die sie betreuenden elidischen Priester haben sich schon vorher fortgesetzt schwerer Kultfrevel

---

38 Dietrich, *Samuel* (Anm. 3), 14.
39 Dass in diesen letzten Aussagen der Name „Saul" umspielt wird, ist eine Beigabe des Samuel-Saul-Erzählers zur Grunderzählung, vgl. BK 8.1 z.St.
40 Es sind dies: ברא 1Sam 2,29; מִפְרֶקֶת 4,18; שׁתר 5,9; כֹּפֶר 6,18; מְנַעַנְעִים 2Sam 6,5; שַׁל 6,7.

schuldig gemacht. Daraufhin trat ihnen ein „Gottesmann" entgegen[41] und hielt ihnen u. a. vor, sie hätten sich „am Besten aller Opfergaben" *vergriffen* (1Sam 2,29). Es wird hier eine Hif.-Form von ברא verwendet, was unwillkürlich an den theologischen *terminus technicus* des „Schaffens" (I ברא) denken lässt; doch dieser ist sonst nur im Qal und im Nif. belegt, und er passt an unserer Stelle sachlich überhaupt nicht. Kein Wunder, dass es abweichende Lesarten gibt: 4QSam[a] und anscheinend auch *G*-Vorlage schreiben ברך, „segnen", offenbar ebenfalls im Hif. (להבריך); auch dies ist einmalig und ergibt nur schwer einen Sinn („[sich] Segen verschaffen"?). Die modernen Lexika, auch HALAT (147), führen eigens für unsere Stelle eine Wurzel II ברא ein, die aufgrund arabischer Etyma (in der Bedeutung „sehr fett" bzw. „frei von Krankheit sein") mit „sich mästen" zu übersetzen sei. Demnach hätten sich die Eliden „an Opfergaben gemästet"; in der Tat war Derartiges zuvor beschrieben worden (1Sam 2,12–16).

– Zwei Kapitel später kommen die Eli-Söhne ums Leben. Als ihr Vater diese Nachricht und speziell die vom Verlust der Lade erhält, fällt er rücklings vom Stuhl und bricht sich sein מַפְרֶקֶת (1Sam 4,18). HALAT (585) meint aufgrund syrischer, arabischer, jüdisch-aramäischer und mittelhebräischer Analogien, die alle "Scheitel" zu meinen scheinen, die Bedeutung "Genick" festlegen zu können. Die LXX gibt das Wort mit νῶτος, "Rücken", wieder, was ebenfalls sinnvoll wäre.

– Unter den Instrumenten der Kapelle, die laut 2Sam 6,5 die Lade-Prozession nach Jerusalem hinein begleitet und die David und Israel zum Tanzen animiert hat, figurieren u. a. מְנַעַנְעִים. Die Spezialuntersuchung von Johannes Braun zählt sie "zu den Überresten der kanaanäischen Musiktradition, und dieser Kulturkontext scheint ihre alleinstehende Erwähnung im AT zu rechtfertigen"[42]. Gemäss HALAT (570) ist das Hapaxlegomenon vom Verb נוע herzuleiten. Dieses bedeutet im Qal "schwanken, umherschweifen", im Nif. "geschüttelt werden", im Hif. "aufrütteln, schütteln" (HALAT 644). Demnach wäre jenes Instrument zu schütteln gewesen. HALAT aber (570) spricht überraschend von einem "Schlaginstrument", dann, einleuchtender, von einer "Rassel" bzw. dem "äg. Sistrum". Letzteres ist laut Brockhaus (Bd. 17, 1973, 466) eine "Rassel, ein Handgriff mit Metallbügel, gegen den beim Schütteln [!] lose eingelassene Querstangen ... klirren". LXX überträgt das Wort mit κύμβαλα, "Zimbeln": metallene Becken, die aneinandergeschlagen, nicht aber "geschüttelt" werden. Noch weiter weg vom hebräischen Lexem begibt

---

41 In *Samuel* (s. Anm. 3), 123 f, habe ich nachzuweisen versucht, dass die Gottesmann-Rede in 1Sam 2,27–36 nicht, wie manche meinen, komplett dtr ist, sondern einen älteren, dtr bearbeiteten Kern enthält; zu ihm gehört die im Folgenden behandelte Stelle.
42 Johannes Braun, Die Musikkultur Altisraels / Palästinas. Studien zu archäologischen, schriftlichen und vergleichenden Quellen (OBO 164), Fribourg / Göttingen: Universitätsverlag / Vandenhoeck & Ruprecht, 1999, 42.

sich der Targum mit der Wiedergabe durch *rᵉbiʿin*, "Trommeln"[43]. Wahrscheinlich drückt sich in diesen Abweichungen die gleiche Absicht aus wie in der Parallelstelle 1Chr 13,8 (und ebenso in der Beschreibung des Tempelorchesters in Ps 150): Dort fehlen die „Rasseln" (wie auch die „Zypressenholzklappern", עֲצֵי בְרוֹשִׁים) aus 2Sam 6,5, also just die volkstümlich-rustikalen Instrumente aus der Ladeumzugs-Kapelle. Offenbar meinte man später, Musik zu Ehren Gottes sollte seriöser und feierlicher sein als die, zu der seinerzeit David und Israel tanzten.

4.3. Der Sauliden-Erzählkranz

Diese von mir als eine der vom "Höfischen Erzähler" benutzten Quellen postulierte Sammlung hat teilweise sehr alte Nordreichstraditionen in sich aufgenommen, die ein facettenreiches Bild der ersten israelitischen Königsfamilie bieten. Insgesamt ist sie indes deutlich prodavidisch-judäisch geformt, womit sie ideologisch und wohl auch zeitlich in die Nähe des „Höfischen Erzählwerks" (Ende 8. Jh.) zu stehen kommt. In ihr finden sich nicht weniger als fünfzehn Hapaxlegomena[44], von denen hier nur ganz wenige diskutiert werden können.

– Ein alter Traditionssplitter ist die Nachricht von einem Metallbearbeitungsmonopol, das die Philister sich in der Anfangszeit Sauls gegenüber den Israeliten gesichert hatten. Dort heisst es, in einem mit seltenen und altertümlichen Wörtern gespickten Vers[45]: „Der Preis war ein Pim für Pflugspitzen und Pflugscharen und ein Drittelschekel für das Schärfen der Äxte und das Richten eines Rindersteckens" (1Sam 13,21). Von Interesse sind hier zwei ‚echte' Hapaxlegomena: פְּצִירָה und פִּים. Das erste Lexem bedeutet nach HALAT (898) „Preis"; es sei ein Derivat der Wurzel פצר und meint ursprünglich „das Auferlegte". Die Bedeutung des zweiten Lexems war lange unklar. Erst vor relativ kurzer Zeit wurden „bei Ausgrabungen – etwa in Geser und Lachisch – Gewichtssteine gefunden, die die althebräische Aufschrift *p-j-m* (wahrscheinlich *pajim*) tragen. Das Wort könnte semitisch die Bezeichnung für ‚Zweidrittel' (eines Schekels) sein, ist aber mögli-

---

43 Braun, ebd.
44 Es sind dies, in der kanonischen Abfolge: תְּשׁוּרָה 1Sam 9,7; חוֹת 13,6; פִּים 13,21; פְּצִירָה 13,21; יַעֲרָה 14,27; חֵלֶק 17,40; יַלְקוּט 17,40; שָׁלִישׁ 18,6; פֶּשַׁע 20,3; מַרְדוּת 20,30; שׂרף 31,12; בִּתְרוֹן 2Sam 2,29; שְׁלִי 3,21; עפר 16,13; יגה 20,13.
45 Ich bin auf die Stelle bereits in Abschnitt 1 („Textfehler") zu sprechen gekommen. Die obige Übersetzung stammt aus Dietrich, *Samuel* (BK 8.2/1); ebd. 28 finden sich die textkritischen Begründungen.

cherweise philistäischen Ursprungs[46]. Anscheinend war der *pjm* faktisch der Schekel von Aschdod; dieser machte etwa 4/5 seines ugaritischen Pendants aus und 2/3 des israelitischen Schekels. Von solchen Seitenreferenzen her kommt man auf ein Gewicht des *pjm* von 7,2 bis 7,8 Gramm; der Schekel wog knapp 11,5 Gramm"[47]. So wurde mit Hilfe der Archäologie eine alte, mit der Zeit offenbar in Vergessenheit geratene Gewichtsbezeichnung wiederentdeckt und damit ein biblisches Hapaxlegomenon aufgeklärt.

– Zwei weitere Hapaxlegomena finden sich in 1Sam 17,40. Der Vers gehört zu einer von zwei Versionen der David-Goliat-Geschichte: derjenigen, in der David als Hirtenknabe den philistäischen Vorkämpfer überwältigt[48]. Zuerst erfährt man, dass er im Bachbett zwischen den beiden Schlachtreihen „fünf glatte (חַלֻּקֵי) Steine" aufliest. Die Wurzel I חלק, von der HALAT (311) das Adjektiv ableitet, bezeichnet in Jes 41,7 im Hif. das "Glattschlagen" von Metall mit einem Hammer; verschiedentlich hat sie, im Qal wie im Hif., einen Beiklang von "glatt = falsch sein" (HALAT 309), was für todbringende Schleudersteine ja durchaus passt. David tut die Steine „zu der Hirtenausrüstung, die ihm gehörte, genauer: in die Tasche (יַלְקוּט)"[49]. Das Wort ist laut HALAT (395) auf das Verb לקט, "sammeln, auflesen", zurückzuführen (HALAT 508). Laut LXX hat David die Steine εἰς τὴν συλλογήν gelegt, "in die Sammlung": vielleicht in der Annahme, ein Hirte möchte wohl stets ein Sortiment von Schleudersteinen mit sich führen. In Wahrheit ist יַלְקוּט ein Gefäss *zum* Sammeln, eine "Tasche" eben, in der David zuvor den ihm vom Vater mitgegebenen Proviant transportiert haben mag.

– In 1Sam 31,12 findet sich die auffällige Mitteilung, die Jabeschiten hätten, nachdem sie die von den Philistern an der Stadtmauer von Bet-Schean zur Schau gestellten Leichname Sauls und seiner Söhne entwendet hatten, diese in Jabesch "verbrannt" (וישרפו אתם). Nun war die Verbrennung von Toten damals nicht nur unüblich, sondern ein ausgesprochenes Sakrileg (vgl. Am 2,1). Gleichwohl übersetzt die LXX ohne Zögern: καὶ κατακαίουσιν αὐτούς. HALAT (1267) hingegen postuliert eine eigene Wurzel II שרף mit der Bedeutung "einbalsamieren", die einzig hier (und in Abwandlungen in Jer 34,5) belegt sei. Sie sei gleichzusetzen mit סרף: einem weiteren Hapaxlegomenon, das in Am 6,10 im Zusammenhang mit Totensalbung gebraucht werde. Beide Verben seien denominiert von einem

---

46 Vgl. hierzu und zum Folgenden M.A. Powell, „Weights and Measures," *ABD* VI, 897–908, bes. 906.

47 Dietrich, *Samuel* (BK 8.2/1), Neukirchen-Vluyn: Neukirchener, 2011, 51.

48 Vgl. Walter Dietrich, *Samuel* (BK 8.2/5), Neukirchen-Vluyn: Neukirchener, 2012, 326–332.

49 Das Hapaxlegomenon wird kaum durch den vorangehenden (!) Ausdruck כלי הרעים אשר לו erklärt (so HALAT 395 und viele andere); vielmehr ist es per Waw-explicativum daran angeschlossen.

Substantiv סרף od. שְׂרָף, "Harz, Balsam" – doch ist ein solches biblisch nicht belegt, muss vielmehr vom Mittelhebräischen her erschlossen werden. Angesichts dieser Sachlage stellt sich die Frage, ob hier nicht Hapaxlegomena erst durch die moderne Lexikographie geschaffen werden und man nicht besser beim wohlbelegten "Verbrennen" bleiben sollte: in diesem Fall als einer äusserst ungewöhnlichen Handlung, die womöglich durch den fortgeschrittenen Verwesungsprozess erzwungen worden war.

4.4. Die Freibeuter-Erzählungen

Dies ist ein weiterer, von mir postulierter „Erzählkranz", den der „Höfische Erzähler" verwendet und zur Grundlage seiner Darstellung des Aufstiegs Davids in 1Sam 16–2Sam 5 gemacht hat. Er birgt sechs Hapaxlegomena[50], von denen hier zwei näher betrachtet seien. Beide stammen aus der anderen, älteren Version der David-Goliat-Geschichte: derjenigen vom Sieg des bis dahin namenlosen Schleudersoldaten David über einen Furcht erweckenden philistäischen Recken.

– Dieser wird eingangs vorgestellt: mächtig gross und beängstigend bewaffnet (1Sam 17,4–7). Zu seiner Ausrüstung gehören "bronzene Beinschienen". MT bietet einen Singular (מִצְחַת נְחֹשֶׁת), doch der ist widersinnig und mit LXX[BA] (κνημῖδες χαλκαί) in einen Plural bzw. Dual zu korrigieren. מִצְחָה nun ist ein Hapaxlegomenon. Es ist offensichtlich eine Ableitung von מֵצַח, "Stirn" (vgl. HALAT 589 f) – ein Wort, das übrigens in 1Sam 17 ebenfalls auftaucht: als der Punkt, an dem Goliat von Davids Stein getroffen wird. Offenbar nahmen die Hebräer es zu Hilfe, um einen Rüstungsgegenstand zu benennen, der ihnen (und dem ganzen Orient) unbekannt war – bis er ihnen an den Beinen griechischer Söldner entgegentrat[51]. Diese hatten ihn, natürlich, *vorn* am Schienbein montiert, was wohl zur sprachlichen Verbindung mit der ebenfalls nach *vorn* weisenden Stirn führte[52].

---

50 Es sind dies: מִצְחָה 1Sam 17,6; ברה 17,8; חָרִיץ 17,18; נחץ 21,9; מַחֲבֹא 23,23; חרץ 2Sam 5,24.

51 Beinschienen waren "commonplace in the Aegean world": David Toshio Tsumura, *The First Book of Samuel* (NICOT), Grand Rapids: Eerdmans, 2007, 443, mit Verweis auf die Ilias, 18.613; 19.370; 21.592. Ebenso bereits Kurt Galling, „Goliath und seine Rüstung," *Volume du congrès international pour l'étude de l'ancien testament (Genève 1965)* (VT.S 15), Leiden: Brill, 1966, 150–169, hier 165.

52 Aus der semantischen Ähnlichkeit bzw. Verwandtschaft beider Lexeme resultierte eine originelle Forschungshypothese: David habe mit seinem Stein gar nicht die Stirn Goliats getroffen, sondern hinter eine seiner Beinschienen, was den Hünen ins Stolpern und schliesslich zu Fall brachte: Ariella Deem, „'And the Stone Sank into his Forehead'. A Note on I Samuel XVII, 49," *VT* 28 (1978), 349–51.

– In seiner Herausforderungsrede verwendet Goliat einen schwer verständlichen Ausdruck: בְּרוּ לָכֶם אִישׁ. Die LXX schreibt: ἐκλέξασθε ἑαυτοῖς ἄνδρα, „wählt euch einen Mann aus". Fand sie in der Vorlage vielleicht noch eine Form von בחר vor, und in MT wäre das ח weggefallen? Oder soll man ברו von ברר (HALAT 155: "ausscheiden, sichten") ableiten? Freilich müsste dann korrekt בֹּרוּ punktiert sein. HALAT nun (148) kreiert ein eigenes Verb – womit wir erneut vor dem Phänomen eines 'lexikogenen Hapaxlegomenons' stehen. בְּרוּ soll Imp. pl. Qal eines Verbs II ברה sein, "e. בְּרִית ... eingehen m. jmd." Demnach sollten also die Israeliten "einen Bund eingehen" mit einem, der gegen Goliat zu kämpfen wagte. M. E. ist das in vieler Hinsicht zu weit hergeholt; besser folgt man LXX und nimmt für MT eine Verschreibung bzw. Fehlpunktierung an.

4.5. Die Abschalom-Novelle

Diese höchst kunstvolle, zeitnahe Erzählung umfasst den Grundbestand von 2Sam 13–19 (20?). Es finden sich darin fünf Hapaxlegomena[53], von denen hier drei behandelt werden.

– מַשְׂרֵת in 2Sam 13,9 bezeichnet offenbar eine Küchengerätschaft, in der Tamar ihrem Halbbruder und späteren Vergewaltiger Amnon das von ihm gewünschte Gebäck reicht. Laut HALAT (606) handelt es sich um ein Derivat von שׂרת oder סרת, doch erstaunlicherweise gibt es beide Verben nicht[54]. Schon die griechischen Übersetzer hatten Schwierigkeiten mit dem Wort. Das beginnt bereits im vorangehenden V.8, wo Tamar zunächst den Teig für das Gebäck zubereitet: so MT und auch LXX[B] (σταῖς). LXX[L] dagegen bietet dort στέαρ, "Fett"[55]. In V.9 dann, wo in MT das Wort erst wirklich steht, umschreibt LXX[L] es mit ἀποχέασις, was soviel heisst wie "Ausschütte" (in figura etymologica zum nachfolgenden Verb ἀποχέω). LXX[B] dagegen übersetzt es mit τήγανον, "Tiegel", mit dem sonst hebräisch מַחֲבַת, „Backblech"[56], wiedergegeben wird. Es verwundert kaum, dass das fragliche Wort immer wieder Emendationsversuche herausgefordert hat; Stoebe[57] führt sie auf,

---

53 Es sind dies: מַשְׂרֵת 2Sam 13,9; מִיכָל 17,20; שִׁפוֹת 17,29; שׁוֹבֶךְ 18,9; לאט 19,5.
54 In KAHAL ist dies geändert.
55 In *Septuaginta Deutsch. Erläuterungen und Kommentare*, Bd. 1, ed. Martin Karrer / Wolfgang Kraus, Stuttgart: Deutsche Bibelgesellschaft, 2011, 831, wird dies so erklärt: "Verschreibung durch Metathesis und Tilgung des מ von משרת 'Pfanne' (so MT) zu שתר, 'Fett'".
56 Vgl. HALAT 537.
57 Hans Joachim Stoebe, *Das zweite Buch Samuelis* (KAT 8.2), Gütersloh: Gütersloher Verlagshaus, 1994, 320.

lehnt sie aber aus gleichem Grund ab wie McCarter[58]: "The rare word ... seems to be firmly attested in Postbiblical Hebrew and Aramaic (independent of references to the present passage) as a term for a pan". So ist es, und die entsprechenden Nachweise finden sich bei HALAT.

– Worin hat sich Abschalom mit seinem langen Haar verfangen? MT sagt: "im שׂוֹבֶךְ einer Terebinthe" (2Sam 18,9). HALAT (1223) gibt für das Hapaxlegomenon die Übersetzung "Geäst" an und verweist dazu auf ein Verb שׂבך. Dieses ist freilich im biblischen Hebräisch nicht belegt (HALAT 1214), doch gibt es Analogien in einigen benachbarten Sprachen, darunter auch alten (wie Akkadisch), die alle auf ein semantisches Feld weisen: "verflechten, umgarnen, befestigen". Was letzte Zweifel schwinden lässt, ist das im AT neunmal belegte, ebenfalls von שׂבך abzuleitende Nomen שְׂבָכָה mit der Grundbedeutung "Flechtwerk" (vgl. HALAT 1214). Abschalom hat sich also im "Geflecht einer Terebinthe" verfangen, was natürlich das Astwerk oder Geäst des Baumes meint.

– Nach 2Sam 19,5 „verhüllte" David, als er vom Tod Abschaloms erfuhr, sein Antlitz und weinte. Das hier verwendete Verb לאט ist gemäss HALAT (488) gleichbedeutend mit dem besser belegten לוט, „einwickeln, verhüllen". Anscheinend haben wir es mit einer altertümlichen Nebenform zu tun.

4.6. Die Texte des „Höfischen Erzählers"

Dem Hauptverfasser der Samuelbücher, der wohl gegen Ende des 8. Jh.s die Geschichte der frühen israelitischen Königszeit erstmals im Zusammenhang niederschrieb und dazu nicht nur zahlreiche Quellen aufnahm, sondern auch eigene Texte schrieb, lassen sich immerhin sieben Hapaxlegomena zuordnen[59]. Dies ist insofern bemerkenswert, als die nächste grosse Redaktion, die deuteronomistische, nicht mehr eines aufweist[60]! Offenbar lässt die sprachliche Originalität, die den älteren Bestand der Samuelbücher auszeichnet, in den jungen Schichten nach.

---

58 P. Kyle McCarter, *II Samuel* (AnB 9), New York a.o.: Doubleday, 1984, 317.

59 Es sind dies: אלה 1Sam 17,39; עין 18,9; לַהֲקָה 19,20; פּוּקָה 25,31; שָׁבָץ 2Sam 1,9; אנש 12,15; חַיּוּת 20,3. Freilich ist hier zuweilen möglich, dass das betreffenden Wort nicht auf den Gesamterzähler, sondern auf eine von ihm benutzte Quelle zurückzuführen ist.

60 Eine Ausnahme könnte das Verb II כהה („schelten, hindern") in 1Sam 3,13 sein, sofern man der verbreiteten Annahme folgt, das jetzige Orakel an den jungen Samuel in 3,12–14 sei ein redaktioneller (m. E. von DtrP stammender) Ersatz für eine ältere Version. Doch könnten darin immer noch ältere Elemente enthalten sein.

– In 1Sam 17,39 versucht Saul, den jungen Hirten David für den Zweikampf mit Goliat zu wappnen, indem er ihm seine eigene Rüstung anlegt. (Die ganze Szene mit der Rüstungsanprobe hat m. E. der Höfische Erzähler eingefügt, um das hervorzuheben, was seiner Meinung nach der Skopus der Geschichte ist: dass nicht Waffen den Sieg bringen, sondern das Mit-Sein Gottes[61].) Doch schnell stellt sich heraus, dass David „unfähig war (וַיֹּאֶל) zu gehen, denn er hatte es noch nicht probiert". So legt er die schwere Rüstung ab und begibt sich mit Stock und Schleuder in den Kampf. Das Verb, das hier mit „unfähig sein" wiedergegeben wird, ist nur hier in dieser Bedeutung belegt. Es gibt zwar noch zwei andere homonyme Wurzeln – die bekannte für „verfluchen" (I אלה) und eine seltene für „wehklagen" (II אלה) –, doch passen beide nicht in den hiesigen Zusammenhang[62]. Das brachte die antiken Übersetzer zum Raten: Die meisten LXX-Versionen schreiben ἐκοπίασεν, „er versuchte (zu gehen)", LXX^L hingegen ἐχώλαινεν, was wohl gleichbedeutend ist mit χωλεύω, „lahm sein, hinken", und jedenfalls abzuleiten von χωλός, „lahm", woraufhin altlateinische Handschriften bieten: *claudicare coepit*, „er begann zu hinken". HALAT (50) hingegen postuliert aufgrund einer arabischen Analogie *'alā*, „zögern", die hebräische Wurzel III אלה mit der Bedeutung „unfähig sein"[63]. Diesmal, so wird man zugeben müssen, handelt es sich nicht um ein ‚lexikogenes Hapaxlegomenon'.

– Nach dem durch David herbeigeführten Sieg Israels über die Philister im Tal Ela werden die heimkehrenden Krieger von jubelnden Frauen begrüsst, die David als noch grösseren Helden rühmen als Saul. Daraufhin gibt der Höfische Erzähler Einblick in das Innere des Königs: Er sei ergrimmt und habe gedacht, nun müsse man David nur noch das Königtum geben (1Sam 18,8). „Und von diesem Tag an und fortan *beäugte* Saul David" (18,9). In meinem Kommentar findet sich dazu die Textnote: „*M* hat hier im Ketib עֹון, die Wurzel für ‚Schuld': wohl eine Fehllesung. Das Qere (עֹוֵן) und *G* (ὑποβλεπόμενος) setzen die Wurzel עין, ‚Auge', voraus. Davon ist hier in einem hapax legomenon ein Verb denominiert"[64], das man sachgemäss mit „(misstrauisch) beäugen" wiederzugeben hat. Es scheint, als zeige sich der Höfische Erzähler hier als Wortschöpfer; doch gibt es laut HALAT (773) analoge Verbbildungen nicht erst in nachbiblischen Sprachen (Mittelhebräisch, Jüdisch-

---

61 Vgl. Dietrich, *Samuel* (BK 8.2/5), Neukirchen-Vluyn: Neukirchener, 2012, 329. 332.

62 Dies gegen Gesenius[18] (59), wo zwar vermerkt wird, dass ein „ar. LW [Lehnwort, W.D.] *'alā* unterlassen, v. etw. abstehen – n. manchen Wz. zu וַיֹּאֶל 1S 17,39" sei, dann aber auf II אלה verwiesen wird, womit man zu der wenig überzeugenden Übersetzung gelangen würde: „David wehklagte zu gehen".

63 KAHAL 27 folgt dem im Prinzip mit dem etymologischen Hinweis: „Arab. *'lw* zögern, aufgeben, lassen".

64 Dietrich, *Samuel* (BK 8.2/5), Neukirchen-Vluyn: Neukirchener, 2012, 399.

Aramäisch und Syrisch), sondern schon im Ugaritischen („*'n* sehen, wahrneh-men")[65]. Gleichwohl bleibt die Anschaulichkeit des Ausdrucks im gegebenen Kontext bemerkenswert.

– David hinterlässt, als er vor Abschalom aus Jerusalem weicht, dort zehn Nebenfrauen (2Sam 15,16), zu denen sein Sohn und Gegner, wie berichtet wird, prompt „eingeht" (16,22). Bei der Rückkehr in seine Residenz findet David diese Frauen vor, lässt sie wegsperren und versorgen, hat aber keinen Umgang mehr mit ihnen; so „wurden sie zu Eingeschlossenen bis zum Tag ihres Todes: eine Wit-wenschaft auf Lebenszeit (חַיּוּת)"[66] (2Sam 20,3). Dieser Satz ist, wie der ganze Motivzug von den Abschalom vorübergehend überlassenen Nebenfrauen Davids, vom Höfischen Erzähler formuliert[67]. Es klingt aus ihm etwas wie Mitgefühl mit diesen namenlosen, im Machtspiel der Männer zu Objekten degradierten Frauen. Wie das Verb עין vom Nomen עַיִן, so ist das Nomen חַיּוּת vom Verb חיה abgeleitet – ein neuerlicher Hinweis auf die sprachschöpferische Kraft des Höfischen Erzählers: diesmal umso mehr, als es für diese Wortbildung keine Vorbilder in älteren se-mitischen, sondern nur Nachbildungen in jüngeren Sprachen gibt (Mittelhebrä-isch, Jüdisch-Aramäisch, Mandäisch: HALAT 298).

– Ein weiterer, ähnlicher Fall scheint das Vorkommen des Nomens פּוּקָה, "Anstoss", in 1Sam 25,31 zu sein. Nur an dieser, vom Höfischen Erzähler gestal-teten Stelle in Abigajils Rede an David gibt es diese Nominalbildung vom Verb I פוק, "taumeln". Das Nomen meint das, was das Taumeln auslöst: in diesem Fall unnötiges Blutvergiessen. Für diese Ausdrucksweise führt HALAT (869 f) keinerlei Parallelen aus anderen Sprachen an.

– Für ein anderes, dem Höfischen Erzähler zuzuschreibendes Hapaxlego-menon hingegen – das Verb I אנש (Nif.) zur Beschreibung des „Kränkelns" eines Kindes in 2Sam 12,15 – gibt es Analogien in alten (Akkadisch) wie in jungen (Arabisch, Syrisch) semitischen Sprachen (vgl. HALAT 70)[68]. Hier ist interessant, dass die LXX das Wort durch ἀρρωστέω, „kraftlos od. schwach sein, insb. krank

---

65 In KAHAL (402) kann daraufhin die etymologische Angabe sehr knapp bleiben: „denom. v. עַיִן"; beim Nomen steht dann der Hinweis „sem.", d. h. allgemeinsemitisch.

66 Diese Zeitspanne bezieht sich nicht auf das Leben Davids, sondern auf das der Nebenfrauen.

67 Dies habe ich näher begründet in meinem Aufsatz: „Die Fünfte Kolonne Davids beim Ab-schalom-Aufstand," In *Seitenblicke. Literarische und historische Studien zu Nebenfiguren im zweiten Samuelbuch* (OBO 249), ed. Walter Dietrich, Fribourg/Göttingen: Universitätsverlag/Van-denhoeck & Ruprecht, 2011, 91–120 = Walter Dietrich, *Die Samuelbücher im deuteronomistischen Geschichtswerk. Studien zu den Geschichtsüberlieferungen des Alten Testaments II* (BWANT 201), Stuttgart: Kohlhammer, 2012, 227–253.

68 In KAHAL (39) ist nur das Akkadische und daneben das Ugaritische erwähnt.

od. kränklich sein"[69], völlig zutreffend wiedergibt, während es in 4QSamᵃ ausgelassen ist – man könnte meinen, weil es nicht verstanden wurde, nach Annahme der massgeblichen Bearbeiter jedoch aufgrund von "haplography (ויאנש ויבקש) owing to both *homoioarkton* and *homoioteleuton*"[70].

Die übrigen Hapaxlegomena sind: אֲגוֹרָה 1Sam 2,36; גְּזֵרָה 2Sam 12,31; חַשְׁרָה 2Sam 22,19; טַבָּחָה 1Sam 8,13; מַלְבֵּן 2Sam 12,31; נהה 1Sam 7,2; קַץ 2Sam 21,16; שׂסף 1Sam 15,33; תפל 2Sam 22,27.

5. Résumé

Um das *Ergebnis dieser Untersuchung* in wenigen Sätzen zusammenzufassen: Die jüngsten Schichten der Samuelbücher bergen so gut wie keine Hapaxlegomena, die älteren hingegen beträchtlich viele. Was den Höfischen Erzähler betrifft, weisen sie auf eine erhebliche Sprachkraft hin, in den von ihm benutzten Quellen darüber hinaus auf eine gewisse Altertümlichkeit sowohl der Sprache als auch der übermittelten Sachverhalte. Die antiken Versionen sahen sich dadurch zuweilen vor Probleme gestellt, denen sie mit hoher Einfühlsamkeit beizukommen suchten. Die moderne Lexikographie vermehrt durch selbstinduzierte Hapaxlegomena mitunter die Probleme, verfügt aber in Gestalt der vergleichenden Semitistik über ein probates Mittel zu ihrer Lösung.

---

69 Menge-Güthling, *Griechisch-deutsches und deutsch-griechisches Wörterbuch*, Berlin-Schöneberg: Langenscheidt, ³1925, 109.
70 *Qumran Cave 4 XII. 1–2 Samuel* (DJD XVII), ed. Frank Moore Cross a.o., Oxford: Clarendon Press, 2005, 144.

Bernd Janowski
Die lebendige *næpæš.*
Das Alte Testament und die Frage nach der „Seele"

Alfred Marx zum 70. Geburtstag

1. Abschied von der Seele? – Vorbemerkungen

Es lassen sich nur wenige Begriffe nennen, die „für die Selbstdeutung des Menschen von größerer Tragweite gewesen sind"[1] als der Begriff „Seele". Seit geraumer Zeit ist der Seelenbegriff allerdings aus der Philosophie, der Theologie und der Psychologie weitgehend verschwunden, ohne dass er in eine andere Disziplin eingewandert und dort zu einer vergleichbaren Bedeutung aufgestiegen ist. Er sei, so heißt es, zu diffus und zu sehr durch religiöse Interpretamente wie die Unsterblichkeitsidee belastet, als dass er mit heutigen neurobiologischen, medizinischen und psychologischen Erkenntnissen in Einklang zu bringen ist. Die neuzeitliche Begriffsgeschichte von „Seele", so beschreibt H. Holzhey diesen Prozess, präsentiert sich

> „als eine Geschichte der Schwächung und des Erlöschens einer Überzeugung, deren Inhalt – bei aller Variabilität im Detail – die Existenz einer unvergänglichen Entität (Kraft, Macht) ist, die den Menschen zu einem individuellen Selbst macht, den Körper eines Lebewesens zu einem lebendigen, die Welt zu einer organischen Totalität, in der alles mit allem in Beziehung steht"[2].

Bei dem seit Descartes propagierten Abschied von der Seele handelt es sich „nicht um einen in jeder Hinsicht kontinuierlichen Prozess, auch wenn man sich das Zurücktreten als eine fortwährende Marginalisierung vorstellen mag"[3]. Mit Abschieden ist es aber so eine Sache. Sie können endgültig sein wie der Abschied der Hinterbliebenen von einem geliebten Menschen, der gestorben ist. Sie können

---

1 Rolf Schönberger, Art. "Seele," In: Petra Kolmer / Armin G. Wildfeuer (Hg.), *Neues Handbuch philosophischer Grundbegriffe* 3 (Freiburg / München: Karl Alber, 2011), 1956–1970, hier: 1956. – Ich danke meinen Kollegen/innen Chr. Frevel (Bochum), K. Liess (München), H. Niehr (Tübingen) und M.S. Smith (New York) dafür, dass sie einzelne Aspekte der folgenden Überlegungen mit mir diskutiert und mir zusätzliche Hinweise gegeben haben.
2 Helmut Holzhey, Art. "Seele IV," HWP 9, 1995, 26–52, hier: 26.
3 Schönberger, aaO 1964.

aber auch vorläufig sein wie der Abschied von jemandem, den man bei anderer Gelegenheit wieder trifft. Gilt das auch für den Seelenbegriff oder ist es bereits ausgemacht, dass seine Marginalisierung auch sein Exitus ist[4]?

Wenn ich im folgenden im Blick auf den alttestamentlichen Begriff *næpæš* nicht von „Seele" spreche, so nicht, um den Seelenbegriff endgültig zu verabschieden – schließlich zieht er in hellenistischer Zeit mit der *Septuaginta* und der *Sapientia Salomonis* in die Sprache der Bibel ein und wirkt von da aus im Zusammenhang mit seiner philosophischen Herkunftsgeschichte intensiv auf die abendländische Geistesgeschichte ein[5]. Mir geht es vielmehr darum zu fragen, ob das Alte Testament von einer (unsterblichen) „Seele" des Menschen im Unterschied zu seinem Leib spricht oder ob es das, was in der abendländischen Tradition seit Pythagoras und vor allem seit Heraklit mit „Seele" bezeichnet wird[6], gar nicht kennt, weil es anthropologisch anders ansetzt. Mit unserem Begriff „Seele" geht jedenfalls eine kulturell geprägte und sprachlich vermittelte Vorstellung vom Menschen einher[7], die nicht unbesehen auf das Alte Testament übertragen werden sollte. Ausgehend von der Andersartigkeit der alttestamentlichen Anthropologie frage ich zunächst nach der Bedeutung von *næpæš* im Alten Testament (II) und kehre danach noch einmal zum Thema „Seele" zurück (III). Den Schluss bildet eine Übersicht zur Lexikographie von *næpæš* (IV). Im Einzelnen gliedert sich der Aufsatz wie folgt:

---

4 S. dazu die Überlegungen bei ders., aaO 1966 ff.

5 S. dazu unten 166 ff.

6 S. dazu die Hinweise unten Anm. 49.

7 S. dazu den Überblick bei Hans-Peter Hasenfratz, *Die Seele: Einführung in ein religiöses Grundphänomen* (Zürich: TVZ, 1986), ferner Friedo Ricken / Burkhard Mojsisch u. a., Art. "Seele," HWP 9, 1995, 1–89 und für die dogmen- und theologiegeschichtlichen Aspekte Christian Link, Art. "Seele II/2–3," RGG⁴ 7, 2004, 1101–1105.

2. *næpæš* – semantische und thematische Aspekte

2.1. Vorüberlegungen

2.1.1 Gen 2:7 als *locus classicus*

Zu den grundlegenden Charakteristika alttestamentlicher Anthropologie zählt der die personale Identität konstituierende Zusammenhang von Leib und „Seele" (*næpæš*) oder – wie wir genauer sagen müssten – von Leib und „Leben(skraft)"[8].

---

8 Hebr. *næpæš* bedeutet nicht (unsterbliche) „Seele", sondern „Leben(skraft), Vitalität", s. dazu Hans Walter Wolff, *Anthropologie des Alten Testaments. Mit zwei Anhängen neu herausgegeben von B. Janowski* (Gütersloh: Gütersloher Verlagshaus, [8]2010), 33 ff; Claus Westermann, Art. "næpæš," THAT 1, [5]1995, 71–96; Horst Seebass, Art. "næpæš," ThWAT 5, 1986, 531–555; *ders.*, Art. "Seele I/2," RGG[4] 7, 2004, 1091 f; Rainer Albertz, Art. "Mensch II," TRE 22, 1992, 464–474, hier: 466; Werner H. Schmidt, "Anthropologische Begriffe im Alten Testament," In: ders., *Vielfalt und Einheit alttestamentlichen Glaubens 2* (Neukirchen-Vluyn: Neukirchener Verlag, 1995), 77–91, hier: 90; Otto Kaiser, *Der Gott des Alten Testaments: Theologie des Alten Testaments Bd.2*, UTB 2024 (Göttingen: Vandenhoeck & Ruprecht, 1998), 291 ff; Robert A. di Vito, "Alttestamentliche Anthropologie und die Konstruktion personaler Identität," In: B. Janowski / K. Liess (Hg.), *Der Mensch im alten Israel: Neue Forschungen zur alttestamentlichen Anthropologie*, HBS 59 (Freiburg / Basel / Wien: Herder, 2009), 213–241, hier: 223 ff; Bernd Janowski, *Konfliktgespräche mit Gott: Eine Anthropologie der Psalmen* (Neukirchen-Vluyn: Neukirchener Verlag, [4]2013), 204 ff; ders., "Was ist der Mensch? Grundzüge einer biblischen Sicht des Menschen," BiKi 67 (2012), 4–9; Christian Frevel / Oda Wischmeyer, *Menschsein: Perspektiven des Alten und Neuen Testaments*, NEB.Themen 11 (Würzburg: Echter, 2003), 27 f.29 f (Frevel); Kathrin Liess, *Der Weg des Lebens: Psalm 16 und das Lebens- und Todesverständnis der Individualpsalmen*, FAT II/5 (Tübingen: Mohr Siebeck, 2004), 16 ff; Andreas Wagner, "Körperbegriffe als Stellvertreterausdrücke der Person in den Psalmen," In: ders., *Beten und Bekennen: Über Psalmen* (Neukirchen-Vluyn: Neukirchener Verlag, 2008), 289–317, hier: 307 ff; ders., "Wider die Reduktion des Lebendigen: Über das Verhältnis der sog. anthropologischen Grundbegriffe und die Unmöglichkeit, mit ihnen die alttestamentliche Men-

Wie dieser Zusammenhang zustande kommt, lässt sich Gen 2,4b–7, dem anthropologischen *locus classicus* der nichtpriesterlichen Schöpfungsgeschichte ent-
nehmen:

4b Am *Tag, als* JHWH Elohim Erde und Himmel machte,

5 <u>während</u> noch kein einziges Gesträuch des Feldes
      auf der Erde entstanden
      und noch kein einziges Kraut des Feldes gesprosst war,
      <u>weil</u> JHWH Elohim es noch nicht hatte regnen lassen auf
      die Erde
6 und kein Mensch da war, den Ackerboden zu bearbeiten,
      <u>wobei</u> ein Wasserstrom aus der Erde aufzusteigen
      und die ganze Oberfläche des Ackerbodens zu tränken
      pflegte,

} Umstands-
   sätze

---

schenvorstellung zu erfassen," In: ders. (Hg.), *Anthropologische Aufbrüche: Alttestamentliche und
interdisziplinäre Zugänge zur historischen Anthropologie*, FRLANT 232 (Göttingen: Vandenhoeck &
Ruprecht, 2009), 183–199, hier: 190 ff; ders., *Gottes Körper: Zur alttestamentlichen Vorstellung der
Menschengestaltigkeit Gottes* (Gütersloh: Gütersloher Verlagshaus, 2010), 130 f; Martin Rösel, "Der
hebräische Mensch im griechischen Gewand: Anthropologische Akzentsetzungen in der Septuaginta," In: B. Janowski / K. Liess (Hg.), *Der Mensch im alten Israel. Neue Forschungen zur alttestamentlichen Anthropologie*, HBS 59 (Freiburg / Basel / Wien: Herder, 2009), 69–92; ders., "Von
der Kehle zur Seele: Neue Akzente im Menschenbild der Septuaginta," BiKi 67 (2012), 30–35; Peter
Marinkovic, "Seele – Geist ohne Körper? Exegetische Anmerkungen zum Personverständnis im
Judentum der persischen und hellenistischen Zeit," In: G. Gasser / J. Quitterer (Hg.), *Die Aktualität
des Seelenbegriffs: Interdisziplinäre Zugänge* (Paderborn: Schöningh, 2010), 309–326, hier: 317 ff;
ders., " *næpæš– psyche – immortalitas:* Hoffnung auf Unsterblichkeit in der biblischen Tradition
der hellenistisch-römischen Zeit?," in: Amei Lang / Peter Marinkovic (Hg.), *Bios – Cultus – (Im)
mortalitas: Zu Religion und Kultur – Von den biologischen Grundlagen bis zu Jenseitsvorstellungen*
(Rahden/Westf.: Verlag Marie Leidorf GmbH, 2012), 187–198; Norbert Kilwing, "*næpæsch* und
ψυχή: Gemeinsames und Unterscheidendes im hebräischen und griechischen Seelenverständ-
nis," In: Carmen Diller u. a. (Hg.), *Studien zu Psalmen und Propheten*, FS H. Irsigler, HBS 64
(Freiburg / Basel / Wien: Herder, 2010), 377–401 und Peter Schwagmeier, "Was steht da, wenn da
,Seele' steht?", Bibel heute 189 (2012), 11–13. Die Polemik gegen diese Interpretation von Oswald
Loretz, "Die postmortale (himmlische) Theoxenie der *npš* ,Seele, Totenseele' in ugaritisch-bibli-
scher Sicht nach Psalm 16,10–11," UF 38 (2006), 445–497, hier: 467 ff führt weder im Blick auf die
Gesamtentwicklung des europäischen Seelenbegriffs seit Homer (s. dazu die Hinweise unten
Anm. 48–49) noch im Blick auf die Interpretation der relevanten alttestamentlichen Belege weiter,
s. dazu auch im Folgenden. Dualistische „Seelen"-Vorstellungen begegnen unter Rekurs auf die
platonische Anthropologie erst in späthellenistischer Zeit, z.B. in SapSal 9,14 f u. ö., s. dazu unten
166 ff.

7 *da formte* JHWH Elohim den Menschen aus Erdkrume vom
und blies in seine Nase den Hauch des Lebens (*nišmat ḥajjim*)
Da wurde der Mensch zu einem lebenden Wesen (*næpæš ḥajjāh*)[9].

Der Verbalsatz Gen 2,7 besteht aus *zwei Teilsätzen*, die jeweils ein Handeln JHWHs beschreiben – JHWH „formte" (*jāṣar*) den Menschen zunächst wie ein Tongebilde „aus (feuchter) Erdkrume vom Ackerboden" (Gebundenheit des *'ādām* an die *ʾaḏāmāh*)[10] und „blies" (*nāpaḥ*) dann „Lebensatem in seine Nase" (Abhängigkeit des *'ādām* vom Schöpfer) – und einer *Folgeschilderung*, die besagt, dass der erschaffene Mensch nicht ein vitales Selbst *hat*, sondern ein vitales Selbst *ist*: „Da wurde der Mensch zu einem lebenden Wesen / Lebewesen (*næpæš ḥajjāh*)"[11]. Der Zusammenhang zwischen der Formung des Menschen aus „Erdkrume vom Ackerboden" (*'āpār min-hā'aḏāmāh*) und der Einhauchung des „Lebensatems" (*nišmat ḥajjim*) durch Gott ist dabei so eng wie möglich, d. h. die Erschaffung des Menschen vollzieht sich in einer materialen Herstellung (Formung) *und* einer Belebung (Einhauchung), wodurch der Mensch *insgesamt* zu einer *næpæš ḥajjāh* wird[12]. Gottes „Lebensatem" ist die Grundbedingung des physischen Lebens, ohne

---

9 Zur Struktur des Satzes Gen 2,4b-7 s. Manfred Weippert, "Schöpfung am Anfang oder Anfang der Schöpfung? Noch einmal zu Syntax und Semantik von Gen 1,1–3," ThZ 60 (2004), 5–22, hier: 15 ff.

10 Zur Bedeutung von *'āpār* s. Othmar Keel/Silvia Schroer, *Schöpfung: Biblische Theologien im Kontext altorientalischer Religionen* (Göttingen/Freiburg, Schweiz: Vandenhoeck & Ruprecht/Academic Press, [2]2008), 145 und Joachim Waschke, "Der Mensch ‚aus Staub' und ‚Gottes Ebenbild': Anmerkungen zu unterschiedlichen anthropologischen Perspektiven," In: Armenuhi Drost-Abgarjan u. a. (Hg.), *Vom Nil an die Saale* (FS A. Mustafa) (Halle: Universität Halle-Wittenberg, 2008), 489–505, hier: 498 ff.

11 Vgl. Wolff, "Anthropologie" (s. Anm. 8), 25 f, ferner Seebass, "*næpæš*" (s. Anm. 8), 546; ders., *Genesis I: Urgeschichte (1,1–11,26)* (Neukirchen-Vluyn: Neukirchener Verlag, 1996), 106 f u. a. In Gen 1,20 f.24.30; (2,19?;) 9,10.12.15.16; Lev 11,10.46 und Ez 47,9 dient *næpæš (ha)ḥajjāh* zur Bezeichnung der Tierwelt, vgl. Wolff, aaO 50 f. Die Wendung *næpæš ḥajjāh* in Gen 2,19 halten Reinhard Feldmeier / Hermann Spieckermann, *Der Gott der Lebendigen: Eine biblische Gotteslehre*, Topoi Biblischer Theologie 1 (Tübingen: Mohr Siebeck, 2011), 209 Anm. 23 für einen Nachtrag, anders Seebass, *Genesis I*, 100 z.St.

12 Vgl. Thomas Hieke, "Staub vom Ackerboden oder weniger als Gott? Menschenbilder des Alten Testaments in spannungsvoller Beziehung," LebZeug 53 (1998), 245–261, hier: 245.247 ff; Andreas Schüle, *Der Prolog der hebräischen Bibel: Der literar- und theologiegeschichtliche Diskurs der Urgeschichte (Genesis 1–11)*, AThANT 86 (Zürich, 2006), 162 f; Waschke, "Mensch" (s. Anm. 10), 500 f und Kilwing, "*næpæsch* und ψυχή" (s. Anm. 8), 385 f. Auf wunderbare Weise kann nach der Totenerweckungserzählung 1 Kön 17,17–24 die *næpæš* wieder in das „Innere" des atemlos gewordenen (V.17b: „Seine Krankheit wurde so schwer, dass kein Atem [*nešāmāh*] mehr in ihm war") und damit (!) dem Tode nahe gekommenen Menschen zurückkehren, so dass dieser wieder lebendig wird: „JHWH hörte auf Elia, und das Leben (*næpæš*) kehrte in sein Inneres zurück, und er lebte" (V.22), s. dazu Westermann, "*næpæš*" (s. Anm. 8), 73 und Winfried Thiel, *Könige*, BK IX/2,1 (Neukirchen-Vluyn: Neukirchener Verlag, 2000), 70 f.76 f.

den Mensch und Tier nicht lebensfähig sind (vgl. Gen 7,22[13]; Ps 104,29 f: $rû^a\d{h}$)[14]. Schematisch lässt sich der in Gen 2,7 beschriebene Schöpfungsvorgang demnach folgendermaßen darstellen:

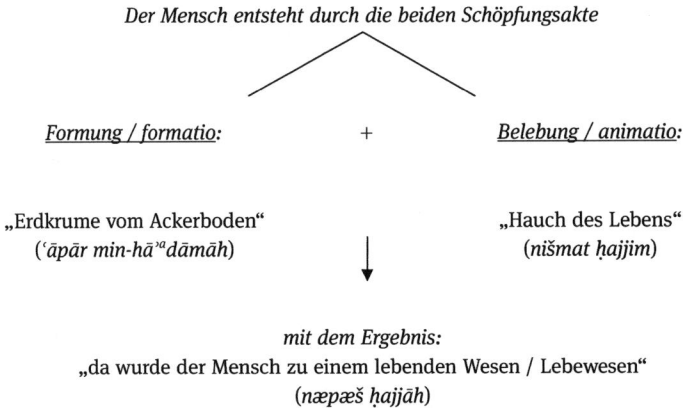

Der Mensch entsteht durch die beiden Schöpfungsakte

Formung / formatio: +   *Belebung / animatio:*

„Erdkrume vom Ackerboden"   „Hauch des Lebens"
(*'āpār min-hā'ªdāmāh*)   (*nišmat ḥajjim*)

mit dem Ergebnis:
„da wurde der Mensch zu einem lebenden Wesen / Lebewesen"
(*næpæš ḥajjāh*)

O. Loretz vertritt demgegenüber die These, dass in Gen 2,7 „die *npš* zu einem Tongebilde hinzukommt. Dieser Vorgang impliziert von Anfang an wieder eine zukünftige Trennung der beiden Elemente des Menschen (Gen 3:19) ... "[15], schematisch:

---

13 Zur Streichung von *rû^a\d{h}* in der Wendung „Alles, in dessen Nase Lebenshauch (*n^ešāmāh*) ist" s. Seebass, *Genesis I* (s. Anm. 12), 205 z.St.

14 Vgl. Otto Kaiser / Eduard Lohse, *Tod und Leben*, Biblische Konfrontationen (Stuttgart u. a.: Kohlhammer, 1997), 33: "Die konkrete Bindung des Lebens an das Atmen hat bei den Semiten wie bei den Griechen mit ihrer Rede von der Psyche dazu geführt, dem Wort ‚(Kehle) Atem' die Bedeutung ‚Lebensprinzip, Person, Selbst, Seele' beizulegen", s. dazu auch Hedwig Lamberty-Zielinski, Art. " *n^ešāmāh*," ThWAT 5, 1986, 669–673, hier: 670 f; *Kilwing*, aaO 384 ff; *Feldmeier / Spieckermann*, aaO 205 ff; Edward Noort, "‚Was ist der Mensch?' Gen 2,7 und die theologische Anthropologie," In: Stefan Beyerle / Axel Graupner / Udo Rüterswörden (Hg.), *Viele Wege zu dem Einen: Historische Bibelkritik – Die Vitalität der Glaubensüberlieferung in der Moderne*, BThSt 121 (Neukirchen-Vluyn: Neukirchener Verlag, 2012), 1–22, hier: 5 ff u. a. Aufgrund des in Gen 2,7 formulierten kreativen Zusammenhangs von *Lebensatem* (*nišmat ḥajjim*) und *Lebewesen* (*næpæš ḥajjāh*) erklärt sich auch die Parallelität von *næpæš* „Leben(digkeit), Vitalität" und *ḥajjim* „Leben" in Dtn 30,6; 2 Sam 11,11; Jon 4,3.8; Ps 7,6; 26,9; 49,19; 66,9; 88,4; Hi 3,20; 9,21; 10,1; Spr 3,22 und Klgl 3,58. Mit dem Lebensatem ist auch die Fähigkeit des Menschen zum Loben Gottes verbunden, vgl. Ps 150,6 und dazu Frank-Lothar Hossfeld / Erich Zenger, Psalmen 101–150, HThK.AT (Freiburg / Basel / Wien: Herder, 2008), 871 ff (Zenger).

15 Loretz, "Theoxenie" (s. Anm. 8), 472 Anm. 84.

| *Erschaffung* | *Sterben / Tod* |
| Tongebilde (1) + *næpæš* „Seele" (2) | Erde ← 1 │ 2 → Gott |

Die *næpæš* kommt nach Gen 2:7 aber nicht zu einem Tongebilde hinzu, sondern sie ist das lebendige *Resultat* zweier Schöpfungsakte des *Deus faber*: der Formung der „Erde vom Ackerboden" und deren Belebung durch den „Hauch des Lebens". Das so entstandene „Lebewesen" (*næpæš ḥajjāh*) und nicht nur ein Teil desselben kehrt beim Tod zum Ackerboden bzw. zur Erdkrume zurück, von dem/der es genommen ist:

> Im Schweiß deines Angesichts wirst *du* Brot essen,
> bis *du* zurückkehrst zum Ackerboden (*ᵃdāmāh*), von dem *du* genommen bist.
> Ja, Erdkrume (*ᶜāpār*) bist *du*,
> und zur Erdkrume (*ᶜāpār*) wirst *du* zurückkehren. (Gen 3,19).

2.1.2 *næpæš* in Gen 35:18

Auch Gen 35,18, der zweite *næpæš*-Beleg, dem Loretz eine zentrale Bedeutung für seine These beimisst, ist m. E. anders zu verstehen:

> Als ihr (sc. der Rahel) Leben (*næpæš*) dahinschwand (*jāṣāʾ*), denn
>   sie starb (*mût*),
> nannte sie seinen Namen ‚Sohn meiner Trauer',
> aber sein Vater nannte ihn ‚Sohn zur Rechten' (Benjamin).

Loretz zufolge belegt Gen 35,18 die „Vorstellung, daß beim Tod eines Menschen seine *npš* ‚Seele' den Leib verläßt und zum Totengeist (*npš*, *npš mt*) wird"[16]. Demnach besage der Text „klar, daß der Mensch beim Tod in einen Teil zerfällt, der so schnell wie nur möglich begraben werden muß, und in einen Totengeist, der in der Unterwelt haust"[17]. Dass die „Seele" beim Tod eines Menschen dessen Leib verlässt, steht aber nicht in Gen 35:18, sondern vielmehr, dass Rahels Leben (*næpæš*) dahinschwand. Die Wendung *jāṣāʾ* „hinausgehen, verlassen" + *næpæš* „Leben" meint hier nicht, dass die „Seele" den Leib Rahels verlässt – vom „Leib" Rahels ist keine Rede –, sondern dass Rahels Leben „dahinschwindet" (// *mût* „sterben")[18]. Wohin Rahel bzw. ihre *næpæš* nach ihrem Tod geht, wird nicht gesagt,

---

16 Ders., aaO 475.
17 Ders., ebd.
18 Vgl. Sir 38,23 hebr., s. dazu auch Ges[18] 481 s.v. *jāṣāʾ* qal 1 g und Horst-Dietrich Preuß, Art. " *jāṣāʾ*," ThWAT 3, 1982, 795–822, hier: 801. Das „Hinausgehen" (*jāṣāʾ*) der *næpæš* ist ein Zustand,

ebenso wenig, dass sie zu einem Totengeist wird, der in der Unterwelt haust[19]. „Eine lebendige, ja immer lebenshungrige *näfäsch* ist der Mensch, solange er lebt, aber eben nur solange"[20].

Exkurs 1: Hat akk. *napištu* die Bedeutung „Seele"?

Die These von O. Loretz wird von Überlegungen M. Dietrichs zur „Dichotomie von ‚Leib' und ‚Seele' in der mesopotamischen Literatur"[21] flankiert. Allerdings kann Dietrich keinen überzeugenden Beleg für seine Auffassung beibringen, dass *napištu* „Kehle, Leben"[22], das akkadische Äquivalent von hebr. *næpæš*, die Bedeutung „Seele" hat. Dietrich diskutiert unter der Überschrift „Das Begriffspaar ‚Leib' und ‚Seele'"[23] zunächst zwei Handerhebungsgebete (Ištar 10 und Ištar 2)[24], in denen der Begriff *napištu* gar nicht vorkommt (!), von ihm aber als Parallelbegriff zu dem „immateriellen *libbu* ‚Leib, Inneres; Herz, Gemüt, Sinn'" und als Gegen-

---

der dem (drohenden) Tod unmittelbar vorhergeht, vgl. Hhld 5,6 („meine *næpæš* ging hinaus") und dazu Othmar Keel, *Das Hohelied*, ZBK.AT 1 (Zürich: TVZ, 1986), 183.

19 In dieses Bild passt auch Jer 31,15, wonach in Rama „eine Stimme" // „ein Klagelied" der toten, um ihre verlorenen Kinder weinenden Rahel gehört wird. Zum einen ist im Text nicht von der *næpæç* Rahels bzw. von ihrer *næpæš* im Grab die Rede und zum anderen ist mit „Rahel" eine symbolische Größe gemeint, in der „sich das Volk unter dem Aspekt der bevorzugenden, besonders auswählenden Zuneigung (verkörpert), freilich mit der schmerzlich klaffenden Lücke einer fehlenden Generation" (Georg Fischer, Jeremia 26 – 52, HThK.AT, Freiburg / Basel / Wien: Herder, 2005, 157).

20 Silvia Schroer / Thomas Staubli, *Die Körpersymbolik der Bibel* (Darmstadt: Wissenschaftliche Buchgesellschaft, ²2005), 53.

21 S. dazu Manfried Dietrich, "Die Dichotomie ‚Leib' und ‚Seele' in der mesopotamischen Literatur," *MARG* 20 (2010), 19 – 36, hier: 27 ff.

22 S. dazu Wolfram von Soden, "Die Wörter für Leben und Tod im Akkadischen und Semitischen," AfO.B 19 (1982), 1 – 7, hier: 4 ff; Michael P. Streck, Art. "Person," RlA 10 (2004), 429 – 431 und neuerdings Ulrike Steinert, *Aspekte des Menschseins im Alten Mesopotamien: Eine Studie zu Person und Identität im 2. und 1. Jt. v. Chr.*, CM 44 (Leiden / Boston: Brill, 2012), 271 ff und dies., "‚Zwei Drittel Gott, ein Drittel Mensch': Überlegungen zum altmesopotamischen Menschenbild," In: B. Janowski (Hg.), *Der ganze Mensch: Zur Anthropologie der Antike und ihrer europäischen Nachgeschichte* (Berlin: Akademie Verlag, 2012), 59 – 81.

23 S. dazu *Dietrich*, aaO 30 ff.

24 Zu diesen beiden Texten s. Annette Zgoll, Die Kunst des Betens: Form und Funktion, Theologie und Psychagogik in babylonisch-assyrischen Handerhebungsgebeten an Ištar, AOAT 308 (Münster: Ugarit Verlag, 2003), 41 ff.191 ff und Anna Elise Zernecke, Gott und Mensch in Klagegebeten aus Israel und Mesopotamien: Die Handerhebungsgebete Ištar 10 und Ištar 2 und die Klagepsalmen Ps 38 und Ps 22 im Vergleich, AOAT 387 (Münster: Ugarit Verlag, 2011), 77 ff.

begriff zu den „materiellen Begriffe(n) SU (= *zumru*) und UZU (= *šīru*)"[25] einfach eingetragen wird. Das ist methodisch mehr als eigenartig.

Die „Dichotomie ‚Leib' – ‚Seele'"[26] sieht Dietrich dann vor allem in dem Ištar-Baghdad-Hymnus *Groneberg, Lob der Ištar*, 112 als gegeben, wenn der leidgeprüfte Beter folgendermaßen klagt:

77 Warum, Ištar, soll nicht länger währen das (: mein) Leben?
78 Ich bin total erschöpft: Bis wann, Ištar, dauert noch die Vorenthaltung der Erlösung?
79 Ausgestreckt sind meine Arme in Klagen,
80 im Wind fliegt meine Seele (*napištu*) davon wie ein Vogel[27]!

An diese Übersetzung knüpft Dietrich eine weitreichende These:

> „Der Beter spürt, dass sein Kräfte, das Leid zu ertragen, schwinden. Er fürchtet, dass sein *napištum* ‚Lebensodem', hier im Sinne von ‚Seele' (sic!), seinen Leib verläßt und wie ein Vogel davonfliegt. Das Bild des Vogels für seine Seele verbindet die in Mesopotamien verbreitete Vorstellung, dass eine Gottheit die Möglichkeit hat, sich wie ein Vogel in der Vertikalen fortzubewegen. Das Bild des Vogels für die ‚Seele' erinnert an die landläufige Vorstellung, dass der *eṭemmu* ‚Totengeist' vogelgestaltig durch die Totenwelt schwebt ... "[28]

Auch in diesen Text trägt Dietrich seine Dichotomie-These unter der Hand ein, indem er behauptet, dass *napištu* „hier im Sinne von ‚Seele'" zu verstehen sei. Wie kommt Dietrich zu dieser Behauptung? Die Antwort ist einfach: weil er von vornherein von der Gleichung *napištu* = „Seele" ausgeht, ohne alternative Übersetzungen und Interpretationen zu diskutieren. Diese allerdings gibt es, z. B. bei M. P. Streck:

77 Zu wenig ist mir, Ištar, nicht lang genug das Leben.
78 Ich bin müde geworden, Ištar. Bis wann noch?
   Löse mir mein Dahinschwinden.
79 Ausgestreckt sind meine Hände, zitternd meine Arme.
80 Im Wind ist mein Leben (*napištu*) wie ein Vogel aufgestiegen[29].

---

25 Dietrich, aaO 30. *zumru* bedeutet „Leib, Körper", *šīru* dagegen „Fleisch, Leib; Eingeweide-Omen".
26 Ders., aaO 31.
27 Übersetzung ders., aaO 31 f.
28 Ders., aaO 32 (mit anschließendem Hinweis auf B. Meissner), vgl. aaO 33: „Ein Beter bittet seine Schutzgöttin, ihn vor dem bevorstehenden Tod zu bewahren; dabei verwendet er für den Übergang der ‚Seele' in den Totengeist das Bild des davonfliegenden Vogels."
29 Übersetzung Michael P. Streck, "Die Klage ‚Ištar Bagdad'," In: W. Sallaberger u. a. (Hg.)., *Literatur, Politik und Recht in Mesopotamien*, FS C. Wilcke, Orientalia Biblica et Christiana 14 (Wiesbaden: Harrassowitz, 2003), 301–312, hier: 308, vgl. auch Brigitte Groneberg, *Lob der Ištar:*

Selbst wenn Dietrichs Übersetzung zutreffen sollte – aber schon das ist fraglich –, ist noch nicht ausgemacht, dass auch seine Interpretation richtig ist. Wesentlich näher liegt es, für *napištu* mit W. von Soden, M.P. Streck, B.G.M. Groneberg, U. Steinert u. a.[30] von der Bedeutung „Leben" auszugehen und in dem Vogelbild von Z.80 eine *Metapher für Vergänglichkeit*[31], d. h. für das – im buchstäblichen Sinn – *entschwindende* Leben zu sehen. Davon, dass der *napištu*-Beleg in dem Ištar-Baghdad-Hymnus *Groneberg*, Lob der Ištar, 112 zeigt, dass „die Dichotomie zwei Elemente miteinander verbindet, von denen der ,Leib' dem Verfall preisgegeben, todgebunden war, die ,Seele' dagegen unsterblich"[32], kann jedenfalls keine Rede sein. Vielmehr „weisen *Näfäš* und *napištu* die gleiche semantische Linie Kehle – Atem – Leben – Person auf"[33]. (*Ende des Exkurses*)

Kehren wir von hier aus zur alttestamentlichen Problematik zurück. Auf die Frage, wohin die *næpæš* beim Tod des Menschen geht, gibt das Alte Testament keine explizite Antwort; jedenfalls werden die Bewohner der Scheol „nirgends als *npšwt*, sondern als *mtjm* (Dtn 18,11; Jes 8,19) oder *rp'jm*, d. h., Ermattete"[34] bezeichnet. Auf der anderen Seite zeigen Texte wie Ps 16,10; 30,4; 56,14 oder 86,13, in denen der Beter um die Bewahrung seiner *næpæš* vor der Scheol bittet bzw. für die Errettung seiner *næpæš* aus der Scheol dankt, dass *næpæš* und Tod/Scheol in Zusammenhang gebracht werden[35]. Es ist in diesen Belegen aber nirgends davon die Rede, dass sich die *næpæš* bei ihrer – drohenden bzw. überwundenen – Unterweltsexistenz vom Leib des Beters gelöst hätte. Mit *næpæš* ist jeweils die Lebendigkeit des ganzen (!) Menschen gemeint, nicht seine unsterbliche „Seele" im Gegensatz zum vergänglichen Leib.

Gebet und Ritual an die babylonische Venusgöttin, CM 8 (Groningen 1997: Styx Publications), 113: „im Wind geht entlang mein Leben wie ein Vogel" (Z.80) und dazu Streck, aaO 311.

30 S. dazu die Hinweise oben Anm. 22.

31 Vgl. Streck, aaO 304, der Z.80 folgendermaßen kommentiert: „unter Verwendung des konventionellen Einzelelementes Wind für Gewalt eine kreative Satzmetapher; Bedeutung: mein Leben ist haltlos". Zu vergleichen ist auch das Vogelbild im Handerhebungsgebet Ištar 2, Z.63 f: „Mein Herz flattert, fliegt hin und her wie ein Vogel des Himmels. / Ich klage wie eine Taube bei Tag und Nacht", s. dazu Zgoll, *Kunst des Betens* (s. Anm. 24), 90 und Zernecke, *Gott und Mensch* (s. Anm. 24), 119.157.181. Als alttestamentliche Sachparallele ist auf das Vogelbild in dem Klagelied Ps 102,7 f (im Kontext von V.2–8) hinzuweisen, s. dazu Janowski, *Konfliktgespräche mit Gott* (s. Anm. 8), 33 ff.119 f.178.

32 Dietrich, aaO 33.

33 Steinert, *Aspekte des Personseins* (s. Anm. 22), 274, vgl. 292 f. Im Unterschied zu *næpæš* wird *napištu* aber nicht mit Verben verwendet, die Emotionen wie Zorn, Angst, Freude oder Verlangen/ Begehren ausdrücken, s. dazu *dies.*, ebd.

34 Vgl. Kilwing, "*næpæsch*" (s. Anm. 8), 392 ff.

35 S. dazu unten 155 ff.

Exkurs 2: *næpæš* met „Person eines Toten"

Es gibt aber *næpæš*-Belege, die für die Frage nach der Korrelation von *næpæš* und Tod von Interesse sind und die im Zusammenhang mit dem Thema „Verunreinigung an Toten" stehen. So haben H.W. Wolff[36] und C. Westermann[37] die These vertreten, dass das Syntagma *næpæš* met die „Leiche" bezeichnen kann, wobei die Herleitung aus der allgemeinen Bedeutung *næpæš* „Person" das Wahrscheinlichste zu sein scheint. Wegen der konstitutiven Verbindung von *næpæš* mit dem Lebensbegriff hat demgegenüber D. Michel[38] eine andere Interpretation dieser Wendung vorgeschlagen. Wie Wolff geht auch Michel von Num 6,6[39] aus, wo im Kontext der Bestimmungen für den Nasiräer die Wendung „*næpæš* eines Toten" (*næpæš* met) begegnet:

> Während aller Tage seines Nasiräats für JHWH darf er zur *næpæš* eines Toten nicht hineingehen.

Da *næpæš* feminin ist, interpretiert Michel die besagte Wendung zu Recht als „*næpæš* eines Toten". Daraus ergibt sich die Folgerung, dass nach altisraelitischer Vorstellung auch ein Toter eine *næpæš* besitzt. Dies dürfte nach Michel auch für die Sachparallelen[40] anzunehmen sein, wobei es bis auf Lev 19,28:

> Wegen eines Toten (*næpæš*)[41] sollt ihr euch keine Einschnitte an eurem Körper machen. Ihr sollt euch keine Tätowierungen anbringen lassen

immer um die Verunreinigung durch die *næpæš* eines Toten geht. Wie kommt es zu dieser Vorstellung? Zur Beantwortung geht Michel von den Anweisungen zur Herstellung und Verwendung eines besonderen Reinigungswassers in Num 19,14 – 16 aus[42]:

---

36 Wolff, *Anthropologie* (s. Anm. 8), 50.

37 Westermann, " *næpæš*" (s. Anm. 8), 90 f.

38 Diethelm Michel, *næpæš* als Leichnam?, ZAH 7 (1994), 81–84.

39 Vgl. auch Lev 21,1 „An der Lebenskraft (*næpæš*) eines seiner (gestorbenen) Stammesgenossen darf man sich nicht verunreinigen" und Lev 21,11: „Und keiner Person eines Toten (*kâl-napšôt met*) darf er sich nähern, auch an Vater oder Mutter darf er sich nicht verunreinigen." Zu der merkwürdigen Pluralform *kâl-napšôt met* s. Andreas Ruwe, *„Heiligkeitsgesetz" und „Priesterschrift": Literaturgeschichtliche und rechtssystematische Untersuchungen zu Leviticus 17,1–26,2*, FAT 26 (Tübingen: Mohr Siebeck, 1999), 248 und Kilwing, aaO 392 Anm. 84.

40 Lev 19,28; 21,1; 22,4; Num 5,2; 6,11; 9,6.7.10; 19,11.13 und Hag 2,13, s. dazu Seebass, "*næpæš*" (s. Anm. 8), 550 f.

41 Wohl Breviloquenz für *næpæš* met.

42 Zu diesem Text s. zuletzt Christian Frevel, "Struggling with the Vitality of Corpses: Understanding the Rationale of the Ritual in Numbers 19", in: Jean-Marie Durand / Thomas Römer / Jörg

14 Dies ist die Tora:
Wenn ein Mensch (*'ādām*) in einem Zelt stirbt (*mût*), so wird jeder, der in das Zelt eintritt, und jeder, der in dem Zelt ist, sieben Tage unrein.
15 Und jedes offene Gefäß, auf dem sich nicht ein verschnürter Deckel befindet, wird unrein.
16 Jeder, der auf offenem Feld einen Schwerterschlagenen oder einen Toten oder Menschenknochen oder ein Grab berührt, wird sieben Tage unrein.

Ausschlaggebend für Michels Interpretation dieses Textes ist die Bestimmung über die Unreinheit eines jeden nicht mit einem verschnürten Deckel verschlossenen Gefäßes (V.15). „Sie kann doch wohl", so Michel,

„dadurch entstehen, daß sich etwas Bewegliches von dem Leichnam löst und in ein Gefäß hineinzuschlüpfen trachtet. (…) Man stellte sich also offenbar vor, nach dem Tode versuche die *næpæš*, sich einen neuen, Körper' zu suchen und in ihn hineinzuschlüpfen – und sei es ‚nur' ein offenes Gefäß "[43].

Schwierig an dieser Deutung, die für *næpæš* auf die Annahme eines „Totengeistes hinausläuft"[44], ist allerdings die Tatsache, dass die Wendung „*næpæš* eines Toten" im Text selber nicht auftaucht, sondern lediglich von der Kontamination eines Zeltes, seiner Bewohner und der darin vorhandenen Gefäße durch den Tod eines Menschen die Rede ist. Daher empfiehlt es sich, für *næpæš* in der Wendung „*næpæš* eines Toten" entweder mit Wolff und Westermann an der Bedeutung „Leichnam" festzuhalten[45] oder – was m.E. wahrscheinlicher ist – von der Bedeutung „Lebenskraft, Person" auszugehen und die Wendung *næpæš met* mit „Person eines Toten" zu übersetzen[46]. Allerdings bedarf es noch eingehender Diskussionen darüber, welche Art von Personauffassung hier vorliegt. (*Ende des Exkurses*)

Festzuhalten ist nach diesen Überlegungen, dass der Gebrauch des Begriffs *næpæš* auf die Grenze des Lebens bezogen ist und „*næpæš* … das Leben dem Tode

Hutzli (éds.), *Les vivants et leurs morts*, OBO 257 (Fribourg / Göttingen: Academic Press / Vandenhoeck & Ruprecht, 2012), 199–226, hier: 208ff.222ff.
43 Michel, aaO 83, s. zur Diskussion Seebass, " *næpæš*" (s. Anm. 8), 550f und Frevel, aaO 222ff.
44 Dafür gibt es allerdings einen eigenen Terminus, s. dazu Seebass, aaO 551; Frevel, aaO 225 u.a.
45 So Angelika Berlejung, "Variabilität und Konstanz eines Reinigungsrituals nach der Berührung eines Toten in Num 19 und Qumran: Überlegungen zur Dynamik der Ritualtransformation," ThZ 65 (2009) 289–331, hier: 294 Anm. 12; 297 mit Anm. 17.
46 Vgl. auch Dagmar Kühn, *Totengedenken bei den Nabatäern und im Alten Testament: Eine religionsgeschichtliche und exegetische Studie*, AOAT 311 (Münster: Ugarit Verlag, 2005), 130ff. In der neupunischen Inschrift KAI 128,3 bedeutet die Wendung *npš mt* „Denkmal eines Toten", s. dazu dies., aaO 189. Zu den altaramäischen *nbš/npš*-Belegen s. unten 150ff.

gegenüber (ist)"[47] – und zwar in Rettung und Bewahrung wie in Bedrohung und Vernichtung.

2.2 Von der „Kehle" zur „Person"

Im Unterschied zu ψυχή in den homerischen Epen, wo dieser Begriff nie für den lebenden Menschen und dessen Aktivitäten gebraucht wird, sondern als εἴδωλον „Abbild" des gestorbenen Menschen immer im Zusammenhang mit dem Tod erscheint (Il. 23,72; Od. 11,83 u. ö., s. Abb.1)[48], tritt die *næpæš* nach dem Alten Tes-

Abb.1: Tod des Sarpedon, attisches Vasenbild (5. Jh. v. Chr.)

---

47 Westermann, " *næpæš*" (s. Anm. 8), 88.
48 S. dazu Bruno Snell, Die Entdeckung des Geistes: Studien zur Entstehung des europäischen Denkens bei den Griechen (Göttingen: Vandenhoeck & Ruprecht, 1975), 18 ff.25 f; Thomas Jahn, Zum Wortfeld "Seele – Geist" in der Sprache Homers, Zetemata 83 (München: C.H. Beck, 1988); Susanne Gödde, Art. "Seele I/3," RGG[4] 7, 2004, 1092 f; Walter Burkert, Griechische Religion der archaischen und klassischen Epoche (Stuttgart: Kohlhammer, [2]2011), 299 ff; Martin F. Meyer, "Der Wandel des Psyche-Begriffs im frühgriechischen Denken von Homer bis Heraklit," ABG 50 (2008), 9 – 28 u. a. – Die Abbildung zeigt, wie die Leiche des Zeussohns Sarpedon, der als Befehlshaber der mit den Trojanern verbundenen Lykier im Kampf mit Patroklos fällt, von Hypnos (Schlaf) und Thanatos (Tod) weggetragen wird. Dabei verlässt die ψυχή den Leib des Patroklos und wird von diesem Augenblick an als εἴδωλον bezeichnet, vgl. Burkert, aaO 299.

tament „während der ganzen Lebenszeit des Menschen voll in Erscheinung, ja sie ist der bestimmende Faktor des Lebens in seinen emotionalen Äußerungen und geistigen Bezügen"[49]. Sie ist aber weder – und das verbindet sie mit dem frühgriechischen ψυχή-Begriff – der Hauptsitz des Bewusstseins noch repräsentiert sie den Menschen nach seinem Tod[50]. Wenn für ihre Eigenschaften und Aktivitäten ein zusammenfassender Begriff genannt werden soll, dann ist es, wie der folgende Überblick zeigt, derjenige des „(individuellen) Lebens" oder der „Lebenskraft".

2.2.1. Überblick

Wie die im Anschluss an H.W. Wolff, C. Westermann und H. Seebass geführte Diskussion[51] gezeigt hat, hat der Begriff *næpæš* einen organischen Fixpunkt, der für seine psychosomatischen Bedeutungsaspekte[52] grundlegend ist und immer wieder durchscheint. Ein Überblick ergibt folgendes Bild:

1. *Kehle, Schlund*
næpæš bezeichnet ursprünglich die „Kehle" oder den „Schlund" (Jes 5,14; 58,3 – 12 [5mal][53]; Hos 9,4; Hab 2,5; Jon 2,6; Ps 69,2; 107,5.9; Spr 25,25 u.ö.) und deren Funktion: die Atmung, aber nicht den äußeren „Hals" (*ṣawwār*)[54]:

---

49 Kilwing, " *næpæš* und ψυχή" (s. Anm. 8), 389. Dass der Mensch nur *eine* Seele (ψυχή) besitzt, und diese seine Person in ihrer Gesamtheit repräsentiert, ist in der europäischen Tradition zum ersten Mal bei Pythagoras und vor allem bei Heraklit fassbar, der von der „Tiefe" der ψυχή spricht. Die Opposition Körper *vs.* Seele taucht dann erst im späten 5.Jh. v.Chr. auf, s. dazu Burkhard Gladigow, Art. "Seele," HrwG 5 (2001), 53 – 56; Walter Burkert, "Mikroskopie der Geistesgeschichte: Bruno Snells ‚Entdeckung des Geistes' im kritischen Rückblick," In: ders., *Kleine Schriften 8: Philosophica* (Göttingen: Vandenhoeck & Ruprecht, 2008), 277 – 292, hier: 279 f.287 ff; ders., *Griechische Religion*, 446 ff.475 f.479 ff; Jan Bremmer, "Die Karriere der Seele: Vom antiken Griechenland ins moderne Europa," In: Janowski, *Der ganze Mensch* (s. Anm. 22), 173 – 198; Meyer, aaO 15 ff; Marinkovic, "Seele" (s. Anm. 8), 312 ff und die Beiträge In: Dorothea Frede / Burkhard Reis (ed.), *Body and Soul in Ancient Philosophy* (Berlin / New York: Walter de Gruyter, 2009) und In: Katja Crone / Robert Schnepf / Jürgen Stolzenberg (Hg.), *Über die Seele*, suhrkamp taschenbuch 1916 (Berlin: Suhrkamp, 2010). Zu dem komplexen Problem s. aus religionswissenschaftlicher Sicht Hasenfratz, *Seele* (s. Anm. 7), 68 ff.
50 Vgl. Bremmer, aaO 173.
51 S. dazu die Hinweise oben Anm. 8.
52 Zur Frage, ob *næpæš* auch „Leichnam" bedeutet, s. oben 141 – 142. Zur *næpæš* Gottes (Am 6,8; Jes 42,1; Jer 51,4 u.ö.) s. Seebass, " *næpæš*" (s. Anm. 8), 551.
53 S. dazu Thomas Staubli, "Maat-Imagery in Trito-Isaiah: The Meaning of Offering a Throat in Egypt and in Israel," In: *M. Nissinen / Ch.E. Carter* (ed.), *Images and Prophecy in the Ancient Eastern Mediterranean*, FRLANT 233 (Göttingen: Vandenhoeck & Ruprecht, 2009), 41 – 50, hier: 43 ff.

> Darum öffnet die Unterwelt weit ihren Rachen (*næpæš*)
> und sie reißt ihr Maul auf, ins Maßlose,
> so dass seine (sc. des Volkes) Pracht und seine Menge hinabsteigt
> und seine lärmende Schar verschmachtet vor Durst. (Jes 5,14)

> So dient ihr Brot nur ihrer Kehle (*næpæš*),
> nichts davon kommt in das Haus JHWHs. (Hos 9,4)

> Wasser umschlossen mich bis an die Kehle (*næpæš*),
> das Urmeer umringte mich,
> Tang war um mein Haupt geschlungen. (Jon 2,6)

Die Bedeutung „Atem" (Hi 41,13, vgl. Jes 3:20 [?][55], Jer 2,24; 4,31) ergibt sich aus der Tatsache, dass die Bewegung der Kehle mit dem Atmen zusammenhängt (vgl. das dreimalige Vorkommen des Verbs *npš* nif. „aufatmen" in Ex 23,12; 31,17 und 2 Sam 16,14) und der Mensch mit dem Tod zu atmen aufhört:

> Sechs Tage sollst du dein Werk tun,
> aber am siebten Tag sollst du aufhören,
> damit ruht dein Rind und dein Esel
> und aufatmet (*npš* nif.) der Sohn deiner Magd und der Fremde. (Ex 23,12)[56]

> Zwischen mir und den Israeliten ist er (sc. der Sabbat) ein Zeichen auf ewig,
> denn in sechs Tagen hat JHWH den Himmel und die Erde gemacht,
> am siebten Tag aber ruhte er und atmete auf (*npš* nif.). (Ex 31,17)[57]

> So kam der König und das ganze Volk, das er bei sich hatte, ermüdet ... an
> und dort konnte er aufatmen (*npš* nif.). (2 Sam 16,14).

2. Verlangen, Begehren

Mit der Körperfunktion „Atem" hängt der Bedeutungsaspekt „Verlangen, Begehren" zusammen, das sich als *Appetit/Hunger* (Spr 13,25), als *Gier* (Ex 15,9; Dtn 12,20; Ez 16,27; Ps 27,12; 41,3) oder als *Wunsch/Sehnsucht* (Ps 35,25, vgl. Gen 23,8; 2 Kön 9,15) äußert und für das eine bestimmte Intentionalität kennzeichnend ist[58]:

---

54 Vgl. *Seebass*, aaO 538 f. Nach Kilwing, "*næpæsch* und ψυχή" (s. Anm. 8), 381 Anm. 24 käme dafür allenfalls Ps 105,18 (*næpæš* // *rægæl* „Fuß") in Frage, s. aber Seebass, aaO 539.

55 Wörtlich: „Häuser = Behälter von Lebenskraft / Atem (?)", vgl. Seebass, aaO 539.

56 Zur Interpretation von Ex 23,10–12 s. Alexandra Grund, *Die Entstehung des Sabbats: Seine Bedeutung für Israels Zeitkonzept und Erinnerungskultur*, FAT II/75 (Tübingen: Mohr Siebeck, 2011), 22 ff („aufatmen" im Sinne einer „vollständige[n] Erneuerung der Lebenskraft" [29]), ferner Norbert C. Baumgart, "Ein Gott, der Atem gibt: Zu intertextuellen Zusammenhängen im Pentateuch," BN 143 (2009), 45–68, hier: 49 ff („verschnaufen").

57 S. dazu Grund, aaO 282 f, ferner Baumgart, aaO 46 ff und Kilwing, aaO 382.

58 Zu diesen und weiteren Belegen s. Seebass, aaO 540 ff. Unter ihnen stechen Ps 42,2 f und Ps 84,3 hervor, s. dazu im Folgenden.

Der Gerechte isst bis zur Sättigung seines Appetits (næpæš),
aber der Bauch der Frevler wird Mangel haben. (Spr 13,25)[59]

2 Selig, wer auf den Geringen achtet:
   Am Tag des Unheils wird JHWH ihn retten.
3 JHWH wird ihn behüten und ihn am Leben erhalten,
   und er wird glücklich gepriesen im Land –
   ja, du wirst ihn nicht preisgeben der Gier (næpæš) seiner Feinde.
4 JHWH wird ihn stützen auf dem Siechbett –
   sein ganzes Lager hast du gewendet in seiner Krankheit. (Ps 41,2–4)

(8) Da redete Chamor mit ihnen: „Das Verlangen (næpæš) meines Sohns
Sichem hängt an eurer Tochter. Gebt sie ihm zur Frau (9) und verschwägert
euch mit uns … " (Gen 34,8 f)

3. Vitales Selbst

Anstelle der Übersetzung von næpæš mit „Seele" hat H. Seebass zu Recht dafür
plädiert, dass es sich bei dem Begriff um „die Vitalität, die sprudelnde Lebens-
energie, die Leidenschaftlichkeit"[60] handelt. Dafür spricht, dass die næpæš JHWH
lobt/„segnet" bzw. zum Loben/„Segnen" aufgefordert wird (Ps 103,1 f.22; 104,1.35,
vgl. Jes 61,10; Ps 34,3; 35,9 u. ö.), dass sie „fett gemacht/gestärkt" wird (Spr 11,25;
13,4), dass sie auf JHWH „hofft" bzw. „wartet" (Ps 33,20; 130,5 f; Klgl 3,25) oder dass
sie als Lebenskraft „zurückgebracht" wird (Ps 19,8; 23,3; Spr 25,13; Ruth 4,15; Klgl
1,11.16 u. ö.):

1b Segne, meine næpæš, JHWH
    und alle meine Innereien seinen heiligen Namen!
2   Segne, meine næpæš, JHWH
    und vergiss nicht alle seine Wohltaten! (Ps 103,1b-2)

    Gut ist JHWH zu dem, der auf ihn hoffte,
    zu dem (leʿnæpæš), der ihn sucht. (Klgl 3,25)

1b JHWH ist mein Hirte, ich habe keinen Mangel,
2   auf Weideplätzen mit frischem Grün lässt er mich lagern,
    an Wasser der Ruhe führt er mich,
3   meine Lebenskraft (næpæš) bringt er zurück (šûb pol.).
    Er führt mich auf Bahnen der Gerechtigkeit
    um seines Namens willen. (Ps 23,1b-3)[61]

---

59 S. dazu auch Arndt Meinhold, *Die Sprüche: Teil 1*, ZBK.AT 16/1 (Zürich: TVZ, 1991), 228: „Es geht
um das Stillen leiblicher Bedürfnisse", vgl. Spr 10,3.
60 Seebass, aaO 544.
61 S. dazu Bernd Janowski, "Der gute Hirte: Psalm 23 und das biblische Gottesbild," In: *Ex oriente
Lux. Studien zur Theologie des Alten Testaments*, FS R. Lux, ABG 39, hg. von Angelika Berlejung und
Raik Heckl (Leipzig: EVA, 2012), 247–271, hier: 253 ff.

Es gibt etwa 30 Belege, an denen sich ein Subjekt (Agens) selber als Objekt (Patiens) behandelt und dieses Objekt mit *næpæš* ausgedrückt wird[62], z. B.:

(Du,) der sich selbst (*næpæš* + Suffix 3.m.sg.) zerreißt in seinem Zorn (Hi 18,4)

Da *næpæš* und „Leben(skraft/-erhaltung)" öfter synonym gebraucht werden und *næpæš* das vitale Selbst bezeichnen kann[63], kann es auch die Funktion des Personalpronomens[64] übernehmen. Die Übergänge sind aber fließend, z. B.:

Sag doch, du (Saraj) seiest meine (sc. Abrams) Schwester, damit es mir um deinetwillen gut gehe und durch dich meine *næpæš*/ich am Leben bleibe (*ḥājāh*). (Gen 12,13)

(19) Wahrhaftig hat dein Knecht ja in deinen Augen Gunst gefunden, so dass dein Gunsterweis, den du mir erwiesen hast, groß war, um meine *næpæš*/mich am Leben zu erhalten (*ḥjh* hiphil). Ich aber, ich vermag nicht, mich aufs Gebirge zu retten, sondern das Unheil würde sich an mich heften, und ich würde sterben. (20) Sieh doch, diese Stadt (da) ist nahe, um dorthin zu fliehen, und sie (das) ist ja nur eine Kleinigkeit. Lass mich doch dorthin mich retten. Ist sie (das) nicht eine Kleinigkeit? Aber meine *næpæš*/ich würde am Leben bleiben (*ḥājāh*)! (Gen 19,19 – 20)

Wer hätte den Staub Jakobs berechnet,
und ‹wer zählt› die ‹Lagerung› Israels?
Sterben möge meine *næpæš*/ich den Tod von Aufrechten,
und meine Nachkommenschaft sei wie (jen)es! (Num 23,10)[65]

Um deines Namens willen, JHWH, mögest du mich beleben (*ḥjh* pi.)!
In deiner Gerechtigkeit wirst du meine *næpæç* /mich aus der Not herausführen! (Ps 143,11)[66]

---

62 S. dazu Ernst Jenni, "Nifʿal und Hitpaʿel im Biblisch-Hebräischen," In: ders., *Studien zur Sprachwelt des Alten Testaments III*, hg. von Hanna Jenni u. a. (Stuttgart u. a.: Kohlhammer, 2012), 131–303, hier: 247 ff.

63 S. dazu mit weiteren Belegen Seebass, aaO 545 f.

64 S. dazu die Übersicht bei Westermann, "*næpæš*" (s. Anm. 8), 90, ferner Wolff, *Anthropologie* (s. Anm. 8), 51 ff.

65 Horst Seebass, *Numeri 3. Teilband: Numeri 22,2 – 36,1*, BK IV/3 (Neukirchen-Vluyn: Neukirchener Verlag, 2007), 11 übersetzt: „Sterben möge mein Ich den Tod von Aufrechten".

66 In Ps 143 kommt *næpæš* 5mal in verschiedenen Bedeutungsnuancen vor (V.3.6.8.11.12), s. dazu Monika Müller, "Die Vergewisserung einer Beziehung: Eine Auslegung zu Ps 143 und seine liturgische Verortung," BN 151 (2011) 71–94, hier: 73 f.79.87.88.

Exkurs 3: *npš* im Ugaritischen

An die bisherige Übersicht lässt sich die Bedeutung von ug. *npš* gut anschließen[67]. Im Ugaritischen hat das Lexem *npš* fünf bzw. sechs Bedeutungen, je nachdem ob man die Bedeutungen 3 und 4 im DULAT 636 einzeln zählt oder zusammenfasst. Im Folgenden beschränke ich mich auf ausgewählte Beispiele aus dem Ba'al-Zyklus (KTU 1.1–1.6) und dem Aqaht-Epos (KTU 1.17–1.18–1.19)[68]:

1. *Kehle*

Wie hebr. *næpæš* bedeutet auch ug. *npš* ursprünglich „Kehle, Schlund", z. B.:

> Du (sc. Ba'al) wirst hinabsteigen (7) in den Rachen (*npš*) des göttlichen Mot,
> in den (8) Schlund (*mhmrt*) des Geliebten Els, des Helden. (KTU 1.5 I 6–8)[69]

2. *Appetit, Verlangen, Begehren*

Mit dem organischen Fixpunkt „Kehle, Schlund" hängt der Bedeutungsaspekt „Appetit, Verlangen, Begehren" zusammen, z. B.:

> Mein Appetit (*npš*) ist der Appetit (*npš*) des Löwen (15) in der Wüste,
> ja, der Appetit (*brlt*) des Delphins (16) im Meer. (KTU 1.5 I 14–16)[70]

In seiner Rede an seine Frau sagt Aqaht:

> (16) „Höre, o Dame Danatiya!
> Richte her (17) ein Böckchen von der Herde
> für den Appetit (*npš*) des Koschar- (18) und-Chasis,
> für das Verlangen (*brlt*) des Gewandten (19) mit Künstlerhänden."
> (KTU 1.17 V 16–19)[71]

---

67 Zum Folgenden s. DULAT = Gregorio del Olmo Lete / Joaqín Sanmartín, *Dictionary of the Ugaritc Language in the Alphabetic Tradition*, Part Two, HdO 67 (Leiden / Boston: Brill, 2003), 636 f s.v. npš I; 638 s.v. npšn.
68 KTU = Manfried Dietrich / Oswald Loretz / Joaqín Sanmartín, *Cuneiform Alphabetic Texts from Ugarit, Ras Ibn Hani and Other Places* (KTU: second, enlarged edition) (Münster: Ugarit Verlag, 1995).
69 Vgl. Simon B. Parker (ed.), *Ugaritic Narrative Poetry*, Writings from the Ancient World 9 (Society of Biblical Literature: Scholars Press, 1997), 141 (M.S. Smith); O. Loretz / M. Dietrich, *Mythen und Epen IV*, TUAT III/6 (Gütersloh: Gütersloher Verlagshaus, 1997), 1174 und DULAT 636 s.v. npš I/1.
70 Vgl. Parker, aaO 142 (Smith); Loretz / Dietrich, ebd. (mit der Übersetzung „Rachen") und DULAT 637 s.v. npš I/2.
71 Vgl. Parker, aaO 58 (S.B. Parker); Loretz / Dietrich, aaO 1269 und dazu den Ausführungsbericht KTU 1.17 V 21–25. Sehr problematisch ist der von DULAT 638 s.v. npšn aufgeführte Beleg bn[p]šny KTU 1.2 III 20, s. dazu Parker, aaO 97 (M.S. Smith: „with my desire") und Loretz / Dietrich, aaO 1128

3. Lebenskraft

Die in DULAT 637 s.v. *npš* 3 („breath, force, soul") und s.v. *npš* 4 („soul, spirit, life") aufgeführten *npš*-Belege lassen sich mit der Übersetzung „Lebenskraft" wiedergeben[72], z. B.:

> (Mit) Lebenskraft (*npš*) möge Danil leben, (37) [der Held des Rāp]iu,
> (mit) Verlangen (*brlt*) der Mann, der Held des Harnamiten!
> (KTU 1.17 I 36 – 37)[73]

> (Mit) Lebenskraft (*npš*) möge Puch[at] leben, (37) die Wasserträgerin,
> die Schöpferin vom Vlies (38) den Tau,
> die Kennerin des Gangs der Sterne[74]!

4. Lebewesen, Person(en)

In einem Brief des Königs von Ugarit an den Pharao schreibt er diesem, dass er für das Wohlergehen seines Oberherrn betet:

> (17) ... Und für
> (18) das Leben der Person (*ḥy. npš*) bete ich
> (19) vor Baʿ[al] Ṣapon, meinem Herrn,
> (20) und (für) die Länge der Tage meines Herrn
> (21) vor Amun und vor den
> (22) Göttern Ägyptens, die beschützen mögen
> (23) die Person (*npš*) der Sonne, des Großkönigs,
> (24) meines Herrn. (KTU 2,23.17 – 24)[75]

---

und zur Diskussion M.S. Smith, *The Ugaritic Baal Cycle, Vol.I: Introduction with Text, Translation and Commentary of KTU 1.1 – 1.2*, VTS 55 (Leiden / New York / Köln: Brill, 1994), 253 f.

72 So auch briefl. M.S. Smith („,life-force' or the like"), s. oben Anm. 67.

73 Vgl. Parker, aaO 53 (S.B. Parker) und Loretz / Dietrich, aaO 1263, die jeweils „By my life / By my soul" bzw. „Bei meinem Atem! / bei meinem Leben!" übersetzen. Aber weder *npš* noch *brlt* hat ein Suffix der 1.c.sg., vgl. DULAT 637 s.v. *npš* 3.

74 Vgl. Parker, aaO 77 (S.B. Parker) und Loretz / Dietrich, aaO 1303, die wieder ein Suffix der 1. Person postulieren. Zu diesen beiden Belegen s. jetzt M.S. Smith, *Poetic Heroes: The Literary Commemoration of Warriors and Warrior Culture in the Early Biblical Worlds* (Grand Rapids, MI: Eerdmans, 2013) (im Druck).

75 S. dazu H. Niehr, „Königtum und Gebet in Ugarit. Der König als Beter, das Gebet für den König und das Gebet zum König," In: *Ich will dir danken unter den Völkern: Studien zur israelitischen und altorientalischen Gebetsliteratur* (FS B. Janowski zum 70. Geburtstag), hg. von Alexandra Grund, Annette Krüger und Florian Lippke (Gütersloh: Gütersloher Verlagshaus, 2013), 603 – 622, hier: 608.

Auch außerhalb der Gebetsliteratur ist diese Bedeutung von *npš* belegt:

> Bericht von Personen (*npš*), die den Königspalast betreten haben.
> (KTU 4.338.1)[76]

5. Ein Stück von Innereien
Diese Bedeutung von *npš* begegnet v. a. in Verwaltungstexten[77].
(*Ende des Exkurses*)

4. Individuelles Leben
næpæš in der Bedeutung „individuelles Leben" meint nicht Leben allgemein, sondern das in den Individuen (Tier oder Mensch) enthaltene Leben (Gen 9,10; 19,17 u. ö.). *næpæš* ist in diesen Belegen bevorzugt Objekt, nicht Subjekt der Handlung, z. B.:

> 8 Und Gott sprach zu Noah und zu seinen Söhnen bei ihm folgendermaßen:
> 9 „Ich aber, siehe, ich bin dabei, meinen Bund aufzurichten mit euch und mit eurem Samen nach euch
> 10 und mit jeglichem lebenden Wesen (*kål- næpæš haḥajjāh*), das bei euch ist
> an Fluggetier, an Vieh und an allen Wildtieren der Erde bei euch aus allen, die aus der Arche herausgegangen sind. (Gen 9,8–10)
> 35 Denn wer mich findet, hat Leben (*ḥajjīm*) gefunden,
> und er hat Wohlgefallen von JHWH erlangt.
> 36 Wer mich aber verfehlt, behandelt sein Leben (*næpæš*) gewalttätig;
> alle, die mich hassen, lieben den Tod. (Spr 8,35 f)
> Saul bekannte: „Ich habe Schuld. Komm zurück mein Sohn David, ich will dir forthin nichts Böses mehr antun, weil mein Leben (*næpæš*) heute in deinen Augen so wertvoll geachtet war. Ich weiß, ich habe wie ein Narr gehandelt und habe große und schwere Fehler gemacht." (1 Sam 26,21)[78]

Die *næpæš* in der Bedeutung „individuelles Leben" wird nicht nur geschont wie in 1 Sam 26,21, sondern auch geachtet (Ps 31,8; Hi 9,21 u. ö.), gerettet (von Gott)[79] oder im „Beutel der Lebendigen" verwahrt (1 Sam 25,29). *Vice versa* gehören hierher auch alle die Belege, die von der Bedrohung der *næpæš* handeln wie in der Wendung „nach dem Leben (*næpæš*) trachten" (1 Sam 20,1; 22,23; 1 Kön 19,10 u. ö.),

---

76 Vgl. DULAT ebd. s.v. *npš* 5.
77 Vgl. DULAT ebd. s.v. *npš* 6.
78 Zum Motiv der „Kostbarkeit des Lebens" s. Bernd Janowski, "Die Kostbarkeit des Lebens: Zur Theologie und Semantik eines Psalmenmotivs," In: ders., *Die Welt als Schöpfung: Beiträge zur Theologie des Alten Testaments 4* (Neukirchen-Vluyn: Neukirchener Verlag, 2008), 249–265.
79 Zu den zahlreichen Belegen s. Seebass, "*næpæš*" (s. Anm. 8), 547.

bei Tötungsdelikten[80] oder in der Talionsformel (Ex 21,23 – 25; Lev 24,18.20, vgl. Dtn 19,21):

> David floh von … in Rama; er kam und klagte vor Jonathan: „Was habe ich nur getan? Wo liegt meine Schuld, wo mein Verfehlen nach Meinung deines Vaters, dass er mir nach dem Leben (*næpæš*) trachtet?" (1 Sam 20,1)

> Sie gaben Josua die Antwort: „Es wurde deinen Sklaven tatsächlich mitgeteilt, was JHWH, dein Gott, seinem Vertrauten Mose befohlen hatte – euch das ganze Land zu geben und vor euch alle Bewohner des Landes zu vernichten. Wir hatten große Angst vor euch um unser Leben (*næpæš* pl.). So haben wir diese Zuflucht genommen." (Jos 9,24)

> 22 Und wenn Männer raufen und (dabei) eine schwangere Frau stoßen, so dass ihre eibesfrucht abgeht, aber (sonst) kein Unglücksfall passiert, soll er mit einer Zahlung belegt werden, so wie der Mann der Frau (sie) ihm auferlegt, und er soll sie durch Schiedsrichter geben.
> 23 Falls aber ein Unglücksfall passiert, sollst du geben:
>   Leben für Leben (*næpæš taḥat næpæš*),
> 24 Auge für Auge,
>   Zahn für Zahn,
>   Hand für Hand,
>   Fuß für Fuß
> 25 Brandmal für Brandmal,
>   Wunde für Wunde,
>   Strieme für Strieme. (Ex 21,23 – 25)[81]

Wo das individuelle Leben seinen Ort im menschlichen oder tierischen Körper hat[82], beantworten Dtn 12,23, vgl. Lev 17,14, und vor allem Lev 17,11 mit hinlänglicher Deutlichkeit mittels der Gleichung Blut = *næpæš*:

> Nur beherrsche dich und genieße kein Blut,
> denn das Blut ist das Leben (*næpæš*),
> und du sollst nicht das Leben/die Lebenskraft (*næpæš*)
> zusammen mit dem Fleisch verzehren. (Dtn 12,23)

> Denn das Leben (*næpæš*) des Fleisches – im Blut ist es.
> Und ich (sc. JHWH) selbst habe es auf den Altar gegeben,
> um für eure *napšôt*/für euch persönlich Sühne zu erwirken;

---

80 S. dazu ders., aaO 547 f.

81 S. dazu Eckart Otto, *Theologische Ethik des Alten Testaments* (Stuttgart / Berlin / Köln: Kohlhammer, 1994), 73 ff; Axel Graupner, "Vergeltung oder Schadensersatz? Erwägungen zur regulativen Idee alttestamentlichen Rechts am Beispiel des *ius talionis* und der mehrfachen Ersatzleistung im Bundesbuch," EvTh 65 (2005), 459 – 477 u. a.

82 S. zu dieser Problematik auch Kilwing, "*næpæsch* und ψυχή" (s. Anm. 8), 389 ff.

denn das Blut ist es, das durch das (in ihm enthaltene) Leben (*næpæš*) sühnt. (Lev 17,11)[83]

5. Lebewesen, Person

Aus der Bedeutung „individuelles Leben" ergibt sich der Übergang zum Aspekt „lebendes Individuum, Einzelwesen, Person, jemand", der in kasuistischen Rechtssätzen (Gen 17,14; Ex 12,15 f u. ö.) oder in Opferbestimmungen begegnet, wenn der betreffende Täter bzw. Akteur möglichst allgemein eingeführt werden soll (Lev 2,1; 4,2; 5,1 u. ö.), sodann bei Personenzählungen (Jos 10,28.30.32 u. ö.) und schließlich bei der Nennung von Familienangehörigen (Gen 36,6) oder von Abhängigen (Gen 12,5), z. B.:

> Wenn jemand (*næpæš*) JHWH ein Speisopfer darbringen will, so soll es aus Grieß bestehen; er soll Öl darauf gießen und Weihrauch dazutun. (Lev 2,1)

> Die (Stadt) Makkeda hatte Josua an diesem Tag eingenommen. Er schlug sie mit der Schneide des Schwertes. Ihren König hatte er der Vernichtung geweiht, die (Bewohner) und alles Leben/alle Personen (*næpæš*), das/die in dieser (Stadt) war/en. Er hatte keinen Entkommenen übriggelassen. Er verfuhr mit dem König von Makkeda, wie er mit dem König von Jericho verfahren war. (Jos 10,28)

> Und Abram nahm Saraj, seine Frau, und Lot, seinen Brudersohn, und all ihre Habe, die sie erworben hatten, und die Lebewesen (*næpæš*), die sie in Haran gemacht hatten. So zogen sie aus, um ins Land Kanaan zu gehen, und sie kamen ins Land Kanaan. (Gen 12,5)

Exkurs 4: *nbš/npš* im Kontext des aramäischen Totenkults

Zu diesem Bedeutungsaspekt von *næpæš* läßt sich auch das sam'alische *nbš* „Person" in der Totenkultstele aus Zincirli BASOR 356 (2009) 53 f (8. Jh. v. Chr.) vergleichen. Sie zeigt neben bzw. unterhalb der Inschrift eine Speisetischszene, die ein bekanntes Motiv des Totenkults aufnimmt: Kuttamuwa, der verstorbene Diener Panamuwas II (ca. 740 – 733 v. Chr.), sitzt vor einem mit Speisen und Gefäßen gedeckten Tisch und hält in seiner Rechten eine Trinkschale und in seiner Linken (wohl) einen Pinienzapfen (s. Abb.2)[84]. Der erste *nbš*-Beleg findet sich in Z.5:

---

83 S. dazu Bernd Janowski, Sühne als Heilsgeschehen: Traditions- und religionsgeschichtliche Studien zur priesterschriftlichen Sühnetheologie, WMANT 55 (Neukirchen-Vluyn: Neukirchener Verlag, ²2000), 242 ff.
84 Die Abbildung stammt aus Eudora J. Struble / Virginia Rimmer Herrmann, "An Eternal Feast at Sam'al: The New Iron Age Mortuary Stele from Zincirli in Context", BASOR 356 (2009), 15 – 49, hier: 19 (Zeichnung: Karen Reczuch).

(1–2) Ich bin KTMW, der Diener des PNMW, der ich mir (schon) zu meinen Lebzeiten eine Stele (*nṣb*) erworben hatte. Und ich habe sie im Bezirk meiner Fortdauer aufgestellt. (2–3) Und das Festopfer dieses Bezirkes beträgt: ein Stier für den Hadad (von?) QRPDL (3–4) und ein Widder für den Vorsteher des Mahles (4) und ein Widder für Schamasch (5) und ein Widder für den Hadad des Weinberges und ein Widder für Kubaba und ein Widder für meine Person (*nbš*), die in der Stele (*nṣb*) (präsent) ist[85].

Abb. 2: Totenkultstele aus Zincirli (8. Jh. v. Chr.)

Der zweite *nbš*-Beleg (+ Suff. 1. c.sg.: *nbšy*) findet sich in Z. 11 derselben Inschrift und bedeutet möglicherweise „(Toten-)Stele":

(6–8) Und jetzt: Wer auch immer von meinen Söhnen oder von den Söhnen eines (anderen) Mannes diesen Bezirk besitzen wird, (8–10) der muss fürwahr jährlich das Beste dieses Weinberges als Darbringung nehmen (10–11) und (hier) bei/an meiner Totenstele (*nbš*) schlachten. (12–13) Und er soll für mich eine Keule bestimmen.

---

85 Übersetzung Ingo Kottsieper, "Eine sam'alische Totenkultstele aus Zincirli," In: Bernd Ja-nowski / Daniel Schwemer (Hg.), *Grab-, Sarg-, Bau- und Votivinschriften*, TUAT.NF 6 (Gütersloh: Gütersloher Verlagshaus, 2011), 321–323, hier: 322f, s. dazu auch Dagmar Kühn, "Eine Wohnstatt für die *nebesch* des Kuttamuwa,", Welt und Umwelt der Bibel Nr. 53 (2009), 74. Anders Herbert Niehr, "Religion in den Königreichen der Aramäer Syriens," In: Corinne Bonnet / Herbert Niehr, *Religionen in der Umwelt des Alten Testaments II*, Kohlhammer Studienbücher 4,2 (Stuttgart: Kohlhammer, 2010), 282ff und Frevel, "Vitality of Corpses," (s. Anm. 42), 223, die jeweils mit "Totengeist" übersetzen.

Den doppelten Sprachgebrauch von *nbš* erklärt I. Kottsieper folgendermaßen: „Die Stele hat ... seine (sc. des Verstorbenen) Person (*nbš*) an Stelle des verendeten Körpers aufgenommen (Z.5) und kann dann selbst als seine *nbš* bezeichnet werden (Z.11)"[86]. Konstitutiv dafür dürfte der enge Zusammenhang zwischen der Person (*nbš*) des Verstorbenen und der ihn repräsentierenden Stele sein. Dieser Zusammenhang bliebe aber auch gewahrt, wenn man *nbšy* Z.11 als Personalpronomen versteht und übersetzt: „und (hier) bei mir schlachten".

Dieselbe Bedeutung von aram. *nbš/npš* dürfte in der älteren Inschrift der Hadad-Statue KAI 214,17.21 f (frühes 8. Jh. v.Chr.) vorliegen, wo der Nachkomme und Thronfolger Panamuwas I. aufgefordert wird, den königlichen Totenkult zu vollziehen:

> (15) Und wer auch immer von meinen Söhnen das Szepter ergreift und sich auf meinen Thron setzt und (sein) Macht festigt (16) und opfert dem Hadad und wenn er den Namen des Hadad anruft und (17) ... dann soll er sprechen: "Die Person (*nbš*) des Panamuwa soll mit dir essen und die Person (*nbš*) des Panamuwa soll mit dir trinken". Immerzu soll er die Person (*nbš*) des Panamuwa zusammen mit (18) Hadad anrufen[87].

Auch hier handelt es sich bei *nbš* wohl um die "Lebenskraft, Person" eines Verstorbenen – und zwar eines Verstorbenen, der durch eine ihn darstellende Statue repräsentiert wird[88]. Dem Urteil von Chr. Frevel: "In sum: *npš/nbš* stands for aspects of the deceased which endure after death and have the ability to represent him"[89] kann man – jenseits der Frage einer sachgemäßen Übersetzung dieses Terminus – jedenfalls nur zustimmen. (*Ende des Exkurses*);

---

86 Ders., aaO 322. Anders Smith, *Poetic Heroes* (s. Anm. 74), der für Z.5 im Anschluss an D. Pardee eine andere Übersetzung vorschlägt: "a ram for my *nbš* that (will be in proximity) to this stele" und kommentiert: "If correct, the point is not that the *nbš* resides in the stele, but comes to the stele marked as the place for the ritual performed on is behalf" (im Druck).

87 Herbert Niehr, "Zum Totenkult der Könige von Sam'al im 9. und 8. Jh. v.Chr,", SEL 11 (194), 57–73, hier: 59 ff und ders., "Religion," 281, der *nbš* auch hier mit "Totengeist" übersetzt.

88 In KAI 215,21 könnte *npš* "Stele" bedeuten, allerdings ist der Text schwierig zu rekonstruieren, s. dazu Herbert Niehr, "Ein weiterer Aspekt zum Totenkult der Könige von Sam'al," SEL 18 (2001), 83–97, hier: 93.

89 Frevel, aaO 223. Die damit angesprochene Problematik bedarf einer eingehenden Diskussion. Sie dürfte in den Kontext der Politischen Theologie gehören, insofern bei einer Amtsperson (König, Würdenträger, Diener u.a.) zwischen einem *natürlichen* und einem *politischen Körper* unterschieden wird, vgl. Niehr, "Ein weiterer Aspekt," 86: "Der König als Mensch ist ein *body natural*, der König als Amtsperson ist ein *body politic*." Während der *body natural* durch den Tod vergeht, wird "das bleibende Element des Königtums, der *body politic*, ... durch ein Bild repräsentiert" (ebd.). Diesem Bild gelten alle kultischen und memorativen Maßnahmen.

Soweit der lexikographische Überblick. Um die Bedeutung von *næpæš* noch etwas zu profilieren, seien im Folgenden zwei charakteristische Themenkomplexe angeführt, in denen dieser Begriff eine zentrale Rolle spielt.

2.2.2. Textbeispiele

Der eine Themenkomplex betrifft den Zusammenhang von *næpæš* und Unterwelt / Gottesferne, der andere den Zusammenhang von *næpæš* und Tempel / Gottesnähe.

1. *næpæš und Gottesferne / Unterwelt*
Aufgrund der für das Alte Testament kennzeichnenden „axiologische(n) und theologische(n) *Asymmetrie von Leben und Tod*"[90] stehen sich næpæç und Unterwelt/Gottesferne diametral gegenüber. Deshalb hofft der Beter darauf, dass JHWH, der Gott des Lebens, ihn bzw. seine *næpæš* nicht der Unterwelt // Grube überlässt:

> 9 Darum freute sich mein Herz (*leb*) und jubelte meine Ehre (*kābôd*),
>   auch mein Fleisch (*bāśār*) wohnt in Sicherheit.
> 10 Ja, du überlässt[91] mich/mein Leben (*næpæš*) nicht der Unterwelt,
>   du lässt es nicht zu, dass dein Frommer die Grube sieht. (Ps 16,9 f)[92]

Wie dieser Text zeigt, ist die *næpæš* „das genaue Subjekt der Klagelieder des Psalters"[93] – und wie wir ergänzen können: auch der Danklieder des einzelnen. Als „vitales Selbst" ist sie nicht nur das ,Organ'[94] des Mitgefühls (Hi 30,25), der Leidenschaft (Ps 103,3; Spr 19,2) und der Freude (Jes 61,10; Sir 51,29), sondern auch das Subjekt von Kummer, Leid, Verzagtheit und Mühsal. Nimmt man die Belege aus dem Jeremia-, dem Jona- und dem Hiobbuch hinzu, so ergibt sich das folgende, unvollständige Bild:

---

90 Martin Leuenberger, *Gott in Bewegung: Religions- und theologiegeschichtliche Beiträge zu Gottesvorstellungen im alten Israel*, FAT I/76 (Tübingen: Mohr Siebeck, 2011), 84 (Hervorhebung im Original).

91 Im Sinn des „Auslieferns", s. dazu Ernst Jenni, *Die hebräischen Präpositionen Bd.3: Die Präposition Lamed* (Stuttgart: Kohlhammer, 2000), 88 (Nr. 3172).

92 S. dazu Kathrin Liess, *Der Weg des Lebens: Psalm 16 und das Lebens- und Todesverständnis der Individualpsalmen*, FAT II/5 (Tübingen: Mohr Siebeck, 2004), 211 ff.

93 Wolff, *Anthropologie* (s. Anm. 8), 44.

94 Genaugenommen ist die *næpæš* kein Körperorgan wie das Herz oder die Leber, sie hat aber einen organischen Fixpunkt, wie die Bedeutung „Kehle, Schlund" (s. oben 144 f) zeigt.

- sie ist schreckensstarr (Ps 6,4),
- sie lechzt nach Gott (Ps 42,2, vgl. Ps 107,9),
- sie dürstet nach Gott (Ps 42,3; 63,2, vgl. Ps 143,6.8),
- sie ist hungrig (Ps 107,9),
- sie sehnt sich/schmachtet nach den Vorhöfen des Tempels (Ps 84,3, vgl. Ps 119,81),
- der Beter schüttet seine næpæš aus (Ps 42,5, vgl. Ps 141,8: Bitte, dass die næpæš nicht weggeschüttet werden möge)[95],
- sie zerfließt (Ps 42,6.7.12; 43,5, vgl. Ps 119,28),
- sie vergeht vor Qual (Ps 107,28),
- sie begehrt auf (Ps 42,6.12; 43,5),
- sie ist niedergebeugt (Ps 57,7, vgl. Ps 44,26: bis in den Staub),
- sie ist unruhig (Ps 116,7),
- sie ist schwach (vor Kummer) (Ps 31,10, vgl. Jon 2,8),
- sie ist sorgenvoll (Ps 13,3) und verzagt (Jon 2,8),
- sie ist untröstlich (Ps 77,3),
- sie ist erschöpft und wehrlos (Jer 4,31),
- sie ist verstoßen (Ps 88,15),
- sie ist verfolgt (Ps 7,6)
- sie leidet unter Bedrängnissen (Ps 31,8, vgl. Ps 143,11.12; Gen 42,21) und Mühsal (Jes 53,11),
- sie fühlt sich von Feinden bedrängt, die dem Beter nach dem Leben trachten (Ps 17,13, vgl. Ps 22,21; 31,14; 35,4.7.12; 38,13; 40,15; 54,5; 56,7; 57,5; 59,4; 63,10; 70,3; 71,10; 86,14; 94,21; 119,109; 143,3),
- sie wird von Löwen zerrissen (Ps 7,3), ist dem Raubtier preisgegeben (Ps 74,19),
- sie ist bitter (Ri 18,25; 1 Sam 1,10; 22,2; 2 Sam 17,8; Jes 38,15; Hi 3,20; 7,11; 10,1 u. ö.)[96],
- sie ist gesättigt mit Übeln (Ps 88,4) und Spott (Ps 123,4),
- sie klebt am Staub (Ps 119,25),
- sie wohnt im Land des Schweigens (Ps 94,17),
- sie wird der Scheol nicht überlassen/ausgeliefert (Ps 16,10).

Greifen wir aus diesem Belegmaterial einige charakteristische Beispiele heraus. Nach Ps 88,4 (innerhalb der Notschilderung V.2–10aα) ist die *næpæš* so mit Übeln „gesättigt", dass das Leben (*hajjîm*) – in Parallele zu *næpæš*[97]! – des Beters die Unterwelt „berührt":

---

95 S. dazu unten 158 ff.

96 S. dazu Westermann, " *næpæš* " (s. Anm. 8), 79 f.80 f; Seebass, "*næpæš*" (s. Anm. 8), 545 und di Vito, "Alttestamentliche Anthropologie" (s. Anm. 8), 228 f. Die Belege aus dem Hiobbuch (3,20; 7,11 u. ö.) bilden dabei insofern eine gewisse Ausnahme, als es bei ihnen nicht um die Gottesferne, sondern um die *bedrängende Gottesnähe* geht, s. dazu den Überblick bei Bernd Janowski, ",Die Erde ist in die Hand eines Frevlers gegeben' (Hi 9,24): Die Frage nach der Gerechtigkeit Gottes im Hiobbuch," In: H. Lichtenberger / H. Zweigle (Hg.), *Wo ist Gott? Die Theodizee-Frage und die Theologie im Pfarramt*, Theologie Interdisziplinär 7 (Neukirchen-Vluyn: Neukirchener Verlag, 2009), 1–18.

97 S. dazu oben Anm. 14.

Notschilderung I

2	bei Tag habe ich geschrien, (jeweils) in der Nacht vor dir.
3	Es komme vor dich mein Gebet,
	neige dein Ohr meinem Schrei!
4	Denn gesättigt mit Übeln ist mein Leben (*næpæš*),
	und mein Leben (*ḥajjīm*) hat die Unterwelt berührt.
5	Zugezählt worden bin ich denen, die in die Grube hinabsteigen,
	ich bin geworden wie ein Mann ohne Kraft.
6	Unter den Toten (bin ich) ein Freigelassener,
	wie Erschlagene, die im Grab liegen,
	an die du nicht mehr gedacht hast,
	sind sie doch von deiner Hand abgeschnitten.
7	Versetzt hast du mich in die tiefste Grube,
	an finstere Orte, in (Meeres-)Tiefen.
8	Auf mir hat gelastet dein Grimm,
	und mit allen deinen Brechern hast du (mich) überwältigt. – *Sela*
9	Entfernt hast du meine Vertrauten von mir,
	zum Abscheu für sie hast du mich gemacht,
	zum Gefangenen/gefangen (bin ich) – und ich kann nicht heraus!
10aα	Mein Auge ist dahingeschwunden vor Elend.

Appellation an JHWH

10aβ.b	Ich habe dich gerufen, JHWH, an jedem Tag,
	ich habe ausgebreitet zu dir meine Hände.
11	Für die Toten solltest du ein Wunder tun
	oder werden Totengeister sich erheben, dich zu preisen? – *Sela*
12	Wird im Grab erzählt deine Güte,
	deine Treue am Ort des Untergangs?
13	Wird kund in der Finsternis dein Wunder
	und deine Gerechtigkeit im Land des Vergessens?

Notschilderung II

14	Ich aber, zu dir, JHWH, habe ich um Hilfe gerufen,
	und (jeweils) am Morgen gelange mein Gebet zu dir!
15	Wozu, JHWH, verstößt du mein Leben/mich (*næpæš*),
	verbirgst du dein Gesicht vor mir?
16	Elend bin ich und todkrank von Jugend auf,
	getragen habe ich deine Schrecken, ich erstarre (?).
17	Über mich sind hinweggegangen deine Zornesgluten,
	deine Schrecken haben mich zum Verstummen gebracht.
18	Umgeben haben sie mich wie Wasser jeden Tag/allezeit,
	umzingelt haben sie mich insgesamt.

19 Entfernt hast du von mir Freund und Gefährten,
    meine Vertrauten – (da ist) Finsternis(ort)! (Ps 88)

„Satt" (śābaʿ V.4a) ist dieser Beter nicht durch ein erfülltes Leben (Gen 25,8; 35,29; 1 Chr 23,1 u. ö.)[98] oder durch eine besondere Gottesgemeinschaft (Ps 16,11[99], vgl. Ps 17,15; 63,6 u. ö.)[100], sondern durch die „Übel", die ihn von Gott getroffen haben[101]. Für ihn wird es – sollte JHWH nicht doch noch eingreifen – kein „Erwachen" geben, weil sein Leben die Unterwelt „berührt" (nāgaʿ) hat und „Finsternis" sein einziger Gefährte ist (V.19). Die Schrecken der Scheol werden dabei in bedrückenden Bildern geschildert. So zeigen die Ortsangaben „Grube" (V.5), „Grab" (V.6, vgl. V.12), „tiefste Tiefen" (V.7), „finstere Orte" (V.7, vgl. V.13) und „(Meeres-)Tiefen" (V.7, vgl. V.18), dass sich der Beter in räumlicher Nähe zur Unterwelt (vgl. V.4) und entsprechend in unüberwindbarer Distanz zu JHWH und der Welt der Lebenden befindet. Sachgemäß sind deshalb die Vergleiche mit den Toten: Der Beter ist denen zugezählt, die in die Grube hinabsteigen (V.5a), er ist wie ein Mann ohne Kraft (V.5b), unter den Toten ein Freigelassener (V.6aα) und gleicht Erschlagenen, die im Grab liegen (V.6aα)[102].

Besonders aufschlussreich für die Leben/Tod-Problematik ist Ps 42/43, wo næpæš zum anthropologischen Leitbegriff wird und der Beter seiner eigenen næpæš gegenübertritt. Die erste Strophe dieses Klagegebets (V.2–6) beginnt mit einem Tiervergleich (V.2), der die existentielle Not des Beters in ein eindrückliches *Sehnsuchtsbild* (lechzende Hirschkuh) fasst, und dieses Bild in jedem der fünf Verse mit *Wasserbildern* – Wasserbäche / Durst / Tränen / Ausschütten / Zerfließen – fortsetzt:

---

98 S. dazu Georg Warmuth, "Art. śābaʿ usw.," ThWAT 7, 1993, 693–704, hier: 702.
99 Ps 16,11 (im Gegensatz zu V.10 mit seiner Unterweltstopik!) liest sich wie eine Kontrastformulierung zu Ps 88,4, s. dazu oben 157.
100 Zu dieser Form der „Sättigung" s. Warmuth, aaO 696 ff.
101 Vgl. Ps 123,3 f, wo das Gottesvolk bzw. dessen næpæš „satt" ist vom Spott // der Verachtung der Hochmütigen. Von diesem Sprachgebrauch her ist auch die Wendung vom „Ausschütten" (śāpak) der næpæš zu verstehen, s. dazu unten 161 f.
102 Zur Interpretation von Ps 88,2–10aα s. Bernd Janowski, "Die Toten loben JHWH nicht: Psalm 88 und das alttestamentliche Todesverständnis," In: ders., *Der Gott des Lebens: Beiträge zur Theologie des Alten Testaments 3* (Neukirchen-Vluyn: Neukirchener Verlag, 2003), 201–243, hier: 207 ff.

Klage (= Situation der trostlosen Gegenwart)

2 Wie eine Hirschkuh lechzt an Wasserbächen,
   so lechzt *mein Leben* (*næpæš*) nach dir, Gott[103].
3 Es dürstet *mein Leben* (*næpæš*) nach Gott, dem lebendigen Gott:
   wann werde ich kommen und ‹sehen›[104] das Gesicht Gottes?
4 Es wurden mir meine Tränen (zu) Brot bei Tag und bei Nacht,
   wenn man zu mir sagt den ganzen Tag:
   „Wo ist dein Gott?"

Erinnerung (= Blick in die heilvolle Vergangenheit)

2 Daran[105] denke ich
   und schütte aus *mein Leben* (*næpæš*) in/bei mir,
   dass ich ‹im Kreis der Edlen› zum Haus Gottes zog
   unter der Stimme des Jubels und Dankes einer feiernden Schar.

Hoffnung (= Sehnsucht nach dem rettenden Gott)

2 Was zerfließt du[106], *mein Leben* (*næpæš*),
   und was begehrst du auf gegen mich[107]?
   Harre auf Gott,
   denn ich werde ihm wieder danken,
   der Rettung ‹meines› Gesichts ‹und› meinem Gott[108]. (Ps 42,2–6)

---

103 In V.2a wird *ʿārag* „lechzen" (zur Bedeutung s. Joachim Schaper, "Wie der Hirsch lechzt nach frischem Wasser": Studien zu Ps 42/43 in Religionsgeschichte, Theologie und kirchlicher Praxis, BThSt 63, Neukirchen-Vluyn: Neukirchener Verlag, 2004, 48 ff) mit der Präp. *ʿal* „auf, über" und in V.2b mit der Präp. *ʾæl* „zu" konstruiert. Statt einer Emendation von *ʿal* zu *ʾæl* ist MT m. E. beizubehalten, vgl. auch Takako Aoki, „Wann darf ich kommen und schauen das Angesicht Gottes?": Untersuchungen zur Zusammengehörigkeit beziehungsweise Eigenständigkeit von Ps 42 und Ps 43, ATM 23 (Münster: LIT Verlag, 2008), 56 f. Wenn man die lokale Bedeutung von *ʿal* ansetzt, könnte man paraphrasierend übersetzen: „Wie eine Hirschkuh (nach Wasser) lechzt an (*ʿal*) Wasserbächen", vgl. Ps 137,1 vom Sitzen „an" (*ʿal*) den Kanälen Babylons. Zum „Lechzen" der Tierwelt nach JHWH s. noch Joel 1,20, wo offenbar auf Ps 42,2f angespielt wird, s. dazu Jörg Jeremias, Die Propheten Joel, Obadja, Jona, Micha, ATD 24/3 (Göttingen: Vandenhoeck & Ruprecht, 2007), 19. Aoki, aaO 78 f übersetzt an beiden Stellen mit „schreien".
104 MT liest hier *rʾh* nif., s. dazu Thomas Dockner, *„Sicut cerva … ": Text, Struktur und Bedeutung von Psalm 42 und 43*, ATSAT 67 (St. Ottilien: EOS Verlag, 2001), 12 ff und unten Anm. 121.
105 *ʾelæh* hat eine kataphorische, d. h. auf den anschließenden *kî*-Satz verweisende Funktion, vgl. Dockner, aaO 179.
106 Zur Bedeutung von *šîʿḥ* hitpol. s. ders., aaO 180 f.
107 Oder: „was bist du leidenschaftlich erregt gegen mich?", zu *hāmāh* s. Ges[18] 280 s.v. *hāmāh* 3a und Andreas Baumann, "Art. *hāmāh* usw.," ThWAT 2, 1977, 444–449, hier: 446.
108 MT: „der Rettung seines Gesichts" und andere Satzabgrenzung („mein Gott" zu Beginn von V.7), zu den textkritischen Problemen s. Dockner, aaO 17 f und Aoki, aaO 61 ff; zur Bedeutung von *panîm* „Gesicht" in Ps 42,3.6.12; 43,5 s. bes. Friedhelm Hartenstein, *Das Angesicht JHWHs: Studien*

Mit V.2 wird der Grundton des Psalms, nämlich die Sehnsucht nach dem lebendigen Gott, angeschlagen – und zwar mit dem elementaren Bild der nach Wasser
suchenden Hirschkuh, das mehrfach auch auf hebräischen Namenssiegeln des 8.
und 7. Jh. v. Chr. erscheint (s. Abb.3)[109].

Abb.3: Wasser oder Futter suchende Hirschkuh, judäisches Namenssiegel (8. Jh. v. Chr.)

Die Relation von Bild (Siegel) und Text (Ps 42,2) dürfte darin bestehen, dass

> „die *Verwundbarkeit* der Hirschkuh dem menschlichen *Gefährdungsbewusstsein* einen An-
> knüpfungspunkt gab. Indem sie sich mit einer nach Wasser bzw. Futter suchenden Hirsch-
> kuh, also einem unter möglicher *elementarer Bedrohung* stehenden Tier, identifizieren,
> bringen sich die Besitzer der Siegel und die Autoren sowie die Beterinnen und Beter des
> Psalms als verletzliche, vom Untergang bedrohte Kreaturen zur Sprache, die gleichwohl ihre
> Hoffnung auf Gott setzen"[110].

Das Besondere an Ps 42 ist nun, dass der Beter seiner eigenen *næpæš* gegenübertritt. Das geschieht in V.5f (sowie in dem Kehrvers 42,12 und 43,5). Zunächst
wird aber die *Ferne Gottes* und das Dürsten des Beters bzw. seiner *næpæš*[111] nach
Gott thematisiert (V.2–4). Dabei wird die Not des Beters, die durch die unentwegte

---

zu seinem höfischen und kultischen Bedeutungshintergrund in den Psalmen und in Exodus 32–34,
FAT I/55 (Tübingen: Mohr Siebeck, 2008), 180 f.
109 S. dazu Othmar Keel / Christoph Uehlinger, Göttinnen, Götter und Gottessymbole: Neue
Erkenntnisse zur Religionsgeschichte Kanaans und Israels aufgrund bislang unerschlossener
ikonographischer Quellen, Mit einem Nachwort von Florian Lippke (Fribourg: Academic Press,
⁶2010), 209 f mit Abb.200b-d, ferner Schaper, Hirsch (s. Anm. 101), 72 ff. Die obige Abbildung (Keel
/ Uehlinger, aaO 209 Nr. 200b) trägt die Beischrift „Yirmeyahu gehörig".
110 Schaper, aaO 77 (Hervorhebung im Original).
111 Sowohl in V.2 („lechzen") als auch in V.3 („dürsten") schwingt dabei die Bedeutung „Kehle"
mit.

Spottfrage seiner Umgebung „Wo ist dein Gott" (V.4b) noch gesteigert wird, in ein existentielles Bild gefasst, wonach sein Hunger nach einem gotterfüllten Leben durch Tränen ‚gestillt' wird.

Mit V.5 ändert sich die Situation, weil sich der Beter jetzt an vergangene Zeiten erinnert, als er in der Gemeinschaft der Tempel-Wallfahrer die *Nähe Gottes* erlebt hatte. In diesem Zusammenhang ist davon die Rede, dass er seine *næpæš* in/bei sich „ausschüttet" (*šāpak*). Auch wenn V.5 „die Entschlossenheit des Beters widerspiegelt, seine Not durch die Erinnerung an die in der Vergangenheit erfahrene heilvolle Nähe Gottes zu überwinden"[112], ist aufgrund des Klagekontextes (V.1–4!) mit C. Westermann u. a.[113] davon auszugehen, dass sich das Syntagma *šāpak* + *næpæš* auf die Klage des Beters bezieht, der im Vergleich mit der heilvollen Vergangenheit seiner trostlosen Gegenwart inne wird und deshalb seine *næpæš* in/bei sich „ausschüttet", d. h. sein Leben beklagt. „Die Klage, in der man ‚sich ausspricht', in der man ‚alles los werden will', ist selbst die Bewegung des Ausschüttens"[114].

Als Sachparallelen lassen sich mit C. Westermann 1 Sam 1,15 f und Hi 30,16 anführen, auch wenn die Formulierungen im Vergleich zu Ps 42,5 Nuancierungen aufweisen:

> 15 Nein, mein Herr, eine Frau hart bedrückten Gemütes bin ich,
>   und Wein und Bier habe ich nicht getrunken,
>   sondern ich habe ausgeschüttet (*šāpak*) mein Leben (*næpæš*)
>   vor (*lipnê*) JHWH.
> 16 Halte deine Magd nicht für eine nichtswürdige Person!
>   Wegen der Fülle meiner Klage (*śîaḥ*) und meines Kummers
>   (*kaʿas*) habe ich bis jetzt geredet. (1 Sam 1,15 f)
>   Doch jetzt hat sich mein Leben (*næpæš*) ausgeschüttet (*šāpak* hitp.)
>   gegen mich,
>   die Tage meines Elends (*jᵉmê-ʿonî*) packen mich. (Hi 30,16)

---

112 Aoki, *"Wann darf ich kommen"* (s. Anm. 101), 82, vgl. aaO 131 und Hans Joachim *Kraus*, *Psalmen 1: Psalmen 1–59*, BK XV/1 (Neukirchen-Vluyn: Neukirchener Verlag, ⁶1989), 475 u. a.
113 So Westermann, „ *næpæš*" (s. Anm. 8), 81, vgl. Willy Schottroff, *„Gedenken" im Alten Orient und im Alten Testament: Die Wurzel zākar im semitischen Sprachkreis*, WMANT 15 (Neukirchen-Vluyn: Neukirchener Verlag, ²1967), 115.132 u. ö.; Seebass, *"næpæš"* (s. Anm. 8), 544; Rüdiger Liwak, "Art. *šāpak* usw.," ThWAT 8, 1995, 428–438, hier: 434 f; Dockner, *„Sicut cerva ... "* (s. Anm. 102), 180 u. a.
114 Westermann, ebd.

Während in der Antwort Hannas an Eli in 1 Sam 1,15 f vom „Ausschütten" der *næpæš*, d. h. vom Ausbreiten der inneren Not vor JHWH[115], in Parallele zum „Klagen" die Rede ist, steht *næpæš* in Hi 30,16 „zugleich für das Ich des Klagenden und für dessen Leben ... quasi als sein eigenes Objekt ... "[116]. Hierher sind auch die *šāpak*-Belege in Ps 69,2; 102,1 und Ps 143,3 zu stellen:

> Vertraut auf ihn (sc. auf JHWH) zu jeder Zeit, Volk,
> schüttet aus (*šāpak*) vor ihm euer Herz (*leb*),
> Gott ist Zuflucht für uns. – *Sela* (Ps 62,9)

> Gebet eines Armen, wenn er kraftlos ist
> und vor JHWH seine Klage (*śîªḥ*) ausschüttet. (Ps 102,1)

> Ich schütte aus (*šāpak*) vor ihm (sc. JHWH) meine Klage (*śîªḥ*),
> tue kund vor ihm meine Drangsal (*ṣārāh*). (Ps 142,3)

Im Unterschied zu den genannten Belegen ist für Ps 42,5 die Parallelität von *šāpak* (+ *næpæš*) und *zākar* „erinnern, gedenken" zu beachten. Denn die Erinnerung des Beters ergreift und hält das fest, was an der *heilvollen Vergangenheit* (V.5) für die *trostlose Gegenwart* (V.1–4) bedeutsam ist – nämlich die Nähe des lebendigen Gottes –, um zu einem angemessenen Verhalten zu finden[117]. Der Beter stößt also auf die Asymmetrie von Einst und Jetzt, was ihn zu einer Neubestimmung seiner Situation *coram Deo* bringt. Diese Neubestimmung äußert sich in den Fragen von V.6a, mit denen er seine *næpæš* als Gegenüber anspricht („du") und sie auffordert, auf Gott zu harren, für dessen Rettung sie ihm wieder dankbar sein wird (V.6b, vgl. V.5b). So gelangt die lechzende (V.2), dürstende (V.3) und klagende *næpæš* (V.5aβ) an einen Punkt oder besser: an einen Ort, an dem die Trostlosigkeit der Gegenwart überwunden und an dem sie die Rettung durch den lebendigen Gott erfahren wird.

2. *næpæš und Gottesnähe / Tempel*
Die Pointe von Ps 42,2–6 besteht darin, dass JHWH seine rettende Gegenwart in der Gottesschau im Tempel gewährt (vgl. V.3aβ.b → V.6b). Von dieser Gottesgegenwart im Tempel, nach der sich die *næpæš* verzehrt, spricht auch der nachexilische Zionspsalm Ps 84[118]:

115 Vgl. Walter Dietrich, *Samuel 1: 1 Sam 1–12*, BK VIII/1 (Neukirchen-Vluyn: Neukirchener Verlag, 2011), 47.
116 Hans Strauß, *Hiob, 2. Teilband: 19,1–42,17*, BK XVI/2 (Neukirchen-Vluyn: Neukirchener Verlag, 2000), 204.
117 Vgl. Schottroff, aaO 115.
118 Zu Ps 84 s. zuletzt Hermann Spieckermann, "Der theologische Kosmos des Psalters," BThZ 21 (2004), 61–79, hier: 68 ff und Kristinn Ólason, "‚Wohl denen, die in deinem Haus wohnen': Beobachtungen zu Ps 84," In: *Studien zu Psalmen und Propheten*, FS Hubert Irsigler, HBS 64, hg. von

Wohnen im Haus JHWHs

2 Wie lieblich sind deine Wohnungen,
JHWH Zebaoth!
3 Gesehnt, ja sogar verzehrt hat sich meine *næpæš* nach den
Vorhöfen JHWHs,
mein Herz und mein Leib jubeln dem lebendigen Gott zu.
4 Sogar der Sperling hat ein Haus gefunden
und die Schwalbe: sie hat ein Nest für sich,
wo sie ihre Jungen hingelegt/-gesetzt hat bei deinen Altären[119].
JHWH Zebaoth, *mein König und mein Gott*[120].
5 Wohl denen, die in deinem Haus wohnen,
immerdar preisen sie dich! – *Sela*

Wallfahrt zum Zion

2 Wohl den Menschen, deren Stärke in dir ist,
gebahnte Wege[121] in ihrem Herzen!
3 Ziehen sie durch das Tal der Dürre,
machen sie es zu einem Quellgrund,
sogar mit Segnungen[122] bedeckt es der Frühregen.
4 Sie gehen von Kraft zu Kraft,
‹sie schauen›[123] Gott in Zion. – *Sela*

Carmen Diller u. a. (Freiburg / Basel / Wien: Herder, 2010), 93–113, vgl. auch Bernd Janowski, "Der Ort des Lebens: Zur Kultsymbolik des Jerusalemer Tempels," In: J. Kamlah (Hg.), *Tempelbau und Tempelkult: Zur Architektur und kultischen Ausstattung von Tempeln in der Levante (2.–1. Jt. v. Chr.)* (Wiesbaden: Harrassowitz, 2012), 363–397.

119 Oder: „auf deine Altäre", s. dazu Ólason, aaO 95. Zum Verständnis des Vogelbilds s. zuletzt Jutta Krispenz, "Am heiligen Ort: Der Hof im Tempel als mythischer Raum," In: Michael Fieger / Jörg Lanckau (Hg.), *Erschaffung und Zerstörung der Schöpfung: Ein Beitrag zum Thema Mythos* (Bern u. a.: Peter Lang, 2011), 45–64, hier: 60 ff.

120 V.4b dürfte ergänzender Zusatz sein, vgl. Ólason, aaO 98.

121 Oder: „Pilgerwege", s. zu diesem Syntagma Frank-Lothar Hossfeld / Erich Zenger, Psalmen 51–100, HThK.AT (Freiburg / Basel / Wien: Herder, 2000), 509 (Zenger); Spieckermann, aaO 68 Anm. 22 und Ólason, aaO 103.

122 Zur steigernden Pluralform *bᵉrākôt* s. Ólason, aaO 104 f.

123 Zur dogmatischen Korrektur des MT (*rʾh* nif. + Präp. *ʾæl*) s. Hossfeld / Zenger, ebd.; Spieckermann, aaO 68 Anm. 24; Hartenstein, *Angesicht JHWHs* (s. Anm. 106), 8 mit Anm. 22; Janowski, *Konfliktgespräche mit Gott* (s. Anm. 8), 92 mit Anm. 166 und ausführlich Oliver Dyma, *Die Wallfahrt zum Zweiten Tempel: Untersuchungen zur Entwicklung der Wallfahrtsfeste in vorhasmonäischer Zeit*, FAT II/40 (Tübingen: Mohr Siebeck, 2009), 306 ff.

Manifestationen der Gegenwart JHWHs

2   JHWH, Gott Zebaoth,
     höre doch mein Gebet,
     vernimm doch, Gott Jakobs! – Sela
3   Unseren Schild sieh an, o Gott,
     und blick an das Angesicht deines Gesalbten[124]!
4   Ja, besser ist ein Tag in deinen Vorhöfen
     als tausend, die ich erwählt habe;
     (besser) stehen an der Schwelle im Haus meines Gottes,
     als wohnen in den Zelten des Frevels.
5   Denn Sonne und Schild ist JHWH Gott,
     Gnade und Ehre gibt JHWH,
     nicht versagt er Gutes denen, die in Makellosigkeit wandeln.
6   JHWH Zebaoth,
     wohl dem Mensch, der auf dich vertraut!

Ps 84 spricht von einer auf das Zionsheiligtum ausgerichteten Bewegung, die sowohl eine emotionale (*Sehnsucht:* V.2–5) wie eine reale Bewegung (*Wallfahrt:* V.6–8) ist[125]. Mit der Gottesschau auf dem Zion – V.8: „Sie gehen von Kraft zu Kraft, ‹sie schauen› Gott in Zion"– verbindet sich nach V. (9 f.)11–13 eine grundlegende Bestimmung der menschlichen Existenz, wenn in V.11 der *Jerusalemer Tempel* als Ort der Fülle (1 Tag :: 1000 Tage, Haus Gottes :: Zelte des Frevels), in V.12a der *Gott dieses Ortes* als richtende und schützende („Sonne und Schild")[126] wie als anziehende und königlich-herrschaftliche Macht („Gnade und Ehre") und in V.12b die *Menschen* als „Gottes-Pilger"[127] und Empfänger all dieses „Guten" gepriesen werden. So beschreibt V.12

> „die Audienz bei JHWH als Beschenktwerden mit ‚Gutem', d. h. mit allem, was ein Menschenleben braucht, damit es gelingt und glücklich wird. Mehr noch: Wer zur Audienz zugelassen wird, hat die Chance, JHWHs ‚Gnade' und Anteil an seiner ‚Herrlichkeit zu erlangen, d. h. von ihm in ein besonderes Dienst- und Schutzverhältnis aufgenommen zu werden. V.12a faßt dies mit den zwei Metaphern ‚Sonne' und ‚Schutzschild' zusammen"[128].

---

124 Zur Fortschreibung V.9 f. s. Hossfeld / Zenger, aaO 512 ff (Zenger) und Ólason, aaO 97.

125 Vgl. Spieckermann, aaO 68 ff. und Dyma, aaO 295 ff.

126 S. dazu Bernd Janowski, "JHWH und der Sonnengott: Aspekte der Solarisierung JHWHs in vorexilischer Zeit," In: ders., *Die rettende Gerechtigkeit: Beiträge zur Theologie des Alten Testaments 2* (Neukirchen-Vluyn: Neukirchener Verlag, 1999), 192–219, hier: 199.206.213 und Othmar Keel, *Die Geschichte Jerusalems und die Entstehung des Monotheismus, Teil 1–2* (Göttingen: Vandenhoeck & Ruprecht, 2007), 281.

127 Hossfeld / Zenger, aaO 516 (Zenger).

128 Bernd Janowski / Erich Zenger, "Jenseits des Alltags: Fest und Opfer als religiöse Kontrapunkte zur Alltagswelt im alten Israel," In: Bernd Janowski, *Die Welt als Schöpfung: Beiträge zur*

Die im Heiligtum erfahrbare Gottesnähe ist das Lebensziel des Beters, der sich mit seiner *næpæš* nach den Vorhöfen JHWHs verzehrt und dessen Herz und Leib dem lebendigen Gott zujubeln (V.3). Diese Gottessehnsucht fasst Ps 63,2 – wie schon Ps 42,3[129] – in das Bild vom „Dürsten" (*ṣāma'*)[130] der *næpæš* nach Gott, das nur durch diesen selbst gestillt werden kann:

2 Gott, mein Gott, ich suche dich[131],
    gedürstet hat nach dir mein Leben (*næpæš*),
    geschmachtet hat nach dir mein Leib
    im dürren und erschöpften Land, ohne Wasser.
3 So habe ich im Heiligtum nach dir geschaut,
    um zu sehen deine Macht und deine Herrlichkeit.
4 Denn deine Güte ist besser als Leben,
    meine Lippen sollen dich rühmen.
5 So segne ich dich mein Leben lang,
    in deinem Namen erhebe ich meine Hände. (Ps 63,2 – 5)

Wie dieser Text zeigt, ist die Tempeltheologie von anthropologischer Relevanz: Dass es der Tempel ist, nach dessen Gott sich die *næpæš* des Beters sehnte, hängt mit der kosmologischen Funktion dieses Ortes und der Wirkmächtigkeit des hier präsenten Lebens- und Rettergottes zusammen[132]. Von ihm geht – wie paradox formuliert wird – die „Güte" aus, die besser ist als „Leben" (V.4a). Durch das Meditieren und Rezitieren dieses Textes „lebt" der bedrängte Beter in der Nähe des Leben spendenden Tempelgottes.

  Blicken wir zurück: Nach dem Zeugnis des Alten Testaments bedeutet *næpæš* nicht „Seele" als eine vom Körper losgelöste bzw. diesem gegenüber selbständige

---

Theologie des Alten Testaments 4 (Neukirchen-Vluyn: Neukirchener Verlag, 2008), 39 – 78, hier: 75 (Zenger).

129 S. dazu oben 158 ff.

130 S. dazu Lothar Ruppert, "Dürsten nach Gott: Ein psalmistisches Motiv im religionsphäno- menologischen Vergleich," In: *Die alttestamentliche Botschaft als Wegweisung*, FS H. Reinelt, hg. von Josef Zmijewski (Stuttgart: Verlag Katholisches Bibelwerk, 1990), 237– 251, hier : 211 ff.

131 Das Verb *šḥr* qal/pi. drückt „ein intensives Tun aus: eine Intensivierung des ‚Auf-etwas-aus-Seins' (*qal*), ein (angestrengtes) ‚Suchen nach' (*pi*)" (Lothar Ruppert, "Art. *šḥr* II," ThWAT 7, 1993, 1222– 1226, hier: 1223). *šḥr* pi. ist „immer eindringliches, die Not wendendes Suchen, mit dem Konnotat des sehnsüchtigen Verlangens, des Ausschau-Haltens" (ders., aaO 1224).

132 S. dazu Janowski, Ort des Lebens (s. Anm. 116), 377 ff und Erich Zenger, "‚Ich liebe den Ort, da deine Herrlichkeit wohnt' (Ps 26,8): Tempeltheologische Semiotisierung des Alltags im Psalter," In: Othmar Keel / Erich Zenger (Hg.), *Gottesstadt und Gottesgarten: Zu Geschichte und Theologie des Jerusalemer Tempels*, QD 191 (Freiburg / Basel / Wien: Herder, 2002), 180– 206, hier: 180 ff.185 ff, der zu Recht auf die den Text strukturierende Bedeutung des Begriffs *næpæš* auf- merksam macht (186 f).

Entität wie bei den Pythagoräern und Platon, sondern „Leben, Lebenskraft" – und zwar „streng konzentriert auf die Grenze des Lebens; *næpæš* ist das Leben dem Tod gegenüber"[133]. Dieses „Leben" ist eine Gabe Gottes (vgl. Gen 2,7), die für alles Weltverhalten des Menschen die elementare, psychosomatische Voraussetzung bildet. Das Alte Testament sieht den Menschen „in ein Geschehen der Lebens-gewährung einbezogen, das er und alles Lebendige nicht selbst in der Hand hat, sondern das Jahwe frei zu Ereignis bringt – stetig, von jeher und auch künftig"[134]. Der Vergleich der nach Gott „lechzenden" *næpæš* mit der nach Wasser „dürs-tenden" Hirschkuh in Ps 42,2[135] bringt dieses Geschehen der Lebensgewährung ebenso elementar wie tiefsinnig zum Ausdruck.

3. Auf dem Weg zur Seele – Ausblick

Die Geschichte des *næpæš*-Begriffs ist damit allerdings noch nicht zu Ende. Neue Aspekte kommen in hellenistischer Zeit in der Übersetzung der *Septuaginta* sowie in der *Sapientia Salomonis* hinzu. Wie M. Rösel[136] dargelegt hat, wurden die Konnotationen des hebräischen Lexems *næpæš* von der Septuaginta weitgehend übernommen, was offenbar darauf zurückzuführen ist, „dass die alte, vorplato-nische Vorstellung von ψυχή dem nahe kommt, was in der Hebräischen Bibel unter *næpæš* verstanden wird"[137]. Allerdings ist das Bild nicht einheitlich, weil die Septuaginta – etwa in den Büchern *Genesis* und *Sprüche* – Pointierungen einge-bracht hat, die den Text für die philosophische Prägung von ψυχή öffnen[138]. Rösel spricht im Blick auf die Übersetzung von *næpæš* in der Septuaginta deshalb von einer „Misch-Anthropologie"[139], die zum einen an den alttestamentlichen Sprachgebrauch von *næpæš* anknüpft und zum anderen – z.T. unter Aufnahme

133 *Westermann, næpæš*, 88.
134 Odil H. Steck, *Welt und Umwelt* (Stuttgart / Berlin / Köln: Kohlhammer, 1978), 143.
135 S. dazu oben 158 ff.
136 S. dazu Martin Rösel, "Die Geburt der Seele in der Übersetzung: Von der hebräischen *näfäsch* über die *psyche* der LXX zur deutschen Seele," In: Andreas Wagner (Hg.), *Anthropologische Aufbrüche: Alttestamentliche und interdisziplinäre Zugänge zur historischen Anthropologie*, FRLANT 232 (Göttingen: Vandenhoeck & Ruprecht, 2009), 151–170; ders., "Mensch" (s. Anm. 8), 69 ff, ferner die bei Rösel, "Geburt der Seele," 162 Anm. 38 genannten Arbeiten von N.P. Bratsiotis, D. Lys, J. Scharbert und H. Gzella.
137 Rösel, "Geburt der Seele," 161.
138 S. dazu die Beispiele bei ders., aaO 162 ff.
139 Ders., "Mensch," 81.

dichotomischer Aspekte[140] – die in der griechischen Philosophie beheimatete Seelenvorstellung rezipiert.

Dualistische Seelenkonzepte, die sich an die platonische Anthropologie anlehnen, tauchen auch in der *Sapientia Salomonis* (letztes Viertel des 1. Jh.s v.Chr / 2. Hälfte des 1. Jh.s n.Chr.) auf und zwar in SapSal 8,19 f und vor allem in SapSal 9,14 f:

19	Ich war ein Kind mit guten Anlagen,
	und hatte dann auch eine gute Seele (ψυχή ἀγαθή) erhalten.
20	Besser gesagt: Da ich gut war, kam ich in einen unbefleckten
	Leib (σῶμα ἀμίαντον). (8,19 f)
2	Denn die Berechnungen der Sterblichen gehen nicht auf,
	und auf unsere Gedanken können wir uns wahrlich nicht verlassen!
3	Denn unser vergänglicher Leib (σῶμα) beschwert unsere Seele (ψυχή),
	und als unser irdisches Zelt (γεῶδες σκῆνος) belastet er unseren
	Geist (νοῦς), der sich um so vieles sorgt. (9,14 f)[141]

Da es innerhalb des ersten Buchteils SapSal 1,1– 6,21 auch andere ψυχή-Belege gibt, die an den alttestamentlichen Sprachgebrauch von *næpæš* anknüpfen[142], stellt sich das Gesamtbild ähnlich differenziert dar wie im Fall der Septuaginta-Übersetzung. Wirkungsgeschichtlich ist jedenfalls festzuhalten, dass „Hieronymus in seiner Vulgata-Übersetzung dem LXX-Sprachgebrauch fast durchgängig mit ‚anima' und Martin Luther mit ‚Seele' gefolgt sind"[143]. Damit war der Weg für die Karriere der „Seele" in der abendländischen Geistes- und Kulturgeschichte vorgezeichnet[144].

Was also bleibt als Fazit nach unseren Überlegungen zum Thema „Das Alte Testament und die Frage nach der ‚Seele'"? Doch der endgültige Abschied von der „Seele"? Ja und Nein! *Ja*, wenn man versucht, den alttestamentlichen Begriff *næpæš* mit Hilfe von metaphysischen Konzeptionen zu erklären, die der Philosophiegeschichte des Abendlands entstammen. *Nein*, wenn man die Potenzen, die

---

140 S. dazu die Beispiele bei ders., "Geburt der Seele," 163.168 f.

141 Übersetzung von Hans Hübner, *Die Weisheit Salomos*, ATD Apokryphen Bd.4 (Göttingen: Vandenhoeck & Ruprecht, 1999), 121. Das anthropologische Konzept dieses Textes ist sogar dreiteilig (Leib – Seele – Geist), s. dazu auch die Interpretation von ders., aaO 130 und Helmut Engel, *Das Buch der Weisheit*, NSK.AT 16 (Stuttgart: Verlag Katholisches Bibelwerk, 1998), 157 f. Sehr wahrscheinlich liegt dabei eine literarische Abhängigkeit von Platons Phaidon 81c vor.

142 S. dazu Mareike V. Blischke, *Die Eschatologie in der Sapientia Salomonis*, FAT II/26 (Tübingen: Mohr Siebeck, 2007), 65 ff.180 ff.

143 Rösel, "Geburt der Seele" (s. Anm. 119), 167 f.

144 S. dazu Gladigow, "Seele" (s. Anm. 49), 53 ff und Bremmer, "Karriere der Seele" (s. Anm. 49), 185 f.186 ff.

in den antiken Diskursen über die „Seele" (ψυχή/*anima*) zu Tage treten, aufnimmt und wirkungsgeschichtlich einzuordnen versucht. Ob dabei „der traditionelle Begriff der Seele trotz allem für die Psychologie als Abgrenzung zum Leib, als konstantes Substrat psychischer Prozesse sowie als Einheitsgrund psychischen Lebens bedeutsam bleiben wird, erscheint doch eher zweifelhaft"[145].

Es geht ja um die Frage, was der Mensch ist und wie er sich selbst versteht. Bei der Antwort auf diese Frage ist immer mit kulturell geprägten und sprachlich vermittelten Vorstellungen vom Menschen zu rechnen, die nicht im Verhältnis 1::1 von einer Kultur oder Sprache auf die andere übertragbar sind. Wenn wir für *næpæš*, so meine Empfehlung, auf die Übersetzung „Seele" verzichten und von den oben skizzierten Bedeutungsaspekten[146] ausgehen sollten, mag das für manch einen ein herber Verlust sein, der nicht hinnehmbar ist. Dann aber muss man zeigen können, dass die Übersetzung „Seele" für *næpæš* nicht nur Hand und Fuß hat, sondern unhintergehbar ist. Solange das nicht gelingt, gibt es m.E. keine Alternative zum Verzicht auf diese Deutung[147]. Im übrigen ist der Gewinn, der mit diesem Verzicht, einhergeht, nicht zu übersehen. Er besteht in der Erkenntnis, dass der Begriff *næpæš* von seiner Grundbedeutung „Kehle, Schlund" bis zu seinen Bedeutungen „vitales Selbst", „Leben(skraft)", „individuelles Leben, Person" ein ganzes Spektrum von Aspekten umfasst, die den Menschen des alten Israel in seiner psychosomatischen Ganzheit in den Blick zu nehmen erlauben[148]. Diese Erkenntnis zurückzugewinnen und für die gegenwärtige Anthropologie fruchtbar zu machen, dürfte eine große Bereicherung sein.

4. Anhang: Zur Lexikographie von *næpæš*

Wie die Untersuchungen von H.W. Wolff, C. Westermann und H. Seebass gezeigt haben, ist die gängige Übersetzung von *næpæš* mit „Seele" mit großer Skepsis zu

---

145 Thomas Krüger, "*ach ja die seele*: Der Verlust der Seele – ein Gewinn für die theologische Anthropologie?," In: ders., *Das menschliche Herz und die Weisung der Seele: Studien zur alttestamentlichen Anthropologie und Ethik*, AThANT 96 (Zürich: TVZ, 2009), 83–89, hier: 83 f. Das Urteil von Th. Krüger bedarf allerdings der Differenzierung, wie die jüngste Diskussion zum Seelenbegriff in Philosophie, Theologie und Psychologie zeigt, s. dazu die Beiträge bei Crone / Schnepf / Stolzenberg (Hg.), *Seele* (s. Anm. 49) u. a.
146 S. dazu oben 144 ff.
147 Anders offenbar Reinhard Feldmeier / Hermann Spieckermann, *Der Gott der Lebendigen: Eine biblische Gotteslehre*, Topoi Biblischer Theologie 1 (Tübingen: Mohr Siebeck, 2011), 205 Anm. 12, die im Übrigen die ψυχή-Belege der Septuaginta zu eindimensional sehen.
148 S. dazu auch Silvia Schroer / Thomas Staubli, *Die Körpersymbolik der Bibel* (Gütersloher Verlagshaus: Gütersloh, ²2005), 53 f.

betrachten. Die folgende Zusammenstellung gibt eine Übersicht über die Lexikographie von *næpæš* und problematisiert noch einmal den Übersetzungsvorschlag „Seele" (die Bedeutungsangabe „Seele" wird dabei durch Fettdruck hervorgehoben).

1) W. Baumgartner / J.J. Stamm / B. Hartmann, Hebräisches und aramäisches Lexikon zum Alten Testament: Unveränderter Nachdruck der 3. Auflage (1967 ff), Bd.1 (Leiden / Boston: Brill, 2004), 672–674 (HALAT):
   1. *Kehle*
   2. *Hals*
   3. *Atem*
   4. *lebendes Wesen*
   5. *Mensch(en), Leute*
      a) (einzelner) Mensch
      b) **Seelenzahl**[149]
   6. *Persönlichkeit* (ca. 220mal)
      a) betont: ich (selber)
      b) Umschreibung des Reflexivpronomens, oft betont: selber
      c) jedermann
      d) // *rûᵃḥ*
   7. *Leben* (ca. 280mal)
   8. ***Seele** als Sitz und Träger von Gefühlen und Empfindungen*[150]
      a) Verlangen, Gier; Eifer, Leidenschaft
      b) Stimmung, wie einem zumute ist
      c) Empfinden, Geschmack
      d) Wille
   9. ***Toten-Seele***[151], *Toter, Leichnam*
   10. *Verschiedenes*
      a) *båttê hannæpæš*
      b) *Grabmal* (nicht im AT)

2) D. Clines (ed.), *The Dictionary of Classical Hebrew, Vol. 5* (Sheffield: Sheffield Academic Press, 2001), 724–734 (DCH):
   1. palate, throat, gullet
   2. neck

---

149 Gemeint ist die Anzahl von Personen oder von Vieh bei Zählungen, s. dazu oben 152.
150 Nach HALAT 673 s.v. *næpæš* 8 ist *næpæš* in der Bedeutung „Seele" der „Sitz u.(nd) Träger v.(on) Gefühlen u.(nd) Empfindungen: a) Verlangen, Gier; Eifer, Leidenschaft, b) Stimmung, wie einem zumute ist, c) Empfinden, Geschmack, d) Wille".
151 S. dazu oben 141 f.

3. appetite, hunger, desire, wish
4. **soul**, heart, mind[152]
5. breath, last breath, **soul**[153]
6. life, lives; **soul**[154]; eternal life
7. being, creature(s)
8a. person, individual
8b. persons, people
8c. perh. deceased person, (dead) body
8d. perh. specif. slave
9a. *næpæš* with pronominal suffix, as personal pronoun
9b. as reflexive pronoun, oneself
9c. as possessive pronoun
10. sustenance
11. perfume
12. sepulchre, (funerary) monument

3) W. Gesenius, Hebräisches und Aramäisches Wörterbuch über das Alte Testamen, 18. Aufl., bearbeitet und herausgegeben von H. Donner, 4. Lfg. (Berlin / Heidelberg / New York: Springer, 2007), 833 – 836 (Ges[18]):
1. *Kehle, Gurgel, Rachen*
2. *Hals*
3. *Hauch, Atem*
4. *Gier, Begierde, Verlangen* (nicht immer sicher von 6 zu unterscheiden)
5. *Bezeichnung für das, was Mensch und Tier zu Lebewesen macht:* herkömmlich **Seele** (verschieden von ψυχή, *anima*), auch Leben, Lebenskraft, mit Sitz im Blut[155]
6. *als Träger von Gefühlen, Empfindungen, Affekten:* **Seele**, Gefühl, Gemüt, *animus*[156]

---

152 DCH 725 f s.v. *næpæš* 4 („soul, heart, mind") führt die Belege auf, die *næpæç* „as seat of desire, will, feelings and emotions" meinen, und fügt hinzu, dass der Unterschied zu den Bedeutungsaspekten 3 („appetite, hunger, desire, wish") und 9 („pronominaler Gebrauch) nicht immer klar ist.

153 Nach DCH 728 s.v. *næpæš* 5 ist *næpæš* in der Bedeutung von „breath, last breath, soul" als „inner being" zu verstehen.

154 Nach DCH 728 s.v. *næpæš* 6 ist *næpæš* in der Bedeutung von „life, lives; soul" als „the vital self" zu verstehen; der Unterschied zum Bedeutungsaspekt 9 („pronominaler Gebrauch) ist nicht immer klar.

155 Nach Ges[18] 834 s.v. *næpæš* 5 ist die herkömmliche Übersetzung „Seele" „versch.(ieden) v.(on) ψυχή, *anima*" – eine Begründung wird allerdings nicht gegeben.

156 Nach Ges[18] 835 s.v. *næpæš* 6 ist *næpæš* „Träger v.(on) Gefühlen, Empfindungen, Affekten (vgl. *leb*)" und bedeutet „Seele, Gefühl, Gemüt, *animus*, z. B. Liebe, Sehnsucht, Freude, Wohlgefallen, Frömmigkeit, Verachtung, Betrübnis, Trauer, Verbitterung u. a., auch v.(on) den Äußerungen d.(er)

7. *Person*
   a) Kollektiver Singular vor allem bei Zählungen (vgl. dtsch. **Seelenzahl**[157])
   b) Bezeichnung für Sklaven
   c) Indefinitpronomen: (irgend) jemand
   d) *næpæš met:* „Seele" eines Toten, jem. totes, ein Toter[158]
8. *in Formeln der Selbstaufforderung*
9. *suffigiert als Umschreibung von Pronominalbegriffen*
10. *Gottes eigene næpæš* (alle Stellen überwiegend nach 5,6 und 9 zu übersetzen)

4) H.W. Wolff, Anthropologie des Alten Testaments. Mit zwei Anhängen neu herausgegeben von B. Janowski (Gütersloh: Gütersloher Verlagshaus, [8]2010), 33–55:
   1. Kehle
   2. Hals
   3. Begehren
   4. **Seele**[159]
   5. Leben
   6. Person
   7. Pronomen

5) C. Westermann, "Art. *næpæš*," THAT 1, [5]1995, 71–96:
   1. *Konkrete Grundbedeutung*
      a) Hauch / Atem
      b) Kehle / Schlund
   2. *Gier / Begier / Verlangen*
      a) Hunger
      b) Rachedurst
      c) Begehr / Wunsch / Belieben

Affekte: weinen, segnen; seltener i.(n) b(e)z.(ug) a.(uf) Gesinnung u.(nd) Stimmung: Belieben, Gutdünken, i.(n) b(e)z.(ug) a.(uf) Erkennen, Wissen, Denken".

157 Vgl. oben Anm. 147.

158 S. dazu oben 141 f.

159 Nach Wolff, *Anthropologie* (s. Anm. 8), 43 führt „ein kleiner Schritt … von der *næpæš* als spezifischem Organ und Akt des Begehrens zu der erweiterten Bedeutung, bei der *næpæš* Sitz und Akt auch anderer seelischer Empfindungen und Gemütszustände wird". Dazu zählt Wolff Ex 23,9; Hi 19,2; 30,25 und zahlreiche Psalmen-Belege (Ps 6,3; 42,6 f.12; 43,5 u. a.), in denen mit *næpæš* die „seelische Stimmung" gemeint ist. Auch die Emotionen des Hasses, der Liebe, der Trauer, der Freude, des Jubels, gehören hierher, „wobei noch zu fragen ist, ob in solchen Fällen der Sitz der seelischen Stimmungen und Gemütswallungen noch zusammengesehen wird mit der Kehle als dem Ort vitaler Bedürfnisse und deren Schluchzen, Hecheln und Jauchzen" (ders., aaO 44).

d) negative Aspekte

e) feste Redewendungen

3. *Seele*

a) begehrend

b) hungrig / satt

c) betrübt / freudig[160]

d) hoffend

e) liebend / hassend

f) lebendig

4. *Leben*

a) Rettung / Bewahrung / Erhaltung

b) Bedrohung / Verlust

5. *Lebewesen / Mensch*

a) in Gesetzen

b) bei Zählungen

c) allgemeine Wendungen

d) pronominaler Gebrauch

6. næpæš (met): Leiche

7. Theologischer Gebrauch

a) Gottes *næpæš*

b) Gottes Handeln an der næpæç des Menschen: rettend / segnend / strafend

c) Verhalten der næpæç des Menschen zu Gott

6) H. Seebass, "Art. *næpæš*," ThWAT 5, 1986, 531–555:

1. *Schlund, Rachen, Kehle*

2. *Verlangen, Begehren*

Exkurs: Zur Übersetzung „**Seele**"[161]

---

160 Auch nach Westermann, " *næpæš*" (s. Anm. 8), 79 (unter *næpæš* 3c) ist „erst in der Stellengruppe, die von der *næpæš* Betrübtsein und Kummer (seltener Freudigkeit und Trost) auszusagen weiß, ... die Übersetzung mit ,Seele' entsprechend dem dt. Wortgebrauch eindeutig und in jedem Fall möglich". In der Zusammenfassung zu den Beleggruppen 3c-d wird diese These allerdings noch einmal eingeschränkt: „Die Wiedergabe von *næpæš* mit „Seele" ist „im Dt. zum Teil nur ein Notbehelf ... Nur in 3c-d deckt sich der Sprachgebrauch von dt. ,Seele' und hebr. *næpæš* einigermaßen" (ders., aaO 84). Charakteristisch ist für die unter 3c-d aufgeführten *næpæš*-Belege das „intensive Ausgerichtetsein auf etwas" (ders., ebd.), und zwar in einem mehr passiven (dürsten, darben u.a.) oder in einem mehr aktiven Sinn (hassen, verabscheuen u.a.); ausschlaggebend ist also die „Intensität des Empfindens" (ders., ebd.). Damit stehen die Beleggruppen 3c-d der Beleggruppe 2 („Gier, Begier, Verlangen") nahe.

161 Den Interpretationen von Wolff und Westermann hat sich schließlich Seebass, " *næpæš*" (s. Anm. 8), 543 ff angeschlossen, wobei er gegenüber Westermann „das Ich oder das Selbst, wie vor

3. *das vitale Selbst, Reflexivpronomen*
4. *Individuiertes Leben*
5. *Lebewesen, Person*
6. *næpæš Gottes*

Wie diese Übersicht zeigt, gibt es hinsichtlich der Übersetzung von *næpæš* mit
„Seele" große Übereinstimmungen (die folgenden Zahlenangaben beziehen sich
auf die jeweiligen Bedeutungsebenen in HAL usw.). Sie wird vor allem für *næpæš*
als *Sitz von Gefühlen und Empfindungen* erwogen (HALAT 8 / DCH 4 – 5 / Ges[18] 6 /
Wolff 4 / Westermann 3 / Seebass 2: Exkurs), dabei aber als „Notbehelf" deklariert.
Daneben spielt die traditionelle „*Seelenzahl*" (HALAT 5b / Ges[18] 7a), die herkömmliche Übersetzung „*Seele, auch Leben, Lebenskraft, mit Sitz im Blut*" (DCH 6 /
Ges[18] 5) und die ominöse „*Totenseele*" (Ges[18] 7d) eine Rolle. Zusammenfassend
lässt sich sagen, dass *næpæš* in der Bedeutung „Seele" „über den Bereich emo-
tionaler seelischer Regungen ... nicht hinaus(geht)"[162] und vor allem nicht mit dem
Topos der „Unsterblichkeit der Seele" in eins gesetzt werden darf. Dafür lässt sich
alttestamentlich kein Beleg beibringen.

---

allem in der Poesie gebräuchlich, als das Subj.(ekt) von Kummer, Betrübtsein u. a." (ders., aaO 543)
ansetzt. Zusammenfassend: „So wie *næpæš* nicht einfach ‚Leben' heißt, sondern die Individuation
von Leben meint, als welches es faktisch vorkommt, so bezeichnet *næpæš* nicht die Seele als eine
Nuance u. a., sondern die Seelenkraft, das Sprudeln von Personalität, die alle tristesse bannende
Energie. (...) Nicht allgemein die Seele und nicht bloß der Nahrungsbedarf sind angesprochen,
sondern der ganze Mensch als *næpæš*, als Lebensfreude und Vitalität" (ders., aaO 544 f).
162 Wolff, aaO 44.

Eran Shuali*

Comment le verbe כִּלְכֵּל a-t-il pris le sens de *supporter?* La lexicalisation de l'emploi métaphorique en hébreu ancien

Introduction

Comme son double titre l'indique, cette étude se donne deux objectifs, tous les deux ayant trait au travail du lexicographe des langues anciennes et plus particulièrement de l'hébreu ancien. Sa première tâche proprement lexicographique sera de comprendre quel était le sens d'un mot choisi – en l'occurrence, le verbe hébreu *kilkēl* (כ.ו.ל. *pilpel*) – dans certains textes bibliques et post-bibliques où il apparaît. Sans être une tentative exhaustive de définition, elle se concentrera seulement sur l'un des sens que les lexicographes, les exégètes et les traducteurs donnent parfois à ce verbe, à savoir, le sens de *supporter*, et ainsi elle tentera d'apporter un complément aux travaux lexicographiques qui ont déjà été faits sur ses autres acceptions[1].

Plus précisément, nous verrons que dans la littérature vétéro- et intertestamentaire le verbe כִּלְכֵּל désigne le fait de supporter de deux manières différentes: tantôt ce sont des métaphores jouant sur son sens concret de *contenir* qui lui donnent ce sens, tantôt il l'a par lui-même. De plus, nous remarquerons que les textes dans lesquels on trouve chacun de ces deux types de désignation se distinguent par l'époque dont ils émanent: dans la plupart des textes plus anciens il est assez clair que le verbe garde son sens concret et ne désigne le fait de supporter que par le biais d'une métaphore, alors que dans les textes plus tardifs il semble le signifier littéralement. Ces observations nous amèneront donc à supposer que cette signification qui avait été d'abord attribuée

---

* Je remercie Jan Joosten, Christophe Rico, Nanine Charbonnel, Leonid Kogan et Abraham Tal pour leurs remarques sur cet article.

1 Ce verbe a été étudié par A. Baumann dans son article sur la racine «כול – *kwl*,» *TDOT* 7:85–89; et par Alexander Rofé dans «A Neglected Meaning of the Verb כול and the Text of 1QS VI:11–13,» in Michael Fishbane and Emanuel Tov, eds., *Sha'arei Talmon: Studies in the Bible, Qumran, and the Ancient Near East Presented to Shemaryahu Talmon* (Winona Lake: Eisenbrauns, 1992), 315–321. Rofé affirme explicitement ne pas être concerné dans son article par le développement sémantique qui a donné au verbe le sens de supporter aussi bien que d'autres sens dérivés (*ibid*, 319), tandis que l'analyse des emplois figuratifs du verbe faite par Baumann reste sommaire (A. Baumann, «*kwl*,» 88–89).

au verbe dans le contexte de certaines métaphores, a été, par la suite, pleinement lexicalisée étant conçue dorénavant comme un sens propre du verbe.

Une analyse plus détaillée de la plupart des occurrences du verbe confirmera cette hypothèse en montrant que même quelques emplois plus anciens du verbe qui ne paraissent pas forcément figuratifs au premier abord, devraient bien être compris comme tels en vue des contextes littéraires immédiats ou plus larges qui sont les leurs. Ainsi, après avoir examiné l'ensemble des passages où כִּלְכֵּל semble signifier *supporter* et avoir déterminé dans lesquels ceci constituait son sens littéral et dans lesquels il ne l'était pas encore, nous pourrons estimer à quelle époque s'est produite la lexicalisation de cette valeur du verbe[2].

Finalement, ayant décrit et délimité les deux temps de ce déplacement de sens qui sont attestés dans les sources à notre disposition, nous essayerons de comprendre comment celui-ci a eu lieu. Dans cette perspective, sera avancé l'argument que les auteurs qui ont fait un usage métaphorique du verbe et ceux qui l'ont employé littéralement l'avaient connu différemment, et que c'est aux origines et aux natures différentes de leurs connaissances du verbe que sont dues leurs compréhensions dissemblables de son sens. Tandis que pour les premiers, des métaphores employant le verbe constituaient un moyen conventionnel d'expression dans un contexte précis, les derniers connaissaient ce verbe principalement, comme il sera montré, à travers les textes dans lesquels ils puisaient des expressions sans toujours faire attention à toutes leurs nuances. Nous verrons donc que la volonté d'employer un vocable considéré comme classique dans des circonstances linguistiques différentes, était à l'origine de l'évolution sémantique qu'il a connue.

En tout dernier lieu, cette hypothèse sur le processus de lexicalisation de l'emploi métaphorique du verbe examiné servira pour faire des observations plus générales sur ce processus, pertinentes peut-être aussi pour d'autres cas de ce phénomène linguistique fort fréquent[3]. Plus précisément, elles chercheront à

---

2 «If we are to interpret accurately biblical texts written over a period of many centuries, it is obviously important to be able to tell when semantic change has occurred, but it may sometimes be equally important to establish that it has not.» George Bradford Caird, *The Language and Imagery of the Bible* (London: Duckworth, 1980), 79. Et aussi: «(...) we must also take into account the consensus that at a given point in time surrounds a word's meaning.» Kirsten Nielsen, *There is Hope for a Tree: The Tree as metaphor in Isaiah*, Journal for the Study of the Old Testament Supplement Series 65 (Sheffield: Sheffield Academic Press, 1989), 64.

3 Une vision sans doute radicale sur la fréquence de ce phénomène est exprimée par Nietzsche dans un paragraphe qui a souvent été cité à ce propos: «Qu'est-ce donc que la vérité ? Une multitude mouvante de métaphores, de métonymies, d'anthropomorphismes, bref, une somme de relations humaines qui ont été poétiquement et rhétoriquement haussées, transposées, ornées, et qui, après un long usage, semblent à un peuple fermes, canoniales et contraignantes:

définir dans quelles circonstances et par quels types d'usage des métaphores peuvent devenir des expressions littérales. Ainsi, ces observations pourraient éclairer un point obscur des théories sur l'évolution des métaphores, qui décrivent en détail les différents degrés de banalisation que les expressions métaphoriques connaissent avant de devenir littérales[4], mais ne montrent pas par quels mécanismes peut avoir lieu le passage d'un degré de littéralité à un degré supérieur[5]. Et quant au lexicographe des langues anciennes qui travaille sur une expression ayant connu une évolution semblable, ces observations, qui sont le second objectif de cette étude, pourraient peut-être lui rendre service dans la tâche de distinguer les usages métaphoriques propres à une expression qui l'intéresse de ses emplois déjà littéraux, et ainsi aider les lecteurs de textes

---

les vérités sont des illusions dont on a oublié qu'elles le sont, des métaphores qui ont été usées et qui ont perdu leur force sensible, des pièces de monnaie qui ont perdu leur empreinte et qui entrent dès lors en considération, non plus comme pièces de monnaie mais comme métal.» Friedrich W. Nietzsche, «Introduction théorétique sur la vérité et le mensonge au sens extramoral,» I, in *Le livre du philosophe*, trad. Angèle Kremer-Marietti ([Paris:] Aubier-Flammarion, 1969), 181–183; voir aussi pp. 179, 185, 189–191, 195, 207. Voir une présentation des positions semblables chez d'autres auteurs et une mise en garde contre certaines conclusions qu'ils en tirent dans Janet Martin Soskice, *Metaphor and Religious Language* (Oxford: Clarendon, 1989), 78–83.

4 La conception la plus répandue de l'évolution des métaphores distingue dans ce processus trois étapes possibles: celle de la métaphore vivante, celle de la métaphore usée – à laquelle Charles Bally donne le nom évocateur d'*image affective*, c'est-à-dire, une image qui est sentie comme telle mais ne se présente pas à l'esprit – et celle de la métaphore morte. Voir par exemple Charles Bally, *Traité de stylistique française* (Heidelberg: C. Winter; Paris: Klincksieck, 1909), 1:193–196; Michel Le Guern, *Sémantique de la métaphore et de la métonymie* (Paris: Larousse, 1973), 82–89; et un ouvrage dédié au langage figuratif dans la Bible, George Bradford Caird, *The Language and Imagery of the Bible*, 66. En revanche, dans son livre *The Centrality of Metaphors to Biblical Thought: A Method for Interpreting the Bible* (Lewiston, NY: E. Mellen Press, 1990), 72–80, Peter W. Macky, propose un schème plus nuancé comportant cinq catégories nommées: *novel metaphors, familiar metaphors, standard metaphors, hidden metaphors* et *retired metaphors*. Pour une présentation récente des principaux travaux sur les métaphores à la fois en linguistique générale et en études bibliques, voir Martin G. Klingbeil, «Metaphors that Travel and (almost) Vanish: Mapping Diachronic Changes in the Intertextual Usage of the Heavenly Warrior Metaphor in Psalms 18 and 144,» in Pierre Van Hecke and Antje Labahn, eds., *Metaphors in the Psalms* (Leuven: Uitgeverij Peeters, 2010), 115–119.

5 Un tel mécanisme est expliqué par Le Guern dans sa présentation du processus de la lexicalisation du mot latin *testa* – le nom d'un petit pot de terre cuite, qui en Gaule a été utilisé métaphoriquement et sans doute humoristiquement pour désigner la tête d'homme, et dont est dérivé en français le mot concret pour désigner cette même partie du corps. Il y écrit: «il y a tout lieu de penser que le petit pot appelé testa était sinon inconnu, du moins très rare en Gaule à l'époque de la colonisation romaine; c'est la rareté des emplois du sens propre qui fait oublier cette valeur quand l'emploi du sens figuré est fréquent.» Michel Le Guern, *Sémantique*, 87.

anciens à comprendre avec plus de précision la pensée de leurs auteurs et la constitution de leurs univers conceptuels.

Nous commencerons par une présentation du verbe כִּלְכֵּל et de ses significations, suite à laquelle seront examinés successivement ses emplois métaphoriques évidents et ses emplois au sein d'énoncés métaphoriques plus difficiles à reconnaître comme tels. Et en dernier lieu, nous procéderons à l'analyse des occurrences où le verbe signifie *supporter* littéralement.

I. Les sens littéraux de כִּלְכֵּל

Il est bien connu que dans son acception la plus courante en hébreu biblique, le verbe כִּלְכֵּל désigne le fait de *subvenir aux besoins de* quelqu'un en général[6], ou plus particulièrement, de subvenir à ses besoins alimentaires[7]. En effet, ce sens semble être clairement attribué au verbe en quatorze de ses vingt-quatre occurrences dans le canon hébraïque de l'Ancien Testament. À celles-ci il faudrait ajouter deux des quatre occurrences du verbe dans les manuscrits hébreux du livre de Ben Sira parvenus jusqu'à nous[8], et au moins trois de ses onze occurrences dans les manuscrits de la Mer Morte[9]. Or, malgré sa fréquence, cette signification ne semble pas être le sens premier du verbe, mais un sens qui en dérive[10] – sans doute un emploi métaphorique lexicalisé. Et bien que nous ne soyons pas en mesure d'indiquer avec certitude quelle est la métaphore qui a pu octroyer au verbe cette signification précise et qui était déjà entièrement effacée au moment de la rédaction des livres les plus anciens de l'Ancien Testament, nous pouvons l'imaginer vu le sens originel du verbe, à savoir, le sens de *contenir*. *Contenir quelqu'un*, peut-être au sens de *l'accueillir chez soi*, signifiait donc métaphoriquement lui fournir ce dont il avait besoin pour subsister[11].

En effet, en quatre versets de l'Ancien Testament, le verbe כִּלְכֵּל désigne manifestement le fait de contenir quelque chose, en insistant, comme l'a

---

6 Gn 50:21; Rt 4:15; 2 S 19:33, 34; 20:3; 1 R 4:7 (cf. 1 R 5:7); Ne 9:21.

7 Gn 45:11; 47:12; 1 R 5:7; 17:4, 9; 18:4, 13.

8 Si 25:22 (manuscrit C); Si 45:24 (manuscrit B).

9 1QS III,17; 1Qh[a] XVII, 34 et 36, et peut-être 4Q405 18,2. Certaines phrases comportant le verbe sont trop fragmentaires pour que l'on puisse y déterminer son sens.

10 Voir Alexander Rofé, «A Neglected Meaning,» 319; A. Baumann, «kwl,» 87.

11 Le verbe akkadien *Kullu* qui est apparenté à כִּלְכֵּל, a connu une évolution semblable: signifiant premièrement *tenir*, l'on trouve parmi ses nombreux sens dérivés celui de *fournir*; voir *CAD*, 8:508–518. Je remercie Leonid Kogan pour avoir attiré mon attention sur la ressemblance de l'histoire du verbe akkadien avec celle du verbe hébreu.

remarqué Alexander Rofé, sur le fait que rien ne déborde[12]. Ainsi, dans le discours de Salomon au moment de l'inauguration du Temple, dont l'un des messages principaux est que ce n'est pas Dieu lui-même qui réside dans le Temple, mais seulement son nom qui s'y trouve[13], l'auteur met dans la bouche du roi le propos suivant:

כִּי הַאֻמְנָם יֵשֵׁב אֱלֹהִים עַל־הָאָרֶץ
הִנֵּה הַשָּׁמַיִם וּשְׁמֵי הַשָּׁמַיִם לֹא יְכַלְכְּלוּךָ
אַף כִּי־הַבַּיִת הַזֶּה אֲשֶׁר בָּנִיתִי:

Est-ce que vraiment Dieu pourrait habiter sur la terre ?
Les cieux eux-mêmes et les cieux des cieux *ne peuvent te contenir!*
Combien moins cette maison que j'ai bâtie! (1 R 8:27)[14]

Salomon avance donc l'argument que même le ciel immense n'étant pas suffisamment grand pour contenir Dieu tout entier, il est évident qu'un bâtiment de dimensions humaines ne pourra aucunement être commensurable avec Lui. Et cette même affirmation est reprise dans le passage parallèle du livre des Chroniques (2 Ch 6:18), aussi bien que précédemment dans le même livre, au moment du recrutement des ouvriers et de l'achat des matériaux pour la construction du Temple (2 Ch 2:5). Dans ce passage des Chroniques, il est intéressant de constater que l'affirmation exerce une autre fonction argumentative: elle semble être la raison pour laquelle le Temple de Jérusalem doit être de grandes dimensions. Puisque le Dieu d'Israël est plus grand que tous les autres dieux, si grand que le ciel tout entier ne peut le contenir – dit l'auteur des

---

12 En analysant Jr 2:13, Rofé souligne que la description des citernes comme fêlées, que l'on trouve dans ce verset, ne fait pas référence à leur capacité de *contenir* l'eau, mais à leur imperméabilité. Voir Alexander Rofé, «A Neglected Meaning,» 315–316.

13 Cela me semble être le fil conducteur du discours (1 R 8:14–53). En effet, il est précisé sept fois au cours du passage que la *maison* a été bâtie pour le *nom* de YHWH (16, 17, 18, 19, 20, 44), en accord avec la prophétie prononcée par Nathan à David (2 S 7:13), à laquelle Salomon fait explicitement référence (1 R 8:15–20, 24–26). De plus, le Temple est désigné comme le lieu dont YHWH a dit «Ici sera mon nom» (29), tandis que le ciel est appelé à trois reprises le *lieu de la demeure* de YHWH (30, 43, 49). Cette distinction est particulièrement centrale dans la description fonctionnelle de la prière adressée au Temple (29, 30, 35, 38, 42, 44, 48) ou faite dans le Temple (33). D'après les paroles de Salomon, YHWH veille sur le Temple (29) de son demeure céleste, d'où il écoutera et exaucera (וְאַתָּה תִּשְׁמַע הַשָּׁמַיִם – 32, 34, 36, 39, 43; וְשָׁמַעְתָּ הַשָּׁמַיִם – 45, 49) les prières qui seront adressées au Temple en des situations diverses. Il me semble significatif que contrairement aux Israélites qui étendront dorénavant leurs mains vers le Temple en priant (38), Salomon lui-même, qui n'a apparemment pas besoin de la médiation du Temple, étende ses mains au cours de cette prière directement vers le ciel (22, 54).

14 Traduction française de la *TOB*.

Chroniques en étoffant le texte du livre des Rois[15] – le Temple lui aussi doit être grand[16].

Un autre emploi de כִּלְכֵּל au sens de *contenir*, qui est indépendant des trois occurrences que nous venons d'étudier, se trouve en Jr 20:9. C'est dans un passage poétique que Jérémie raconte comment la parole de Dieu qu'il avait été séduit de recevoir faisait de lui un sujet de ridicule, si bien qu'il a résolu de ne plus la proclamer – une démarche qui était pourtant destinée à l'échec (Jr 20:7–9). Et c'est ainsi qu'il décrit cette tentative de taire la prophétie:

וְאָמַרְתִּי לֹא־אֶזְכְּרֶנּוּ וְלֹא־אֲדַבֵּר עוֹד בִּשְׁמוֹ
וְהָיָה בְלִבִּי כְּאֵשׁ בֹּעֶרֶת עָצֻר בְּעַצְמֹתָי
וְנִלְאֵיתִי כַּלְכֵל וְלֹא אוּכָל:

Je me disais: Je ne penserai plus à lui, je ne parlerai plus en son Nom;
mais c'était en mon cœur comme un feu dévorant, enfermé dans mes os.
Je m'épuisais à le contenir, mais ne n'ai pas pu. (Jr 20:9)[17]

La parole divine semble être présentée ici comme un liquide brûlant, telle la lave volcanique, qui coulait à l'intérieur du prophète cherchant à jaillir de sa bouche sans qu'il puisse l'en empêcher[18].

Une indication supplémentaire quant à la signification du verbe כִּלְכֵּל dans ce dernier verset, est le fait que ce verset trouve un parallèle proche, et par sa formulation et par son imagerie, qui emploie le verbe הֵכִיל (כ.ו.ל. Hiphil). Ce verbe, analysé par la plupart des grammairiens comme relevant de la même racine que כִּלְכֵּל, désigne le fait de contenir non seulement dans le cadre de telles métaphores, mais aussi dans des contextes concrets et donc plus clairs le fait de contenir. Par exemple, les cuves fabriquées pour le palais de Salomon sont décrites ainsi:

וַיַּעַשׂ עֲשָׂרָה כִיֹרוֹת נְחֹשֶׁת
אַרְבָּעִים בַּת יָכִיל הַכִּיּוֹר הָאֶחָד

Il fit dix cuves de bronze. Chaque cuve *pouvait contenir* quarante baths (1 R 7:38)[19].

---

15 1 R 5:15–20.
16 2 Ch 2:4.
17 Traduction française de *La Bible de Jérusalem*.
18 La colère divine est présentée comme du liquide brûlant à plusieurs autres endroits: Es 42:25; Jr 7:20; 44:6; Ez 21:36; 22:20, 22, 31; Ne 1:6; So 3:8; Lm 2:4; 4:11; 2 Ch 34:25. Pour une analyse de ce verset voir aussi Alexander Rofé, «A Neglected Meaning,» 316.
19 Traduction française de la *TOB*.

Et de même, Jérémie compare le Dieu d'Israël délaissé par son peuple et les dieux païens qu'ils se sont mis à adorer, à des masses d'eau de nature différente:

כִּי־שְׁתַּיִם רָעוֹת עָשָׂה עַמִּי
אֹתִי עָזְבוּ מְקוֹר מַיִם חַיִּים
לַחְצֹב לָהֶם בֹּארוֹת
בֹּארֹת נִשְׁבָּרִים אֲשֶׁר לֹא־יָכִלוּ הַמָּיִם:

Car mon peuple a commis un double péché:
ils m'ont abandonné, moi qui suis une source d'eau vive,
pour se creuser des citernes,
des citernes crevassées, qui *ne retiennent pas* l'eau. (Jr 2:13)[20].

Dans les deux cas, l'emploi du verbe pour décrire des récipients de liquides ne laisse pas de doute quant à sa signification.

Et en effet, nous pouvons rapprocher Jr 20:9 de l'affirmation suivante du même prophète:

וְאֵת חֲמַת יְהוָה מָלֵאתִי
נִלְאֵיתִי הָכִיל
שְׁפֹךְ עַל־עוֹלָל בַּחוּץ
וְעַל סוֹד בַּחוּרִים יַחְדָּו

Je suis rempli de la colère de Yahvé,
je suis las de la *contenir!*
Déverse-la donc sur l'enfant dans la rue,
et aussi sur les réunions des jeunes gens. (Jr 6:11)[21].

La ressemblance entre les deux affirmations saute aux yeux. Dans les deux, les verbes כַּלְכֵּל et הָכִיל à l'infinitif absolu suivent le verbe נִלְאֵיתִי – je m'épuisais à / je suis las de. Et dans les deux, abstraction faite de quelques nuances, l'image est similaire: une substance divine placée à l'intérieur du prophète se répand en dehors de lui malgré tous ses efforts pour la retenir à l'intérieur. Il semble donc judicieux d'en conclure que l'auteur de Jérémie considérait les deux verbes comme des synonymes ou tout au moins des quasi-synonymes, car il n'est pas aisé de discerner la nuance sémantique qui a pu lui faire préférer l'un à l'autre dans chacun des deux passages[22].

---

20 Traduction française de Louis Segond. Voir l'analyse d'Alexander Rofé mentionnée précédemment en note 12.

21 Traduction française de *La Bible de Jérusalem*.

22 Il existe d'autres verbes quadrilitères qui ne diffèrent sémantiquement que guère des verbes trilitères dont ils dérivent, par exemple: פָּצַץ – פִּצְפֵּץ, גָּלַל – גִּלְגֵּל. Voir à ce sujet Igal Yannay, «Augmented Verbs in Biblical Hebrew,» in *Hebrew Union College Annual* 45 (1974), 74–75. Pour

II. Les emplois métaphoriques

Comme le montrent les exemples parcourus jusqu'à présent, les verbes הֵכִיל et כִּלְכֵּל sont employés dans l'Ancien Testament le plus souvent non pas pour désigner des réalités concrètes, mais dans la représentation des images à portée métaphorique, particulièrement celles des choses divines. En fait, cinq seulement des douze occurrences du verbe au *hiphil* décrivent des objets tangibles, et sans doute il ne faudrait en compter que trois, puisque deux de ces occurrences constituent des réécritures plutôt fidèles des versets du livre des Rois faites par l'auteur des Chroniques[23]. Et le verbe au *pilpel*, pour sa part, n'est jamais employé dans un contexte concret.

Hormis les énoncés métaphoriques employant הֵכִיל ou כִּלְכֵּל et étudiés ci-dessus[24], il faudrait faire mention de quelques autres images au sein desquelles apparaît le verbe au *Hiphil*. Ainsi, au cœur d'un long passage allégorique qui présente Jérusalem et Samarie comme deux sœurs qui sont des «filles perdues»[25], le prophète Ézéchiel prononce la phrase suivante:

כּוֹס אֲחוֹתֵךְ תִּשְׁתִּי
הָעֲמֻקָה וְהָרְחָבָה
תִּהְיֶה לִצְחֹק וּלְלַעַג
מִרְבָּה לְהָכִיל:

La coupe de ta sœur, tu la boiras;
elle est profonde, elle est large.
Elle sera l'occasion de rire et de moquerie,
à cause de sa grande *contenance*. (Ez 23:32)[26]

---

une explication de l'étymologie du sens premier des verbes au *Pilpel* et au *Hiphil*, qui sont probablement dérivés du verbe au *Qal* – כָּל attesté en Es 40:12 aussi bien que dans un ostracon trouvé à Yavneh-Yam et dans le calendrier de Gézer, voir Alexander Rofé, «A Neglected Meaning,» 318.

23 1 R 7:26 = 2 Ch 4:5, 1 R 7:38; 1 R 8:64 = 2 Ch 7:7.

24 1 R 8:27; Jr 6:11; 20:9; 2 Ch 2:5; 6:18.

25 La clé de l'allégorie qui s'étale tout au long du chapitre 23 du livre d'Ézéchiel, est explicitement donnée au verset 4: וּשְׁמוֹתָן שֹׁמְרוֹן אָהֳלָה וִירוּשָׁלַם אָהֳלִיבָה. Même si la *BHS* a raison de dire que cette identification aussi bien que celle de l'une des sœurs avec Samarie au verset 33, sont des additions postérieures (voir *ad locos*), le récit qui fait passer en Égypte les premiers actes de prostitution commis par les sœurs et qui fait venir leurs amants d'Assyrie et de Babylone, semble quand même censé d'être une allégorie facilement interprétable pour ses lecteurs.

26 Traduction française de la *TOB*.

La compréhension du verset tel qu'on le trouve dans le texte massorétique n'est pas aisée, mais sa traduction grecque semble permettre de reconstruire un texte à la fois plus ancien et plus cohérent. La voici:

τὸ ποτήριον τῆς ἀδελφῆς σου πίεσαι
τὸ βαθὺ καὶ τὸ πλατὺ
τὸ πλεονάζον τοῦ συντελέσαι

La coupe de ta sœur, tu [la] boiras,
[la coupe qui est] profonde et large,
abondante d'achever.

Cette version dont la fin peu intelligible semble refléter une technique de traduction très littérale, laisse donc transparaître la *Vorlage* que les traducteurs avaient probablement sous les yeux. Nous pouvons supposer que les mots: תִּהְיֶה לִצְחֹק וּלְלַעַג – *elle sera l'occasion de rire et de moquerie*, absents dans la Septante, sont une addition tardive destinée à expliciter l'image, et que le vocable מרבה est, en réalité, un participe féminin du verbe הִרְבָּה (ר.ב.ה. *hiphil*) décrivant *la coupe* comme il a été traduit par les Septante, et doit donc être vocalisé מַרְבָּה. La *Vorlage* reconstruite devrait donc se lire ainsi:

כּוֹס אֲחוֹתֵךְ תִּשְׁתִּי
הָעֲמֻקָה וְהָרְחָבָה
מַרְבָּה לְהָכִיל:[27]

La coupe de ta sœur, tu [la] boiras
[la coupe qui est] profonde et large
[et qui] *contient* beaucoup.

Il est clair que cette coupe ne *contient* pas concrètement de liquide, mais métaphoriquement une grande quantité de malheurs[28].

Un autre usage métaphorique du verbe הֵכִיל, qui est particulièrement important pour la suite de notre propos, se rencontre à la fin d'une prophétie de Joël annonçant le jour de YHWH[29]. Le prophète y dit:

---

27 Voir BHS, *ad locum*.
28 Dans la plupart de ses emplois métaphoriques dans l'Ancien Testament, *la coupe* symbolise le mauvais sort induit par la colère divine: Es 51:17, 22; Jr 25:15, 17, 28; 49:12; Ha 2:16; Ps 11:6; 75:9; Lm 4:21. Seulement en trois occurrences dans les Psaumes, elle semble être une métaphore d'un sort bon: Ps 16:5; 23:5(?);116:13. Comparez aussi à Mt 26:39; Mc 14:36; Lc 22:42.
29 Jl 2:1–11.

וַיהוָה נָתַן קוֹלוֹ לִפְנֵי חֵילוֹ
כִּי רַב מְאֹד מַחֲנֵהוּ
כִּי עָצוּם עֹשֵׂה דְבָרוֹ
כִּי־גָדוֹל יוֹם־יְהוָה וְנוֹרָא מְאֹד
וּמִי יְכִילֶנּוּ:

(...) le Seigneur donne de la voix à la tête de son armée.
Ses bataillons sont très nombreux,
puissant est l'exécuteur de sa parole.
Grand est le jour du Seigneur, redoutable à l'extrême;
qui *peut le supporter?* (Jl 2:11)[30].

Le caractère métaphorique de l'emploi du verbe הָכִיל dans ce verset ne saute peut-être pas aux yeux lors d'une lecture rapide du verset isolé de son contexte, et en effet il ne semble pas être reflété dans la plupart de ses traductions tant anciennes que modernes, dont celle de la *TOB* qui est citée ci-dessus. Depuis la Vulgate, il est de coutume de traduire la question rhétorique par laquelle se termine cette prophétie de Joël, en employant une expression non-métaphorique, telle que le verbe *supporter* en français, qui rend pourtant bien la signification globale de cette proposition[31]. Or, quand on porte son attention sur l'imagerie utilisée par Joël tout au cours de cette prophétie, il semble bien plus probable que le verbe figure ici au sein d'une métaphore consciemment faite qui joue sur son sens littéral de *contenir*.

En effet, dans tout ce passage les événements du jour de YHWH sont décrits comme l'invasion d'une armée caractérisée notamment par sa *grandeur*, tant par le nombre des soldats que par leur puissance. Ainsi, la bande des exécuteurs du jour de YHWH est décrite comme *un peuple nombreux* (רַב) *et puissant* (וְעָצוּם), *tel qu'on n'en a jamais vu, tel qu'après lui il n'y en aura plus jamais, jusqu'aux années des générations les plus lointaines*; et un peu plus loin, *comme un peuple puissant* (עָצוּם) *rangé en bataille*[32]. On remarquera que non seulement l'adjectif רַב traduit par la *TOB* par *nombreux* invoque la grandeur, mais aussi le participe passif עָצוּם qui désigne une chose grande soit au sens propre soit par sa force[33]. De plus, il est précisé qu'en s'avançant vers les villes nul des envoyés de YHWH *ne bouscule*

---

30 Traduction française de la *TOB*.
31 Le verbe est traduit ainsi par la Vulgate et le Targoum Jonathan, ainsi que par la *TOB*, Louis Segond, *La Bible de Jérusalem*, Émile Osty, *The King James Bible, The English Standard Version, The New International Version* et Martin Luther.
32 Jl 2:2, 5; traduction française de la *TOB*.
33 Voir *DCH* 6:532.

son voisin, chacun va son chemin[34] – une image qui semble impliquer que les rangs seront serrés, et donc les soldats nombreux.

L'imagerie de la grandeur est aussi très présente dans le dernier verset de cette prophétie, qui est celui qui nous intéresse: les bataillons (מַחֲנֶה, littéralement le *camp*) de YHWH sont dits *très nombreux*; *l'exécuteur de sa parole* est qualifié de עָצוּם; et *le jour de YHWH* est caractérisé comme étant lui-même *grand* (גָדוֹל). Et si l'on comprend le verbe הֵכִיל littéralement, comme signifiant *contenir*, la question clôturant la prophétie semble elle aussi cohérente avec cette même imagerie. En effet, à la fin de cette description du jour grandement terrible qui est à venir, le prophète se tourne vers ses auditeurs comme pour leur demander qui parmi eux est de taille à *contenir* en lui les événements de ce jour vu leur immensité effarante.

À cette analyse littéraire du texte, nous pouvons aussi ajouter un témoignage ancien qui confirme la conclusion sur la signification du verbe הֵכִיל dans ce verset. En effet, au moins une traduction ancienne semble avoir interprété le verbe littéralement. Il s'agit de la Septante qui a rendu les derniers mots du verset par: καὶ τίς ἔσται ἱκανὸς αὐτῇ; – *et qui est suffisant pour lui?* et a conservé ainsi l'effet métaphorique de l'emploi du verbe הֵכִיל[35].

---

34 Jl 2:8; traduction française de *La Bible de Jérusalem*.

35 Une autre occurrence du verbe au *Hiphil* où l'on lui donne souvent le sens de *supporter* se trouve en Am 7:10 [c'est le cas dans la Septante, la Vulgate, le Targoum Jonathan et toutes les traductions modernes que j'ai consultées; voir la liste en note 31]. Ce verset fait partie d'un rare passage narratif qui interrompt la chaîne prophétique du livre et relate un incident conflictuel entre le prophète et un prêtre de la ville de Beth-El nommé Amatsia. Le passage se compose de deux parties: un message envoyé au roi du royaume du nord, Jéroboam II, par ledit Amatsia au sujet d'Amos, et un échange verbal entre le prophète et le prêtre. Le message au roi commence par les affirmations suivantes:

קָשַׁר עָלֶיךָ עָמוֹס בְּקֶרֶב בֵּית יִשְׂרָאֵל
לֹא־תוּכַל הָאָרֶץ לְהָכִיל אֶת־כָּל־דְּבָרָיו

Et ceci est traduit par Louis Segond ainsi:
Amos conspire contre toi au milieu de la maison d'Israël;
le pays ne peut *supporter* toutes ses paroles.

Or, en comparant l'argument d'Amatsia dans ce message aux paroles qu'il adresse par la suite directement à Amos, l'objectif de la démarche d'Amatsia se trouve éclairé ainsi que la signification précise du verbe הֵכִיל dans sa bouche. En effet, face à face avec Amos, Amatsia l'incite à partir en exil au royaume de Juda [vs. 12], et il justifie sa revendication en évoquant les mêmes faits qu'il a mentionnés dans son message au roi qui était destiné à mettre le prophète en cause, à savoir qu'Amos avait prophétisé spécifiquement contre le roi lui-même et plus généralement contre la souveraineté du royaume du nord [11 et 13]. À la lumière de cette demande explicite, on peut mieux comprendre ce qu'Amatsia voulait sans doute suggérer prudemment au roi de faire. Disant que le royaume ne pouvait *contenir* les paroles d'Amos, il

Quelques remarques générales peuvent être faites sur les emplois manifestement métaphoriques des verbes כִּלְכֵּל et הֵכִיל. D'abord, nous constatons que
dans toutes les métaphores où figure l'un des deux verbes, son objet est divin,
c'est-à-dire, ce qui est contenu, ou beaucoup plus souvent, ce qui ne peut pas
être contenu, c'est Dieu lui-même, sa colère, des actions faites par Lui ou, dans
un seul cas, les bienfaits divins considérés abstraitement et indépendamment du
Dieu d'Israël[36]. Quant à ce qu'elles semblent vouloir dire[37], nous remarquons que
toutes ces métaphores accentuent la grandeur de Dieu, surtout par rapport à la
petitesse de l'homme. De plus, à part la métaphore de 1 R 8:27 qui est reprise
deux fois dans les Chroniques, il semble que toutes les métaphores décrivent,
plus particulièrement, la grandeur de la colère de Dieu ainsi que celle de ses
effets, tels que la parole menaçante mise dans la bouche de Jérémie, le
malheureux sort infligé à Samarie, ainsi que les événements du jour de YHWH
tel qu'il est décrit dans le livre de Joël. Et ces métaphores, cela ne peut pas passer
inaperçu, se trouvent toutes dans le corpus prophétique.

Les métaphores employant les verbes כִּלְכֵּל et הֵכִיל ne se ressemblent donc
pas seulement sur le plan rhétorique, en raison du choix similaire de vocabulaire
et d'imagerie qui y a été fait; elles se ressemblent également, nous venons de le
voir, sur le plan thématique. Et ces ressemblances, aussi bien que la concen-

---

semble vouloir dire que le royaume ne pouvait laisser agir dans son territoire un homme qui
avait prononcé de telles paroles et qui envisageait sans doute de continuer à le faire. Son
affirmation devrait donc être comprise comme une métonymie dans laquelle les paroles
renvoient à celui qui les a prononcées. Ainsi, si l'on donne au verbe son sens littéral, le seul qui
est attesté par ailleurs à l'époque de la rédaction du passage en question [celle du prophète ou
de ses disciples, à savoir, le VIIIe siècle; voir Tchavdar S. Hadjiev, *The Composition and Redaction
of the Book of Amos* (Berlin: Walter de Gruyter, 2009), 78–88], la phrase où il figure semble
parfaitement intelligible et l'ensemble de ce court passage trouve plus de cohérence.

36 C'est le cas de Jr 2:13. Voir la remarque suivante concernant l'emploi de langage
métaphorique au sujet de Dieu dans la Bible: «Were it not for metaphor, argue many scolars,
little, if anything, could be said regarding God. (...) [Another] approach manitains that since God
cannot be understood directly, we can only speak of him indirectly. Thus, according to this
theory, it is also our cognitive condition that necessitates speech via metaphorical images. Put
differently: were it not for metaphor, God would remain an ineffable subject, perhaps altogether
unthinkable.» David H. Aaron, *Biblical Ambiguities: Metaphor, Semantics, and Divine Imagery* (2d
edition; Boston, Leiden: Brill, 2002), 9-11.

37 «I. A. Richards propose d'appeler «teneur» (*tenor*) l'idée sous-jacente, et «véhicule» (*vehicle*)
l'idée sous le signe de laquelle la première est appréhendée.» Paul Ricœur, *La métaphore vive*
(Paris: Éditions du Seuil, 1975), 105. Ricœur, pour sa part, propose les termes français de *thème*
et de *phore* comme traductions des termes de Richards. Voir aussi le terme d'*intenté* qu'il emploie
d'après Émile Benveniste; *ibid*, 93.

tration de ces métaphores surtout dans un seul type de littérature, semblent suggérer que dans ce type de littérature elles constituaient ce que l'on appellera d'après Peter Macky des *métaphores habituelles*. En effet, Macky donne le nom de *Familiar Metaphors* à des métaphores qui ne sont pas innovantes et donc inattendues et frappantes, mais qui ne sont pas non plus ce qu'il appelle des *métaphores standard* pour lesquelles il existe une interprétation figée connue par tous. Les lecteurs reconnaissent ces métaphores facilement comme telles puisqu'elles leur sont déjà familières, mais ils doivent toujours les examiner par l'imagination afin de comprendre ce que l'auteur voulait y dire. Macky constate, en outre, que des métaphores de ce genre sont très fréquentes dans la Bible[38].

Or, malgré les ressemblances entre les différentes métaphores que nous avons examinées en ce qui concerne le vocabulaire employé, l'imagerie et la thématique, nous constatons que, hormis les réécritures que l'on trouve dans les Chroniques, ces métaphores ne sont ni citations ni paraphrases les unes des autres, mais des compositions sans doute originales. Et le fait que ces images semblables exprimées par les mêmes mots apparaissent sans interdépendance directe sous la plume de différents auteurs lorsqu'ils abordaient les mêmes thèmes, peut être dû à la nature même des conceptions sous-jacentes à ces thèmes. En effet, il y a dans différents écrits de l'Ancien Testament de nombreuses indications qui suggèrent que les notions mêmes de Dieu et de la colère de Dieu étaient, pour employer le terme de George Lakoff et Mark Johnson, métaphoriquement structurés[39]. Dieu semble avoir été conçu, parmi bien d'autres manières, à travers la métaphore: *Dieu est grand*[40], et sa colère à travers la métaphore: *la colère de Dieu est un liquide*[41]. Et le fait donc que ces

---

38 Peter W. Macky, *The Centrality of Metaphors*, 75–76.

39 George Lakoff and Mark Johnson, *Metaphors We Live By* (Chicago & London: The University of Chicago Press, 1980); traduction française: *Les métaphores de la vie quotidienne*, trad. Michel de Fornel, (Paris: Les Éditions de Minuit, 1985).

40 Cette conception se reflète, par exemple, dans les nombreuses phrases attribuant à Dieu l'adjectif *grand* pour décrire autre chose que la grandeur spatiale. Dans des expressions telles que: «(...) le Dieu grand, puissant et redoutable, l'impartial et l'incorruptible» [Dt 10:17], «(...) Dieu grand et redoutable, qui gardes l'alliance et la fidélité envers ceux qui l'aiment et qui gardent ses commandements» [Ne 1:5; tr. fr. de la *TOB*], la *grandeur* semble être conçue comme une qualité abstraite de Dieu, de même que l'impartialité, la fidélité et la puissance qui lui est, elle aussi, attribuée métaphoriquement. En fait, il est vraisemblable que cette qualité correspondait dans l'esprit des écrivains vétérotestamentaires à ce que nous pourrions appeler la dignité ou la majesté de Dieu, étant donné qu'ils attribuaient l'adjectif *grand* fréquemment aussi à des rois, des prêtres et d'autres notables.

41 Cette métaphore est attestée, par exemple, par les verbes qui décrivent souvent la colère divine: מָלֵא – *être plein de*, מִלֵּא – *remplir*, נִתַּךְ – *se déverser*, שָׁפַךְ – *déverser*, שָׁתָה – *boire*. Il est intéressant de remarquer que ces verbes sont associés à la colère de Dieu surtout dans les livres

conceptions métaphoriques soient si répandues pourrait bien expliquer comment des auteurs différents mais ayant des systèmes conceptuels semblables à propos de Dieu, pouvaient imaginer, indépendamment les uns des autres, Dieu et sa colère comme des choses qui pouvaient ou non être *contenues*.

III. Les occurrences au sein de métaphores cachées

Les caractéristiques spécifiques de l'emploi métaphorique des verbes כִּלְכֵּל et הֵכִיל que nous avons dégagées dans la section précédente en nous fondant sur les énoncés dont la métaphoricité était manifeste, vont maintenant pouvoir nous aider à comprendre la nature de deux autres emplois de ces verbes. Ces emplois se trouvent eux aussi dans la littérature prophétique et ressemblent sur plus d'un point à leurs emplois dans les métaphores que nous avons examinées plus haut, mais une différence majeure les rend plus difficiles à évaluer. En effet, les passages dans lesquels se trouvent ces emplois ne développent pas d'imagerie telle que celles de la grandeur ou de la liquidité. Et pour cette raison, on peut avoir l'impression en les lisant que les énoncés dans lesquels les verbes figurent n'exploitent pas leur sens premier de *contenir*, pour créer un effet de surprise en présentant ce dont ils parlent sous un angle inhabituel[42], mais emploient les verbes comme s'ils signifiaient tout simplement *supporter*. Cependant, l'analyse de ces énoncés dans leurs contextes aussi bien que dans le contexte plus large du traitement métaphorique des thèmes de la colère divine et des événements eschatologiques dans la littérature prophétique, peut nous montrer qu'ils sont ce que Peter Macky appelle des *métaphores cachées*[43], c'est-à-dire, des expressions reflétant des notions métaphoriques qui sont inscrites dans le langage[44]. Or, de telles expressions, aussi conventionnelles qu'elles puissent être, sont toujours senties comme figurées par les locuteurs, qui restent donc conscients de ce qu'en

---

prophétiques où l'on trouve aussi les métaphores employant les verbes כִּלְכֵּל et הֵכִיל concernant ce même sujet.

42 «En effet, on est plus vivement frappé d'une expression, quand on voit qu'elle est tout autre qu'on se l'était imaginé, et l'esprit semble dire: Comme c'est vrai! Je me trompais. Il y a aussi de l'élégance à faire entendre ce qu'on ne dit pas (...). On y trouve une connaissance nouvelle et une métaphore.» Aristote, *La Rhétorique*, III, 11, 1412a, trad. Norbert Bonafous (Paris: Durand, 1856), 343.

43 Peter W. Macky, *The Centrality of Metaphors*, 79–80, 137–162.

44 La place importante de telles notions dans le langage est soulignée notamment par George Lakoff et Mark Johnson, *Metaphors We Live By*.

elles au moins un mot – dans les énoncés en question, ces mots étant les verbes כִּלְכֵּל et הֵכִיל – est employé d'une façon qui diverge de son usage littéral[45].

Le premier des deux cas de ce type se trouve, comme trois des exemples que nous avons vus plus haut, dans le livre de Jérémie, où au cours d'un passage qui oppose la puissance de Dieu à la futilité des idoles, le prophète dit au sujet du premier:

מִקִּצְפּוֹ תִּרְעַשׁ הָאָרֶץ
וְלֹא־יָכִלוּ גוֹיִם זַעְמוֹ

La terre tremble devant sa colère
et les nations *ne supportent pas* sa fureur (Jr 10:10)[46].

La traduction française de Louis Segond citée ici rend donc le verbe par *supporter*, et en ceci elle suit une longue tradition. Non seulement est-il rendu ainsi par toutes les traductions modernes que j'ai consultées[47], mais c'est aussi de cette manière qu'il semble avoir été compris par les principales traductions anciennes. Cette proposition étant absente de la Septante, sa première traduction grecque, celle de Théodotion, rend le verbe par ουχ υποισουσιν – *ils ne supporteront pas*[48]. De la même manière, le Targoum Jonathan le rend par ולא יכלון (...) לסוברא – *ils ne pourront supporter*; et la Vulgate par *non sustinebunt* – *ils ne supporteront pas*.

Cependant, ce qui peut indiquer que l'emploi du verbe soit métaphorique pour les locuteurs de l'époque et que le verbe y garde donc son sens premier, c'est le fait même qu'il est employé au sujet de la colère divine. En effet, la grande récurrence de métaphores qui présentent la colère de Dieu comme un liquide dans la littérature prophétique atteste que la liquidité appartenait alors à ce que Max Black a appelé *le système de lieux communs associés* à la notion de la colère divine[49]. Or, l'habitude de lier ces deux notions faisait non seulement

---

45 «In calling [a] sentence a case of metaphor, we are implying that at least one word (...) is being used metaphorically in the sentence, and that a least one of the remaining words is being used literally. Let us call the [first] word (...) the *focus* of the metaphor, and the remainder of the sentence in which that word occurs the *frame*.» Max Black, «Metaphor,» in *Models and Metaphors: Studies in Language and Philosophy* (Ithaca, NY: Cornell University Press, 1962), 27–28.

46 Traduction française de Louis Segond.

47 *TOB, La Bible de Jérusalem*, Émile Osty, *The English Standard Version, King James, The New International Version* et Martin Luther.

48 Voir Joseph Ziegler, ed., *Septuaginta Gottingensis*, vol. 15 – *Ieramias, Baruch, Threni, Epistula Ieremiae* (Göttingen: Vandenhoeck & Ruprecht, 1957), *ad locum.*

49 Max Black, «Metaphor,» 40. Dans un article postérieur, Black a préféré intituler cette même notion *le complexe implicatif*; voir «More About Metaphor,» *Dialectica* 31, n° 3–4, 442.

composer des métaphores expressives de ce type, comme celles que nous avons vues, mais aussi employer un vocabulaire associé aux liquides au sujet de la colère de Dieu sans que cela serve un but rhétorique ou littéraire précis. En effet, on trouve dans le livre de Jérémie même ainsi que dans des livres postérieurs, plusieurs énoncés où la colère de Dieu est dite, par exemple, être *déversée* sur les hommes ou les *remplir*, sans que ces expressions s'insèrent pour autant dans une imagerie plus développée[50]. Et dans ces expressions – sans doute comme dans celle de Jr 10:10 – il est clair que les verbes n'acquièrent pas de sens nouveau, mais qu'ils sont compris selon leur sens habituel et constituent ainsi des métaphores cachées.

Le verbe au *Pilpel* se trouve, lui aussi, employé dans une occurrence au sein de ce qui paraît être une métaphore cachée, et ceci au cours d'une prophétie eschatologique de Malachie annonçant la venue du messager de Dieu, à propos duquel le prophète déclare:

וּמִי מְכַלְכֵּל אֶת־יוֹם בּוֹאוֹ
וּמִי הָעֹמֵד בְּהֵרָאוֹתוֹ
כִּי־הוּא כְּאֵשׁ מְצָרֵף וּכְבֹרִית מְכַבְּסִים:

Qui *supportera* le jour de sa venue?
Qui se tiendra debout lors de son apparition?
Car il est comme le feu d'un fondeur, comme la lessive des blanchisseurs. (Ml 3:2)[51]

L'emploi du verbe כִּלְכֵּל dans ce verset ressemble manifestement à l'emploi du verbe הֵכִיל dans l'annonce du jour de YHWH par le prophète Joël étudié plus haut[52]. Dans les deux cas, le verbe apparaît au sein d'une question rhétorique ayant une structure syntaxique similaire: *Et qui* + verbe + COD, et destinée à accentuer l'incapacité des hommes à faire face aux événements eschatologiques prochains. Pourtant, alors qu'en Joël la question s'intègre dans toute une imagerie de la grandeur des événements en question et semble donc être une expression métaphorique employée délibérément, rien dans le contexte du passage de Malachie n'indique que le verbe y garde son sens premier de *contenir* dans le cadre d'une métaphore[53], et qu'il ne signifie pas littéralement *supporter*.

---

50 Voir Jr 10:25; 42:18; Ez 7:8; 9:8; 14:19; 20:8, 13, 21, 33, 34; 30:15; Jb 21:20; Est 3:5; 5:9; 2 Ch 12:7; 34:21.

51 Traduction française de la *TOB*.

52 Voir pp. 181–83.

53 Des événements eschatologiques sont qualifiés de *grands* par plusieurs prophètes: Jr 30:7; Os 2:2; Jl 3:4; 4:14; So 1:14. Cependant, la seule mention de *grandeur* du jour de YHWH dans le livre de Malachie, en Ml 3:23 (cf. Jl 3:4), ne se trouvant pas dans le même passage prophétique que notre verbe, n'aide guère à interpréter la manière dont il est employé dans le présent verset.

De plus, nous constaterons que dans ce passage de Malachie la métaphore principale qui concerne l'action du messager de Dieu à laquelle les hommes seront incapables de faire face – celle de la purification par le feu et par la lessive, ne relève aucunement du registre quantitatif qui est celui du verbe כִּלְכֵּל, qui ne semble donc pas y être associé. En fait, les deux questions rhétoriques posées avant la description métaphorique de l'œuvre du messager – *qui supportera / contiendra le jour de sa venue?* et *qui se tiendra debout lors de son apparition?* – semblent être rattachées discursivement plutôt à ce qui les précède, à savoir, au fait que la venue du messager a été *cherchée* et *désirée* par les destinataires de la prophétie[54]. C'est au moyen de ces questions dont la réponse est censée être évidente, que le prophète tente de faire voir à ses auditeurs toute l'absurdité de leur désir, qui, une fois exaucé, rendra imminents leur jugement et leur châtiment[55].

Ne figurant donc pas au sein d'une métaphore destinée à contribuer à la composition de l'image des événements eschatologiques dans ce texte, les deux verbes employés dans les questions rhétoriques se trouvant dans ce verset – כִּלְכֵּל et עָמַד, semblent avoir été choisis par l'auteur non pas pour les images qu'ils véhiculaient, mais en vertu de leur conventionalité dans les propos prophétiques au sujet de l'incapacité des hommes à faire face à Dieu. Ainsi, dans le livre de Jérémie, comme nous l'avons vu, les verbes כִּלְכֵּל et הֵכִיל avaient été employés métaphoriquement à trois reprises pour indiquer que l'on ne pouvait faire face à la colère de Dieu[56], alors que Joël avait utilisé le verbe au Hiphil pour dire que le jour de YHWH ne pourrait être supporté par les hommes. De même, dans plusieurs prophéties qui décrivent les événements eschatologiques comme l'offensive d'une armée ou l'assaut d'un lion, le verbe עָמַד désigne par métonymie le fait de ne pas y survivre[57]. Or, bien que le caractère imagé que ces verbes pouvaient avoir ne soit pas mis en relief dans ce passage de Malachie, le fait que les deux y soient employés dans un contexte proche de celui où ils étaient employés de façon clairement métaphorique et au sein d'énoncés à formulation semblable, pourrait indiquer qu'ils n'avaient pas, à ce stade, de

---

54 *Et soudain il entrera dans son sanctuaire, le Seigneur que vous <u>cherchez</u>; et l'Ange de l'alliance que vous <u>désirez</u>, le voici qui vient!* (Ml 3:1, tr. fr. de *La Bible de Jérusalem*).

55 Nous noterons que les versets 3 et 4 de notre chapitre qui soulignent l'aspect bénéfique de la purification qui sera accomplie par le messager, diffèrent à la fois en ton et en genre littéraire de l'ensemble du passage, si bien que certains commentateurs les ont considérés comme des ajouts postérieurs à la rédaction. Pour une bibliographie sur cette question, voir Andrew E. Hill, *Malachi: A New Translation with Introduction and Commentary* (The Anchor Bible; New York: Doubleday, 1998), 275.

56 Jr 6:11; 10:10; 20:9.

57 Jr 49:19; 50:44; Ez 13:5; Am 2:15; Ne 1:6.

nouveaux sens indépendants qui pouvaient s'employer librement[58]. Nous pouvons supposer que si l'on pouvait comprendre dans ce verset que le verbe כִּלְכֵּל désignait le fait de *supporter* et le verbe עָמַד – le fait de *survivre*, c'est parce que dans des contextes et au sein d'énoncés similaires c'était ce qu'ils désignaient habituellement, et non pas du fait que leurs sens propres l'impliquaient.

Or, il y a dans ces énoncés ce qui semble être un bon indice en faveur de cette hypothèse. En effet, comme nous l'avons pu constater, dans tous les énoncés qui désignaient la capacité de contenir quelque chose, que ce soit concrètement ou métaphoriquement, et où כִּלְכֵּל et הֵכִיל étaient conjugués, on les a trouvés au yiqtol[59], et cela est aussi vrai pour tous les emplois métaphoriques du verbe עָמַד que nous avons mentionnés. Et en fait, il n'est aucunement étonnant que ce soit cette forme qui soit choisie par les différents auteurs, puisque c'est elle qui exprimait normalement en hébreu biblique la modalité potentielle[60]. En revanche, dans les deux questions rhétoriques de notre verset, les verbes sont au participe – ce qui pour כִּלְכֵּל ainsi que pour son synonyme au Hiphil constitue la seule occurrence au participe dans l'Ancien Testament[61].

En fait, il semblerait que l'auteur de Malachie choisisse cette forme, qui exprimait souvent en hébreu biblique le *futurum instans*[62], pour insister sur l'imminence de la venue du messager, qui avait été soulignée aussi par les premiers mots de la prophétie: הִנְנִי שֹׁלֵחַ מַלְאָכִי – *Voici que je vais envoyer mon*

---

58 L'expression עָמַד בְּ- aura en hébreu mishnique et talmudique le sens indépendant de *supporter* ou de *surmonter* une chose difficile. Voir les deux exemples suivants:

אין גוזרין גזירה על הצבור אלא אם כן רוב צבור יכולין לעמוד בה

L'on n'impose pas une règle au public à moins que la majorité puisse la **supporter.** (*b. B. Bat.* 60b)

עשרה נסיונות נתנסה אברהם אבינו ועמד בכלם

Dix épreuves ont été données à Abraham notre père, et il les a toutes **surmontées.** (*m. 'Avot* 5:3).

59 1 R 7:26, 38; 8:27; Jr 2:13; 10:10; Jl 2:11; 2 Ch 2:5; 4:5; 6:18. Ailleurs, la *capacité de contenir* est exprimée encore plus explicitement par une construction comportant le verbe הֵכִיל à l'infinitif précédé des verbes conjugués: -קָטֹן מִ – *trop petit pour...* (1 R 8:64) et יָכוֹל– *(ne) peut...* (Am 7:10; 2 Ch 7:7).

60 Voir Jan Joosten, *The Verbal System of Biblical Hebrew: A New Synthesis Elaborated on the Basis of Clasical Prose* (Jérusalem: Simor, 2012), 273–274, où 1 R 8:27 est donné en exemple de cet emploi modal du *Yiqtol*.

61 Le verbe כִּלְכֵּל se trouve au participe en Si 25:22 au sens de *pourvoir aux besoins de*, et en Si 49:9 et 4Q402 4,6 probablement au sens déjà lexicalisé de *supporter*.

62 Voir Jan Joosten, *The Verbal System*, 241–242.

messager[63]. Cependant, bien que pouvant décrire des actions comme proches dans le futur en les présentant justement comme si elles se déroulaient dans le présent[64], le participe en hébreu biblique était, de par sa nature, dépourvu de nuances modales. Donc, si l'on prenait en compte l'usage du participe dans ces questions, on devrait les comprendre comme signifiant non pas: *qui peut supporter le jour de sa venue?* et *qui peut survivre à son apparition?* mais: *qui est-ce qui va supporter le jour de sa venue?* et *qui est-ce qui va survivre à son apparition?* comme si le prophète cherchait à identifier dans la foule les personnes qui seraient amenées à le faire. Or, l'explication juxtaposée à ces questions rhétoriques – *car il est comme le feu d'un fondeur, comme la lessive des blanchisseurs* – indique clairement que ce n'était pas ce que l'auteur voulait dire.

En effet, ce qui peut expliquer que l'auteur de Malachie omette d'exprimer le caractère potentiel des actions désignées par les deux verbes dans ces questions, c'est que pour lui ce caractère était évident. Comme ces verbes étaient habituellement utilisés sous une modalité potentielle dans des contextes semblables, l'auteur pouvait sentir que la potentialité était impliquée par les verbes eux-mêmes, et donc que la signification globale d'énoncés comme ceux qu'il écrivait ne changeait pas si, au lieu du Yiqtol, on employait le participe afin d'accentuer l'imminence des événements à venir. Et ce constat peut affirmer l'hypothèse selon laquelle pour l'auteur de Malachie les deux verbes ne signifiaient pas supporter et survivre littéralement. Car si à son époque ces sens avaient été déjà lexicalisés, les verbes auraient pu les avoir dans des contextes variés. Dans certains de ces contextes, on aurait en effet employé les verbes pour désigner des actions conçues comme potentielles, mais dans bien d'autres on aurait été amené à les utiliser pour faire référence à des actions envisagées sous d'autres modalités, par exemple, pour décrire des faits réels passés ou présents ou bien pour donner des ordres. La potentialité n'aurait pu alors être considérée comme inhérente aux verbes eux-mêmes, si bien que pour désigner des actions potentielles – comme celles que Malachie voulait mettre sous les yeux de ses auditeurs – elle aurait dû être exprimée d'une manière ou d'une autre.

Pour conclure cette analyse des énoncés dans lesquels les verbes כִּלְכֵּל et הֵכִיל ont été employés non pas pour présenter les sujets traités sous une nouvelle lumière due au fait qu'ils s'y appliquaient par métaphores, mais au contraire parce que les verbes étaient considérés comme idiomatiques dans le traitement de ces mêmes sujets, il faut d'abord préciser que ce type d'emploi ne peut être dissocié de l'usage de ces verbes dans le cadre d'imageries cohérentes et

---

63 Traduction française de *La Bible de Jérusalem.*
64 Voir Jan Joosten, *The Verbal System*, 241–242.

délibérément élaborées. En effet, ces deux types d'emploi présentent des caractéristiques fort semblables: ils apparaissent surtout dans un même genre de discours – le discours prophétique, par rapport au même sujet, à savoir, la colère de Dieu, et dans des énoncés qui expriment la même conception selon laquelle l'homme est incapable de faire face à cette colère.

Donc, toutes ces occurrences des deux verbes dans les Prophètes, que nous avons été amenés à regrouper en deux catégories distinctes puisque des méthodes différentes étaient requises pour évaluer en chacune d'elles la nature de l'emploi des verbes et leur sens pour les auteurs qui s'en servaient, attestent en fait l'existence d'un seul usage commun dans le langage de ces auteurs. En effet, elles indiquent que dans les discours prophétiques il était coutume d'exprimer la conception que les hommes ne pouvaient supporter la colère de Dieu, en employant métaphoriquement les verbes כִּלְכֵּל et הֵכִיל. Et cet usage était suffisamment conventionnel pour qu'il se fasse non seulement lorsque la présence d'autres métaphores semblables le rendait approprié, mais aussi quand il n'était pas provoqué par le contexte. Or, le fait que des expressions du deuxième type, qui pouvaient paraître énigmatiques à ceux qui ne connaissaient pas l'usage commun qui les avait occasionnées, soient mises par écrit dans des textes qui étaient abondamment lus et étudiés, jouait, comme nous le montrera la suite, un rôle important dans l'attribution ultérieure d'un sens nouveau à l'un des deux verbes.

IV. Le nouveau sens de כִּלְכֵּל

Contrairement au verbe הֵכִיל qui, même dans l'état de développement de l'hébreu qui se présente dans les textes de Qumrân, ne désigne l'action de *supporter* que par des métaphores soit explicites soit cachées qui se fondent sur son sens premier de *contenir*[65], plusieurs occurrences du verbe כִּלְכֵּל indiquent qu'à partir d'une certaine phase de l'évolution de la langue hébraïque, ce verbe désignait cette même action littéralement, et donc que ce sens avait été pleinement lexicalisé. Il n'est, bien évidemment, pas possible de conclure dans tous ces cas avec le même degré de certitude, qu'en employant le verbe l'auteur n'était pas du tout conscient de son sens premier, mais au moins deux de ces occurrences semblent l'attester de manière fort probable.

Un premier type de confirmation de la lexicalisation du nouveau sens est l'emploi du verbe dans le livre de Ben Sira, écrit très probablement au premier

---

65 Voir 1QS XI,20; 4Q431 1,5; 4Q491 11i17. Ces trois énoncés semblent être modelés sur ceux de Jl 2:11 et Ml 3:2. Le verbe au *Hiphil* n'est pas attesté dans les manuscrits hébreux du livre de Ben Sira.

quart du deuxième siècle avant notre ère[66], au sein d'un passage métaphorique avec les imageries duquel le sens de *contenir* ne pourrait s'accorder, ce qui atteste qu'il ne pouvait se présenter *à l'esprit d'une façon sensible et concrète*[67]. La péricope dans laquelle le verbe apparaît, Si 6:18-22, traite de la sagesse et se compose de cinq versets qui sont tous conservés en hébreu, à l'exception du premier dont nous n'avons que la fin. La voici en hébreu, avec les noms des témoins textuels cités entre parenthèses[68]:

(C) 6:18		תשיג חכמה (...)
(C) 6:19	כחורש וקוצר קרב אליה	וקוה לרוב תבואתה
	כי בעבודתה מעט תעבוד	ולמחר תאכל פריה
(A) 6:20	עקובה היא לאויל	ולא יכלכלנה חסר לב
(A) 6:21	כאבן משא תהיה עליו	לא יאחר להשליכה
(A) 6:22	כי המוסר כשמה[69] כן הוא	ולא לרבים היא נְכֹחָה

6:18 (...) tu obtiendras la sagesse.
6:19 Comme un laboureur et comme un moissonneur approche-toi d'elle
    et espère en l'abondance de sa récolte.
    Car pour sa culture tu travailleras peu,
    et demain tu mangeras ses fruits.
6:20 Elle est tortueuse pour le sot,
    et celui qui manque d'intelligence ne la *supporte* pas.
6:21 Elle est pour lui comme une lourde pierre
    et il ne tarde pas à la rejeter,
6:22 car la discipline mérite bien son nom
    et elle n'est pas évidente pour la multitude[70].

---

66 Patrick W. Skehan and Alexander A. Di Lella, *The Wisdom of Ben Sira* (The Anchor Bible; New York: Dobleday, 1987), 9–10.

67 Charles Bally, *Traité de stylistique française*, vol. 1, 198. Voir la remarque suivante de Janet Martin Soskice: «Three rough guidelines can be given for distinguishing living from dead metaphors. The first is that one recognizes a dissonance or tension in a living metaphor whereby the terms of the utterance used seem not strictly appropriate to the topic at hand (...). This is illustrated by the occurrence of mixed metaphors like 'Jesus was an oasis of calm in a torrent of angry faces» and «All our black sheep have come home to roost». Janet Martin Soskice, *Metaphor and Religious Language*, 73.

68 Pancratius C. Beentjes, *The Book of Ben Sira in Hebrew: A Text Edition of All Extant Hebrew Manuscripts and a Synopsis of All Parallel Hebrew Ben Sira Texts* (Leiden: Brill, 1997), *ad locos*.

69 Il s'agit d'un jeu de mots: le substantif מוסר – *la discipline*, est pris pour le participe du verbe הוּסַר (ס.ו.ר). *Hophal*), et signifierait *ce qui est retiré / écarté*. Voir *La Sagesse de ben Sira*, traduction de l'hébreu, introduction et annotation par Charles Mopsik (Lagrasse: Verdier, 2003), 98, note 1.

70 *La Sagesse de ben Sira*, trad. Charles Mopsik, 97–98.

La péricope commence par une prescription de s'initier à la connaissance de la sagesse dès sa jeunesse (6:18)[71]. De cette phrase il ne reste en hébreu que la fin, mais son contenu est donné par la Septante[72]. Ensuite, cette prescription de ne pas s'attarder à s'instruire est expliquée au moyen de deux métaphores, dont la première présente les grands bienfaits qui résultent d'une instruction entreprise à un jeune âge et qui surpassent largement les efforts qui y sont investis (6:19), alors que la seconde décrit les tentatives, destinées à l'échec, de connaître la sagesse tardivement (6:21–22a). Et la péricope se termine par le constat de l'auteur qu'en réalité peu de gens suivent son conseil et que pour la plupart d'entre eux la sagesse reste indécelable (6:22b).

La proposition qui nous intéresse constitue le second hémistiche du verset 20 qui se situe entre les deux métaphores qui forment le corps de l'argument de la péricope. En ce qui concerne son contenu, introduisant la figure du sot et de celui qui manque d'intelligence ce verset fait manifestement partie de la description de la formation entreprise trop tard, et non pas de celle qui a été commencée à temps. Cependant, en examinant l'imagerie du verset 20, nous constatons que la transition entre ces deux passages, se fait graduellement au sein de ce verset même. En effet, le premier hémistiche du verset affirme que pour le sot la sagesse est עקובה – un adjectif peu fréquent dans la littérature hébraïque parvenue jusqu'à nous, mais dont le sens concret apparaît très clairement en Es 40:4[73]: il désigne le terrain accidenté, c'est-à-dire, la terre non-plate. Ainsi, tout en restant dans l'imagerie de la métaphore agricole du verset 19, cet hémistiche tente de présenter de façon imagée la difficulté de s'initier à la sagesse sur le tard et la vanité d'une telle tentative, en les opposant à la facilité et à la profitabilité de la tâche si l'on s'y met dès la jeunesse. Pour celui qui avait commencé tôt, la sagesse ressemble à un champ fertile et facile à cultiver, tandis que pour celui qui s'est attardé, elle est comme une terre incultivable. En revanche, l'affirmation que l'on trouve dans le second hémistiche du verset – *et celui qui manque d'intelligence ne peut la supporter* (לא יכלכלנה) – ne relève plus du même champ conceptuel d'images agricoles. En fait, en marquant le point de

---

71 Skehan et Di Lella font l'hypothèse que l'école dans laquelle Ben Sira a lui-même enseigné la sagesse était destinée aux jeunes (voir Si 51:23–28), entre autres du fait qu'il s'adresse dans de nombreuses sentences à: *mon fils* (בני); Patrick W. Skehan and Alexander A. Di Lella, *The Wisdom of Ben Sira*, 12.

72 τέκνον, ἐκ νεότητός σου ἐπίλεξαι παιδείαν, καὶ ἕως πολιῶν εὑρήσεις σοφίαν. *Mon fils! dès ta jeunesse choisis l'instruction et jusqu'à tes cheveux blancs tu trouveras la sagesse* (tr. fr. de La Bible de Jérusalem).

73 כָּל־גֶּיא יִנָּשֵׂא וְכָל־הַר וְגִבְעָה יִשְׁפָּלוּ וְהָיָה הֶעָקֹב לְמִישׁוֹר וְהָרְכָסִים לְבִקְעָה: – *Que toute vallée soit comblée, toute montagne et toute colline abaissées, que **les lieux accidentés** se changent en plaine et les escarpements en large vallée* (tr. fr. de La Bible de Jérusalem).

transition entre les deux images de la péricope, elle semble avoir pour fonction d'introduire la métaphore qui va suivre, celle de la sagesse comme une lourde pierre à porter que celui qui n'est pas habitué à sa charge, l'ayant soulevée, ôte vite de ses épaules. Donc, comme la proposition comportant le verbe כִּלְכֵּל est fortement liée rhétoriquement à l'image soigneusement développée de l'homme portant une lourde pierre, il me semble invraisemblable que l'auteur, qui est si attentif à l'expressivité des métaphores dans cette péricope, ait l'intention d'esquisser en elle l'image de tout autre chose, à savoir, du fait de *contenir* la sagesse. La juxtaposition de cette proposition à l'image qui la suit, me semble attester plutôt que pour Ben Sira le verbe כִּלְכֵּל ne véhiculait aucune image particulière[74].

Deux remarques supplémentaires peuvent, à mon avis, appuyer les conclusions de cette analyse. Premièrement, si la reconstruction d'une proposition légèrement lacunaire de 4Q405 par ses éditeurs est juste[75], on trouve en hébreu post-biblique une occurrence de כִּלְכֵּל où ce verbe décrit une action dont l'objet

---

74 Bien que le sens du verbe כִּלְכֵּל en Ps 112:5 ne soit suffisamment clair pour constituer une preuve de sa lexicalisation, il me semble que son emploi dans ce texte doit être rapproché de celui qui en est fait dans le passage que nous venons d'étudier. Le texte de Ps 112:5–6 est le suivant:

טוֹב־אִישׁ חוֹנֵן וּמַלְוֶה
יְכַלְכֵּל דְּבָרָיו בְּמִשְׁפָּט:
כִּי־לְעוֹלָם לֹא־יִמּוֹט
לְזֵכֶר עוֹלָם יִהְיֶה צַדִּיק:

Bienheureux l'homme qui prend pitié et prête,
qui *règle* ses affaires avec droiture.
Non, jamais il ne chancelle,
en mémoire éternelle sera le juste. [tr. fr. de *La Bible de Jérusalem*]

L'image décrite ici semble être celle du juste qui *supporte*, c'est-à-dire, qui *porte* ses affaires avec droiture, si bien qu'il ne chancelle jamais. Et cette interprétation est confirmée par le Targoum des Psaumes, qui rend la phrase par: יסובר מילוי כהלכתא. Les significations qui sont données au verbe par la plupart des traductions anciennes et modernes, y compris celle qui est citée, me semblent difficiles à retenir, ne serait-ce qu'elles ne sont attestées dans aucun autre texte biblique. Voir aussi Charles Augustus Briggs et Emilie Grace Briggs, *A Critical and Exegetical Commentary on the Book of Psalms*, vol. II, 386. Si le verbe כִּלְכֵּל a ici en effet le sens lexicalisé de *supporter*, on pourrait compter ceci parmi les éléments tardifs dans la langue de ce psaume; voir Avi Hurvitz, *Beyn Lashon LeLashon: LeToldot Leshon HaMiqra Biymei Bayit Sheni* (Jerusalem: Bialik Institute, 1972), 174 [en hébreu]. Je remercie Jan Joosten pour m'avoir signalé cette dernière référence. Voir aussi Si 49:9 (manuscrit B): וגם הזכיר את איוב נֹ[ב]יֹא [[ ]] המכלכל כל דֹ[רכי צ]דֹק.
75 Voir l'explication du choix des éditeurs dans Esther Eshel et al., eds., *DJD* XI (Oxford: Clarendon Press, 1998), 357, L. 5.

est le mot משא lui-même. En effet, dans cet hymne trouvé à Qumrân louant des
êtres divins (אלהים), il est dit:

לכ]לכלם משאי כול (...)[76]

Comme le précisent les éditeurs du texte, le mot משא peut avoir des sens
différents, tels *que fardeau, tâche, soulèvement, parole* ou même *parole d'éloge*, et
la partie du texte dans laquelle figure cette proposition est trop fragmentaire
pour en comprendre la signification[77]. Néanmoins, quel que soit le signifié précis
désigné ici par le substantif משא, il me semble difficile de douter que le lien avec
le verbe נָשָׂא – porter, dont il dérive, soit plus ou moins senti au moment de la
rédaction de cet hymne, étant donné la grande fréquence de ce verbe dans les
textes vétérotestamentaires ainsi que dans ceux de la secte de Qumrân même.
Donc, pour l'auteur de cet hymne, comme pour Ben Sira, le verbe כִּלְכֵּל n'était pas
incompatible avec l'idée de porter, ce qui semble attester qu'il ne pouvait
véhiculer une image d'un ordre tout à fait différent, telle que l'image de *contenir*.

Deuxièmement, concernant le passage de Ben Sira, on peut se demander
pourquoi, si la proposition: *et celui qui manque d'intelligence ne peut la
supporter*, est en effet destinée à introduire l'image de la pierre à porter et y est
donc liée rhétoriquement, l'auteur n'a pas employé simplement le verbe נָשָׂא au
lieu de כִּלְכֵּל. En effet, נָשָׂא qui est utilisé très souvent dans l'Ancien Testament
métaphoriquement pour désigner le fait de *supporter* une chose pénible[78], aurait
eu l'avantage de correspondre parfaitement à l'image développée. D'ailleurs,

---

76 4Q405 23i5; la traduction anglaise proposée dans les *DJD* est la suivante: *in order that] they
be steadfast in the tasks of all things*; voir *ibid*, 356.

77 *Ibid*, 357, L. 5.

78 Voir, par exemple, Gn 4:13; Lv 10:17; Es 1:14; Pr 30:21 et beaucoup d'autres occurrences
signalées dans: אברהם אבן־שושן, קונקורדנציה חדשה לתורה, נביאים וכתובים (ירושלים: קרית־ספר, 1993),
ad locum. Voir aussi Si 13:2. כִּלְכֵּל est mis en parallèle avec נָשָׂא en Pr 18:14:

רוּחַ־אִישׁ יְכַלְכֵּל מַחֲלֵהוּ   וְרוּחַ נְכֵאָה מִי יִשָּׂאֶנָּה

Il me semble que les deux verbes sont utilisés ici comme des quasi-synonymes, et que le verset
devrait donc être traduit: *L'esprit de l'homme peut* **supporter** *sa maladie, tandis qu'un esprit
attristé – qui pourrait le* **supporter**? Néanmoins, on ne peut pas totalement exclure une
interprétation imagée de cette sentence, qui se traduirait donc: *L'esprit de l'homme peut* **contenir**
(c'est-à-dire, *retenir*) *sa maladie, mais un esprit abattu – qui le* **relèvera**? C'est ainsi que la
plupart des traducteurs modernes semblent avoir interprété ce verset. Nous remarquerons que si
dans ce verset כִּלְכֵּל signifiait en effet *contenir*, ce serait le seul cas attesté où le verbe se
comprendrait ainsi par rapport à un objet qui ne soit pas divin.

Ben Sira lui-même l'emploie dans un autre passage également au sujet de la sagesse, à propos de laquelle il prescrit:

ומשאה תשא נפשכם:[79]

(...) si bien que son fardeau, votre âme le *portera*. (Si 51:26)

Sans prétendre pouvoir répondre pleinement à cette question, il me semble qu'une raison possible pourrait être d'ordre poétique. En effet, il se peut que le choix du vocabulaire dans cette proposition soit motivé, entre autres choses, par la volonté de créer une allitération, en l'occurrence en ל qui est répété quatre fois dans cette proposition:

ולא יכלכלנה חסר לב

Et cela me semble d'autant plus probable que le verset précédent est lui aussi très riche en allitérations[80].

Un deuxième exemple de l'emploi du verbe כִּלְכֵּל, tiré cette fois-ci d'un texte trouvé à Qumrân, montre sans doute de la façon la plus immédiate qu'au moment de la rédaction du texte en question – 4Q185, écrit avant la fin du premier siècle avant notre ère[81] – le verbe signifiait tout simplement *supporter* sans aucune métaphoricité sous-entendue. La phrase comportant le verbe qui nous intéresse se lit ainsi:

(...) ומי יכלכל לעמוד לפני מלאכיו כי באש להבה ישפט] ועמ]ו רוחתיו[82]

---

79 Manuscrit B; Pancratius C. Beentjes, The Book of Ben Sira in Hebrew, *ad locum*.

80 Le verset 19 présente des allitérations en ר, ק et ע:

כחורש וקוצר קרב אליה   וקוה לרוב תבואתה
כי בעבודתה מעט תעבוד (...)

81 Le manuscrit trouvé est daté de la fin de l'époque hasmonéenne. John Strugnell, «Notes en marge du volume V des 'Discoveries in the Judaean Desert of Jordan',» *Revue de Qumrân* 7 (1970), 269.

82 4Q185 1–2 i 8–9. Nous citons ici, comme dans la suite de l'étude de ce texte, son édition la plus récente: Herman Lichtenberger, «Der Weisheitstext 4Q185 – Eine neue Edition,» in Charlotte Hempel, Armin Lange and Hermann Lichtenberger, eds., *The Wisdom Texts from Qumran and the Development of Sapiential Thought* (Leuven: Leuven University Press / Peeters, 2002), 127–50; le texte hébreu se trouvant pp. 130–132. La lecture de Lichtenberger aussi bien que sa reconstruction des passages lacunaires diffèrent quelquefois, de peu ou de beaucoup, de celles que l'on trouve dans l'édition officielle du texte: John M. Allegro, ed., *DJD* V (Oxford: Clarendon Press, 1968), 85–87; aussi bien que de celles de John Strugnell, «Notes en marge du volume V,» 269–273. Nous signalerons ces différences lorsqu'elles seront pertinentes pour notre étude. En

Et qui *supporterait* de se tenir debout face à ses anges, car par le feu brûlant il jugera[et avec] lui ses esprits?!

Comme la proposition circonstancielle de cause qui clôt cette phrase insiste sur le caractère douloureux du jugement dans lequel les anges joueront un rôle, il semble évident que le verbe désigne ici le fait de *supporter* ou *d'être en mesure de*, comme dans les nombreux cas examinés plus haut. Or, la structure syntaxique de la proposition principale atteste que cette désignation ne pouvait se faire au moyen d'une métaphore même cachée, car le verbe כִּלְכֵּל y qualifie non pas un nom, comme dans toutes les phrases examinées jusqu'à présent, mais un verbe, en l'occurrence, le verbe לעמוד – *se tenir debout*, ici à l'infinitif construit. En effet, il est difficile de concevoir comment l'auteur du texte aurait pu se représenter l'image de *contenir* une action telle que celle de rester debout. Selon la formulation de Janet Martin Soskice, le réseau initial d'implications dans lequel la métaphore s'insérait, a complètement disparu[83].

Outre une preuve supplémentaire de la lexicalisation du sens originellement métaphorique du verbe à une époque plutôt tardive de l'évolution de l'hébreu ancien, cette phrase peut aussi nous montrer de façon particulièrement claire comment le verbe était connu des locuteurs à cette époque et dans quels contextes il était employé. En effet, l'ensemble du texte d'instruction ou de sagesse dans la première partie duquel figure cette phrase, est écrit dans ce que Thomas Tobin a appelé un style anthologique[84], et cela est encore plus marqué

---

l'occurrence, à la fois Allegro et Strugnell complètent la lacune de la ligne 9 ainsi: ישפטו[ו – *ils jugeront*, contrairement à Lichtenberger qui conjecture que le verbe était au singulier. Quoi qu'il en soit, il est clair d'après les deux versions que les anges sont impliqués dans le jugement, soit en l'accomplissant eux-mêmes soit en tant qu'auxiliaires de Dieu dans sa fonction de juge.

83 «As the metaphor becomes commonplace, its initial web of implications becomes, if not entirely lost then difficult to recall.» Janet Martin Soskice, *Metaphor and Religious Language*, 73. Pour Soskice, vérifier si une métaphore renvoie à un modèle plus large, est le moyen le plus important pour déterminer si elle est vive ou morte.

84 Thomas H. Tobin, «4Q185 and Jewish Wisdom Literature,» in Harold W. Attridge, John J. Collins and Thomas H. Tobin, eds., *Of Scribes and Scrolls: Studies on the Hebrew Bible, Intertestamental Judaism and Christian Origins, Presented to John Strugnell on the Occasion of his Sixtieth Birthday,* College Theology Society Resources of Religion 5 (Lanham: University Press of America, 1990), 146. Tobin donne une liste concise de mots et d'expressions qui semblent avoir été empruntés par l'auteur de 4Q185 au corpus vétérotestamentaire, et notamment à la littérature de sagesse; voir ibid, 146–147. Voir aussi Donald J. Verseput, «Wisdom, 4Q185, and the Epistle of James,» Journal of Biblical Literature 117, n° 4 (1998), 696–700. Une tentative plus ample de trouver les sources d'influence possibles du texte, a été faite par Matthew J. Goff, *Discerning Wisdom: The sapiential Literature of the Dead Sea Scrolls,* Supplements to Vetus Testamentum 116 (Leiden: Brill, 2007), 122–145.

dans le passage eschatologique qui constitue la première partie du texte tel qu'il est parvenu jusqu'à nous[85]. Ce passage pourrait peut-être effectivement être qualifié, d'après Donald Verseput, de *pastiche d'allusions vétérotestamentaires*[86]. Afin de mettre cela en évidence, je présenterai ce passage en mettant en relief seulement les expressions non-banales pour lesquelles on trouve une ou des correspondances dans l'Ancien Testament.

7 [...................................] ואין כח לעמוד לפניה ואין מקוה

8 לזעם] אף אלהינו] ומי יכלכל לעמוד לפני מלאכיו כי באש[87]

9 להבה ישפט] ועמ]ו רוחתיו ואתם בני אדם א]ין כח]כי הנה

10 כחציר יצמח ופארתו[88] יפרח כציץ חסדו נשב]ה בו] רוחו

11 ויבש עגזו וציצו תשא רוח עד אייקום לעמ]דו מל]בד

12 [ו]יבקשוהו ולא ימצאהו ואין מקוה vacat ולא ימצא כי רוח

13 והוא כצל ימיו על האר]ץ] (...)

7 [...] *et il n'y a pas de force pour se tenir debout* face à elle et *il n'y a pas d'espoir*[89]

8 en ce qui concerne la colère [de notre Dieu]. *Et qui supporterait de se tenir debout face à ses anges*, car par *le feu*

9 *brûlant il jugera*[et avec] lui ses esprits. Et (pour) vous, fils d'homme, *il n'*[*y a pas de force*]. Car voici

10 comme *l'herbe* il pousse, et sa gloire fleurira *comme une fleur. Son éclat – son vent soufflera* [*sur lui*]

11 et son foin[90] *se séchera* et *le vent* emportera *ses fleurs* là où rien ne subsiste [...][91]

---

85 L'écrit de sagesse le plus étendu trouvé à Qumrân: 4QSapiential Work A, a probablement commencé lui aussi par un passage eschatologique traitant du jugement divin; John J. Collins, *Jewish Wisdom in the Hellenistic Age* (Edinburgh: T&T Clark, 1998), 116–117. Pour une présentation de ce passage de 4QSapiential Work A, voir Daniel J. Harrington, *Wisdom Texts from Qumran* (London & New York: Routledge, 1996), 41. D'après Harrington, l'introduction eschatologique de 4QSapiential Work A, fournit la perspective théologique dans laquelle les conseils du sage devaient être interprétés, une remarque qui est sans doute pertinente aussi pour 4Q185.

86 Donald J. Verseput, «Wisdom, 4Q185, and the Epistle of James,» 696.

87 Allegro y voit plutôt כאש – *comme du feu*. Nous y reviendrons par la suite.

88 Allegro lit ici מארצו – *de sa terre*.

89 Strugnell interprète le phonème מקוה comme un participe *Piel*, auquel il donne le sens de *supporter* du verbe correspondant en araméen; voir John Strugnell, «Notes en marge du volume V,» 269. En revanche, en ligne 12 il traduit la même expression par: «nor is there a hope for him»; voir *ibid*, 272.

90 Le mot עגזו est un *hapax legomenon* en hébreu. Pour ses interprétations possibles, voir John Strugnell, «Notes en marge du volume V,» 269–270.

12 [*Et*] *ils le chercheront mais ne le trouveront pas, et il n'y a pas d'espoir* vacat
Et on ne trouvera que du vent.

13 Et lui, *ses jours sur la terre sont comme de l'ombre.* (...)

On trouve dans ce court passage trois formules isolées qui semblent être empruntées à des sources bibliques. Premièrement, l'expression ואין כח לעמוד – *et il n'y a pas de force pour se tenir debout*, se trouvant en ligne 7 et peut-être reprise partiellement en ligne 9, apparaît en tant que telle en Esd 10:13 et en Dn 11:15. Deuxièmement, l'expression אש להבה – *un feu brûlant,* en lignes 8–9, figure en Lm 2:3 dans un contexte de vengeance divine aussi bien qu'en Os 7:6[92]. Dans les deux cas, elle est précédée de la préposition כ- – *comme,* qui est lue par Allegro à la place de ב- – *par* dans notre texte aussi. Et troisièmement, l'association des deux verbes בָּקֵשׁ et מָצָא entretenant des rapports de concession, que l'on trouve en ligne 12, apparaît plusieurs fois dans différents livres de l'Ancien Testament[93].

En outre, il est possible d'identifier de courts passages vétérotestamentaires, allant d'un à quelques versets, dans lesquels l'auteur de 4Q185 puise plusieurs expressions, ce qui peut attester que sa démarche était consciente. Ainsi, à la fois l'expression ואין מקוה– *et il n'y a pas d'espoir,* aux lignes 7 et 12, et la tournure כצל ימיו על הארץ – *ses jours sur la terre sont comme de l'ombre,* à la ligne 13, proviennent selon toute probabilité de 1 Ch 29:15, étant donné qu'elles en constituent une reprise presque littérale[94]. De plus, un passage d'Isaïe qui, lui aussi, met en scène un événement eschatologique comme cette partie de 4Q185, et qui était fréquemment cité dans de tels contextes dans la littérature inter- et néotestamentaire[95] – à savoir, Es 40:1–8 – fait l'objet d'un travail plus élaboré de paraphrase dans notre texte. L'auteur qumrânien en reprend le vocabulaire:

---

91 Les différents éditeurs sont d'accord que mot אייקום est étrange. Pour sa traduction, j'ai suivi Florentino Garcia Martínez and Eibert J. C. Tigchelaar, eds., *The Dead Sea Scrolls Study Edition* (Leiden: Brill, 1997–1998), 1:379. Le sens des deux derniers mots de la ligne, tels qu'ils sont reconstruits par Lichtenberger, est quelque peu obscur.

92 Voir aussi Es 4:5.

93 Par exemple: 2 S 17:20; Es 41:12; Jr 5:21; 29:13; Ez 26:21; Os 2:9; Am 8:12; Ps 37:36; Ct 3:1, 2; 5:6; 2 Ch 15:4.

94 L'énoncé négatif אין מקוה n'est attesté que dans ce verset des Chroniques. En revanche, l'énoncé affirmatif יש מקוה apparaît en Esd 10:2 aussi bien qu'en 1QH[a] XI,20; XIV,6; XVII,14; XXII,7. Dans les Chroniques l'on trouve כְּצֵל יָמֵינוּ עַל־הָאָרֶץ, à la 1ère personne du pluriel et non pas à la 3ème du singulier. Quant à l'emprunt de cette expression, voir John Strugnell, «Notes en marge du volume V,» 270; Matthew J. Goff, *Discerning Wisdom,* 127–128.

95 Voir Donald J. Verseput, «Wisdom, 4Q185, and the Epistle of James,» 697, note 22, et la bibliographie qui y est donnée.

חציר, ציץ, חסד, רוח, יבש aussi bien que la tournure נשבה בו רוחו[96], pour en faire une image agricole semblable à celle du texte biblique, mais non pas identique[97]. Et plus loin dans le texte, il reprend sans doute au même passage d'Isaïe aussi les deux mots דרך / מסלה – chemin / route, dont il transpose le sens en les employant pour décrire des modes de vie humaine[98].

Ayant constaté cette technique de composition utilisée par l'auteur de 4Q185, nous avons de bonnes raisons de croire que la phrase qui nous intéresse est, elle aussi, une paraphrase consciente d'un verset biblique – Ml 3:2, étudié plus haut – avec lequel elle présente plusieurs traits communs, à la fois en ce qui concerne son message et son imagerie et en ce qui concerne son vocabulaire et sa formulation[99].

[100](...) וּמִי מְכַלְכֵּל אֶת־יוֹם בּוֹאוֹ וּמִי הָעֹמֵד בְּהֵרָאוֹתוֹ כִּי־הוּא כְּאֵשׁ מְצָרֵף

(...) ומי יכלכל לעמוד לפני מלאכיו כי באש להבה ישפט

Comme en Malachie, notre phrase a pour but d'annoncer les horreurs du jugement divin qui s'accomplira en présence des anges[101]. Et, de la même façon que dans le propos du prophète, cela est exprimé au moyen d'une question rhétorique qui met en cause la capacité des hommes à faire face aux événements eschatologiques. Plus précisément, trois éléments dans cette phrase rappellent la formulation de Malachie. Premièrement, elle commence par les mêmes mots

---

96 En Es 40:7 il est écrit: כִּי רוּחַ יְהוָה נָשְׁבָה בּוֹ. En outre, si l'on rattache le troisième mot de la ligne 10, dont la lecture est contestée (voir note 88), à la proposition qui la précède, il paraît que l'expression יפרח כציץ חסדו est, elle aussi, une reprise de la métaphore d'Isaïe וְכָל־חַסְדּוֹ כְּצִיץ הַשָּׂדֶה – *et toute sa grâce est comme la fleur des champs* (tr. fr. de *La Bible de Jérusalem*).

97 Thomas H. Tobin, «4Q185 and Jewish Wisdom Literature,» 146; Donald J. Verseput, «Wisdom, 4Q185, and the Epistle of James,» 697–698; Matthew J. Goff, *Discerning Wisdom*, 126–128.

98 Ces mots apparaissent en II,1–2; Donald J. Verseput, «Wisdom, 4Q185, and the Epistle of James,» 698.

99 La ressemblance entre les deux phrases est signalée par Herman Lichtenberger, «Der Weisheitstext 4Q185,» 147, Zeile 8; et par Matthew J. Goff, *Discerning Wisdom*, 125, note 14.

100 Pour une traduction française de ce verset, voir ci-dessus.

101 Tobin maintient que la conception selon laquelle les anges avaient un rôle dans le jugement divin n'avait apparu au sein du judaïsme du deuxième Temple qu'avec la littérature apocalyptique et les écrits de la secte de Qumrân. En effet, il conclut de la présence de ce thème en 4Q185 que son auteur connaissait et adhérait à des conceptions semblables à celles qui se trouvent exprimées en Dn 12:1–4 et en maint endroit dans 1 Énoch, et il se sert de ce constat pour situer la rédaction du texte dans le temps et dans un milieu précis. Thomas H. Tobin, «4Q185 and Jewish Wisdom Literature,» 150–152. Pourtant, il ne signale pas que ce thème est également présent dans le passage de Ml 3:1–5, dont l'énoncé principal qui atteste de cette conception en 4Q185 semble dépendre d'un verset.

que l'énoncé de Malachie: וּמִי suivi du verbe כְּלְכֵּל[102]. Deuxièmement, le verbe
עָמַד y est également employé pour tracer l'image de *ne pas pouvoir rester debout*
à cause des anges[103]. Et troisièmement, l'incapacité à supporter les anges est
expliquée de la même façon par une comparaison de leur action au feu[104]. Or,
non seulement ces trois éléments de la formulation de Ml 3:2 sont présents dans
cette courte phrase, mais ils apparaissent aussi dans le même ordre.

De plus, la plus grande différence de construction entre cette phrase de
4Q185 et celle de Malachie – la subordination du verbe עָמַד au verbe כְּלְכֵּל et, par
conséquent, l'absence d'un complément d'objet direct nominal propre à ce
dernier – peut s'expliquer à la lumière de son contexte immédiat. En effet,
quelques mots plus haut, en employant une autre expression reprise à l'Ancien
Testament l'auteur a écrit: ואין כח לעמוד לפניה[105], un énoncé semblable à la
première moitié de notre phrase à la fois par l'image qu'il trace – celle des
hommes qui ne peuvent rester debout au moment des événements eschatologiques, et par sa structure syntaxique, car dans les deux cas le verbe עָמַד est à
l'infinitif et il est subordonné à une expression désignant l'incapacité et suivi
d'un complément introduit par la préposition לְפְנֵי. Cherchant à créer une
structure parallèle à celle de l'énoncé précédent, l'auteur semble donc avoir
assimilé le verbe כְּלְכֵּל à l'expression ואין כח, tous deux désignant, à ses yeux,
sous des nuances légèrement différentes, simplement l'incapacité de faire une
chose.

L'emploi du verbe כְּלְכֵּל par l'auteur de 4Q185 permet de comprendre mieux
que les autres exemples où le verbe a le sens lexicalisé *de supporter,* comment il
est arrivé que son sens premier de *contenir* ne soit plus présent à l'esprit des
locuteurs et que le sens nouveau soit pris pour un sens littéral. En effet, il est très
clair que l'auteur de 4Q185 se sert du verbe non pas par un choix spontané de

---

102 Nous avons vu qu'une question semblable est posée aussi en Jl 2:11, où le verbe au *Hiphil*
est employé. Il est intéressant de remarquer que l'auteur de 4Q185 emploie le verbe au *Yiqtol*, ce
qui était sans doute plus idiomatique que l'emploi du participe par Malachie. Voir ci-dessus.
103 Cette image a été rapprochée de celles de Ne 1:6; Ps 76:8; 130:3; voir Herman Lichtenberger,
«Der Weisheitstext 4Q185,» 132, 147, Zeile 8; Matthew J. Goff, *Discerning Wisdom*, 125, note 14.
104 Comme il a déjà été dit, Allegro lit ici כאש.
105 Plusieurs conjectures ont été faites quant au mot ou aux mots auxquels renvoyaient les
nombreux suffixes de la 3ème personne du féminin singulier dans ce texte. Selon Strugnell il
s'agirait soit de *la sagesse* (חכמה) soit de *la Loi* (תורה); John Strugnell, «Notes en marge du
volume V,» 269. Acceptant l'analyse de Strugnell pour la plupart des cas, Lichtenberger est d'avis
que le suffixe en I,7 renvoyait plutôt à l'un des deux mots נקמה *(la vengeance)* ou חמה *(la colère)*
qui apparaissent hors contexte deux lignes plus haut, ce qui conviendrait, en effet, beaucoup
mieux au message eschatologique du passage; Herman Lichtenberger, «Der Weisheitstext
4Q185,» 146.

vocabulaire, mais en pensant à une phrase biblique spécifique qu'il connaissait en bloc[106], qu'il l'ait cherchée dans un rouleau ou dans sa mémoire[107]. Et le sens qu'il attribue au verbe reflète la signification globale que celui-ci avait dans le contexte limité de la phrase à laquelle il puise. Ainsi, il semble ignorer momentanément ou faire abstraction des nuances de métaphoricité que le verbe présente dans d'autres passages bibliques qu'il connaissait sans aucun doute, comme cela peut arriver lorsque l'on emploie une expression recherchée qui n'est pas courante dans sa bouche et que l'on ne rencontre pas souvent. Et s'il pouvait «oublier» le sens premier du verbe alors qu'il pensait à son usage en Ml 3:2, c'est que dans ce verset biblique la métaphore qui joue sur le sens premier du verbe pour lui attribuer sa signification de *supporter,* n'est, comme nous l'avons vu, aucunement explicitée étant devenu un lieu commun connu de tous.

Conclusion

Les textes hébreux qui sont parvenus jusqu'à nous depuis l'Antiquité, nous permettent de voir le verbe כִּלְכֵּל à deux moments distincts de son évolution sémantique. D'une part, nous le voyons employé peu avant ou peu après l'exil de Babylone au sein d'un type précis de métaphores qui jouent sur son sens premier de *contenir* pour décrire de façon imagée la supériorité de Dieu et pour susciter de la crainte vis-à-vis de sa colère. D'autre part, nous voyons que dans l'hébreu du deuxième Temple, le verbe désignait l'action abstraite de *soutenir* ou de *supporter* et s'employait dans des contextes divers.

En effet, les attestations de ces deux types d'usage nous permettent de supposer ce qui est advenu au verbe entre ces deux époques et comment a émergé sa nouvelle acception. Il semblerait que l'usage métaphorique spécifique du verbe, courant autour de l'ère de l'exil notamment dans les discours prophétiques, a par la suite été oublié. Plus tardivement, les locuteurs de l'hébreu de l'époque du Second Temple ayant connu cet usage à travers les textes, ont essayé d'employer le verbe comme ils pensaient que leurs ancêtres

---

106 Quant au phénomène des *pseudo-classicismes*, voir Jan Joosten, «Pseudo-classicisms in Late Biblical Hebrew, in Ben Sira, and in Qumran Hebrew», in T. Muraoka, J. F. Elwolde, eds., *Sirach, Scrolls and Sages: Proceedings of a Second International Symposium on the Hebrew of the Dead Sea Scrolls, Ben Sira, and the Mishnah, Held at Leiden University, 15–17 December 1997* (Leiden: Brill, 1999), 146–159.

107 Je pencherais plutôt pour la deuxième option, étant donné la grande diversité de sources des citations se trouvant dans ce passage, et aussi vu la «correction» de la syntaxe verbale de Malachie en employant כִּלְכֵּל non pas au participe, mais au *Yiqtol*.

l'avaient employé. Or, comme dans les textes le verbe figurait le plus souvent dans le cadre de métaphores concernant l'incapacité des hommes à *supporter* la colère divine et ses effets, ils ont retenu que le verbe désignait cette action non pas métaphoriquement mais littéralement, et c'est ainsi qu'ils l'utilisaient dans leur propre langage et dans leurs écrits.

À partir du cas précis de la lexicalisation de cet emploi métaphorique du verbe כִּלְכֵּל, une conclusion peut être tirée concernant l'usage des métaphores en général et leur lexicalisation éventuelle. Une grande partie des métaphores que nous utilisons ne sont pas des créations originales de notre imagination, mais des formes d'expression connues dans certains contextes. Elles viennent à notre esprit quand nous nous exprimons sur un sujet précis, en même temps que le vocabulaire qu'il est de coutume d'employer en le traitant et les idées reçues qu'il est habituel de répéter le concernant. Et en effet, une lexicalisation complète d'un emploi métaphorique, suite à laquelle le mot ou l'expression en question acquiert un sens indépendant qui peut s'employer dans une variété de contextes différents, peut se produire lorsque l'on pense à la métaphore originelle en dehors de son contexte thématique, linguistique, culturel, rhétorique ou littéraire naturel. Elle peut avoir lieu, par exemple, quand on essaie d'utiliser une expression recherchée que nous avons apprise de façon non-naturelle, telle qu'une expression que nous avons trouvée dans les livres.

Par conséquent, dans les recherches lexicographiques sur les langues anciennes, ce qui peut aider à faire la différence entre les occurrences métaphoriques d'un mot ou d'une expression et ses occurrences lexicalisées, c'est l'identification du contexte thématique, linguistique, culturel, rhétorique ou littéraire précis dans lequel l'emploi métaphorique a été courant. Ayant identifié ce contexte, il serait raisonnable de présumer que des occurrences de ce mot ou de cette expression qui sont difficiles à évaluer mais qui figurent dans le même contexte, et peut-être aussi dans des contextes assez proches, ont été senties par les locuteurs comme métaphoriques, alors que ses occurrences dans de tout autres contextes sont des usages faits suite à l'oubli de son caractère métaphorique.

Part II: **Hebrew and Greek**

Jan Joosten

The Interplay between Hebrew and Greek in Biblical Lexicology: Language, Text, and Interpretation

"Biblical lexicology: Hebrew and Greek" – the title of the present collection – can only designate two scientific endeavors, not one. Each of the two branches requires its own set of competences. And each entails its own unique challenges. Specialists in one rarely are specialists in the other. The one is a part of Semitics, the other – arguably – of classics.

Nevertheless, they are not entirely distinct. They are, to begin with, typologically somewhat similar. Both are extremely complex undertakings, whose success is never assured. Both involve trying to define the meaning of words in ancient writings, without much external data. Both deal with texts that are considered canonical in faith communities that are still very much around today[1]. The two endeavors also overlap. Because of the way the biblical corpus evolved in Antiquity, Hebrew and Greek philology meet in the field of textual criticism. The textual history of the Hebrew Bible and the Septuagint bleed into one another in various ways, many of which are relevant to lexicographical research[2]. An even broader area of overlap is that of of exegesis. Hebrew works and Greek works are part of the same variegated fabric of exegetical writings explaining and interpreting ancient Jewish scriptures[3]. This too interferes with lexicology. The meaning of a word and its explanation in later writings – although theoretically distinct – are often difficult to tell apart. The upshot of all these considerations is that the two disciplines are, to a certain extent, intertwined. Lexicographers of the Hebrew Bible expressly consult the Septuagint as one of their sources. Likewise, lexicographers of the Septuagint do at least sometimes take the Hebrew text into account – even if the precise role of the Hebrew in Sep-

---

1 The canonical status of the biblical texts should not, of course, form an obstacle to scientific inquiry. Nonetheless, every philologist of the Bible remembers the criticism Jerome attracted when he translated a certain Hebrew word in a novel way (probably substituting *hedera* for *cucurbita* in Jon 4:6, for Hebrew קיקיון), see Augustine, Ep. II 82, § 35.
2 See James Barr, Comparative Philology and the Text of the Old Testament (Oxford: OUP, 1968; reprinted with a postscript: Winona Lake: Eisenbrauns, 1987).
3 See, e. g., *Hebrew Bible/Old Testament. The History of its Interpretation, Vol. I, Part 1: Antiquity* (Göttingen: Vandenhoeck & Ruprecht, 1996).

tuagint lexicography remains a delicate question[4]. Although theoretically distinct, the two fields of research feed into one another: new results in the one may have repercussions on the other. It is to this interrelatedness of Hebrew and Greek lexicography that this paper will be devoted. The underlying thesis is that each side will gain from more intensive collaboration and exchanges.

1. The Septuagint as a source of information on the meaning of Hebrew words

Let us begin with the relatively less problematic issue of using lexical information from Greek in semantic investigations on Biblical Hebrew. The status of the Septuagint in lexicographical research on the Hebrew Bible is widely recognized. The classic statement is that of Wilhelm Gesenius, who famously reduced the number of sources to be consulted by Hebrew lexicographers to three:

1) The biblical usage itself, as it arises out of the contexts where a word is used;
2) Jewish tradition as codified in the ancient translations, commentaries and dictionaries;
3) Comparisons with cognate languages[5].

In detailing the second point, the use of traditional Jewish knowledge, he starts with the Septuagint and underlines the importance it has because of its great age. When the Septuagint was produced, Hebrew was still a living and spoken

---

4 See the discussion between Boyd-Taylor and Muraoka on methodological issues: Cameron Boyd-Taylor, "The Evidentiary Value of Septuagintall Usage for Greek Lexicography", *BIOSCS* 34 (2001): 47–80; Takamitsu Muraoka, "Recent Discussions on Septuagint Lexicography With Special Reference to the So-called Interlinear Model", in *Die Septuaginta – Texte, Kontexte, Lebenswelten* (ed. Martin Karrer, Wolfgang Kraus; WUNT I, 219; Tübingen: Mohr, 2008), 221–235.
5 "Forschen wir den letzten Quellen unserer Kenntnis der hebräischen Wortbedeutungen nach, so lassen sich diese au folgende *drei* zurückführen: 1) der *Sprachgebrauch des A.T.* selbst, soweit er aus dem Zusammenhange der einzelnen Stellen und der Vergleichung aller derer in welchen ein Wort oder eine Phrase vorkommen, erkannt wird; 2) die *traditionelle Kenntniss* der hebräischen Sprache, welche sich bei den *Juden* erhalten hat, und theils in *alten Uebersetzungen,* theils in den *jüdischen Commentarien* und *Wörterbüchern* niedergelegt ist; 3) die Vergleichung der *stammverwandten Sprachen,* welche zwar alle in den uns vorliegenden Denkmäler jünger sind, als das A.T., aber zum Theil reicher, als das biblische Hebräisch, und entweder lebende durch einheimische Grammatiker lexicalisch bearbeitete Sprachen, oder wenigstens in mehrere Schriftstellern erhalten sind, so dass über die Bedeutungen der wörter verhältnismässig seltener als im Hebräischen Zweifel obwalten können". Wilhelm Gesenius, *Hebräisches und chaldäisches Handwörterbuch über das Alten Testament* (Leipzig: Vogel, 1857[5]), III.

language[6]. The translators may have had access to linguistic knowledge that was later forgotten. Almost in the same breath, however, Gesenius expresses his mistrust toward most of the lexical information that can be gained from the Greek version. The translators' knowledge of Hebrew was partial and imperfect.

The somewhat ambivalent view of the Septuagint expressed by Gesenius continues to dominate in more recent lexicographical research. Many new meanings of Hebrew words have been suggested on the basis of information drawn from the Septuagint. James Barr collected a significant number of such proposals in his book *Comparative Philology and the Text of the Old Testament* published in 1968[7]. But Barr didn't commit to any of them. Moreover, few of those "new meanings" made it into the mainstream continental dictionaries of Biblical Hebrew, although it is to be said that the Sheffield Hebrew Dictionary is more open in this respect. Septuagint renderings are very often the earliest witness to the correct interpretation of Hebrew words. But its authority is hard to assess. The Greek translators seem to have had access to lexical information of good quality. But they also err often enough. Some Hebrew words are rendered with such a wide range of equivalents that it appears the translators are simply guessing[8]. Thus, even the felicitous renderings of the Septuagint may elicit skepticism. When a Hebrew word is translated correctly, is it because the translators disposed of authentic linguistic knowledge, or because they guessed the meaning correctly from the context?

In spite of widespread skepticism, much of it justified, no Hebrew lexicographer has been emboldened to jettison the Septuagint altogether. The guidelines fixed by Gesenius still hold.

---

6 This was true even according to Gesenius' now outdated view according to which Hebrew died out some time in the Hasmonean Age. See in more detail, Jan Joosten, "Wilhelm Gesenius and the history of Hebrew in the Biblical period", forthcoming in a volume to be edited by Stefan Schorch in the BZAW series.

7 See above, note 2.

8 See Emanuel Tov, "Did the Septuagint Translators Always Understand Their Hebrew Text?" in *De Septuaginta. Studies in honour of John William Wevers on his sixty-fifth birthday* (ed. Albert Pietersma, Claude Cox; Missisauga, Ontario: Benben, 1984), 53–70, reprinted in E. Tov, *The Greek and Hebrew Bible. Collected Essays on the Septuagint* (Leiden: Brill, 1999), 203–218.

1.1 New Hebrew Words Recovered on the Basis of the Septuagint

An obvious place where the Septuagint becomes relevant for the study of Hebrew words is when textual criticism leads to the recovery of new words on the basis of the Greek translation. An interesting example is found in 1 Kgs 1:36. After David, at the instigation of Nathan, has instructed his men to install Solomon on the throne, Benaiah expresses himself as follows:

> 1 Kgs 1:36
> אָמֵן כֵּן יֹאמַר יְהוָה
> Amen: thus may YHWH say.

MT's "Thus may YHWH *say*" is weak both stylistically and substantially. One expects an assertion that God will bless the initiative, be pleased by it, or bring it about. A number of divergent readings are attested in the versions[9]. The most interesting reading is found in the Septuagint[10]:

> Γένοιτο· οὕτως πιστώσαι κύριος
> Let it be. Thus may the Lord *confirm*.

This reading is contextually much better than that of the MT. Moreover, it is probably not a facilitating reading created by the translator. Instead, the Greek verb almost certainly reflects a form of the root אמן "to be firm". The equivalence between אמן and πιστόω is well attested in the Septuagint[11]. And the roots אמר and אמן are confused in other biblical passages[12].Thus it appears that the *Vorlage* of the Old Greek read:

> אמן כן יאמן יהוה
> Amen, thus may YHWH confirm.

---

9 See BHS and C. F. Burney, *Notes on the Hebrew text of the books of Kings* (Clarendon; Oxford, 1903), 9. A full discussion of the readings and the way they relate to one another will be contained in the 1 Kings volume of the Oxford Hebrew Bible, which Jan Joosten, Jean Koulagna and Matthieu Richelle are preparing in the framework of the *Groupe de Recherches sur la Septante et le Judaïsme Ancien*, Strasbourg.

10 The Septuagint evidence is itself complicated because the Lucianic text has a doublet which also diverges from the MT, see James A. Montgomery, Henry S. Gehman, *The Book of Kings* (ICC; Edinburgh: T. &. T. Clark, 1950), 85.

11 See, e.g., 2 Sam 7:16; 1 Kgs 8:26; 2 Chr 1:9; Ps 78(77):8.

12 See e.g. Jer 15:11, MT versus the Septuagint; Hos 12:1 MT versus Septuagint and Targum.

It is impossible to know the stem form of the verb אמן intended in this clause. Most likely it was – in our terms – either a *piel* or a *hiphil*. Since the *hiphil* is elsewhere used in the meaning 'to trust, to believe', the piel is perhaps more likely. In any case, there are no attestations in the biblical corpus of a hiphil or piel of אמן meaning 'to confirm'. This helps to explain the MT: the rare יַאֲמֵן "may he confirm" was inadvertently read as יאמר "may he say", substituting a frequent verb for a rare one.

If these text-critical considerations are accepted, dictionaries of Biblical Hebrew should be enriched with a notice that אמן, piel or hiphil, means 'to confirm'. The interest of such an addition emerges in the light of Qumran Hebrew. One of the non-biblical texts discovered in the caves attests the piel of אמן with the meaning 'to confirm, to ratify (a covenant)':

4QBark^c (4Q436) 1:4
ובריתכה אמנתה לי
And your covenant you have confirmed unto me.

The usage is unique in the Scrolls. Rabbinic Hebrew adds a few attestations:

Tos. *Ter.* I, 4
אביו שאמן אחריו
His father who confirmed (his utterance) after him (the minor)[13].

The verb is not an Aramaism. One might be tempted to explain it as a late Hebrew innovation. However, the textual data suggest that it is rather to be viewed as the continuation of a rare early usage.

It is difficult to estimate how many Hebrew words or meanings could be added to the biblical lexicon if textual emendations were taken into account. Perhaps the number would be rather small. As the connections with later texts show, even a small amount of supplementary data can be significant.

1.2 Authentic Lexical Information Known to the Translators

Far more common is the use of the Septuagint in recovering the meaning of Hebrew words by the help of their Greek equivalent. Much of this work has been done centuries ago, and is nowadays part and parcel of the lexicographical tra-

---

13 For other attestations, see Marcus Jastrow, *A Dictionary of the Targumim, the Talmud Babli and Yerushalmi, and the Midrashic Literature* (1903; reprinted New York: Pardes, 1950).

dition[14]. Nevertheless, new discoveries remain to be made. New texts may throw a different light on Greek equivalents that had never been taken seriously[15]. Or research on non-Tiberian traditions of Hebrew may turn out to work hand-in-hand with the Septuagint[16]. In such cases, research on the Hebrew side works as a catalyst in showing the relevance of Septuagint renderings for the definition of Hebrew word meanings.

In other cases, research on the Greek side may play a similar role. The Septuagint is a difficult corpus. Sometimes it is necessary to do some lexicography on Greek words before they can be used in Hebrew lexicography. An example will illustrate what such cases may involve. In a doctoral dissertation on *Laws on Loans in the Bible* submitted to the Hebrew University in 2010, Avi Shveka has proposed to redefine the meaning of חבל I, qal[17]. Instead of 'to take or hold a pledge' – the meaning proposed in all modern dictionaries – he argues the verb should be understood to mean 'to distrain, to distress'; it does not refer to action undertaken by a creditor who seeks a guaranty that his loan will be repaid, but to action of a creditor whose loan is overdue and who makes life miserable for his debtors until they pay[18]. The main evidence for this reinterpretation comes from Job and Ezekiel, where חבל is referred to as an action that is inherently reprehensible:

Ezek 18:16

וְאִישׁ לֹא הוֹנָה חֲבֹל לֹא חָבָל וּגְזֵלָה לֹא גָזָל

He does not wrong anybody, *exacts no pledge* and commits no robbery.

The exegetical relevance of this reinterpretation is greatest in legal passages in Exodus and Deuteronomy. Instead of excluding certain objects from being taken as security, the laws in effect, according to the new proposal, forbid the use of excessive force in recovering debts. To my mind, there is a lot to say in

---

14 See, e.g., Takamitsu Muraoka, "Apports de la LXX dans notre compréhension de l'hébreu et du grec, et de leur vocabulaire", in *L'apport de la Septante aux études sur l'Antiquité. Actes du colloque de Strasbourg 8 et 9 novembre 2002* (ed. Jan Joosten, Philippe Le Moigne; Lectio Divina 203; Paris: Cerf, 2005), 57–68.

15 See, e.g., Elisha Qimron, "The Biblical Lexicon in Light of the Dead Sea Scrolls", *DSD* 2 (1995): 295–329.

16 See Zeev Ben-Hayim, "Traditions in the Hebrew Language, with Special Reference to the Dead Sea Scrolls", *Scripta Hierosolymitana* 4 (1958): 200–214, in particular 212–214.

17 See Avi Shveka, "Biblical Laws of Loans: A Comparative Perspective" (PhD diss., Hebrew University, 2010), 17–43.

18 Shveka follows an interpretation known from ancient Jewish sources and more recently defended also by Shalom M. Paul, *Amos* (Hermeneia; Minneapolis: Fortress, 1991), 83–85.

favor of the thesis argued by Shveka. In fact, there is a bit more to say for it than he realizes. With regard to the Septuagint, Shveka merely states that it inaugurates a long tradition, continued by all modern dictionaries, of taking the verb in the meaning of 'to take or hold a pledge'. Ostensibly, this judgment is correct. Throughout the Septuagint, with one or two exceptions, Hebrew חבל I qal is rendered systematically with the verb ἐνεχυράζω[19]:

> Ezek 18:16 LXX
> καὶ ἄνθρωπον οὐ κατεδυνάστευσεν καὶ ἐνεχυρασμὸν οὐκ ἐνεχύρασεν καὶ ἅρπαγμα οὐχ ἥρπασεν
> [He] did not oppress a person and *did not exact a pledge* and did not commit robbery (NETS).

According to the lexicon of Liddell, Scott and Jones, the meaning of the Greek verb is, indeed, 'to take a pledge, take in pledge'.

As all Septuagint scholars know, the meanings given in LSJ do not always apply to the Septuagint – even when, as in this case, biblical passages are expressly mentioned in the lexicon article. One of the main problems is that LSJ is oriented toward the vocabulary of classical literature, while the Septuagint often uses post-classical and non-literary Greek. As was demonstrated by Adolf Deissmann at the end of the 19th century, and more recently by John Lee and others, much of the vocabulary of the Septuagint finds its closest analogue in documentary papyri of the Ptolemaic age. The distinction is relevant in the present case. In the papyri, ἐνεχυράζω does appear to mean 'to take a pledge' once or twice. But far more often the verb appears in contexts where a different meaning is required. In such contexts, it occurs together with the verbs περισπάω 'to vex', εἰσβιάζομαι 'to force one's way into (a house)', ἀποβιάζομαι 'to treat with violence', or ὑβρίζω 'to insult'. In an IOU dated 182 or 158 B.C.E., the debtor writes that if he does not pay the debt in time, ἐξέσται σοι ἐνεχυράζειν με παντὶ τρόπωι ᾧ ἐὰν αἱρεῖ "you may – – me in any way you choose"[20]. Clearly, the meaning 'to take a pledge' does not apply here and the meaning 'to distrain, to pressurize' is much more apposite. It appears that in Hellenistic usage, the meaning of the verb evolved from 'to take a pledge' to 'to distrain', no doubt because the exaction of "pledges" was often used by creditors as a means to exert pressure on their debtors. In light of the usage dominating in the papyri, the Septuagint occurrences may have to be rendered differently. The earliest readers of

---

19 The only exceptions are Prov 20:16; 27:13.

20 See *Sammelbuch griechischer Urkunden aus Ägypten, Vierundzwanzigster Band (Nr. 15875– 16340)* (ed. Hans-Albert Rupprecht; Joachim Hengstl; Wiesbaden: Otto Harrassowitz, 2003), n° 16296.

the Septuagint may have understood the verse in Ezekiel quoted above to mean: "He did not oppress a person and *did not pressurize anyone to pay a debt...*" Indeed, one passage strongly favors the post-classical interpretation:

> Judith 8:16
> ὑμεῖς δὲ μὴ ἐνεχυράζετε τὰς βουλὰς κυρίου τοῦ θεοῦ ἡμῶν, ὅτι οὐχ ὡς ἄνθρωπος ὁ θεὸς ἀπειληθῆναι
> Do not *try to bind* (?) the purposes of the Lord our God, for God is not like a human being, to be threatened... (NRSV)[21].

Judith here protests against the promise of Uzziah, the town elder, to surrender after holding out five more days against the Assyrians. Judith's claim is that one cannot force God to act in this way. The meaning 'to take a pledge' does not fit the passage at all. Different modern translations have sought more or less plausible interpretations: the NRSV reflects the idea that a pledge may bind one to a course of action. The notion of distrainment or pressurizing, however, accords much better with the context: in Judith's eyes, the people of Bethulia are treating God as a recalcitrant debtor, whom they are forcing to pay up. If the verb ἐνεχυράζω indeed means 'to distrain, to pressurize' in the Septuagint, then the Greek version confirms the interpretation of Hebrew חבל proposed by Shveka. Admittedly, even if all of this is true, one may still doubt whether the Greek rendering is based on sound knowledge of Biblical Hebrew rather than on contextual exegesis of the biblical passages in which the Hebrew verb occurs.

The example shows that, if one considers the Septuagint to be relevant at all, the analysis of the Greek data should be done according to state of the art in Septuagint studies. Over and beyond this, the example illustrates the heuristic value of a more comprehensive approach to biblical lexicography. In the end, a skeptical lexicographer may estimate that the meaning of ἐνεχυράζω in the Septuagint is hard to define, that the contribution of the Greek rendering to the understanding of חבל I is therefore problematic, and that the true lexical meaning of the Hebrew remains in doubt. Even such agnosticism will have to recognize the value of the detour through Septuagint lexicography. It is relevant to observe that the semantic development from 'to take a pledge' to 'to pressurize' is a plausible one, as the Greek data illustrate[22]. Even if חבל strictly means 'to take a pledge', it would be easy to imagine that, in Ancient Israel as in Ptolemaic

---

21 Cf. NETS: "do not hold to account the purposes of the Lord, our God".

22 Reading through the Greek papyri using the verb ἐνεχυράζω gives one a feel for the realities involved in the kind of transactions regulated in biblical laws on loans. "Real-world" implications may not belong to lexicography in the strict sense of the word, but they are certainly relevant for the exegete.

Egypt, the taking of pledges would often be done for no other reason than to put additional pressure on a debtor suspected of being on the verge of defaulting on his debt.

2. The study of Hebrew meanings and its use in Septuagint lexicography

A more controversial question is that of the use of Hebrew in determining the meaning of Septuagint words. Although lexicographers have often defined the meaning of Septuagint words on the basis of the purported meaning of the Hebrew, this practice has been widely criticized[23]. In recent publications there has been something of a backlash. Nowadays, Septuagint lexicographers for the most part keep their distance from the Hebrew. The meaning of the Greek words – so goes the theory – is to be determined solely on the basis of Hellenistic Greek usage and the biblical context. For the most part, this is a healthy attitude. Particularly in cases where one suspects that a Hebrew word has tainted the meaning of its Greek equivalent, this should be demonstrated solely on contextual grounds. The Septuagint does contain a number of "Greek words with Hebrew meanings" (to use David Hill's celebrated phrase), such as κτίζω 'to create' or δόξα 'glory', which have taken on a new meaning more or less unattested in non-biblical Greek. But this new meaning can be established only on the basis of the contexts in which the Greek word occurs[24]. If we decide to translate the Greek verb εὐλογέω, normally meaning 'to praise', as 'to bless' in the Septuagint, this is not because it translates Hebrew ברך, but because it occurs constantly in contexts where the meaning 'to praise' does not fit and the meaning 'to bless' is required.

Nevertheless, the purist exclusion of the Hebrew from Septuagint lexicography is not warranted in all cases. In a recent article, I have argued that Hebrew can play a part in Septuagint lexicography, although a limited one[25]. Alongside

---

23 See, e.g., G. B. Caird, "Towards a Lexicon of the Septuagint I," *JThS* 19 (1968): 453–475; idem, "Towards a Lexicon of the Septuagint II," *JThS* 20 (1969): 21–40; Katrin *Hauspie*, "The LXX Quotations in the LSJ Supplements of 1968 and 1996," in *Biblical Greek Language and Lexicography. Essays in Honor of Frederick W. Danker* (ed. B.A. Taylor *et al.*; Grand Rapids: Eerdmans, 2004), 108–125.
24 The most convincing evidence of semantic development comes from cases where the new meaning is attested in texts that were originally written in Greek.
25 Jan Joosten, "Source-language Oriented Remarks on the Lexicography of the Greek Versions of the Bible," *EThL* 81 (2005): 152–164.

lexicographical information on Hellenistic Greek, and alongside analysis of the Biblical context, study of the source text may function as a heuristic tool. It will help in determining which meaning the translators were thinking of when they rendered a word in a given way. This can prove to be particularly helpful with Greek words that are polysemic. This will again be illustrated by a single example. Consider the Greek verb κατακρατέω in the following passage in the Minor Prophets:

> Mic 1:9
> ὅτι **κατεκράτησεν** ἡ πληγὴ αὐτῆς, διότι ἦλθεν ἕως Ιουδα καὶ ἥψατο ἕως πύλης λαοῦ μου, ἕως Ιερουσαλημ
> For her plague **has become grievous**; for it has come even to Juda; and has reached to the gate of my people, even to Jerusalem (Brenton).
>
> כִּי אֲנוּשָׁה מַכּוֹתֶיהָ כִּי־בָאָה עַד־יְהוּדָה נָגַע עַד־שַׁעַר עַמִּי עַד־יְרוּשָׁלָ͏ם
> For her wound is **incurable.** It has come to Judah; it has reached to the gate of my people, to Jerusalem (NRSV).

In the Septuagint, κατακρατέω is practically always used as a transitive verb meaning 'to seize, to lay hold of, to gain mastery of'. Thus NETS has translated "her blow has taken hold" suggesting a kind of ellipsis. The Syrohexapla likewise translates *'eḥdat mḥota dilah* "her blow has *seized*". In the present passage, however, the verb seems to be intransitive; at least, there is no obvious direct object. Brenton renders the verb "to become grievous", and Muraoka in his lexicon proposes the gloss 'to intensify'[26]. The latter meanings are attested in classical Greek, but not elsewhere in the Septuagint[27]. The lexicographer faces conflict: the context seems to impose the intransitive reading 'to become strong', while the Septuagint lexicon favors the transitive meaning 'to seize, to overpower'. At this point, a look at the Hebrew may be helpful.

At first blush, the information to be gained from the Hebrew is inconclusive. Hebrew אנש means 'to be weak, to be sick', and the passive participle is used to qualify medical conditions that are serious. If anything, the meaning of the Hebrew would seem to strengthen the intransitive reading of Greek κατεκράτησεν. A closer look shows that the Hebrew root אנש may not have been well known to the translators: אנוש is rendered στερεός 'hard' in Jer 15:18, (Theodotion), and ανιστημι 'to raise' in Jer 30:12; it is confused with אנוש 'human being' in Isa

---

26 Takamitsu Muraoka, *A Greek-English Lexicon of the Septuagint* (Leuven: Peeters, 2009).

27 There are two apparent exceptions, but they are both problematic and should not be fielded in favor of the meaning "to become strong": for Nah 3:14, *Les Douze Prophètes 4–9* (ed. Marguerite Harl *et al.*; La Bible d'Alexandrie XXIII 4–9; Paris: Cerf; 1999), 228; for 1 Kgs 12:24u, see Muraoka, *Lexicon*, 374 ("he put his foot down").

17:11; Jer 17:9, 16. If κατεκράτησεν reflects אנושה, one would have to treat the Greek rendering as a guess.

There is another possibility, however. Perhaps instead of the root אנש 'to be weak', the translator thought of what we would define as the root אנס with *samekh*. In the Qumran scrolls, confusion of *shin/sin* and *samekh* is frequent; the root אנס is at times written with a *shin:*

> 1QS VII 12
> ואשר יהלך לפני רעהו ערום ולוא היה אנוש
> 4Q261 f5a_c:6 היה אנוש
> Anyone who walks about naked in the presence of a comrade, unless he be *forced.*

Confusion of *shin/sin* and *samekh* is well attested also in the Septuagint[28]. Thus the confusion seems plausible. According to a recent study by David Talshir, the root אנס, in post-biblical Hebrew and Jewish Aramaic, expressed the meanings: 'to despoil, to extort, *to seize, to subjugate*, to prevent, to force, to rape a woman'[29]. He lists several passages in which the verb has an impersonal subject overpowering a personal object: חלמי אנסני "my dream overpowered me" (4Q531 f22:9); משתיא אנסיה "(his) drinking overpowered him" (BGit 68b). This is very close to the meaning expressed by Greek κατακρατέω in some Septuagint passages:

> Mic 4:9 LXX
> **κατεκράτησάν** σου ὠδῖνες ὡς τικτούσης
> Pangs as those of a woman in childbirth **have overcome you**[30].

All this leads up to the hypothesis that the translator in Mic 1:9 identified אנושה (disregarding the *waw*, and perhaps analyzing the *he* as a suffix pronoun) as a form of the verb אנס and translated accordingly. Although the verb אנס is poorly attested in the Hebrew Bible, it may well have been part of the translator's mental lexicon. The Septuagint translators rather often render the biblical text after Late Hebrew or Aramaic[31].

---

28 In the book of Micah, see Mic 5:4, where נסיכי "princes" is rendered δήγματα "bites" after the root נשך.
29 David Talshir, "On the use of אנס in Aramaic and in Hebrew", *Meghillot* 3 (2005): 205–229.
30 See also 1 Mac 6:54, κατεκράτησεν αὐτῶν ὁ λιμός, "hunger overpowered them".
31 See the studies of the present author gathered in Jan Joosten, *Collected Studies on the Septuagint. From Language to Interpretation and Beyond* (FAT I, 83; Tübingen: Mohr-Siebeck, 2012), 25–120.

If this is correct, it follows that the translator intended the clause κατεκράτη-σεν ἡ πληγὴ αὐτῆς to mean: "the plague has overcome her", taking the personal pronoun as the object of the verb[32].That this meaning could indeed be perceived by a Greek reader in Antiquity is shown in the commentary of Cyril of Alexandria. Cyril first quotes the lemma according to the received Septuagint text, but in his commentary reorders the text to κατεκράτησεν αὐτῆς ἡ πληγή, showing that to him the pronoun is indeed governed by the verb. From here, he goes on to explain that the verse refers to Sennacherib who, "having *occupied* all Samaria and ravaged Judea, besieged Jerusalem"[33].

As should be clear, the argument is not that the meaning of the Hebrew verb may be transferred to the Greek. The argument is that given the polysemy of certain Greek words, and given the obscurity of some Septuagint contexts, lexicographers should be open to all the help they can get. Study of the Hebrew may indicate which meaning of a Greek word the translators were thinking of when they used it in the translation. It may seem perilous to try and penetrate the mind of the translators, to guess why they chose the words they chose. Often enough, the process of translation remains a mystery. Once in a while, however, close philological study may throw light on this or that Greek equivalent. Such occasions should not be neglected, nor shamefully hidden from sight, but carefully exploited for a better understanding of the version and its vocabulary. This point keeps its validity even if the present example should be judged not to be convincing.

2.1 From Hebrew to Greek, and back

The Greek may illuminate the Hebrew, and vice versa. In some cases, the process operates in the two directions simultaneously. It is not rare that comparative study of Hebrew words in the Bible and their Greek equivalents in the Septuagint leads to a better understanding of both. This may happen in surprising ways, as may be illustrated with a few additional remarks continuing the example in Mic 1:9 discussed above.

According to a note in the Syrohexapla, Symmachus and Theodotion diverged from the Septuagint in their rendering of the Hebrew adjective אנושה. The Syriac equivalent is *qaṭīrāytā* 'forcible', which in other passages corresponds to Greek βίαιος. On this basis, scholars retrovert the same Greek adjective in Mic

---

32 This was correctly understood by Giguet, who in his French translation writes: "la plaie l'accable". See P. Giguet, *La Sainte Bible. Traduction de l'Ancien Testament d'après les Septante,* Tome III (Paris: Poussielgue, 1872), 633.
33 PG 71, col. 656.

1:9 as well. βίαιος is attested for both Aquila and Theodotion in a few other places where the Hebrew text has אנוש. As is well known, Aquila and Theodotion
usually practice stereotyped translation, associating one and only one Greek
word with any one Hebrew word – Symmachus is less systematic in this regard.
It is fairly certain, therefore, that Aquila and Theodotion rendered each occurrence of the adjective אנוש with Greek βίαιος[34]. What is the meaning of this
Greek word? Muraoka in his lexicon provides the gloss: 'possessed of great
power', and translates 'strong, powerful', including a passage from Theodotion
in Job 34:6 where the Hebrew has אנוש. In light of the usage of the word in
non-translated Greek[35], this is certainly a possible interpretation. The *recentiores*
would have associated the Hebrew word not with weakness, as we would do
today on the basis of etymology, but with strength, presumably on the basis of
the contexts in which it occurs[36].

It is also possible, however, that Greek βίαιος was chosen to render Hebrew
אנוש because it expressed the meaning 'forced, constrained'. This second meaning too is well attested in all varieties of Greek. It opens up the possibility that
the rendering is not in fact based on contextual exegesis, but on identification
of the roots אנש and אנס, in the same way as was argued for the translator of
Micah in the preceding section. Aquila and Theodotion may have considered
that אנוש equaled אנוס 'forced'. A blow described as אנוש would be a blow
from which there is no escape.

In light of these considerations, it is interesting to look again at some data
from Qumran Hebrew. Alongside the passage in the Rule Scroll where אנוש with
shin/sin almost certainly means 'forced', the adjective אנוש occurs in two passages in the Hodayoth where it qualifies the noun כאוב 'pain':

> 1QHa XIII 30 (+4Q429 f2:11) ותהי לכאוב אנוש ונגע נמאר
> And (the poison) will become a – pain and a grievous sore.

> 1QHa XVI 28–29 כי פרח נגֹ֯[י]֯עֹֿי למרורים וכאוב אנוש
> For my sores have burst into a – pain that cannot be stopped.

In these passages, all interpreters have given the adjective its biblical meaning of
'serious, incurable'. Although again possible, this identification is less than cer-

---

34 See N. Turner, J. Reider, *An Index to Aquila* (Leiden: Brill, 1966). Note that in Jer 30:12, two
different renderings of אנוש are attributed to Aquila: a) ἀπεγνωσμένον 'desperate' (reflecting
contamination with the Hebrew root יאש, cf also Ps 69:21 and the Vulgate rendering of Jer
15:18); b) βίαιον.
35 And also in Aquila himself, for βίαιος is also the rendering of Hebrew גבור, see Gen 10:8 etc.
36 Note also the rendering תקיף 'strong' in Targum Jonathan to Jer 15:18 ; 17:9; 30:12.

tain. In light of the Greek data from Aquila and Theodotion, one might suppose that Qumran Hebrew knew only one root אנש / אנס "to force, etc.". The association with pain would be based on biblical passages such as Isa 17:11 or Jer 30:15, but the interpretation of the adjective may be more indebted to post-biblical Hebrew and Aramaic.

In modern dictionaries – BDB, KBL³, SHD, Gesenius[18] – the adjective אנוש is routinely translated as 'incurable' (or 'unheilbar' in German). This rendering probably goes back to the Vulgate's *insanabilis* in Jer 30:12, 15. Jerome appears to have adopted this interpretation from Symmachus, for whom the equivalence between אנוש and ἀνίατος is attested in Jer 15:18 and 30:12. As long as it is not taken too literally, the rendering is contextually serviceable, particularly in passages where the adjective qualifies wounds or afflictions. But what is it based on? Where did Symmachus, if indeed he is the first to have proposed this translation, get his idea? Perhaps, he derived it from the context; in Jer 15:18 reads הָרְפֵא מֵאֲנָה אֲנוּשָׁה וּמַכָּתִי "my wound is –, it refuses to be healed". I wonder, however, whether Symmachus' choice may not, at least partly, have been inspired by the identification of the roots אנש and אנס: an 'incurable' wound is a wound that cannot be stopped, a wound that is forced on one and from which there is no escape.

The discussion of this example has come full circle. Our starting point was the problem of the Greek verb κατακρατέω in Mic 1:9. The possibility that the translator thought of the verb אנש / אנס 'to overpower' throws light on the meaning of this Greek verb. Going on from here, the question was raised whether at some stage in the interpretation of the Hebrew Bible, the verbs אנש and אנס may have been amalgamated more generally. The data in the late Greek translations of Aquila and Theodotion suggest that this was indeed the case. If so, this might have implications for Hebrew lexicography, not of the Bible, but of Qumran Hebrew: instead of two roots, אנש and אנס, this state of the language may know only one verb in two spellings. Finally, one might ask whether Symmachus, Jerome and, in their wake, modern dictionaries of Hebrew, do not also reflect this confusion, thus straying from the true interpretation of the biblical words.

Conclusion

Although recently engaged in a major lexical enterprise[37], the present author cannot look back, like some of the other distinguished contributors to the present volume, on any amount of experience as a working lexicographer. His forays into Hebrew and Greek semantics are those, mostly, of an exegete trying to interpret ancient texts. As an avid and assiduous user of Hebrew and Greek dictionaries, he is grateful to those who spend many years of their productive scholarly lives working in the field of lexicology. He is neither competent, nor desirous to formulate fundamental criticism of the teams producing or having produced dictionaries of biblical and peri-biblical corpora. The above remarks are more in the way of wishful thinking.

As has been illustrated by the help of a few examples, lexicological and lexicographical research on biblical texts would profit if there were more exchanges and more conversation between specialists of Hebrew and specialists of biblical Greek. The study of biblical Hebrew vocabulary can derive immense benefits from bringing the Septuagint into the picture, not perfunctorily but according to the best and latest practices established in the field. Similarly, lexicographers of Septuagintal literature should keep an eye on the Hebrew text, again not just in a superficial way, but with full awareness of the exegetical ins and outs, including the history of interpretation up to the early middle ages. What would be involved is probably out of reach to any one individual, interdisciplinary collaboration would be called for.

Contrary to expectation, perhaps, research on the meaning of Hebrew and Greek words in biblical texts, although stretching back many centuries, hasn't come to the end of the road. As the present volume shows, many new discoveries remain to be made. Various factors are changing our understanding of the biblical corpora, not just on the philosophical and hermeneutical levels, but in regard to philological minutiae as well. The discovery of the Dead Sea Scrolls has been an important catalyst, non-Tiberian Hebrew traditions are attracting renewed attention, Semitic studies are in a flux, Septuagint research is experiencing a real revival. An important worry is how to raise students to take care of all of this knowledge in the next generation. The most immediate challenge, however, is to keep an eye on the whole in spite of increasing demands of specialization: Old Testament scholars, Qumranologists, and Septuagint experts – not to speak of Hebraists, New Testament Scholars, specialists of Second Temple Judaism, etc. – need to speak to one another. The whole is greater than the sum of the parts.

---

37 See the contribution of Eberhard Bons to the present volume.

Part III: **Greek**

Gilles Dorival
La lexicographie de la Septante entre Sem et Japhet

En Genèse 9,25–27, Noé maudit son fils dernier-né, Cham, qui a vu sa nudité alors qu'il était ivre. Il annonce que Cham sera le serviteur de ses deux fils aînés, Sem et Japhet. Il ajoute à propos de ce dernier: «Qu'il habite dans les habitations de Sem». Pour Bar Qappara, qui a été actif entre 180 et 220 à Césarée de Palestine et qui recommandait l'étude du grec, ce verset signifie que les mots de la Loi peuvent être prononcés dans la langue de Japhet, c'est-à-dire en grec, dans les tentes de Sem, c'est-à-dire en Israël[1]. Vers 300, rabbi Yuda commentait ainsi: «de ce verset nous apprenons qu'une traduction est permise»[2]. Cette position d'ouverture à la langue grecque a sûrement été minoritaire chez les Sages. Toutefois ce n'est pas ce point qui retiendra l'attention ici, mais la portée des propos de Bar Qappara et Yuda pour la lexicographie biblique: à leurs yeux, Sem et Japhet symbolisent respectivement la langue source des Ecritures, l'hébreu, et la langue cible par excellence, le grec. D'où la question: du point de vue lexicographique, comment la langue de Sem et la langue de Japhet s'articulent-elles entre elles?

1. Le modèle interlinéaire et le modèle socioculturel

Au moins à première analyse, on peut répartir les lexicographes modernes de la Septante en deux catégories: ceux qui privilégient la langue source, l'amont, et ceux qui accordent la priorité à la langue cible, l'aval. Le modèle interlinéaire défendu depuis une quinzaine d'années par Albert Pietersma, Cameron Boyd Taylor et de nombreux chercheurs anglophones défend la priorité de l'original hébreu sur la LXX[3]. La traduction de la LXX est en relation de dépendance par

---

1 Talmud de Jérusalem *Megillah* 1,11, p. 71b; voir aussi *Bereshit Rabbah* 38,8.
2 Bereshit Rabbah 36,8.
3 Albert Pietersma, «A New Paradigm for Addressing Old Questions: The Relevance of the Interlinear Model for the Study of the Septuagint», In *Bible and Computer*, ed. Johann Cook (Leiden: Brill, 2002), 337–364; Albert Pietersma, Benjamin G. Wright, eds, *A New English Translation of the Septuagint and other Greek Translations Traditionally Included under that Title* (New York/Oxford: Oxford University Press, 2007), XVI-XVII; Cameron Boyd-Taylor, «A Place in

rapport à l'hébreu. Cette dépendance se manifeste dans le fait qu'elle ne peut pas être lue indépendamment de l'hébreu, parce que les influences qu'elle a subies la rendent souvent incompréhensible pour quiconque ne fait pas référence au texte source. Les deux textes doivent donc être maniés ensemble. La traduction répond en fait à un but pédagogique: celui de servir, aux côtés de l'original hébreu, comme une aide écrite à la fois pour étudier la langue hébraïque et pour comprendre le texte biblique. Le terme d'interlinéarité a renvoyé un temps à l'existence d'un document interlinéaire réel, mais il est employé à présent dans le sens métaphorique d'une relation de dépendance et de soumission. Les traducteurs fournissent des équivalents mot-à-mot de l'hébreu quand cela est possible, paraphrasent les passages difficiles ou obscurs, ajoutent des explications quand l'hébreu risque d'être mal compris. Pour respecter la relation de dépendance de la LXX par rapport à l'hébreu, la New English Translation of the Septuagint (NETS) ne propose pas une traduction directe du texte grec, mais part de la traduction de l'hébreu telle que la propose la New Revised Standard Version (NRSV) et lui apporte les modifications qu'impose la LXX. Le *Lexicon* de Johan Lust, Erik Eynikel et Katrin Hauspie repose sur une position linguistique très proche[4].

Selon les tenants de la priorité du texte hébreu, l'entreprise française de la Bible d'Alexandrie et les travaux du grand lexicographe qu'est Takamitsu Muraoka accordent la priorité au texte cible, puisqu'ils utilisent, pour établir le sens des mots de la LXX, les textes, les papyri et les inscriptions de l'époque hellénistique et romaine[5]. On pourrait qualifier leur modèle linguistique de socioculturel. La Bible d'Alexandrie est critiquée parce qu'elle serait une traduction selon les Pères, qu'elle utilise en effet dans son annotation. Toutefois, au moins dans le cas du Pentateuque il serait plus juste de parler d'une traduction selon Philon d'Alexandrie et les lecteurs juifs hellénophones de la LXX, Nouveau Testament compris.

Les deux modèles lexicographiques ainsi dégagés ne vont pas sans poser problème. Le modèle interlinéaire rend problématique l'établissement d'un

---

the Sun: The Interpretative Significance of LXX-Psalm 18:5c», *BIOSCS* 31 (1998), 71–105 (la LXX comme «métaphrase», comparée à la manière dont le texte d'Homère était manipulé dans les écoles d'Egypte, tantôt rendu mot-à-mot dans la langue de la koiné tantôt paraphrasé) et «Lexicography and Interlanguage – Gaining our Bearings», *BIOSCS* 37 (2004), 55–72 (la LXX comme «interlangage», un concept emprunté à Gideon Toury, *Descriptive Translation Studies and Beyond* (Amsterdam: John Benjamins Publishing Company, 1995)).

4 Johan Lust, Erik Eynikel, Katrin Hauspie, *A Greek-English Lexicon of the Septuagint*, 2 vol. [α-ι, κ-ω] (Stuttgart: Deutsche Bibelgesellschaft, 1992–1996).

5 Takamitsu Muraoka, *A Greek-English Lexicon of the Septuagint* (Louvain/Paris/Walpole (MA): Peeters, 2009).

lexique de la LXX, puisque le grec est sous la dépendance de l'hébreu. Il est nécessaire et suffisant de connaître le sens des mots hébreux pour connaître le sens des mots grecs correspondants. En conséquence, un mot grec donné n'a pas forcément la signification qu'il a habituellement en grec, mais celle du mot hébreu qui lui correspond. Ainsi, selon Albert Pietersma, dans les Psaumes, ἔλεος ne signifie pas «pitié», mais «bienveillance, gentillesse», comme חסד qui lui correspond[6]. Mais, comme l'a montré Jan Joosten, dans le même livre des Psaumes, le verbe ἐλεέω et l'adjectif ἐλεήμων évoquent l'idée de pitié, à l'instar des mots hébreux qu'ils traduisent, les verbes חנן et רחם, l'adjectif חנון; il n'y aucune raison de penser qu' ἔλεος ait un autre sens que les mots qui lui sont apparentés[7]. De plus, le modèle interlinéaire est incapable de rendre compte des variations de traduction: en Genèse 31,19, תרפים est traduit par εἴδωλα; le traducteur de 1 Règnes ne se rappelait peut-être plus cette traduction, mais pourquoi a-t-il transcrit sous la forme θεραφίν en 15,23 et traduit par κενοταφία en 19,13 et 16? Le modèle interlinéaire ne permet pas non plus de mettre en évidence les innovations lexicographiques: κλητή, en Lévitique 23,3, correspond à מקרא («appelé»), mais il ne peut ici avoir ce sens; il est en fait un adjectif substantivé qui désigne un jour où le peuple est appelé à un rassemblement public[8]. Enfin le modèle interlinéaire n'a que faire des traditions d'interprétation, dont l'existence est pourtant plus que probable à l'époque de la traduction.

De son côté, le modèle socioculturel poussé à l'extrême risque de passer à côté de ce qui fait la coloration juive des mots de la LXX, dans la mesure où il s'efforce de leur donner l'un des sens usuels qu'ils ont dans les documents d'époque hellénistique. De plus, il est impuissant face aux décalques de traduction. Par exemple, le mot εἰρήνη est l'équivalent fixe de שלום en Juges (texte du *Vaticanus*) et 1–4 Règnes, dans des tours qui décalquent des expressions hébraïques de salutation, par lesquelles on demande des nouvelles. En 2 Règnes 11,7, David interroge Ouri «pour la paix de Joab et pour la paix du peuple et pour la paix de la guerre»; pour le traducteur bilingue, David demande des nouvelles de Joab, du peuple et de la guerre; «la paix de Joab» et «la paix du peuple» devaient paraître un peu mystérieuses à un lecteur grec, et «la paix de la guerre», franchement énigmatique. On peut se demander d'ailleurs si le mot grec

6 Albert Pietersma, *A New English Translation of the Bible: The Psalms* (Oxford/New York: Oxford University Press, 2000), XXII.
7 Jan Joosten, «חסד 'bienveillance' et ἔλεος 'pitié'. Réflexions sur une équivalence lexicale dans la Septante», In *«Car c'est l'amour qui me plaît, non le sacrifice...»*. Recherches sur Osée 6,6 et son interprétation juive et chrétienne, ed. Eberhard Bons (Leiden/Boston: Brill, 2004), 25–42.
8 Cécile Dogniez, «Les noms de fêtes dans le Pentateuque grec», *JSJ* 37 (2006), 344–366, en particulier 351.

a encore un sens au niveau du grec et s'il ne fonctionne pas plutôt comme le symbole du mot hébreu[9]. Ce qu'on note encore, c'est que ce sémitisme n'a pas été admis par les traducteurs du Pentateuque, qui ne rendent pas littéralement שלום, mais emploient des verbes comme ἀσπάζεσθαι ou ὑγιαίνειν. Enfin le modèle socioculturel au sens strict ne recourt pas aux traditions d'interprétation. Il partage cette carence avec le modèle interlinéaire. Toutefois, les traditions d'interprétation peuvent faire partie d'un modèle socioculturel élargi, dans la mesure où elles appartiennent à l'environnement culturel des traducteurs.

Est-il possible de proposer un modèle qui ne tombe pas dans les difficultés rencontrées par les deux premiers modèles? Emanuel Tov formule souvent l'idée qu'il faut traduire la LXX en donnant aux mots les sens qu'ils avaient pour les traducteurs. On ne peut qu'être d'accord avec ce point de vue. Mais nous ne sommes pas dans la tête des traducteurs et nous ne sommes jamais sûrs que le sens que nous retenons est bien celui des traducteurs. Il n'y a en fait que deux moyens pour déterminer le sens des mots de la LXX: regarder le sens de leurs correspondants hébreux et examiner leurs emplois dans la documentation grecque de l'époque. La thèse défendue ici est qu'il faut tantôt donner la priorité à la langue de départ, tantôt à la langue d'arrivée, tantôt aux deux à la fois. Qu'est-ce à dire?

2. Sem

Le modèle interlinéaire qui privilégie Sem rend bien compte des translittérations, des sémitismes, des stéréotypes et des homophonies. Les translittérations ne sont pas autre chose que des mots hébreux présents dans la traduction grecque. Elles montrent que, pour les traducteurs, toutes les réalités bibliques n'ont pas leur équivalent grec. Diverses sortes de translittérations peuvent être distinguées: pour nous en tenir au Pentateuque, dans le domaine des plantes, σαβέκ (TM סבך) est la plante du sacrifice d'Isaac (Genèse 22,13); dans le domaine des unités de mesure, l'ἵν (TM הין) équivaut à environ 6,5 litres et l'οἰφί (TM איפה) à 45 litres; en Exode, le γόμορ (TM חמר) est un solide; le mot hébreu est parfois traduit par κόρος (Lévitique et Nombres); dans le domaine des denrées alimentaires, la nourriture miraculeuse du désert se dit μάν ou μάννα; il y a aussi la boisson alcoolisée σίκερα; dans le domaine religieux, on peut signaler les θεραφίν, les

---

9 Voir Emanuel Tov, «Three dimensions of Words in the Septuagint», *RB* 83 (1976), 529–544 (= *The Greek and Hebrew Bible. Collected Essays on the Septuagint* (Leiden/Boston/Köln: Brill, 1999), 85–94, en particulier 88–89).

χερουβίν, la fête appelée πάσχα, le nom d'agent γειώρας et σάββατα. Certains de ces mots sont translittérés de l'araméen: γειώρας, μάννα (mais pas μάν), πάσχα, σάββατα et σίκερα. Il se peut que deux mots soient translittérés de l'égyptien: Μωυσῆς and θῖβις[10]. Il faut noter que ces mots entrent partiellement dans le lexique grec: dans les manuscrits, ils reçoivent un accent; souvent, ils sont précédés de l'article τό ou τά; certains sont déclinés (γειώρας, Μωυσῆς, σάββατα); certains ont des dérivés (σαββατίζειν). Pour évaluer l'importance du phénomène des translittérations, il faut signaler que le phénomène inverse se produit: il arrive que la LXX traduise des mots que les traductions modernes translittèrent: en Genèse 3,20, Eve est appelée Ζωή, «Vie»; en Genèse 11,28, Ur, la cité d'Abraham, devient χώρα, «territoire». Dans la Genèse, environ trente noms géographiques sont traduits. De tels exemples montrent que les anciens traducteurs ont parfois considéré que la Bible hébraïque était plus traduisible que nous ne le pensons aujourd'hui. Deux points mériteraient d'être approfondis. Tout d'abord, la répartition inégale des translittérations dans les livres bibliques: comme l'a signalé Henry St. John Thackeray, elles sont assez peu nombreuses dans le Pentateuque, Isaïe, la première moitié de Jérémie, les XII, totalement absentes de la deuxième moitié d'Ezéchiel, de Psaumes, de Proverbes, de Job, des livres classés par les Sages parmi les Ecrits, mais elles sont très fréquentes en Juges, 3–4 Règnes, 1–2 Paralipomènes, Esdras[11]. En second lieu, pourquoi certains mots sont-ils tantôt translittérés tantôt traduits[12]? On peut être tenté d'expliquer ce phénomène par le fait que les livres bibliques ont été traduits par des traducteurs différents. Cette explication est pertinente dans bon nombre de cas, mais pas toujours. Par exemple, si l'on prend le couple γόμορ/κόρος, l'explication fonctionne pour le Pentateuque: le premier mot est attesté six fois en Exode et le second seulement en Lévitique 27,16 et Nombres 11,32; mais elle ne vaut pas pour Ezéchiel, où les deux mots sont attestés à deux versets de distance (γόμορ en 45,11; κόρος en 45,13); le traducteur connaît-il les deux traductions du Pentateuque et aurait-il voulu les reproduire? Une telle explication est bien subtile.

---

10 Yvan Koenig, «Quelques 'égyptianismes' de la Septante», *BIFAO* 98 (1998), 223–233.

11 Henry St. John Thackeray, *A Grammar of the Old Testament in Greek according to the Septuagint* Vol. I. *Introduction, Orthography and Incidence* (Cambridge: Cambridge University Press, 1909; réimpr. Hildesheim/New York: Georg Olms, 1978), 32–36.

12 Les exemples sont: αἰλάμ/ναός et d'autres mots; βαμά/ἄλσος et d'autres mots; γεδδούρ/ληστήριον et d'autres mots; γόμορ/κόρος; δαβείρ/ναός; ἐφούδ/ἐπωμίς; θεραφίν/εἴδωλον et d'autres mots; μάναα/δῶρον ou θυσία; ναγέβ/ἔρημος et d'autres mots; ναζίρ ou ναζιραῖος/εὐξάμενος ou un autre mot; νέβελ/ἀγγεῖον ou ἀσκός; σαβαώθ/παντοκράτωρ ou τῶν δυνάμεων; σεφηλά/πεδινή; σίκερα/μέθυσμα ou μέθη.

Dans les sémitismes, l'influence de la langue source ne concerne pas la littéralité des mots, comme dans les translittérations, mais leur signification: le mot grec a plus ou moins le sens du mot hébreu. Les sémitismes se subdivisent en aramaïsmes, lorsque des mots et des tours grecs reflètent une influence de la langue araméenne ou encore lorsque des mots hébreux ont été compris comme des mots araméens, et en hébraïsmes, lorsque l'influence est celle de l'hébreu biblique et postbiblique. Des expressions comme «pécher devant Dieu», «regarder devant Dieu», «s'approcher devant Dieu», où «devant» est un ajout qui exprime le respect pour la personne divine, sont des aramaïsmes; elles sont présentes également dans les targums araméens, qui les généralisent, et elles reflètent l'influence du langage de la cour de l'époque perse, où l'on ne parle pas au roi, mais devant le roi[13]. En ce qui concerne les hébraïsmes, voici plus d'un siècle qu'Henry Barclay Swete a dressé une liste d'une trentaine de mots qui reçoivent dans la LXX de nouvelles significations dues au modèle hébreu, comme ἅγιον, ἁμαρτωλός, ἀρετή, ἀφόρισμα, ἄφρων; en fait, dans tous ces cas, il ne s'agit pas tant de nouvelles significations que de nouveaux contextes d'emploi; et le sens se laisse assez facilement déduire du contexte[14]. Un peu plus tard, Henry St. John Thackeray a dressé une autre liste de mots ou expressions dans lesquels l'influence de l'hébreu est évidente. Par exemple, en Deutéronome 28,1, διδόναι, qui signifie normalement «donner», a le sens de τιθέναι, «placer», sous l'influence de נתן; en Exode 13,10, où il faut observer un rituel «de jours en jours», le mot ἡμεραί a le sens d' «années», et non de «jours»; toutefois, dans le contexte, le lecteur grec comprend que les jours en question forment une longue série de jours[15]. Certaines expressions physiognomoniques, qui se réfèrent à une partie du corps humain, sont traduites littéralement; le résultat est parfois acceptable, comme, en Genèse 24,57, «interroger la bouche de quelqu'un» au sens d'«interroger quelqu'un»; d'autres fois, la traduction fait problème, comme, en Genèse 19,21, «admirer la face de quelqu'un» signifiant «prendre en compte quelqu'un»; toutefois, θαυμάζειν a, en grec classique, le sens d' «honorer», qui est proche de la signification hébraïque. Les pages de Thackeray sont précieuses en ce qu'elles montrent que des tours souvent considérés comme des sémitismes ne le sont pas; par exemple, διδόναι + infinitif, au sens de «permettre», est classique. Cependant, du point de vue du locuteur grec, d'autres sémitismes sont moins acceptables. Par exemple, dans la religion grecque, les ἀναθέματα sont

---

13 Jan Joosten, «L'agir humain *devant* Dieu. Remarques sur une tournure remarquable de la Septante», *RB* 113 (2006), 5–17.
14 Henry Barclay Swete, *An Introduction to the Old Testament in Greek* (Cambridge: Cambridge University Press, 1902; réimpr. New York: Ktav Publishing House, 1968), 307.
15 Henry St. John Thackeray, *op. cit.* note 11, 39–46.

des offrandes commémoratives consacrées aux dieux dans les temples. Dans le Pentateuque, ἀνάθεμα traduit חרם: le rite biblique consiste à détruire des objets, et non à les conserver. De la sorte, une nouvelle signification voit le jour, mais ce nouveau sens peut être déduit du contexte. Même dans le cas de sémitismes avérés, les lecteurs grecs ne sont pas sans ressources. Par exemple, πληροῦν τὰς χεῖρας, «remplir les mains» (Exode 32,29, Nombres 7,88), est la traduction littérale de l'hébreu, qui signifie «consacrer, habiliter»; apparemment, l'expression grecque n'a pas ce sens; mais le contexte d'emploi est tel que le lecteur comprend que ce remplissage des mains n'est pas un acte ordinaire, mais une métaphore qui désigne l'acceptation d'une responsabilité particulière au nom de Dieu; en Nombres, l'expression est employée en parallèle du verbe «oindre», dont elle apparaît comme synonyme. Il arrive cependant que certaines traductions littérales soient presque incompréhensibles. Par exemple, en Nombres 1,2; 4,22 et 26,2, que signifie l'ordre de Dieu: «Prends le commencement de toute l'assemblée d'Israël»? A cette expression obscure, les traducteurs ont préféré ailleurs en Nombres (4,2; 31,26 et 49) «Prends la somme totale de l'assemblée», avec le mot κεφάλαιον au lieu d'ἀρχή. Ce changement de traduction permet de rendre compréhensible ce qui ne l'était pas. On note au passage que le modèle interlinéaire ne permet pas de rendre compte de la variation de traduction. Au total, on peut être d'accord avec Chaim Rabin qui, à propos des sémitismes, a mis en avant la notion de «tolérance sémantique»: même si les mots sont employés de manière nouvelle, leur sens nouveau est en général compris grâce au contexte. De plus l'acceptabilité de la LXX augmente au fur et à mesure qu'augmente la quantité des textes traduits: il se crée une sorte de sous-langage (il vaudrait mieux dire une stylistique) qui se comprend de mieux en mieux[16].

Comme les hébraïsmes, les traductions stéréotypées dénotent une influence de la langue source. Cette notion est apparue dès 1912 chez Martin Flashar[17]. Mais elle n'a pris que peu à peu de l'importance, notamment grâce à Emanuel Tov[18]. On désigne par ce terme deux phénomènes voisins qui relèvent, chez les traducteurs, de la volonté de traduire de manière cohérente: (1) Un même mot hébreu tend à être rendu par un même mot grec. Par exemple le mot ברית est traduit par διαθήκη plus de 260 fois; il n'y a que trois exceptions (Genèse 14,13; 1

---

16 Chaim Rabin, «The Translation Process and the Character of the Septuagint», *VT* 11 (1961), 201–221.

17 Martin Flashar, «Exegetische Studien zum Septuagintapsalter», *ZAW* 32 (1912), 81–116, 161–189, 241–268, en particulier 105 (*stereotypen Übersetzungen*)

18 Emanuel Tov, *The Text-Critical Use of the Septuagint in Biblical Research* (Jérusalem: Simor, 1981), 54–57.

Règnes 11,11; 2 Paralipomènes 16,13)[19]. On peut encore citer ἀδελφός/אח, θεός/
אלהים), κύριος/יהוה, νόμος/תורה. (2) Une même famille de mots hébreux tend à
être rendue par une même famille de mots grecs. Par exemple, les mots de la
famille de טוב sont rendus par ἀγαθός et ἀγαθύνειν. Ces traductions stéréotypées
sont susceptibles d'aboutir à des sémitismes sémantiques: c'est le cas d'ἀγαθύνειν, qui veut dire normalement «faire du bien à quelqu'un»; mais, en Ruth
3,16, Booz «mangea, but et son cœur ἠγαθύνθη», littéralement «fut rendu bon»;
l'hébreu signifie en fait «se réjouit»; le grec n'exclut pas cette signification, mais
elle n'a rien d'évident, même dans le contexte. L'exemple de κοίτη est plus
difficile encore; en grec, ce mot désigne la couche et, par euphémisme, les
relations sexuelles; mais ces sens ne conviennent pas en Nombres 5,20, où il est
dit, à propos de la femme adultère, qu'un homme autre que son mari lui a
«donné sa κοίτη»; le mot grec est la traduction stéréotypée de שכב et de ses
dérivés nominaux. Quelle est cette couche que l'homme donne à la femme
adultère? En Lévitique 15,16, il est question de «couche de semence» (κοίτη
σπέρματος/שכבת זרע), qu'on comprend comme la semence qui est répandue sur
la couche, «les pertes séminales», ou la semence émise pendant les relations
sexuelles, «épanchement de semence», «sperme»; en Nombres 5,20, le mot
κοίτη a le sens de sperme à lui tout seul. Certes une telle signification ne saute
pas aux yeux, mais le TM lui-même n'a pas un sens évident, au point qu'on a
imaginé l'existence de deux racines שכב, l'une signifiant «coucher», l'autre
«s'épancher»[20].

Dans les pages de sa grammaire où il réfléchit sur l'élément sémitique dans
le grec de la LXX, Henry Saint John Thackeray a attiré l'attention sur une
tendance qu'on peut observer dans les livres qui suivent le Pentateuque et Josué:
les traducteurs préfèrent, parmi les mots grecs, ceux qui ont des sonorités
semblables à celles des mots hébreux[21]. Ici l'influence de l'hébreu sur le grec ne
concerne pas la signification, comme dans les sémitismes, mais uniquement les
sonorités, autrement dits les mots en tant que phonèmes. Par exemple, les mots
ἀλαλάζειν, ἀλαλαγμός, ὀλολύζειν, ὀλολυγμός, «hurler, hurlement», sont homophones de ילל, «crier», et יללה, «cri»; or, ces mots se correspondent dans les
Prophètes; aussi bien les mots grecs que les mots hébreux sont des onomato-

19 Sur cette équivalence, voir Adrian Schenker, «Διαθήκη pour ברית. L'option de traduction de
la LXX à la double lumière du droit successoral de l'Egypte ptolémaïque et du livre de la
Genèse», In Lectures et relectures de la Bible. Festschrift P.-M. Bogaert, eds. Jean-Marie Auwers,
André Wénin (Leuven: Peeters, 1999), 126–131.
20 James Barr, Comparative Philology and the Text of Old Testament (Oxford: Clarendon Press,
1968), 137.
21 Henry St. John Thackeray, op. cit. note 11, 36–38.

pées. Thackeray propose une liste d'une quarantaine de mots homophones, dont il dit qu'elle est sans aucun doute susceptible d'être étendue. De fait, les savants postérieurs ont élargi le nombre des mots homophones[22]. La question est de savoir si ces repérages sont pertinents: Emanuel Tov affirme que la reconnaissance d'une homophonie suppose que le sens des mots hébreu et grec homophones soit différent; car si les mots hébreu et grec ont le même sens, l'homophonie peut être accidentelle, comme par exemple dans le cas de עולה et de ὁλοκαύτωμα, qui désignent une offrande entièrement brûlée: le mot grec est un excellent équivalent du mot hébreu et il a été choisi pour cette raison, et non pour des raisons d'homophonie[23]. Dans le même esprit, James Barr a émis des doutes sur beaucoup d'exemples d'homophonies et ne retient qu'un petit nombre de cas possibles[24]. On peut cependant se demander si ces réserves ne sont pas hypercritiques: le traducteur peut choisir un mot grec parce qu'il est un bon équivalent d'un mot hébreu et aussi parce qu'il lui est homophone. Sans doute la question mériterait-elle d'être réexaminée.

3. Japhet

Le modèle socioculturel qui privilégie la langue cible convient bien aux traductions conjecturales et au procédé de traduction que l'on propose d'appeler les «hellénismes». Lorsque les traducteurs étaient en présence d'un texte hébreu à leurs yeux difficile ou problématique, ils ont proposé des traductions conjecturales, qui se divisent en plusieurs catégories, comme l'a bien montré Emanuel Tov[25]. La plus importante d'entre elles consiste dans les traductions

---

22 Par exemple Charles T. Fritsch, «Homophony in the Septuagint», In *Proceedings of the Sixth World Congress of Jewish Studies* (Jérusalem: Jerusalem Academic Press, 1977), 115–120 (liste de 76 mots grecs ayant des consonances voisines de celles des mots hébreux). Voir aussi George B. Caird, «Homoeophony in the Septuagint», In *Jews, Greeks and Christians. Essays in Honor of W. D. Davies*, eds. Robert Hamerton-Kelly, Robin Scroggs (Leyde: Brill, 1976), 74–88; Jan de Ward, «Homoeophony in the Septuagint», *Biblica* 62 (1981), 551–556.

23 Emanuel Tov, «Loan-Words, Homophony, and Transliterations in the Septuagint», *Biblica* 60 (1979), 216–238 (= *op. cit.* note 9, 165–182). Tov s'interroge sur l'homophonie תך/τόκος, «oppression/usure» (Psaumes 54 (55),12 et 71 (72),14), parce que, dans le contexte des deux psaumes, le mot grec peut être un bon équivalent du mot hébreu.

24 James Barr, «Doubts about Homophony in the Septuagint», *Textus* 12 (1985), 1–78.

25 Emanuel Tov, «Did the Septuagint Translators Always Understand Their Hebrew Text?», In *De Septuaginta. Studies in Honour of John William Wevers on His Sixty-Fifth Birthday*, eds. Albert Pietersma, Claude E. Cox (Mississauga [Ont.]: BenBen Publications, 1984), 53–70 (= *op. cit.* note 9, 203–218). E. Tov range les translittérations parmi les traductions conjecturales, mais une

contextuelles: par exemple, le mot ארמן est rendu par ἄμφοδον (Jérémie 17,27; 49,27 [30,16]), ἄντρον (3 Règnes 16,18), βάρις (Psaumes 47 (48),4), βασίλειον (Proverbes 18,19), γῆ (Jérémie 9,20 [21]), ἐναντίον (4 Règnes 15,25), θεμέλιον (Isaïe 25,2), ναός (Jérémie 30 (37),18), οἶκος (Isaïe 32,14), πόλις (Isaïe 34,13), πυργόβαρις (Psaumes 121 (122),7), χώρα (Amos 3,9; 10; 11; Michée 5,4 [5]). Tov note avec pertinence que l'établissement d'une traduction conjecturale n'est jamais sûr parce qu'elle peut en fait dépendre d'un autre modèle hébreu ou encore d'une tradition ancienne d'interprétation. De fait, le nombre de ces traductions conjecturales est appelé à se réduire au fur et à mesure que la tradition de lecture dont dépend la LXX sera mieux connue.

Les hellénismes sont des traductions marquées par la prégnance du contexte socioculturel grec. Elles ajoutent à l'original hébreu. Par exemple, dans le livre des Nombres, δῆμος rend presque toujours le mot משפחה et est nettement distingué de la tribu, φυλή, qui correspond à מטה. Les traducteurs renvoient ainsi à une réalité politique grecque de l'époque classique et hellénistique, où les tribus et les dèmes sont des divisions et des subdivisions des cités d'Athènes, de Rhodes et d'Alexandrie[26]. De la sorte, la LXX transpose le modèle de l'organisation civique sédentaire en usage dans de grandes cités grecques à la description d'une population nomade errant dans le désert: les fils d'Israël forment ainsi l'équivalent d'une cité en déplacement. On peut trouver que cette transposition est une réussite. On peut aussi estimer qu'elle va trop au delà des réalités bibliques.

En Nombres 1,18, Moïse et Aaron passent en revue les fils d'Israël; ils accomplissent un acte qui n'est pas clair en hébreu, mais que les targums et les traductions modernes comprennent comme un enregistrement. Selon la LXX, «ils mettaient sur des tablettes» les noms des soldats. Elle utilise le verbe ἐπαξονεῖν, dont le sens premier est «placer sur des axes». Dans le vocabulaire politique grec, les ἄξονες étaient les quatre côtés d'une pièce de bois de section carrée sur laquelle étaient gravées les lois de Solon; la pièce de bois tournait sur un axe; de la sorte, chacun pouvait consulter les lois; à Rome, un dispositif de ce genre existait dans le cas des lois privées. Ainsi, Moïse et Aaron transposent au cas des soldats hébreux une pratique attestée dans le monde gréco-romain pour les lois.

---

translittération n'est pas une traduction. Outre les traductions contextuelles, E. Tov signale les manipulations contextuelles (sur les consonnes de l'hébreu), la prise en considération du parallélisme, l'emploi d'un terme général qui convient dans le contexte et les traductions étymologiques.

26 Voir Gilles Dorival, «Le lexique de l'administration et de la politique» In *Handbuch zur Septuaginta. IV Sprache*, eds. Eberhard Bons, Jan Joosten (sous presse).

Il serait utile d'établir une liste des hellénismes, qui ne sont sans doute pas très nombreux. On se limitera à un exemple dans le Pentateuque et un autre exemple dans un corpus biblique plus large. En Nombres 11,20, le peuple est dégoûté de la manne; Seigneur annonce qu'il va lui donner à manger de la viande pendant un mois, jusqu'à ce qu'elle lui sorte par les narines: «elle sera pour vous un choléra». Le TM utilise ici le mot זרא, employé ici et en Siracide 39,27, qui signifie, semble-t-il, «dégoût», «horreur». En grec, il y a deux choléras: le choléra «humide», caractérisé par une forte excrétion des humeurs par en haut et par en bas, ainsi que par des vomissements, des coliques et des spasmes; le choléra «sec» offre les mêmes symptômes, à l'exception des coliques et des vomissements[27]. Normalement, le choléra sans adjectif désigne le choléra humide, tandis que l'autre forme de choléra est accompagnée de l'adjectif «sec». Voilà pourquoi, ici, le choléra a toutes chances d'être le choléra humide. Les médecins de l'Antiquité signalent, entre autres causes, l'excès de nourriture[28]. Ainsi, dans la LXX, le peuple est puni par Seigneur d'une maladie qu'il s'inflige à lui-même en mangeant trop de viande. Ici, l'hellénisme consiste dans l'adoption du vocabulaire médical grec. Là encore, on peut trouver que la LXX outrepasse les données bibliques et accorde un peu trop au contexte civilisationnel grec. Néanmoins, si l'on recourt au modèle interlinéaire élargi, qui intègre les traditions d'interprétation, cette conclusion sera fortement nuancée: chez les Sages, le mot זרא reçoit un sens médical, celui d'enflure des parois abdominales ou celui de ver solitaire et parasite (*Nombres Rabbah* 7, 40 – 41); certes, ces sens ne sont pas ceux de la LXX; mais il se pourrait bien qu'il ait existé une exégèse ancienne, présente dans la LXX et certains rabbins, qui donnait un sens médical à זרא [29].

Le verbe ἀγχιστεύω et les noms apparentés sont présents dans le Pentateuque, Josué, 2–3 Règnes, 2 Esdras et Ruth. Cette famille de mots, qui signifie «agir en tant que plus proche parent», correspond normalement à la racine גאל, «racheter», qui est traduite plus souvent par λυτροῦν et sa famille. De fait, λυτροῦν est un bon équivalent de גאל: les deux mots ont le même sens. Pourquoi cette variation de traduction? La LXX distingue le rachat sans autre précision et le rachat qui fait intervenir le plus proche parent. En grec classique, le plus proche parent intervient dans le domaine de l'héritage et dans le domaine de la vengeance légalement autorisée. On retrouve ces emplois dans la LXX, notamment dans le cas du proche parent qui réclame le sang, celui que les traductions

---

27 Pseudo-Galien, *Médecin* (= *Introductio sive medicus*) 1, 14, 736.
28 Alexandre de Tralles, *Thérapeutiques* 2, 321.
29 Leo Prijs, *Jüdische Tradition in der Septuaginta* (Leiden: Brill, 1948), 21–22.

modernes appellent souvent le vengeur du sang. Mais la LXX élargit les domaines d'intervention du plus proche parent: dans le Pentateuque, il a le droit et le devoir d'acheter la propriété du parent pauvre qui est contraint de vendre son bien (Lévitique 25,25 et 26); dans le livre de Ruth, il a le droit d'acquérir le champ d'une veuve dont il est le plus proche parent et le devoir de l'épouser[30].

4. Sem et Japhet

La LXX présente des procédés de traduction où il est impossible de décider qui l'emporte, la langue source ou la langue cible. Plus exactement, la langue source est prévalente en un sens, mais la langue cible l'est en un autre. Les deux modèles fonctionnent conjointement. Ces procédés sont les néologismes, les traductions décalées et les traductions multiples. Les néologismes peuvent être analysés comme des mots «forgés pour exprimer des idées sémitiques», selon l'expression de Henry Barclay Swete, qui dressait une liste de 5 mots, ἀκροβυστία, ἀναθεματίζειν, ὁλοκαύτωμα, σκανδαλίζειν, σπλαγχνίζειν[31]. Mais, dans le même temps, les néologismes vont dans le sens de la langue grecque, qui est caractérisée par un fort renouvellement de son vocabulaire à l'époque hellénistique et romaine. C'est ainsi qu' ὁλοκαύτωμα est un néologisme qui ne peut déconcerter le lecteur grec, puisque que le verbe ὁλοκαυτέω figure chez Xénophon, comme le rappelle Takamitsu Muraoka dans son *Lexicon*. Le plus célèbre des néologismes de la LXX est sans doute θυσιαστήριον: ce mot a été forgé sur θυσία, qui désigne l'offrande apportée par les fidèles au Seigneur; le sens du mot ne fait aucune difficulté par le lecteur grec: c'est le lieu qui recueille les offrandes, l'«autel à offrandes»; en fabriquant ce mot dont la grécité est incontestable, les traducteurs distinguent l'autel du désert, qui est unique et réservé à l'unique Seigneur, du βωμός païen, qui est le mot adopté pour les multiples autels des multiples dieux. Du point de vue sémantique, plusieurs faits méritent d'être soulignés: tantôt le sens du néologisme va de soi au niveau de la langue grecque (ὁλοκαύτωμα); tantôt le contexte d'emploi permet de comprendre le sens: en 2 Maccabées 6,8, σπλαγχνίζειν ne peut que signifier «manger les entrailles d'une bête sacrifiée»; tantôt, enfin, la détermination de la signification demande une vraie réflexion: c'est le cas d' ἀναθεματίζειν, dont le sens «maudire» repose sur une évolution sémantique du substantif ἀνάθεμα propre à

---

30 Gilles Dorival, «ἀγχιστεία ἀγχιστεύς ἀγχιστευτής ἀγχιστεύω», In *Historical and Philological Lexicon of the Septuagint*, eds. Eberhard Bons, Jan Joosten (sous presse).
31 Henry Barclay Swete, *op. cit.* note 14, 307.

la LXX; il désigne les êtres humains, les animaux, les objets qui, dans un contexte de victoire militaire, sont offerts à Dieu au point d'être détruits complètement et qui sont donc maudits. Pour nous en tenir aux exemples de Swete, les deux derniers cas demandent apparemment de la réflexion: σκανδα- λίζειν est formé sur σκάνδαλον qui est lui-même un néologisme de la LXX, tandis qu' ἀκροβυστία est composé de deux éléments, ἀκρο- qui désigne l'extrémité, et -βυστία, qui n'est pas connu par ailleurs. Mais σκάνδαλον figure dans le *P. Cair. Zen.* 608, 7 du IIIᵉ siècle avant notre ère au sens de «piège» et l'élément σκανδαλ- est présent dans le composé σκανδάληθρον attesté chez Aristophane, qui désigne la tige qui sert de détente à un piège; il se pourrait bien que σκάνδαλον soit ancien en grec; seuls les hasards de la transmission des textes explique-raient son absence dans la littérature classique. En ce qui concerne ἀκροβυστία, le contexte d'emploi permet de comprendre qu'il ne peut s'agir que du prépuce (voir Genèse 17,11); de plus, ce mot fait écho à ἀκροποσθία, qui est le nom du prépuce chez Aristote; enfin un Grec ne pouvait pas ne pas rapprocher l'élément -βυστία du verbe βύω, «bourrer, remplir»: de fait le prépuce se situe sur la partie «remplie» du pénis. Le nombre des néologismes de la LXX est compris entre 287 et 1900, sur un ensemble de 9500 mots[32]. Ces néologismes mériteraient une étude systématique, qui est aujourd'hui possible grâce aux lexiques de Johan Lust *et alii* et de Takamitsu Muraoka.

Le phénomène des mots grecs employés de manière légèrement décalée est rarement décrit par les lexicographes de la LXX, sans doute parce qu'il est d'une grande finesse linguistique et qu'il peut susciter le reproche de surinterprétation. Pour rendre une réalité biblique, les traducteurs utilisent un mot grec qu'ils emploient de manière légèrement inhabituelle. De la sorte, ils montrent que la réalité biblique n'a pas de vrai équivalent en grec, tout en opérant une véritable traduction. La réalité biblique est hellénisée, mais en même temps elle est différenciée de la réalité grecque. Par exemple, dans la religion grecque, τὰ σωτήρια désigne le sacrifice du salut, que l'on offre en action de grâces pour une guérison ou un heureux retour. Un sacrifice analogue existe dans la Bible hébraïque, où il porte le nom de שלמים. La traduction littérale de l'hébreu serait σωτηρία. Or, la LXX propose toujours le substantif singulier τὸ σωτήριον. De la sorte, par le truchement du radical σωτηρ-, elle évoque le sacrifice du salut des

---

[32] 287 selon Christian Schröder, «Alphabetische Zusammenstellung auffälliger Neologismen der Septuaginta», In *In Brennpunkt: Die Septuaginta. Studien zur Entstehung und Bedeutung der Griechischen Bibel*, eds. Hanz-Josef Fabry, Ulrich Offerhaus (Stuttgart/Berlin/Köln: Kohlhammer, 2001), 61–69; 1900 selon Takamitsu Muraoka, *op. cit.* note 5, XIII; le chiffre probable est 850.

Grecs, mais, grâce au singulier, elle suggère que le sacrifice biblique du salut n'est pas exactement identique au rite grec[33].

Parfois, la LXX donne des traductions multiples d'un même mot hébreu. Serait-ce que, comme la langue française, le grec n'aime pas la répétition d'un même mot dans le même ensemble textuel et a le souci de varier? Peut-être cette explication vaut-elle dans quelques cas. Mais, ailleurs, elle ne convient pas. En Nombres 35, les fils d'Israël reçoivent l'ordre de réserver aux lévites quarante-huit villes, ainsi que le מגרש qui les entoure; ce substantif est relativement clair en hébreu, où il désigne la zone immédiatement extérieure aux murs des villes, dans laquelle les habitants mènent paître leurs troupeaux (verbe גרש). Il ne semble pas que la langue grecque ait un correspondant pour cette réalité hébraïque. La LXX propose quatre traductions: aux v. 2 et 7, τὰ προάστια, «les banlieues»; au v. 3, τὰ ἀφορίσματα, «les <lieux> mis à part»; au v. 4, τὰ συγκυροῦντα, «les <lieux> contigus»; au v. 5, τὰ ὅμορα, «les <lieux> limitro-phes». Les première, troisième et quatrième traductions renvoient à l'organisa-tion de l'espace, la deuxième est de type interprétatif: au lieu d'être décrit en termes d'espace, le מגרש est défini par sa fonction, qui consiste dans une mise à part pour les lévites. Le souci de variation pourrait être invoqué pour la première catégorie de traduction; ce n'est pas le cas pour la seconde catégorie, qui correspond à un changement de registre langagier. Un tel procédé correspond-il à la prévalence de la langue source, dans la mesure où, si un même mot hébreu est rendu par plusieurs termes grecs, c'est qu'aux yeux des traducteurs il n'aurait pas de véritable équivalent en grec et qu'il n'est pas traduisible? Mais une telle explication n'est sans doute pas juste, tout d'abord parce qu'il aurait été facile de translittérer מגרש, ensuite parce que les quatre traductions sont de vraies tentatives de traduction. Dès lors, on peut suggérer que la multiplicité des traductions s'explique ainsi: face à une réalité biblique considérée comme n'ayant pas de vrai équivalent grec, les traducteurs ont considéré que la moins mauvaise approximation de celle-ci consistait à combiner plusieurs traductions: le מגרש est une sorte de banlieue, un espace qui est contigu et limitrophe aux villes, enfin un lieu qui est mis à part. Donc, en un sens, la priorité est donnée à l'original hébreu, puisqu'il est considéré comme n'ayant pas de vrai équivalent en grec; mais, en un autre sens, le fait qu'il donne lieu à quatre traductions

---

33 Autre exemple: la phase préparatoire de tout sacrifice consiste à apporter l'offrande. Dans la religion grecque, cet apport est désigné par le verbe ἐπιφέρειν. Ce verbe est employé par la LXX, mais jamais dans un contexte de sacrifice. A sa place, elle utilise les verbes ἀναφέρειν et προσφέρειν, qui font clairement écho au verbe grec tout en s'en distinguant: il est ainsi suggéré que l'apport sacrificiel biblique est différent de l'apport grec, tout en relevant du même grand rituel.

différentes qui, chacune, définit un élément caractéristique montre que l'adaptation à la langue d'arrivée est ressentie comme prioritaire.

Il n'est facile de proposer un modèle qui formalise les données complexes qui précèdent. Il s'agit en fait de conjuguer l'approche descendante (top-down) et l'approche ascendante (bottom-up). Un élément de complexité particulier tient à la tradition d'interprétation qui peut se situer en amont de la LXX (et dont celle-ci dépend) ou en aval (les targums, les Sages). Toute suggestion de formalisation sera la bienvenue.

Cécile Dogniez
Quelques remarques sur le vocabulaire du travail dans la Bible à l'épreuve de la traduction des Septante

La tentation d'appréhender le travail dans l'Antiquité – sous le prétexte que le travail est une réalité vieille comme le monde – à la lumière de nos modes de pensée et de notre expérience propre est le premier risque qui menace toute étude sur cette question. Or nous savons que le travail – que ce soit dans le monde grec ancien ou dans celui de la Bible hébraïque – n'est pas pensé selon les catégories qui sont aujourd'hui les nôtres. Une autre difficulté – outre la connaissance très imparfaite que nous avons de cette réalité dans les mondes antiques malgré les témoignages littéraires, et quelque fois les sources documentaires, que nous possédons[1] –, tient à la complexité de cette catégorie qui revêt une diversité d'aspects, tant les activités et les finalités qui s'y rapportent peuvent être plurielles et spécifiques à la fois.

Dans la présente étude, loin de vouloir essayer de cerner tous les contours de la conception du travail dans la Bible grecque des Septante – le sujet est trop vaste –, nous nous efforcerons de réfléchir sur quelques particularités dans l'énonciation de ce thème dans ce corpus en nous attachant au lexique utilisé pour traduire ce que dit le texte hébreu en la matière.

---

[1] Les travaux sur les rapports de dépendance sociale et sur les différents aspects de l'organisation du travail dans l'Orient ancien sont nombreux. Pour l'Egypte, citons par exemple l'ouvrage collectif édité par B. Menu, *L'organisation du travail en Egypte ancienne et en Mésopotamie. Colloque Aidea – Nice 4–5 octobre 2004* (Le Caire: Institut français d'archéologie orientale, 2010), avec une riche bibliographie sur la documentation papyrologique concernant les contrats de travail aux pages 95 à 106. Sur l'étude d'I. Biezunska-Malowist, *L'esclavage dans l'Egypte gréco-romaine*, 2 vol. (Wroclaw: 1974, 1977), portant sur l'esclavage et l'exploitation du travail, voir par exemple le compte rendu de P. Lévêque, *Revue des Etudes Grecques* 92 (1979), 231–238. Enfin nous renvoyons sur ce sujet de l'esclavage dans l'Antiquité à l'abondante bibliographie donnée par L. H. Feldman dans son article sur «Josephus' Vocabulary for Slavery», paru dans L. H. Feldman, *Studies in Hellenistic Judaism* (Leiden, New York, Köln: E.J. Brill, 1996), 84–85. Sur le vocabulaire de l'esclavage dans le livre grec de Ruth en particulier, nous renvoyons aux études d'E. Bons, «Le vocabulaire de la servitude dans la Septante du livre de Ruth», *JSJ* 33 (2002), 153–163 et d'I. Assan-Dhote, J. Moatti-Fine, «'Moi je serai comme une de tes esclaves!' (Rt 2, 13). *Paidiskè* dans la Bible grecque: esclave et concubine, esclave et mère porteuse», M. Loubet, Pralon, eds., *Eukarpa. Etudes sur la Bible et ses exégètes: en hommage à Gilles Dorival* (Paris: Editions du Cerf, 2011), 37–44.

Nous reviendrons brièvement sur quelques choix lexicaux majoritaires auxquels ont eu recours les traducteurs grecs. Nous essaierons de voir s'il y a ou non équivalence exacte entre le lexique hébreu et le lexique grec. Mais l'essentiel de notre propos portera sur l'examen d'un certain nombre de passages dans la Bible grecque où cette notion de travail reçoit une autre connotation que celle que donne à lire le texte massorétique. La Septante, à l'exception de certains livres comme celui d'Isaïe par exemple, est, en règle générale, une traduction plutôt fidèle de son modèle. Or, malgré cette correspondance assez exacte entre les deux textes, on peut noter quelques écarts. Ce sont ces différences ayant trait au lexique relatif au travail qui retiendront ici notre attention, afin de voir s'il s'agit de modifications délibérées ou non de la part du ou des traducteurs et s'il y a des changements de sens par rapport à l'hébreu. Nous essaierons ainsi de comprendre ce que disent ces divergences lexicales sur cette idée du travail dans le monde juif parlant grec à l'époque hellénistique.

Il importe avant tout de rappeler ici ce que J.P. Vernant[2] a mis en lumière à propos de la pensée et de la langue grecques mais qui, nous semble-t-il, peut également s'appliquer au monde de la Bible hébraïque, à savoir qu'il n'y a pas de notion générale, unique, correspondant à ce que nous, modernes, appelons au sens abstrait «le travail», ni non plus un seul terme pour exprimer cette notion contemporaine. Ce qui ne nous empêche nullement, cependant, de réfléchir – en évitant tout anachronisme – sur la représentation dans la Bible de ce que nous nommons le travail, étant donné que ce livre évoque à plusieurs reprises à la fois les diverses formes d'activités auxquelles s'adonnent Israël ou les autres peuples, et la condition laborieuse de l'homme qu'impliquent certains travaux exigeant un effort pénible.

Quelques choix lexicaux majoritaires

La racine hébraïque עבד est la plus fréquemment employée dans la Bible pour exprimer le travail, ou plus précisément la notion de «service» à l'égard de quelqu'un impliquant une dépendance, que ce soit celle des sujets vis-à-vis d'un roi, d'un serviteur vis-à-vis de son maître, ou même celle de l'homme à l'égard de la divinité. C'est donc le travail pour autrui – il n'est pas question du travail pour

---

2 «Travail et nature dans la Grèce ancienne», *Journal de psychologie* (1955), 1–29 repris dans *Mythe et pensée chez les Grecs. Etudes de psychologie historique* (Paris: F. Maspero, 1965), 196–217.

soi – qui est au cœur de cette représentation du travail comme service. Mais cette racine עבד est polysémique puisqu'elle dénote plusieurs types de «service», à la fois le service et la servitude, mais aussi le travail et le culte. S. Daniel a souligné que, dans l'ensemble, face à cette diversité d'usages, les traducteurs du Pentateuque grec comme ceux des autres livres n'ont pas «cherché à reproduire cette ambiguïté attachée à la racine hébraïque»[3] et ont pris soin d'en distinguer les différents aspects sémantiques, qu'ils soient cultuels ou profanes.

Ainsi, lorsque le verbe עבד est utilisé pour exprimer un service, un travail quelconque, et en particulier l'action de servir, de travailler la terre, c'est-à-dire la cultiver, tous les traducteurs grecs emploient le verbe grec ἐργάζεσθαι. On trouve du reste cette équivalence lors de la première occurrence de עבד en Gn 2,5 où il est dit que, lorsque Dieu fit le ciel et la terre, «il n'y avait pas d'homme pour servir la terre» (LXX ἐργάζεσθαι, «travailler»). Il en va de même pour le substantif עבדה rendu en grec à l'aide du nom ἔργον, au singulier ou au pluriel et, plus rarement, du substantif ἐργασία. Ces termes, employés dans la Septante conformément à leur usage en grec classique, définissent d'une façon très générale toute sorte d'action, mais aussi le résultat de l'action. Utilisés pour exprimer l'aspect concret de l'activité humaine que nous qualifions aujourd'hui de «travail», ces mots ἔργον et ἐργάζεσθαι se distinguent généralement des termes δουλεύειν, δουλεία et δοῦλος que la Septante réserve la plupart du temps aux formes d'asservissement, par exemple celui d'un peuple à l'égard d'un autre[4], ou aux formes de servitude, entendues au sens fort d'esclavage individuel ou collectif[5], qu'exprime dans certains cas la racine עבד[6]. Même si la chose semble aller de soi, il n'est peut-être pas inutile de rappeler que le terme δοῦλος et les mots apparentés servent à l'origine à désigner dans la langue grecque l'état de celui qui n'est pas libre, par opposition à l'ἐλεύθερος, avant d'évoquer la condition de l'esclave assujetti à son maître et au profit duquel ce dernier exécute sa tâche, son travail. Dans la Septante δουλεύειν constitue donc une

---

3 S. Daniel, *Recherches sur le vocabulaire du culte dans la Septante* (Paris: Klincksieck, 1966), 55.

4 Voir par exemple l'asservissement de rois en Gn 14,4; d'une nation en Gn 15,14.

5 Voir par exemple en Ex 14,5; 21,2.6; Lv 25,39; Is 14,3.

6 Le traducteur grec opère parfois une différenciation lexicale très subtile entre ἐργάζεσθαι et δουλεύειν au point même d'employer l'un et l'autre verbe dans le même contexte pour le même hébreu עבד selon l'intention de son discours. C'est le cas par exemple pour décrire la condition de Jacob, à la fois travailleur à gages et esclave de Laban en Gn 29,27 avec l'emploi de ἐργασία, alors qu'il emploie δουλεύειν en Gn 29,15, ou encore pour préciser le statut de l'esclave hébreu, véritable «esclave» en Lv 25,39 (avec l'emploi du verbe δουλεύειν comme en Ex 21,6; Dt 15,12.18), mais aussi au «travail» pour son maître (ἐργάζεσθαι) en Lv 25,40. Sur ces passages, voir S. Daniel, *op. cit.*, 56–58.

bonne traduction pour traduire עבד, lorsqu'il s'agit d'une complète soumission, d'un service imposé, d'un travail obligatoire, de l'exploitation d'un salarié.

Rappelons également que lorsque la racine hébraïque עבד ne désigne ni ce que nous appelons à proprement parler le travail, qu'il soit agricole, artisanal ou domestique, ni l'asservissement ou l'esclavage, mais tout simplement le service cultuel, assimilé dans la langue hébraïque à un travail de «service» à l'égard de la divinité, les traducteurs grecs ont recours à une terminologie bien spécifique qui exclut toute connotation d'asservissement. Ils emploient, lorsqu'il s'agit du peuple, λατρεύειν, «rendre un culte», et λατρεία «culte, rite», empruntés au lexique classique mais d'usage peu fréquent pour dire d'abord «travailler pour un salaire» (λάτρον signifiant «salaire»[7]) et dans quelques rares cas «servir les dieux»[8], rendre un culte à une divinité[9], ou λειτουργεῖν et λειτουργία appartenant à la langue grecque du service public, militaire ou cultuel[10], pour nommer, dans la Bible, le service que rend la classe sacerdotale, prêtres ou lévites, dans le sanctuaire[11]. Λειτουργία et λειτουργεῖν semblent alors ne plus

---

7 La Septante utilise l'autre mot μισθός pour désigner «les gages», «le salaire», versés pour tout travail à un homme entré au service d'un propriétaire. La loi biblique ne précise pas le montant fixe du salaire – ce peut être un paiement en nature. En revanche elle est très stricte sur le versement de celui-ci qui n'autorise aucun délai comme le prescrit l'injonction «et le salaire du salarié ne restera pas à dormir chez toi jusqu'au matin» de Lv 19,13 et Dt 24,14–15; sur le rappel de cette loi dans le grec de Mal 3,5, voir la note *ad loc.* de L. Vianès, *Malachie*, La Bible d'Alexandrie 23.12 (Paris: Les Editions du Cerf, 2011). Sur l'interprétation de cette loi juive à l'époque des Tannaïm, voir J.H. Heinemann, «The Status of the Labourer in Jewish Law and Society in the Tannaitic Period», *HUCA* 25 (1954), 274 s.

8 Voir les quelques exemples donnés par A. Hilhorst, «'Servir Dieu' dans la terminologie du judaïsme hellénistique et des premières générations chrétiennes de langue grecque», in *Fructus centesimus: Mélanges G.J.M. Bartelink*, eds. A.A.R. Bastiaensen, A. Hilhorst, C.H. Kneepkens (Steenbrugge: 1989), 184.

9 Sur ce vocabulaire, voir par exemple C. Dogniez, M. Harl, eds., *Le Pentateuque d'Alexandrie* (Paris: Les Editions du Cerf, 2001), Glossaire, 876–878; S. Daniel, *op. cit.*, 66–76. Dans le Deutéronome, en particulier, ce verbe λατρεύειν traduit עבד lorsqu'il s'agit du service des idoles. Mais on trouve par exemple un emploi de λατρεύειν en un sens politique en Dt 28,48. Il faut toutefois exclure de ces emplois religieux, majoritaires dans la Septante, l'expression ἔργον λατρευτόν pour traduire l'hébreu עבדה מלאכת lorsqu'il s'agit de l'interdiction de tout travail susceptible d'apporter un profit quelconque (voir par exemple P. Harlé, D. Pralon, *Le Lévitique*, La Bible d'Alexandrie 3 (Paris: Les Editions du Cerf, 1988, 188 et S. Daniel, *op. cit.*, 333).

10 Sur cette fonction publique et officielle que désignent λειτουργία et λειτουργεῖν dans les papyrus, voir par exemple G. Dorival, *Les Nombres*, La Bible d'Alexandrie 4 (Paris: Les Editions du Cerf, 1994), 116.

11 Sur cet usage prépondérant dans la Septante, voir par exemple C. Spicq, *Notes de lexicographie néo-testamentaire*, OBO 22/1 (Göttingen: 1978), 475–478 et S. Daniel, *op. cit.*, 76–78;

avoir dans la Septante aucun rapport étymologique avec l'idée de travail, d'œuvre, mais paraissent se rapporter davantage à l'exercice d'une fonction religieuse. De la même manière, quelques emplois du verbe ἐργάζεσθαι prennent également en de très rares cas cette connotation religieuse lorsque le contexte est celui du service officiel des Lévites, par exemple en Nb 3,7; 8,11. Force est donc de constater qu'il y a dans la Septante plusieurs manières de dire le «travail» des Lévites – il consiste d'ailleurs généralement en de véritables travaux de déménagement de la Tente du Témoignage –, comme c'est aussi le cas en hébreu qui a recours à trois racines différentes, עבד, צבא et שרת.

En outre, il importe de préciser que, d'une part, δουλεύειν n'a pas toujours dans la Septante cette valeur péjorative de soumission contrainte et d'esclavage qu'il a dans la langue grecque mais qu'il a, dans quelques cas, un sens plus neutre, voire parfois laudatif[12] et, d'autre part, qu'il comporte quelques emplois religieux[13]. Ce qui laisse entendre que la polysémie de la racine עבד se retrouve parfois dans les emplois variés de δουλεύειν et de δοῦλος dans la Bible grecque.

Le vocabulaire du travail est riche dans la Bible hébraïque et comporte d'autres mots que ceux de la racine עבד. De la même façon, la terminologie utilisée par les traducteurs de la Septante pour rendre ces diverses notions de travail, que ce soit une activité agricole, artisanale, domestique, une tâche servile ou un labeur qui exige douleur et peine, est elle aussi variée. Nous reviendrons sur certains de ces termes, hébreux ou grecs, au fur et à mesure des exemples que nous avons choisi d'étudier.

L'énonciation du travail propre au grec

Gn 3,17: la peine au travail

Le premier exemple concerne inévitablement le passage bien connu de Gn 3,17 sur la malédiction de la terre qui intervient dans le récit après la faute d'Adam. Le texte massorétique dit ceci: «Parce que tu as écouté la voix de ta femme et que

---

104–111. Sur les emplois juifs et païens du verbe λειτουργεῖν, voir aussi A. Hilhorst, «Servir Dieu», 186–189.

12 Sur cette extension favorable, voir par exemple S. Daniel, *op. cit.*, 62–64.

13 Voir par exemple Ez 20,40 à propos de la restauration du service de Dieu sur la montagne sainte ou Ml 3,14.18 dans l'expression «servir Dieu»: cf. S. Daniel, *op. cit.*, 66–76; A. Hilhorst, «Servir Dieu», 179–181. On notera de même cette valeur nouvelle, positive, du mot δοῦλος employé dans le poème du Serviteur en Is 49,3.5 alors que dans les autres poèmes, en Is 42,1 et 52,13, c'est παῖς qui est utilisé.

tu as mangé de l'arbre dont je t'avais interdit de manger, maudit soit le sol à cause de toi (בעבורך)». La fin du texte grec se lit ainsi «... maudite soit la terre en tes travaux (ἐν τοῖς ἔργοις σου)». L'écart ainsi constaté se caractérise par l'introduction en grec de la notion de «travail».

Qu'une telle énonciation soit délibérée ou non de la part du traducteur – soit parce qu'il avait sous les yeux, ou même seulement à l'esprit, une forme de עבדה, au lieu de בעבורך, soit parce qu'il a lu, volontairement ou par suite d'une erreur, une forme hébraïque où le ר et le ד sont inversés –, on ne peut pas pour autant y voir un énoncé stipulant la malédiction du travail, en particulier du travail agricole. Il s'agit bien en effet ici dans le grec du travail de la terre, nommé à l'aide du terme ἔργον[14] et l'ensemble du passage, même en hébreu[15], induit de toute façon ce contexte agricole. Par ailleurs, nous avons vu que l'agriculture est censée avoir été déjà pratiquée dans le jardin d'Eden bien avant la faute d'Adam, comme le mentionne Gn 2,5.15.

Ainsi la formulation du grec ici – et il en sera de même en 8,21 – n'énonce nullement, semble-t-il, le travail comme une malédiction, conséquence inéluctable de la faute d'Adam. Ce serait prêter là au judaïsme hellénistique dont la Septante est l'une des œuvres les plus représentatives une conception négative du travail manuel, sous le prétexte que la terminologie utilisée est celle des auteurs grecs classiques qui n'auraient que dédain et mépris à l'égard du travail[16]. J.P. Vernant a du reste attiré l'attention sur le fait que la représentation du travail dans la Grèce ancienne est plus complexe qu'il n'y paraît au premier abord et que, lorsque le travail reçoit une image négative chez les Grecs, celle-ci ne concerne généralement pas le travail de la terre qui ne constitue pas à proprement parler un métier, ni un savoir-faire au même titre que les métiers artisanaux[17].

---

14 Rappelons en ce sens que ἔργον et le verbe ἐργάζεσθαι sont pour ainsi dire toujours utilisés pour parler du travail agricole – il ne semble pas y avoir dans la Septante d'autres mots pour dire cela.

15 Voir Gn 3,23.

16 C'est contre les conceptions de G. Bertram sur ce sujet (TWNT Stuttgart: 1935, II, 640, *s.v.* ἔργον) que F. Gryglewicz a rédigé son article «La valeur morale du travail manuel dans la terminologie grecque de la Bible», *Biblica* 37 (1956), 314–337.

17 Voir, sur ce point, en particulier, J.P. Vernant, *Mythe et pensée chez les Grecs*, 220–221. Sur la valeur honorable du travail agricole chez Homère ou Hésiode, par exemple, voir A. Aymard, «Hiérarchie du travail et autarcie individuelle dans la Grèce archaïque», *Etudes d'Histoire ancienne*, Paris (1967), 321–322.

La traduction grecque du passage de Gn 3,17 pris ici comme exemple précise, explicite, me semble-t-il, la formulation plutôt elliptique du TM[18]: la malédiction de la terre n'est pas prononcée pour elle-même, d'une façon générale et une fois pour toutes, mais elle s'applique bien entendu aux tâches auxquelles vont désormais s'adonner les hommes sur cette terre et qui, dorénavant, se feront au prix d'un effort. Ce n'est pas le travail de la terre qui est maudit ici dans la Septante, mais la terre à l'occasion du travail de l'homme qui désormais sera pénible[19].

Gn 47,21: l'asservissement par le travail

En Gn 47,21, l'écart dans le texte grec par rapport au texte massorétique porte sur l'énonciation de l'asservissement du peuple égyptien par Joseph. Au lieu du TM «(Joseph) fit passer (le peuple) dans les villes (העביר אתו לערים)», la Septante donne: «il asservit à (Pharaon) le peuple dont il fit des serviteurs (τὸν λαὸν κατεδουλώσατο αὐτῷ εἰς παῖδας)». L'hébreu ne paraît pas très clair[20]. Du reste le Pentateuque samaritain confirme le texte de la Septante, souvent adopté dans bon nombre de traductions modernes de l'hébreu.

Avec l'emploi de cet intensif καταδουλοῦσθαι, le grec énonce ici une forme de travail bien spécifique: «asservir» les Egyptiens, ce n'est rien d'autre que les «faire travailler» pour le compte de Pharaon. Pour éclairer le sens de ce verbe, on peut par exemple se référer au passage en grec d'Ex 1,13–14, concernant cette fois non plus les Egyptiens, mais les fils d'Israël, qui nous renseigne fort bien sur la nature du travail dont il s'agit.

Le verbe καταδουλοῦσθαι traduit en effet en Ex 1,14 et 6,5 la racine עבד exprimant cet état de servitude d'Israël entre les mains des Egyptiens mais tout le passage détaille explicitement, en grec et en hébreu, à la fois les différents types de travaux imposés – travaux de terrassement et travaux agricoles (les travaux les plus durs, mortier, briques et tous les travaux dans les champs) – et

---

18 Pour J.W. Wevers, *Notes on the Greek Text of Genesis* (Atlanta, GA: 1993), 46, l'écart avec le TM s'explique plutôt par le soin qu'a mis le traducteur à éviter la répétition du TM qui donne deux fois, en début et en fin de phrase, la justification de la malédiction.
19 H. Arendt ne dit pas autre chose à propos de Gn 3,17: «la malédiction est généralement mal comprise...la peine du travail est le résultat du péché originel... L'homme non déchu eût travaillé dans la joie mais il eût travaillé», *Condition de l'homme moderne*, trad. G. Fradier, Paris: 1988,154, note 1.
20 C'est du moins l'opinion de J. W. Wevers, *op. cit.*, 800.

les conditions de travail, qui se résument à un seul mot, celui de «violence» (βίᾳ et μετὰ βίας en Ex 1,13 et 14).

La conception du travail évoquée ici en grec avec le verbe καταδουλοῦσθαι peut encore être davantage précisée par l'emploi de deux autres verbes introduits par le traducteur grec en Ex 1,13–14, lesquels ajoutent à l'état d'asservissement par le travail deux connotations très fortes, celle de la douleur avec la présence de l'intensif κατοδυνᾶν en Ex 1,14 («[les Egyptiens] faisaient de leur vie une souffrance par les travaux les plus durs»), mais aussi dès Ex 1,13 celle de l'oppression avec le verbe καταδυναστεύειν, à nouveau un intensif avec le préfixe κατα- en une équivalence unique avec le hiphil de la racine עבד que donne ici le TM. Comme le remarque J. Pons, avec ce verbe «nous sommes au niveau même de l'oppression: c'est proprement 'tyranniser, abuser du pouvoir'»[21]. Avec l'emploi de καταδουλοῦσθαι, les traducteurs de la Genèse et de l'Exode parlent bien ici, me semble-t-il, du travail, mais du travail en termes d'oppression et de domination et soulignent expressément le rapport de forces – avec ce que cela comporte comme violence et comme souffrance – qui entre en jeu dans cette relation de «service» contraint entre un serviteur et son maître, que ce soit entre les Egyptiens et Pharaon ou entre Israël et les Egyptiens[22].

Gn 49,15: le travail du cultivateur

La différence qui existe entre le grec et l'hébreu de Gn 49,15 constitue un autre exemple qui nous permet d'appréhender d'une certaine façon la représentation du travail que nous donne à lire la Septante à travers le lexique utilisé. Dans ce passage des bénédictions de Jacob sur ces fils, le grec dit qu'Issachar «est devenu un cultivateur (ἐγενήθη ἀνὴρ γεωργός)», une qualification absente ici du TM pour lequel Issachar est «devenu esclave à la corvée (לְמַס־עֹבֵד)». La Septante, conformément à l'exégèse traditionnelle de cette prédiction en milieu juif[23], refuse nettement d'attribuer un tel destin d'asservissement à cette tribu d'Israël et substitue à cette soumission à la corvée un sort beaucoup moins funeste et plus noble, celui du travail du «cultivateur». On se souvient en effet que ce terme classique γεωργός qualifie de façon laudative Noé en Gn 9,20. Ce qui, certes, semble ne pas être le cas lorsque cette même activité agricole caractérise Caïn

---

21 J. Pons, *L'oppression dans l'Ancien Testament* (Paris: Letouzey & Ané, 1981), 146. J. Pons rappelle que le mot καταδυναστεύειν n'est pas fréquent en grec classique mais qu'il est attesté au sens de «opprimer» dans les papyrus.
22 Sans analyser Gn 47,21, S. Daniel étudie également le lexique d'Ex 1,13–14: *op. cit.*, 58–59.
23 Comme S. Daniel le souligne pour les Targums ou chez Rachi, *op. cit.*, 60.

par rapport à Abel en Gn 4,2, mais c'est alors le tour participial, littéralement «Caïn était travaillant la terre (ἦν ἐργαζόμενος τὴν γῆν)», qui est utilisé, en un décalque de la syntaxe hébraïque, et constitue plutôt une description péjorative de Caïn (c'est ainsi du moins que le comprendra Philon d'Alexandrie en *Agric* 20 – 25). Dans le grec de Gn 49,15, en revanche, le travail du cultivateur est ainsi explicitement valorisé par rapport à l'état de servitude que sont les travaux forcés ou la soumission à la corvée qu'exprime le texte massorétique.

Dt 20,11: l'exploitation tributaire

On retrouve ce même évitement de la mention des travaux forcés dans le règlement concernant les villes étrangères assiégées mais qui n'offrent aucune résistance à Israël dans le grec de Dt 20,11: la double expression de l'hébreu «le peuple te devra la corvée et le travail (יהיו לך למס ועבדוך)» est adoucie en grec et rendue avec un lexique qui correspond sans doute davantage à la situation politique de l'époque. Le grec dit: «ils te paieront tribut et te seront soumis (ἔσονταί σοι φορολόγητοι καὶ ὑπήκοοι σου)», introduisant ici une exploitation tributaire et non plus servile. En réalité, la marque de l'esclavage n'est plus le travail imposé mais devient le versement du tribut par celui qui est soumis. Il convient sans doute de préciser que le sens du mot hébreu מס, parfois traduit par le simple ἔργον, par exemple en Ex 1,11 pour évoquer les travaux infligés par Pharaon aux Hébreux, peut avoir évolué vers celui de «tribut», puisque dans la forme lucianique d'Est 10,1 le terme מס «corvée», est rendu par τέλη au sens de «taxes»[24]. De la même façon, mais à l'inverse, on peut se demander si le terme φόρος «taxe, tribut, impôt», ne prend pas parfois en grec ce sens de «corvée» puisqu'en 3 R 9,21, dans ce même contexte de peuples soumis, l'expression hébraïque למס־עבד est traduite par εἰς φόρον δουλείας «à la corvée servile»[25].

Jon 4,10: la peine affective

En Jon 4,10 une divergence entre le grec et l'hébreu porte sur le sens donné à une autre racine hébraïque importante, renvoyant à ce même champ sémantique du travail. Il s'agit de עמל qui, certes, compte relativement peu d'occurrences dans le

---

24 Voir la note de C. Cavalier, *Esther*, La Bible d'Alexandrie 12 (Paris: Les Editions du Cerf, 2012), 234.
25 Voir la note sur Dt 20,11, M. Harl, C. Dogniez, *Deutéronome*, La Bible d'Alexandrie 5 (Paris: Les Editions du Cerf, 1992), 240.

texte massorétique mais désigne le travail sous son aspect péjoratif en énonçant, plus que tous les autres termes, ce qu'il y a d'aliénant, de douloureux et qui est source de peine et de fatigue lors de cette activité humaine. On retrouve ici l'étymologie de notre mot français «travail» [26] qui vient du bas latin *tripalium* désignant un instrument de torture formé de trois pieux. Selon l'hébreu de Jon 4,10, le ricin n'aurait coûté aucun travail à Jonas qui se lamente. Le traducteur des Douze Petits Prophètes, pour traduire cette forme עמלת, emploie l'expression οὐκ ἐκακοπάθησας «tu n'as subi aucun mauvais traitement», entendue plutôt au sens psychologique: «tu n'as pas été malheureux». Il y a là assurément un léger changement de registre puisque certains manuscrits grecs ainsi que Justin (*Dial.* 107,4) ont éprouvé le besoin de revenir plus précisément au sens concret de l'hébreu en utilisant la forme ἐκοπίασας «tu as travaillé, tu as pris de la peine». L'emploi de ce verbe grec κοπιᾶν évoquant cette fatigue au travail est en effet plus littéral pour rendre l'hébreu עמל. On trouve d'ailleurs cette équivalence, par exemple en Jg 5,26 B, pour nommer les «travailleurs» (κοπιώντων), ou en Ps 126,1 pour qualifier le travail des maçons (ἐκοπίασαν)[27]. Le grec de Jon 4,10 n'énonce donc nullement cette idée de travail présente dans le texte massorétique et ne retient, non sans ironie, que la peine affective.

---

26 Cette nuance d'effort douloureux est encore présente aujourd'hui dans la langue française avec l'emploi du mot «travail» pour décrire les souffrances de l'accouchement. En hébreu, c'est le terme עצב qui désigne ce type de douleurs. Le grec λύπη est un bon équivalent en Gn 3,16 à propos de l'enfantement d'Eve mais en 1 Par 4,9, pour ce même contexte, le traducteur transcrit l'hébreu sous la forme γαβης.

27 La traduction en grec des différents noms de métiers dans la Bible mériterait une étude lexicale à part. Que l'on songe au passage de Sir 38,25–34 sur les métiers manuels ou aux artisans de l'Exode: par exemple le forgeron, χαλκεύς, en Sir 38,28 ou le potier, κεραμεύς, en Sir 38,29, le brodeur, ποικιλτής, en Ex 26,36, le brocheur, ῥαφιδευτής, en Ex 27,16, le lissier, ὑφάντης, en Ex 26,1, le lapidaire, λιθουργικός, en Ex 28,11 ou le parfumeur, μυρεψός, en Ex 30,25. Remarquons que le traducteur de l'Exode substitue parfois au nom du simple artiste en hébreu celui plus spécifique de l'artisan ou encore le nom des travaux (voir A. Le Boulluec, P. Sandevoir, *L'Exode*, La Bible d'Alexandrie 2 (Paris: Les Editions du Cerf, 1998, la note sur Ex 28,6 et Ex 35,35). Ailleurs, certains métiers précis comme celui des bûcherons en 2 Par 2,9 ou des tisserands en Is 19,10 sont tout simplement nommés des ἐργαζόμενοι, des «travailleurs», tandis que le fondeur d'or conserve la désignation spéciale qu'il a en grec, χρυσοχόος, en Is 40,19; 46,6 par exemple.

Μοχθεῖν et μόχθος dans l'Ecclésiaste

Dans l'Ecclésiaste, qui offre une image très pessimiste du travail[28] parce que, «en plus d'être aliéné et aliénant (4,4–6), [il] rappelle constamment la finitude humaine (11,6)»[29], la racine עמל compte le plus grand nombre d'occurrences. Dans ce livre où l'auteur se demande constamment quel profit il y a à se donner tant de peine au travail – ainsi en Ecc 2,18–20 «Je déteste tout le travail que je fais ici-bas, et que je laisse à mon successeur (18). Et qui sait s'il sera sage ou fou? Et il sera maître de tout mon labeur, où j'ai mis de la peine, et de la sagesse pendant ma vie. Cela aussi est vanité (19). J'en viens à me décourager pour toute la peine que j'ai prise sous le soleil (20)» – la Septante a recours à un lexique très négatif et de sens très fort, appartenant à la langue grecque classique, surtout celle des poètes et des tragiques: μοχθεῖν pour traduire le verbe hébreu et μόχθος pour traduire le substantif; ce sont là deux mots grecs qui expriment avec force cette souffrance, ce tourment et cette peine, mais pas nécessairement consécutifs aux durs travaux du corps[30].

F. Vinel a bien montré que, avec le choix lexical de μόχθος associé à l'emploi de tout un lexique riche et varié décrivant de façon hyperbolique la souffrance et l'épuisement, la version grecque de l'Ecclésiaste accentuait cette «perception négative de l'existence»[31]. Il semble en effet que le terme μόχθος «le tourment», suggérant la douleur[32] de la fatigue et de la peine, soit encore plus fort et d'une autre nature que le mot grec πόνος qui exprime généralement le dur effort, l'accablement de la peine.

---

28 Le livre des Proverbes, en revanche, offre une vision plus positive du travail. En Prov 31,18, par exemple, le traducteur grec accentue même ce thème du travail dans le portrait qu'il dresse de la maîtresse de maison.

29 Cf. A. Da Silva, «La conception du travail dans la Bible et dans la tradition chrétienne occidentale», *Théologiques* 3 (1995), 96.

30 Sur ce point, voir par exemple la bibliographie donnée par F. Gryglewicz, «La valeur morale du travail manuel», 314–337, sp. 319, note 5. Sur les emplois de μόχθος dans la Septante pour traduire d'autres mots hébreux, voir F. Gryglewicz, 321 avec les notes.

31 F. Vinel, *L'Ecclésiaste*, La Bible d'Alexandrie 18 (Paris: Les Editions du Cerf, 2002), 76–77.

32 Sur la nature du lien entre les deux sphères sémantiques, celle du travail et celle de la douleur, voir par exemple C. Jourdan-Annequin, «Travail et discours mythique», in J. Annequin, E. Geny, E. Smadja, eds., *Le travail. Recherches historiques. Table ronde de Besançon*, 14 et 15 novembre 1997 (Paris: 1999), 30, citant F. Mawet, *Recherches sur les oppositions fonctionnelles dans le vocabulaire homérique de la douleur (autour de πῆμα – ἄλγος)*, (Bruxelles: Palais des Académies, 1979) pour πόνος.

Πόνος et κόπος dans la Bible grecque

Πόνος est en effet un terme souvent utilisé dans la Bible grecque pour rendre la racine hébraïque עמל lorsqu'elle a non le sens de «travail» mais celui de «peine», comme en Gn 41,51 pour parler des peines de Joseph, ou en Jb 3,10 et 5,6 pour signifier la souffrance de Job. Dans le grec d'Ex 2,11, par exemple, domine cette nuance psychologique du mot πόνος, en correspondance avec un autre mot hébreu appartenant au vocabulaire du travail, סבלת, un substantif qui désigne l'oppression pesante que subissent les Hébreux en Egypte[33], autrement dit leur servitude au travail. On retrouve également cette même connotation psychologique propre au grec en Nb 23,21, où la combinaison de πόνος et de μόχθος évoque le «tourment» de Jacob et l' «accablement» d'Israël, là où le TM a recours à deux substantifs évoquant non le travail, même sous son aspect pénible, mais l'iniquité (און) et le mal (עמל).

Mais le premier sens de πόνος, celui de travail à connotation péjorative[34], dans tout ce qu'il a de fatiguant et pénible, est bien attesté dans la Septante. Dans le livre de la Sagesse en 5,1; 10,10, πόνος nomme ce labeur qui épuise; en 19,16, πόνος au pluriel désigne explicitement les corvées d'Egypte. Remarquons en passant que ce type de vocabulaire qui associe travail et peine véhicule en grec comme en hébreu une même conception quasi universelle, mais pas nécessairement toujours péjorative, du travail. Ainsi, en une acception courante dans la Septante et bien attestée en grec classique, πόνος désigne par métonymie et de façon plus positive le fruit du labeur, de la peine, les produits du travail. Il traduit alors, en une bonne équivalence lexicale, le mot hébreu יגיע qui connote ce même effort requis par le travail et, de là, en quelques rares occurrences, le fruit du travail dont l'homme jouit. On trouve ainsi πόνος pour ce même substrat hébreu, avec cette connotation positive en Dt 28,33; Ps 77,46; 108,11; 127,2; Os 12,9; Ag 1,11; Jr 20, 5; Ez 23, 29.

Si, dans la Septante comme dans la langue grecque classique, πόνος nomme à la fois le travail, la peine que l'on prend à ce travail et le produit qui en résulte, il n'en va pas de même pour κόπος, un terme moins usité dans la Septante; en grec ce mot désigne bien l'effort du travailleur, la peine, la souffrance, la fatigue liée au travail qu'il fournit – et c'est bien ainsi qu'il est utilisé en Gn 31,42 «Dieu a

---

33 Cf. A. Le Boulluec, P. Sandevoir, *L'Exode*, La Bible d'Alexandrie 2, 83. L. Ramlot, «Le travail selon la Bible», *Bible et vie chrétienne* 75 (1967), 45, signale ce mot סבלת parmi le vocabulaire du travail.

34 Sur cette connotation péjorative de πόνος dérivé de πένης, πενία, «pauvreté», voir par exemple F. Gryglewicz, «La valeur morale du travail manuel», 319.

vu la souffrance de mes mains» – mais il ne semble guère employé au sens de fruit du labeur. On le trouve cependant deux fois dans la version grecque en ce sens dérivé par métonymie: en 2 Esd 15,13[35], «que Dieu secoue hors de sa maison et de ses biens tout homme qui ne tiendra pas sa parole (ἐκ τοῦ οἴκου αὐτοῦ καὶ ἐκ κόπου αὐτοῦ)», – ici le substrat hébreu יגיע s'entend selon cette deuxième acception de «produit qui résulte du travail» – et en Sir 14,15 où il est employé avec πόνος: «Est-ce que tu ne laisseras pas à d'autres le fruit de ton labeur et le fruit de tes peines à la décision du sort? (τοὺς πόνους σου καὶ τοὺς κόπους σου)».

A moins de désigner le produit qui résulte du travail, le vocabulaire πόνος et κόπος [36], dans la version grecque, souligne moins le travail en lui-même que l'aspect de peine, de fatigue et de souffrance qui s'y attache. Ces mots κόπος et πόνος sont de signification très proche dans la Septante au point que, dans les manuscrits, ils sont parfois remplacés l'un par l'autre[37]. Ils ne marquent donc pas de gradation dans la peine au labeur.

Mais κόπος et πόνος ne sont pas les deux seuls équivalents du terme hébreu יגיע. Deux autres mots grecs sont utilisés selon les différentes acceptions du mot: en Jb 10,3 et 39,11 ἔργον nomme concrètement le travail, alors qu'en Is 55,2; Jr 3,24 et Ez 23,29 (comme double traduction, semble-t-il) μόχθος souligne le tourment lié au travail, davantage que κόπος et πόνος et avec une intensité de caractère tragique si l'on songe à la force de ce mot dans le grec de l'Ecclésiaste.

Na 2,14: l'introduction en grec du motif de la renommée du travail

Prenons maintenant l'exemple d'un autre lieu dans la Bible où la Septante, plutôt que de remplacer, de souligner ou d'adoucir tel ou tel aspect associé à la notion de travail telle qu'elle est énoncée en hébreu, introduit au contraire de façon explicite l'idée de travail, alors que le texte massorétique donne à lire autre chose. Il s'agit de Na 2,14 où le Seigneur tout-puissant menace Ninive en ces termes: «je ferai disparaître de la terre ta proie et, assurément, on n'entendra

---

35 Voir la note sur κόπος de T. Janz, *II Esdras (Esdras-Néhémie)*, La Bible d'Alexandrie 11.2 (Paris: Les Editions du Cerf, 2010), 280.

36 La double expression κόπος καὶ πόνος «souffrance et peine», toujours donnée dans cet ordre, revient plusieurs fois dans la Septante, en Ps 9,28 (TM 10,7); 89(90),10; Hab 1,3 et Jr 20,18, pour traduire des termes hébreux différents, tels אָוֶן, עָמָל, יָגוֹן. On trouve parfois les deux mots l'un près de l'autre, par exemple en Sir 14,15 et en Jr 51,33 (TM 45,3).

37 C'est ce que fait remarquer F. Gryglewicz, «La valeur morale du travail manuel», 319 pour Job 3,10; Ps 9,35; 54,11; Sg 10,10 et Sir 29,4 par exemple.

plus parler de tes œuvres (τὰ ἔργα σου))». Certes le texte massorétique présente ici une difficulté portant sur la forme du mot hébreu מלאך «messager», jugée incorrecte mais maintenue par D. Barthélemy qui traduit ainsi: «je supprimerai de la terre tes rapines et l'on n'entendra plus la voix de tes messagers»[38].

Il est difficile d'affirmer en toute certitude qu'il y a dans le grec de Na 2,14 une modification délibérée de l'hébreu, mais on peut sans doute faire l'hypothèse soit d'un autre substrat, soit d'une autre lecture, bien qu'aucun autre témoin ne vienne confirmer cette leçon de la version grecque. Le traducteur grec des Douze Prophètes a en effet pu lire le mot hébreu מלאכה qui signifie le travail, l'affaire, l'œuvre à accomplir à la place de מלאך, «messager». מלאכה, qui appartient au vocabulaire du travail et le désigne non, semble-t-il, en tant que mission[39] mais comme activité à accomplir ou encore en tant qu'ouvrage ou produit manufacturé, est très fréquent dans la Bible et la Septante le traduit le plus souvent par ἐργασία ou par ἔργον selon l'acception de l'hébreu.

Ἐργασία qui renvoie à l'action a en effet «un sens plus large et plus abstrait que ἔργον, lequel s'applique plutôt à des ouvrages précis, considérés en tant que réalisations matérielles»[40]. Ainsi, en Gn 2,2, ἔργον, au pluriel, désigne le travail, les œuvres, que Dieu acheva au sixième jour pour se reposer au septième jour[41], tandis que ἐργασία, en Jon 1,8, nomme selon le grec, non la mission du prophète comme l'hébreu מלאכה, mais son activité, son travail, sur lequel l'interrogent les matelots.

---

38 D. Barthélemy, *Critique textuelle de l'Ancien Testament. 3, Ezéchiel, Daniel et les 12 Prophètes*, OBO 50/3 (Fribourg-Göttingen: 1992), 812–815.

39 Sur le rejet d'une telle interprétation de ce mot hébreu מלאכה, voir E.L. Greenstein, «Trans-Semitic Idiomatic Equivalency and the Derivation of Hebrew ml'kh», *Ugarit-Forschungen* 11 (1979), 329–337. Je dois cette référence à J. Joosten. Qu'il en soit remercié.

40 S. Daniel, *op. cit.*, 56. Sur cette valeur neutre de ἔργον, voir F. Gryglewicz, «La valeur morale du travail manuel», 325.

41 C'est le travail de Dieu, son activité créatrice durant six jours, qui justifie dans la Torah la loi du travail des six jours suivie de l'injonction du repos sabbatique (Ex 20,9; 23,12; 31,15; 34,21; 35,2; Lv 23,3; Dt 5,13 avec l'emploi du lexique grec ποιεῖν ἔργα, «travailler», et καταπαύειν/κατάπαυσις, ἀναπαύειν/ἀνάπαυσις pour signifier l'arrêt du travail, le repos). Mais sans doute faut-il voir ici la trace d'une idéologie libératrice très ancienne d'un système d'exploitation par le travail (cf. A. Caquot, «L'attitude des Religions sémitiques à l'égard des métiers manuels», *3e et 4e Colloques d'Histoire des Religions organisés par la Société Ernest Renan* (Orsay: 1979, 5). Sur cette dialectique révolutionnaire du travail et du repos, voir par exemple D. Nocquet, «Travail des hommes, écho du labeur de Dieu. Réflexions sur la notion de travail dans l'Ancien Testament», *Autres Temps. Cahiers d'éthique sociale et politique* 63 (1999), 19–29, sp. 25–26.

Rappelons que les mots de ce lexique du travail, à la fois l'hébreu מלאכה[42] et le grec ἔργον et ἐργασία, sont très importants mais qu'ils n'ont en eux-mêmes aucune connotation négative ou dépréciative. Dans la Septante, en tout cas, ἔργα renvoie aussi bien aux œuvres divines qu'aux œuvres des nations ou des adversaires d'Israël comme ici en Na 2,14. De la même façon ἐργασία est d'un emploi neutre auquel seul le contexte confère telle ou telle nuance; c'est par exemple ce terme qu'utilise le traducteur grec en Gn 29,27, comme équivalent de עבדה cette fois, pour «faire dire à l'astucieux Laban que Jacob n'avait pas 'été esclave' (δουλεύειν) chez lui», mais avait accompli un simple travail (ἐργασία)[43]. Mais ce mot désigne aussi dans la Septante à la fois ce qu'a fait Ruth, en 2,12, et qui lui est justement rétribué par Dieu et les œuvres ou le travail des idoles que condamne très violemment le Seigneur en particulier en Is 1,31 et 41,24 – dans ces trois exemples, il convient de préciser que ἐργασία traduit un autre équivalent hébreu, le substantif פעל, qui désigne également le travail[44]. On voit donc que l'écart qui existe en Na 2,14 entre l'hébreu et le grec porte sur la renommée des œuvres de Ninive dont seul le contexte indique qu'elles sont néfastes.

Certes la mention de «la voix des messagers» du TM disparaît dans la Septante, mais l'introduction du motif de la renommée du travail ne surprend nullement le lecteur et vient même accentuer cette fin du renom de Ninive plusieurs fois affirmée dans la version grecque, en Na 1,12, «et l'on n'entendra plus bruit de toi» et en 3,19, «tous ceux qui entendent nouvelle à ton propos battront des mains contre toi»[45].

Is 5,10: le travail des animaux

Dans le dernier exemple que nous avons choisi d'examiner, la divergence entre le texte hébreu et le texte de la version grecque porte sur l'énonciation non du travail humain ni même divin, mais sur le travail des animaux. Dans un contexte

---

42 Il faudrait ici ajouter le terme hébreu מעשה qui désigne largement le labeur des hommes en tant qu'activité productrice et créative et à la connotation parfois positive ou négative lorsqu'il est suivi de l'expression deutéronomiste «de tes/ vos mains». Ce lexique ambivalent est majoritairement rendu dans la Septante avec le mot ἔργον. Dans l'Ecclésiaste, on trouve surtout ποίημα «œuvre, ouvrage», et deux fois ποίησις au sens de «façon», en Ex 28,8 et 36,12 (TM 39,5).
43 Cf. S. Daniel, *op. cit.*, 86; voir aussi 57.
44 Sur cet autre vocabulaire hébraïque du travail, voir par exemple P. Humbert, «L'emploi du verbe *pāʿal* et de ses dérivés substantifs en hébreu biblique», *ZAW* 65 (1953), 35–44.
45 Voir M. Harl *et al.*, *Les Douze Prophètes. Aggée, Abdiou, Jonas, Naoum, Ambakoum, Sophonie*, La Bible d'Alexandrie 23.4–9 (Paris: Les Editions du Cerf, 1999), *ad loc.*

de malédiction divine contre les transgresseurs et ceux qui ne pratiquent pas la justice, le grec d'Is 5,10 se lit ainsi: «Là en effet où travailleront dix attelages de bœufs, on produira une seule jarre (οὗ γὰρ ἐργῶνται δέκα ζεύγη βοῶν, ποιήσει κεράμιον ἕν), et qui sème six artabes produira trois mesures». En ce lieu, le texte massorétique ne mentionne nullement le travail des animaux mais prévient seulement que «dix arpents de vigne (עשרת צמדי־כרם) ne donneront qu'un tonnelet». Même si la traduction grecque du livre d'Isaïe est bien connue pour sa liberté par rapport à son modèle, peut-on essayer de comprendre l'écart que nous avons ici?

Le mot hébreu כרם «vigne» est parfaitement identifié dans les versets précédents du chant de la vigne où il revient à plusieurs reprises (v.1.2.3.4.5.6.7): le traducteur grec le traduit par ἀμπελών. Le mot hébreu צמד signifie une «paire», une «couple», et s'emploie généralement à propos d'animaux, par exemple d'ânes en Jg 19,3.10; 2 Sam 16,1 et plus souvent de bœufs en 1 Rois 19.19.21; Jb 1,3; 42,12. Dans toutes ces occurrences la Septante rend le mot par ζεῦγος signifiant «le joug», l'«attelage» de deux animaux mais aussi, «une couple, une paire» d'animaux. Dans le livre d'Isaïe, le mot צמד figure trois fois, et il est bien identifié par le traducteur grec en Is 21,7 et 9 puisqu'il est traduit par δύο («deux cavaliers), puis par le terme technique συνωρίς («des chevaux d'attelage»). Dans notre passage, et de façon assez exceptionnelle, semble-t-il, le mot hébreu צמד ne concerne pas des animaux mais il est associé à un mot qui évoque une terre cultivable – un champ comme en 1 Sam 14,14, ou la vigne comme ici –, et désigne une unité de mesure, un «arpent» de terre ou de vigne. On peut donc imaginer que le traducteur grec ne connaissait pas cet autre emploi fort rare du mot hébreu au sens de mesure au carré, de surface, et qu'il a opté pour l'acception plus courante du mot, applicable aux animaux. Mais on peut également faire l'hypothèse que l'introduction de la mention de l'attelage des bœufs avec l'ajout du verbe ἐργάζεσθαι[46] est délibérée et ne fait qu'expliciter ce que dit l'hébreu de façon elliptique. Il y aurait dans le grec d'Isaïe un retour en quelque sorte au sens étymologique du mot hébreu qui désigne l'arpent de terre, en tant qu'il représente précisément la surface de travail, l'aire de labour d'une paire (de bœufs). Les dix arpents de vigne correspondraient au travail de labour par jour de dix attelages de bœufs[47]. Ce qui importe ici, en hébreu – et le

---

46 Sur le travail des animaux exprimé à l'aide du verbe ἐργάζεσθαι, voir par exemple Dt 15,19; 21,3 et Is 30,24 (il s'agit là précisément du labour des bœufs). Voir sur ce point, F. Gryglewicz, «La valeur morale du travail manuel», 325.

47 Sur cette estimation, voir H. Wilberger, *Isaiah 1–12. A Commentary* (Minneapolis; 1991), 199. On peut aussi se référer ici aux «douze paires de bœufs» (δώδεκα ζεύγη βοῶν) qui labourent le champ d'Elisée lorsque Elie le rencontre en 3 R 19,19.

grec va tout à fait en ce sens en introduisant de façon parfaitement appropriée cette image du joug du labeur –, c'est de montrer le lien qu'il y a entre la loi divine et l'activité humaine. On retrouve cette même menace sur la production du travail contre ceux qui ne respectent pas l'alliance divine, mais en des termes différents, en Lv 26,20[48] et en Dt 28,38[49]. Le châtiment divin atteint l'homme dans ce qu'il a de plus précieux, son travail.

Conclusion

Nos remarques sur l'énonciation du travail à partir de quelques exemples pris dans le texte grec de la Septante, assurément trop peu nombreux, sont loin d'épuiser le sujet dont les implications sont d'ordre à la fois technique, politique, économique, psychologique, etc. Elles permettent cependant, nous semble-t-il, de mettre en évidence des pratiques de traduction propres aux traducteurs grecs, même s'il importe de préciser qu'il faudrait toujours examiner les livres de la Bible grecque un par un, mais aussi de confirmer certaines hypothèses générales en matière de lexicographie. On constate en effet que malgré le souci de bien distinguer les différents champs sémantiques que recouvre le lexique du travail dans la Bible, en particulier le registre polysémique du «service» inhérent à la racine hébraïque עבד, les traducteurs de la Bible grecque conservent parfois l'ambivalence de la notion dans la variété des emplois de certains termes. En outre, on ne peut pas dire que le lexique de cette Bible juive offre une image négative du travail. Certes il en accentue certains aspects, celui de l'oppression ou de la souffrance liées à cette activité humaine ou, au contraire, en adoucit la formulation pour l'adapter à la situation politique de l'époque. Mais lorsqu'il y a des écarts par rapport au texte hébreu, ce qui retient particulièrement l'attention, c'est l'étroite dépendance avec le contexte des choix lexicaux; le plus souvent, ils ne font qu'expliciter, semble-t-il, un substrat jugé parfois trop elliptique.

---

48 Lv 26,20, traduction BA 3: «et votre force ne vous servira de rien, et votre terre ne donnera pas de quoi semer, et l'arbre de votre champ ne donnera pas son fruit».
49 Dt 28,38, traduction BA 5: «Tu emporteras dans la plaine beaucoup de semence et tu en rapporteras peu parce que la sauterelle la mangera».

Kyriakoula Papademetriou

The dynamic semantic role of etymology in the meaning of Greek biblical words. The case of the word ἐκκλησία

The semantic role of etymology in diachronic perspective

Pre-scientific etymology

Etymology, as an interest for the word meaning, is probably as old as language. Both in the Bible and in Homer there are many instances where a connection is attempted between a noun and its meaning. Proper names, mainly, are interpreted through their purported original meaning, which is detected in their phonetic forms and associated with legends and mythology[1]. In those ancient times, the term etymology referred to an etiological approach of designations. But this is not the whole content of etymology.

Setting out from an "etymology" of etymology, the Greek word ἐτυμολογία is composed of the adjective ἔτυμος, -ον, which means "true, genuine"[2], and in its neuter form, τὸ ἔτυμον, means "the truth", combined with the verb λέγω (n. λόγος), "to speak". Thus, at first, etymology meant speaking about the truthfulness of things, particularly about the true meaning of words, whereby the true meaning of the things, designated by the words, was revealed[3]. For the people of archaic times the noun had an ontological sense, it referred to the essence of the referent, since the human word possessed an extraordinary power, which under certain circumstances became even sacred or magic. Therefore, as becomes evident from the etymology of "etymology" as well as from the prac-

---

1 Cf. for the name of Odysseus: *Od.* 19.406–7; for the name of Telemachus: *Il.* 4.353–54; *Odysee*, 2.332–3; 15.10; for the name of Skamander: *Il.* 20.74. See more in Evanthia Tsitsibakou-Vasalos, *Ancient Poetic Etymology. The Pelopids: Father and Sons* (Stuttgart: Fr. Steiner Verlag), 2007.
2 Cf. Homer, *Il.* 10.534: ψεύσομαι ἦ ἔτυμον ἐρέω ("shall I be wrong, or speak the truth?").
3 See Scholia in Dionysii Thracis *Artem Grammaticam*, in *Grammatici Graeci* (ed. G. Uhlig; Lipsiae, 1883), v. I, 3.309.2–14: Τί ἐστιν ἐτυμολογία; Ἀνάπτυξις τῶν λέξεων ἁρμόζουσα τῇ φωνῇ, δι' ἧς καὶ τὸ ἀληθὲς σαφηνίζεται ("What is etymology? Unfolding the words in their own dialect, by which the truth is illustrated").

tice of ancient etymologies, any interest in the word meaning was clearly philosophical and theological.

This philosophical interest explains the attraction etymology exercises on the human mind, but, furthermore, it could point towards the delusion that risks occurring in such an arbitrary procedure as well. Plato was the first who dealt with the reliable use of etymology in the form of a grammatical practice[4]. The main question was if the words were imposed on things by nature or by convention namely, a philosophical issue, since it pertained to the original imposition of the words, to the creation of the language, to a *glossogony*, so to speak. However, all considered that etymology was a legitimate strategy both for philosophical and rhetorical reasons[5].

Aristotle was the first who clarified that the imposition of words should not be regarded as the ontological but as the methodological basis on which the relation between referent and cognition is shaped; according to Aristotle each name was a symbol[6]. The Stoics were those who studied etymology in grammatical terms and regarded it as a literary criterion for discerning the purity of the language, its *hellenicity*; nevertheless, they believed that language is both natural and transcendent, and such as it recovers the truth of the things[7]. During the Hellenistic period, when knowledge of the Greek language (Greek literacy) started being considered as a qualification, grammarians distinguished the epistemological from the rhetorical and philosophical use of etymology; etymology was used as a methodological tool for recovering the proper use of language[8].

The Romans were interested in etymology, as well. Varro sought to combine the two aspects of etymology and discerned two kinds of etymology, *voluntaria*, which is based on mythology and on allegory, and *naturalis*, which is based on linguistic conventions. He stated that "after words are imposed on things according to the often arbitrary human will (*voluntas*), forms are derived in order to produce *sententia*, when united with one another systemically"[9].

---

4 Plato, in his work *Cratylus*.

5 See Dialexeis, in *Die Fragmente der Vorsokratiker* (eds. H. Diels-W. Kranz; Berlin: ⁶1954), v. II 345: etymology is connected with the rhetorician's artificial memory. See also Hippon in idem, v. I (Berlin: ⁹1960), 386. Cf. Plato, *Phaedrus*, 260e.

6 Aristotle, *On Interpetation* 16a.

7 See *Stoicorum veterarum fragmenta* (ed. I. Ab Arnim; Stuttgart: B.G. Teubner, 1964), v. II, 44.

8 See Dionysios Thrax, *Ars Grammatica*, in *Grammatici Graeci* (ed. G. Uhlig; Lipsiae: 1883), v. I, 1α'.

9 Varro, *De lingua latina*, VII.1. Generally for etymology in the late antiquity see more in Mark Amsler, *Etymology and Grammatical Discourse in Late Antiquity and the Early Middle Ages* (Studies in the History of the Language Sciences 44; Amsterdam: J. Benjamins Publishing, 1989), 15–57.

The Stoic-Varronian etymological model dominated in the following centuries, but it also received intense criticism. From a philosophical perspective Sextus Empiricus and from a grammatical perspective. Quintilian both rejected the claim that language by its nature reflects reality and introduced the criterion of the usage (*consuetudo*), which they considered as the appropriate criterion on which the study of the word meaning should be based.

Christian thought on etymology was influenced mainly by the Platonic view which was mediated through Neo-Platonism. According to this each word encompasses a true meaning, which can be unfolded by studying the grammatical elements of the word. Augustine presents a similar view, when he states that the words are signs, which should be interpreted by grammatical rules and verified by social conventions[10].

Thus, Plato, Skeptics (like Sextus Empiricus) and Augustine, setting out from different philosophical principles, converge to the same critique. They all conclude that etymology is determined by linguistic convention and usage and that it is only an ancillary mean of detecting the word meaning. These etymological theories dominated throughout Medieval Period with some variations. Grammarians and commentators, not only pagans, but also Christians, used etymology mainly as a technical mean of restoring the original language (Latin or Greek) and offering new exegesis on the texts. Etymology served as a way for defining words, not only grammatically, but historically, mythographically and exegetically as well.

Scientific etymology

The deficiencies of this etymological approach were clearly revealed in 19th century, when previous philosophical theories were put aside and theoretical hypotheses took their place thus founding comparative linguistics. Historical linguistics emerged as a separate discipline, through which new rules and methodological approaches were set so as to establish a profound research mode of the lexicological origin and development of words, based on variation and alteration within the internal system of each language. Thus, etymology could no longer be rejected as a subjective theory, as had been the case up to then, and gained validity as a form of historical scientific exploration of word derivation. However, etymology as an interpretative method endured a fierce blow from modern linguistics, when Saussure posited the arbitrary nature of

---

10 Augustine, in his work *De Dialectica*.

the "linguistic sign", mentioned the priority of synchrony against diachrony and analyzed the importance of the words' current usage against their meaning derivation[11].

Nowadays etymology constitutes an integral and indispensable part of each grammar, the *Etymologicon*, which informs us about the formation of words on the basis of production and composition. But as a discipline, etymology covers a wide range of issues related to the history and the development of language and word formation. It is subdivided into the following fields of research: a) analysis of the words into their constituent elements and finding the root-meanings, b) reconstruction of both form and sense of the words in a proto-language c) tracing the changes of words' forms and meanings in the perspective of the historical development of a language, d) identification of loan words from other languages and their semantic adaptations, and e) after identifying the crucial influence of social structure on the structure of the language, etymology has to examine the implications of this influence and the chain reactions it might have caused in the development of the various word significations.

Since etymology is associated with meaning, lexicology and lexicography closely related to it, since it offers solid ground on which the history and background of the of the words are presented[12]. Semantics is, also, connected to etymology, from a historical perspective, since it is a useful tool for the diachronic examination of word significations. But could interpretation and exegesis similarly benefit from etymology within the context of a synchronic consideration of texts' language? Actually, biblical scholars have quite often used etymology the way pre-scientific etymological practice had been passed on to them, as it has already been analyzed above; that is, by essentially associating the original meaning of the word with its referent and, then, being guided through the exegetical process by this original meaning, which was, in fact, largely questionable.

The danger of etymologizing for the interpretation of words was raised by James Barr[13]. He stressed the necessity for biblical scholars to be aware of the linguistic resources and he concluded that etymology is not a safe way for interpreting words in their context and that the semantic value of words should be

---

11 For the etymological theories in this period see Brigitte Nerlich, *Semantic Theories in Europe, 1830–1930. From etymology to contextuality* (Studies in the History of the Language Sciences 59; Amsterdam: J. Benjamins, 1992).

12 See Yakov Malkiel, *Essays on Linguistic Themes* (Berkeley and Los Angeles: University California Press, 1968), 175–198.

13 James Barr, *Semantics of Biblical Language* (Oxford: 1961), 107–60. Cf. idem, "Etymology and the Old Testament" in *Language and Meaning. Studies in Hebrew Language and Biblical Exegesis* (ed. J. Barr; Qudtestamentische Studiën, Deel XIX; Belgium: Brill, 1974), 1–28.

determined occording to their current usage and not to their derivation. His major argument was the Saussurian principle that etymology belongs to diachrony, which involves to the development of a language, while contextual semantics is an integral part of, which involves the static current usage of the words. Barr's critique awakened biblical scholars' interest in and awareness of linguistics, so as to avoid any etymological fallacy.

However, neither Saussure nor Barr rejected the important role of etymology for the study of language. They merely limited the predominance etymology held after the establishment of historical linguistics in the 19th century and they reduced it to an ancillary discipline in the search for meaning of words in context.

The dynamics of language according André Martinet

Meanwhile, further developments in modern linguistics after Saussure highlighted the role of etymology and limited some extreme reservations that have been stated against the validity of etymology. Linguists like André Martinet stressed the functionality of language and discerned in diachronic development a dynamic which legitimately discontinued the stability of any synchronic situation[14] to such an extent that both diachrony and synchrony could no longer be autonomously studied. In brief, this statement goes as follows:

According to Saussure[15] the system of language and its history, namely its synchronic and diachronic perspective, despite their interdependence, are actually separate and should be considered as such. Just like in the case of a chess game, in order to watch the game at a certain point, someone does not need to have watched the whole course of the game or the moves that have led the players to that point (that is to know the "history" of the game are, the same applies in language, too; in order to describe a certain synchronic linguistic case, someone does not need to refer to its history. It is merely sufficient to identify the interrelationships developed among linguistic elements. In other words, the native speaker of a language is not actually aware of theevolutionary succession which generated the linguistic system; synchrony is "the genuine and the singular reality for the speaking community". Due to this fact, any linguist who wants to understand a certain synchronic point "must delete the past". Therefore, the synchronic system appears as static and stable, while , on the

---

14 Against the static character of the synchrony was the School of Prague and linguists as Eugeniu Coseriu and Hansjakob Seiler.

15 F. de Saussure, *Cours de Linguistique Générale* (1915; repr. Paris: 1968), 141–260.

other hand, the diachronic process appears to be dynamic containing the evolutionary process under which it was formulated.

Nevertheless, it is a general linguistics principle that languages change through time they never cease to function. This means that they go through a gradual change, not at all abrupt, since a common language is an absolutely essential element in keeping it functional, while at the same time it facilitates mutual understanding within the context of social life. On the other hand, as Martinet argues[16], the evolution of a language depends on the evolution of the communicative needs of the community which uses it; in turn, the evolution of both is directly associated with the intellectual, social and economic development of this community. Thus, it will take centuries or even millennia for any changes in the language to take effect. Moreover, because linguistic evolution, as every other human behavior, is governed by the law of minimum effort, as well as by the law of language economy, these changes are put into effect with minimal innovation.

Therefore, according to Martinet's statement, the boundaries between diachrony and synchrony are not so clearly distinct, because of the perpetual evolution that any language goes through. Each change, prior to formulating a transition from one stage to the other, namely prior to becoming a diachronic fact, sets off as a synchronic process in coexistence with a given synchronic status, both of the original form, which is going to change, and of the form which is changing. This change involves as in a conflict among several features within the system creating several variations of the linguistic elements. Thus, synchrony also displays a dynamic character, since processes of linguistic changes potentially developed within it. As for diachrony, it constitutes a series of successive synchronies. Moreover, as Martinet suggests, if we understand how synchrony functions dynamically, we will able to understand how changes occur in diachrony, caused by respective dynamics deriving of the same linguistic system.

On the other hand, socio-linguistics has recently reached the same concludion by studying the phenomenon of synchronic linguistic diversity and linguistic change. The research opened up the way towards the cancellation of clearly defined boundaries ended up cancelling the watertight distinction between synchrony and diachrony[17].

---

16 André Martinet, *Éléments de Linguistique Générale* (Paris: Armand Colin/Masson, 1970, ⁴1996), pp. 172–81; cf. pp. 28–9. 33–4.
17 Theodosia Pavlidou, *Κοινωνιογλωσσολογία (Socio-Linguistics)*, no pages (cited in 2006–2008, Centre for the Greek Language) : http://www.greek-language.gr/greekLang/modern_greek/tools/lexica/glossology/show.html?id=102. See also William Labov, *Principles of Linguistic Change, 1, Internal Factors* (Cambridge, Mass.-Oxford: Blackwell, 1994).

Greek as a language and supporting etymological analysis

Furthermore, Martinet states that if we could examine the language of a community which would be rigorously unique and thoroughly homogeneous, we might ascertain that the differences emerging within it represent various successive stages of the same usage and not several usages that coexist. In this perspective, it is interesting examine Greek as a language. Indeed, the Greek language as a whole has always kept its feature of a unique national language, bearing uninterrupted both oral and written tradition as well as historic continuity[18]. In terms of structure, it is easy for anyone to go back to its earlier periods and ascertain the historic relation of words and structures others prior to them. At the same time, it is difficult to discern can be regarded as new or old elements in each linguistic phase, when each element appeared and prevailed, what was coined and what was eradicated in the long linguistic tradition of the people.

The point I wish to make here is that in the case of the Greek language and within the above mentioned theoretical framework, diachrony, including etymology, might be taken seriously into account for clarifying the contemporary meaning of words. After having analyzed the way a certain word is used in its current as well as in other contemporary contexts, we might examine the diachronic evolution of its meaning by studying the various usages of this word during precedent periods or by even exploring the meaning of its root. This examination will not be hypothetical or subjective at all, because we will verify each usage in its context, not only within the contemporary but also within the ancient text, while analyzing the usage based on historical and contemporary social data.

Moreover, the study of Modern Greek words' usage could also provide us with more evidence to help us clarify the word meaning. Regarding the words used in the New Testament, such an attempt may lead us to concrete results, since the language used in its texts – the so-called Koine – constitutes an authentic part of contemporary vernacular Greek. At the beginning of the 20th century Thumb[19] emphasized on the usefulness of Modern Greek for the understanding of the biblical language, and subsequently many scholars recognized the importance of his study[20]. Thus, we can orientate towards a certain field of

---

18 See Robert Browning, *Medieval and Modern Greek* (Cambridge University Press, 1983), 2–3. Cf. Georgios Babiniotis, *Συνοπτική Ιστορία της Ελληνικής Γλώσσας [Concise History of the Greek Language]* (Athens: ³1998), 81.

19 A. Thumb, *Die griechische Sprache im Zeitalter des Hellensmus: Beiträgezur Geschichte und Beurteilung der Koine* (Strassbourg: 1901), 1–27.

20 Among them J. H. Moulton, "The Science of Language and the Study of the New Testament" in idem, *The Christian Religion in the Study and in the Street* (London: 1919), 134–36. More see in

meaning to which the word is semantically referred and trace up to today various usages of this word which have generated similar, modified or even opposite, but still systematically justifiable, meanings.

Regarding the words used in the text of the Septuagint, it would be appropriate, at this point, to highlight some issues. First of all, the Septuagint text is a translation, that is a technical philological work, the language of which is mostly artificial and does not reflect common contemporary usage. Secondly, the translators were men highly educated with a thorough knowledge of the Greek language and culture, so they must have been interested in the proper use of the language and they must have known how to use it properly. Thirdly, the social and cultural environment in which the translators lived and worked (Alexandria of 3rd century B.C.E.), was a world that cherished scholarship and acknowledged the preciousness of speech. All these factors can lead us to the conclusion that the etymological consciousness of the translators was really deep and, surely, this played a specific role in the way they used the words. Therefore, it is important if one decides to explore the meaning of their texts to take into account the etymology of the Greek words they choose to use.

The case of the word *ἐκκλησία*

Barr's criticism

As an example I will refer to the meaning of the word ἐκκλησία as it is used in the Greek Bible. Barr[21] has criticized the way T. F. Torrance associates the etymology of the Greek word ἐκκλησία (from ἐκκαλέω, -ῶ "call out") with the etymology of the Hebrew word *qāhāl*, of which ἐκκλησία is a translation, (*qāhāl* from a conjectural root *qwl* "call") and thereby suggests that ἐκκλησία is used as the proper translation for indicating the community called by God in order to constitute His people. It could be stated that this connection he establishes is disputable, since, firstly, because the derivation of *qāhāl* from *qwl* is quite uncertain, and secondly, *qāhāl* merely means gathering, without presenting any equivalence to ἐκκλησία, in several Old Testament passages.

Nevertheless, Barr has further challenged the assertion that the word ἐκκλησία might have obtained a special use in the Septuagint associated with its orig-

---

G. H. R. Horsley, *New Documents Illustrating Early Christinity. Volume 5. Linguistic Essays* (Maquarie University, 1989), 70 ff.

21 J. Barr, *The Semantics*, 119–29.

inal classical meaning essentially preparing the ground for its New Testament use ἐκκλησία. He maintains is that the biblical word ἐκκλησία is merely used designating the notion of meeting and gathering of men, without any particular character. Therefore, etymologizing this word could be needless, or even misleading, when it could guide to false meanings, for example that ἐκκλησία is a name used for the people of God, Israel.

However, at this point we ought to pay attention to the dynamic character of etymology that might play a role, according to Martinet's conclusions, in an effort of semantically elucidating of the current meaning of the word. We ought also to be aware that misleading as the etymologizing of a word may be, equally misleading may also be an imprecise perception of its etymology. Thus, first we will examine the original meaning of the word ἐκκλησία, as well as its ancient Greek usage and then we will study it not only synchronically but also contextually up until New Testament times.

The original sense of the word and the ancient Greek usage

The noun ἐκκλησία, a word deriving from ἐκ and καλῶ, literally means a public gathering summoned by a herald[22]. At an early point, the word evolved into a technical term used to describe the regular assembly of the whole body of citizens in a democratic city (δῆμος), which decided for public affairs. This meaning maintains an immediate and actual reference to the etymology of the word, as such an official takes place after an official calling out of the citizens, who were named ἔκκλητοι "the ones being summoned"[23].

The first occurrence of the word is in Herodotus' and Thucydides' texts, although it is known that the ἐκκλησία had first been established by Solon (594 B.C.E) as the congregation of all the citizens, who participated equally in the decision process of the Athenian democracy.

Aristotle adapted this term to Homeric congregations[24], although the corresponding word in Homer's texts is ἀγορά or ἄγυρις. By examining the aforemen-

---

22 J. H. Moulton-G. Milligan *The Vocabulary of the Greek Testament Illustrated from the Papyri and Other Non-literary Sources* (London: 1930).

23 See H. Liddell and R. Scott, *Greek-English Lexicon* (n. ed. by H. St. Jones; 1925 ff.): "ἐκκλησία, ἡ, (ἔκκλητος) an assembly of the citizens regularly summoned, the legislative assembly". For the socio-historical data see G. Glotz, *The Greek City and its Institutions* (London-New York: 1929).

24 Aristotle, *Politics*, 3.1285a: δηλοῖ δ᾽ Ὅμηρος· ὁ γὰρ Ἀγαμέμνων κακῶς μὲν ἀκούων ἠνείχετο ἐν ταῖς ἐκκλησίαις, ἐξελθόντων δὲ καὶ κτεῖναι κύριος ἦν ("as Homer proves, for Agamemnon en-

tioned usage of the word in ancient Greek texts it becomes obvious that the original meaning encompassed the semantic features of legality, publicity and political quality.

These features, according to the ancient Greek evidence, were preserved in any usage of the word ἐκκλησία throughout Antiquity and they distinguished this word from any other synonymous used for denoting a simple gathering or meeting, such as the words σύλλογος, σύναξις, συνάθροισις, συνέδριον, some of which are also used in the Septuagint. Usually, it was coupled with the word δῆμος, which is, also, a word for a public assembly although mainly of the inhabitants of a city without bearing any legal features[25]. The gathering of the citizens as a δῆμος was characterized by its jurisdiction to confer and decide as an ἐκκλησία.

The contemporary usage

It has been argued by some scholars that since the Hellenistic and early Roman period the ἐκκλησία had lost its actual civic and democratic power, and that the word came to simply denote any assembly of people[26]. Nevertheless, the suggestion for any mitigating of the meaning of the word during Hellenistic times, even within the context of colloquial Greek is not sufficiently documented. The study of this period's contemporary texts, not only the literary ones[27] but also the non-literary documents of the Hellenistic times hardly corroborates this suggestion. A host of inscriptions deriving from the Eastern Kingdoms of the descendants of

---

dured being reviled in the assemblies but when they were on an expedition had authority to put a man to death").

25 Cf P. Louw and E. A. Nida, *Greek-English Lexicon of the New Testament Based on Semantic Domains* (New York: ²1989), v. I, 11.78.

26 See G.E.M. De St Croix, *The Class Struggle in the Ancient Greek World* (Ithaca: Cornell University Press, 1981), 527–533. Also, A.H.M. Jones, *The Greek City from Alexander to Justinian* (Oxford: Clarendon Press, 1971), 177.

27 See Polybius, *Histories*, 4.34.6; 6.12.4, where the duties of the consuls are described καὶ μὴν ὅσα δεῖ διὰ τοῦ δήμου συντελεῖσθαι τῶν πρὸς τὰς κοινὰς πράξεις ἀνηκόντων, τούτοις καθήκει φροντίζειν καὶ συνάγειν τὰς ἐκκλησίας, τούτοις εἰσφέρειν τὰ δόγματα, τούτοις βραβεύειν τὰ δοκοῦντα τοῖς πλείοσι ("Again as concerns all the affairs of state administered by the people it is their duty to take these under their charge, to summon assemblies, to introduce measures and to preside over the execution of the popular decrees"). Also, see Plutarchus, *T. Grachus*, 16; *Demetrius*, 38.8: ἐκ τούτου τὸν Σέλευκον ἐκκλησίαν ἀθροίσαντα πάνδημον εἰπεῖν ὅτι βούλεται καὶ διέγνωκε τῶν ἄνω πάντων τόπων Ἀντίοχον ἀποδεῖξαι βασιλέα ("consequently, Seleucus called an assembly of the entire people and declared it to be his wish and purpose to make Antiochus king of all Upper Asia").

Alexander the Great include the word ἐκκλησία in contexts which leave no doubt about as to the official and institutional character of this assembly of the citizens[28].

Characteristic evidence comes from Egypt, from the city of Ptolemais of Hermiou, from 278/77 B.C.E.: it is a decree of the βουλή and the δῆμος, in which it is mentioned that some citizens, who rioted and disturbed the βουλαί and the ἐκκλησίαι (in plural, which alludes to repeated behavior), even during elections, were punished. Clearly, the *ἐκκλησία in this instance* is juxtaposed to the political institution of βουλή and it bears the meaning of the joint parliamentary body of the city; also, it is said that one of the responsibilities of the ἐκκλησία was holding elections, a purely political task.

1 ἔδοξεν τῆι βουλῆι καὶ τῶι δήμωι· Ἑ[ρ]μᾶς
  Δόρκωνος Μεγιστεὺς εἶπεν· ἐπειδὴ πρυτάνεις
  οἱ σὺν Διονυσίωι Μουσαίου τοῦ ὀγδόου ἔτους,
  ...
  Νεοπτόλεμος Θεοδώρου Καρανεύς, καλῶς καὶ ἀξίως
  τῆς πόλεως προέστησαν ὁρῶντές τινας τῶν πολιτῶν
  [μ]ὴ ὀρθῶς ἀνα[στρ]εφομένους καὶ θόρυβον οὐ τὸν τυχόντα παρ[έ]-
10 [χ]οντας ἐν τ[αῖς] βουλαῖς [καὶ] ἐν ταῖς ἐκκλησίαις, [μ]άλιστα δὲ
  ἐν ταῖς ἀρχα[ιρεσίαις μέχρι βίας καὶ] ἀσ[ε]βείας, προεληλυθότας,
  ἐπέστησαν τῆι κακ[ίαι, κολάζοντ]ε[ς τοῖς] ἐκ τῶν νόμων ἐπιτίμοις,
  δι' ὃ συμβέβηκεν τὴν πό[λ]ι[ν εὐνομωτέραν γεγο]νέναι ...[29]

Indeed, although the form of the classic Greek city had lost its rigorous political meaning, the civic and political character of citizen assemblies sense does not appear to have been altered and the meaning of the word ἐκκλησία preserved its basic semantic features, certainly in the East[30]. It is noteworthy that François Chamoux in his work for the Hellenistic civilization argues explicitly:

---

28 There is a great number of similar inscriptions, mainly from Asia Minor but as well as from Egypt (see all the known Collections of the Inscriptions). For a small sample see F. W. Danker, *A Greek-English lexicon of the New Testament and other early Christian literature*, 3rd ed. [BDAG] (Chicago and London: The University of Chicago Press, 2000).

29 W. Dittenberger, *Orientis Graeci Inscriptiones Selectae (OGIS)* (2 vols.; Leipzig 1903–1905), 1.48: "The *βουλή* and *the δῆμος* decided: Hermas, son of Dorco, from Megiste said· because the *πρυτάνεις*, who were with Dionysius Musaeus in the eighth year, [...] Neoptolemos, son of Theodorus from Karana headed the city good and worthy, when they saw some of the citizens misbehaving and disturbing too much amid the βουλαί and ἐκκλησίαι, even reaching violence and impiety during the elections, they intercepted the wickedness by imposing the legitimate punishment; for this reason, the city became well functioning according to the rule of law".

30 The historical evidence is adequately presented in Francois Chamoux, *Hellenistic Civilization* (transl. by Michel Roussel; Blackwell Publishing Company, 2002), ch. 6 "The Survival of the

"The political organization of cities underwent no radical change after Alexander. As described above from the example of Apollonia on the Pontus, the popular Assembly and the Council (whatever the diverse designations of those two institutions) remained everywhere the two basic instruments of the State's authority, with the magistrates constituting the executive"[31].

Particularly for the city of Hellenistic Alexandria, D. Graham J. Shipley and Mogens H. Hansen contend that "Its civic structure was based on Athens, with hereditary citizenship, deme membership, an assembly, a council, and elected magistrates"[32].

Therefore, during the period when the Hebrew Bible was translated into Greek and particularly within the local area where the translation took place, the ἐκκλησία was acknowledged as an actual political institution, the name of which called to mind and corresponded exactly to the process of its function, i.e. to an act of consultation of the people after being summoned.

The Septuagint usage

In the Septuagint text the word ἐκκλησία occurs seventy-three times, five times in original Greek and sixty-eight times as a translation of the Hebrew word *qāhāl* (קָהָל)"assembly, congregation". The word *qāhāl* is also translated thirty-six times as the Greek word συναγωγή "gathering, congregation"[33], six times as ὄχλος and in unique occurrences as σύστασις, συνέδριον and πλῆθος[34]. The word συναγωγή, which derives from the verb συνάγω "to bring together", is used in the Septuagint text not only as a translation of *qāhāl*, but also of other Hebrew

City", 165–213. D. Graham J. Shipley with Mogens H. Hansen, "The Polis and Federalism", in *The Cambridge Companion to the Hellenistic World*, ed. Glenn R. Bugh (Cambridge University Press, 2007), 52–72. See also recently Young-Ho Park, "Paul's ἐκκλησία as a civic assembly" (Ph.D. diss., Faculty of the Division of the Humanities, Department of New Testament and Early Christian Literature; Chicago, Illinois: Dec. 2012), p. 34 ff.

31 Fr. Chamoux, *Hellenistic Civilization*, p.187.

32 D. G. J. Shipley with M. H. Hansen, "The Polis and Federalism", in *The Cambridge Companion to the Hellenistic World*, p. 65.

33 Συναγωγή is used, also, by Septuagint as a translation of the Hebrew word *'eda* (עֵדָה)"gathering by appointment or agreement" (cf Ps 21 [22]:17). More see in W. Schrage, "συναγωγή", *Theological Dictionary of the New Testament (TDNT)* (eds. G. Kittel and G. Friedrich, transl. G. W. Bromiley; Grand Rapids, Michigan: Wm. B. Eerdmans Publishing Company, 1964), 7. 798–841.

34 See H.-J. Fabry, קָהָל in *Theological Dictionary of the Old Testament (TDOT)* (eds. G. J. Botterweck, H. Ringen, H.-J. Fabry; Grand Rapids, Michigan: Wm. B. Eerdmans Publishing Company, 1974-), 12.561.

words, not only denoting the gathering of the people, but also any other type of gathering, such as of water (Lev 11:36; Prov 3:20; Isa 19:6; 37:25), of stones (Job 8:17), of bulls (Ps 67[68]:30) etc. Thus, συναγωγή is rather common designation, whereas ἐκκλησία is much more specific. On the other hand, the political origin of the meaning of the word ἐκκλησία does not quite have a relation with the historico-religious nuances that the word *qāhāl* , when used to describe the congregation of the Jewish people, could convey. Therefore, the connotation of the Greek word should only be linked with the Greek institution and attributed to a process.

The question arising from this is if the etymological and technical sense of the Greek word ἐκκλησία was a determinant factor in its specific usage in the Septuagint text. In order to achieve a better understanding of the potential relation between the Greek usage and the usage of the word in the Septuagint text, it would be appropriate to consider the semantic postulates[35], which emerge from the semantic relations of the word and which might concur with the meaning of the word as it is used in the Septuagint context.

The civic and democratic quality of the word ἐκκλησία implies the ideas of self-government, member equality, and conciliarity; it also presupposes freedom of speech and collective judgment. Certainly, all these constituted elements of the ancient and contemporary Greek culture; however they had no religious character, as did the "theocratic" government of Israel. Still, these semantic features could offer a clear description, in contemporary Greek terms, of the presence of a socio-religious body, which includes similar institutions of collective governance, be they political, religious, or even both. Additionally, the word ἐκκλησία could have been used by the translators for making a conceptual analogy.

In the Septuagint text the word *qāhāl* is translated as ἐκκλησία mainly in Deuteronomy (except 5:22; 33:4), Judges, Samuel, Kings, Chronicles, Ezra, Nehemiah, twice in Ezekiel and unique instances in Joshua, Psalms Job, Micah, Joel, and Lamentations. In the Pentateuch it is generally translated as συναγωγή, and as such also occurs in some Psalms (67[68]:31, 85[86]:14). The fact that the word ἐκκλησία is mainly used in the so-called historical books, which tackle issues of the legal and political organization of Israel, might be indicative and advocate for the specialized meaning of the Greek word. Moreover, it is remarkable that

---

35 The semantic or meaning postulates, according to Rudolf Carnap's definition (*Meaning and necessity*, 2nd ed. Chicago: Chicago University Press, 1956), is regarded as an alternative theory to the semantic componential analysis and it is preferred when we are interested only in the necessary semantic relations of the words. See J. Lyons, *Linguistic Semantics: An Introduction,* Cambridge: Cambridge University Press, 1995, p. 126 f.

there is an almost exclusive usage of the word throughout Deuteronomy, a book that contains the rules of the worship and the law of the state of Israel transmitted in written and aimed at studying[36], i. e. in an official way. In addition, the translation of the Hebrew text of Deuteronomy into Greek affirms a good knowledge of Greek, both literary and vernacular[37], thus the special use of the word ἐκκλησία is justified.

A possible explanation for the usage of the word ἐκκλησία in the Septuagint text might be given on the basis of an effort made towards the development of a political identity for the Jewish people. While previously in the Tetrateuch the word συναγωγή was used, later, in Deuteronomy, where the organization of Israel as a state was described and a more political language was required for a more appropriate understanding on behalf of the contemporaries, the use of the word ἐκκλησία was preferred. It is remarkable that the word συναγωγή occurs in Deuteronomy only once in the singular (5:22) and once in the plural form (33:4) with reference to the assembly of Israel during the time when the Law was delivered to Moses, as it had been described in Exodus.

Contextual analysis

Looking into the usage of the word ἐκκλησία in the Septuagint text, aiming at a semantic analysis of the surface structure of the sentences, we may ascertain that the word ἐκκλησία is especially used in the following contexts:

– Referring to as a body with power and whenever it is not quoted independently, it is usually coupled with a genitive that it is to be recognized rather as a genitive of quality than of content or even possessive. Thus, this genitive of quality may serve as an adjective, which attributes some new features to the ordinary meaning of the word: ἐκκλησία of the people of the God (Jd 20:2) or ἐκκλησία of Israel (1 Kings 8:14.22.55; 12:3; 1 Ch 13:2; 2 Ch 6:3.12,13; 20:5; 23:2) or ἐκκλησία κυρίου (De 23:1 [2]. 2 [3]; 1 Ch 28:8; Mi 2:5) and ἐκκλησία θεοῦ (Ne 13:1).

– Construed with the verb ἐκκλησιάζω "call on the assembly", which is a classical technical verb denoting a legal and political gathering of the people. Its use in the following passage might be considered as a process of semantic

---

36 See W. Schrage, "'Ekklesia' and 'Synagoge': zum Ursprung des urchristlichen Kirchenbegriffs", *Zeitschrift für Theologie und Kirche* 60 (1963): 180–81, where there is a survey of the scholar suggestion that Septuagint used this term for the designation of Israel as the chosen people, especially at the time the Law is given in Deuteronomy.
37 See La Bible d' Alexandrie LXX, vol. 5. Le Deutéronome, par C. Doigniez et M. Harl, Paris: Les Éditions du Cerf, 1992, 29–40.

transition from the general meaning of the word συναγωγή to the specialized meaning of the word ἐκκλησία: namely, a συναγωγή, i.e. an assembly, as well as all the leaders of Israel ἐκκλησιάζονται, are gathered after being officially ordered so as to become an ἐκκλησία:

Judges (A) 20:1

καὶ ἐξῆλθον πάντες οἱ υἱοὶ Ἰσραὴλ καὶ ἐξεκκλησιάσθη πᾶσα ἡ συναγωγὴ ὡς ἀνὴρ εἷς ἀπὸ Δαὰν καὶ ἕως Βηρσαβεὲ καὶ γῇ Γαλαὰδ πρὸς Κύριον εἰς Μασσηφά 20:2 καὶ ἔστη τὸ κλίμα παντὸς τοῦ λαοῦ πᾶσαι αἱ φυλαὶ Ἰσραὴλ ἐν τῇ ἐκκλησίᾳ τοῦ λαοῦ τοῦ Θεοῦ τετρακόσιαι χιλιάδες ἀνδρῶν πεζῶν σπωμένων ῥομφαίαν

"and all the sons of Israel came out, from Dan and up to Bersabee, and the land of Galaad, and all the congregation assembled like one man to the Lord at Massepha (20:2 A) And the region of all the people stood, and the tribes of Israel in the assembly of the people of God, four hundred thousand men, foot-soldiers drawing a sword" (NETS).

– Mentioned to in parallel with the leadership of Israel as a large governing body along with the king and the leaders: namely, it is not"the leaders of the ἐκκλησία" but "the leaders or the king and the ἐκκλησία".

2 Chronicles 30:2

καὶ ἐβουλεύσατο ὁ βασιλεὺς καὶ οἱ ἄρχοντες καὶ πᾶσα ἡ ἐκκλησία ἡ ἐν Ιερουσαλὴμ ποιῆσαι τὸ Φασὲκ τῷ μηνὶ τῷ δευτέρῳ

"and the king and the rulers and all the assembly in Jerusalem took counsel to hold the phasek (Heb. Passover) in the second month" (NETS).

2 Chronicles 30:4

καὶ ἤρεσεν ὁ λόγος ἐναντίον τοῦ βασιλέως καὶ ἐναντίον τῆς ἐκκλησίας

"and the plan was pleasing both to the king and to the assembly" (NETS).

2 Chronicles 30:25

καὶ ηὐφράνθη πᾶσα ἡ ἐκκλησία οἱ ἱερεῖς καὶ οἱ Λευῖται καὶ πᾶσα ἡ ἐκκλησία Ιούδα καὶ οἱ εὑρεθέντες ἐξ Ισραὴλ καὶ οἱ προσήλυτοι οἱ ἐλθόντες ἀπὸ γῆς Ισραὴλ καὶ οἱ κατοικοῦντες ἐν Ιούδα

"and the whole assembly was glad: the priests and the Leuvites and all the assembly of Ioudas and those present from Israel and the guests who had come from the land of Israel and those who dwelt in Ioudas" (NETS).

Cf. 2 Ch 28:14; 29:23.

– Construed with verbs which describe an official process of a socio-political action, like διατίθεμαι διαθήκην "make a covenant", βουλεύομαι "decide", παρίσταμαι "be present" the similar ones.

2 Chronicles 23:3

καὶ διέθεντο πᾶσα ἐκκλησία Ἰούδα διαθήκην ἐν οἴκῳ τοῦ Θεοῦ μετὰ τοῦ βασιλέως

"and the all the assembly of Ioudas made a covenant with the king in the house of God" (NETS).

2 Chronicles 30:2
καὶ ἐβουλεύσατο ὁ βασιλεὺς καὶ οἱ ἄρχοντες καὶ πᾶσα ἡ ἐκκλησία ἡ ἐν Ἰερουσαλὴμ ποιῆσαι τὸ Φασὲκ τῷ μηνὶ τῷ δευτέρῳ
"and the king and the rulers and all the assembly in Ierousalem took counsel to hold the phasek (Heb. Passover) in the second month" (NETS).

2 Chronicles 30:23
καὶ ἐβουλεύσατο ἡ ἐκκλησία ἅμα ποιῆσαι ἑπτὰ ἡμέρας ἄλλας καὶ ἐποίησαν ἑπτὰ ἡμέρας ἐν εὐφροσύνῃ
"and the assembly decided to hold it together for seven more days and they celebrated for seven days with gladness" (NETS).

2 Chronicles 6:3
καὶ ἐπέστρεψεν ὁ βασιλεὺς τὸ πρόσωπον αὐτοῦ καὶ εὐλόγησεν τὴν πᾶσαν ἐκκλησίαν Ἰσρα-ὴλ καὶ πᾶσα ἐκκλησία Ἰσραὴλ παρειστήκει
"And the king turned his face and blessed all the assembly of Israel and all the assembly of Israel stood by" (NETS).

Cf. 2 Chronicles 6:12. 13; 1 Kings 8:14.

– Construed with adverbial designations of time (ἡμέρα τῆς ἐκκλησίας, the day of the ἐκκλησία) and of place ἐνώπιον (in front of), ἐν μέσῳ (in the midst) and as well as similar ones, which point to fixed statutes of an official institution

Deuteronomy 4:10
ἡμέραν ἣν ἔστητε ἐναντίον Κυρίου τοῦ Θεοῦ ὑμῶν ἐν Χωρὴβ τῇ ἡμέρᾳ τῆς ἐκκλησίας ὅτε εἶπεν Κύριος πρός με ἐκκλησίασον πρός με τὸν λαόν καὶ ἀκουσάτωσαν τὰ ῥήματά μου
"about the day when you stood before the Lord your God at Choreb, on the day of the as-sembly, when the Lord said to me 'Assemble the people to me, and let them hear my words" (NETS).

Cf. also Deuteronomy 9:10; 18:16

Nehemiah 8:2
καὶ ἤνεγκεν Ἔσδρας ὁ ἱερεὺς τὸν νόμον ἐνώπιον τῆς ἐκκλησίας ἀπὸ ἀνδρὸς καὶ ἕως γυναι-κὸς καὶ πᾶς ὁ συνίων ἀκούειν ἐν ἡμέρᾳ μιᾷ τοῦ μηνὸς τοῦ ἑβδόμου
"and Esdras the priest brought the law before the assembly, from man to woman, and every person who understands, to listen on the first day the seventh month" (NETS 2 Esdr 18:2).

– Mentioned in contexts implying legal or political actions as if it were a parlia-mentary or a judiciary body

Deuteronomy 23:2–3
οὐκ εἰσελεύσεται θλαδίας καὶ ἀποκεκομμένος εἰς ἐκκλησίαν Κυρίου 23:3 οὐκ εἰσελεύσεται ἐκ πόρνης εἰς ἐκκλησίαν Κυρίου

Deut 23:1 "A castrated male and one made a eunuch shall not enter the assembly of the Lord". 23:2 "One from a prostitute shall not enter the assembly of the Lord" (NETS).

Ezra 10:8

καὶ πᾶς ὃς ἂν μὴ ἔλθῃ εἰς τρεῖς ἡμέρας ὡς ἡ βουλὴ τῶν ἀρχόντων καὶ τῶν πρεσβυτέρων ἀναθεματισθήσεται πᾶσα ἡ ὕπαρξις αὐτοῦ καὶ αὐτὸς διασταλήσεται ἀπὸ ἐκκλησίας τῆς ἀποικίας

"Anyone who does not come within three days, as the council of the rulers and the elders (demands), all his property will be anathematized, and he himself banned from the assembly of the exile (NETS 2 Esdr 10:8).

Nehemiah 5:7

καὶ ἐβουλεύσατο καρδία μου ἐπ᾽ ἐμέ καὶ ἐμαχεσάμην πρὸς τοὺς ἐντίμους καὶ τοὺς ἄρχοντας καὶ εἶπα αὐτοῖς ἀπαιτήσει ἀνὴρ τὸν ἀδελφὸν αὐτοῦ ὑμεῖς ἀπαιτεῖτε καὶ ἔδωκα ἐπ᾽ αὐτοὺς ἐκκλησίαν μεγάλην

"and my heart deliberated with me, and I quarreled with the distinguished and the rulers and I said to them 'Will a man demand back of his brother? You are demanding back'. And I held a great assembly for them" (NETS 2 Esdr 15:7).

Cf. Nehemiah 5:13

Nehemiah 13:1

ἐν τῇ ἡμέρᾳ ἐκείνῃ ἀνεγνώσθη ἐν βιβλίῳ Μωυσῆ ἐν ὠσὶν τοῦ λαοῦ καὶ εὑρέθη γεγραμμένον ἐν αὐτῷ ὅπως μὴ εἰσέλθωσιν Ἀμμανῖται καὶ Μωαβῖται ἐν ἐκκλησίᾳ Θεοῦ ἕως αἰῶνος

"On that day there was read from the book of Moyses in the hearing of the people, and there was found written in it that Ammanites and Moabites should not enter in the assembly of God forever" (NETS 2 Esdr 23:1).

Michaias 2:5

διὰ τοῦτο οὐκ ἔσται σοι βάλλων σχοινίον ἐν κλήρῳ ἐν ἐκκλησίᾳ Κυρίου

"Therefore you will have no one to cast the line by lot in the assembly of the Lord" (NETS).

Joel 2:16

συναγάγετε λαόν ἁγιάσατε ἐκκλησίαν ἐκλέξασθε πρεσβυτέρους

"Gather the people. Sanctify an assembly; welcome the aged" (NETS).

Furthermore, there are a number of Septuagint passages, mainly in Psalms, where the word ἐκκλησία implies a religious institution, which is authorized for religious, but also social and, in a way, civic affairs, like feasts and public worship or the implementation of the Law[38]. Since Psalms is predominantly considered as a liturgical book, the religious nuances are plausible and as such comprehensible.

Actually, it is quite consistent for a theocratic nation like ancient Israel to have closely interwoven both civic and social affairs closely with the religious ones; and it is mostly because of this that the word ἐκκλησία could not be

---

38 See Ps 21[22]:22.25; 25[26]:12; 34 [35]:18; 67[68]:26 (in plural); 106[107]:32; 149:1.

used with the clear political sense it held in Greek. The major criticism made against the Greek meaning of the word in Septuagint is that there is no religious sense in it. Nevertheless, this criticism could be mitigated, if we consider that the Septuagint usage is implemented in terms of an analogous and, if applicable, metaphorical manner of handling the term. In other words, the translation of the Hebrew Bible was itself constituted a process of Hellenization and acculturation fitted into the political framework of the Hellenistic world.

The book of Proverbs quotes the word only once jointly with the word συναγωγή: Prov 5:14 παρ' ὀλίγον ἐγενόμην ἐν παντὶ κακῷ ἐν μέσῳ ἐκκλησίας καὶ συναγωγῆς "I was almost in every evil situation, in the midst of an assembly and congregation" (NETS). The translator uses both words for denoting the assembly: ἐκκλησία for qāhāl and συναγωγή for 'edā. He may intend to denote any kind of public gathering, simultaneously creating a verbal variation through synonyms. This seems more probable than a hendiadyn figure (i. e. the gathering of the assembly)[39].

Similar usage of the word is presented in the book of 1 Maccabees. In 1 Macc 2:56 ἐκκλησία is mentioned as an institutional body in front of which someone should bear witness to his case and receive a heritage of land or the official body which deliberates on and decides about a war or a feast or about political affairs in general (1 Macc 4:49; 5:16; 14:9.19).

In the books of the Septuagint which are preserved or written in Greek the word ἐκκλησία eminently displays its civic semantic features, since it is used to represent a consulting body of the people, in which the wise man should "open his mouth" (Sir 15:5; 21:17; 24:2) or a judicial body, in front of which a wife, who left her husband, should be brought for inquisition (Sir 23:24) as well as a body responsible for the political decision making. Furthermore, a duty of the ἐκκλησία was to establish which should be considered as its members' good deed and to declare their praise (Sir 31:11; 39:10; 44:15).

Philo's and Josephus' use

Philo and Josephus use the word ἐκκλησία to denote the congregation of Israel, as well as several assemblies convened for some special purposes[40]. A number of these references are quotations from the Old Testament passages, mostly from

---

39 So Park, "Paul's ἐκκλησία", 83. Schmidt, *TDNT* 3:528 has another explanation: "The translator is not sure how to handle two terms which obviously mean the same thing".

40 See Philo, *De Abrahamo*, 20; *De specialibus legibus*, 1.325; 2.44. Josephus, *Jewish Antiquities*, 4.309; 9,250; *Jewish War*, 1.654,666; 4.162, 255.

Deuteronomy which are aligned with their usage in the Septuagint. Nevertheless, they use ἐκκλησία even in cases where the Septuagint text suggests συναγωγή[41]. It is evident, particularly in Josephus, that in many cases the word is cited with connotations similar to its classical Greek meaning and that it is used as a well-known and familiar term to the contemporary readers.

In any case, during the Hellenistic and Greco-Roman period the word ἐκκλησία did not simply mean a meeting, but it always maintained the civic connotations of its Greek origin. In most cases that the word appears to denote an assembly without bearing any special features of the Greek ἐκκλησία, we could talk about a metaphor that attributes extra features to the notion of the simple meeting; e. g. ἐκκλησία πονηρευομένων "ἐκκλησία of evildoers" (Ps 25 [26]:5), ἐκκλησία ὄχλου "ἐκκλησία of mob" (Sir 26:5), ἐκκλησία προφητῶν "ἐκκλησία of prophets" (1 Sam 19:20), ἐκκλησία πιστῶν "ἐκκλησία of troops loyal to the leader" (1 Macc 3:13). Finally, we cannot exclude an unreflected usage of the word which depends on the quality of the translation.

Conclusion

It is true that one could hardly assert that in the Septuagint there is a consistent use of the word ἐκκλησία in its classical meaning. Nevertheless, there is sufficient evidence to support the fact that the word ἐκκλησία preserves its basic semantic load in the Septuagint usage, as we have already shown above, albeit in an attenuated form of its features as a technical political term.

The word ἐκκλησία in the Septuagint text is not exclusively used for religious matters, but also for secular meetings like the preparation of a war or plans to avoid a danger. The ἐκκλησία it was convened at regular intervals, it was assembled in an official manner, it served for the expression of political identity of the people of Israel. Therefore is no strong rationale not to designated ἐκκλησία as an institutional body, which could have been successfully aligned with the contemporary technical Greek term denoting the civic assembly.

Indeed, one who is aware of the basic distinction between the meanings of the Greek words συναγωγή 'the gathering of people', and ἐκκλησία 'the legislative body of citizens, could perceive this distinction in the way these words are used in the Septuagint text. Certainly, Certainly, within the context of the Septuagint text all the semantic features of the original Greek word ἐκκλησία could not

---

41 See Philo, *On the Decalogue*, 32.45; *De posteritate Caini*, 143. Josephus, *Jewish Antiquities*, 3.292; 4.22.

have been kept and it was not used as a technical term, since a technical term requires a corresponding cultural background which was not the case in ancient Israel. However, it is fair to support that the Greek educated translators employed sufficient semantic features of the word, adjusted them to their culture, and rendered some aspects of the institutional Jewish assembly more intelligible by making them accessible to the contemporary Hellenized world. In this way, the ἐκκλησία τοῦ δήμου (of the people) became the ἐκκλησία κυρίου (of Lord).

Thus, through the Septuagin text a new meaning was created, the ἐκκλησία κυρίου, which later, within the Greco-Roman context, could be elaborated by Paul and other New Testament writers to establish the term of the Christian ἐκκλησία[42].

A general conclusion

Instead of any other general conclusion in this paper I would cite the ascertainment of a distinguished linguist, Stephen Ullmann, that "a series of tests designed to study the influence of context has shown that there is usually in each word a hard core of meaning which is relatively stable and can only be modified by the context within certain limits"[43]. Consequently, we might work on the synchronic level of our text, without leaving aside the diachronic examination of the words. Etymology through its dynamic character in the semantic development so as to gain a more elucidated, clear and insightful understanding of elucidation of the meanings.

---

42 The Christian elaboration of the term ἐκκλησία, especially by Paul, has received a large discussion and debate. See representatively Paul Trebilco, "Why Did the Early Christians Call Themselves Ἡ Ἐκκλησία?" *New Testament Studies (NTS)* 57, 3 (2011): 440–60; and George H. van Kooten, "Ἐκκλησία τοῦ θεοῦ: The 'Church of God' and the Civic Assemblies (ἐκκλησίαι) of the Greek Cities in the Roman Empire: A Response to Paul Trebilco and Richard A. Horsley", *New Testament Studies (NTS)* 58, 4 (2012): 522–548.
43 S. Ullmann, *Semantics: An Introduction to the Science of Meaning* (Oxford: 1962), 49.

Romina Vergari

Aspects of Polysemy in Biblical Greek: the Semantic Micro-Structure of Κρίσις

Introduction

This paper deals with data concerning the semantic *micro-structure* of the equivalent κρίσις in the translated texts of the Septuagint. The investigation is limited to the textual *corpus* constituted by the books of Pentateuch and Isaiah[1]. The data should be regarded as the preliminary results of a research project concerning a broader portion of the Septuagint lexicon, that is, nouns associated with

---

1 The decision to limit the corpus to this portion corresponds to the need to carry out the investigation within a language which presents, as far as possible, homogeneous features. Therefore, we had to take into account two aspects: the structural, functional and stylistic features of the Greek as well as the technique adopted by the translators. Such methodological requirements led us to base the analysis on the classification of the books of the Septuagint drawn up by S.J. Thackery, as part of his still fundamental *A Grammar of the Old Testament in Greek according to the Septuagint* (Cambridge: Cambridge University Press, 1909, reprinted in 2003, Olms: Hildesheim). According to Thackeray, among the translations, only the books of Pentateuch, Joshua (only partially) and Isaiah express a good κοινή Greek (13–14). Inclusion in this corpus of the book of Isaiah projects us into the question of the historical and linguistic relationship between the translation of the Pentateuch and the translations of the other parts of the Hebrew Bible. Herein the tricky question of dependency cannot be discussed, see, however: Isac L. Seeligmann, *The Septuagint Version of Isaiah. A Discussion of Its Problems* (Leiden: Brill, 1948); R. Hanhart and H. Spieckermann (eds.), *The Septuagint Version of Isaiah and Cognate Studies* (Forschungen zum Alten Testament 40; Tübingen: Mohr Siebeck, 2004); E. Tov, "The impact of the LXX Translation of the Pentateuch on the Translation of other books", in *Mélanges Dominique Barthelemy* (Edited by P. Casetti, O. Keel and A. Schenker; Freiburg: Editions Universitaires, 1981), 577–592; Ronald L. Troxel, *LXX-Isaiah as Translation and Interpretation: The Strategies of the Translator of the Septuagint of Isaiah* (JSJSup 124; Leiden/Boston: Brill, 2008); and J. Barr, "Did the Greek Pentateuch really serve as a Dictionary for the Translation of the Later Books?", in *Hamlet on a Hill. Semitic and Greek Studies Presented to Professor T. Muraoka on the occasion of his Sixty-Fifth Birthday.* (Edited by M. F. J. Baasten and W. Th. Van Peursen. Leuven-Paris-Dudley: Peeters), 523–543. In particular, Barr cautions against committing firmly to the view of priority of the Pentateuch's translation (arguing that even though the vocabulary of the Septuagint includes a large element of stereotyping, often the renderings of the Pentateuch itself are very mixed and lack uniformity both with respect to common and widespread terms and to rare and "difficult" ones). As for the book of Isaiah, he agrees with Thackeray, recognizing that it largely shows common features with the Pentateuch. He points out, however, that: "all similarities between usage in Isaiah and usage in the Pentateuch can work equally well in the opposite way", Barr, *op.cit.*, 540.

the notion of 'law'. The aims of such an analysis are, on one hand, to provide a description of word meaning consistent with a lexicological pattern which takes into account both the flexibility that the noun demonstrates in context (ranging from *vagueness* to *polysemy*)[2] and the syntagmatic processes of semantic composition (such as *sense selection, sense modulation* and *sense coercion*)[3]. On the other hand, we wish to show how the same degree of context-dependence applies to more extended paradigmatic meaning structures such as word-field. The data will also make it possible to investigate whether different semantic Hebrew equivalents match the patterns of polysemy shown by the noun in Greek.

In this paper, the cluster of sense-nodules associated with the word κρίσις (i. e. the relatively autonomous units of sense capable of playing an independent role in the semantic processes) will be discussed[4].

---

2 On the multi-level phenomenon of polysemy see A. Blank, "Polysemy in the lexicon and in discourse", in *Polysemy. Flexible Patterns of Meaning in Mind and Language* (Edited by B. Nerlich, Z. Todd, V. Herman and D.D. Clarke; Trend in Linguistics Studies and Monograph 142; Berlin/New York: Mouton de Gruyter, 2003), 267–293. For a conceptual typology of these variants see D. Geeraerts, "Vagueness's puzzles, polysemy vagaries", *Cognitive Linguistics* 43/3 (1993), 223–272.

3 See: F. Recanati, *Literal Meaning* (Cambridge: Cambridge University Press, 2004) and idem, "Pragmatic Enrichment and Conversational Implicature", in *Routledge Companion to the Philosophy of Language* (Edited by G. Russell and D. Graff Fara; London: Routledge, 2012), and J. Pustejovsky, *The generative Lexicon* (Cambridge, Mass.: The MIT Press, 1995); idem, "Type Construction and the Logic of Concepts", in *The Language of Word Meaning* (Edited by P. Bouillon and F. Busa; Cambridge, Mass.: Cambridge University Press, 2001), 91–123; idem, "Type Theory and Lexical Decomposition", *Journal of Cognitive Science* 6 (2006), 39–76; J. Pustejovsky and A. Rumshisky, "Between chaos and structure: interpreting lexical data through a theoretical lens", *International Journal of Lexicography* 21 (2008), 337–355; J. Pustejovsky and E. Ježek, "Semantic Coercion in Language: Beyond Distributional Analysis", *Italian Journal of Linguistics/Rivista italiana di Linguistica* 20 (2008), 175–208.

4 We decided to limit the semantic analysis to the relation Noun-Adj. and Verb-Dir. Obj. The Greek Septuagint is based upon the text edited by Alfred Rahlfs available in *Accordance*, which includes the Kraft/Taylor/Wheeler Septuagint Morphology Database with lemma and grammatical tagging information for each word in the text. Essential resources consulted for assigning values to the word occurrences were: T. Muraoka, *A Greek-English Lexicon of the Septuagint* (Leuven: Peeters, 2009); J. Lust, E. Eynikel, K. Hauspie, *A Greek-English Lexicon of the Septuagint* (Stuttgart: Deutsche Bibelgesellschaft, 2003; E. Hatch and H. A. Redpath, *A Concordance to the Septuagint and the other Greek Versions of the Old Testament* (Oxford: Clarendon, 1897–1906; rev. 2nd ed.; Grand Rapids: Baker, 1998. English translations used for the texts provided are based on *A New English Translation of the Septuagint and the Other Greek Translations Traditionally Included under That Title* (Edited by A. Pietersma and Benjamin G. Wright, New York/Oxford: Oxford University Press, 2007, 2nd repr. with corrections and emendations, 2009).

1. Methodological Remarks

The methodological approach generally used will be that of *Corpus based descriptive lexical Semantics*.

From a strictly structuralist perspective, the analytical unit in lexical semantics has to be the *lexeme*, that is, an abstract representation (pertinent to the linguistic and, more specifically, to the idiolinguistic dimension) of the conceptual content (pertinent to the cognitive sphere). Indeed, the notion proper to the *lexeme* coincides with the meaning of the *lemma* with which it is associated in the language-lexicon as a whole. According to this descriptive approach, the *lexical field* is a set of *lemmata* that must possess two essential requirements, one syntactical and the other logical-semantic. On the one hand, words must be connected in a *paradigmatic relation*, in other words they must share an associative mechanism because they occur in the same syntactical contexts. On the other hand, a *semantic relation* of *hyperonymy/hyponymy* or *holonymy/meronymy* must exist between the concept that defines the overall field-content (not necessarily lexically represented) and the lexemes that belong to the same field, whereas the lexemes should be characterized by a semantic relation of reciprocity as *co-hyponymy, co-meronimy, synonymy* or *opposition*. The underlying theoretical presupposition is that a lexeme can be described in *componential terms* as the summation of simple pertinent semantic features and that this configuration pertains permanently to the *lemma* and forms the basis for all the meaning relations that can be built within the lexicon. Such relations therefore reproduce the abstract system of opposition and reciprocal content delimitation that pertain between lexemes. These assumptions also permit the definition of the lexical field as a *structured organization of lexemes*.

The approach described above lacks flexibility however. The notion of *dimension* enables a better comprehension of the complexity involved[5]. Although the framework hitherto represented is extremely rigorous, nevertheless it seems inadequate to describe highly complex lexical fields, as those connected with abstract notions and moreover fails to convey the *vagueness* and *polysemy* which words exhibit in their actual use in context.

---

5 According to Coseriu, the dimension should be viewed as: "el punto de vista o el criterio de una oposición (...) el contenido con respecto al cual ella se establece y que, por lo demás, no existe – en la lengua considerada – sino en virtud, precisamente, del hecho de que a él se refiere una oposición, o sea, del hecho de que es soporte implícito de una distinción, funcional", E. Coseriu, *Principios de Semántica Estructural* (Madrid: Biblioteca Románica Hispánica, 1977).

Given the limitations of structural semantics, the approach elaborated by the English scholar, Allan Cruse, has been adopted for this study. This model is capable of describing word-meaning both in its unvarying aspect, for which the structural terms mentioned above still hold, and in its variability, which is deeply context-dependent; the term *context* is here used in its broader sense, referring to linguistic, pragmatic and even cultural characterization.

Cruse starts from the statement that "in principle word meaning may be regarded as infinitely variable and context sensitive". Nevertheless, he argues that regions of higher semantic density are capable of forming more or less well-defined "lumps" of meaning with greater or lesser stability under contextual change. He calls the process of congelation into lumps *nodulation*, and the lumps thus formed *sense-nodules*. Such relatively autonomous units of sense play "an independent role in various semantic processes"[6]. Finally, the meaning of a word turns out to be the conceptual content made accessible by the use of that word (as opposed to any other) in particular contexts.

The semantic unit, which Cruse refers to as *sense nodule*, can be compared to what Geeraerts describes as a particular portion of information, part of the semantic structure of the word itself and which shows a certain degree of independence from the context[7]. By detecting *sense nodules*, we can thus delineate the semantic micro-structure of a polysemous word and distinguish between what, in the use of a given word, is a particular interpretation – generated *ad hoc* in accordance with the specificity of the context (in the broad meaning of the term, including encyclopedic and situational information) – and those which are more likely to be stored in the speaker's memory, leaving some trace on the linguistic system because more stable in shifting contexts.

The introduction of such a notion has remarkable theoretical and methodological implications for the branch of semantics which deals with sense relations and lexical fields. By using such parameters of logical, linguistic and referential nature, it is possible to describe classes of sense nodules with similar features, that is, to group sense nodules which produce similar results when tested for discreteness and contextual dependence. Such classes are called *sub-senses*, *facets* or *ways-of-seeing*[8].

---

6 A. Cruse, "Aspects of the micro-structure of word meanings", in *Polysemy: Theoretical and Computational Approaches* (Edited by Y. Ravin and C. Leacock; Oxford: Oxford University Press, 2000), 30–51, here 30.

7 D. Geeraerts, "Vagueness's puzzles, polysemy vagaries", *Cognitive Linguistics* 4/3 (1993), 223–272.

8 A word with sub-senses has an overall meaning that is vague and general. This "superordinate" sense never arises in context, but rather is activated by a pressure exerted by the context.

By introducing into the semantic description of word meaning a degree of flexibility and dynamism, we not only account adequately for the context-sensitivity of word-meaning, but also, given the cognitive nature of these sense nodules, can adopt them as the parameters of the contrastive and interlinguistic approach required by the present study. Lexical fields thus consist of a range of lexemes which embody in language, and from time to time in the *corpus* examined, lexical representations of such *sense nodules*. We can now move to an examination of the data.

2. The semantic micro-structure of κρίσις

The noun κρίσις exhibits a rich referential polysemy structured as follows: ACTION – SPEECH ACT – PROCESS – ABSTRACT ENTITY[9]. The meanings associated with this word are wide-ranging within the semantic sphere of the administration of justice and designate different aspects of the judicial proceedings necessary to enforce individual rights. As such, they originate from a dispute in which one party proceeds against another, appealing to an individual or a body which holds the authority and the legitimacy to pass judgement. The pro-

---

Often, the sub-senses show a mutual taxonomic relation; in this case semantic discontinuity correlates to referential discontinuity. The facets are other types of semantic sub-units that do not imply a different referent; they focus rather, on different aspects of it, relevant to mutually exclusive categories in an ontology of reference, as e.g. [ABSTRACT] vs [CONCRETE] vs [ANIMATED] vs [HUMAN]. Finally, the ways-of-seeing are discontinuities which do not imply either differences of reference or differences in the semantic category attributed to the referent; they are, rather, different ways of accessing in it. Although Cruse is critical of the possibility of strictly limiting the number of such perspectives, he finally accepts the parallel with the four qualia roles (formal, constitutive, agentive, telic) identified by Pustejovsky, *op.cit.*, 1995; they play a role in processes of semantic composition, in particular, they govern "the ways in which predicates can attach themselves to nouns", see W. Croft and A. Cruse, *Cognitive Linguistics* (Cambridge: Cambridge University Press, 2004), 137.

9 For a discussion on structuring systems see L. Talmy, *Towards a Cognitive Semantics: Language Speech and Communication* (Cambridge Mass.: The MIT Press, 2000) and M. Prandi, *The Building Blocks of Meaning. Ideas for a philosophical grammar* (Amsterdam/Philadelphia: John Benjamins, 2004); for the feature Aktionsart in NPh, see Simon C. Dik, *Theory of Functional Grammar: The Structure of the Clause* (2nd rev. ed.; Berlin/New York: Mouton de Gruyter, 1997); for the functional development of the notion of Seisart see J. Rijkhoff, *The noun phrase* (Oxford Studies in Typology and Theoretical Linguistics; Oxford: Oxford University Press, 2002) and idem, "Layers, levels and contexts in Functional Discourse Grammar", in *The noun phrase in Functional Discourse Grammar* (Edited D. García Velasco and J. Rijkhoff; Trends in Linguistics; Berlin: Walter de Gruyter, 2008), 63–116.

ceedings end with the pronouncement of a verdict which is binding on both parties.

The referential polysemy of κρίσις covers each of the eventive structures represented in Figure 1.

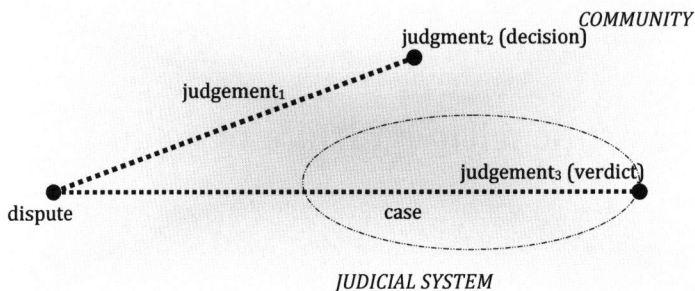

Figure 1 – The referential polysemy of κρίσις

As will be demonstrated through an analysis of its syntagmatic and paradigmatic relations within the *corpus*, the word cannot be defined as a technical term *tout court*. However, in some cases, its usage suggests the existence of a legal or judicial system known to the authors and their audience alike. Such a system includes at least: a) a group of human beings who identify themselves as a community; b) an abstract body of regulations (with an *erga omnes* coercive force), whose function it is to regulate the behavior of the individual and bring him to justice and to acknowledgment of the truth; c) office holders responsible for settling disputes and enforcing individual rights, when they are denied, of passing judgments and imposing binding measures which regulate the behavior of individuals on the basis of the same body of regulations; d) a specific space-time context in which those eligible to pass judgment, perform their function.

2.1 Action

The sense nodule 'dispute' is triggered by the combination with κρίνειν 'to judge', προσάγειν 'to bring', 'to bring to one's notice', προσέχειν 'to pay attention'. Thanks to the syntagmatic operation of sense modulation, these predicates are capable of selecting the meaning 'event' in the semantic range of κρίσις. Let us dwell for a moment on the paradigmatic relations activated by this sense nodule.

Table 1

κρίνειν 'to judge'	κρίσις 'dispute', 'case'
	ῥῆμα 'case (verbally presented)'

The context in table 1 occurs two times: Gen 19:9, Isa 49:25. Use of κρίσις 'dispute' overlaps with ῥῆμα 'case' (Exod 18:22; 18:26; Hebrew *dābār*), becoming its contextual synonym.

In Gen 19:9, the sense is metaphorical; Lot does all he can to protect his two guests from the violence which a group from Sodoma intend to inflict on them. This is not only an act of opposition to abuse, but also a moral act of justice, intended to prevent a serious breach in the duty of hospitality. Though he lives in Sodoma, Lot does not belong to the people of Sodoma and this is precisely the point at stake. The natives deny he has the authority to settle disputes and to pass judgments because he is an alien in Sodoma (εἰς ἦλθες παροικεῖν, μὴ καὶ κρίσιν κρίνειν "as one you came to reside as an alien; surely not also to pass judgment"), but, finally, God himself miraculously intervenes in favor of the guests. The natives' behavior causes exemplary punishment to befall the town, the complete destruction of which is sign of the universality of YHWH's moral law.

Table 2

προσάγειν 'to bring' + ἔναντι κυρίου	κρίσις 'case'
	δῶρον 'gift'
	θυσία 'sacrifice'
	κάρπωμα 'cultic offering'
	ὁλοκαύτωμα 'wholly burnt offering'

The context set out in table 2 occurs in Num 27:5. In this context κρίσις is defined by its paradigmatic relations with a set of eventive nouns that can be defined as trivalent regarding the valency pattern: someone who gives rise to the action, an object which is brought or led, and finally someone to whom the action is addressed. In most cases προσάγειν modulates the metonymic sense "entity" in its direct object, but something different happens in combination with κρίσις; the semantic structures of the items combined give rise to the metaphorical reading 'to bring the case before', which is highly characteristic of legal discourse.

Since in Num 27:5 the third constituent of the predicate (encoded by the phrase ἔναντι κυρίου 'before the Lord') refers to God, we deduce that God himself can issue a judgment in cases involving individual rights. This intervention, however, requires mediation; thanks to a direct dialogic relation, Moyses has the ability to perform this function and thus can bring before God a case in which the rights of an individual are at stake.

Table 3

προσέχειν 'to pay attention'	κρίσις 'case'
	λόγος 'speech', 'discourse'
	νόμος 'law'

The context in table 3 occurs only once, in Isa 1:23; the MT reads *wərîḇ 'almānāh lō' yāḇô' 'ălêhem* 'the widow's cause never reaches them'. In this passage, God blames the ἄρχοντες of Israel because their corruption harms widows, one of the weakest groups in the community; consequently, God himself undertakes to intervene in defence of their rights.

Here the word κρίσις (like νόμος 'law') is used as a hyponym of λόγος, through its *facet* [CONTENT]. Both λόγος and κρίσις exhibit the same referent; but while the former designates an act of speech in general, the latter refers to a specific kind of "reported" speech with a specific predicative force, i.e. it is meant to be uttered within a juridical environment (*agentive quale*), with the purpose of the acknowledgement and enforcement of individual rights (*telic quale*).

2.2 Process

The sense nodule 'decision', 'judgement' arises, in certain contexts, from combination with the predicates ἐκζητεῖν 'to ask for', ἐκκλίνειν 'to pervert', ἐπερωτᾶν 'to consult', and with the adjective modifiers ἀληθινός 'true', 'truthful' and δίκαιος 'righteous'. We will now discuss the semantic relations activated by this nodule.

Table 4

ἐκζητεῖν 'to ask for'	κρίσις 'judgement'
'to engage oneself in'	κρίμα s. 'justice'
	κρίσις s. 'justice'
	νόμος s. 'law'
	δίκαιος n. s. 'what is just'
	κακός n. s. 'what is morally bad'

ἐκζητεῖν 'to ask for'	κρίσις 'judgement'
'to look for'	θεός 'God (YHWH)'
	φίλος m.'friend'
	χίμαρος 'goat'

Through the paradigmatic structure shown in table 4, we can first of all highlight how the sense modulation goes in the opposite direction to that previously observed: it is the argument here that selects the predicate's meaning, particularly where the object of the verb is an animated entity. In this case, the verb's meaning will be 'to look for'. Where the object doesn't satisfy this requirement, the verb adjusts its meaning by use of a metaphorical extension 'to strive to know', 'to engage oneself devotedly in' or 'to perform'. It is worth noting that the diagram presents strong evidence of the polysemy of κρίσις: in the same combination, in fact, we find the lexeme with the meaning 'right', 'justice' (Isa 1:17), which will be discussed in detail later; Exod 18:15 is an instance of the latter sense:

Exod 18:15
παραγίνεται πρός με ὁ λαὸς ἐκζητῆσαι κρίσιν παρὰ τοῦ θεοῦ
'the people come to me (Moyses) to seek judgment from God'[10].

If we have established that Moyses is the trustworthy interpreter of God's teachings, we must add that this role depends on his privileged relationship with God: he indeed addresses the Lord without further mediation as in the case of Salpaad's daughters above mentioned (Num 27:5); where he obtains from God a judgement concerning rights. The knowledge of God's judgment in specific cases involves thus a two-step process: the people bring their case to Moyses, and then he discusses the case directly with YHWH, receiving his verdict.

Table 5

ἐκκλίνειν 'to pervert'	κρίσις 'judgement'
'to bend out from the regular path'	ὁδός 'road'

The context in table 5 is the most frequent in the Pentateuch (Exod 23:2; Deut 16:19; 24:17; 27:19). While in some textual instances, a specific juridical environ-

---

10 Translations of reference are *A new English Translation of the Septuagint* (NETS) for the Septuagint text, and *The New Jewish Publication Society of America Tanakh* (TNK) for the Masoretic text; if different translations will be suggested, it will be emphasized in the text.

ment is expressly represented, in others, its existence and its functions (e. g. individuals or a community responsible for passing judgement and established as such) are only implied, if required at all.

On one hand, in the latter cases, κρίσις refers to the faculty of making considered decisions or coming to sensible conclusions, something every human being is capable of in his private or public life; on the other hand, in those contexts which assume a juridical context—namely passages from the Deuteronomic Code (Deut 4:44–26:19) and from the Covenant Code (Exod 20:22–23:19)—the noun refers rather to the faculty of deciding a case or passing judgments with coercive value by those who are appointed to do so. In the following passages, mention is made of wrong attitudes which can cause the process to be distorted and compromise its outcome.

The perversion of a judgement, in short, is caused by the corruption of those responsible for executing it, those who allow themselves to accept gifts or illicit favours[11]. In this situation, the judgment is not straightforward, but deviates to some extent (hence, the metaphorical sense of the combination). Typically, in a litigation, gifts come from the wealthier party, while the socially weaker party eventually succumbs to the law of the stronger; once again, the widow (χήρα), the orphan (ὀρφανός), the foreigner (προσήλυτος) prototypically belong to this second group (Deut 24:17).

Independence must also be a distinguishing feature of the judge and the judging body: they cannot be uncritical or conformist in their attitude but must oppose any decision which, on the basis of law, is unjust or incomplete[12].

Table 6

ἀληθινός 'true' , 'truthful'	κρίσις 'judgement'
	βουλή 'decision'
	ἔργον 'action'
	καρδία 'attitude'
	θεός 'God (YHWH)'
	κύριος 'the Lord (YHWH)'

---

11 "You shall appoint for yourselves judges and officers (γραμματοεισαγωγεῖς) in all your cities (…) they shall judge the people with righteous judgment (κρινοῦσιν τὸν λαὸν κρίσιν δικαίαν). They shall not pervert judgment (οὐκ ἐκκλινοῦσιν κρίσιν), they shall not take gifts (οὐδὲ λήμψονται δῶρον). For gifts blind the eyes of the wise, and nullify the words of the righteous (τὰ γὰρ δῶρα ἐκτυφλοῖ ὀφθαλμοὺς σοφῶν καὶ ἐξαίρει λόγους δικαίων)" (Deut 16:18–19).

12 "You shall not be with the majority for wrongdoing (οὐκ ἔσῃ μετὰ πλειόνων ἐπὶ κακίᾳ). You shall not associate with a crowd (μετὰ πλήθους) to turn side with the majority so as to pervert judgment (ὥστε ἐκκλῖναι κρίσιν)" (Exod 23:2).

ἀληθινός 'true' , 'truthful'	κρίσις 'judgement'
'not fraudulent'	μέτρον 'linear measure' σταθμίον 'unit of measurement for solids'
'good'	ὁδός 'way'

Table 7

δίκαιος 'righteous', 'unbiased'	κρίσις 'judgement'
	κρίμα 'judgement' ῥῆμα 'statement' ἀνήρ 'man' ἄνθρωπος 'man' βασιλεύς 'supreme ruler, king' κύριος 'the Lord (YHWH)'
'unaltered'	ζυγός 'balance' σταθμίον 'standard weight for balances' χοῦς 'liquid measure'

Among the operations of semantic composition which govern sense modulation in a given context, the one that occurs between a noun and its adjectival modifiers is described in literature as an operation of sub-selection. The phenomenon occurs where there are many senses available for an adjective, in which case the noun selects the one which syntagmatically fits best. More particularly, the noun modulates only the portion that satisfies its selectional requirement.

In table 6, among the selectees of ἀληθινός we find μέτρον 'linear measure' and σταθμίον 'unit of measurement for solids'. Combined with these nouns, ἀληθινός means 'unaltered'. We are now better able to understand how a judgement can be defined as 'just' and, consequently, which sense is sub-selected by κρίσις: a judgement is ἀληθινός when it is truthful, correct and impartial.

The meaning of δίκαιος is modulated in the same way (table 7); moreover, it should be remarked that while ἀληθινός has paradigmatic relations with words relevant to the inner world of the individual (βουλή 'decision', καρδία 'heart', 'attitude'), δίκαιος is instead correlated to a class of events that have a social and interpersonal dimension, more or less associated with the juridical context (i.e. κρίμα 'judgement', ῥῆμα 'word', 'statement').

Both adjectives select animate entities; for instance, in Gen 6:9 Noe is called a 'righteous man'. Let us compare the Septuagint reading with the MT:

Gen 6:9
Νωε ἄνθρωπος δίκαιος, τέλειος ὢν ἐν τῇ γενεᾷ αὐτοῦ· τῷ θεῷ εὐηρέστησεν Νωε
Noe was a righteous man, being perfect in his *generation*; Noe was well pleasing to God.
Nōaḥ ʾîš ṣaddîq tāmîm hāyāh bədōrōtāyw ʾet hāʾēlōhîm hithallek Nōaḥ
Noah was a righteous man; he was blameless in his age; Noah walked with God.

The text of the Septuagint simply glosses that a man who is righteous and perfect is pleasing to God (εὐαρεστεῖν) on account of his righteousness (as justice and faithfulness belong to YHWH himself). The MT supplies a more exhaustive reading, giving the reason why he is considered righteous, i. e. because 'Noah walked with God'.

A similar metaphor is available in Greek, in combinations such as φυλάσσειν τὸν ὁδόν κυρίου / τοὺς ὁδοὺς κυρίου; many times νόμος occurs in these contexts as well (Exod 13:10; Lev 19:19, 19:37), never corresponding to *tôrāh*, as expected, but rather to *ḥuqqāh*.

Thus, we deduce from the text that human justice arises from adherence to the precepts of God. This adherence is not thought of in terms of theoretical acknowledgment but as a distinctly practical activity.

2.3 Speech act

Besides indicating a process, κρίσις as 'decision' or 'sentence', is also capable of referring to the final act in this process, which normally entails a speech act. This event occurs when binding instructions are legitimately pronounced.

Selectors of this contextual sense are: ἀναγγέλλειν 'to make public announcement', δεικνύναι 'to show by way of instruction', διαλέγεσθαι 'to explain', διδάσκειν 'to teach', ποιεῖν 'to put into effect', φυλάσσειν 'to keep', 'to perform'.

Table 8

ἀναγγέλλειν 'to announce'	κρίσις 'sentence'
	ἀγγελία 'message', 'piece of news'
	διαθήκη 'covenant'
	ἔσχατος n. pl. 'what will happen later in the future'
	καινός n. pl. 'novelty', 'what has not yet happened'
	κακός n. s. 'what is morally bad'
	λόγος 'speech', 'discourse'
	πλάνησις 'misleading message'
	πρότερος n. 'events of the past', 'the past'
	ῥῆμα 'statement'

ἀναγγέλλειν 'to announce'	κρίσις 'sentence'
'to declare'	ἀλήθεια 'what is in accordance with reality'
	δικαιοσύνη 'righteousness'
	δόξα 'glory'

The context in table 8 occurs in Deut 17:9. In this combination κρίσις establishes a quasi-synonymy with λόγος 'speech' or more precisely a relation of co-hyponymy, as both words belong to the class 'speech act'. On one hand, λόγος is a prototypical instance of a speech act, which is not further specified. On the other hand, κρίσις is characterized by a telic and agentive predicative force (different from that previously observed), since, in this case, the word refers to a very specific pronouncement uttered by a competent person or group – in this particular case, the Leuites (οἱ ἱερεῖς οἱ Λευῖται) and the judge (κριτής) – at the conclusion of proceedings.

Table 9

δεικνύναι 'to show by way of instruction'	κρίσις 'sentence'
(+ speech act)	δικαίωμα 'ordinance'
	κρίσις s. 'judgment' (Isa 40:14)
	ῥῆμα 'word', 'statement'
'to show evidence of' (+ attitude)	θυμός 'wrath '
'to show', 'to cause to be seen'	αἷμα 'blood'
(+ entity)	γῆ 'region'
	ἱερόν 'temple'
	καρπός 'fruit'
	ξύλον 'piece of wood'
	οἶκος 'house', 'room'
	πρόσωπον 'face'
	πῦρ 'fire'
	φῶς 'light'

The verb δεικνύναι 'to show' (table 9) prototypically selects entities as direct objects. The verb also undergoes metaphorical extension in combination with nouns which belong to the semantic category of emotions or attitudes, such as θυμός 'wrath' (Isa 48:9).

As the table shows, the verb exhibits a regular pattern of polysemy in its distribution. Let us dwell for a moment on the particular class of objects which refers to speech acts as ῥῆμα 'word', 'statement' (Num 23:3), or by means of presupposition as κρίσις 'sentence' (Deut 4:5) and δικαίωμα 'ordinance' (Deut 4:5). These selectees exploit only a portion of the meaning available in the verb, namely that which refers to the process of content transmission. Since, in these combinations, the content transmitted is verbal rather than visual, the specific sense that emerges in context, being modulated by the semantic structure of the object, is respectively 'to say', 'to report' or 'to teach'.

Since in Deut 4:5, Moyses acts as an intermediary between the community of Israel and YHWH, we can therefore outline, as follows, the vectors in the cycle of content transmission:

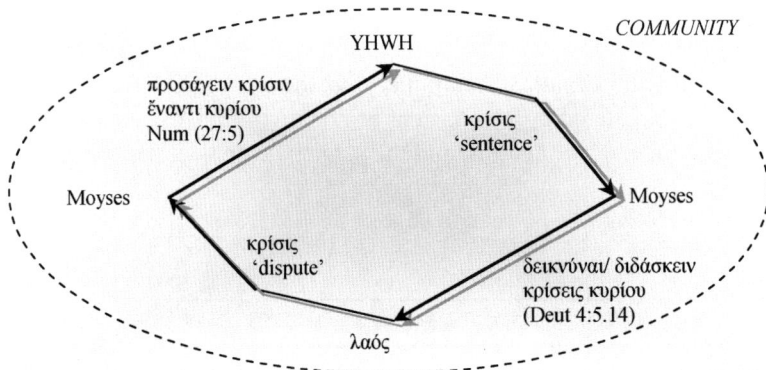

Figure 2 – Content Transmission of κρίσις

Figure 2 helps us appreciate how the meaning of κρίσις varies according to context, depending on who pronounces it.

However, it can be argued from the textual data, that God himself, under certain circumstances, may intervene in the administration of justice – without any necessity for intermediaries – passing judgments in cases involving individual rights. If those in charge of judging fail to settle a controversy on the basis of the rules of νόμος – as in the inheritance dispute narrated in Num 27:1–11 – Moyses submits the matter to God, by means of a direct dialogue with him (προσάγειν κρίσιν ἔναντι κυρίου). God assesses the case and passes a judgement appropriate to their needs; Moyses, in turn, reports (δεικνύναι) the contents of the divine decision to the parties with an immediate impact on those concerned (effectiveness *inter partes*):

Num 27:7
(καὶ ἐλάλησεν κύριος πρὸς Μωυσῆν λέγων) ὀρθῶς θυγατέρες Σαλπααδ λελαλήκασιν. δόμα δώσεις αὐταῖς κατάσχεσιν κληρονομίας ἐν μέσῳ ἀδελφῶν πατρὸς αὐτῶν καὶ περιθήσεις τὸν κλῆρον τοῦ πατρὸς αὐτῶν αὐταῖς

(And the Lord spoke to Moyses, saying:) Salpaad's daughters have spoken correctly. You shall give to them as a gift a possession of inheritance in the midst of their father's brothers, and you shall confer the allotment of their father on them.

The verdict is then immediately reformulated by God with binding effectiveness *erga omnes:*

Num 27:8–11
καὶ τοῖς υἱοῖς Ισραηλ λαλήσεις λέγων·Ἄνθρωπος ἐὰν ἀποθάνῃ καὶ υἱὸς μὴ ᾖ αὐτῷ, περιθή-
σετε τὴν κληρονομίαν αὐτοῦ τῇ θυγατρὶ αὐτοῦ·ἐὰν δὲ μὴ ᾖ θυγάτηρ αὐτῷ, δώσετε τὴν κληρονομίαν τῷ ἀδελφῷ αὐτοῦ· ἐὰν δὲ μὴ ὦσιν αὐτῷ ἀδελφοί, δώσετε τὴν κληρονομίαν τῷ
ἀδελφῷ τοῦ πατρὸς αὐτοῦ· ἐὰν δὲ μὴ ὦσιν ἀδελφοὶ τοῦ πατρὸς αὐτοῦ, δώσετε τὴν κληρονομίαν τῷ οἰκείῳ τῷ ἔγγιστα αὐτοῦ ἐκ τῆς φυλῆς αὐτοῦ, κληρονομήσει τὰ αὐτοῦ. καὶ ἔσται
τοῦτο τοῖς υἱοῖς Ισραηλ **δικαίωμα κρίσεως,** καθὰ συνέταξεν κύριος τῷ Μωυσῇ
You shall speak to the sons of Israel, saying, "If a person dies, and he has no son, you shall
confer his inheritance on his daughter. Now if he has no daughter, you shall give the inheritance to his brother. Now if he has no brothers, you shall give his inheritance to his father's
brother. Now if there are no brothers of his father, you shall give the inheritance to his near-
est relative from his tribe; he shall inherit what is his. And this shall be for the sons of Israel
a rule of law, just as the Lord instructed Moyses".

By means of induction, the abstract rule of law (δικαίωμα κρίσεως) is formulated from a specific judgment, whose effectiveness is guaranteed by its authoritative source, *i.e.* God himself. In this process of content transmission, Moyses, as the person appointed by God, conveys both the verdict to the parties and the rules of law to all the community.

Table 10

διδάσκειν 'to teach'	κρίσις *pl.* (κυρίου) 'sentence', 'precept'
+ κυρίου	δικαίωμα 'ordinance'
	ἐντολή 'commandment'
	ἔνταλμα 'command', 'precept'
	κρίμα 'injunction to be observed'
– κυρίου	ᾠδή 'song'

In the context in table 10 (instantiated in Deut 4:14), the sense discussed above, is also selected by the verb διδάσκειν. Since, once again, this responsability is entrusted to Moyses by God himself (ἐμοὶ ἐνετείλατο κύριος), it is arguable that his role towards the people is not limited to the mere disclosure and dissem-ination of content, but expands to include an educative function.

Table 11

ποιεῖν 'to put into effect', 'to comply with'	κρίσις *pl.* (+ κυρίου) 'sentence', 'precept'
+ κυρίου	δικαίωμα *pl.* 'ordinance'
	ἐντολή *pl.* 'commandment'
	θέλημα *pl.* 'desire'
	κρίμα *pl.* 'injunction to be observed'
	λόγος *pl.* 'speech', 'divine message'
	ὁδός *pl.* 'path'
	πρόσταγμα *pl.* 'precept'
	ῥῆμα *pl.* 'precept'
	διαθήκη *sing.* 'covenant'
	κρίσις *sing.* 'what is just' (Gen 18:19)
	νόμος *sing.* 'law'
– κυρίου	ἀγαθός *neu. sing.* 'what is morally good'
	ἀρεστός *neu. sing./pl.* 'what is morally pleasing'
	καλός *neu. sing.* 'what is morally acceptable'

As shown in table 11, κρίσις 'judgment' or 'precept' legitimately belongs to the class of direct objects selected by ποιεῖν and φυλάσσειν. In the context taken into account here, a further morphological specification, the plural form, makes selection of the sense 'precept' easier. To abide by the law or the covenant of God (in this case νόμος and διαθήκη exhibit a genuine referential synonymy) basically means adapting one's behavior to the body of his judgements, statutes, precepts with *erga omnes* binding effectiveness.

Table 12

ἐπερωτᾶν 'to consult'	κρίσις 'response'
	ἐγγαστρίμυθος 'ventriloquist'
	θεός 'deity other that YHWH'
	ἀνήρ 'man'
	νεκρός 'corpse'
'to ask questions'	πατήρ 'father'

The context in table 12 projects the use of κρίσις into a divinatory framework[13], not found elsewhere in our corpus-based analysis. The verb ἐπερωτᾶν 'to consult' typ-

---

13 The context refers to the practice of consulting the priest's *'ēpod*, which contained the *'ûrîm* and the *tummîm* (Exod 28:39; Lev 8:8). For a detailed discussion on the meaning and use of such

ically selects human beings – ἀνήρ 'man', πατήρ 'father' or ἐγγαστρίμυθος 'ventriloquist', via an implication describable as 'the opinion of' or 'the response of'. As in the episode narrated in Num 27:21, κρίσις is modified by the complement τῶν δήλων. In this case the implication turns out to be explicit.

2.4 Abstract entity

The divine origin of the judgement, highlighted in the passages discussed above, plays a fundamental role in the semantic relationship between the senses associated with the decision-making process to those associated with the notions of right, righteousness and justice. The idea of the law finally corresponds to the whole body of God's judgments, and the justice is conceived as the practice and enforcement of law.

In the Pentateuch, as previously demonstrated, conceptualization of this kind predominates; the collective plural form κρίσεις refers to body of divine verdicts (Lev 25:18; Deut 4:5; 11:1.32; 30:10.16). Nevertheless, the concept of an abstract prescriptive principle which governs action is not unknown, as is evident in the use of the singular form κρίσις as a mass noun (Gen 18:19.25; Deut 10:18). Maximum use of the meaning 'justice' as the principle that permeates the law and human behavior is made in the book of Isaiah[14]. Selectors of the contextual sense are: ἐκφέρειν 'to spread', 'to extend', τιθέναι 'to establish', 'to set'.

Table 13

ἐκφέρειν 'to spread', 'to extend'	κρίσις 'right' 'justice'
	ἔκστασις 'consternation' ὄνομα 'fame'
'to bring out', 'to take'	ἄρτος 'bread' λίθος 'stone'

---

instruments, see J. Lindblom, "Lot-Casting in the Old Testament", *Vetus Testamentum* 12 (1962) 164–178; C. Houtman, "The Urim and Thummim: A New suggestion". *Vetus Testamentum* 40 (1990), 229–232; C. Van Dam, *The Urim and Thummim: A Means of Revelation in Ancient Israel,* Winona Lake: Eisenbrauns, 1997; A. M. Kitz, "The Hebrew Terminology of Lot Casting and Its Ancient Near Eastern Context", *Catholic Biblical Quarterly* 62/2 (2000), 207–214.

14 It must be said that in the book of Isaiah other uses are not totally extraneous, an instance is Isa 58:4 εἰς κρίσεις καὶ μάχας νηστεύετε 'you fast for quarrels and fights', MT *lārîḇ ûmaṣṣāh tāṣûmû;* here the plural and the combination with μάχας forces the selection of the sense 'dispute'.

ἐκφέρειν 'to spread', 'to extend'	κρίσις 'right' 'justice'
	σκεῦος 'tool'
'to carry'	μόσχος 'calf'
'to produce'	βλαστός 'bud' βοτάνη 'herbage'

Table 13 shows that the meaning of the verb ἐκφέρειν is syntagmatically determined by the direct object with which it combines. Typically, ἐκφέρειν 'to bring out' selects concrete entities (as ἄρτος, λίθος, σκεῦος), associating the idea of transport with that of movement from a given place; when it combines with an animate entity (as μόσχος), the verb takes on the nuance, 'to carry out'. When the subject cannot fulfill the task required by the verb due to the position it occupies in the hierarchy of animacy – as in the case of γῆ in Gen 1:12, or ῥάβ- δος in Num 17:23 – under these circumstances, the verb reaches semantic agreement through the sense 'to produce'. Furthermore, in the distribution of ἐκφέρειν, there is a paradigmatic sub-structure consisting of abstract entities – ἔκστασις 'consternation' (Num 13:32) , ὄνομα 'fame' (Deut 22:19) and κρίσις as well:

> Isa 42:3
> κάλαμονγὰρ τεθλασμένον οὐ συντρίψει καὶ λίνον καπνιζόμενον οὐ σβέσει, ἀλλὰ εἰς ἀλή-
> θειαν ἐξοίσει κρίσιν
> A bruised reed he will not break, and a smoking wick he will not quench, but he will *extend right to truth*.

Thus, the metaphorical reading 'to extend right to truth' is generated in context, triggered by the semantics of the object and by the pressure exerted by the phrase εἰς ἀλήθειαν; such a deed is specifically ascribed to God himself as supreme judge (ὁ κρίνων πᾶσαν τὴν γῆν "the one who judges all the earth" Gen 18:25; described according to the characteristic features mentioned above ὅστις οὐ θαυμάζει πρόσωπον οὐδ' οὐ μὴ λάβῃ δῶρον 'who does not marvel at a person, neither will he take a bribe' Deut 10:18), or his servant (ὁ παῖς μου Isa 42:1).

Table 14

ποιεῖν	κρίσις	'to do justice'
'to make', 'to perform'	διαθήκη 'covenant' πόλεμος 'war' ἐπισκοπή 'visit'	

ποιεῖν	κρίσις	'to do justice'
'to put into effect', 'to comply with'	ἀλήθεια 'faithfulness' δικαιοσύνη 'justice' κρίσις *sing.* 'what is just' ἔλεος 'mercy' δικαίωμα *pl.* 'ordinance' ἐντολή *pl.* 'commandment' κρίσις *pl.* 'judgement', 'precept' ῥῆμα *pl.* 'precept'	
'to fashion', 'to construct', 'to prepare' (+ artifact)	ἔδεσμα 'dish' κρίκος 'buckle' κιβωτός 'ark' χιτών 'tunic'	

Table 15

ἀνταποδιδόναι	κρίσις	'to repay', 'to revenge'
	ἀνταπόδομα ἀνταπόδοσις δίκη	
'to punish'	ἀδικία 'iniquity' ἁμαρτία 'transgression' πονηρός n.pl. 'what is morally wrong'	

By analyzing data in table 14, we will highlight regular patterns of polysemy in the meaning of ποιεῖν on one hand and will find further evidence for the inherent polysemy of κρίσις on the other. Let us start with the prototypical instances. Combined with an artifact of some kind, the verb activates the basic meaning 'to make', 'to produce', assuming, from time to time, the nuance appropriate to the specific features of the object e. g. ποιεῖν ἔδεσμα 'to make (to cook) a dish' (e.g. Gen 24:4.7.14), ποιεῖν κρίκους 'to make (to chisel) buckles' (Exod 26:11) or ποιεῖν χιτῶνας 'to make (to tailor) tunics' (Exod 28:40). The combination with eventive nouns triggers the sense 'to do', 'to carry out', as in the case of ποιεῖν διαθήκην 'to make a covenant' (Isa 28:15), ποιεῖν γάμος 'to make a wedding (feast)' (Gen 29:22); ποιεῖν ἐπισκοπήν 'to visit' (Isa 23:17); ποιεῖν πόλεμον 'to make war' (Deut 20:12.20). In the specific case of the homogeneous lexical field related to the body of the divine precepts, as discussed before, the sense activated in context is rather 'to perform', 'to follow' or 'to obey'. A further homogeneous group of objects consists of the following nominal forms related to abstract notions used as mass nouns: ἀλήθεια (Gen 47:29), ἔλεος (e.g. Gen 24:12; Exod 20:6), and, finally, κρίσις (Gen 18:19; Isa 1:24). If, in the case of attitudes (as ἔλεος), the meaning exhibited can be glossed as 'to show', in the other cases the verb develops the sense 'to spread', 'to cause to become popular'. The enforcement of what is right is a function undertaken eminently by God himself.

The expression ποιεῖν κρίσιν, like its synonymous ἀνταποδιδόναι κρίσιν, ends up being the equivalent of ἐκδικεῖν 'to revenge', since the assertion of right and justice may imply punishment, should God's declare that the party concerned is guilty. This is the case in the following:

Isa 1:24
οὐ παύσεται μου ὁ θυμὸς ἐν τοῖς ὑπεναντίοις, καὶ κρίσιν ἐκ τῶν ἐχθρῶν μου ποιήσω
For my wrath on my adversaries will not abate, and I will *execute* judgment *of* my foes!

However, since the vengeance of God leads essentially to the assertion of the right, those who are part of the redeemed (οἱ λελυτρωμένοι Isa 35:9) conceive it as an event of salvation:

Isa 35:4
ἰδοὺ ὁ θεὸς ἡμῶν κρίσιν ἀνταποδίδωσιν καὶ ἀνταποδώσει, αὐτὸς ἥξει καὶ σώσει ἡμᾶς
Look, our God is repaying judgment; yes, he will repay; he himself will come and save us

Let us dwell for a moment on the Hebrew counterpart of these texts. The MT reads:

Isa 1:24
wə'innāqmāh mē'ôyḇāy
I will wreak vengeance on my enemies

Isa 35:4
hinnēh 'ĕlōhêḵem nāqām yāḇô' gəmûl 'ĕlōhîm hû' yāḇô' wəyōša'ăḵem
Behold your God! Requital is coming, The recompense of God, He himself is coming and *he will save you.*

In the first passage, we find the stem *nqm* in *niph'al* 'to avenge oneself'; in the second, there is the noun *nāqām*, which refers both to human revenge and to divine vengeance (*HALOT* 6342). By choosing the equivalent κρίσις instead of ἐκδίκησις (as for instance in Deut 32:35; Isa 59:17) or ἐκδικεῖν (as in Gen 4:24; Exod 21:20.21; Num 31:2; Deut 32:43), the Greek version seems to add a reference to the juridical context which is not present in the MT; the Septuagint text thus suggests that the vengeance of God may be understood as the execution a verdict of conviction at the end of a trial.

As we have previously noted, the establishment of justice, and the consequent state of equity, is a function almost exclusively reserved to God or to a subject whom he delegates to fulfill the task in his place (in Isa 42:1 ὁ παῖς μου); such a state, however, may change due to human intervention. The following combinations identify the correct attitudes of man towards the law and right order: οἶδα 'to know', φυλάσσειν 'to keep'.

Table 16

οἶδα 'to have learnt'	κρίσις 'right'
	ἀγαθός *neu. sing.* 'what is morally good'
	κακός *neu. sing.* 'what is morally bad'
	σύνεσις 'understanding'
'to be familiar with'	θεός 'God (YHWH)'
	Ιωσηφ 'Ioseph'
'to have experienced'	παιδεία 'punishment'
	εἰρήνη 'peace', 'well-being'
	κοίτη 'nuptial bed', 'sex'
	πονηρία 'evilness'

In the distribution of οἶδα, regular patterns of selectional polysemy can be detected; when the verb combines with eventive nouns such as παιδεία 'punishment' (Deut 11:2) or κοίτη 'nuptial bed (sexual intercourse)' (Num 31:18), its contextual meaning can be glossed as 'to have experience of'; however when combined with animate nouns, specifically human beings, the sense will be rather 'to become acquainted with', e.g. Ιωσηφ (Exod 1:8). Besides these uses, we typically find the verb in combination with mass nouns related to abstract notions, such as ἀγαθόν 'what is good' (Num 14:23; Deut 1:39), κακόν 'what is evil' (Deut 1:39), σύνεσις 'understanding' (Isa 56:11), εἰρήνη 'peace' (Isa 59:8). Finally, there is κρίσις, present in Isa 51:7; let us compare the Greek text and its Hebrew counterpart.

Isa 51:7
ἀκούσατέ μου, οἱ εἰδότες κρίσιν, λαός μου, οὗ ὁ νόμος μου ἐν τῇ καρδίᾳ ὑμῶν
Hear me, you who know judgment, my people, you in whose heart is my law.

MT *šim'û 'ēlay yōd'ê ṣedeq 'ām tôrātî ḇəlibbām*
Listen to me, you who know (the) righteousness, people who lay my instruction to heart.

The noun κρίσις, as equivalent of *ṣedeq* is rather unusual compared to the typical rendering δικαιοσύνη. In the Septuagint, we can find just one other instance, namely Isa 11:4 (in this case the entire passage presents some difficulties, since the noun occurs as accusative-adverbial modifier of κρίνειν, with a quite odd dative complement ταπεινῷ, in order to render the Hebrew phrase wəšāp̄aṭ bəṣedeq dallîm). Observing the lexical relations described in table 16, we can see that the notion of "knowing" is mostly shaped as the ability to distinguish between what is good and what is bad (cfr. Num 14:23, Deut 1:39, Isa 56:11), and the presence of κρίσις in this network of relationships is not surprising. Nevertheless, the absence of δικαιοσύνη deserves a comment; the Greek reading seems indeed suggest a specific interpretation of justice, limited and focused on the ability to judge well.

Table 17

φυλάσσειν 'to keep'	κρίσις s. 'righteousness'
	ἀλήθεια 'faithfulness' δικαιοσύνη 'justice' νόμος 'law' διαθήκη 'covenant'
'to observe'	δικαίωμα 'ordinance' ἐντολή 'commandment' κρίμα 'injunction to be observed' κρίσις pl. 'sentence', 'precept' λόγος 'speech', 'divine message' μαρτύριον 'instruction' νόμιμον 'statute' ὁδός pl. 'path' πρόσταγμα 'precept' φύλαγμα 'what is to be observed'
'to watch over'	ἄκρα 'citadel' ἔπαλξις 'battlements' κτῆνος 'cattle' ὀχύρωμα 'fortress'

Table 16 shows some paradigmatic relations which are highly relevant to the semantic micro-structure of κρίσις: first of all κρίσις 'right' is quasi-synonymous with νόμος (κυρίου), διαθήκη (κυρίου) or δικαιοσύνη 'justice'; secondly, this specific sense, which we have tried to show is inherent to the semantics of the noun, is auto-metonymous with κρίσις 'judgment' or 'precept', formerly discussed. This extension can be described, therefore, as a metonymy, as the following instances show:

Isa 56:1
φυλάσσεσθε κρίσιν ποιήσατε δικαιοσύνη

keep judgment, do righteousness

Deut 30:16
φυλάσσεσθαι τὰ δικαιώματα αὐτοῦ (κυρίου) καὶ τὰς κρίσεις αὐτοῦ (κυρίου)
keep his statutes, and his judgements

As *holonym* the word covers the range of content that has binding value, inasmuch as it is issued by God himself; this content has the function of steering the members of the people of Israel toward justice and truth.

Man is thus called to know, practice and comply with the law; however, adherence to the law is not the only option. Individuals or the community as a whole may be negative towards it, going as far as to reject it, both in practice and in principle. This behavior is expressed by the verb ἐγκαταλείπειν 'to disregard' (Isa 58:2).

Conclusion

In the present article, we sought to propose a corpus-based description of the semantic micro-structure of κρίσις, consistent with the principles of flexibility of word-meaning in context and processes of semantic composition and modulation. In applying this dynamic model to the study of the Greek biblical lexicon, we adopted two main methodological strategies. On one hand, we took into account the three different dimensions of lexicographical description described by Tov, namely: "the meaning of the words in the pre-Septuagintic stage, the meaning in the Septuagint itself as intended by the translators, and the meaning of the words as quoted from the LXX"[15] (Tov 1999:94), limiting, for the moment, our investigation into the second dimension proposed. On the other hand, we constantly bore in mind the words of the lexicologist Alan Cruse, as follows: "It is clear that the terms of sense relations such as antonymy and hyponymy cannot be lexemes (cf. Lyons) nor even senses. In fact, no simple unit can be identified which can fulfil this role: the terms of such relations are any nodules of sense with a sufficient degree of discreteness in particular contexts. [...] The same degree of context-dependence applies to more extended paradigmatic meaning structures such as word-field"[16].

---

15 E. Tov, "Three Dimensions of Words in the Septuagint", in *The Greek and Hebrew Bible. Collected Essays on the Septuagint* (Vetus Testamentum Supl. 72; Leiden/Boston/Köln: Brill, 1999), 85–94, in particular 94.
16 Cruse, *op.cit.*, 2000, 50.

At the conclusion of this analysis, it will be helpful to provide the following summary of our findings. The research patterned an inventory of sense-nodules associated with the word; each of them is described according to its syntagmatic properties (its *philonyms*), its semantic relations (its *synonyms, holo/meronyms,* and so on), its Masoretic Text's equivalent/s, its distribution within the corpus. This system of registration strives to include a considerable number of relevant parameter in order to provide a good basis for discussion concerning the question of variety and constancy in vocabulary use in the Septuagint, as it has been set by Barr on several occasions. Limiting ourselves for the moment to the case of κρίσις, the next step that has to be done in this direction is to determine how far the use here depicted is in general use outside the Septuagint.

κρίσις

– ACTION (VERBALLY PRESENTED) 'dispute'; 'case'

Philonyms:
ἀφαιρεῖν 'to take away' (Isa 40:27)
κρίνειν 'to judge' (Gen 19:9, Isa 11:4, 49:25)
προσάγειν 'to bring (to notice)' (Num 27:5)
προσέχειν 'to pay attention' (Isa 1:23)

Synonym:
ῥῆμα 'case'

MT equivalents: *rîḇ* ; *mišpāṭ*

– ACTION (SPEECH ACT) 'sentence'; 'response'

Philonyms:
ἀναγγέλλειν 'to make public announcement' (Deut 17:9, Isa 41:1)
διαλέγεσθαι 'to speak about' (Isa 63:1)
ἐπερωτᾶν 'to consult' (Num 27:21)
σωτήριος n. gen. 'acquittal' (Isa 63 :1)

Hyperonym: λόγος 'message'
Meronym: ῥήματα 'words'.

MT equivalent: *mišpāṭ*

- SPEECH ACT (CONTENT) 'precept'

Philonyms:
δεικνύναι 'to show by way of instruction' (Deut 4:5)
διδάσκειν 'to teach' (Deut 4:14)
ποιεῖν 'to practice' (Lev 25:18, Deut 4:5, 11:32, 30:10)
φυλάσσειν 'to comply with' (Deut 11:1, 30:10, 30:16)
κύριος g. '(of the) Lord (YHWH)' (Lev 25:18, Deut 4:5, 4:14, 11:1; 11:32, 30:10, 30:16)

Co-meronyms: ἐντολή pl. 'commandment', κρίμα pl. 'injunction to be observed ',
δικαίωμα pl. 'ordinance', πρόσταγμα pl. 'precept'; holonyms: νόμος 'law',
διαθήκη 'covenant'

MT equivalent: *mišpāṭ*

- PROCESS 'judgement'

Philonyms:
ἐκζητεῖν 'to ask for' (Exod 18:15)
ἐκκλίνειν 'to pervert' (Exod 23:2, Deut 16:19, 24:17, 27:19, Isa 10:2)
ἀληθινός 'truthful' (Isa 59:4)
δίκαιος 'righteous' (Deut 16:18, Isa 58:2)

Co-hyponym: βουλή 'decision'

MT equivalent: *mišpāṭ*

- ACTION 'requital', 'right punishment'

Philonyms:
ἀναμένειν 'to anticipate eagerly the coming of' (Isa 59:11)
ἀνταποδιδόναι 'to mete out as recompense' (Isa 35:4)
ποιεῖν 'to do justice' (Gen 18:25, Deut 10:18, Isa 1:24)
μέγας 'great' (Exod 6:6)

Quasi-synonym: ἐκδίκησις 'vengeance' or ἐκδικεῖν 'to avenge'

MT equivalents: *šep̄eṭ, nqm* Niphʿal, *nāqām*

– ABSTRACT ENTITY 'right'; 'righteousness'; 'justice'

Philonyms:
ἀφαιρεῖν 'to take away' (Isa 40:27)
δεικνύναι 'to show by way of instruction' (Isa 40:14)
ἐγκαταλείπειν 'to disregard' (Isa 58:2)
ἐκζητεῖν 'to engage oneself in' (Isa 1:17)
ἐκφερέιν 'to spread' (Isa 42:3)
οἶδα 'to have learnt' (Isa 51:7)
ποιεῖν 'to put into effect' (Gen 18:19)
τιθέναι 'to establish' (Isa 42:4)
φυλάσσειν 'to keep' (Isa 56:1)

Co-hyponyms: ἀλήθεια 'faithfulness'; ἀγαθός n. s. 'what is morally good'; quasi-synonym: δικαιοσύνη 'justice'; νόμος 'law'

MT equivalents: *mišpāṭ, ṣedeq.*

Part IV: **Projects**

Abraham Tal
The Historical Dictionary of the Hebrew Language: a Presentation

Within the limits of a lecture delivered at a multi-participants conference, I shall try to make a short sketch of the nature of the Historical Dictionary of the Hebrew Language, with special reference to the problem of Biblical Hebrew within its wingspan. I underline the word "problem", because this dictionary is – for the time being – a non-biblical lexicon.

The founding fathers, who conceived the dictionary back in the fifties of the previous century, adopted the idea put forward in the thirties of the same century by the poet Hayyim Nahman Bialik to compile an "academic" dictionary of the Hebrew language based upon a study of its entire vocabulary, i. e. a work that will encompass all strata of Hebrew during its first three thousands years of existence[1]. Though on different fundaments, Bialik echoed a desideratum expressed Leopold Zunz who made manifest his frustration vis-à-vis the lack of such a dictionary[2]. The idea was subject of deliberation at several occasions in the sessions of the ועד הלשון העברית, "Committee for the Hebrew Language", an institution founded at the dawn of the 20th century, whose purpose was to adapt Hebrew to the needs of modern life, and therefore visualized the dictionary as an instrument of language programming. David Yellin, the president of the "Committee" (till 1945), even attempted to promote the idea (followed later by Naftali Herz Tur-Sinai in 1952), albeit without significant progress.

It was only in the year 1954, soon after the foundation of the "Academy of the Hebrew Language", that a project concerning the dictionary was initiated. An editorial board was constituted with the explicit task to compile "a historical dictionary of the Hebrew language". After debates that lasted five years the Academy appointed Zeev Ben-Hayyim to the task of compiling a comprehensive dictionary, which would encompass the whole history of Hebrew. Ben-Hayyim accepted the assignment a year later, after he examined the work of several European institutions, and presented in the year 1959 to the plenary of the Academy

---

1 Published in his דברים שבעל פה, vol. I, 1935, pp. 108–109. According to his vision the purpose of the "academic" dictionary is to form the basis of the renewal of ancient Hebrew as a spoken language in a modern society.
2 In his "Wünsche für ein Wörterbuch der hebräischen Sprache", *ZDMG* 10 (1856), 501–512.

his plan, which was adopted and continues to constitute the blue print of the dictionary to this very day[3].

To be sure, lexicographical compositions in Judaism were produced ever since the list of "difficult" words in the Talmud was composed by Zemah Ben Palṭoi, head of the academy of Pumbedita in Babylon in the 10th century. The list is no longer extant, and all we know about it comes from several quotations made by R. Nathan Ben Yechiel mi-Romi of the 11th century in his well-known Aruk (ערוך). The latter is indeed a full dictionary, but Hebrew wasn't its object as such. Concerned with the understanding of the Talmud, the work of R. Nathan was mostly dedicated to "foreign" words: Aramaic, Greek, Latin, Persian, etc[4].

The first instrument dealing with Hebrew proper is a list of *hapax legomena*, named "Interpretation of isolated seventy words" (כתאב אלסבעין לפט'ה), composed by the celebrated R. Saʿadya Gaon in the 10th century (actually the list comprises 86 words). Another work of the same author is his famous Sefer ha-Egron (ספר האגרון). This too, is not exactly a dictionary according to our notions of dictionaries, but rather an instrument made for poets, a kind of "book of rhymes", the words being arranged in alphabetical order of their first and last letters. In any case, its contribution to the knowledge of normative Hebrew was remarkable and so was it with regard to the diffusion of the notion of the Hebrew root[5]. The first step towards the compilation of a Hebrew dictionary may be considered the work of the 10th century R. Yehuda Ḥayyuǧ, who adopted the theory of the triliteral root, studied the structure of "defective" roots and arranged them in alphabetical order[6]. Obviously, his aim was rather to prove the viability of the principle of the root in Biblical Hebrew.

The corollary of this activity is the famous work of R. Yona Ibn Ǧanaḥ "The book of roots" (ספר השורשים, 11th century)[7]. This book, although it discusses

---

3 Proceedings of the Academy of the Hebrew Language, 6 (1959), 87.

4 See Alexander Kohut's introduction to his edition of the ערוך: *Aruch Completum sive Lexicon vocabula et res, quae in Libris Targumicis, Talmudicis et Midraschicis continentur*, by Nathan Ben Yechiel (vol. I; repr. New York: Pardes, 1955), xiii-xix.

5 Nevertheless, Saʿadya's root was not yet the triliteral root of the later grammarians. This issue was still a matter of dispute, and many combats took place at the time among contemporary grammarians, such as Dunash ben Labraṭ (Saʿadya's disciple) and his rival, Menaḥem ben Saruq. They too had not recognized the principle of triliterality of the Hebrew root.

6 Originally written in Arabic and translated into Hebrew by R. Moses Giqaṭilla: שלשה ספרי דקדוק, (Three grammatical treatises), the first two of which deal with the Hebrew roots. The work was published by John W. Nutt, *Two Treatises on Words Containing Feeble and Double Letters* (London and Berlin: Asher, 1870).

7 The Arabic original was edited by Adolf Neubauer, The Book of Hebrew Roots by Abu'l-Walid Marwan ibn Janah, called Rabbi Jonah (Oxford: Clarendon Press, 1875). Later, W. Bacher edited

every biblical root, cannot be considered a dictionary in the modern sense of the word, since its purpose is not a description of the words position in the lexical system of the language, nor does it define the meaning of the words methodically. Ibn Ğanaḥ used the lexical definition just as a means of grammatical argumentation, in order to prove either the common origin of apparently different words or their affiliation to different roots. However, the impact of his book was remarkable, and we may say that the methodically treated vocabulary of Hebrew started with Ibn Ğanaḥ, who opened the way to the compilations of modern dictionaries. Many medieval scholars left their enlightening traces on this way, but it was undoubtedly the work of R. David Qimḥi (12th to 13th centuries), named Sefer ha-Shorashim as well[8], that become the source of knowledge for the many non-Jewish scholars who, from the days of the Renaissance on, dealt with Hebrew lexicography. Qimḥi's work was a real dictionary. He had nothing to prove anymore, since the idea of the triliteral Hebrew root was already widely accepted. His purpose was to provide scholars with a dictionary whose main aim is meaning. Later, his work became a model for lexicographers and even the great Thesaurus of Wilhelm Gesenius wasn't clear of its influence.

A multitude of Hebrew dictionaries were produced during the last centuries. All of them, however varied with regard to the area covered, shared one characteristic: they were all specialized works devoted to a certain category of literature, whether Bible or Talmud, etc., none of them has ever attempted to cluster the entire Hebrew vocabulary, from the beginning of the existence of Hebrew literature to the time of its compilation. In fact, none of them ever aimed at describing the history of the Hebrew vocabulary. Their aim was rather to render the old books intelligible, although historical-comparative references were given, as far as their area of interest is concerned. Such is Gesenius' revolutionary *Hebräisches und Chaldäisches Handwörterbuch über das Alte Testament* (Leipzig, 1810) and all its followers. Moreover, Jacob Levy's excellent *Wörterbuch über die Talmudim und Midraschim* (1876 – 89), and Marcus Jastrow's popular *Dictionary of the Targumim, the Talmud Babli and Yerushalmi, and the Midrashic Literature* (1886 and 1903) brought Hebrew and Aramaic under the same roof, as the corpora of interest dictated. Like the works of their numerous foregoers[9], they had a philological-exegetical goal rather than a historical-linguistic one[10].

---

the Hebrew translation of R. Judah ibn Tibbon: Sepher Haschoraschim, Würzelwörterbuch der hebräischen Sprache, etc. (Berlin: M'kize Nirdamim, 1896).

8 J.H.R. Biesenthal, Sefer ha-shorasim le-rabi David ben Yosef Kimhi ha-Sefaradi = Rabbi Davidis Kimchi Radicum liber sive Hebraeum bibliorum lexicon, etc. (Berlin: G. Bethge, 1847).

9 A complete to date list is given in the 1906 English version of Jewish Encyclopedia, see http://www.jewishencyclopedia.com/articles/5180-dictionaries-hebrew.

A complete dictionary, by means of which one can observe written Hebrew over the centuries, was not undertaken before the dawn of the 20th century, when the challenge was taken up by Eliezer Ben-Yehuda, the pioneer of Modern Hebrew. His 16-volume work, inspired by the concept of the unity and historical continuity of Hebrew across the ages, is the first of its genre. But, one has to keep in mind the author's purpose: to restore the status of Hebrew as the spoken language of the Jewish people in its own territory. Having been used for ages mainly for liturgy and learning, Hebrew was no longer an instrument for conversation. Consequently, Ben-Yehuda put himself at work elaborating a modern instrument of verbal and written communication, using material dormant for millennia. He invented or, shall I say re-invented, hundreds of words by which he hoped to adapt an ancient language to modern needs, for, according to his views, the new has to be based on the old. This was actually the role of his dictionary: to display this continuity. Consequently, from the pure linguistic point of view, the dictionary suffers from an inherent flaw: *it represents an extra-linguistic idea.*

The editorial board was immediately faced with the question of the structure of the planned dictionary. They considered two distinct ways of compilation. The first one envisages a comprehensive vocabulary embracing all epochs of the Hebrew history, in similarity with the Oxford English Dictionary, i.e. a lexicon of all Hebrew words from the biblical times up to these days. The other way is to edit a continuous series of dictionaries of shorter periods, the so-called "period dictionaries"[11], which, put together, would provide the image of the whole extent of the lexicon. An eloquent endeavor in this direction is the "Trésor de la Langue Française", whose extent is the language of French during the 19th and the 20th centuries. The Editorial board opted for the first way of compilation; say a comprehensive dictionary, which will encompass the whole history of Hebrew, taking into account the evolution of meaning, use and combinatory position of every lexeme along the ages.

However, for practical purposes during the preliminary stages of work, a division has been made, dictated by the extent of knowledge of each period of the

---

10 A remarkable turning from this lexicological stream was made by Elias Levitas. In the introduction to his Sefer ha-Tishbi he criticized the tendency of his predecessors, mainly of the author of the Aruk, Nathan ben Yehiel of Rome, to treat only Talmudic and Midrashic words that need clarification: המלות החמורות הנמצאות בתלמוד ובמדרשים... רק לבאר איזה דין... ולא לבאר המלה ההיא, "the difficult words found in the Talmud and Midrashim... just in order to explain a certain rule..., not to explain the word for its own sake" (Eliyahu Baḥur, *Opusculum recens Hebraicum Eliia Levita Germano... cui titulum fecit Tishbi...* etc. (Isnae in Algauia, 1541), introduction, unnumbered page.
11 E.g., A. Craigie, "The Value of the Period Dictionaries", *Transactions of the Philological Society*, 36 (1937), 53–62.

language. In order to avoid vicious circles, a non-linguistic principle of division has been adopted, i.e., a division based on chronological-literary principles as follows:

- Division a: the pre biblical period.
- Division b: the biblical period.
- Division c: from the 2nd century B.C. (the close of the biblical period) to the beginning of the C.E. (the Dead Sea literature).
- Division d: from the 1st century C.E. to the 3rd century (Hebrew replaced by Aramaic as a spoken language).
- Division e: from the 3rd to the 6th centuries (the Talmud and the old Midrash).
- Division f: from the 6th to the 8th centuries (the liturgy and the late Midrash).
- Division g: from the 8th to the 11th centuries (the Ge'onic, Karaite and grammatical-masoretic literature).
- Division h: from the 11th century (medieval and rabbinic literature) to the 18th century (the Enlightenment).
- Division i: from the 18th to the 20th centuries.

Another and even more important factor is what is called "the state of the art". It is unnecessary to insist on how far knowledge of the various branches of Hebrew literature has progressed and advanced since Ben-Yehuda, in both quantity and quality. Many ancient pieces, previously unknown, or extant only in fragmentary state are now available. Let me remind two major discoveries of the 20th century:

1) The Cairo Geniza that revealed an abundance of literary, halakhic, legal, historic, etc. documents hidden for centuries. For example a poet like יניי, known for centuries only from quotations made during the middle ages and just from one liturgical poem, extant in a prayer book. More than 800 poems of his authorship have been discovered in the Geniza and published recently. A multitude of Hebrew words, concealed for centuries, come to surface. From these compositions we got acquainted with unknown Hebrew words like עלק, in the sense of 'to enflame', עקב, meaning 'to give a name', פרד, 'to run', etc.

2) The Dead Sea scrolls have revolutionized our knowledge of the Hebrew language as it was practiced at the beginning of our era. Dozens of manuscripts and thousands of fragments have presented unknown words like שדך, 'peace of mind'; בסרון, 'disdain'; סרך, 'order', etc.

On the other hand, the Geniza has revealed many known compositions in a state of transmission much more reliable, i.e., closer to the original, than their copies, handed down by generations of copyists, as was the case with most halakhic and midrashic compositions. As if the Geniza has disclosed a forgotten face of Hebrew literature, prior to the late process of distortion caused by endless stages of transmission. Guttenberg's invention of printing, with all its blessings, had a very unwanted impact over the texts in the sense that the printers contributed heavily to the deterioration of the texts, as far as language is concerned in the first place. Modern Philology has shown how manuscripts antecedent of printed editions are far more reliable (see below).

Given that the divisions a and b regard the pre-biblical and the biblical period, which are best lexicographically covered by various dictionaries authored by the best scholars, Ben-Hayyim took a very brave decision: to *temporarily* exclude the Bible from the projected dictionary. He understood that lexicographic processing of Biblical Hebrew is not the most urgent task, given that over the centuries the most qualified brainpower in the field has consecrated its intellectual capabilities in order to elucidate the Biblical Hebrew lexicon. Learned scholars yielded a great deal of invaluable dictionaries, the product of which will be synthesized and included in the Historical Dictionary at a later stage. Moreover, the Hebrew Bible was transmitted during the ages at a satisfactory level of accuracy, fairly represented by the consecutive editions of *Biblia Hebraica*, even by the Daniel Bomberg printed editions מקראות גדולות (1516 – 7; 1524 – 6).

Ben-Hayyim recognized that, for the present, the most urgent endeavor is the lexicon of the language which developed *after* the biblical period, since the lexicographic treatment of this Hebrew suffers from many flaws and displays a distorted image of the post-biblical *Wortschatz*. Moreover, the transmission of the texts is in a disastrous state of preservation, ever since printed editions were initiated[12].

Accordingly, the upper chronological limit was established at the 2nd century B.C.E., with Ben-Sira as its representative[13]. Biblical books allegedly belonging to the same period, such as Daniel and Ecclesiastes, are excluded, since they belong to the stratum of biblical literature, and, as such they are treated in all the existing biblical Dictionaries. Obviously, the delimitation in question is *not* entirely chronological.

Ben-Hayyim divided the work into three main sections, according to the stages of development of Hebrew and to the linguistic environment in which Hebrew acted (as he envisaged them in his lecture delivered at the 8th congress for

---

[12] Many printers are business people, therefore money minded. They endeavor to provide the public with accessible books, which are easy to digest and easy to sale. They hire a learned person who collects manuscripts, studies them, and collates one manuscript destined to satisfy the avidity of contemporary bibliophiles (or should I say bibliomaniacs), who pay for the delight to have them in their libraries. Actually, even authentic researchers and *hommes de lettres* fell into the trap of these standardized printed editions and yield lexicons and grammars based on untrustworthy material. See Kutscher's article mentioned below in note 15.

13 The Academy published a sample edition: *The Book of Ben Sira, Text, Concordances and Analysis of the Vocabulary* (Jerusalem, 1973) [in Hebrew].

Jewish Studies in Jerusalem 1981)[14]. Each section was allocated to a team of scholars specialized in its specific domain.

Section one encompasses the period from the second century B.C.E. up to the 11th century C.E., when Hebrew functioned, whether being spoken or written with another Semitic language in the background: Aramaic (and later Arabic). Hebrew developed in a linguistically cognate environment. This section is dedicated to what is usually called Rabbinic Hebrew: the Mishna, the midrashic compositions, the Talmud and the early Liturgy, on the one hand, and the compositions of the Hellenistic, Roman and Byzantine periods, such as the Qumran material, etc.

Section two covers the period between the 12th and the 18th centuries, regarding two major geographic areas, only one of which is Arabic-speaking, the other having European languages as background.

Section three, which starts with the Enlightenment, is marked by an intense activity in the sphere of belles-lettres, secular scholarship etc., which changed both sources of inspiration and linguistic habits. Most compositions were written by people who spoke Italian, Ladino, German, Russian, and mainly Yiddish. All this influenced visibly the character of Hebrew. Obviously, Hebrew functioned as a literary language on a non-Semitic background.

The work was pursued in several stages.

The first stage was to elaborate a detailed catalogue of all Hebrew written works, of whatever literary genre. In the first section, this meant generating a list of every composition, no matter its state of transmission, from the 2nd century C. E. up to the 11th century. The list constituted the foundations on which an index was based, which contains a file for every piece. The data collected in these files concerns the time of composition, state of transmission manuscript or publication (whether critical or diplomatic). The files are arranged in chronological order, forming a sort of abridged history of Hebrew literature. As far as the second and third sections are concerned, the catalogue has no aspirations to comprehensiveness. Given the enormous quantity of compositions produced since the 11th century, a list of selected pieces is being worked out.

The second stage is the textual stage. For the lexicographic treatment of the ancient texts manuscripts have been preferred to the printed editions produced during the previous centuries. Whenever a critical edition of a text exists, it is

---

14 Reprinted in his collected papers *The Struggle for a Language* (Jerusalem: The Academy of the Hebrew Language, 1992), 1–22 [in Hebrew].

compared with the manuscript on which it is based. This implies major philological as well as lexicographical work, since very often linguistic considerations
prompt philological decisions, and vice-versa. The treatment consists of comput-
erizing every text, so that a grammatical analysis could classify every word according to its root on the one hand, and according to its semantic status on
the other hand.

So far matters look familiar. After all, this is what such kind of lexicography
deals with: elaborating lists of compositions to be included, registering their lexemes, parsing their words, and composing the entries according to the principles
established either at the beginning or in the course of the work.

Less familiar, however, is the peculiar state of the texts that constitute the
backbone of the dictionary. I shall try to present two factors that affect the character of the compositions of the first section, especially those which belong to
the Roman and Byzantine period.

One factor is inherent to the linguistic environment of the Land of Israel in
the first centuries of the Christian era: the co-existence of Hebrew and Aramaic.
This factor was determinative in the formation process of the Talmud and the
Midrash, which were molded as a mixture of Hebrew and Aramaic. Since our
purpose is not a glossary of given texts, but a dictionary of a language as wit-
nessed by some texts, it was essential to eliminate the material that does not belong to the domain of our concern. There is no great difficulty in identifying entire Aramaic phrases and even single words given their specific features, which
may be determined without any doubt. However, one has to keep in mind that
these are two sister-languages with a great deal of common words in their vocabulary and only their specific grammatical form can reveal their origin.
Thus, the Hebrew הצלם, 'the image', is easily distinguishable from its Aramaic
correspondent צלמא. But, when the word is not articulated and unvocalized,
how can one distinguish between the Hebrew צֶלֶם and the Aramaic צְלֵם? Most
texts are unvocalized, and this presents a major difficulty.

Moreover, the co-existence of the two languages in the same territory undoubtedly led to reciprocal influence, manifested mainly in their vocabulary.
Many loanwords and even more calques must have been literally invading
each other. How can one isolate interpolated Aramaic words from real loanwords
that have been incorporated into Hebrew, becoming a part of its vocabulary? This
is important, for only the last category is to be included into the database of the
dictionary. The rules of inclusion/exclusion formed in the course of time a rather
voluminous manual, to be constantly consulted.

The second factor is the state of accuracy of ancient compositions such as
the Mishna, the Talmud, etc., which have reached us by a long process of transmission during which they deteriorated greatly. Many scribes, whether ignorant

or "over-learned," contributed to the degradation of their text substituting genuine Mishnaic forms and words for their biblical correspondent[15].

A good illustration is the printed editions of the Jerusalem Talmud, whose language, a western Aramaic dialect, quite often strangely resembles that of the eastern Aramaic Babylonian Talmud. This is the result of a metamorphosis. Most of the modern printed editions are photomechanical reproductions of the Vilna edition (1926), which is a copy of the Zhitomir print (1860 – 67). This is in turn a copy of the Cracow edition (1610), which is a reproduction of the first printed edition, made by Daniel Bomberg in Venice in 1523. The latter is apparently a copy of the unique manuscript comprising the full text: the famous Leiden manuscript Or. 4720 (Scalliger 3)[16].

One can follow the stages of the metamorphosis. The Babylonian Talmud being the major factor in Jewish education for centuries[17], the rabbis were experts in its form and language. They, sometimes unconsciously, sometimes deliberately, "corrected" the Jerusalem Talmud and altered its language and even its contents. The Leiden manuscript is therefore the best source for this composition, especially when its evidence is corroborated with the fragments from the Cairo Geniza[18].

The problem is therefore to find the best sources for a given composition. Indeed, the dictionary has greatly benefited from the collective effort of many generations of scholars, who from the days of "Wissenschaft des Judentums" on, endeavored to reveal forgotten manuscripts and evaluate them by producing critical and annotated editions.

On the other hand, one may ask the question whether a historical dictionary should include only "original" forms, stemming from "kosher" manuscripts, and completely disregard corrupted forms, even though they become popular by intensive and lasting use, part and parcel of the subsequent literature. This is the case, for example with the verb התאכל (to be consumed), which in late editions changed to התעכל, through an over-learned emendation. Learned people, who were aware of the deformations caused by the loss of the gutturals, produced

---

15 A survey of the deteriorated state of the printed editions of these texts is given by Y.E. Kutscher in his לשון חז"ל in *Henoch Yalon Jubilee Volume*, eds. Saul Lieberman & alii (Jerusalem: Kiryat Sepher, 1963), 246 – 280 [in Hebrew].

16 Copied in Rome, in the year 1289.

17 The process that enthroned the Babylonian Talmud is discussed in Louis Ginsberg, *A Commentary on the Palestinian Talmud*, vol. I, (New York: The Jewish Theological Seminary of America, 1941), xli-xlvi.

18 Although many Babylonian Aramaic forms and words invaded these fragments too, as one may infer from their edition: Louis Ginsberg, *Yerushalmi Fragments from the Genizah*, vol. I, (New York: The Jewish Theological Seminary of America, 1909), *passim*.

this hyper-correction (if indeed it *is* hyper-correction). Should we ignore the form with the Ayin i. e. התעכל, although it penetrated all kinds of literature? An examination of the material leads to interesting considerations.

The root אכל, originally 'to eat', occurs several times in the Bible in the metaphorical sense 'to consume', 'devour', 'kill' dependent on its operating agent. Thus, when it occurs with 'sword' it denotes 'killing': הלנצח תאכל חרב, "shall sword devour forever?" (2 Sam 2:26); וחרבי תאכל בשר, "my sword shall devour flesh" (Deut 32:42); חֶרֶב תְּאֻכְּלוּ "you shall be devoured by sword" (Isa 1:20), etc. This kind of collocations which personifies the sword occurs 13 times in the Bible.

To be sure, Hebrew does have a verb which expresses straightforwardly the notion of slaughter, namely שחט, usually in reference to animals to be eaten or sacrificed: ההולך לשחוט את פסחו, "he who goes to slaughter his Pesach lamb" (Mishna Pesachim III, 7), etc., but also with regard to humans, e.g., וישחט מלך בבל את בני צדקיהו, "The king of Babylon slew the sons of Zedekiah" (Jer 52:10). In any case, the שחיטה, 'slaughtering' is not explicitly performed by an instrument, even though it is implied. The only exception is the case of Abraham who uses a מאכלת, 'knife' (?): ויקח את המאכלת לשחט את בנו, "and he took the knife to slay his son" (Gen 22:10). It is noticeable that the instrument Abraham uses for slaughtering his son, the מאכלת, belongs to the root אכל too!

Likewise, 'fire' prefers the root אכל to express 'burning', e.g., ומראה כבוד יהוה כאש אכלת בראש ההר, "the appearance of the glory of the Lord was like a devouring fire on the top of the mountain" (Exod 24:17); ותצא אש מלפני יהוה ותאכל אותם וימתו, "and fire came forth from the presence of the Lord and devoured them" (Lev 10:2). Obviously, the most popular passage is Exod 3:2: הסנה בער באש והסנה איננו אֻכָּל, "the bush was burning in fire, yet it was not consumed". This association is particularly present when offerings are involved, e. g., ותצא אש מלפני יהוה ותאכל על המזבח את העלה, "and fire came forth from before the Lord and consumed the burnt offering" (Lev 9:24); ותעל אש מן הצור ותאכל את הבשר ואת המצות "and there sprang up fire from the rock and consumed the flesh and the unleavened cakes" (Judg 6:21); ותפל אש יהוה ותאכל את העלה, "fire of the Lord fell, and consumed the burnt offering" (1 Kgs 18:38); אשר תאכל האש את העלה על המזבח, "which the fire has consumed the burnt offering on the altar" (Lev 6:3), etc. The pair occurs in less solemn occasions too, for example Exod 22:5, which is completely secular: כִּי־תֵצֵא אֵשׁ וּמָצְאָה קֹצִים וְנֶאֱכַל גָּדִישׁ אוֹ הַקָּמָה אוֹ הַשָּׂדֶה שַׁלֵּם יְשַׁלֵּם

"When fire breaks out and catches in thorns so that the stacked grain or the standing grain or the field is consumed, he that kindled the fire shall make full restitution for the consumed grain".

There is no need to say that Biblical Hebrew does have a verb which express-es straightforwardly the notion of burning, namely שׂרף, e.g., עריכם שרפות אש, "your cities are burned with fire" (Isa 1:7), etc., 125 times in the Bible.

The root אכל occurs in the same environment in the so-called "Rabbinic He-brew".

Mishna Bava Qamma VI, 4 says: השולח את הבעירה ואכלה עצים, "He who causes a fire to break out, which consumed wood". Mishna Tamid, which deals with the daily offering says in II, 5: וְהָאֵבָרִים וְהַפְּדָרִים שֶׁלֹּא נִתְאַכְּלוּ מִבָּעֶרֶב מַחֲזִירִין אוֹתָם לַמַּעֲרָכָה הִצִּיתוּ שְׁתֵי הַמַּעֲרָכוֹת בָּאֵשׁ: 'The limbs and pieces of fat which had not been con-sumed (נִתְאַכְּלוּ) the preceding evening they put back onto the altar fire, they kin-dled the two altar fires.' Mishna Tamid I, 5 describes the way the priest clears the ashes of the burnt sacrifices from the altar: וּפִינָה אֶת הַגֶּחָלִים הֵילָךְ [וְהֵילָךְ] וְחָתָה מִן הַמְּאוּכָּלוֹת הַפְּנִימִיּוֹת וְיָרַד, "and he cleared away the cinders from one side and the other, scooped up the *innermost ashes*, and came down". By המאוכלות, *innermost ashes*, the Mishna refers to the parts of the sacrificed animal, which the fire con-sumed. The passive participle of the doubled conjugation Pi'el is used to repre-sent an accomplished fact, described in Lev 6:3 as follows: ולבש הכהן מדו בד ומכנסי בד ילבש על בשרו והרים את הדשן אשר תאכל האש את העלה על המזבח ושמו אצל המזבח, "and the priest shall put on his linen garment, and put his linen breeches upon his body, and he shall take up the ashes to which the fire has consumed the burnt offering on the altar, and put them beside the altar". Now, the Mishna relates about the ashes of the animal as המאוכלות, the passive participle of Pi'el which represents the accomplishment of the act requested in Leviticus: 'con-sumed by fire'. This is repeated in the Halakhic Midrash Sifra, sect. צו I, 2. The relation between Leviticus and the tractate Tamid is further treated by the Jeru-salem Talmud in Yoma II, 1, explaining that המאוכלות in the Mishna is related to האשׁ אשר תאכל in Lev 6:3. The consumed parts of the offering, the המאוכלות, are the result of the action which is expressed by the frequent verb נתאכל, as we have seen in Tamid II, 5 הָאֵבָרִים וְהַפְּדָרִים שֶׁלֹּא נִתְאַכְּלוּ מִבָּעֶרֶב, "the limbs and pieces of fat which *had not been consumed* the preceding evening".

There is no doubt that all these sources use the root אכל in order to express consuming by fire. What we encounter here is a biblical metaphor which gener-ated a Halakhic term, extensively used in connection with the rules concerning offerings and sacrifices.

A variant denotation developed in the Mishna is 'to digest'. Tractate Bera-khot VIII, 7 reads: עַד אֵמָתַי הוּא מְבָרֵךְ עַד כְּדֵי שֶׁיִּתְאַכֵּל הַמָּזוֹן שֶׁבְּמֵעָיו, "until when may he recite the grace [ברכת המזון, obligatory blessing after a meal]? Until the food has been digested in his intestines".

The Babylonian Talmud quotes the same Mishnayot, introducing a slight modification. The verb אכל changes into עכל. Whether as a scribal over-learned way of copying or not, the simple fact is that a new root, עכל, appears and reappears in numerous instances all over the Babylonian Talmud, wherever burnt offerings, digestion, etc. are involved, not just eating; e. g. in tractate Zevahim, the Babylonian Talmud 64a reads: ההפנימיות המעוכלות in tractate Yoma, 45a the Babylonian Talmud says איברין ופדרין שלא נתעכלו, "the limbs and the fat which were not consumed [on the altar]"; in Berakhot, 51b the Babylonian Talmud quotes the Mishna: עד כדי שיתעכל המזון שבמעיו, substituting שיתעכל for שֶׁיִּתְאַכֵּל, etc. There is only one instance of Aleph, איברין ופדרין שלא נתאכלו, in the same context in Berakhot 26b. The Aramaic portions of Babylonian Talmud also have אתעכל in the same sense, e. g. הוה מיעכל, "was consumed [by fire]" (Shevu'ot, 17b).

Evidently, one may ask whether this new spelling is a simple corruption or it reflects a tendency to create an artificial differentiation between 'eating' and other ways of 'consuming', whether by burning or by rotting, was at work.

Furthermore, the Babylonian Talmud extended the use of עכל from the domain of burnt offerings to the domain of money allotted for the redemption of the firstborn, which is also a kind of offering (וכל בכור אדם בבניך תפדה, "every first-born of man among your sons you shall redeem" – Exod 13:13). A human firstborn should be redeemed instead of being sacrificed as is the firstling of an animal. When the money destined for redemption is spent for other purposes, the Talmud says: נתעכלו המעות, "the money has been consumed" (tractate Bechorot, 49a).

As mentioned above, the Babylonian Talmud was for centuries the core of Jewish education. There is no wonder that its innovations influenced learned as well as less learned persons, especially scribes, who copied ancient documents for learning. This happened, e. g. to the Tosephta, a collection of apocryphal halakhot, not included in the codex which we know as the Mishna. The Tosephta includes all these halakhot, many of them collected from quotations in the Babylonian Talmud, and therefore bear its imprints. Accordingly, we find עכל in Tosephta tractates Menachot VI, 5; Sanhedrin IX, 8; Kippurin II, 11, etc.

Another composition heavily influenced by the Babylonian Talmud is Avot d'Rabbi Nathan. This is a collection of *dicta*, resembling the tractate Avot in the Mishna, but known from its printed editions as a supplement to Babylonian Talmud. It is dated to the 6th century C.E., but reached us by much later revisions. It would be unsurprising to find there the verb עכל, following Babylonian Talmud orthography. However, it merits our attention, since the verb occurring in this instance reflects the sense "to digest": וכשהיו מרבין לאכול מבשר הקדשים היו שותים את מי השילוח ומתעכל במעיהן כדרך שהמזון מתעכל, "when [the priests] were eating the meat of the offerings, they were drinking water from the Shiloah and [the meat] was digested in their intestines, the way food is digested" (Avot d'Rabbi Nathan 35).

This particular type of consume, namely within the digestive system, generated a very productive verb in Modern Hebrew: עיכל, 'to digest', largely represented in dictionaries. The modern dictionary *Rav-Millim*, for instance, defines it as 'to process and disintegrate food until it is absorbed in blood and body'. The same עיכל is used in Modern Hebrew for 'eaten by rust'[19].

We witness a (scribal?) intervention, which resulted in two differentiated orthographies: אכל for eating food, and עכל for consuming, digesting, even *vernichten*. Obviously, the differentiation in question does not reflect a living language phenomenon, but had an important effect on the living contemporary Hebrew. The digestive system is מערכת העיכול in Modern Hebrew. Moreover, the same verb occurs in a metaphoric sense, expressing an idea that is assimilated in spite of its uncommon character: קשה לעכל את הרעיון, "it is difficult to *digest* the idea" (probably the English use of *digest* in the sense of assimilation of new information was the agent of this use).

The predilection of later scribes for the Ayin, which frequently supplanted an original Aleph, is recognizable in the famous case of the title ארכי דיינין, "the elder among the judges", a function designated by coupling the Greek ἀρχή and the Hebrew/Aramaic דיין. Some manuscripts of Mishna Avot VIII, 1 still preserve this ancient form, ארכי דיינין, which became unintelligible to later generations[20]. They attributed the Greek word to the Hebrew ערך, 'to prepare', 'arrange' which occurs in Job in connection with משפט, 'justice': הנה נא ערכתי משפט, "Behold, I have prepared my case" (Job 13:18) and changed the title into the much more diffused עורכי דיינים. Its prototype seems to be found in the Midrash Genesis Rabba (6th century) sect. 50, which interprets ולוט ישב בשער סדום in Gen 19:1 as relating the high status of Lot among the people of Sodom: אותו יום מינוהו ארכי יודיקי, "that day they appointed him as *archijudex*". Obviously, sitting at the gate was a function reserved for judges (or personalities of high position: 2 Sam 19:9; 1 Kgs 22:10). The same homily is re-told in the later Midrash collection שכל טוב (12th century), only this time ארכי is transformed into ערכי, typical to late sources. Apparently, in the order of events in this metamorphosis the substitution of the Hebrew דיין for the Latin loan יודיקי preceded the replacement of the Greek loanword ארכי by the Hebrew עורך[21].

---

19 This apparently reflects for example the French "mangé de rouille". Cf. "Les portes des maisons s'ouvrent de nouveau faisant crier leur gonds mangés de rouille" (Charles-Ferdinand Ramuz, *La grande peur dans la montagne* (Paris: Grasset, 1926), 37.
20 MS Parma (de Rossi 138). MS Cambr. Add. 470.1 already has ערכי, while in the Kaufmann manuscript (A50), a later hand changed the initial Aleph into Ayin.
21 See E. Y. Kutscher, *Words and their History* (Jerusalem: Kiryath-Sepher, 1961), 89–91 [in Hebrew]. Interestingly enough, the prefix ארכי was maintained as is in Jewish sources when no as-

This transformation is possibly reflected in a very solemn liturgical piece, attributed to the 7th century poet Elazar Haqaliri, לאל עורך דין, which enumerates the qualities of God when He judges the humanity on the Rosh Hashana.

Finally a modern term was born: עורך דין, used in Modern Hebrew for 'lawyer'. Its earliest evidence occurs in an article published in the Neo-Hebrew periodical *Hammeliṣ* of 29.8.1861 which says: שכר לו עורך דין (אדוואקאט) איש נוצרי להצדיקו בריבו, "he hired a Christian advocate to plead for him in the trial". The author put אדוואקאט 'advocate' in parenthesis in order to show to the reader that עורך דין is an uncommon term which needs clarification. Two years later (16.7.1863) the same periodical uses a plural form (whether correct or not): עורך דינים, in parallel with the well-known terms סנגורים, 'defense attorneys' and קטגורים, 'prosecutors'.

Most interesting is the case of the spelling עקילס for Ἀκύλας, the famous translator of the Bible into Greek. This is a Greco-Latin name, recorded several times in the New Testament as such, e. g. Acts 18:2, 18:26, etc. It has an initial Alpha, with a *spiritus lenis*, therefore has nothing to do with the Semitic laryngeal fricative Ayin. According to the database of the Historical Dictionary, out of 36 occurrences, only two are spelled with an initial Aleph, by late Midrashim. The remaining 34 occurrences are spelled exclusively with a Ayin, whether in old or young sources[22].

There is a lesson that may be learned from the above discussion: sometimes disregarding inferior sources may lead to the omission of real lexical units, which although born in sin, acquired a *Sitz im Leben* and are part and parcel of the current vocabulary.

The presence of the biblical vocabulary in Post-Biblical Hebrew is manifest not only in overt cases, which are natural, but also in lexemes, in which its existence is somehow concealed under unorthodox orthographies, made with or without intention.

The case of verb עכל is therefore an illustration of the fact that even a non-biblical dictionary cannot escape biblical lexemes in disguise.

---

sociation with ערך was occasioned by the environment: ארכיסטראטיגוס (< ἀρχιστρατηγός – Genesis Rabba, ch. 50), ארכיליסטיס (< ἀρχιληστής – Genesis Rabba, ch. 58), ארכידיקי (< ἀρχίδικος), etc. (S. Krauss, *Griechische und Lateinische Lehnwörter im Talmud, Midrasch und Targum*, vol. II, (Berlin, 1899), 130 – 31).

22 Numerous similar cases of preference for ה or ע in spelling Greek or Latin word with an initial vowel, e. g., the snake חכינה in the Jerusalem Talmud (Pe'ah 17d, etc.) and its correspondent עכנאי in the Babylonian Talmud (Berachot 19a), both express ἔχιδνα respectively ἔχις (S. Krauss *ibid.*, 250, 415).

Sometimes we find biblical vocables that adopt different meanings in later compositions, though their form is maintained intact. One illustrating example is the word עֲלוּקָה, a *hapax* occurring in Prov 30:15: לעלוקה שתי בנות הב הב. The ancient translations render the word as 'leech': βδέλλα in the Septuagint, עלקא in the Peshitta, *sanguisuga* in the Vulgata, and this is also the meaning of עלוקהto this very day. However, the database of the Historical Dictionary reveals 48 cases in which עלוקה denotes 'hell', e. g., in a prayer by the 5th century poet Yosse b. Yosse: בהבדילו בין מים למים הסיק עלוקה תפתה לבלי חק, "when (God) separated the waters from the waters (Gen 1:6), he kindled the עלוקה, a Tophet (תָּפְתֶּה, Isa 30:33) without limit (Isa 5:14)"[23]. The association of עלוקה with 'hell' is founded on the following verse (Prov 30:16), which starts with the insatiable שאול, rendered as ᾅδης by the Septuagint, and as *infernus* by Jerome. This triggered a homily in the Babylonian Talmud: לעלוקה שתי בנות הב הב מאי הב הב אמר מר עוקבא שתי בנות שצועקות מגיהנום, '... what is meant by הב הב, it is (the voice of) two daughters who cry from Gehenna' (tractate Avoda Zara 17a). Mar 'Uqba plays on the verb הבהב, 'burning'[24], which suggests the unquenched fire of hell: he joins two consecutive imperatives of יהב 'give' in order to produce the quadriliteral root which achieves the homily. Thus, a midrashic word-play, which includes a slight distortion of the text, emanates polysemy.

Ezek 1:14 has a much disputed *hapax:* בָּזָק. It follows ברק, 'lightening' (v. 13), in a rather complex description of the מרכבה, the heavenly 'chariot', in which much 'fire' is involved. The ancient translations rendered the word as 'lightening': ברקא in the Targum, זיקתא in the Peshitta, and *fulgus* in the Vulgata[25], which is apparently the reason of the emendation of בזק to ברק. However, the root exists in the Aramaic of the Jerusalem Talmud (Bava Metsi'a 11a): דבזק as an explanation of the Mishnaic והבריקה, 'blinded by a lightening' (Bava Metsi'a VI, 3)[26]. Liturgical Hebrew made extensive use of the word from the Byzantine period on, sometimes in its biblical environment, which became a recurrent collocation: כמראה הבזק, e. g. Yannay (5th century) says כמראה הבזק in a hymn dedicated to Pentecost, and Haqalir (7th century) uses the same expression in a poem

---

23 A. Mirski, *Yosse ben Yosse Poems* (Jerusalem: Bialik Institute, 1977), 126 [in Hebrew].
24 E.g., היו מהבהבין אותו באור כדי לקיים בו מצוות קלי, "they did parch it in fire, so as to carry out the requirement that it be parched with fire" (Lev. 2:14). See also Z. Ben-Hayyim, עלק, *Leshonenu* 14 (1946), 196–197 [in Hebrew].
25 The Septuagint has no equivalent for verse 14. See recent discussion in *Septuaginta Deutsch, Erläuterungen und Kommentare zum griechischen Alten Testament*, vol. II (Stuttgart: Deutsche Bibelgesellschaft, 2011), 2860.
26 E.g., *Biblia Hebraica* (Kittel), ad loc. But see J. Blau, "Zum Hebräisch der Übersetzer des AT", *VT* 6 (1956), 97–99.

for Rosh Hashana. However, the same Haqalir dismantles the biblical collocation in another poem for Rosh Hashana: טסות כבזק "they glide like a lightening". The plural בזקים that occurs in a poem of Yannay proofs that בזק has now attained the status of an independent lexeme, no longer subordinated to the collocation with כמראה or in other association with Ezek 1:14. Such is the case of 41 records out of 71 in the Academy's database. No wonder that in Modern Hebrew בזק is an autonomous lexeme, normally functioning as a determinative element denoting celerity: מבצע בזק is a swift operation. In במהירות הבזק the second word intensifies the first one, both denoting 'very quickly', etc.

The third stage consists of lemmatization. At this stage the computer generates the lemma, i. e. the main entry under which all words belonging to the family are assembled. The historical dictionary established the root as lemma, given that Hebrew, as well as any Semitic language, lives and respires within the space of the root. This is the very spirit of the language. The root is an abstraction, with no meaning and no lexical status. However, every word is the product of a root, appearing under a distinct grammatical form; whether a conjugation when a verb; or a nominal pattern. All grammatical forms are distinct from each other by a formative, which may be a prefix, a suffix, an infix or a certain distribution of vowels and reduplication of radical consonants. I don't reveal secrets; these are well-known facts. All I am trying to do is to show how this particularity of Hebrew causes difficulties in the process of computerization. The computer, in order to classify a word with its root, has to dissociate all its affixes so that only the root remains. It has to detach the initial מ and the final ת from the word מחברת. Similarly, it has to detach the suffix ‏ים– from חברים, and the infix ו (I call it thus for the sake of simplicity) together with the suffix ת from חוברת, so that all these words are grouped together under the root חב"ר. This is not too difficult to learn for an intelligent, well-educated computer. However, there are many difficulties in teaching a computer to distinguish between a radical letter and a prefix in many cases. Actually, there is no automatic way to discern between ת as the first radical of the word תחום, 'area', the root of which is תח"ם, and the same ת when a prefix in the word תרומה, 'offering', whose root is רו"ם.

Another great difficulty is the great number of homographs, a particularity of written Hebrew. With the system of vocalization, conceived during the early middle ages, we know how to distinguish between words that do not differ from each other in consonants, for instance between the verb סָבַל, 'to suffer' and the noun סֵבֶל, 'suffering' or between two different nouns like בֹּקֶר, 'morning', vs. בָּקָר, 'cattle'. Not to mention the homographic בְּקֹר, 'in chill'.

Given that the morphological structure of Hebrew consists in consonantal roots from which words are formed by means of affixes and infixes, it was necessary to establish a list of such additions to the root in order to enable the computer to define automatically the root of every word:

a) Lexical particles: mono-literal words having their own meaning and function, which never occur alone, but are always prefixed to the following word, e.g. the conjunction ו, the prepositions מ, ל, כ, ב, etc.,

b) The verbal and nominal affixes that determine time: כתבתי, conjugation: נפעל, and respectively gender: חברה, number: חברים, and status: החבר.

c) Pronominal elements that define possession: ביתי or object: הושיעני.

Unfortunately, a perfect classification is impossible in this way, since a great deal of homographs remains, independent on additional letters. Such is e.g. למד which may signify לָמַד, לִמֵּד, or לָמֵד. The computer wasn't able to discern between these different verbal conjugations. Though nowadays progress has been made in teaching the computer to take into consideration the context, still, this has not progressed in the measure of zero-error which is the dictionary's requirement.

Instead, we combined automation with human intelligence. Within the framework of the lemmatization process, a form-bank has been compiled from the very start, on the base of forms already existing in the processed texts (a form being defined as a string of letters between spaces), and the corresponding items listed by the lexicographer. The first text was analysed manually, and yielded the primary form-bank, which was applied to the second text. The computer produced lemmata for some of the second text on the basis of the primary form-bank. For the rest, lemmata were determined manually. These became a supplement to the form-bank, which thus increased in quantity of forms and was applied to the third text, and so on. In a quite short time the computer was able to analyse any text with a very small error margin.

In the year 1988, the editorial board published a concordance of the Tanaitic period (200 B.C. – 300 C.E.), presenting every word in its context. It was published under the form of microfiches, obviously a clumsy way to retrieve data, since apart from its reduced dimensions; nothing differentiates a microfiche from a printed concordance. One always gets a kind of linear information: form, root, limited context, etc.

Lately, works are carried out that aim at putting the entire database at the disposal of the public. At the site of the Academy of the Hebrew Language a retrieval program is being prepared, which will enable the researcher to arrange entries in every conceivable way: alphabetically, chronologically, statistically, etc. The context will be as big as the researcher asks, so that meaning could be better defined. Moreover, lexical combinations could be identified and collocations pinpointed. I refer to those phrases which we are used to call recurrent combinations. They are unidiomatic but enough frequent to form a lexical unity. Sequels of words that always come together without any change in their meaning (unlike idioms). Only a computer can isolate such pairs in order to be listed by the lexicographer. For example, the adjective נאה, 'beautiful'. In Modern Hebrew one can use it in conjunction with a man, a woman, a house, a day, etc., but never with a horse, a window or a car, for which יפה is employed. These preferences are a significant part of the lexicon. I hope that with our retrieval program things will be obvious.

Two and a half years ago, at the "Internationale Fachkonferenz" in Halle, dedicated to the two centuries anniversary of Gesenius' Hebräisch-Deutsch Handwörterbuch, I ventured to express my hopes that the web site of the Historical Dictionary of Hebrew will be ready "by the end of the year". Well, I must realize that these hopes were only partly fulfilled: the site is only partially ready, i. e., it still needs improvements as far as friendly approach is concerned. The database is accessible and the user is provided with the information he looks for, within the limits of the so far existent material.

H. G. M. Williamson
Semantics and Lexicography: A Methodological Conundrum

The purpose of the present chapter is to draw attention to the importance of rigorous research in the semantics of Classical Hebrew for lexicography. I propose to do this by way of an introduction to the Semantics of Ancient Hebrew Database project (SAHD), with which I have been involved over many years and of which I am the secretary. I shall therefore first explain briefly some of the reasons why this project was initiated and describe its working methods, and then reflect a little on its implications for modern lexicography.

Recognizable research on semantics can effectively be traced back as far as the work of the great medieval Jewish scholars, though it must in fact also have been considered from much earlier times, not least by those to whom we owe the ancient versions. And since the Renaissance, as a survey of the major Dictionaries could rapidly demonstrate, it is a question which has become increasingly complex as new sources of evidence and new linguistic methods have come into play.

Not surprisingly, the flood of potentially relevant published material has grown to the point where no individual can hope to master it all, so that there is a danger that valuable work will be lost sight of and, equally serious, that many scholars engaged in commentary writing or other forms of research will find themselves reinventing the wheel. More seriously, though, different methods are favoured by different scholars, and none of the aids which are currently available embraces them all. To give a well-known example, the recently completed Sheffield Dictionary[1] is of great value for those who favour an approach to semantics based on syntagmatics, but those who believe that comparative philology also has a role to play will find little help.

But beyond these well-known concerns, there is so much more to semantics than the writing of dictionaries. The need to study lexemes within their semantic fields is now well established, but less attention is generally given to such mat-

---

1 David J. A. Clines, ed., *The Dictionary of Classical Hebrew*, vols. 1–5 (Sheffield: Sheffield Academic Press, 1993–2001) and vols. 6–8 (Sheffield: Sheffield Phoenix Press, 2007–2011). While the Dictionary is thus now complete, Clines has announced in the Preface to volume 8 that a revision of volume 1 is planned, because it was not uniform with the later volumes, together with a ninth volume containing addenda and corrigenda, and a complete English-Hebrew index.

ters as the meaning of the same lexeme within different social registers, within different regional or dialectal settings, or in diachronic terms. If Ancient Hebrew spans some one thousand years, more or less, it should be expected that there will be considerable variation to be found within it. Furthermore it is important to be candid about the difficulties we face with regard to the semantics of Ancient Hebrew by contrast with many other languages, namely the very limited quantity of data in the case of most lexemes, the textual uncertainties resulting from the manual transmission of the text over many centuries, and the difficulties of knowing even roughly what is the correct date of much of the Biblical literature. These uncertainties should not stop us from doing what we can, but they impose inevitable limitations on the application of some forms of semantic research, such as the full application of the method of componential analysis that is much favoured in our field in Italy, for instance.

The SAHD project

It was concerns such as these which first led Professor J. Hoftijzer of Leiden University to identify the need for a semantics database. In collaboration with some other European colleagues, he secured funding for a three-year project to explore the questions in greater detail and to consider how such a database could best be organized[2]. Many of these early deliberations have been published[3], and on the basis of these consultations detailed guidelines were drawn up and agreed by the executive committee[4]. The procedures adopted may be summarized as follows, though it will be appreciated that this is only a brief outline.

First, since 1995 a number of centres and some individuals have set to work on agreed semantic fields. The level of activity varies according to each centre's ability to secure funding, and the participation of new centres is a regular item on the committee's agenda. Nevertheless, it has to be admitted that progress is generally far slower than had been originally hoped or than remains desirable.

---

2 J. Hoftijzer, "An ESF Network on the Semantics of Classical Hebrew," *ZAH* 5 (1992), 85–86.
3 Many of the papers from the first two workshops were published in *ZAH* 6/1 (1993) and 7/1 (1994), and from the third (together with other material) in Takamitsu Muraoka, ed., *Studies in Ancient Hebrew Semantics*, Abr-Nahrain Sup 4 (Louvain: Peeters, 1995). For brief updates subsequently, see Takamitsu Muraoka, "Ancient Hebrew Semantics Database," *ZAH* 10 (1997), 98, and "Further Progress on the Ancient Hebrew Semantics Database Project," *ZAH* 17–20 (2004–2007), 247–48.
4 The chair of the committee also acts effectively as editor of the project. Professor Hoftijzer was succeeded in this role by Professor Takamitsu Muraoka, and Professor Holger Gzella succeeded Professor Muraoka on the latter's retirement.

Once the lexemes within the chosen semantic field have been formally assigned, material on them is assembled within a uniform format and in seven sections, the first six of which cover each of the approaches to semantics which are generally used, even though few if any scholars use them all at the same time. I should make clear at this point, of course, that Ancient Hebrew is deemed to cover everything, including inscriptions, down to and including the Dead Sea Scrolls.

(1) *Root and comparative material:* this covers both etymological proposals and suggestions based on comparative Semitic philology, as well as supplying the raw comparative data even if the matter is non-controversial. Neither here nor elsewhere are co-workers required to evaluate the strength of any given proposal, though of course if their research throws up relevant considerations that may be included. The main aim is to provide a database which will be of service to other scholars who require information on a given lexeme for whatever purpose. Thus from an agreed corpus of secondary literature (including standard reference works, commentaries, journal runs and monograph series from 1945 onwards) as well as other scattered suggestions that they may pick up, the primary aim is to be comprehensive in the bibliographical collection and description of data. As with other sections, so here the database is divided into A and B parts. Proposals which have been generally discounted for whatever reason are included in the B section, while those which are possible or at least are still on the table are entered under A. I stress, however, that even what seem to us at present to be wild or just plain silly suggestions are all meant to be recorded. Who knows whether future discovery will not lead to a reappraisal of the present consensus? A database should be exactly what it says; it is not a dictionary which gives the lexicographer's best judgment with which someone else may, of course, disagree.

(2) *Formal characteristics:* this section is generally brief and descriptive, but of course morphology can play a part in semantics in certain circumstances. It can be informative for etymology, for instance, while note needs sometimes to be taken of lexemes that occur only in specific or a severely limited number of forms, for reasons that may reward investigation.

(3) *Syntagmatics* is also descriptive, but its importance for semantics can scarcely be overemphasized. While by no means sufficient on its own, the use of a lexeme within each individual context is often a primary determinant of meaning. One has only to think of issues such as which prepositions a verb may govern, or of which actions a noun can serve as subject, to see the point.

(4) *The ancient versions.* This was once a primary means for determining the meaning of words, particularly rare ones, though it has tended to fall from view somewhat in recent times. It so happens that this has been a particular research strength of some of our most productive co-workers, who are able to integrate the kind of listings that one may find in Hatch and Redpath[5] with the more far-reaching discussions of the versions themselves in contemporary research. Given that there is no equivalent for Hatch and Redpath for the other versions, this will provide useful information in its own right, of course, in addition to locating current work within its ancient tradition. And here I should mention that there are cases where co-workers can quickly identify, whether in this section or in others, aspects of the topic which have never been adequately treated in the past, and MRN (= more research needed) is an acceptable abbreviation within the database. It should help future users to identify where there are gaps in our knowledge so that they can concentrate on these rather than redoing what may have been adequately done in the past.

(5) *Lexical/Semantic field.* As already mentioned, one of the strengths of our project is that co-workers work within semantic fields so as to be able to refine the meaning of words in accordance with their synonyms, antonyms and so on. This is one of the most accessibly valuable results of the database work and I shall return to some examples of its importance later. Much valuable work has been done in recent years on this basis, but it has hardly penetrated any of the standard reference works currently available. It is just one more example of the advantage of the database approach.

(6) *Exegesis.* This is a bit of a catch-all, and at the regular meetings of co-workers which we hold where they can discuss methods and problems the question often arises as to what it should cover. Our working definition is broad: an opportunity to bring in from whatever source information which scholars have found to be illuminating as one may cull it from commentaries, monographs, and articles. Nor should one overlook the importance of *realia*, which for want of anywhere better also come in here. Archaeological discoveries and iconography are examples. Needless to say, this is another section where generous use can be made of the A and B categories.

---

5 Edwin Hatch and Henry A. Redpath, *A Concordance to the Septuagint and the Other Greek Versions of the Old Testament (Including the Apocryphal Books)* (3 vols.; Oxford: Clarendon Press, 1897–1906).

The final section is simply entitled "summary". Here co-workers can express their conclusions if they feel able to do so, though of course that is not a requirement. A full bibliography is also attached, as befits the nature of the project.

There can be no doubt that for practical reasons (mainly the difficulty of raising adequate finance to maintain many full-time co-workers) progress has been much slower than was originally anticipated. Despite this there are valuable results to report. Three full volumes of printed entries have appeared, and a fourth is on its way. The first is a collection of entries by S. Bindi (Florence), J. K. Aitken (Cambridge) and A. Salvesen (Oxford), this having been explicitly published as something of a "shop-window" for the project[6]. Two further volumes have also been published, these being in each case a collection of semantically related lexemes as analysed by a single scholar[7].

The project does not expect to publish the majority of its results in hard copy, however, but rather as on-line files accessed via the project's website: http://www.sahd.div.ed.ac.uk/. Entries are currently mounted at each co-worker's home institution with a link from the main project website making them easily accessible. The reason for preferring this form of publication in the long run is obvious: it is in the nature of the project that it will need regular updating, and furthermore new data may call for the revision of previously formulated opinions. Such updating calls for care in processing, of course, because the original authors have the right to retain academic credit for their work. In an on-line format, however, this can be made clear without too much difficulty.

It should be noted *en passant* that of course this is by no means the only current project relating to Ancient Hebrew semantics. Some of the more extensive series, such as the *ThWAT*[8], contain a good deal of relevant information in their entries, those engaged in Bible translation work, at the Bible Society or the Wycliffe Bible Translators, for instance, have a practical interest in the subject and publish some of their results (though usually and inevitably at a briefer

---

6 Takamitsu Muraoka, ed., *Semantics of Ancient Hebrew*, Abr-Nahrain Sup 6 (Louvain: Peeters, 1998).

7 James K. Aitken, *The Semantics of Blessing and Cursing in Ancient Hebrew*, Ancient Near Eastern Studies Sup 23 (Louvain: Peeters, 2007), and John E. Hartley, *The Semantics of Ancient Hebrew Colour Lexemes*, Ancient Near Eastern Studies Sup 33 (Louvain: Peeters, 2010). A further volume, edited by Graham I. Davies, on lexemes relating to deliverance is at an advanced stage of preparation.

8 G. Johannes Botterweck, Helmer Ringgren and Heinz-Josef Fabry, eds., *Theologisches Wörterbuch zum Alten Testament*, 8 vols. (Stuttgart: Kohlhammer, 1970–1995) (ET, *Theological Dictionary of the Old Testament*, 15 vols. [Grand Rapids: Eerdmans, 1974–2006]).

and more accessible level)[9], and individual scholars frequently take a lexeme or semantic field for particular analysis[10]. But attention should be drawn here in particular to another electronic project which is not as widely known as it might be, but which in some respects helpfully complements the SAHD. I refer to the work of many of our Dutch colleagues in Het Oudtestamentisch Werkgezelschap on what is called the כלי *Database: Utensils in the Hebrew Bible*, edited by Johannes C. de Moor in cooperation with Bob Becking and Marjo C. A. Korpel, and available at http://www.otw-site.eu/KLY/kly-intro.php. About 50 lexemes are here presented, and in one or two cases there is overlap with lexemes already studied by SAHD. There is clearly considerable common ground between the two projects, though the כלי project is more limited in the range of lexemes it analyses and is more related specifically to the Biblical world. While it too clearly works to a standard template for entries, it is not identical, so that one may also speak of an element of complementarity.

Most of us involved in SAHD were unaware of the progress of this project until its site went "live" in 2011 and examples were circulated among colleagues. Whatever may be the history behind all this, there is now friendly contact between the two projects and it is anticipated that they will move forward in close co-operation.

Some results: כֶּתֶר, נֵזֶר and עֲטָרָה

Based on some of the conclusions drawn by colleagues working in Oxford, I propose now to explore how the positive results of current semantics research can pose acute problems for lexicographers.

For three years Dr. Alison Salvesen worked for the project on lexemes related to kingship. Some of her database entries are available in hard copy and others

---

9 See, for instance, the *Semantic Dictionary of Biblical Hebrew*, edited for the United Bible Society by Reinier de Blois and available via their website http://www.ubs-translations.org, and the UBS's journal *The Bible Translator*. For some further references, see Gene L. Green, "Lexical Pragmatics and the Lexicon," *Bulletin for Biblical Research* 22 (2012), 315–33.
10 See recently, for example, Francesco Zanella, *The Lexical Field of the Substantives of "Gift" in Ancient Hebrew*, SSN 54 (Leiden: Brill, 2010); Daniel C. Leavins, *Verbs of Leading in the Hebrew Bible* (Piscataway, NJ: Gorgias, 2011); Matthew R. Schlimm, *From Fratricide to Forgiveness: The Language and Ethics of Anger in Genesis*, Siphrut 7 (Winona Lake, IN: Eisenbrauns, 2011); Stephen L. Sheed, *Radical Frame Semantics and Biblical Hebrew: Exploring Lexical Semantics*, BibInt Series 108 (Leiden: Brill, 2011); Stefan C. Reif, "On Some Considerations of the Word Ma'aseh," in *Studies on the Text and Versions of the Hebrew Bible in Honour of Robert Gordon*, ed. Geoffrey Khan and Diana Lipton, VTSup 149 (Leiden: Brill, 2012), 337–51.

electronically. Among the lexemes she researched are three that are generally translated "crown", namely כֶּתֶר, נֵזֶר, and עֲטָרָה[11]. Investigation quickly shows how unsatisfactory this English gloss can be.

In some ways the simplest to deal with is *keter*[12]. It occurs only three times, all in the book of Esther (plus once in a fragment from Qumran that reveals nothing else of help) and is always in the construct state before *malkût*, so that it is clearly used in a royal context[13]. In Est. 1:11 it is worn by Vashti, in 2:17 by Esther, and at 6:8 (where there is in any case some textual uncertainty) by either a man whom the king wishes to honour or his horse. It should thus not be identified with any item used exclusively for the reigning monarch, such as the upright *tiara*, a fabric cap depicted frequently in association with many figures with the top flopped forward, but upright only in connection with the king.

Etymology is uncertain—Salvesen has no less than six suggestions in the B category[14]! Her own preference is to link it with the verbal root *ktr* "to surround", which obviously suits some sort of headdress well. Perhaps more helpful, however, is the observation that the word must be related in some way with Greek κίταρις/κίδαρις, which seems to derive from Semitic (note Aramaic *kitra'*). From this we may learn more about the form of the item in that it is applied in classical sources to some kind of headband worn around (not identified with) the crown or *tiara*. It could be worn by, but was not restricted exclusively to, the Achaemenid king. Since the word is found only in Esther, as already mentioned, this seems very suitable. Thus a *keter* is best defined as a headband or fabric fillet which could be worn alone or around a crown or *tiara*. It could be distinguished in some way, perhaps by colour, dye, or decoration, in cases where it was distinctly royal, as the Esther occurrences make clear by the addition of *malkût*, and it could be worn by a king but not exclusively so.

In the light of Salvesen's work it is not clear how this might best be rendered in English. "Headband" sounds too common; "turban" would be better, though a *keter* would not have resembled it in all aspects by any means; "crown" is clearly misleading; "tiara" and "diadem" both have some historical claims to carrying

---

11 See Muraoka, ed., *Semantics*, 67–73, 89–100, and 106–13; also Alison G. Salvesen, "The Trappings of Royalty in Ancient Hebrew," in *King and Messiah in Ancient Israel: Papers from the Oxford Old Testament Seminar*, ed. John Day, JSOTSup 270 (Sheffield: Sheffield Academic Press, 1998), 119–141 (121–30).

12 See also Alison G. Salvesen, "כֶּתֶר (Esther 1:11; 2:17; 6:8): Something to do with a Camel?" *JSS* 44 (1999), 35–46.

13 There is a marked contrast in this with the regular use in post-Biblical Hebrew for "crownlets" that decorate the tops of some letter shapes.

14 It should be noted in particular that no satisfactory Old Persian derivation has been found.

this sense[15]; "tiara" is historically best but nowadays it is generally considered to be something more solid, so that to use it without explanation would be misleading; "diadem" is therefore perhaps the closest, though even that is far from precise; commentary rather than translation therefore seems to be required.

Moving on to *nezer* we may note that it is used in two related but distinct ways, as some type of headdress worn by the king or the high priest and in relation to the consecrated hair of the Nazirites. The extent to which these two are related either etymologically or semantically is fiercely disputed, but we do not, perhaps, need to enter into that debate here (Salvesen offers a very full summary of the discussion); I shall focus only on the first of the two senses.

It is possible that the item in question developed over time, as we shall see, so that it becomes difficult to know how far the implications about form in one passage may be applied to others. In the case of the High Priest's *nezer*, it is said in Exod 39:30–31 to have been made of gold, to have an engraving on it ("Holy to the Lord") and to have been fastened to the turban (מצנפת) with a blue cord (see too Exod 28:36–38, though the word *nezer* itself does not occur there); Exod 39:6 agrees with this location, the turban being on the head and the holy *nezer* on the turban; so too Lev 8:9. The word seems to be used in closest association, if not apposition, with ציץ, from which one may deduce either that it was flower-shaped or that it sparkled; the latter is attractive in view of the fact that the *nezer* will gleam (יציץ) (not "blossom") in Ps 132:18[16]. Opinion is thus divided as to whether it was rosette-shaped or whether, as several ancient sources suggest, it was more like a gold plate. Either way, it was clearly of modest size and was fastened to a more substantial head-garment.

This at once makes some sort of sense of the first of the very few applications to royalty, for in 2 Sam 1:10 we read that an Amalekite brought Saul's *nezer* that was on his head to David after Saul had been killed in battle. Clearly this will not have been a crown in any conventional sense, therefore, but if it could be worn in battle it must have been slight enough not to encumber a warrior.

---

15 The concise *OED* gives for "diadem" (*inter alia*): "1 a crown or headband worn as a sign of sovereignty. 2 a wreath of leaves or flowers worn round the head", and for "tiara": "1 a jewelled ornamental band worn on the front of a woman's hair. 2 ... 3 *hist.* a turban worn by ancient Persian kings".

16 This may also be the implication of the simile at Zech 9:16, which speaks of "the (gem)stones of the *nezer* מתנוססות on his land"; most commentators take the verb as "gleaming" or the like, but it is not entirely certain; cf. Wilhelm Rudolph, *Haggai—Sacharja 1–8—Sacharja 9–14—Maleachi*, KAT 13/4 (Gütersloh: Gerd Mohn, 1976), 185, and Carol L. and Eric M. Meyers, *Zechariah 9–14: A New Translation with Introduction and Commentary*, AB 25C (New York: Doubleday, 1993), 158–59.

At 2 Kgs 11:12 (2 Chron. 23:11) the *nezer* was "put on" the young Joash by Je-hoiada the priest. This says nothing about its form, but it implies in the context that it was thought to symbolize Joash's royal legitimacy since as a second object of the same verb we have "the testimony" (ויתן עליו את־הנזר ואת־העדות). A similar deduction might be made from Ps 89:40 (parallel with ברית) and 132:18 (contrast-ing with the disgrace of the king's enemies). This sense of "insignia" may be re-lated to the evidence Salvesen collects from the word's lexical field that it is gen-erally used in contexts where cultic or ritual concerns are prominent. In priestly usage this would not be surprising, and something of that sense may also have been present for royal usage.

If Zech 9:16 is rightly understood to mean that by that time the *nezer* could have gemstones embedded in it, it is clear that the form had become more elab-orate in its ornamentation. That is typical for items of insignia, of course, as many modern examples could attest. It does not, however, indicate that we should render "crown", as most modern translations seem to do, for that gives a quite misleading impression. Salvesen contents herself in her conclusion with a descriptive phrase: "a visible sign that the wearer had been consecrated to God; a sign on the head marking out the bearer as being in a special relation-ship to the Deity" (p. 98), while her final usage is "diadem". I am not aware of any sensible English equivalent; "metal fillet" is close, except that a fillet usually surrounds the head completely, unlike a *nezer*. Might one coin the term "head-plaque"?

Finally, we come to the word *ʿaṭārâ*, which is the commonest of our three lex-emes. At first it looks as though it might approach closer to our English gloss "crown", for it can be made of gold (2 Sam 12:30; 1 Chr 20:2; Ps 21:4; Esth 8:15) or of silver and gold (Zech 6:11) and have jewels (again 2 Sam 12:30; 1 Chr 20:2). It can be worn on the head, as all the same references indicate (and see too Ezek 16:12; Job 19:9; Lam 5:16), and its cognate verb *ʿāṭar*, "surround", sug-gests that it could be cylindrical, like a modern crown. It could be worn by a king, as several of the references already supplied make clear, and see too Jer 13:18; Ezek 21:31 (ET, 26).

Other passages show that more needs to be said, however. Without difficulty we should note on the one hand that the word is often used figuratively, usually in contexts which have ceremony and rejoicing as the point of connection; in this, therefore, it should be distinguished from *nezer*, which, as mentioned above, is more associated with cult and ritual (such a distinction emerges with greater clarity when semantic fields are studied as a whole).

Beyond this, however, though fully in line with such figurative uses, we should observe first that an *ʿaṭārâ* could be made of flowers (Isa 28:1, 3, 5), still worn on the head (v. 1); this equates more to English "garland" or "wreath" (note that at Prov 4:9 it stands in parallel with לִוְיָה, another word for a garland worn on the head; cf. Prov 1:9), with the former being preferable here because of its more joyful overtones. Second, the ‘ʿᵃṭārâ can be worn by many more than just the king, including at least (i) women in different capacities (at Jer 13:18 it relates still to royalty in the person of the queen mother, while at Ezek 16:12 and 23:42 it concerns a token of favour by a lover for the woman with whom he is associated, whether licitly or not), (ii) revellers (Isa 28), (iii) a bridegroom (Ct 3:11—though referring to "Solomon", the use is in connection with his wedding day rather than more specifically with his royalty), (iv) a high priest (at least so far as the difficult text of Zech 6:11, 14 currently goes[17]), and (v) a loyal subject, as a reward (Esth 8:15).

This quick survey indicates that ‘ʿᵃṭārâ does duty for both English "crown" and "garland", and although it is more usually the case that (on the basis of how the item is made) "crown" is more commonly the sense in obviously royal contexts and "garland" in others, this distinction is not absolute. The feature which seems to hold the vast majority of cases together, including those that are purely figurative, either by directly positive statement or by inference from the anticipated outcome of reversal, is honour, victory, joy, and celebration[18]. It is thus distinguished from *nezer* in both form and symbol.

Having now summarized some of the principal conclusions of Salvesen's research into the semantics of these three words, it is clear that they differ quite sharply the one from the other in the form that the items take, in the identity of those who wear them, and in what they seem chiefly to signify. I have found it next to impossible to find satisfactory English equivalents, and even those that approximate in some respects fail completely in others; thus *keter:* diadem; *nezer:* "head-plaque"; *ʿᵃṭārâ:* "crown or garland".

I do not need to belabour the point that no lexicographer can adequately gloss these terms, so that even the best approximations will be severely misleading without extensive additional commentary, which exceeds the possibilities for most dictionaries. Merely to clarify how far we still need to travel even when working within these restrictions may be made clear by the following summary of the renderings in some of the standard dictionaries of Biblical or Classical Hebrew:

---

17 For discussion, with abundant additional bibliography, see Wolter H. Rose, *Zemah and Zerubbabel: Messianic Expectations in the Early Postexilic Period*, JSOTSup 304 (Sheffield: Sheffield Academic Press, 2000), 46–59.

18 In both respects (i.e. crown/garland, and association with victory and celebration) Salvesen observes that it comes close in meaning to Greek στέφανος.

	BDB	HAL	DCH
כֶּתֶר	crown	hoher Turban Kopfschmuck	crown, turban, decoration (on horse)
נֵזֶר	(consecration) crown (Naziriteship)	(Weihe, Weihung) Kranz, Diadem, Stirnreif	(consecration, separation, Naziriteship) (hair of consecration) crown, diadem
עֲטָרָה	crown, wreath	Kranz, Krone, Diadem	crown, diadem, wreath

Some results: נָבִיא, חֹזֶה and רֹאֶה

The second field of study that I shall summarize much more briefly is that relating to nouns for prophets undertaken by Dr Jonathan Stökl. His database entries on נָבִיא, חֹזֶה, and רֹאֶה are available online via the SAHD website, but one may also profitably consult the published version of his doctoral thesis[19].

I start by noting that most dictionaries render *ḥozeh* and *ro'eh* identically: BDB and DCH have "seer" and HAL and Ges[18] have "Seher". While this is understandable on the basis of the verbs of which these words are, strictly speaking, participles, nevertheless an English or German reader would not realize on this basis that there are two separate words used here, and this problem becomes acute in a verse like 1 Chr 29:29, where both words occur as a qualifier of two different individuals.

The advantage of tackling such a problem by way of semantic field is precisely that one seeks to distinguish between near synonyms. Such words may overlap in some or even many contexts, but as in any language there will not be total interchangeability. Stökl's conclusion is that, where the context makes the point clear, *ḥozeh* is used to refer specifically to official, i.e. court or temple, Judean officials. The large majority of occurrences are in the books of Chronicles, so that he is understandably cautious about committing firmly to the view that in this it also reflects pre-exilic reality; nevertheless, he seems to allow that there is some evidence from occasional references in favour of a positive response to that question[20] while also indicating that it may have been under the later influence

---

19 J. Stökl, *Prophecy in the Ancient Near East: A Philological and Sociological Comparison*, CHANE 56 (Leiden: Brill, 2012), esp. 155–202. There are some respects in which in relation to our particular topic this work supersedes Robert R. Wilson, *Prophecy and Society in Ancient Israel* (Philadelphia: Fortress, 1980), and David L. Petersen, *The Roles of Israel's Prophets*, JSOTSup 17 (Sheffield: JSOT Press, 1981).

20 See *Prophecy in the Ancient Near East*, 194.

of Aramaic that the term became more popular. Related terms from the same root suggest that what the seer saw was visionary, though he also states that it "could include the 'seeing' and subsequent interpretation of ominous signs", which suggests that forms of divination should not be excluded.

The title *ro'eh* is even more rare, with only eleven secure occurrences: it is applied several times to Samuel in 1 Sam 9 and then again several times in Chronicles. This seems to rule out the possibility that the difference between *ḥozeh* and *ro'eh* can be explained simply on diachronic grounds. Although it is not much to go on, the frequent applications to Samuel (in texts of whatever date) suggest that the main difference from *ḥozeh* is that the *ro'eh* was available to the wider public, outside and beyond the court circles.

If Stökl is correct, then it is fully justifiable from one perspective to translate both terms by "seer". But it might be expected that a lexicographer would want to make clear the difference between two overlapping but distinct lexemes. Since we have no equivalents in modern languages for the different roles of court and publicly accessible seers, this can only be done by a paraphrase, which is acceptable in a work of reference but probably falls down when it comes to a formally equivalent as opposed to a dynamically equivalent translation.

The *ro'eh* is associated with the *nabî'* at 1 Sam 9:9, of course: "the one who is now called a prophet was formerly called a seer". Along with others Stökl maintains that this cannot simply be read historically, as though the two terms were of the same meaning but used in different periods; rather, the verse is added to explain a common but unusual term in the story with the term which by the glossator's time had become common. A study of the use of *nabî'*, which occurs over 300 times in the Hebrew Bible (as well as twice in the certainly pre-exilic Lachish Letters), shows that it has a much more complex history, including significant development of meaning through time[21]. While some of his results depend upon questions of dating the relevant literature, it remains clear that significant development in the application of the title took place from either ecstatic or strongly divinatory practice early on to a word that came to signify classical writing prophets by the later period, including "the prophets" as an incipient corpus. Thus again, while we may legitimately translate "prophet", it would be misleading if so simple a gloss were to hide the wide range of practices that this term covered.

---

21 I shall not here discuss the feminine form, נביאה. In addition to Stökl's analysis, I may refer to my own discussion of the word in "Prophetesses in the Hebrew Bible", in *Prophecy and Prophets in Ancient Israel: Proceedings of the Oxford Old Testament Seminar*, ed. John Day, LHB/OTS 531 (New York: Continuum, 2010), 65–80; this includes further bibliography.

The range of issues relating to words for prophets is thus not so acute as those for crowns from a lexicographical point of view, but in some ways that is even more telling for my main point[22]. While doubt remains over some lexemes, we generally have a well-established set of lexicographical English or other modern language equivalents for Classical Hebrew words. Semantics muddies these waters in two ways, however. First, it adds a surprisingly large degree of additional precision to our understanding of what the lexemes signify, and this sometimes leaves us without any secure equivalent at all, or at least not one that is not seriously misleading. Second, there is a danger in all lexicography that we tame the foreign language by assimilating it to our own culture and expectations. Semantics is able to show how lexemes give expression to *realia* or practices which are quite foreign to our culture. It is imperative for responsible interpretation that we do not domesticate the language to any degree further than is necessary for comprehension.

---

22 For another telling example of this sort, by a scholar who has also worked for SAHD in the past, see Peter J. Williams, "'Slaves' in Biblical Narrative and in Translation", in *On Stone and Scroll: Essays in Honour of Graham Ivor Davies*, ed. James K. Aitken, Katharine J. Dell, and Brian A. Mastin, BZAW 420 (Berlin: de Gruyter, 2011), 441–52.

Stefan Schorch
Lexicon of Samaritan Hebrew According to the Samaritan Pentateuch Tradition

1. Introduction: Short Description of the Project

The "Lexicon of Samaritan Hebrew According to the Samaritan Pentateuch Tradition" is a joint project of Moshe Florentin (Tel Aviv University) and myself which was launched this year. The project aims at the creation of a scholarly dictionary of the Samaritan Hebrew dialect[1] which is attested in the Samaritan Pentateuch tradition. It will encompass the manuscripts of the Samaritan Pentateuch, the Samaritan oral reading tradition of the Pentateuch, and the early exegetical traditions within the Samaritan community as preserved in the Samaritan Targum, in the Samaritan Arabic translation, as well as in the traditional trilingual word-lists called *Ham-Melitz*.

The dictionary will feature a comprehensive etymological, morphological, and semantic analysis of each lexeme found in Samaritan Pentateuch (= SP) based on close reading of the Samaritan versions and with cognizance of traditional Samaritan lexicography. Each entry will provide the following data:

1. Lemma; 2. Etymological cognates (including other traditions of Hebrew); 3. Attributed meaning in Samaritan literature (Targum, Arabic translation of the Torah); 4. Morphological inventory; 5. Determination of semantics (with exact references and contextual quotations); 6. Derivates.

2. Samaritan Hebrew

The distinctiveness and importance of the Samaritan Hebrew dialect (= SH) as reflected in the Samaritan version of the Pentateuch and in the Samaritan tradition was first recognized and analyzed by Wilhelm Gesenius (*De Pentateuchi Samaritani origine, indole et auctoritate commentatio philologico-critica*, 1815). However, Gesenius had no firsthand knowledge of the reading tradition of the Pentateuch as passed down through the Samaritan community. Although

---

[1] Although hitherto debate on the question of whether Samaritan Hebrew should be regarded as a dialect in its own right remains to be conclusively settled, there is much evidence in its favor.

some fragments of the Samaritan reading tradition have been published since the 19th century[2], it was Zeev Ben-Hayyim's work which altered its general reception. Particularly significant was his publication of a transcription of the full Samaritan reading of the Torah together with an analytic concordance[3]. Moreover, in his excellent *Grammar of Samaritan Hebrew* (1977; revised English ed. 2000) and in many further publications, Ben-Hayyim systematically defined the grammatical features of the Hebrew language tradition as preserved in the Samaritan reading tradition. He further compared it to other Hebrew language traditions with a particular focus on the Masoretic text, but also the language of the Dead Sea Scrolls, Mishnaic Hebrew, and to early Greek and Latin transcriptions of Hebrew words. Ben-Hayyim concluded that the Samaritan reading of the Pentateuch preserves a type of Hebrew which was spoken among the (proto-)Samaritans between the 2nd century B.C.E. and the 1st century C.E.[4] Additionally, according to Schorch, it seems possible to connect SH with the Hebrew dialect spoken in the geographical region of Ephraim[5]. Thus, the characteristic features of SH can be determined both with regard to the history of the Hebrew language and to Hebrew dialectology[6].

Although the past 50 years have seen great advances in the study of SH in the fields of grammar, comparative language history, and dialectology there has been no similar progress for SH lexicography. There is much still to explore. Even the fact that SH references have been included in some of the newer Biblical Hebrew lexica (i. e., *KBL³* and *GesMD¹⁸*) does not alter this statement. Data

---

2 Petermann, Julius Heinrich: *Versuch einer hebräischen Formenlehre nach der Aussprache der heutigen Samaritaner: nebst einer darnach gebildeten Transscription der Genesis und einer Beilage enthaltend die von dem recipirten Texte des Pentateuchs abweichenden Lesarten der Samaritaner.* Leipzig: Brockhaus, 1868 (Abhandlungen für die Kunde des Morgenlandes; 5,1); recordings by A. Schaade and H. Ritter, published in the appendix to Kahle, Paul E., *The Cairo Geniza.* Oxford: Basil Blackwell, ²1959; Murtonen, Aimo E., *Materials for a Non-Masoretic Hebrew grammar II: An etymological vocabulary to the Samaritan Pentateuch.* Helsinki: 1960.

3 Ben-Hayyim, Zeev, *The Literary and Oral Tradition of the Samaritans,* vol. IV. Jerusalem: The Academy of the Hebrew Language, 1977 [= *LOT IV*].

4 Ben-Hayyim, Zeev, *A Grammar of Samaritan Hebrew: based on the recitation of the Law in comparison with the Tiberian and other Jewish traditions.* Winona Lake, Ind.: Eisenbrauns, 2000 [= GSH], 553–559.

5 Schorch, Stefan, *Die Vokale des Gesetzes: Die samaritanische Lesetradition als Textzeugin der Tora. Band 1: Genesis.* Berlin; New York: de Gruyter, 2004 (BZAW; 339), 35–39.

6 See Schorch, Stefan, "Spoken Hebrew of the Late Second temple period according to the oral and the written Samaritan tradition", in: Jan Joosten / Jean-Sebastien Rey (edd.): *Conservatism and Innovation in the Hebrew Language of the Hellenistic Period : Proceedings of a Fourth International Symposium on the Hebrew of the Dead Sea Scrolls & Ben Sira.* Leiden: Brill 2008 (Studies on the Texts of the Desert of Judah; 73), 175–190, here: 181–183.

referenced in these lexica refer almost exclusively to phonological and morphological features of given Samaritan readings, but not to their semantic value or to their history of interpretation among the Samaritans. Perhaps most problematic from the perspective of SH lexicography however, is the incompleteness of the data provided. Both lexica quote only such SH words with equivalents in the Masoretic text and omit the cases where the Samaritan Pentateuch attests an alternative text.

Yet another book deserves a brief mentioning in this context, namely Murtonen's *Etymological vocabulary to the Samaritan Pentateuch* (1960). The goal of that book, as suggested in the title, appears promising. Admittedly, it does not propose an independent semantic analysis of the SH lexicon as it is a "vocabulary" and not a dictionary or a lexicon. However, Murtonen's work suffers from grave methodical weaknesses, especially with respect to the quality of the transcriptions employed and to the linguistic analysis of the readings the entries are based upon. It is due to this that his *Vocabulary* includes an unseemly amount of ghost entries and incorrect morphological indications. The work was thus justly ignored by the wider academic community as a source for further research.

Despite the fact that phonological and morphological analysis carried out up until now confirms that SH is a key witness for the Hebrew language spoken in the Late Second Temple period and shortly thereafter; there is no dictionary nor any other lexicographical tool which provides complete data for, and a comprehensive analysis of, the SH lexicon.

Fully aware of this lexicographic *desideratum* in the field of SH on the one hand, and, on the other, keen cognizance of the importance of the lexicographical data preserved in the SH tradition for adjacent fields of studies such as Semitic philology, the study of other traditions of Hebrew (especially the Masoretic tradition of Biblical Hebrew, the Hebrew of the Dead Sea Scrolls, and Mishnaic Hebrew), as well as for Samaritan studies itself our project aims to provide the lexicographical data and the tools for subsequent studies.

Notably, the present environment in SP scholarship seems to provide the necessary scientific basis for this goal. Apart from the publication of the Samaritan reading tradition of the Pentateuch by Ben-Hayyim mentioned above, a very reliable edition of the Samaritan Targum has been published by Abraham Tal (1980–1984) and an Arabic Translation of SP was made available by Haseeb Shehadeh in an edition of similarly high standards (1989–2002). Additionally, the Samaritan Targum is fully covered by Abraham Tal's *Dictionary of Samaritan Aramaic* (2000), providing much information necessary for the study of the Samaritan Targum and SP. The textual traditions embedded in the Samaritan reading of the Torah have been analyzed in a book by Stefan Schorch (*Die Vokale des Gesetzes: Die samaritanische Toralesung als Textzeugin der Tora*, 2004) and by

Moshe Florentin and Abraham Tal as part of their synoptic edition of Ms. Nablus 6 of SP jointly with the Masoretic text (*The Pentateuch – The Samaritan version and the Masoretic version*, 2010).

Let us now turn to the manuscript tradition of SP. The current project will have to consider the entire range of the Samaritan manuscript tradition because, unlike the scribal tradition of the Masoretic text, Samaritan manuscripts are so divergent that no two manuscripts (not even of one and the same scribe) are identical in respect of the external form of the written text. Much important information can still be found in the different apparatuses of von Gall's edition (1914–1918) even though his eclectic primary text is of no direct value for the project. The F. Pérez Castro (*Séfer Abiša*, 1959) and L. F. Girón Blanc (*Pentateuco hebreo-samaritano: Genesis*, 1976) editions provide information from further manuscripts not included in the von Gall edition. However, they are both restricted to single books, namely, Genesis and Deuteronomy respectively. The Tal/Florentin edition (2010) mentioned above covers the full extent of the Samaritan Torah but it refers to only one manuscript. The lack of a current edition which covers the entire manuscript tradition of SP will be compensated by cooperation with the "Samaritanusedition" project based at the University of Halle and led by Stefan Schorch who is also one of the two partners on the dictionary project. The "Samaritanusedition" team currently comprises of ten collaborators and is funded by the Deutsche Forschungsgemeinschaft (DFG) for the periods 2007–2010 and 2011–2019. The team is working on a critical *editio maior* of the SP. From its work so far, the team has built up a large collection of digitized Samaritan manuscripts covering all known Hebrew manuscripts of SP until ca. 1500 C.E., electronic transcriptions of the Hebrew manuscripts until ca. 1400 C.E., a database of concurrent readings in the Samaritan Targum and the Samaritan Arabic translations, as well as a database of parallels between SP and passages found in the Septuagint tradition and the Dead Sea Scrolls. Moreover, the *editio maior* relating to the Book of Genesis is already in the proof-reading stage, and the Exodus and Leviticus editions are both well advanced (the former in cooperation with a Hungarian team from the University "Károli Gáspár" Budapest under the direction of József Zsengellér)[7].

By cooperating with the "Samaritanusedition" team these resources can be made available to the dictionary project. Moreover, lest we forget, further tools developed within the framework of the "Samaritanusedition" project, such as

---

7 A detailed description of this project can be found in Schorch, Stefan, "Der Pentateuch der Samaritaner: Seine Erforschung und seine Bedeutung für das Verständnis des alttestamentlichen Bibeltextes". In: Frey, Jörg / Schattner-Rieser, Ursula / Schmid, Konrad (eds.), *Die Samaritaner und die Bibel*. Berlin [u. a.]: de Gruyter, 2012 (Studia Samaritana; 7), 5–30; here: 18–27.

special fonts containing all additional signs of the SH script, could also be shared.

3. The Lexicon of Samaritan Hebrew According to the SP Tradition

Naturally due to the proximity of the Samaritan and the Jewish Pentateuch, the lexicon of SH according to the Samaritan tradition of the Pentateuch has many meeting points and overlaps with the Tiberian tradition of Biblical Hebrew as attested in the Torah (= TH). Thus, in many cases, the difference between the two is merely phonetical, as for instance in the overture of the Pentateuch:

Gen 1:1 SH *bå̄rå̄šət bå̄ra ʔēluwwəm ʔit ʔaššå̄məm wit ʔå̄rəṣ*

TH בְּרֵאשִׁית בָּרָא אֱלֹהִים אֵת הַשָּׁמַיִם וְאֵת הָאָרֶץ

Nevertheless, the numerous and often quite fundamental differences between the two textual corpora establish the language of the Samaritan Pentateuch as a linguistic entity of its own which ought to be described separately from Biblical Hebrew in the Masoretic tradition and which ought to be extended to the lexicon too.

3.1. The Samaritan Hebrew lexicon contains lexemes not found in Masoretic Hebrew

Due to the multifarious differences between the Samaritan and the Jewish Pentateuch, SH contains many lexemes not found in Masoretic Hebrew. Some of these lexemes can even be recognized on the basis of the consonantal framework e.g.,

Gen 23:8 SH אם ישת נפשכם לקבר את מתי מלפני שמעוני

ʔam yåšåt nåfeškimma liqbår ʔit mitti milfåni šēmåʔuni

TH אִם יֵשׁ אֶת נַפְשְׁכֶם לִקְבֹּר אֶת מֵתִי מִלְּפָנַי שְׁמָעוּנִי

"If you will that I should bury my dead out of my sight, hear me".

In Gen 23:8, the vast majority of the manuscripts of the Samaritan Pentateuch contain the reading ישת as against אֶת יֵשׁ in the MT[8], exhibiting one word instead

---

8 Nevertheless, some of the oldest preserved manuscripts of the SP appear to exhibit traces

of two. According to the Samaritan reading tradition, the word is read as *yā̊šå̄t*, which should be analyzed as an infinitive of the verbal root יש"ׁי⁹. Thus, this verb, which is not found in TH, is part of the SH lexicon.

Logically, given that this case is a *hapax legomenon* in the Samaritan tradition, the determination of its meaning presents a difficult task for the lexicographer. Hebrew lexicography's well established method would analyze and combine three kinds of data, namely: (A) the context, (B) the translation of the word in ancient versions, and (C) the etymology.

According to the versions, the expression אם ישׁת נפשׁכם was understood by the Samaritans as "if your soul desires"[10], which would more or less appear to

---

which attest that the reading ישׁ את may not have been unknown in the older manuscript tradition: In Ms. St. Petersburg Russian National Library, Firkowitch Collection IIa 45 (written 1182) and Ms. Cambridge University Library Add. 1846 (supposedly written 11th–12th century), there is an erasure between the שׁ and the ת, i.e. ישׁ\\ת, pointing to the possibility that the respective mss. originally read ישׁ את (or: ישׁאת ?). Ms. Dublin Chester Beatty Library 751 (written 1225) reads ישׁת, attesting a supralinear dot between the שׁ and the ת. Since the Samaritan scribal tradition generally employs a supralinear dot (or a supralinear little stroke) as a text-critical sign by which the scribe indicates that he is familiar with a diverging reading; the writing ישׁת in Ms. Dublin Chester Beatty Library 751 may be taken as a further indication of the existence of the variant ישׁ את among the Samaritans. This evidence from the manuscripts of the Samaritan Pentateuch gets support from Ms. C of the Samaritan Targum which translates the passage in question as אם אית ית נפשׁכן, and from Ms. נ auf die Samaritan Arabic version, which translates: ان كان في نفوسكم, which seems to suppose a Hebrew *Vorlage* close to (or identical with) the Masoretic text, cf. Tal, Abraham, "Divergent Traditions of the Samaritan Pentateuch as Reflected by its Aramaic Targum". *JAB* 1 (1999), 297–314.

9 See Schorch, *Die Vokale des Gesetzes*, 159–160. It should be noted that the Samaritan Targum (with the exception of Ms C, see above) as well as the Samaritan Arabic translation, render this verbal form not as an infinitive but as a perfect, 3rd fem., cf. Ben-Hayyim, *GSH*, 247 and TAL, Abraham / Florentin, Moshe: Tal, Abraham / Florentin, Moshe (eds.), חמישה חומשי תורה, נוסח שומרון ונוסח המסורה: מבוא, הערות, נספחים [The Pentateuch – The Samaritan version and the Masoretic version, Hebr.]. Tel Aviv: The Haim Rubin Tel Aviv University Press, 2010 (= PSM], 641. However, as the Targumic rendering follows the needs of the target language at least to some extent or is otherwise dependent on translation technique, the present Aramaic and Arabic translation naturally do not imply that the translators interpreted their Hebrew *Vorlage* as a perfect. Although the construction אם + infinitive may seem somewhat difficult, it does have parallels in Masoretic Hebrew, cf. Job 9:27 אם אָמְרִי אשׁכחה שׂיחי אעשׂבה פני – "If I say, I will forget my complaint; I will put off my sad countenance." (English translation according to *NRSV*). A further possible parallel is attested in the MT of Ex 7:27; 9:2, where מָאֵן in אם מָאֵן אתָּה is often analyzed as a Pi'el participle (see Gesenius, Wilhelm, *Hebrew Grammar*, ed. E. Kautzsch / A. E. Cowley. Oxford: Clarendon Press, ²1910 [= GKC], § 52 s), although it might be favorable to explain the form as an infinitive, compare below.

10 Cf. Samaritan Targum Ms. J: אם אתריחת נפשׁכן. The main witnesses of the Samaritan Arabic version translate accordingly: ان هويت نفوسكم (= Ms. א, similarly Ms. B).

correspond with the context; although the meaning "desire" the versions apparently attribute to the verbal form in question may be influenced by the connection with the subject נפש, reflecting an idiomatic expression. From the perspective of etymology, the root √yšy is well established in different Semitic languages
(cf. especially Akkadian *išū* "to have"). Thus, the evidence at hand gives some
reason to believe that the SH verb ישה means "to have."

The case of the SH ישת may have demonstrated the fundamental importance
of the vocalization handed down in the traditional Samaritan reading of the
Torah. Even though the verb ישה left traces in the consonantal framework clearly
visible especially when compared with the Masoretic text, it would have been
virtually impossible to correctly recognize and analyze it without reference to
the vocalization. Nevertheless, the vast majority of cases in which the text of
the Samaritan Pentateuch differs from the Masoretic text puts an even greater
emphasis on its reading because the characteristics of SH appear *only* in vocalization – the consonantal framework of the two textual corpora being identical.

A prominent example for this phenomenon can be found in Jacob's blessing
of his sons:

Gen 49:5 SH כלו חמס|מכרתיהם   "**their covenants** finished violence"
              kallu ʔâməs |*makrētiyyimma*|
         TH כְּלֵי חָמָס|מְכֵרֹתֵיהֶם   "**their swords** are weapons of violence"

The Masoretic text in this passage from Jacob's blessing of Simeon and Levi is
not entirely clear, but it is usually understood as suggested by *NRSV* as "weapons
of violence are their swords"[11]. It is the last word, מְכֵרֹתֵיהֶם which puzzles lexicographers and exegetes alike.

---

11 Similarly JPS TaNaKh (1985): "Their weapons are tools of lawlessness;" Luther: "Ihre Schwer-
ter sind mörderische Waffen". The newer French Bible translations, on the other hand, seem
generally to follow the suggestion that *מְכֵרָה is a noun built from the root II *מכר "to plan, counsel" (cf. *HALOT*, s.v.): "leurs accords ne sont qu'instruments de violence" (French Traduction
Œcuménique de la Bible, 1988); "ils s'accordent pour agir avec violence" (French Bible en français courant, 1997). Apart from the methodological difficulty to propose a Hebrew root II *מכר on
the basis of evidence from Geʻez, this suggestion seems contextually problematic because it presupposes the otherwise unattested metaphorical use of כלי "instrument," as already pointed out
by August Dillmann in his commentary on Genesis, who therefore rejected it, cf. Florentin,
Moshe, כלי חמס מכרתיהם [כלי חמס מְכֵרֹתֵיהֶם (בראשית מט, ה) והנוסח השומרוני של התורה] *as reflected
in Samaritan traditions*, Heb.]. Lěšonénu 63 (2000–2001), 189–202; here: 193–194. The French
Bible de Jérusalem (1973) appears to have been aware of this problem and tried to solve it
with the help of a text-critical operation, namely, by emending the first word of the passage
into *כָּלוּ (with SP and LXX συνετέλεσαν): "ils ont mené à bout la violence de leurs intrigues".

The Samaritan text has two variants in this passage as compared with the MT. The initial word is read *כַלּוּ "they finished" (instead of MT כִּלְי) and the final word which is under discussion here is read *makrētīyyimma* i.e., *מַכְרָתֵיהֶם based on the noun *makrət (= *מַכְרָת) in the pl. + suffix 3. pl. masc. Thus, on the basis of a consonantal framework, which is identical, the reading produces a different word. As in the former example, we are again dealing with a *hapax legomenon* here.

The noun *makrət is derived from the root כר"ת "to cut" and corresponds to the nominal pattern *maqtil*[12]. It was understood as a *nomen actionis*[13] according to the Samaritan Targum; although the different manuscripts do not seem to fully agree with respect to its exact meaning. Ms. J, representing the oldest stage of the Samaritan Targum, renders בקיומין "with their covenant-making", obviously on the basis of the idiomatic phrase כרת ברית "to make a covenant", with a supposed ellipsis of the object ברית. However, apart from this understanding, other manuscripts of the Samaritan Targum possibly preserve traces of yet another traditional way of understanding *makrētīyyimma*, namely "their annihilation (of the people of Shekhem)"[14]. And finally, the Samaritan Arabic version translates מכרתיהם with مقاطعها "their swords". However, as this latter understanding only appears in the Samaritan Arabic translation at a period of time when מכרתיהם was understood as "their swords" in both Jewish and Christian exegesis of Gen 49:5[15], the Samaritan Arabic rendering may be influenced by contemporary Jewish or Christian sources. According to the Samaritan Targumic tradition as described above, the oldest and most wide spread way of understanding the word in question here was "their covenant-making".

Of course this conjecture does not answer the question of how the Masoretic text in its present state should be understood.

12 See Ben-Hayyim, *LOT* III/1, 33.

13 For *nomina actionis* of the nominal pattern *maqtil* in Samaritan Hebrew see Macuch, Rudolf, *Grammatik des samaritanischen Hebräisch*. Berlin: de Gruyter, 1969 (Studia Samaritana; 1) [= *GSH*], 403–404 § 134 b.

14 Thus Tal, with regard to Targum Ms. V: במעקרין (see Tal, Abraham, *A Dictionary of Samaritan Aramaic*. Leiden; Boston; Köln: Brill, 2000 [= *DSA*], s.v. מעקר); Ms. A: בקטעותם (see TAL, *DSA* s.v. קטעו). It seems difficult, however, to exclude the possibility that מעקר and קטעו could express the meaning "covenant making," cf. Florentin, כלי חמס מכרתיהם *as reflected in Samaritan traditions*, 201.

15 Cf. Florentin, כלי חמס מכרתיהם *as reflected in Samaritan traditions*, 199.

3.2. The Samaritan Hebrew lexicon contains lexemes exhibiting differences in morphology as compared with their Masoretic counterparts

A substantial number of differences between SH and TH concerns morphology. For example, חשב "skillful workman" (Exod 26:1 etc.) is pronounced *ḥōšēḇ* in TH but is pronounced *ʕaššåb* in SH. The SH noun follows the nominal pattern *qaṭṭāl*, the former TH noun is, of course, a part. act. This opposition between part. act. in one tradition and a 'regular' nominal pattern in the other is a very common phenomenon and occurs in both directions e. g., with regard to the noun מכסה "cover" (Gen 8:13 etc.), SH applies a *Pi'el* participle, while TH exhibits a "regular" noun pattern, i. e. TH *miḵsæ* versus SH *mēkassi*.

Some of these morphological differences concern the different usage of verbal stems – many SH verbs employ the verbal stems differently from their Masoretic counterpart, and *vice versa*. However, what could be observed in the previous example with regard to the application of nominal patterns is true for the employment of verbal stems as well. In many cases the morphological difference has no semantic consequences whatsoever e. g., in TH, the verb מכר "to sell" is used in the *Qal*, in SH, however, it is used in the *Pi'el* e. g.,

Exod 21:7 SH[16] וכי ‏ימכר‏ איש את בתו   "when a man **sells** his daughter"
                        wkī ‏yēmakkər‏ *ʔiš ʔit bittu*
      TH   וְכִי ‏יִמְכֹּר‏ אִישׁ אֶת בִּתּוֹ

While the *Pi'el* of the verb מכר is unknown from TH, its use is quite consistent in SH which attests no single instance of מכר *Qal*. Even in cases where the consonantal framework seems to exclude to *Pi'el*, according to the general rules of TH grammar, SH still applies it e. g.,

Lev 25:16 SH הוא | מכר | לך   "he is **selling** to you"
          ū |*makkər*| *låk*
      TH הוא | מֹכֵר |לְךָ?

Although without the prefix מ-, the word *makkər* is a *Pi'el* participle[16].

---

16 Participial forms *Pi'el* without prefix מ- are not unusual in SH, see Ben-Hayyim, *GSH*, § 2.12.9. A comparable form might be preserved in the MT of Exod 7:27; 9:2 (אִם מָאֵן אַתָּה), where מָאֵן is often explained as a *Pi'el* participle (see GKC § 52 s). It should be noted, however, that the form might be an infinitive, leading to the same construction as attested in SP אם ישת נפשכם (Gen 23:8), compare above.

The verb מכר is one of many attestations of the shift of verbs originally used in the *Qal* which came to be used in the *Pi'el*. This shift is widespread in SH, although SH in other cases preserves the use of the *Qal* in verbs, which in TH came to be used in the *Pi'el*:

Gen 29:25 SH ולמה רמיתני "Why then **have you deceived me?**"
 wlēmå rå̄mītåni
 TH וְלָמָּה רִמִּיתָנִי

The SH reading rå̄mītåni reflects a form of the *Qal*, i.e., it corresponds to TH ‎*רְמִיתָנִי. Thus, II רמה "to betray" is used in SH in the same stem like I רמה "to throw" (cf. Exod 15:1. 21).

Most obviously, in none of the examples quoted so far has the use of a different verbal stem implied any difference in meaning. In the case of many other verbs, however, the application of a different verbal stem may have semantic consequences which ought to be carefully described in a lexicon of Samaritan Hebrew. An interesting example can be found in Gen 45:2 where the MT reads "The Egyptians heard it, and the household of Pharaoh heard it", applying the verb שמע "to hear" in the *Qal* twice. The Samaritan reading, however, reads the first occurrence of this verb in the *Qal* and the second in the *Pi'el*:

Gen 45:2 SH וישמעו מצרים וישמעו בית פרעה
 wyišmā̊ʔu miṣrəm wyēšammā̊ʔu bit få̊ru
 TH וַיִּשְׁמְעוּ מִצְרַיִם וַיִּשְׁמַע בֵּית פַּרְעֹה

Due to the alternation in the use of verbal stems, the Samaritan text should be understood differently from the MT "The Egyptians heard it, and **they let** the household of Pharaoh **hear it**"[17]. Being confronted with this verse the lexicographer should take notice of a meaning of the verb שמע *Pi'el* in SH which is absent in TH, namely, the causative "to make hear".

---

17 Compare Targum Ms. A: ושמעו מצראי וחוו בית פרעה, and the Samaritan Arabic version: فسمع لمصريون واذاعوا في آل فرعون, which both render in the same sense. Interestingly, the Septuagint seems to be based on a similar vocalization of its Hebrew *Vorlage*: ἤκουσαν δὲ πάντες οἱ Αἰγύπτιοι καὶ ἀκουστὸν ἐγένετο εἰς τὸν οἶκον Φαραω.

3.3. Lexemes shared by SH and Masoretic Hebrew have differences in meaning in the two traditions

Up until this point I was looking at differences in the Samaritan and Tiberian Hebrew lexicon based on the existence of a given word in one corpus which is absent in the other (3.1.), or differences in morphology of a certain lexeme (3.2.). A further section of lexical differences between Samaritan and Tiberian Hebrew is comprised of differences in meaning a given lexeme may attest (according to the co-text[18]) or may have acquired (due to its traditional interpretation) in these two Hebrew traditions. Let us turn to an example of this now:

> Deut 32:13   SH   שדה ‏תנופת‎‏ ויאכלהו
> "he will feed him with the **choice** of the field"[20]
> *yåkīlēʔu tēnūfåt šådi*
>
> TH   שָׁדָי ‏תְּנוּבֹת‎‏ וַיֹּאכַל
> "and he did eat the **produce** of the field"

The SP passage quoted above is different from the corresponding MT in several areas starting with the verb which is, according to MT, vocalized in the *Qal*. In the SP, however, it employs the *Hifʿil* and has an additional personal suffix. However, I would like to focus here on the second word where the SP reads *תְּנוּפָה whereas the corresponding word in MT is תְּנוּבָה "produce".

Although both the etymology and the exact meaning of תְּנוּפָה are disputed, the MT as a whole gives one few reasons to doubt that the noun was primarily regarded as a cultic term. It is therefore important to note that the present passage from SP attests a different meaning for תְּנוּפָה which is not related to the cult, a fact which can be easily deduced from the co-text of the verse. As the present use only occurs in Deut 32:13, it is again difficult to determine the exact meaning. The fact that some of the manuscripts of the Samaritan versions apply the term used for "wave-offering" elsewhere doesn't seem very significant, as the rendering may be purely technical. Other manuscripts translate "choice," a rendering which seems fitting both with regard to the co-text of the passage and with respect to the range of meanings implied by the root נו"ף:

---

18 In accordance with the terminology used in German professional language of philology, it seems heuristically helpful and methodologically appropriate to discern between "co-text" and "context": While the latter term concerns the whole range of circumstances which create the environment of a given phenomenon, the former term designates the textual environment only.

HALOT discerns three different lexemes, namely I נוף "to move to and fro", II נוף "to spray", and III נוף "to be high, elevated". Although Köhler and Baumgartner formally linked תְּנוּפָה to I נוף "to move to and fro"[19], they expressed their doubts on this connection:

> "[T]he meaning of the sbst. is disputed, but possibilities include.
> a) traditionally from I נוף hif. [...]: consecration effected by swinging, or brandishing upon the hands before God or the altar [...].
> b) from Arb. nāfa [i.e. to be high, be elevated, surpass] [...] in the sense of uplifted (raised) offering [...].
> c) from Neo-Babylonian nūptu addition, additional payment [...] from which תְּ means special supplement [...] = from Arb. nauf excess, surplus [...].
> d) deciding which proposal to accept is difficult, but the first (a) probably comes into consideration less than seemed apparent for a long time; and the second (b) probably deserves greater preference to the last (c) [...]"[20].

It would thus seem plausible to consider the etymological connection of SH *tēnūfa* in Deut 32:13 with the root listed as III נוף in *HALOT*, "to be high, elevated".

Alternatively, or in combination with the suggested reconsideration of the etymology of תנופה, the meaning of the SH noun *tēnūfa* in Deut 32:13 might be influenced by the meaning of the Samaritan Aramaic root נו"ף "to be high, elevated, blossoming"[21], which opens up the possibility that SH *tēnūfa* in Deut 32:13 means "fruit".

The example of SH *tēnūfa* demonstrates an obvious fact – the determination of the meaning of a given word is largely dependent on the co-texts in which it is used and, therefore, when encountering instances of the same word which appear in new co-texts the lexicographer should adjust the analysis of the meaning accordingly. However, in a corpus of traditional literature or scripture, as the Torah is regarded in both the Samaritan and Jewish communities, a further factor may be very productive in shaping and changing the meaning of a given passage or word of that corpus – namely, interpretation of scripture. In my final example, I would like to draw attention to this phenomenon and its influence on the lexicon of SH:

Gen 49:11 SH עירו | לגפן | אסורי "(Judah is) bound to his city *Gåfən*."
              ʔåsūri | *algåfən* | *ʔīru*
         TH עירה | לַגֶּפֶן | אֹסְרִי "(Judah is) binding his foal to the vine".

---

19 See the last line of the entry I נוף, where תְּנוּפָה is listed as a derivate of this root.

20 *HALOT*, s.v. תְּנוּפָה.

21 See TAL, *DSA*, s.v.

As you can see, the above passage contains divergences in each word. The first word in SP is a passive participle, as against the active participle in MT, the last word is understood as "his city" (i.e. I עיר), as against MT "his foal" (i.e. II עיר [< עַיִר])[22]. On the basis of this text, and in the context of a Samaritan tradition of polemics against the Jews and Jerusalem, גפן comes to be understood as a name of Jerusalem[23]. Of course, one could question whether a Lexicon of Samaritan Hebrew should record a meaning which appears secondary. However, given that the use of גפן became very popular in Samaritan exegesis and later Samaritan literature the dictionary would otherwise be omitting an important piece of information.

4. Significance of the Lexicon of Samaritan Hebrew

4.1. Lexicography

The dictionary will present the lexicon of SH as preserved in the Torah together with a comprehensive semantic analysis, creating an important resource of lexicographical information. On the one hand, it will become be a central tool for any further work at the SP and the Samaritan tradition as a whole (*piyyutim*, commentaries, halakhic and grammatical works etc.). On the other hand, the Samaritan reading of the Torah is one of the witnesses for the Hebrew spoken in the Late Second Temple period and shortly thereafter and is thus a further important step towards the reconstruction of the Hebrew language of this period.

4.2. Etymology

Besides the semantical analysis, the dictionary will also provide a comprehensive etymological analysis for each lexeme. This seems especially important in light of the following considerations:

(a) The Samaritan Hebrew lexicon preserves some rarely used words which are otherwise unknown in Hebrew. Together with its usage in context, the analysis of the etymological background may thus help to establish the morphology of a given lexeme and to determine its meaning.

---

22 Cf. *HALOT*, s.v.
23 See TAL, *DSA*, s.v. גפנה², and cf. Tal / Florentin, *PSM*, 656.

(b) The etymological analysis of the SH lexicon means a further important contribution of Hebrew studies to comparative Semitic studies.

4.3. Textual history

The textual framework of SP represents a certain development in the textual history of the Pentateuch. The closest cognate of this text type can be found in the pre-Samaritan texts from Qumran. It has long been recognized that SH was one of the most influential factors in the process of shaping the characteristics of SP and the dictionary will therefore be an important contribution towards the understanding of that text-historical process.

4.4. History of interpretation

The Samaritan community throughout its history produced a rich literature in the field of interpretation of the Biblical text of SP i.e., especially the Samaritan Aramaic Targum, the Samaritan Arabic translation, Midrashim such as *Tebat Marqe* and *Sefer Asatir*, halakhic compositions, and commentaries (the latter two in Arabic). Research in this field is a still ongoing task but the work suffers as it is often unclear which Biblical *Vorlage* and from which understanding a given interpretation proceeds. The dictionary will become an essential tool in this field. Moreover, as the dictionary will provide information on how a given lexeme is interpreted by the Samaritans, it will provide a framework and a reliable basis from which any further research in Samaritan Biblical interpretation can proceed.

5. Sample Entry: The Root קה"ת

קהת – Although no direct attestation of this verb in other Hebrew traditions or in other Semitic languages seems to be preserved, there is clear evidence that this root belongs to the ancient strata of Semitic and was known in Hebrew beyond SH. The root is the basis of the n.p.m. קְהָת (Gen 46:11; Exod 6:18; Num 3:17 etc.) and תוקהת (Q) – תָּקְהָת (K) (2 Chr 34:22). Additionally, the Aramaic text of Testamentum Levi 66–67 contains a midrash interpreting the biblical name קהת using the Aramaic verb כנש "gather": [וקרא[תי שמה [קהת וחזית]י די לה [תהו]ה כנשת כל [עמא] – "[and] I [call]ed his name [Kohat as] I [saw] that [people] gather to him." This midrashic explanation probably goes back to a Hebrew original based on the verb קהת "to gather", see SCHORCH, *Die hebräische Wurzel QHT*. As for Ancient Canaanite, the root most likely appears in a n.p.m. from Phoenicia, transcribed in a Middle Egyptian source as *I3wmkhtj* (= Ilu-mqht, see ALBRIGHT, *The Egyptian Empire in Asia*, 240 n. 2). Ug. n.p.m. Aqht (see VIROLLEAUD, *La légende phénicienne de Dan'el*, 96). Akk. *qātu* (< *qat'um* < **qahtum*) "hand" seems to be a derivation of this root, see GOETZE, *The etymology of Akk. qātum.*

Nif.: PK 3 pl. m. יקהתו *yiqqåtu.* – "gather" (refl.): ולו יקהתו עמים (Gen 49:10) – "and to him people gather" (MT וְלוֹ יִקְּהַת עַמִּים:). The meaning attributed to the verb קהת in the Samaritan Targumim is דבר hitpa. "be lead" (Mss. JNM) and כנש itpa. "gather" (Mss. CM); the Samaritan Arabic translation renders جمع VIII "gather" (refl.) (א), and كود VII "come together" (B).

Bibliography

Albright, W., "The Egyptian Empire in Asia in the Twenty-first Century B.C." *JPOS* 8 (1928), 240 n. 2); Goetze, A., "The etymology of Akk. qātum 'hand'". *JCS* 2 (1948), 269–270; Schorch, St., "Die hebräische Wurzel QHT". *ZAH* 10 (1997), 76–84; Virolleaud, Ch., *La légende phénicienne de Dan'el.* Paris 1936 (MRS I).

Eberhard Bons

The "Historical and Theological Lexicon of the Septuagint" (HTLS)

Introduction: The Septuagint as a version of the Old Testament in its own right

Until recently, research on the Septuagint (LXX) has only ever played a secondary role in Old Testament exegesis. When carrying out research on the so-called proto-canonical books of the Hebrew Bible scholars are accustomed to focussing on the Masoretic Text (MT). As is well-known, the MT is the result of a process of textual harmonization and standardisation which began in the first centuries C. E. and ended some centuries later with standardised texts copied and distributed within the Jewish communities[1]. For Western biblical scholars, there is no doubt that the Old Testament text originating from this process is the reference when it comes to the biblical text. In this respect, all of the proto-canonical books share the same fate.

If scholars have attributed a secondary role to the LXX, albeit implicitly, it is because they are influenced, at least to some extent, by two decisions of the Western Church at the time of the Reformation. While the Reformed Churches opted for *hebraica veritas*, the Roman Catholic Church went in the opposite direction. At the Council of Trent in 1546, the Vulgate was declared the normative biblical text for teaching and preaching[2].

It is not overstating it to say that these two decisions had a decisive impact on exegetical practice from the XVI century onwards. Catholic and Protestant exegesis still considered the LXX as one of the textual sources of the Bible, even if they concentrated on the Hebrew or Latin texts. However, in privileging *a priori* the Hebrew or the Latin text, the LXX was denied its own particular place in bib-

---

1 For a brief overview of the origins of the Masoretic Text, see the chapter "El Texto bíblico," In Elvira Martín Contreras and Guadalupe Seijas de los Ríos-Zarzosa, *Masora. La transmisión de la tradición de la Biblia Hebrea* (Estella: Verbo Divino, 2010), 23–36.
2 For detailed information on these topics, see e.g. Siegfried Raeder, "The Exegetical and Hermeneutical Work of Martin Luther," In *Hebrew Bible / Old Testament. The History of Its Interpretation. Volume II: From the Renaissance to the Enlightenment*, ed. Magne Sæbø (Göttingen: Vandenhoeck & Ruprecht, 2008), 363–406, esp. 368–370; Jared Wicks, "Catholic Old Testament Interpretation in the Reformation and the Early Confessional Eras," In *ibid.*, 617–648, esp. 627–629.

lical studies. As a consequence, most scholars are not used to considering the writings of the LXX as autonomous texts which, though translated from a Hebrew source, do undeniably have their own theological and literary characteristics and which, for this reason, deserve detailed study in their own right.

To return to Western biblical exegesis, it is to be taken *cum grano salis* that it is only legitimate to quote the LXX in the following circumstances:

1. To correct the MT when the latter appears tricky, untranslatable or even wrong[3].
2. To interpret the New Testament, which used the LXX to formulate christological and ecclesiological concepts, quoting the Greek Old Testament very often, e.g. Ps 2; 109 |110][4].

By concentrating on these two allegedly "legitimate" approaches to the LXX, the study of the Septuagint as a significant document in its own right has been neglected. Moreover, traditional approaches to the LXX are too restrictive. This is evident from historical, text-critical and biblical research of the LXX carried out in the last three decades, whose results converge on similar conclusions:

Although most of the LXX texts are translations of an underlying Hebrew text, they display a wealth of literary and theological features which deserve attention. In addition to the literary and theological features of each of the LXX books, it is noteworthy that the entire collection of translated and non-translated texts is a document of Hellenistic Judaism. As such, it is rooted in a social and cultural environment that is different from Palestinian Judaism. Moreover, with respect to certain theological details, the LXX turns out to be a kind of "update" of the existing Hebrew Scriptures.

The LXX is the textual source not only of the New Testament (NT) authors but also of the so-called Intertestamentary literature, of Philo, Josephus and of the Greek Church fathers. Therefore, it has an impact on the diffusion of Jewish

---

3 For a fairly nuanced position, see e.g. Ernst Würthwein, *Der Text des Alten Testaments. Eine Einführung in die Biblia Hebraica* (Stuttgart: Deutsche Bibelgesellschaft, 5th edit. 1988). On the one hand, he states (p. 82): "Wohl bleibt sie [the LXX] auch uns ein außerordentlich wichtiger und unentbehrlicher Textzeuge, der die Heilung mancher verderbter Stellen möglich macht". On the other hand, he warns against hastily reconstructing the alleged Hebrew source of the LXX (*ibid.*, p. 82f): "Aber nur nach sorgfältiger Vertiefung in ihren Geist, ihre jeweilige Übersetzungstechnik und ihre Geschichte kann man sie zu textkritischen Operationen heranziehen. Vor vorschnellem Retrovertieren in das Hebräische in der Meinung, damit ohne weiteres die hebräische Vorlage zu gewinnen, muß gewarnt werden".

4 The bibliography is abundant, see e.g. the bibliography in Filippo Belli, Ignacio Carbajosa, Carlos Jódar Estrella, Luis Sáncheu Navarro, *L'Antico nel Nuovo. Il ricorso alla Scrittura nel Nuovo Testamento* (Bologna: Dehoniane, 2008), 181–209.

and Christian belief in ancient societies that should not to be underestimated. Suffice to mention concepts like creation, covenant, law or sin, which vehicle Hebrew thought. In other words, even though something of the original sense of the respective words may have been lost in translation, the intention was to make available Jewish ideas to a Hellenistic public.

In addition to its influence on the New Testament and the Greek Church fathers, the LXX plays an important role in ancient Jewish and Christian epigraphy and iconography[5], and, indirectly, in art, literature and music from Antiquity onwards. On the assumption that a text discloses itself, at least in part, insofar as it has its own *Wirkungsgeschichte*, biblical research cannot completely disregard this issue.

To be sure, recent LXX research has produced important results in the form of translations of and commentaries on the Greek Old Testament texts and numerous studies on specific text-critical and exegetical detail problems[6]. However, there is no doubt that a lexicon of the most important and typical words of the LXX, is still missing.

The aim of this paper is to present a new research tool whose first volume is to be published in 2016. In particular, the following questions will be addressed:
1. Why is there a need for a Historical and Theological Lexicon of the Septuagint (HTLS)? How does this lexicon differ from dictionaries of the Septuagint and of the New Testament that are already available?
2. Which issues will be dealt with in the entries of the HTLS? How are these articles structured? What is the underlying understanding of the evolution of the Greek language?
3. What results can be expected? How can the HTLS give us new insights into the terminology of the Septuagint and its impact on later Jewish and Christian theological language?

1. The need for a new research tool

The future "Historical and Theological Lexicon of the Septuagint" is meant to close a gap in the available literature on the vocabulary of the LXX and the NT.

---

5 See e.g. the wealth of epigraphical evidence in the edition by Antonio Enrico Felle, *Biblia epigraphica. La sacra scrittura nella documentazione epigrafica dell'orbis christianus antiquus* (III-VIII secolo) (Bari: Edipuglia, 2006).
6 For the recent evolution of Septuagint research, see e.g. Jennifer M. Dines, *The Septuagint* (London / New York: T&T Clark, 2004), 151–156; Martin Rösel, "Die *graphe* gewinnt Kontur. Die Stellung der Septuaginta in der Theologiegeschichte des Alten Testaments", *Theologische Literaturzeitung* 135 (2010), 639–651.

a) For about two centuries, the only LXX dictionary was the *Novus Thesaurus Philologico-Criticus, sive Lexicon in LXX et reliquos interpretes graecos ac scriptores apocryphos Veteris Testamenti,* published about two centuries ago by J.F. Schleusner[7]. In 1992 and 1996, the Belgian scholars Johan Lust, Erik Eynikel und Katrin Hauspie produced a *Greek English-Lexicon of the Septuagint*[8] which is without doubt very useful for LXX research. It provides the English equivalents of all attested words in the LXX, together with statistical data about the distribution of the words and an excellent bibliography. To some extent this dictionary is comparable to Takamitsu Muraoka's *Greek-English Lexicon of the Septuagint*[9], which is more comprehensive than the dictionary by Lust, Eynikel and Hauspie and whose bibliographical data is more recent. However, these two dictionaries and Schleusner's Thesaurus have two features in common: on the one hand they take into account the complete vocabulary of the LXX but on the other they provide only the most basic information. Thus, the two recent Greek-English dictionaries of the LXX classify the extant occurrences according to semantic criteria and offer the respective English equivalents. The entries in Schleusner's Thesaurus, written in Latin, provide more information, giving not only the Latin equivalents of the Greek word but their Hebrew equivalents according to the MT. It cannot be denied that the material contained in these lexica is essential for the translator. Nonetheless, their aim was not to provide the user with comprehensive information about the pre-history of a LXX word, or its use in non-biblical Greek or about its possible impact on later Jewish and Christian literature.

b) In a certain sense, the New Testament lexica are able to fill some important gaps. This is the case of Ceslas Spicq's *Lexique théologique du Nouveau Testament*[10]. Without any doubt, this research tool has the avantage of taking into account the LXX use of numerous NT words. However, it focusses on NT vocabulary. *Mutatis mutandis* the same applies for the comprehensive *Theologisches Wörterbuch zum Neuen Testament* (ThWNT) edited by Gerhard Kittel und Gerhard Friedrich[11]. This multi-volume dictionary offers useful information about Greek words attested both in the New Testament and in the LXX. Future research would therefore do well to take into consideration its sections on the LXX. However, the *Kittel* is insufficient for several reasons despite its undeniable merits:

7 Leipzig: Weidmann, 1820–1821.
8 Revised edition in one volume, Stuttgart: Deutsche Bibelgesellschaft, 2003.
9 Leuven: Peeters, 2009.
10 Fribourg (Suisse): Éditions universitaires/Paris: Cerf, 1991. An English translation is available: *Theological lexicon of the New Testament*, 3 vols., Peabody: Hendrickson, 1994.
11 10 vols., Stuttgart: Kohlhammer, 1933–1979.

α) It is not necessary to mention the serious objections James Barr has raised against Kittel's dictionary in his book *The Semantics of Biblical Language*[12]. In particular, Barr claimed that the sense of a word is not fixed, but that a given word acquires its meaning only as one element within a sentence. Therefore, caution is needed when authors argue, in particular in the wake of Kittel, that biblical words tend to have the same meaning in different writings or that e.g. the LXX and its vocabulary are to be considered as a *praeparatio evangelii*[13]. A correct methodological approach consists in a more descriptive and unbiased analysis of the linguistic data. More than one scenario is possible: on the one hand, it cannot be ruled out that one and the same word or expression is used in an analogous manner by different writers. On the other hand, it might prove to be the case that different writers used words or expressions in a different manner. Needless to say the situation gets even more complicated if the same author uses one and the same word in various senses.

β) From the point of view of the LXX scholar, the ThWNT is unsatisfactory for another reason. As is well-known, its main purpose was to analyze the NT vocabulary in the context of its specific biblical and Hellenistic background. Therefore, LXX issues are dealt with by Kittel's dictionary only if they contribute to explaining the NT meaning of a given word. However, the LXX contains numerous important words which are absent from the NT, for whatever reason. Other words are attested only rarely in the NT. It is understandable that Kittel's dictionary only mentions them in passing or does not pay attention to them.

This is the case of a series of technical terms of the LXX that appear rarely in the New Testament, e.g. ἀποστάσιον, "certificate of divorce" (e.g. Deut 24:1; Mark 10:4) and γαζοφυλάκιον, "treasury", which is mentioned about 25 times in the LXX and five times in the NT (e.g. 4 Kdgms 23:10; Mark 12:41).

Moreover, some theological or anthropological vocabulary is missing completely from the ThWNT whereas in other cases the entries are very short. E.g., the divine title ἀντιλήμπτωρ "protector", which is very important in the LXX Psalms (e.g. Ps 3:4; 17:3LXX) is not dealt with. Another divine title of the LXX, βοηθός, "helper" (e.g. Exod 15:2; Ps 9:10), which appears only once in the NT (Hebr 13: 6, quotation of Ps 117:6), is the subject of a very short entry by Friedrich Büchsel[14]. As for anthropological terms, no article is devoted e.g. to ἀφθαρσία, "incorruption", a noun which is mentioned en passant in the article φθείρω[15].

---

12 First edition: Oxford: Oxford University Press, 1961.
13 See e.g. Georg Bertram, "Praeparatio Evangelii in der Septuaginta," *Vetus Testamentum* 7 (1957), 225–249, esp. 231.
14 Friedrich Büchsel, art. βοηθέω κτλ., *ThWNT* I, 627–628.
15 Günther Harder, art. φθείρω κτλ., *ThWNT* IX, 94–106, on p. 97, 102.

Interestingly, the article on βιάζομαι, "to urge, to force" written by Gottlob Schrenk[16] does not include a section on the LXX although the verb as well as the corresponding noun βία are attested around 50 times in the LXX (e.g. Exod 1:13; 14:25).

Finally, various key words of Greek culture and religion occur at times in the LXX but do not appear in the NT. In consequence, there was no need to mention them in Kittel's lexicon. E.g., the noun ἄγαλμα, "statue, image" is probably the usual Greek word for the statue of a god. The word is attested only twice in the LXX of Isaiah (Isa 19:3; 21:9), but it is absent from numerous LXX texts which polemicize against images of the gods (e.g. in Isa 44:9–20; Ps 134:14–18[LXX]; Epistle of Jeremiah). For these statues, the LXX prefers to use the word εἴδωλον, which occurs about 90 times (e.g. Exod 20:4). Furthermore, the word ἀρετή, "virtue", a key word in Greek education and ethics, has some scattered attestations in the LXX, at least in books translated from Hebrew (e.g. Isa 42:8; Hab 3:3), and is very rare in the NT as well (e.g. Phil 4:8). Another interesting example is the verb ἀθλέω, "to contend in battle" and the corresponding noun ἆθλον, "prize of contest, struggle". Although the Old Testament reports many struggles and wars, these words nowhere appear in the translated books of the LXX, not even in accounts such as Jacob's struggle with the angel (Gen 32:25) or David's struggle with Goliath (1 Kgdms 17). In these and similar cases the question arises why a very common Greek word did not find its way into the LXX or why it is so rare.

c) Irrespective of whether a word is dealt with by the available biblical lexica, there is no doubt that LXX research has made significant progress in the last decades. One of the major aims of the HTLS is to take into consideration the main achievements of scholarship, especially in the field of the LXX and related disciplines.

α) With regards to LXX studies, nowadays we have at our disposal critical editions which constitute a sound basis for future research. Furthermore, the discovery of the Qumran texts as well as studies on textual criticism and translation techniques shed more light on the differences and divergences between the various editions of the biblical text[17]. As a result, we can define more precisely the literary and theological characteristics of a given edition, over and above the tex-

---

16 Gottlob Schrenk, art. βιάζομαι, βιαστής, *ThWNT* I, 608–613.
17 It might suffice to quote here a publication which had a great impact on text-critical studies: Emanuel Tov, *The Text-Critical Use of the Septuagint in Biblical Research* (Jerusalem: Simor, 1981, ²1997).

tual details. This enables us to take into account concepts and ideas which span more than one biblical book.

β) In the last decades, numerous papyri and inscriptions have been deciphered and made accessible to scholars. It is obvious that many of these scattered documents can contribute to a better understanding of the language of the LXX. This is the case of the divine titles used in the LXX of which many can be better explained against the background of the papyri, e. g. the aforementioned noun ἀντιλήμπτωρ[18]. Something similar might be said of the vocabulary of sin and law. A series of terms appear in the legal language of Ptolemaic Egypt, especially in documents which have been analysed and published in recent time[19]. Generally speaking, the existing lexica do not take into consideration this material in a systematic manner. Both papyri and inscriptions can nowadays be searched easily on the respective electronic databases. Thus, it is possible in only a few minutes to locate words or expressions in a mass of electronically processed data. In the past, word searches of this kind would have been as impossible as looking for a needle in a haystack. Of course, progress is still slow in this field, despite the availability of electronic databases.

In conclusion, current biblical research is aware of the specific place that the LXX has both in the evolution of the text of the Bible and in ancient Jewish and Christian theology. Therefore, we need a research tool which covers a wide range of words and word groups of the LXX, their Greek background and their history in later Jewish and Christian theology.

2. Methodological issues

HTLS articles should address the following questions: 1. Is the word already attested in classical or Hellenistic Greek literature? 2. Is the word attested in the papyri or inscriptions of the Hellenistic or Roman periods? 3. Is the word attested in ancient Jewish literature written in Greek, notably the writings of Philo or Josephus? 4. Is the word attested in the New Testament or in the Early Christian literature up until the end of the II century B.C.E.?

---

18 See e. g. the article by Anna Passoni Dell'Acqua, "La metafora biblica di Dio come roccia e la sua soppressione nelle antiche versioni," *Ephemerides Liturgicae* 91 (1977), 417–453.
19 See Anna Passoni dell'Acqua, "La terminologia dei reati nei προστάγματα dei Tolemei e nella versione dei LXX," In *Proceedings of the XVIII International Congress of Papyrology, Athens 25–31 may 1986*, Vol. II (Athens: Greek Papyrological Society, 1988), 335–350.

One crucial question was how to define the criteria for selecting words or word groups to be included in the lexicon. We are very much aware of the fact that clear-cut criteria do not exist. However, the following questions enabled us to draw up a list:

Which LXX words are given a new, specific meaning that they do not have in classical or Hellenistic Greek? By way of an example, in classical Greek, the verb κτίζω denotes the process of founding a city or a building (e. g. Herodotus, *Hist.* I.168, 170). In biblical Greek, however, the verb mostly refers to God's creative act (e. g. Gen 14:19, 22). That is not to suggest that the verb always has the same meaning in every Jewish or Christian Greek text. On the contrary, it has to be established which meaning prevails in a given context. One cannot rule out the possibility that the verb in one instance means "to create" and in another "to found" (e. g. in 1 Esdr 4:53)[20].

Does the LXX introduce technical terms into religious or legal terminology which become common in later Jewish or Christian texts, whereas they do not have this specific meaning in so-called pagan texts? Example: In Greek a βωμός is a hill or a raised platform, sometimes an altar (Homer, *Il.* 4, 48; 8, 249; Herodotus, *Hist.* I.183; Euripides, *Andromache*, 162). In biblical Greek, however, the noun denotes an altar to foreign deities[21] (e. g. Exod 34:13; exceptions: 2 Macc 13:8; Sir 50:12, 14). As for the verb ἀγχιστεύω, it means "to be near" in classical Greek (e. g. Euripides, *Tro.* 224). Sometimes, the words of the same root also have a moral connotation: neighbours have the duty of helping each other (e. g. Herodotus, *Hist.* V.80). The LXX, however, places the word in the context of redemption: "to exercise the rights and responsibilities of a kinsman, to redeem" (e. g. Lev 25:25).

Can the specific LXX meaning of a word be better explained in the Egyptian context of the papyri? Once again, let us quote the noun ἀντιλήμπτωρ, "protector" which the LXX uses to render words such as *miśgāḇ* "secure height, stronghold" (e. g. Ps 17:3; 45:8, 12[LXX]). In an Egyptian context, however, an ἀντιλήμπτωρ is normally a person, often a high functionary who is called for assistance by a petitioner (e. g. BGU IV.1139).

---

20 For detailed information on the use of κτίζω and its derivatives, see Eberhard Bons and Anna Passoni Dell'Acqua, "A Sample Article: κτίζω – κτίσις – κτίσμα – κτίστης," In *Septuagint Vocabulary. Pre-History, Usage, Reception*, eds. Eberhard Bons and Jan Joosten (SCSt 58; Atlanta, Georgia: Society of Biblical Literature, 2011), 173–187.

21 See Knut Usener, "Die Septuaginta im Horizont des Hellenismus. Ihre Entwicklung, ihr Charakter und ihre sprachlich-kulturelle Position," In *Im Brennpunkt: Die Septuaginta. Studien zur Entstehung und Bedeutung der Griechischen Bibel*, eds. Siegfried Kreuzer and Jürgen Peter Lesch (BWANT 161; Stuttgart: Kohlhammer, 2004), 78–118, esp. 108 f.

Does the LXX employ words in new or specific contexts in such a manner that the word is connected to a particular event or reality? E.g. the verb γογγύζω "to mutter" and its derivations refer to the murmuring of the Israelites in the desert.

Does the LXX employ a vocabulary, e. g. philosophical and anthropological terms, which have no direct equivalent in the Hebrew Bible, but which occur in the translated books? As an example, in classical Greek thinking, humans are considered mortal whereas gods are immortal (e. g. Homer, *Il.* I, 339). Biblical Hebrew, however, has no word for "mortal". Nevertheless, the word θνητός occurs here and there in the translated books, e. g. Isa 51:12; Prov 20:24.

As for the evolution of Greek language, we have to reckon with various phenomena: the LXX introduces "new" meanings, whereas the "older" meanings reappear in later Jewish and Christian texts; the LXX introduces new terminology which has no impact on subsequent Jewish and Christian literature; one and the same word has a typical LXX meaning as well as its "traditional" meaning; the LXX employs words and expressions of colloquial Greek etc. In short, we cannot establish a linear relationship by means of which "Biblical Greek" develops from the LXX. Rather, we have to take into consideration interplay of various factors: the meaning of an underlying Hebrew word, the context of Egyptian Greek, the social environment, rhetorical skill, *koiné* Greek, allusions to Greek literature and mythology, etc.

3. Expected results

How can the HTLS give us new insight into the terminology of the Septuagint and its impact on later Christian theological language? It might suffice to quote some examples:

a) The systematic study of the papyri proves useful insofar as it can provide interesting results:

α) For a long time, scholars were convinced that the word προσήλυτος was a LXX neologism[22]. A recently published article, however, raises doubts as to whether this hypothesis is really viable. In Papyrus Duke Inv. 727, which goes back to the 3rd century B.C.E., the term προσήλυτος seems to denote strangers[23].

---

22 Karl Georg Kuhn, art. προσήλυτος, *ThWNT* VI, 727–745, on p. 730.
23 C. Jakob Butera/David M. Moffitt, "P.Duk. inv. 727: A Dispute with 'Proselytes' in Egypt," In *Zeitschrift für Papyrologie und Epigraphik* 177 (2011), 201–206.

If this hypothesis is correct, the conclusion is clear: when rendering the Hebrew word *ger* the translators did not invent a new Greek noun or adjective but had recourse to a word already existing in their environment.

β) Sometimes the papyri offer the closest parallels to LXX quotations. E.g., the noun βοηθός as a divine title is very rare outside the LXX, Josephus, and later Christian literature. However, in the papyri we find petitions where a human "helper" and sometimes a god is called βοηθός (e. g. UPZ 1.52)[24].

γ) Among the adjectives whose meaning ranges from "unusual" to "wicked", some LXX texts, especially Job, use the neuter of ἄτοπος, normally as the object of a verb like ποιέω and πράσσω. Once again, the papyri provide some material which enables us to shed light on the background to these expressions, as will be shown by Daniela Scialabba in her forthcoming HTLS article. Interestingly, the clause "he has not done anything wrong", put into the mouth of the repentant thief, appears in Luke 23:41.

b) The idea of divine education or correction (παιδεύω, παιδεία) appears several times in the Book of the Twelve Prophets, although the Hebrew text does not necessarily require such a translation. According to Amos 3:7, God does not reveal his council (*sôd*) to the prophets (as in the MT), but his παιδεία. Of course, this variant might be explained by an error, the translator having read the root *ysr*. Be this as it may, it is striking that the idea of divine correction is closely related to another text, Hos 5:2, where God presents himself as the "educator" of his people (παιδευτής). Therefore, the question is whether these and other LXX occurrences of the idea of divine education reveal a specific theological concept. If so, does this concept undergo development in later texts, e. g. in the Psalms of Solomon and in the New Testament? And how can it be situated in the wider context of Jewish-hellenistic theology and Greek education? A futur HTLS article will trace the development of this idea. Of course, texts and ideas are not to be confused. It is all the more indispensable to show how this idea is shaped in a given context[25].

In conclusion, the articles which have been already submitted allow us to formulate the following expectations: the entries of the lexicon will enable us to place LXX words in the larger context of their hellenistic environment, to de-

---

24 For more details, see Eberhard Bons, "The Noun βοηθός as a Divine Title. Prolegomena to a Future HTLS Article". In *The Reception of Septuagint Words in Jewish-Hellenistic and Christian Literature* eds. Eberhard Bons, Ralph Brucker, Jan Joosten (WUNT II/367; Tübingen: Mohr Siebeck, 2013), 53–66.

25 See Patrick Pouchelle, *Dieu éducateur. Une nouvelle approche d'un concept de la théologie biblique entre Bible Hébraïque, Septante et Littérature grecque* (Tübingen: Mohr Siebeck, 2015).

scribe their specific features and the contexts in which they appear, and to give us an idea of their impact on later Jewish and Christian writers.

Bible reference index

Index of Hebrew words

Index of Greek words